ISBN 978-1-5283-9025-5
PIBN 10167785

This book is a reproduction of an important historical work. Forgotten Books uses state-of-the-art technology to digitally reconstruct the work, preserving the original format whilst repairing imperfections present in the aged copy. In rare cases, an imperfection in the original, such as a blemish or missing page, may be replicated in our edition. We do, however, repair the vast majority of imperfections successfully; any imperfections that remain are intentionally left to preserve the state of such historical works.

The date shows when this volume was taken.

To renew this book copy the call No. and give to the librarian

HOME USE RULES.

All Books subject to Recall

All books must be returned at end of college year for inspection and repairs.

Students must return all books before leaving town. Officers should arrange for the return of books wanted during their absence from town.

Books needed by more than one person are held on the reserve list.

Volumes of periodicals and of pamphlets are held in the library as much as possible. For special purposes they are given out for a limited time.

Borrowers should not use their library privileges for the benefit of other persons.

Books of special value and gift books, when the giver wishes it, are not allowed to circulate.

Readers are asked to report all cases of books marked or mutilated.

Do not deface books by marks and writing.

GENERAL

RAILROAD LAWS

OF THE

S TATE OF N EW Y ORK,

WITH

Amendments to and Including the Session of
the Legislature of 1906.
Also Interstate Commerce Acts

COMPILED BY THE RAILROAD COMMISSIONERS

ALBANY
J. B. LYON COMPANY, STATE PRINTERS
1907

APPENDIX.

LAWS APPLICABLE TO RAILROAD COMPANIES

[Compiled by the Board of Railroad Commissioners.]

FIRST — CHAPTER 95, LAWS OF 1890, KNOWN AS THE "CONDEM-NATION LAW," AND "PROCEEDINGS TO CHANGE THE NAME OF A CORPORATION."

SECOND — CHAPTER 563, LAWS OF 1890, KNOWN AS THE "GEN-ERAL CORPORATION LAW."

THIRD — CHAPTER 564, LAWS OF 1890, KNOWN AS THE "STOCK CORPORATION LAW."

FOURTH — CHAPTER 565, LAWS OF 1890, KNOWN AS THE "RAIL-ROAD LAW."

ALSO, OTHER GENERAL LAWS RELATING TO RAILROADS. ALSO, SECTIONS OF THE CODE OF CRIMINAL PROCEDURE AND PENAL CODE RELATING DIRECTLY TO RAILROADS. ALSO, THE RAPID TRANSIT ACT. ALL AS AMENDED TO AND INCLUDING THE SESSION OF THE LEGISLATURE OF 1906. ALSO, THE INTERSTATE COMMERCE ACT, WITH KINDRED ACTS, AS AMENDED TO JUNE 30, 1906.

A FEW CITATIONS TO DECISIONS OF COURTS ARE GIVEN.

*THE CONDEMNATION LAW

CHAP. 95, LAWS OF 1890.

AN ACT to amend the Code of Civil Procedure.

(As amended to and including the session of the Legislature of 1906.)

CHAPTER XXIII OF THE CODE OF CIVIL PROCEDURE

SUPPLEMENTAL PROVISIONS.

TITLE I.

PROCEEDINGS FOR THE CONDEMNATION OF REAL PROPERTY.

Condemnation law.

SECTION 3357. This title shall be known as the condemnation law.

Terms used defined.

§ 3358. The term "person," when used herein, includes a natural person and also a corporation, joint stock association, the state and a political division thereof, and any commission, board, board of managers or trustees in charge or having control of any of the charitable or other institutions of the state; the term "real property," any right, interest or easement therein or appurtenances thereto; and the term "owner," all persons having any estate, interest, or easement in the property to be taken, or any lien, charge, or incumbrance thereon. The person instituting the proceedings shall be termed the plaintiff; and the person against whom the proceeding is brought, the defendant.

Thus amended by chap. 589, Laws of 1896. See said chapter.

Title to real estate, how acquired.

§ 3359. Whenever any person is authorized to acquire title to real property, for a public use by condemnation the proceeding for that purpose shall be taken in the manner prescribed in this title.

* See provisions of Rapid Transit Act, post.

Petition to Supreme Court; petition what to contain.

§ 3360. The proceeding shall be instituted by the presentation of a petition by the plaintiff to the supreme court setting forth the following facts:

1. His name, place of residence, and the business in which engaged; if a corporation or joint-stock association, whether foreign or domestic, its principal place of business within the state, the names and places of residence of its principal officers, and of its directors, trustees or board of managers, as the case may be, and the object or purpose of its incorporation or association; if a political division of the state, the names and places of residence of its principal officers; and if the state or any commission or board of managers or trustees in charge or having control of any of the charitable or other institutions of the state, the name, place of residence of the officer acting in its or their behalf in the proceedings.

Subdivision 1 thus amended by chap. 589, Laws of 1896. See said chapter.

2. A specific description of the property to be condemned and its location, by metes and bounds, with reasonable certainty.

3. The public use for which the property is required and a concise statement of the facts showing the necessity of its acquisition for such use.

4. The names and places of residence of the owners of the property; if an infant, the name and place of residence of his general guardian, if he has one, if not, the name and place of residence of the person with whom he resides; if a lunatic, idiot, or habitual drunkard, the name and place of residence of his committee or trustee, if he has one; if not, the name and place of residence of the person with whom he resides. If a non-resident, having an agent or attorney residing in the state authorized to contract for the sale of the property, the name and place of residence of such agent or attorney; if the name or place of residence of any owner can not after diligent inquiry be

ascertained, it may be so stated with a specific statement of the extent of the inquiry which has been made.

5. That the plaintiff has been unable to agree with the owner of the property for its purchase and the reason of such inability.

6. The value of the property to be condemned.

7. A statement that it is the intention of the plaintiff, in good faith, to complete the work or improvement, for which the property is to be condemned; and that all the preliminary steps required by law have been taken to entitle him to institute the proceeding.

8. A demand for relief, that it may be adjudged that the public use requires the condemnation of the real property described, and that the plaintiff is entitled to take and hold such property for the public use specified, upon making compensation therefor, and that commissioners of appraisal be appointed to ascertain the compensation to be made to the owners for the property so taken.

Notice of presentation of petition; service of petition and notice.

§ 3361. There must be annexed to the petition a notice of the time and place at which it will be presented to a special term of the supreme court, held in the judicial district where the property or some portion of it is situated, and a copy of the petition and notice must be served upon all the owners of the property at least eight days prior to its presentation.

Service, how made.

§ 3362. Service of the petition and notice must be made in the same manner as the service of a summons in an action in the supreme court is required to be made, and all the provisions of articles one and two of title one of chapter five of this act, which relate to the service of a summons, either personally or in any other way, and the mode of proving service, shall apply to the service of the petition and notice. If the defendant has an agent or attorney residing in this state, authorized to contract for the sale of the real property described in the petition, service upon such agent or attorney will be sufficient service upon such defendant. In case the defendant is an infant of the age of fourteen years or upwards, a copy of the petition and notice shall also be served upon his general guardian, if he has one, if not, upon the person with whom he resides.

Duty of general guardian, committee or trustee; court, when to appoint guardian ad litem; when, attorney for defendant.

§ 3363. If a defendant is an infant, idiot, lunatic or habitual drunkard, it shall be the duty of his general guardian, committee or trustee, if he has one, to appear for him upon the presentation of the petition and attend to his interests, and in case he has none, or in case his general guardian, committee or trustee fails to appear for him, the court shall, upon the presentation of the petition and notice, with proof of service, without further notice, appoint a guardian ad litem for such defendant, whose duty it shall be to appear for him and attend to his interests in the proceeding, and, if deemed necessary to protect his rights, the court may require a general guardian, committee or trustee, or a guardian ad litem to give security in such sum and with such sureties as the court may approve. If a service other than personal has been made upon any defendant, and he does not appear upon the presentation of the petition, the court shall appoint some competent attorney to appear for him and attend to his interests in the proceeding.

Appearance of parties; service of papers.

§ 3364. The provisions of law and of the rules and practice of the court, relating to the appearance of parties in person or by attorney in actions in the supreme court, shall apply to the proceeding from and after the service of the petition, and all subsequent orders, notices and papers may be served upon the attorney appearing and upon a guardian ad litem in the same manner and with the same effect as the service of papers in an action in the supreme court may be made.

Answer to petition.

§ 3365. Upon presentation of the petition and notice with proof of service thereof, an owner of the property may appear and interpose an answer, which must contain a general or specific denial of each material allegation of the petition controverted by him, or of any knowledge or information thereof sufficient to form a belief, or a statement of new matter constituting a defense to the proceeding.

Verification of petition and answer.

§ 3366. A petition or answer must be verified, and the provisions of this act relating to the form and contents of the verification of pleadings in courts of record, and the persons by whom it may be made, shall apply to the verification.

Trial of issue and decision thereon.

§ 3367. The court shall try any issue raised by the petition and answer at such time and place as it may direct, or it may order the same to be referred to a referee to hear and determine, and upon such trial the court or referee shall file a decision in writing, or deliver the same to the attorney for the prevailing party, within twenty days after the final submission of the proofs and allegations of the parties, and the provisions of this act relating to the form and contents of decisions upon the trial of issues of fact by the court or a referee, and to making and filing exceptions thereto, and the making and settlement of a case for the review thereof upon appeal, and to the proceedings which may be had, in case such decision is not filed or delivered within the time herein required, and to the powers of the court and referee upon such trial, shall be applicable to a trial and decision under this title.

Provisions applicable.

§ 3368. The provisions of title one of chapter eight of this act shall also apply to proceedings had under this title.

Judgment, entry of; etc.

§ 3369. Judgment shall be entered pursuant to the direction of the court or referee in the decision filed. If in favor of the defendant the petition shall be dismissed, with costs to be taxed by the clerk at the same rates as are allowed, of course, to a defendant prevailing in an action in the supreme court, including the allowances for proceedings before and after notice of trial. If the decision is in favor of the plaintiff, or if no answer has been interposed and it appears from the petition that he is entitled to the relief demanded, judgment shall be entered, adjudging that the condemnation of the real property described is necessary for the public use, and that the plaintiff is entitled to take and hold the property for the public use specified, upon making compensation therefor, and the court shall thereupon appoint three disinterested and competent freeholders, residents of the judicial district embracing the county where the real property, or some part of it, is situated, or of some county adjoining such judicial district, commissioners to ascertain the compensation to be made to the owners for the property to be taken for the public use specified, and fix the time and place for the first meeting of the commissioners. Provided, however, that in any such proceeding instituted within the first or second judicial district, such commissioners shall be residents of the county where the real property, or some part of it, is situated, or of some adjoining county. If a trial has been had, at least eight days' notice of such appointment must be given to all the defendants who have appeared. The parties may waive, in writing, the provisions of this section as to the residence of the commissioners, and in that case they may be residents of any county in the state. Where owners of separate properties are joined in the same proceeding, or separate properties of the same owner are to be condemned, more than one set of commissioners may be appointed. ·

Thus amended by chap. 530, Laws of 1895.

Duty of commissioners; report; compensation.

§ 3370. The commissioners shall take and subscribe the constitutional oath of office. Any of them may issue subpoenas and
administer oaths to witnesses; a majority of them may adjourn
the proceeding before them, from time to time in their discretion.
Whenever they meet, except by appointment of the court or pursuant to adjournment, they shall cause at least eight days' notice
of such meeting to be given to the defendants who have appeared,
or their agents or attorneys. They shall view the premises
described in the petition, and hear the proof and allegations of
the parties, and reduce the testimony taken by them, if any,
to writing, and after the testimony in each case is closed, they,
or a majority of them, all being present, shall, without unnecessary delay ascertain and determine the compensation which
ought justly to be made by the plaintiff to the owners of the
property appraised by them; and, in fixing the amount of such
compensation, they shall not make any allowance or deduction
on account of any real or supposed benefits which the owners
may derive from the public use for which the property is to be
taken, or the construction of any proposed improvement connected with such public use. But in case the plaintiff is a railroad corporation and such real property shall belong to any
other railroad corporation, the commissioners on fixing the
amount of such compensation, shall fix the same at its fair value
for railroad purposes. They shall make a report of their proceedings to the supreme court with the minutes of the testimony
taken by them, if any; and they shall each be entitled to six dollars for services for every day they are actually engaged in the
performance of their duties, and their necessary expenses, to be
paid by the plaintiff; provided, that in proceedings within the
counties of New York and Kings such commissioners shall be
entitled to such additional compensation not exceeding twenty-
five dollars for every such day, as may be awarded by the court.

Thus amended by chap. 384, Laws of 1898, taking effect September 1, 1898.
As to condemning railroad property, see section 7, Railroad Law, *post.*

Confirmation of report; rehearing before commissioners; final order; deposit of money deemed payment.

§ 3371. Upon filing the report of the commissioners, any party may move for its confirmation at a special term, held in the district where the property or some part of it is situated, upon notice to the other parties who have appeared, and upon such motion, the court may confirm the report, or may set it aside for irregularity, or for error of law in the proceedings before the commissioners, or upon the ground that the award is excessive or insufficient. If the report is set aside, the court may direct a rehearing before the same commissioners, or may appoint new commissioners for that purpose, and the proceedings upon such rehearing shall be conducted in the manner prescribed for the original hearing, and the same proceedings shall be had for the confirmation of the second report, as are herein prescribed for the confirmation of the first report. If the report is confirmed, the court shall enter a final order in the proceeding, directing that compensation shall be made to the owners of the property, pursuant to the determination of the commissioners, and that upon payment of such compensation, the plaintiff shall be entitled to enter into the possession of the property condemned, and take and hold it for the public use specified in the judgment. Deposit of the money to the credit of, or payable to the order of the owner, pursuant to the direction of the court, shall be deemed a payment within the provisions of this title.

Offer to purchase by plaintiff; notice of acceptance of offer; costs and allowances.

§ 3372. In all cases where the owner is a resident and not under legal disability to convey title to real property the plaintiff before service of his petition and notice, may make a written offer to purchase the property at a specified price, which must within ten days thereafter be filed in the office of the clerk of the county where the property is situated; and which cannot be given in evidence before the commissioners, or considered by them. The owner may at the time of the presentation of the petition, or at any time previously, serve notice in writing of the acceptance of plaintiff's offer, and thereupon the plaintiff may, upon filing the petition, with proof of the making of the offer and its acceptance, enter an order that upon payment of the compensation agreed upon, he may enter into possession of the real property described in the petition, and take and hold it for the public use therein specified. If the offer is not accepted, and the compensation awarded by the commissioners does not exceed the amount of the offer with interest from the time it was made, no costs shall be allowed to either party. If the compensation awarded shall exceed the amount of the offer with interest from the time it was made, or if no offer was made, the court shall, in the final order, direct that the defendant recover of the plaintiff the costs of the proceeding, to be taxed by the clerk at the same rate as is allowed, of course, to the defendant when he is the prevailing party in an action in the supreme court, including the allowances for proceedings before and after notice of trial and the court may also grant an additional allowance of costs, not exceeding five per centum upon the amount awarded. The court shall also direct in the final order what sum shall be paid to the general or special guardian, or committee or trustee of an infant, idiot, lunatic or habitual drunkard, or to an attorney appointed by the court to attend to the interests of any defendant upon whom other than personal service of the petition and notice may have been made, and who has not appeared, or costs, expenses and counsel fees, and by whom or out of what fund the same shall be paid. If a trial has been had, and all the issues determined in favor of the plaintiff, costs of the trial shall not be allowed to the defendant, but the plaintiff shall recover of any defendant answering the costs of such trial caused by the interposition of the unsuccessful defense, to be taxed by the clerk at the same rate as is allowed to the prevailing party for the trial of an action in the supreme court.

Compensation awarded, etc., to be docketed as a judgment; delivery of possession; issue of writ of assistance.

§ 3373. Upon the entry of the final order, the same shall be attached to the judgment roll in the proceeding, and the amount directed to be paid, either as compensation to the owners, or for the costs or expenses of the proceeding, shall be docketed as a judgment against the person who is directed to pay the same, and it shall have all the force and effect of a money judgment in an action in the supreme court, and collection thereof may be enforced by execution and by the same proceedings as judgments for the recovery of money in the supreme court may be enforced under the provisions of this act. When payment of the compensation awarded, and costs of the proceeding, if any, has been made, as directed in the final order, and a certified copy of such order has been served upon the owner, he shall, upon demand of the plaintiff, deliver possession thereof to him, and in case possession is not delivered when demanded, the plaintiff may apply to the court without notice, unless the court shall require notice to be given, upon proof of such payment and of service of the copy order, and of the demand and non-compliance therewith, for a writ of assistance, and the court shall thereupon cause such writ to be issued, which shall be executed in the same manner as when issued in other cases for the delivery of possession of real property.

Abandonment and discontinuance of proceeding.

§ 3374. Upon the application of the plaintiff to be made at any time after the presentation of the petition and before the expiration of thirty days after the entry of the final order, upon eight days' notice of motion to all other parties to the proceeding who have appeared therein or upon an order to show cause, the court may, in its discretion, and for good cause shown, authorize and direct the abandonment and discontinuance of the proceeding, upon payment of the fees and expenses, if any, of the commissioners, and the costs and expenses directed to be paid in such final order, if such final order shall have been entered, and upon such other terms and conditions as the court may prescribe; and upon the entry of the order granting such application and upon compliance with the terms and conditions therein prescribed, payment of the amount awarded for compensation, if such compensation shall have been theretofore awarded, shall not be enforced, but in such case, if such abandonment and discontinuance of the proceeding be directed upon the application of the plaintiff, the order granting such application, if permitting a renewal of such proceedings, shall provide that proceedings to acquire title to such lands or any part thereof shall not be renewed by the plaintiff without a tender or deposit in court of the amount of the award and interest thereon.

Thus amended by chap. 475, Laws of 1894.

Appeal from final order; stay of proceedings.

§ 3375. Appeal may be taken to the general term of the supreme court from the final order, within the time provided for appeals from orders by title four of chapter twelve of this act; and all the provisions of such chapter relating to appeals to the general term from orders of the special term shall apply to such appeals. Such appeal will bring up for review all the proceedings subsequent to the judgment, but the judgment and proceedings antecedent thereto may be reviewed on such appeal, if the appellant states in his notice that the same will be brought up for review, and exceptions shall have been filed to the decision of the court or the referee, and a case or a case and exceptions shall have been made, settled and allowed, as required by the provisions of this act, for the review of the trial of actions in the supreme court without a jury. The proceedings of the plaintiff shall not be stayed upon such an appeal, except by order of the court, upon notice to him, and the appeal shall not affect his possession of the property taken, and the appeal of a defendant shall not be heard except on his stipulation not to disturb such possession.

Appeal from judgment in favor of defendant.

§ 3376. If a trial has been had and judgment entered in favor of the defendant, the plaintiff may appeal therefrom to the general term within the time provided for appeals from judgments by title four of chapter twelve of this act, and all the provisions of such chapter relating to appeals from judgments shall apply to such appeals; and on the hearing of the appeal the general term may affirm, reverse or modify the judgment, and in case of reversal may grant a new trial, or direct that judgment be entered in favor of the plaintiff. If the judgment is affirmed, costs shall be allowed to the respondent, but if reversed or modified, no costs of the appeal shall be allowed to either party.

New appraisal.

§ 3377. On the hearing of the appeal from the final order the court may direct a new appraisal before the same or new commissioners, in its discretion, and the report of such commissioners shall be final and conclusive upon all parties interested. If the amount of the compensation to be paid is increased by the last report, the difference shall be a lien upon the land appraised, and shall be paid to the parties entitled to the same, or shall be deposited as the court shall direct; and if the amount is diminished, the difference shall be refunded to the plaintiff by the party to whom the same may have been paid, and judgment therefor may be rendered by the court, on the filing of the last report, against the parties liable to pay the same.

Adverse and conflicting claimants to money.

§ 3378. If there are adverse and conflicting claimants to the money, or any part of it, to be paid as compensation for the property taken, the court may direct the money to be paid into the court by the plaintiff, and may determine who is entitled to the same, and direct to whom the same shall be paid, and may, in its discretion, order a reference to ascertain the facts on which such determination and direction are to be made.

Allowance of costs in certain cases.

§ 3379. At any stage of the proceeding the court may authorize the plaintiff, if in possession of the property sought to be
condemned, to continue in possession, and may stay all actions
or proceedings against him on account thereof, upon giving
security, or depositing such sum of money as the court may
direct to be held as security for the payment of the compensation which may be finally awarded to the owner therefor and
the costs of the proceedings, and in every such case the owner
may conduct the proceeding to a conclusion, if the plaintiff
delays or neglects to prosecute the same. When the final award
to any owner is less than fifty dollars, in proceedings to condemn
a right of way, for telephone or telegraph poles and wires, the
allowance of costs, if any, and the amount thereof not exceeding
that prescribed by statute, shall be in the discretion of the court
in any action or proceeding that may have been or may hereafter be stayed, if the telephone or telegraph poles and wires,
in such action or proceeding so stayed, shall have been
erected for more than three years prior to the commencement
thereof.

Thus amended by chap. 774, Laws of 1900, taking effect September 1, 1900.

Entry upon and use of property after answer has been interposed.

§ 3380. When an answer to the petition has been interposed,
and it appears to the satisfaction of the court that the public
interests will be prejudiced by delay, it may direct that the
plaintiff be permitted to enter immediately upon the real property to be taken, and devote it temporarily to the public use
specified in the petition, upon depositing with the court the sum
stated in the answer as the value of the property, and which
sum shall be applied, so far as it may be necessary for that
purpose, to the payment of the award that may be made, and
the costs and expenses of the proceeding, and the residue, if
any, returned to the plaintiff, and, in case the petition should be
dismissed, or no award should be made, or the proceedings

should be abandoned by the plaintiff, the court shall direct that the money so deposited, so far as it may be necessary, shall be applied to the payment of any damages which the defendant may have sustained by such entry upon and use of his property, and his costs and expenses of the proceeding, such damages to be ascertained by the court, or a referee to be appointed for that purpose, and if the sum so deposited shall be insufficient to pay such damages, and all costs and expenses awarded to the defendant, judgment shall be entered against the plaintiff for the deficiency, to be enforced and collected in the same manner as a judgment in the supreme court; and the possession of the property shall be restored to the defendant.

See 111 App. Div. 686; 351 Misc. 333.

Notice of pendency of proceedings; effect thereof; duty of county clerk.

§ 3381. Upon service of the petition, or at any time afterwards before the entry of the final order, the plaintiff may file in the clerk's office of each county where any part of the property is situated, a notice of the pendency of the proceeding stating the names of the parties and the object of the proceeding, and containing a brief description of the property affected thereby, and from the time of filing, such notice shall be constructive notice to a purchaser, or incumbrancer of the property affected thereby, from or against a defendant with respect to whom the notice is directed to be indexed, as herein prescribed, and a person whose conveyance or incumbrance is subsequently executed or subsequently recorded, is bound by all proceedings taken in the proceeding, after the filing of the notice, to the same extent as if he was a party thereto. The county clerk must immediately record such notice when filed in the book in his office kept for the purpose of recording notices of pendency of actions, and index it to the name of each defendant specified in the direction appended at the foot of the notice, and subscribed by the plaintiff or his attorney.

2

Power of court to make all necessary orders, etc.

§ 3382. In all proceedings under this title, where the mode or manner of conducting all or any of the proceedings therein is not expressly provided for by law, the court before whom such proceedings may be pending, shall have the power to make all necessary orders and give necessary directions to carry into effect the object and intent of this title, and of the several acts conferring authority to condemn lands for public use, and the practice in such cases shall conform, as near as may be, to the ordinary practice in such court.

Repeal.

§ 3383. So much of all acts and parts of acts as prescribe a method of procedure in proceedings for the condemnation of real property for a public use is repealed, except such acts and parts of acts as prescribe a method of procedure for the condemnation of real property for public use as a highway, or as a street, avenue, or public place in an incorporated city or village, or as may prescribe methods of procedure for such condemnation for any public use for, by, on behalf, on the part, or in the name of the corporation of the city of New York, known as the mayor, aldermen, and commonalty of the city of New York, or by whatever name known, or by or on the application of any board, department, commissioners or other officers acting for or on behalf or in the name of such corporation or city, or where the title to the real property so to be acquired vests in such corporation or in such city; and all proceedings for the condemnation of real property embraced within the exceptions enumerated in this section are exempted from the operation of this title.

Thus amended by chap. 247, Laws of 1890.

Title, when to take effect.

§ 3384. This title shall take effect on the first day of May, one thousand eight hundred and ninety, and shall not affect any proceeding previously commenced.

TITLE II.

Proceeding on application to sell, mortgage, etc., property.

SECTION 3390. Whenever any corporation or joint stock association is required by law to make application to the court for leave to mortgage, lease or sell its real estate, the proceeding therefor shall be had pursuant to the provisions of this title.

Petition to court; petition, what to contain; verification.

§ 3391. The proceeding shall be instituted by the presentation to the supreme court of the district or the county court of the county where the real property, or some part of it, is situated, by the corporation or association, applicant, of a petition setting forth the following facts:

1. The name of the corporation or association, and of its directors, trustees or managers, and of its principal officers, and their places of residence.

2. The business of the corporation or association, or the object or purpose of its incorporation or formation, and a reference to the statute under which it was incorporated or formed.

3. A description of the real property to be sold, mortgaged or leased, by metes and bounds, with reasonable certainty.

4. That the interest of the corporation or association will be promoted by the sale, mortgage or lease, of the real property specified, and a concise statement of the reasons therefor.

5. That such sale, mortgage or lease has been authorized, by a vote of at least two-thirds of the directors, trustees or managers of the corporation or association, at a meeting thereof, duly called and held, and a copy of the resolution granting such authority.

6. The market value of the remaining real property of the corporation or association, and the cash value of its personal assets, and the total amount of its debts and liabilities, and how secured, if at all.

7. The application proposed to be made of the moneys realized from such sale, mortgage or lease.

8. Where the consent of the shareholders, stockholders or members of the corporation or association, is required by law to be first obtained, a statement that such consent has been given, and a copy of the consent or a certified transcript of the record of the meeting at which it was given, shall be annexed to the petition.

9. A demand for leave to mortgage, lease or sell the real estate described.

The petition shall be verified in the same manner as a verified pleading in an action in a court of record.

Hearing of application.

§ 3392. Upon presentation of the petition, the court may immediately proceed to hear the application, or it may, in its discretion, direct that notice of the application shall be given to any person interested therein, as a member, stockholder, officer or creditor of the corporation or association, or otherwise, in which case the application shall be heard at the time and place specified in such notice, and the court may in any case appoint a referee to take the proofs and report the same to the court, with his opinion thereon.

Court may grant application; appearance on hearing.

§ 3393. Upon the hearing of the application, if it shall appear, to the satisfaction of the court, that the interests of the corporation or association will be promoted thereby, an order may be granted authorizing it to sell, mortgage or lease the real property described in the petition, or any part thereof, for such sum, and upon such terms as the court may prescribe, and directing what disposition shall be made of the proceeds of such sale, mortgage or lease.

Any person, whose interests may be affected by the proceeding, may appear upon the hearing and show cause why the application should not be granted.

Notice to creditors on application of insolvent corporation, etc.

§ 3394. If the corporation or association is insolvent, or its property and assets are insufficient to fully liquidate its debts and liabilities, the application shall not be granted, unless all the creditors of the corporation have been served with a notice of the time and place at which the application will be heard.

Service of notices.

§ 3395. Service of notices, provided for in this title, may be made either personally or, in case of absence, by leaving the same at the place of residence of the person to be served, with some person of mature age and discretion, at least eight days before the hearing of the application, or by mailing the same, duly enveloped and addressed and postage paid, at least sixteen days before such hearing.

Power of court to make all necessary orders.

§ 3396. In all applications made under this title, where the mode or manner of conducting any or all of the proceedings thereon are not expressly provided for, the court before whom such application may be pending, shall have the power to make all the necessary orders and give the proper directions to carry into effect the object and intent of this title, or of any act authorizing the sale of corporate real property, and the practice in such cases shall conform, as near as may be, to the ordinary practice in such court.

Title, when to take effect.

§ 3397. This title shall take effect May first, one thousand eight hundred and ninety, and shall not affect any proceeding previously commenced.

Proceeding-s to Change the Name of a Corporation.

CODE OF CIVIL PROCEDURE.

See section 2410 as to change of name of an individual.

Petition by corporation.

§ 2411. A petition to assume another corporate name may be made by a domestic corporation, whether incorporated by a general or special law, to the supreme court at a special term thereof, held in the judicial district in which its principal business office shall be situated, or, if it be other than a stock corporation, at a special term held in the judicial district in which its certificate of incorporation is filed or recorded, or in which its principal property is situated, or in which its principal operations are or theretofore have been conducted. If it be a banking, insurance or railroad corporation, the petition must be authorized by a resolution of the directors of the corporation, and approved if a banking corporation by the superintendent of banks; if an insurance corporation, by the superintendent of insurance, and if a railroad corporation, by the board of railroad commissioners. The petition to change the name of any other corporation must have annexed thereto a certificate of the secretary of state, that the name which such corporation proposes to assume is not the name of any other domestic corporation or a name which he deems so nearly resembling it, as to be calculated to deceive.

Thus amended by chap. 366, Laws of 1893.

Contents of petition.

§ 2412. The petition must be in writing, signed by the petitioner and verified in like manner as a pleading in a court of record, and must specify the grounds of the application, the name, age and residence of the individual whose name is proposed to be changed, and the name which he proposes to assume, and if the petitioner be a corporation, its present name, and the name it proposes to assume, which must not be the name of any other corporation, or a name so nearly resembling it as to be calculated to deceive; and if it be a railroad corporation, a corporation having banking powers or the power to make loans upon pledges or deposits, or to make insurances, that the petition has been duly authorized by a resolution of the directors of the corporation and approved by the proper officer.

Thus amended by chap. 366, Laws of 1893.

Notice of presentation of petition.

§ 2413. If the petition be to change the name of an infant, and is made by the infant's next friend, notice of the time and place when and where the petition will be presented must be served upon the father, or if he is dead or cannot be found, upon the mother, or if both are dead or cannot be found, upon the general guardian or guardian of the person of the infant, in like manner as a notice of a motion upon an attorney in an action, unless it appears to the satisfaction of the court that the infant has no father or mother, or that both reside without the state or cannot be found, and that he has no guardian residing within this state, in which case the court may dispense with notice or require notice to be given to such persons and in such manner as the court thinks proper. If the petition be made by a corporation located elsewhere than in the city and county of New York, notice of the presentation thereof shall be published once in each week for three successive weeks in the state paper, and in a newspaper of every county in which such corporation shall have a business office, or if it has no business office, of the county in which its principal corporate property is situated, or in which its operations are or theretofore have been principally conducted, which newspaper, if it be a banking corporation, shall be designated by the superintendent of banks, if an insurance corporation, other than a town or county co-operative insurance corporation, by the superintendent of insurance, or if a railroad corporation, by the railroad commissioners. In the city and county of New York such notice shall be published once in each week for three successive weeks in two daily newspapers published in such county. If the petition be made by a corporation, a copy of the petition and notice of motion shall be filed with the secretary of state, and the proposed name shall thereupon be reserved for said corporation until three weeks after the date of such motion, and until three weeks after the date of any adjournment of such motion if notice of such adjournment shall be filed with the secretary of state, and no certificate of incorporation of a proposed corporation, having the same name as the name proposed in such petition, or a name so nearly resembling it as to be calculated to deceive, shall be filed in any office for the purpose of effecting its incorporation, and no corporation formed without the state of New York having the same name or a name so nearly resembling it as to be calculated to deceive shall be given authority to do business in this state.

Thus amended by chap. 89, Laws of 1906, taking effect September 1, 1906.

Order.

§ 2414. If the court to which the petition is presented is satisfied thereby, or by the affidavit and certificate presented therewith, that the petition is true, and that there is no reasonable objection to the change of name proposed, and if the petition be to change the name of an infant, that the interests of the infant will be substantially promoted by the change, and, if the petitioner be a corporation, that the petition has been duly authorized and that notice of the presentation of the petition, if required by law, has been made, the court shall make an order authorizing the petitioner to assume the name proposed on a day specified therein, not less than thirty days after the entry of the order. The order shall be directed to be entered and the papers on which it was granted, to be filed within ten days thereafter in the clerk's office of the county in which the petitioner resides, if he be an individual, or in the office of the clerk of the city court of New York if the order be made by that court, or, if the petitioner be a corporation, in the office of the clerk of the county in which its certificate of incorporation, if any, shall be filed, or if there be none filed in which its principal office shall be located, or if it has no business office, in the county in which its principal property is situated, or in which its operations are or theretofore have been principally conducted, or in the office of the clerk of the county in which the special term granting the order is held; and, if the petitioner be a corporation, that a certified copy of such order shall, within ten days after the entry thereof, be filed in the office of the secretary of state; and also, if it be a banking corporation, in the office of the superintendent of banks, or if it be an insurance corporation, in the office of the superintendent of insurance, or if it be a railroad corporation, in the office of the board of railroad commissioners. Such order shall also direct the publication, within ten days after the entry thereof of a copy thereof in a designated newspaper, in the county in which the order is directed to be entered, at least once if the petitioner be an individual, or if the petitioner be a corporation, once in each week for four succssive weeks. The county clerk, in whose office an order changing the name of a corporation is entered, shall record the same at length in the book kept in his office for recording certificates of incorporation.

Thus amended by chap. 946, Laws of 1895.

When change to take effect.

§ 2415. If the order shall be fully complied with, and within forty days after the making of the order, an affidavit of the publication thereof shall be filed and recorded in the office in which the order is entered, and in each office in which certified copies thereof are required to be filed, if any, the petitioner shall, on and after the day specified for that purpose in the order, be known by the name which is thereby authorized to be assumed, and by no other name. No proceedings heretofore had under sections two thousand four hundred and fourteen and two thousand four hundred and fifteen of the code of civil procedure for the change of the name of a corporation, shall be invalid by reason of the non-filing of an affidavit of the publication of the order changing such name within twenty days from the date thereof.

Thus amended by chap. 264, Laws of 1894.

Substitution of new name in pending action or proceeding.

§ 2416. An action or special proceeding, civil or criminal, commenced by or against a person whose name is so changed shall not abate, nor shall any relief, recovery or other proceeding therein be prevented, impeded or impaired in consequence of such change of name. The plaintiff in the action or the party instituting the special proceeding, or the people, as the case requires, may, at any time, obtain an order amending any of the papers or proceedings therein, by the substitution of the new name, without costs and without prejudice to the action or proceeding.

Thus amended by Chap. 366, Laws of 1893.

Reports by clerks to state officers.

§ 2417. The clerk of each county and of each court, shall annually, in the month of December, report to the secretary of state all changes of names of individuals or of corporations, which have been made in pursuance of orders filed in their respective offices during the past year and since the last previous report, and also report in like manner to the superintendent of banks all changes of the names of banking corporations, and to the superintendent of insurance all changes of names of corporations authorized to make insurances. The secretary of state must cause to be published, in the next volume of the session laws a tabular statement showing the original name of each person and corporation and the name which he or it has been authorized to assume.

Thus amended by Chap. 366, Laws of 1893.

THE GENERAL CORPORATION LAW.

CHAP. 563, LAWS OF 1890.

(Generally amended by Chap. 687, Laws of 1892.)

AN ACT in relation to corporations, constituting chapter thirty five of the general laws.

(As amended to and including the session of the Legislature of 1906.)

[SEE SECTIONS OF CODE OF CRIMINAL PROCEDURE AND PENAL CODE, THIS VOLUME.]

CHAPTER XXXV OF THE GENERAL LAWS.

THE GENERAL CORPORATION LAW.

Short title.

SECTION 1. This chapter shall be known as the general corporation law.

Classification of corporations.

§ 2. A corporation shall be either,

1. A municipal corporation,
2. A stock corporation,
3. A non-stock corporation, or
4. A mixed corporation.

A stock corporation shall be either,

1. A moneyed corporation,
2. A transportation corporation, or
3. A business corporation.

A non-stock corporation shall be either,

    1. A religious corporation, or

    2. A membership corporation.

A mixed corporation shall be either,

    1. A cemetery corporation,

    2. A library corporation,

    3. A co-operative corporation.

    4. A board of trade corporation, or

    5. An agricultural and horticultural corporation.

A transportation corporation shall be either,

    1. A railroad corporation, or

    2. A transportation corporation other than a railroad corporation.

A membership corporation shall include benevolent orders and fire and soldiers' monument corporations.

A reference in a general law to a class of corporations described in accordance with this classification shall include all corporations theretofore formed belonging to such class.

Definitions.

§ 3. 1· A municipal corporation includes a county, town, school district, village and city, and any other territorial division of the State established by law with powers of local government.

2. A stock corporation is a corporation having a capital stock divided into shares, and which is authorized by law to distribute to the holders thereof dividends or shares of the surplus profits of the corporation. A corporation is not a stock corporation because of having issued certificates called certificates of stock, but which are in fact merely certificates of membership and which is not authorized by law to distribute to its members any dividends or share of profits arising from the operations of the corporation.

3. The term non-stock corporation includes every corporation other than a stock corporation.

4. A moneyed corporation is a corporation formed under or subject to the banking or the insurance law.

5. A domestic corporation is a corporation incorporated by or under the laws of the State or colony of New York. Every corporation which is not a domestic corporation is a foreign corporation, except as provided by the code of civil procedure for the purpose of construing such code.

6. The term, directors, when used in relation to corporations, shall include trustees or other persons, by whatever name known, duly appointed or designated to manage the affairs of the corporation.

7. The term, certificate of incorporation, shall include articles of association or any other written instruments required by law to be filed, to effect. the incorporation of a corporation, including a certified copy of an original certificate of incorporation filed for such purpose in pursuance of law.

8. The term, member of a corporation, shall include every person having a right to vote at a meeting of the corporation for the election of directors, other than a person having a right to vote only upon a proxy.

9. The term, office of a corporation, means its principal office within the State or principal place of business within the State, if it has no principal office therein.

10. The term, business of a corporation, when used with reference to a non-stock corporation, includes the operations for the conduct of which it is incorporated.

11. The term, corporate law or laws, when used in any law forming a part of the revision of the general laws of the State of which this chapter is a part, means the general laws of this State relating to corporations included in such revision.

Thus amended by chap. 672, Laws of 1895.

Qualifications of incorporators.

§ 4. A certificate of incorporation must be executed by natural persons, who must be of full age, and at least two-thirds of them must be citizens of the United States and one of them a resident of this State. This section shall not apply to a corporation formed by the reincorporation or consolidation of existing corporations, or to the reorganization of a corporation upon the sale of the property and franchises of a previously existing corporation or otherwise.

Thus amended by chap. 672, Laws of 1895.

Filing and recording certificates of incorporation.

§ 5. Every certificate of incorporation including the corporate name or title and every amended or supplemental certificate, and every certificate which alters the provisions of any certificate of incorporation or any amended or supplemental certificate, hereafter executed shall be in the English language, and except of a religious, cemetery, moneyed, municipal or fire department corporation, shall be filed in the office of the secretary of state, and shall be by him duly recorded and indexed in books specially provided therefor, and a certified copy of such certificate or amended or supplemental certificate with a certificate of the secretary of state of such filing and record, or a duplicate original of such certificate or amended or supplemental certificate shall be filed and similarly recorded and indexed in the office of the clerk of the county in which the office of the corporation is to be located, or, if it be a non-stock corporation, and such county be not determined upon at the time of executing the certificate of incorporation, in such county clerk's office as the judge approving the certificate shall direct. All taxes required by law to be paid before or upon incorporation and the fees for filing and recording such certificate must be paid before filing. No corporation shall exercise any corporate powers or privileges until such taxes and fees have been paid.

Thus amended by chap. 285, Laws of 1902.

Corporate names.

§ 6. No certificate of incorporation of a proposed corporation having the same name as a corporation authorized to do business

under the laws of this state, or a name so nearly resembling it as
to be calculated to deceive, shall be filed or recorded in any office
for the purpose of effecting its incorporation, or of authorizing
it to do business in this state. A corporation formed by the
reincorporation, reorganization or consolidation of other corporations or upon the sale of the property or franchises of a
corporation, may have the same name as the corporation or one
of the corporations to whose franchises it has succeeded. No
corporation shall be hereafter organized under the laws of this
state, with the word trust, bank, banking, insurance, assurance,
indemnity, guarantee, guaranty, savings, investment, loan or
benefit as part of its name, except a corporation formed under
the banking law or the insurance law.

Thus amended by chap. 9, Laws of 1902.

Amended and supplemental certificates.

§ 7. If in the original or amended certificate of incorporation
of any corporation, or if in a supplemental certificate of any corporation any informality exist, or if any such certificate contain
any matter not authorized by law to be stated therein, or if the
proof or acknowledgment thereof shall be defective, the corporators or directors of the corporation may make and file an
amended certificate correcting such informality or defect or
striking out such unauthorized matter; and the certificate
amended shall be deemed to be amended accordingly as of the
date such amended certificate was filed, and upon the filing of
such an amended certificate of incorporation, the corporation
shall then for all purposes be deemed to be a corporation from
the time of filing the original certificate.

The supreme court may, upon due cause shown, and proof
made, and upon notice to the attorney-general, and to such other
persons as the court may direct, and upon such terms and conditions as it may impose, amend any certificate of incorporation
which fails to express the true object and purpose of the corporation, so as to truly set forth such object and purpose.

When an amended or supplemental certificate is filed, an entry shall be made upon the margin of the index and record of the original certificate of the date and place of record of every such amended certificate.

The amendment of a certificate under this section shall be without prejudice to any pending action or proceeding, or to any rights previously accrued.

See subdivision 13, section 2, also section 3, Railroad Law, also chap. 238, Laws 1893, *post*.

Lost or destroyed certificates.

§ 8. If either of the certificates of incorporation shall be lost or destroyed after filing, a certified copy of the other certificate may be filed in the place of the one so lost or destroyed and as of the date of its original filing, and such certified copy shall have the same force and effect as the original certificate had when filed.

Certificate and other papers as evidence.

§ 9. The certificate of incorporation of any corporation duly filed shall be presumptive evidence of its incorporation, and any amended certificate or other paper duly filed or recorded relating to the incorporation of any corporation, or its existence or management, and containing facts required or authorized by law to be stated therein, shall be presumptive evidence of the existence of such facts.

Thus amended by chap. 672, Laws of 1895.

Limitation of powers.

§ 10. No corporation shall possess or exercise any corporate powers not given by law, or not necessary to the exercise of the powers so given. The certificate of incorporation of any corporation may contain any provision for the regulation of the business and the conduct of the affairs of the corporation, and any limitation upon its powers, or upon the powers of its directors

3

and stockholders, which does not exempt them from the performance of any obligation or the performance of any duty imposed by law.

Thus amended by chap. 672, Laws of 1895.

Grant of general powers.

§ 11. Every corporation as such has power, though not specified in the law under which it is incorporated:

1. To have succession for the period specified in its certificate of incorporation or by law, and perpetually when no period is specified.

2. To have a common seal, and alter the same at pleasure.

3. To acquire by grant, gift, purchase, devise or bequest, to hold and to dispose of such property as the purposes of the corporation shall require, subject to such limitations as may be prescribed by law.

4. To appoint such officers and agents as its business shall require, and to fix their compensation, and'

5. To make by-laws, not inconsistent with any existing law, for the management of its property, the regulations of its affairs, and the transfer of its stock, if it has any, and the calling of meetings of its members. Such by-laws may also fix the amount of stock, which must be represented at meetings of the stockholders in order to constitute a quorum, unless otherwise provided by law. By-laws duly adopted at a meeting of the members of the corporation shall control the action of its directors. No by-law adopted by the board of directors regulating the election of directors or officers shall be valid unless published for at least once a week for two successive weeks in a newspaper in the county where the election is to be held, and at least thirty days before such election. Subdivisions four and five of this section shall not apply to municipal corporations.

Thus amended by chap. 672, Laws of 1895.

Enlargement of limitations upon the amount of the property of non-stock corporations.

§ 12. · If any general or special law heretofore passed, or any certificate of incorporation, shall limit the amount of property a corporation other than a stock corporation may take or hold, such corporation may take and hold property of the value of three million dollars or less, or the yearly income derived from which shall be five hundred thousand dollars or less, notwithstanding any such limitations. In computing the value of such property, no increase in value arising otherwise than from improvements made thereon shall be taken into account.

Thus amended by chap. 400, Laws of 1894.

Acquisition of additional real property.

§ 13. When any corporation, except a life insurance corporation, shall have sold or conveyed any part of its real property, the supreme court may, notwithstanding any restriction of a general or special law, authorize it to purchase and hold from time to time other real property, upon satisfactory proof that the value of the property so purchased does not exceed the value of the property so sold and conveyed within the three years next preceding the application.

Thus amended by chap. 228, Laws of 1906.

Acquisition of property without the state.

§ 14. Any·domestic corporation transacting business in other states or foreign countries may acquire and dispose of such property as shall be requisite for such corporation in the convenient transaction of its business. Any domestic corporation establishing or maintaining a charitable, philanthropic or educational institution within this state may also carry on its work and establish or maintain one or more branches of such institution or an additional institution or additional institutions in any other state, the District of Columbia or in any part of the territories or dependencies of the United States of America or in any foreign country and for either of said purposes may take by devise or bequest, hold, purchase, mortgage, sell and convey or otherwise dispose of such real and personal property without this state as may be requisite therefor. But nothing in this section contained shall be construed as exempting from taxation property to any additional amount than is now allowed to such corporation under existing laws.

Thus amended by chap. 178, Laws of 1903.

Certificate of authority of a foreign corporation.

§ 15. No foreign stock corporation other than a moneyed corporation, shall do business in this state without having first procured from the secretary of state a certificate that it has complied with all the requirements of law to authorize it to do business in this state, and that the business of the corporation to be carried on in this state is such as may be lawfully carried on by a corporation incorporated under the laws of this state for such or similar business, or if more than one kind of business, by two or more corporations so incorporated for such kinds of business respectively. The secretary of state shall deliver such certificate to every such corporation so complying with the requirements of law. No such corporation now doing business in this state shall do business herein after December thirty-first, eighteen hundred and ninety-two, without having procured such certificate from the secretary of state, but any lawful contract previously made by the corporation may be performed and enforced within the state subsequent to such date. No foreign stock corporation doing business in this state shall maintain any action in this state upon any contract made by it in this state unless prior to the making of such contract it shall have procured such certificate. This prohibition shall also apply to any assignee of such foreign stock corporation and to any person claiming under such assignee or such foreign stock corporation or under either of them. No certificate of authority shall be granted to any foreign corporation having the same name as an existing domestic corporation, or a name so nearly resembling it as to be calculated to deceive, nor to any foreign corporation, other than a moneyed or insurance corporation, with the word "trust," "bank," "banking," "insurance," "assurance," "indemnity," "guarantee," "guaranty," "savings," "investment," "loan," or "benefit," as a part of its name.

Thus amended by chap. 490, Laws of 1904, see chap. 962, Laws of 1896, *post*.

Proof to be filed before granting certificate.

§ 16. Before granting such certificate the secretary of state shall require every such foreign corporation to file in his office a sworn copy in the English language of its charter or certificate of incorporation and a statement under its corporate seal particularly setting forth the business or objects of the corporation which it is engaged in carrying on or which it proposes to carry on within the State, and a place within the State which is to be its principal place of business, and designating in the manner prescribed in the code of civil procedure a person upon whom process against the corporation may be served within the State. The person so designated must have an office or place of business at the place where such corporation is to have its principal place of business within the State. Such designation shall continue in force until revoked by an instrument in writing designating in like manner some other person upon whom process against the corporation may be served in this State. If the person so designated dies or removes from the place where the corporation has its principal place of business within the State, and the corporation does not within thirty days after such death or removal designate in like manner another person upon whom process against it may be served within the State, the secretary of state may revoke the authority of the corporation to do business within the State, and process against the corporation in an action upon any liability incurred within this State before such revocation, may, after such death or removal, and before another designation is made, be served upon the secretary of state. At the time of such service the plaintiff shall pay to the secretary of state two dollars, to be included in his taxable costs and disbursements, and the secretary of state shall forthwith mail a copy of such notice to such corporation if its address, or the address of any officer thereof, is known to him.

Thus amended by chap. 672, Laws of 1895.

Acquisition of real property in this state by certain foreign corporations.

§ 17. Any foreign corporation created under the laws of the United States, or of any state or territory thereof, and doing business in this state, may acquire such real property in this state as may be necessary for its corporate purposes in the transaction of its business in this state, and convey the same by deed or otherwise in the same manner as a domestic corporation.

Acquisition by foreign corporation of real property in this state.

§ 18. Any foreign corporation may purchase at a sale upon the forclosure of any mortgage held by it, or, upon any judgment or decree for debts due it, or, upon any settlement to secure such debts, any real property within this state covered by or subject to such mortgage, judgment, decree or settlement, and may take by devise any real property situated within this state and hold the same for not exceeding five years from the date of such purchase, or from the time when the right to the possession thereof vests in such devisee, and convey it by deed or otherwise in the same manner as a domestic corporation.

Thus amended by chap. 136, Laws of 1894.

Prohibition of banking powers.

§ 19. No corporation except a corporation formed under or subject to the banking laws, shall by any implication of construction be deemed to possess the power of carrying on the business of discounting bills, notes or other evidences of debt, of receiving deposits, or buying and selling bills of exchange, or shall issue bills, notes or other evidences of debt for circulation as money.

Thus amended by chap. 236, Laws of 1904.

Qualification of members as voters.

§ 20. Unless otherwise provided in the certificate of incorporation, every stockholder of record of a stock corporation shall be entitled at every meeting of the corporation to one vote for every share of stock standing in his name on the books of the corporation; and at every meeting of a non-stock corporation, every member, unless disqualified by the by-laws, shall be entitled to one vote. The stockholders of a stock corporation, by a by-law adopted by vote at any annual meeting, or at any special meeting duly called for such purpose, may prescribe a period, not exceeding forty days prior to meetings of the stockholders, during which no transfer of stock on the books of the corporation may be made. Except in cases of express trust, or in which other provision shall have been made by written agreement between the parties, the record holder of stock which shall be held by him as security, or which shall actually belong to another, upon demand therefor and payment of necessary expenses thereof, shall issue to such pledger or to such actual owner of such stock, a proxy to vote thereon. The certificate of incorporation of any stock corporation may provide that at all elections of directors of such corporation, each stockholder shall be entitled to as many votes as shall equal the number of his shares of stock multiplied by the number of directors to be elected, and that he may cast all of such votes for a single director or may distribute them among the number to be voted for, or any two or more of them as he may see fit, which right, when exercised, shall be termed cumulative voting. The stockholders of a corporation heretofore formed, who, by the provisions of laws existing on April thirty, eighteen hundred and ninety-one, were entitled to the exercise of such right, may hereafter exercise such right according to the provision of this section. A stockholder may, by agreement in writing, transfer his stock to any person or persons for the purpose of vesting in him or them the right to vote thereon for a time not exceeding five years upon terms and conditions stated, pursuant to which such person or persons shall act; every other stockholder, upon his request there-

for may, by a like agreement in writing also transfer his stock to
the same person or persons and thereupon may participate in the
terms, conditions and privileges of such agreement; the certificates of stock so transferred shall be surrendered and cancelled
and certificates therefor issued to such transferee or transferees
in which it shall appear that they are issued pursuant to such
agreement and in the entry of such transferee or transferees
as owners of such stock in the proper books of said corporation
that fact shall also be noted and thereupon he or they may vote
upon the stock so transferred during the time in such agreement
specified; a duplicate of every such agreement shall be filed in the
office of the corporation where its principal business is transacted
and be open to the inspection of any stockholder, daily, during
business hours. No member of a corporation shall sell his vote
or issue a proxy to vote to any person for any sum of money or
anything of value. The books and papers containing the record
of membership of the corporation shall be produced at any meeting of its members upon the request of any member. If the right
to vote at any such meeting shall be challenged, the inspectors
of election, or other persons presiding thereat, shall require such
books, if they can be had, to be produced as evidence of the right
of the person challenged to vote at such meeting, and all persons
who may appear from such books to be members of the corporation
may vote at such meeting in person or by proxy, subject to the
provisions of this chapter.

Thus amended by chap. 355, Laws of 1901.
See section 2 of the amendatory act as to its effect.

Proxies.

§ 21. Every member of a corporation, except a religious corporation, entitled to vote at any meeting thereof may so vote by
proxy.

No officer, clerk, teller or bookkeeper of a corporation formed
under or subject to the banking law shall act as proxy for any
stockholder at any meeting of any such corporation.

Every proxy must be executed in writing by the member him-self, or by his duly authorized attorney. No proxy hereafter made shall be valid after the expiration of eleven months from the date of its execution unless the member executing it shall have speci-fied therein the length of time it is to continue in force, which shall be for some limited period. Every proxy shall be revocable at the pleasure of the person executing it; but a corporation having no capital stock may prescribe in its by-laws the persons who may act as proxies for members, and the length of time for which prox-ies may be executed.

Challenges.

§ 22. Every member of a corporation offering to vote at any election or meeting of the corporation shall, if required by an in-spector of election or other officer presiding at such election or meeting, or by any other member present, take and subscribe the following oath: "I do solemnly swear that in voting at this elec-tion I have not, either directly, indirectly or impliedly received any promise or any sum of money or anything of value to influ-ence the giving of my vote or votes at this meeting or as a con-sideration therefor." Any person offering to vote as proxy for any other person shall present his proxy and, if so required, take and subscribe the following oath: " I do solemnly swear that I have not, either directly, indirectly or impliedly, given any promise or any sum of money or anything of value to induce the giving of a proxy to me to vote at this election, or received any promise or any sum of money or anything of value to influence the giving of my vote at this meeting, or as a consideration there-for." The inspectors or persons presiding at the election may administer such oath, and all such oaths and proxies shall be filed in the office of the corporation.

Thus amended by chap. 355, Laws of 1901.
See section 2 of the amendatory act as to its effect.

Effect of failure to elect directors.

§ 23. If the directors shall **not be elected on the day** designated in the by-laws, or by law, the corporation shall not for that reason be dissolved; but every director shall continue to hold his office and discharge his duties until his successor has been elected.

See section 22, Stock Corporation Law, *post.*

Mode of calling special election of directors.

§ 24. If the election has not been held on the day so designated, the directors shall forthwith call a meeting of the members of the corporation for the purpose of electing directors, of which meeting notice shall be given in the same manner as of the annual meeting for the election of directors.

If such meeting shall not be so called within one month, or, if held, shall result in a failure to elect directors, any member of the corporation may call a meeting for the purpose of electing directors by publishing a notice of the time and place of holding such meeting at least once in each week for two successive weeks immediately preceding the election, in a newspaper published in the county where the election is to be held and in such other manner as may be prescribed in the by-laws for the publication of notice of the annual meeting, and by serving upon each member, either personally or by mail, directed to him at his last known post-office address, a copy of such notice at least two weeks before the meeting.

Mode of conducting special elections of directors.

§ 25. Such meeting shall be held at the office of the corporation, or if it has none, at the place in this state where its principal business has been transacted, or if access to such office or place is denied or cannot be had, at some other place in the city, village or town where such office or place is or was located.

At such meeting the members attending shall constitute a quorum. They may elect inspectors of election and directors and adopt by-laws providing for future annual meetings and election of directors, if the corporation has no such by-laws, and transact any other business which may be transacted at an annual meeting of the members of the corporation.

Qualification of voters and canvass of votes at special elections.

§ 26. In the absence at such meeting of the books of the corporation showing who are members thereof, each person, before voting, shall present his sworn statement setting forth that he is a member of the corporation; and if a stock corporation, the number of shares of stock owned by him and standing in his name on the books of the corporation, and, if known to him, the whole number of shares of stock of the corporation outstanding. On filing such statement, he may vote as a member of the corporation; and if a stock corporation, he may vote on the shares of stock appearing in such statement to be owned by him and standing in his name on the books of the corporation.

The inspectors shall return and file such statements, with a certificate of the result of the election, verified by them, in the office of the clerk of the county in which such election is held, and the persons so elected shall be the directors of the corporation.

Powers of supreme court respecting elections.

§ 27. The supreme court shall, upon the application of any person or corporation aggrieved by or complaining of any election of any corporation, or any proceeding, act or matter touching the same, upon notice thereof to the adverse party, or to those to be affected thereby, forthwith and in a summary way, hear the affidavits, proofs and allegations of the parties, or otherwise inquire into the matters or causes of complaint, and establish the election or order a new election, or make such order and give such relief as right and justice may require.

Stay of proceedings in actions collusively brought.

§ 28. If an action is brought against a corporation by the procurement or default of its directors, or any of them, to enforce any claim or obligation declared void by law, or to which the corporation has a valid defense, and such action is in the interest or for the benefit of any director, and the corporation has by his connivance made default in such action, or consented to the validity of such claim or obligation, any member of the corporation may apply to the supreme court, upon affidavit, setting forth the facts, for a stay of proceedings in such action, and on proof of the facts in such further manner and upon such notice as the court may direct, it may stay such proceedings or set aside and vacate the same, or grant such other relief as may seem proper, and which will not injuriously affect an innocent party, who, without notice of such wrongdoing and for a valuable consideration, has acquired rights under such proceedings.

Directors.

§ 29. The affairs of every corporation shall be managed by its board of directors, at least one of whom shall be a resident of this state. Unless otherwise provided (by law) a majority of the board of directors of a corporation at a meeting duly assembled shall be necessary to constitute a quorum for the transaction of business and the act of a majority of the directors present at a meeting at which a quorum is present shall be the act of the board of directors. The members of a corporation may in by-laws fix the number of directors necessary to constitute a quorum at a number less than a majority of the board, but at least equal to one-third of its number. Subject to the by-laws, if any adopted by members of a corporation, the directors may make necessary by-laws of the corporation.

Thus amended by chap. 737, Laws of 1904.

Directors as trustees in case of dissolution.

§ 30. Upon the dissolution of any corporation, its directors, unless other persons shall be appointed by the legislature, or by some court of competent jurisdiction, shall be the trustees of its creditors, stockholders or members, and shall have full power to settle its affairs, collect and pay outstanding debts, and divide among the persons entitled thereto the money and other property remaining after payment of debts and necessary expenses.

Such trustees shall have authority to sue for and recover the debts and property of the corporation, by their name as such trustees, and shall jointly and severally be personally liable to its creditors, stockholders or members, to the extent of its property and effects that shall come into their hands.

See provisions of the Code of Civil Procedure.
See sections 57 and 61, Stock Corporation Law, chap. 310, Laws of 1886, *post.*

Forfeiture for non-user.

§ 31. If any corporation, except a railroad, turnpike, plankroad or bridge corporation, shall not organize and commence the transaction of its business or undertake the discharge of its corporate duties within two years from the date of its incorporation, its corporate powers shall cease.

Extension of corporate existence.

§ 32. Any domestic corporation at any time before the expiration thereof, may extend the term of its existence beyond the time specified in its original certificate of incorporation, or by law, or in any certificate of extension of corporate existence, by the consent of the stockholders owning two-thirds in amount of its capital stock, or if not a stock corporation, by the consent of two-thirds of its members, which consent shall be given either in writing or by vote at a special meeting of the stockholders called for that purpose, upon the same notice as that required for the annual meetings of the corporation; and a certificate under the seal of the corporation that such consent was given by the stockholders in writing, or that it was given by vote at a meeting as aforesaid, shall be subscribed and acknowledged by the president or a vice-president, and by the secretary or an assistant secretary of the corporation, and shall be filed in the office of the secretary of state, and shall by him be duly recorded and indexed in a book specially provided therefor, and a certified copy

of such certificate, with a certificate of the secretary of state
of such filing and record, or a duplicate original of such certificate, shall be filed and similarly recorded and indexed in the
office of the clerk of the county wherein the corporation has its
principal place of business, and shall be noted in the margin of
the record of the original certificates of such corporation, if any,
in such offices, and thereafter the term of the existence of such
corporation shall be extended as designated in such certificate.
If the term of existence of any domestic corporation shall have
expired and it shall be made satisfactorily to appear to the supreme court that such corporation was legally organized, pursuant to any law of this state, and that it shall have issued its
bonds payable at a date beyond the date fixed in its charter or
certificate of incorporation for the expiration of its corporate
existence, and such bonds shall be unmatured and unpaid, the
supreme court may, upon the application of any person interested
and upon such notice to such other parties as the court may
require, by order, authorize the filing and recording of a certificate reviving the existence of such corporation, upon such conditions and with such limitations as such order shall specify,
and extending such corporate existence for a term not exceeding
the term for which it was orginally incorporated. Upon filing
and recording such certificate in the same manner as certificates
of extension of corporate existence duly issued before the expiration of the existence of a domestic corporation is authorized
by law to be filed and recorded, such corporate existence shall
be revived and extended in pursuance of the terms of such order,
but such revival and extension shall not affect any litigation commenced after such expiration and pending at the time of such
revival. If a corporation formed under or subject to the banking
law, such certificate shall not be filed or recorded unless it shall
have indorsed thereon the written approval of the superintendent
of banks; or, if an insurance corporation, unless it shall have indorsed thereon the written approval of the superintendent of insurance; and, if a turnpike or bridge corporation, it shall not be
filed unless it shall have indorsed thereon or annexed thereto a

certified copy of a resolution of the board of supervisors of each county in which such turnpike or bridge is located, approving of and authorizing such extension. If all the stock of a corporation other than a corporation formed under or subject to the banking law, or an insurance corporation, or a turnpike, plank-road or bridge corporation shall be lawfully owned by another stock corporation entitled by law to take a surrender and merger thereof, the corporate existence of such corporation whose stock is so owned may be extended at any time for the term of the corporate existence of the possessor corporation, by filing in the office or offices in which the original certificate or certificates of incorporation of the first-mentioned corporation were filed a certificate of such extension executed by its president and secretary and by such corporation owning all the shares of its capital stock. Every corporation extending its corporate existence under this chapter or under any general law of the state shall thereafter be subject to the provisions of this chapter and of such general law, notwithstanding any special provisions in its charter, and shall thereafter be deemed to be incorporated under the general laws of the state relating to the incorporation of a corporation, for the purpose of carrying on the business in which it is engaged, and shall be subject to the provisions of such law. The certificate of incorporation of any corporation whose duration is limited by such certificate or by law, may require that the consent of stockholders owning a greater percentage than two-thirds of the stock, if a stock corporation, or of more than two-thirds of the members, if a non-stock corporation, shall be requisite to effect an extension of corporate existence as authorized by this section.

Thus amended by chap. 256, Laws of 1905.

Conflicting corporate laws.

§ 33. If in any corporate law there is or shall be any provision in conflict with any provisions of this chapter or of the stock corporation law, the provisions so conflicting shall prevail, and the provision of this chapter or of the stock corporation law with which it conflicts shall not apply in such a case. If in any such law there is or shall be a provision relating to a matter embraced in this chapter or in the stock corporation law, but not in conflict with it, such provision in such other law shall be deemed to be in addition to the provision in this chapter or in the stock corporation law relating to the same subject-matter, and both provisions shall, in such case, be applicable.

Laws repealed.

§ 34. Of the laws enumerated in the schedule hereto annexed, that portion specified in the last column is repealed. Such repeal shall not revive a law repealed by any law hereby repealed, but shall include all laws amendatory of the laws hereby repealed.

Saving clause.

§ 35. The repeal of a law or any part of it specified in the annexed schedule shall not affect or impair any act done, or right accruing, accrued or acquired, or liability, penalty, forfeiture or punishment incurred prior to May 1, 1891, under or by virtue of any law so repealed, but the same may be asserted, enforced, prosecuted or inflicted, as fully and to the same extent as if such law had not been repealed. All actions and proceedings, civil or criminal, commenced under or by virtue of the laws so repealed, and pending on April 30, 1891, may be prosecuted and defended to final effect in the same manner as they might under the laws then existing, unless it shall be otherwise specially provided by law.

Construction.

§ 36. The provisions of this chapter, and of the stock corporation law, the railroad law, the transporation corporations law, and the business corporations law, so far as they are substantially the same as those of laws existing on April 30, 1891, shall be construed as a continuation of such laws modified or amended according to the language employed in this chapter, or in the stock corporation law, the railroad law, the transporation corporations law, or the business corporations law, and not as new enactments.

References in laws not repealed to provisions of laws incorporated into the general laws hereinbefore enumerated and repealed, shall be construed as applying to the provisions so incorporated.

Nothing in this chapter or in the other general laws hereinbefore specified shall be construed to amend or repeal any provision of the Criminal or Penal Code or to impair any right or liability which any existing corporation, its officers, directors, stockholders or creditors may have or be subject to or which any such corporation, other than a railroad corporation, had or was subject to on April 30, 1891, by virtue of any special act of the legislature creating such corporation or creating or defining any such right or liability, unless such special act is repealed by this chapter.

Law revived.

§ 37. Chapter three hundred of the laws of eighteen hundred and fifty-five, entitled "An act to incorporate the Baptist Historical Society of the city of New York," which was inadvertently repealed by the transportation corporations law, is revived and re-enacted, and shall be of the same force and effect as if it had not been repealed.

When notice or lapse of time unnecessary.

§ 38. Whenever under the provisions of any of the corporate laws a corporation is authorized to take any action after notice to its members or after the lapse of a prescribed period of time, such action may be taken without notice and without the lapse of any period of time, if such action be authorized or approved, and such requirements be waived in writing by every member of such corporation, or by his attorney thereunto authorized.

This section added by chap. 672, Laws of 1895.

As to acts of directors.

§ 39.   Whenever, under the provisions of any of the corporate laws, a corporation is authorized to take any action by the agreement or action of its directors, managers or trustees, such agreement or action may be taken by such directors, regularly convened as a board, and acting by a majority of a quorum, except when otherwise expressly required by law or the by-laws of the corporation and any such agreement shall be executed in behalf of the corporation by such officers as shall be designated by the board of directors, managers or trustees.   At any meeting at which every member of the board of directors shall be present, though held without notice, any business may be transacted which might have been transacted if the meeting had been duly called. Except when otherwise required by law or the by-laws of the corporation, special meetings of the members of the corporation may be called in the same manner as the annual meeting thereof.

Thus amended by chap. 355, Laws of 1901.
See section 2 of the amendatory act as to its effect.

Alteration and repeal of charter.

§ 40.   The charter of every corporation shall be subject to alteration, suspension and repeal, in the discretion of the legislature.

This section added by chap. 672, Laws of 1895.

No contributions for political purposes.

. § 41.   No corporation or joint-stock association doing business in this state, except a corporation or association organized or maintained for political purposes only, shall directly or indirectly pay or use or offer, consent or agree to pay or use any money or property for or in aid of any political party, committee or organization, or for, or in aid of, any corporation, joint-stock or other association organized or maintained for political purposes, or for, or in aid of, any candidate for political office or for nomination for such office, or for any political purpose whatever, or for the reimbursement or indemnification of any person for moneys or property so used. Any officer, director, stockholder, attorney or agent of any corporation or joint-stock association which violates any of the provisions of this section, who participates in, aids, abets or advises or consents to any such violation, and any person who solicits or knowingly receives any money or property in violation of this section, shall be guilty of a misdemeanor and punishable by imprisonment in a penitentiary or county jail for not more than one year and a fine of not more than one thousand dollars. No person shall be excused from attending and testifying, or producing any books, papers or other documents before any court or magistrate, upon any investigation, proceeding or trial, for a violation of any of the provisions of this section, upon the ground or for the reason that the testimony or evidence, documentary or otherwise, required of him may tend to convict him of a crime or to subject him to a penalty or forfeiture; but no person shall be prosecuted or subjected to any penalty or forfeiture for or on account of any transaction, matter or thing concerning which he may so testify or produce evidence, documentary or otherwise, and no testimony so given or produced shall be received against him upon any criminal investigation or proceeding.

This section added by chap. 239, Laws of 1906.

SCHEDULE OF LAWS REPEALED.

Revised Statutes...........Part I, chapter 18............All

LAWS OF	CHAPTER	SECTIONS
1811..................	67..................	All.
1815..................	47..................	All.
1815..................	202..................	All.
1816..................	58..................	All.
1817..................	223..................	All.
1818..................	67..................	All.
1819..................	102..................	All.
1821..................	14..................	All.

LAWS OF	CHAPTER	SECTIONS
1822	213	All.
1836	284	All.
1836	316	All.
1838	160	All.
1838	161	All.
1838	262	All.
1839	218	All.
1842	165	All.
1846	155	All.
1846	215	17, 18.
1847	100	3, 4.
1847	210	All.
1847	222	All.
1847	270	All.
1847	272	All.
1847	287	All.
1847	398	All.
1847	404	All.
1847	405	All.
1848	37	All.
1848	40	All.
1848	45	All.
1848	259	All.
1848	265	All.
1848	360	All.
1849	250	All.
1849	362	All.
1850	71	All.
1850	140	All.
1851	14	All.
1851	19	All.
1851	98	All.
1851	107	All.
1851	487	All.
1851	497	All.

LAWS OF	CHAPTER	SECTIONS
1852	228	All.
1852	372	All.
1853	53	All.
1853	117	All.
1853	124	All.
1853	135	All.
1853	245	All.
1853	333	All.
1853	471	1, 2, 4.
1853	481	All.
1853	502	All.
1853	626	All.
1854	3	All.
1854	87	All.
1854	140	All.
1854	201	All.
1854	232	All.
1854	269	All.
1854	282	All.
1854	312	All.
1855	301	All.
1855	302	All.
1855	390	All.
1855	478	All.
1855	485	All.
1855	495	All.
1855	546	All.
1855	559	All.
1856	65	All.
1857	29	All.
1857	83	All.
1857	185	All.
1857	202	All.
1857	262	All.
1857	444	All.

LAWS OF	CHAPTER	SECTIONS
1857	546	All.
1857	558	All.
1857	643	All.
1857	776	All.
1858	10	All.
1858	125	All.
1859	209	All.
1859	311	All.
1859	455	All.
1860	116	All.
1860	269	All.
1860	523	All.
1861	149	All.
1861	170	All.
1861	215	All.
1861	238	All.
1862	205	All.
1862	248	All.
1862	425	All.
1862	438	All.
1862	449	All.
1862	472	All.
1863	63	All.
1863	134	All.
1863	346	All.
1864	85	All.
1864	337	All.
1864	517	All.
1864	582	All.
1865	234	All.
1865	246	All.
1865	307	All.
1865	691	All.
1865	780	All.
1866	73	All.

LAWS OF	CHAPTER	SECTIONS
1866	259	All.
1866	322	All.
1866	371	All.
1866	697	All.
1866	780	All.
1866	799	All.
1866	838	*All.
1867	12	All.
1867	49	All.
1867	248	All.
1867	254	All.
1867	419	All.
1867	480	All.
1867	509	All.
1867	775	All.
1867	906	All.
1867	937	All.
1867	960	All.
1867	974	All.
1868	253	All.
1868	290	All.
1868	573	All.
1868	781	All.
1869	234	All.
1869	237	All.
1869	605	All.
1869	706	All.
1869	844	All.
1869	917	All.
1870	124	All.
1870	135	All.
1870	322	All.
1870	443	All.
1870	568	All.

Laws of	Chapter	Sections
1870	773	All.
1871	95	All.
1871	481	All.
1871	535	All.
1871	560	All.
1871	657	All.
1871	669	All.
1871	697	All.
1871	883	All.
1872	81	All.
1872	128	All.
1872	146	All.
1872	248	All.
1872	283	All.
1872	350	All.
1872	374	All.
1872	426	All.
1872	609	All.
1872	611	All.
1872	779	All.
1872	780	All.
1872	820	All except 20.
1872	829	All.
1872	843	All.
1873	151	All.
1873	352	All.
1873	432	All.
1873	440	All.
1873	469	All.
1873	616	All.
1873	710	All.
1873	737	All.
1873	814	All.
1874	76	All.

LAWS OF	CHAPTER	SECTIONS
1874	143	All.
1874	149	All.
1874	240	All.
1874	288	All.
1874	430	All.
1875	4	All.
1875	58	All.
1875	88	All.
1875	108	All.
1875	113	All.
1875	119	All.
1875	120	All.
1875	159	All.
1875	193	All.
1875	256	All.
1875	319	All.
1875	365	All.
1875	445	All.
1875	510	All.
1875	586	All.
1875	598	All.
1875	606	All.
1875	611	All.
1876	77	All.
1876	135	All.
1876	198	All.
1876	280	All.
1876	358	All.
1876	373	All.
1876	415	All.
1876	435	All.
1876	446	All.
1877	103	All.
1877	158	All.

LAWS OF	CHAPTER	SECTIONS
1877	164	All.
1877	171	All.
1877	224	All.
1877	266	All.
1877	374	All.
1878	61	All.
1878	121	All.
1878	163	All.
1878	203	All.
1878	210	All.
1878	261	All.
1878	264	All.
1878	316	All.
1878	334	All.
1878	394	All.
1879	214	All.
1879	253	All.
1879	290	All.
1879	293	All.
1879	350	All.
1879	377	All.
1879	393	All.
1879	395	All.
1879	413	All.
1879	415	All.
1879	441	All.
1879	503	All.
1879	505	All.
1879	512	All.
1879	541	All.
1880	5	All.
1880	85	All.
1880	90	All.
1880	94	All.
1880	113	All.

LAWS OF	CHAPTER	SECTIONS
1880	133	All.
1880	155	All.
1880	182	All.
1880	187	All.
1880	223	All.
1880	225	All.
1880	241	All.
1880	254	All.
1880	263	All.
1880	267	All.
1880	349	All.
1880	415	All.
1880	417	All.
1880	484	All.
1880	510	All.
1880	575	All.
1880	582	All.
1880	583	All.
1880	585	All.
1881	22	All.
1881	58	All.
1881	77	All.
1881	117	All.
1881	148	All.
1881	213	All.
1881	232	All.
1881	295	All.
1881	296	All.
1881	311	All.
1881	313	All.
1881	321	All.
1881	337	All.
1881	338	All.
1881	351	All.
1881	399	All.

LAWS OF	CHAPTER	SECTIONS
1881	422	All.
1881	464	All.
1881	468	All.
1881	470	All.
1881	472	All.
1881	485	All.
1881	551	All.
1881	589	All.
1881	649	All.
1881	650	All.
1881	674	All.
1881	685	All.
1882	73	All.
1882	82	All.
1882	140	All.
1882	273	All.
1882	289	All.
1882	290	All.
1882	306	All..
1882	309	All.
1882	349	All.
1882	353	All.
1882	393	All.
1882	405	All.
1883	46	All.
1883	71	All.
1883	102	All.
1883	216	All.
1883	232	All.
1883	237	All.
1883	238	All.
1883	240	All.
1883	287	All.
1883	323	All.
1883	361	All.

LAWS OF	CHAPTER	SECTIONS
1883	381	All.
1883	382	All.
1883	384	All.
1883	386	All.
1883	387	All.
1883	388	All.
1883	409	All.
1883	482	All.
1883	483	All.
1883	497	All.
1884	140	All.
1884	193	All.
1884	208	All.
1884	223	All.
1884	252	All.
1884	267	All.
1884	367	All.
1884	386	All.
1884	397	All.
1884	421	All.
1884	422	All.
1884	439	All.
1884	441	All.
1884	444	All.
1885	84	All.
1885	127	All.
1885	141	All.
1885	153	All.
1885	171	All.
1885	305	All.
1885	369	All.
1885	422	All.
1885	423	All.
1885	489	All.
1885	498	All.

LAWS OF	CHAPTER	SECTIONS
1885	535	All.
1885	540	All.
1885	549	All.
1886	65	All.
1886	182	All.
1886	271	All.
1886	321	All.
1886	322	All.
1886	403	All.
1886	415	All.
1886	509	All.
1886	551	All.
1886	579	All.
1886	586	All.
1886	592	All.
1886	601	All.
1886	605	All.
1886	634	All.
1886	642	All.
1887	450	All.
1887	486	All.
1887	536	All.
1887	570	All.
1887	616	All.
1887	622	All.
1887	724	All.
1888	189	All.
1888	306	All.
1888	313	All.
1888	359	All.
1888	394	All.
1888	447	All.
1888	462	All.
1888	513	All.
1888	514	All.

LAWS OF	CHAPTER	SECTIONS
1888	549	All.
1888	560	All.
1889	57	All.
1889	76	All.
1889.	78	All.
1889	236	All.
1889	242	All.
1889	281	All.
1889	332	All.
1889	369	All.
1889	426	All.
1889	519	All.
1889	524	All.
1889	531	All.
1889	532	All.
1889	564	All.
1890	23	All.
1890	98	All.
1890	119	All.
1890	193	All.
1890	292	All.
1890	416	All.
1890	421	All.
1890	483	All.
1890	497	All.
1890	505	All.
1890	508	All.
1890	543	All.
1891	57	All.
1891	287	All.
1892	2	**All.**

THE STOCK CORPORATION LAW.

CHAP. 564, LAWS OF 1890.

(Generally amended by Chap. 688, Laws of 1892.)

AN ACT in relation to stock corporations, constituting chapter thirty-six of the general laws.

(As amended to and including the session of the Legislature of 1906.)

[SEE SECTIONS OF CODE OF CRIMINAL PROCEDURE AND PENAL CODE, THIS VOLUME.]

CHAPTER XXXVI OF THE GENERAL LAWS.

ARTICLE I.

GENERAL POWERS; REORGANIZATION.

Short title and application of chapter.

SECTION 1. This chapter shall be known as the stock corporation law, but article one shall not apply to monied corporations.

Power to borrow money and mortgage property.

§ 2. In addition to the powers conferred by the general corporation law, every stock corporation shall have the power to borrow money and contract debts, when necessary for the transaction of its business, or for the exercise of its corporate rights, privileges or franchises, or for any other lawful purpose of its incorporation; and it may issue and dispose of its obligations for any amount so borrowed, and may mortgage its property and franchises to secure the payment of such obligations, or of any debt contracted for said purposes. Every such mortgage, except purchase money mortgages and mortgages authorized by contracts made prior to May first, eighteen hundred and ninety-one, shall be consented to by the holders of not less than two-thirds of the capital stock of the corporation, which consent shall be given either in writing or by vote at a special meeting of the stockholders called for that purpose, upon the same notice as that required for the annual meetings of the corporation; and a certificate under the seal of the corporation that such consent was given by the stockholders in writing, or that it was given by vote at a meeting as aforesaid, shall be subscribed and acknowledged by the president or a vice-president and by the secretary or an assistant secretary, of the corporation, and shall be filed and recorded in the office of the clerk or register of the county wherein the corporation has its principal place of business. When authorized by like consent, the directors under such regulations as they may adopt, may confer on the holder of any debt or obligation whether secured, or unsecured, evidenced by bonds of the corporation the right to convert the principal thereof, after two and not more than twelve years from the date of such bonds into stock of the corporation; and if the capital stock shall not be sufficient to meet the conversion when made, the directors shall from time to time, authorize an increase of capital stock sufficient for that purpose by causing to be filed in the office of the secretary of state, and a duplicate thereof in the office of the clerk of the county where the principal place of business of the corporation shall be located, a certificate under the seal of the corporation, subscribed and acknowledged by the president and secretary of the corporation setting forth,

1. A copy of such mortgage; or resolution of directors authorizing the issue of such bonds.

2. That the holders of not less than two-thirds of the capital stock of the corporation duly consented to the execution of such

5

mortgage or resolution of directors authorizing the issue of such bonds by such corporation;

3. A copy of the resolution of the directors of the corporation authorizing the increase of the capital stock of the corporation necessary for the purpose of such conversion;

4. The amount of capital theretofore authorized, the proportion thereof actually issued and the amount of the increased capital stock;

If the corporation be a railroad corporation the certificate shall have endorsed thereon the approval of the board of railroad commissioners. When the certificate herein provided for has been filed, the capital stock of such corporation shall be increased to the amount specified in such certificate.

Thus amended by chap. 745, Laws of 1905.

See sections 8, 44, 45, 46, Stock Corporation Law, subdivision 10, section 4, Railroad Law, *post.*

Reorganization upon sale of corporate property and franchises.

§ 3.   When the property and franchises of any domestic stock corporation shall be sold by virtue of a mortgage or deed of trust, duly executed by it, or pursuant to the judgment or decree of a court of competent jurisdiction, or by virtue of any execution issued thereon, and the purchaser, his assignee or grantee shall have acquired title to the same in the manner prescribed by law, he may associate with him any number of persons, not less than the number required by law for an incorporation for similar purposes at least two-thirds of whom shall be citizens of the United States and one shall be a resident of this state, and they may become a corporation and take and possess the property and franchises thus sold, and which were at the time of the sale possessed by the corporation whose property shall have been so sold, upon making and acknowledging and filing in the offices where certificates of incorporation are required by law to be filed, a certificate in which they shall describe by name and reference to the law under which it was organized, the corporation whose property and franchises they have acquired and the court by whose authority the sale had been made, with the date of the judgment or decree authorizing or directing the same, and a brief description of the property sold, and also the following particulars:

1. The name of the new corporation intended to be formed by the filing of such certificate; and the place where its principal office is to be located.

2. The maximum amount of its capital stock and the number of shares into which it is to be divided, specifying the classes thereof, whether common or preferred, and the amount of, and rights pertaining to, each class.

Thus amended by chap. 80, Laws of 1902.

3. The number of directors, not less nor more than the number required by law for the old corporation, who shall manage the affairs of the new corporation, and the names and post-office address of the directors for the first year. They may insert in such certificate any provisions relating to the new corporation, or its management, contained in any plan or agreement which may have been entered into as provided in section four of this chapter. Such corporation shall be vested with, and be entitled to exercise and enjoy, all the rights, privileges and franchises, which at the time of such sale belonged to, or were vested in the corporation, last owning the property sold, or its receiver, and shall be subject to all the provisions, duties and liabilities imposed by law on that corporation. Any proceedings heretofore taken in substantial compliance with this section. as hereby amended, and any and all incorporations based thereon are hereby ratiffed and confirmed.

Subdivision 3 thus amended by chap. 706, Laws of 1904.

Contents of plan or agreement.

§ 4. At or previous to the sale the purchasers thereat, or the person for whom the purchase is to be made, may enter into a plan or agreement, for or in anticipation of the readjustment of the respective interests therein of any creditors, mortgagees and stockholders, or any of them, of the corporation owning such property and franchises at the time of sale, and for the representation of such interests in the bonds or stock of the new corporation to be formed, and may therein regulate voting by the holders of the preferred and common stock at any meeting of the stockholders, and may provide for, and regulate voting by the holders, and owners of any or all of the bonds of the corporation, foreclosed, or of the bonds issued or to be issued by the new corporation; and such right of voting by bondholders shall be exercised in such manner, for such period, and upon such conditions, as shall be therein described. Such plan or agreement must not be inconsistent with the laws of the state and shall be binding upon the corporation, until changed as therein provided, or as otherwise provided by law. The new corporation when duly organized, pursuant to such plan or agreement and to the provisions of law, may issue its bonds and stock in conformity with the provisions of such plan or agreement, and may at any time within six months after its organization, compromise, settle or assume the payment of any debt, claim or liability of the former corporation upon such terms as may be lawfully approved by a majority of the agents or trustees intrusted with the carrying out of the plan or agreement of reorganization, and may establish preferences in favor of any portion of its capital stock and may divide its stock into classes; but the capital stock of the new corporation shall not exceed in the aggregate, the maximum amount of stock mentioned in the certificate of incorporation.

Thus amended by chap. 354, Laws of 1901.
See section 5 of the amendatory act as to its effect.

Sale of property; possession of receiver and suits against him.

§ 5. The supreme court may direct a sale of the whole of the property, rights and franchises covered by the mortgage or mortgages, or deeds of trust foreclosed at any one time and place to be named in the judgment or order, either in case of the nonpayment of interest only, or of both the principal and interest due and unpaid and secured by any such mortgage or mortgages or deeds of trust. Neither the sale nor the formation of the new corporation shall interfere with the authority or possession of any receiver of such property and francises, but he shall remain liable to be removed or discharged at such time as the court may deem proper. No suit or proceeding shall be commenced against such receiver unless founded on willful misconduct or fraud in his trust after the expiration of sixty days from the time of his discharge; but after the expiration of sixty days the new corporation shall be liable in any action that may be commenced against it, and founded on any act or omission of such receiver for which he may not be sued, and to the same extent as the receiver, but for this section would be or remain liable, or to the same extent that the new corporation would be had it done or omitted the acts complained of.

See chap. 378, Laws 1883, chap. 285, Laws 1884, chap. 310, Laws 1886, chap. 522, Laws 1898, chap. 534, Laws 1898, chap. 404, Laws 1902, section 76 Railroad Law, and section 8, Labor Law, *post*.

Municipalities may assent to plan of readjustment.

§ 6. The commissioners, corporate authorities or proper officers of any city, town or village, who may hold stock in any corporation, the property and franchises whereof, shall be liable to be sold, may assent to any plan or agreement of reorganization which lawfully provides for the formation of a new corporation, and the issue of stock therein to the proper authorities or officers of such cities, towns or villages in exchange for the stock of the old or former corporation by them respectively held. And such commissioners, corporate authorities or other proper officers may assign, transfer or surrender the stock so held by them in the manner required by such plan, and accept in lieu thereof the stock issued by such new corporation in conformity therewith.

Thus amended by chap. 354, Laws of 1901.
See section 5 of the amendatory act as to its effect.
See town bonding acts, *post*.

Combinations abolished.

§ 7. No domestic stock corporation and no foreign corporation doing business in this state shall combine with any other corporation or person for the creation of a monopoly or the unlawful restraint of trade or for the prevention of competition in any necessary of life.

Thus amended by chap. 384, Laws of 1897.
See chap. 962, Laws 1896, and chap. 690, Laws 1899, *post*.

As to proper authorization of mortgages.

§ 8. Whenever any mortgage affecting property or franchises within this state heretofore or hereafter executed by authority of the board of directors in behalf of any stock corporation, domestic or foreign, of any description, recites or represents in substance or effect that the execution of such mortgage has been duly consented to, or authorized by stockholders, such recital or representation in any such mortgage, after public record thereof within this state, shall be presumptive evidence that the execution of such mortgage has been duly and sufficiently consented to, and authorized by stockholders as required by any provision of law. After any such mortgage heretofore or hereafter shall have been publicly recorded for more than one year in one or more of the counties of this state containing the mortgaged premises or any part thereof, and the corporation shall have received value for bonds actually issued under and secured by such mortgage, and interest shall have been paid on any of such bonds according to the terms thereof, such recital or representation of such mortgage so recorded shall be conclusive evidence that the execution of such mortgage has been duly and sufficiently consented to, and authorized by stockholders as required by any provision of law, and its validity shall not be impaired by reason of any defect or insufficiency of consent or authority of stockholders or in filing or recording such consent or authority, and such mortgage shall be valid and binding upon the corporation, and those claiming under it, as security for all valid bonds issued or to be issued thereunder, unless such mortgage shall be adjudged invalid in an action begun as hereinafter, in this section, provided. Notwithstanding the foregoing provisions of this section, the invalidity of any such mortgage heretofore recorded because of insufficiency of consent by stockholders may be adjudged in any action for such purpose begun before the first day of April, nineteen hundred and two, and the invalidity of any such mortgage hereafter recorded, because of insufficiency of consent by stockholders, may be adjudged ·in any action for such purpose begun, within one year after the earliest record of such mortgage in any county in this state, provided in either case that such action shall have been so begun by or in behalf of the corporation by direction of the board of directors acting in their own discretion, or upon the written request of the holders of not less than one-third of the capital stock of the corporation; and in any such action so begun by or in behalf of the corporation, the recitals or representations of the mortgage shall be presumptive evidence only as first above provided. Whenever hereafter, in compliance with any law of this state, the officers of any corporation shall have made and filed and recorded a certificate that the execution of a mortgage hereafter made by the corporation has been duly consented to by stockholders, such certificate shall be conclusive evidence as to the truth thereof, in favor of any and all persons who in good faith shall receive or purchase, for value, any bond or obligation purporting to be secured by such mortgage, at any time when said certificate shall remain of record and uncancelled. Nothing in this section contained shall affect any right or any remedy in respect of any such right of any creditor accrued before this enactment nor shall it dispense with the necessity of obtaining the consent of the board of railroad commissioners to any mortgage by a railroad corporation.

Added by chap. 354, Laws of 1901.
See section 5, said chapter.

ARTICLE II.

DIRECTORS AND OFFICERS; THEIR ELECTION, DUTIES AND LIABILITIES.

Directors.

§ 20. The directors of every stock corporation shall be chosen at the time and place fixed by the by-laws of the corporation by a plurality of the votes at such election. Each director shall be a stockholder unless otherwise provided in the certificate, or in a by-law adopted by a stockholders' meeting. Vacancies in the board of directors shall be filled in the manner prescribed in the by-laws. Notice of the time and place of holding any election of directors shall be given by publication thereof, at least once in each week for two successive weeks immediately preceding such election, in a newspaper published in the county where such election is to be held, and in such other manner as may be prescribed in the by-laws. Policyholders of an insurance corporation shall be eligible to election as directors, whether or not they be stockholders. At least one-fourth in number of the directors of every stock corporation shall be elected annually.

Thus amended by chap. 238, Laws of 1906.
See chap. 317, Laws of 1881, *post*.

Change of number of directors.

§ 21. The number of directors of any stock corporation may be increased or reduced, but not below the minimum number prescribed by law, when the stockholders owning a majority of the stock of the corporation shall so determine, at a meeting to be held at the usual place of meeting of the directors, on two weeks' notice in writing to each stockholder of record. Such notice shall be served personally or by mail, directed to each stockholder at his last known post-office address. Proof of the service of such notice shall be filed in the office of the corporation at or before the time of such meeting. The proceedings of such meeting shall be entered in the minutes of the corporation and a transcript thereof verified by the president and secretary of the meeting shall be filed in the offices where the original certificates of incorporation were filed. Such increase or reduction may also be effected by unanimous consent without a meeting, in which case there shall be filed in the offices herein specified, the unanimous consent of the stockholders in writing, signed by them, or their duly authorized proxies, but no such consent shall be valid unless there is annexed thereto an affidavit of the custodian of the stock book of such corporation stating that the persons who have signed such consent, either in person or by proxy, are the holders of record of the entire capital stock of said corporation issued and outstanding. If a corporation formed under or subject to the banking law, the consent of the superintendent of banks, and if an insurance corporation, the consent of the superintendent of insurance, shall be first obtained to such increase or reduction of the number of directors. This section shall apply to any stock corporation whether organized under a general or special law, and the number of directors may be increased as hereby provided notwithstanding the maximum number of directors now prescribed by law. If the number of directors be increased, the additional directors authorized by such increase shall be elected by the votes of a majority of the directors in office at the time of the increase. If the original or an amended certificate of incorporation of the corporation shall provide that the directors shall be divided into two or more classes, whose terms of office shall respectively expire at different times, the additional directors shall be divided among such classes as nearly as practicable in proportion to the respective numbers of directors constituting each class prior to such increase.

Thus amended by chap. 750, Laws of 1905.

When acts of directors void.

§ 22. When the directors of any corporation for the first year of its corporate existence shall hold over and continue to be directors after the first year, because of their neglect or refusal to adopt the by-laws required to enable the stockholders to hold the

annual election for directors, all their acts and proceedings while
so holding over, done for and in the name of the corporation, de-
signed to charge upon it any liability or obligation for the ser-
‘vices of any such director, or any officer, or attorney or counsel
appointed by them, and every such liability or obligation shall be
held to be fraudulent and void.

See section 23 of General Corporation Law, *ante*.

Liability of directors for making unauthorized dividends.

§. 23. The directors of a stock corporation shall not make dividends, except from the surplus profits arising from the business
of such corporation, nor divide, withdraw or in any way pay to
the stockholders or any of them, any part of the capital of such
corporation, or reduce its capital stock, except as authorized by
law. In case of any violation of the provisions of this section,
the directors under whose administration the same may have happened, except those who may have caused their dissent therefrom
to be entered at large upon the minutes of such directors at the
time, or were not present when the same happened, shall jointly
and severally be liable to such corporation and to the creditors
thereof to the full amount of any loss sustained by such corporation or its creditors respectively by reason of such withdrawal,
division or reduction. But this section shall not prevent a division
and distribution of the assets of any such corporation remaining
after the payment of all its debts and liabilities upon the dissolution of such corporation or the expiration of its charter; nor
shall it prevent a corporation from accepting shares of its capital
stock in complete or partial settlement of a debt owing to the corporation, which by the board of directors shall be deemed to be
bad or doubtful.

Thus amended by chap. 354, Laws of 1901.
See section 5 of the amendatory act as to its effect.

Section 24 repealed by chap. 354, Laws of 1901.

Liability of directors for loans to stockholders.

§ 25. No loan of moneys shall be made by any stock corporation, except a monied corporation, or by any officer thereof

out of its funds to any stockholder therein, nor shall any such corporation or officer discount any note or other evidence of debt, or receive the same in payment of any installment or any part thereof due or to become due on any stock in such corporation, or receive or discount any note, or other evidence of debt, to enable any stockholder to withdraw any part of the money paid in by him on his stock. In case of the violation of any provision of this section, the officers or directors making such loan, or assenting thereto, or receiving or discounting such notes or other evidences of debt, shall, jointly and severally, be personally liable to the extent of such loan and interest, for all the debts of the corporation contracted before the repayment of the sum loaned, and to the full amount of the notes or other evidences of debt so received or discounted, with interest from the time such liability accrued.

See sections of Penal Code as to certain penalties, *post.*

Transfers of stock by stockholder indebted to corporation.

§ 26. If a stockholder shall be indebted to the corporation, the directors may refuse to consent to a transfer of his stock until such indebtedness is paid, provided a copy of this section is written or printed upon the certificate of stock.

Officers.

§ 27. The directors of a stock corporation may appoint from their number a president. and may appoint a secretary, treasurer, and other officers, agents and employes, who shall respectively have such powers and perform such duties in the management of the property and affairs of the corporation, subject to the control of the directors, as may be prescribed by them or in the by-laws. The directors may require any such officer, agent or employe to give security for the faithful performance of his duties, and may remove him at pleasure. The policy holders of an insurance corporation shall be eligible to election or appointment as its officers.

Inspectors and their oath.

§ 28. The inspectors of election of every stock corporation shall be appointed in the manner prescribed in the by-laws, but the inspectors of the first election of directors and of all previous meetings of the stockholders shall be appointed by the board of directors named in the certificate of incorporation. No director or officer of a monied corporation shall be eligible to election or appointment as inspector. Each inspector shall be entitled to a reasonable compensation for his services, to be paid by the corporation, and if any inspector shall refuse to serve, or neglect to attend at the election, or his office become vacant, the meeting may appoint an inspector in his place unless the by-laws otherwise provide. The inspectors appointed to act at any meeting of the stockholders shall, before entering upon the discharge of their duties, be sworn to faithfully execute the duties of inspector at such meeting with strict impartiality, and according to the best of their ability, and the oath so taken shall be subscribed by them, and immediately filed in the office of the clerk of the county in which such election or meeting shall be held, with a certificate of the result of the vote taken thereat.

Books to be kept.

§ 29. Every stock corporation shall keep at its office, correct books of account of all its business and transactions, and a book to be known as the stock-book, containing the names, alphabetically arranged, of all persons who are stockholders of the corporation, showing their places of residence, the number of shares of stock held by them respectively, the time when they respectively became the owners thereof, and the amount paid thereon. The stock-book of every such corporation shall be open daily, during at least three business hours for the inspection of its stockholders and judgment creditors, who may make extracts therefrom. No transfer of stock shall be valid as against the corporation, its stockholders and creditors for any purpose except to render the transferee liable for the debts of the corporation to the extent provided for in this chapter, until it shall have been entered in such book as required by this section, by an entry showing from and to whom transferred. The stock book of every such corporation and the books of account of every bank shall be presumptive evidence of the facts therein so stated, in favor of the plaintiff, in any action or proceeding against such corporation or any of its officers, directors or stockholders. Every corporation that shall neglect or refuse to keep or cause to be kept such books, or to keep any book open for inspection as herein required, shall forfeit to the people the sum of fifty dollars for every day it shall so neglect or refuse. If any officer or agent of any such corporation shall wilfully neglect or refuse to make any proper entry in such book or books, or shall neglect or refuse to exhibit the same, or to allow them to be inspected and extracts taken therefrom as provided in this section, the corporation and such officer or agent shall each forfeit and pay to the party injured a penalty of fifty dollars for every such neglect or refusal, and all damages resulting to him therefrom.

Thus amended by chap. 354, Laws of 1901.
See section 5 of the amendatory act as to its effect.
See 106 App. Div. 349.

Annual report to secretary of state.

§ 30. Every domestic stock corporation and every foreign stock corporation doing business within this state, except moneyed and railroad corporations, shall annually during the month of January, or, if doing business without the United States, before the first day of May, may make a report as of the first day of January, which will state:

1. The amount of its capital stock and the proportion actually issued.

2. The amount of its debts or an amount which they do not exceed.

3. The amount of its assets or an amount which its assets at least equal.

4. The names and addresses of all the directors and officers of

the company, and in the case of a foreign corporation. the name
also of the person designated in the manner prescribed by the code
of civil procedure, as a person upon whom process against the
corporation may be served within this state.

Such report shall be made by the president or a vice-president
or the treasurer or a secretary of the corporation and shall be
filed in the office of the secretary of state. If such report be not
so made and filed, any such officer who shall thereafter neglect
or refuse to make and to file such report, within ten days after
written request so to do shall have been made by a creditor or
by a stockholder of the corporation, shall forfeit to the people
the sum of fifty dollars for every day he shall so neglect or
refuse.

Thus amended by chap. 415, Laws of 1905, taking effect September 1, 1905.
See chap. 690, Laws of 1899, *post*.

Liability of officers for false certificates, reports or public notices.

§ 31. If any certificate or report made or public notice given
by the officers or directors of a stock corporation shall be false
in any material representation, the officers and directors signing
the same shall jointly and severally be personally liable to any
person who has become a creditor or stockholder of the corporation upon the faith of any such certificate, report, notice or
any material representation therein to the amount of the debt
contracted upon the faith thereof if not paid when due, or of
the damage sustained by any purchaser of or subscriber to its
stock upon the faith thereof. The liability imposed by this section
shall exist in all cases where the contents of any such certificate, report or notice or of any material representation therein
shall have been communicated either directly or indirectly to
the person so becoming a creditor or stockholder and he became
such creditor or stockholder upon the faith thereof. No action
can be maintained for a cause of action created by this section
unless brought within two years from the time the certificate,
report or public notice shall have been made or given by the
officers or directors of such corporation.

Alterations or extension of business.

§ 32. Any stock corporation heretofore or hereafter organized under any general or special law of this state may alter its certificate of incorporation so as to include therein any purposes, powers or provisions which at the time of such alteration may apply to corporations engaged in a business of the same general character, or which might be included in the certificates of incorporation of a corporation organized under any general law of this state for a business of the same general character, by filing in the manner provided for the original certificate of incorporation an amended certificate, executed by the president and secretary, stating the alteration proposed, and that the same has been duly authorized by a vote of a majority of the directors and also by vote of stockholders representing at least three-fifths of the capital stock, at a meeting of the stockholders called for the purpose in the manner provided in section forty-five of this chapter, and a copy of the proceedings of such meeting, verified by the affidavit of one of the directors present thereat, shall be filed with such amended certificate.

Thus amended by chap. 751, Laws of 1905.

Sale of franchise and property.

§ 33. A stock corporation, except a railroad corporation and except as otherwise provided by law, with the consent of two-thirds of its stock, may sell and convey its property, rights, privileges and franchises, or any interest therein or any part thereof to a domestic corporation, engaged in a business of the same general character, or which might be included in the certificate of incorporation of a corporation organizing under any general law of this state for a business of the same general character, and a domestic corporation the principal business of which is carried on in, and the principal tangible property of which is located within a state adjoining the state of New York, may with the consent of the holders of ninety-five per centum of its capital stock, sell and convey its property situate without the state of New York, not including its franchises to a corporation organized under the laws of such adjoining state, and such sale and conveyance shall, in case of a sale to a domestic corporation, vest the rights, property and franchises thereby transferred, and in case of a sale to a foreign corporation the property sold in the corporation to which they are conveyed for the term of its corporate existence, subject to the provisions and restrictions applicable to the corporation conveying them. Before such sale or conveyance shall be made such consent shall be obtained at a meeting of the stockholders called upon like notice as that required for an annual meeting. If any stockholder not voting in favor of such proposed sale or conveyance shall at such meeting, or within twenty days thereafter object to such sale, and demand payment for his stock, he may, within sixty days after such meeting, apply to the supreme court at any special term thereof held in the district in which the principal place of business of such corporation is situated, upon eight days' notice to the corporation, for the appointment of three persons to appraise the value of such stock, and the court shall appoint three such appraisers, and designate the time and place of their proceedings as shall be deemed proper, and also direct the manner in which payment for such stock shall be made to such stockholders. The court may fill any vacancy in the board of appraisers occurring by refusal or neglect to serve or otherwise. The appraisers shall meet at the time and place designated, and they or any two of them, after being duly sworn honestly and faithfully to discharge their duties, shall estimate and certify the value of such stock at the time of such dissent, and deliver one copy to such corporation, and another to such stockholder, if demanded; the charges and expenses of the appraisers shall be paid by the corporation. When the corporation shall have paid the amount of such appraisal, as directed by the court, such stockholders shall cease to have any interest in such stock and in the corporate property of such corporation and such stock may be held or disposed of by such corporation.

Thus amended by chap. 130, Laws of 1901.

Not to affect any action or proceeding commenced before chapter 130 became a law.

As to liability of directors or officers to creditors.

§ 34. No director or officer of any stock corporation shall be liable to any creditor of the corporation, because of the creation of any excessive indebtedness, or because of any failure to make or to file an annual report, whether heretofore or hereafter occurring;

(1) In case of any debt, as to which personal liability of directors or officers may be or shall have been waived by such creditor, or by anyone under whom he claims; or by any provision of any instrument creating or securing such debt: or

(2) Unless within three years after the occurrence of the act or the default in respect of which it shall be sought to charge the director or officer, such creditor shall have served upon such director or officer written notice of his intention to hold him personally liable for his claim; provided, nevertheless, that any such liability, because of any such default now existing and not waived as above provided, may be enforced by action begun at any time within the year eighteen hundred and ninety-nine or by action begun thereafter, if within such year written notice of intention to enforce such liability shall have been given as above provided.

Any director or officer, who, because of any such existing or future liability, shall pay any debt of the corporation, shall be subrogated to all rights of the creditor in respect thereof against the corporate property, but not against the stockholders of the corporation; and also shall be entitled to contribution from all other directors and officers of the corporation similarly liable for the same debt, and the personal representatives of any such director or officer who shall have died before making such contribution.

This section added by chap. 354, Laws of 1899.
See other statutes in this book as to liability of directors or officers.

6

ARTICLE III.

Stock; acquirement of stocks and bonds of other corporations; guarantee of bonds of other corporations.

§ 40. The stock of every stock corporation shall be represented by certificates prepared by the directors and signed by the president or vice president and secretary or treasurer and sealed with the seal of the corporation, and shall be transferable in the manner prescribed in this chapter and in the by-laws. No share shall be transferable until all previous calls thereon shall have been fully paid in. Any stock corporation, domestic or foreign, now existing or hereafter organized, except monied corporations, may purchase, acquire, hold and dispose of the stocks, bonds and other evidences of indebtedness of any corporation, domestic or foreign, and issue in exchange therefor its stock, bonds or other obligations if authorized so to do by a provision in the certificate of incorporation of such stock corporation, or in any certificate amendatory thereof or supplementary thereto, filed in pursuance of law, or if the corporation whose stock is so purchased, acquired, held or disposed of, is engaged in a business similar to that of such stock corporation, or engaged in the manufacture, use or sale of the property, or in the construction or operation of works necessary or useful in the business of such stock corporation, or in which or in connection with which the manufactured articles, product or property of such stock corporation are or may be used, or is a corporation with which such stock corporation is or may be authorized to consolidate. When any such corporation shall be a stockholder in any other corporation, as herein provided, its president or other officers shall be eligible to the office of director of such corporation, the same as if they were individually stockholders therein and the corporation holding such stock shall possess and exercise in respect thereof, all the rights, powers and, privileges of individual owners or holders of such stock. Any stock corporation may, in pursuance of a unanimous vote of its stockholders voting at a special meeting called for that purpose by notice in writing signed by a majority of the directors of such corporation stating the time and place and object of the meeting and served upon each stockholder appearing as such upon the books of the corporation, personally or by mail at his last known post-office address at least sixty days prior to such meeting, guarantee the bonds of any other domestic corporation engaged in the same general line of business; and any stock corporation owning the entire capital stock of any other domestic stock corporation engaged in the same general line of business may in pursuance of a two-thirds vote of its stockholders voting at a special meeting called for that purpose by notice in writing signed by a majority of the directors of such corporation, stating the time and place and object of the meeting and served upon each stockholder appearing as such upon the books of the corporation personally, or by mail, at his last known post-office, at least sixty days prior to such meeting, guarantee the bonds of such other corporation.

  Thus amended by chap. 601, Laws of 1902.

Subscriptions to stock.

§ 41. If the whole capital stock shall not have been subscribed at the time of filing the certificate of incorporation, the directors named in the certificate may open books of subscription to fill up the capital stock in such places, and after giving such notices as they may deem expedient, and may continue to receive subscriptions until the whole capital stock is subscribed. At the time of subscribing, every subscriber, whose subscription is payable in money, shall pay to the directors ten per centum upon the amount subscribed by him in cash, and no such subscription shall be received or taken without such payment.

Consideration for issue of stock and bonds.

§ 42. No corporation shall issue either stock or bonds except for money, labor done or property actually received for the use and lawful purposes of such corporation. Any corporation may purchase any property authorized by its certificate of incorporation, or necessary for the use and lawful purposes of such corporation, and may issue stock to the amount of the value thereof in payment therefor, and the stock so issued shall be full paid stock and not liable to any further call, neither shall the holder thereof be liable for any further payment under any of the provisions of this act; and in the absence of fraud in the transaction the judgment of the directors as to the value of the property purchased shall be conclusive; and in all statements and reports of the corporation, by law required to be published or filed, this stock shall not be stated or reported as being issued for cash paid to the corporation, but shall be reported as issued for property purchased.

  Thus amended by chap. 354, Laws of 1901.
  See section 5 of the amendatory act as to its effect.

Time of payment of subscriptions to stock.

§ 43. Subscriptions to the capital stock of a corporation shall be paid at such times and in such installments as the board of directors may by resolution require. If default shall be made in the payment of any installment as required by such resolution, the board may declare the stock and all previous payments thereon forfeited for the use of the corporation, after the expiration of sixty days from the service on the defaulting stockholder, personally or by mail directed to him at his last known post-office address, of a written notice requiring him to make payment within sixty days from the service of the notice at a place specified therein, and stating that, in case of failure to do so, his stock and all previous payments thereon will be forfeited for the use of the corporation.

Such stock, if forfeited, may be reissued or subscriptions therefor may be received as in the case of stock not issued or subscribed for. If not sold for its par value or subscribed for within six months after such forfeiture, it shall be canceled and deducted from the amount of the capital stock. If by such cancellation, the amount of the capital stock is reduced below the minimum required by law, the capital stock shall be increased to the required amount within three months thereafter or an action may be brought or proceedings instituted to close up the business of the corporation as in the case of an insolvent corporation. If a receiver of the assets of the corporation has been appointed, all unpaid subscriptions to the stock shall be paid at such times and in such installments as the receiver or the court may direct.

Increase or reduction of capital stock.

§ 44. Any domestic corporation may increase or reduce its capital stock in the manner herein provided, but not above the maximum or below the minimum, if any, prescribed by general law governing corporations formed for similar purposes. If increased, the holders of the additional stock issued shall be subject to the same liabilities with respect thereto as are provided by law in relation to the original capital; if reduced, the

amount of its debts and liabilities shall not exceed the amount
of its reduced capital, unless an insurance corporation, in which
case the amount of its debts and liabilities shall not exceed the
amount of its reduced capital and other assets.   The owner of
any stock shall not be relieved from any liability existing prior
to the reduction of the capital stock of any stock corporation.
If a banking corporation, whether the capital be increased or
reduced, its assets shall at least be equal to its debts and liabilities and the capital stock, as increased or reduced.   A domestic
railroad corporation may increase or reduce its capital stock in
the manner herein provided, notwithstanding any provision contained herein, or in any general or special law fixing or limiting
the amount of capital stock which may be issued by it.

Thus amended by chap. 354, Laws of 1901.
See section 5 of the amendatory act as to its effect.

Notice of meeting to increase or reduce capital stock.

§ 45.   Every such increase or reduction must be authorized
either by the unanimous consent of the stockholders, expressed
in writing and filed in the office of the secretary of state and in
the office of the clerk of the county in which the principal business office of the corporation is located, or by a vote of the stockholders owning at least a majority of the stock of the corporation, taken at a meeting of the stockholders specially called for
that purpose in the manner provided by law or by the by-laws.
Notice of the meeting, stating the time, place and object, and
the amount of the increase or reduction proposed, signed by the
president or a vice president and the secretary, shall be published once a week, for at least two successive weeks, in a newspaper in the county where its principal business office is located,
if any is published therein, and a copy of such notice shall be
duly mailed to each stockholder or member at his last-known
post-office address at least two weeks before the meeting or
shall be personally served on him at least five days before the
meeting.

Thus amended by chap. 354, Laws of 1901.
See section 5 of the amendatory act as to its effect.

Conduct of such meeting; certificate of increase or reduction.

§ 46. If, at the time and place specified in the notice, the stock-holders shall appear in person or by proxy in numbers representing at least a majority of all the shares of stock, they shall organize by choosing from their number a chairman and secretary, and take a vote of those present in person or by proxy, and if a sufficient number of votes shall be given in favor of such increase or reduction, or if the same shall have been authorized by the unanimous consent of stockholders expressed in writing signed by them or their duly authorized proxies, a certificate of the proceeding showing a compliance with the provisions of this chapter, the amount of capital theretofore authorized, and the proportion thereof actually issued, and the amount of the increased or reduced capital stock, and in case of the reduction of capital stock the whole amount of the ascertained debts and liabilities of the corporation shall be made, signed, verified and acknowledged by the chairman and secretary of the meeting, and filed in the office of the clerk of the county where its principal place of business shall be located, and a duplicate thereof in the office of the secretary of state. In case of a reduction of the capital stock, except of a railroad corporation or a moneyed corporation, such certificate or consent hereinafter provided for shall have indorsed thereon the approval of the comptroller, to the effect that the reduced capital is sufficient for the proper purposes of the corporation, and is in excess of its ascertained debts and liabilities; and in case of the increase or reduction of the capital stock of a railroad corporation or a moneyed corporation, the certificate or the unanimous consent of stockholders as the case may be, shall have indorsed thereon the approval of the board of railroad commissioners, if a railroad corporation; of the superintendent of banks, if a corporation formed under or subject to the banking law, and of the superintendent of insurance, if an insurance corporation. When the certificate herein provided for, or the unanimous consent of stockholders in writing, signed by them or their duly authorized proxies, approved as aforesaid has been

filed, the capital stock of such corporation shall be increased
or reduced, as the case may be, to the amount specified in
such certificate or consent. The proceedings of the meeting
at which such increase or reduction is voted, or, if such increase or reduction shall have been authorized by unanimous
consent without a meeting, then a copy of such consent shall
be entered upon the minutes of the corporation. If the capital stock is reduced, the amount of capital over and above the
amount of the reduced capital shall, if the meeting or consents
so determine or provide, be returned to the stockholders pro rata,
at such times and in such manner as the directors shall determine, except in the case of the reduction of the capital stock of
an insurance corporation, as an alternative to make good an
existing impairment.

Thus amended by chap. 123, Laws of 1904.

Preferred and common stock.

§ 47. Every domestic stock corporation may issue preferred
stock and common stock and different classes of preferred stock,
if the certificate of incorporation so provides, or by the consent
of the holders of record of two-thirds of the capital stock, given
at a meeting called for that purpose upon notice such as is
required for the annual meeting of the corporation. A certificate of the proceedings of such meeting, signed and sworn to by
the president or a vice-president, and by the secretary or assistant secretary, of the corporation, shall be filed and recorded in the
offices where the original certificate of incorporation of such corporation was filed and recorded; and the corporation may, upon
the written request of the holders of any preferred stock, by a two-
thirds vote of its directors, exchange the same for common stock,
and issue certificates for common stock therefor, upon such valuation as may have been agreed upon in the certificate of organization of such corporation, or the issue of such preferred stock, or
share for share but the total amount of such capital stock shall
not be increased thereby.

Thus amended by chap. 354, Laws of 1901.
See section 5 of the amendatory act as to its effect.

Prohibited transfers to officers or stockholders.

§ 48. No corporation which shall have refused to pay any of its notes or other obligations, when due, in lawful money of the United States, nor any of its officers or directors, shall transfer any of its property to any of its officers, directors or stockholders, directly or indirectly, for the payment of any debt, or upon any other consideration than the full value of the property paid in cash. No conveyance, assignment or transfer of any property of any such corporation by it or by any officer, director or stockholder thereof, nor any payment made, judgment suffered, lien created or security given by it or by any officer, director or stockholder when the corporation is insolvent or its insolvency is imminent, with the intent of giving a preference to any particular creditor over other creditors of the corporation shall be valid, except that laborers' wages for services shall be preferred claims and be entitled to payment before any other creditors out of the corporation assets in excess of valid prior liens or incumbrances. No corporation formed under or subject to the banking, insurance or railroad law shall make any assignment in contemplation of insolvency. Every person receiving by means of any such prohibited act or deed any property of the corporation shall be bound to account therefor to its creditors or stockholders or other trustees. No stockholder of any such corporation shall make any transfer or assignment of his stock therein to any person in contemplation of its insolvency. Every transfer or assignment or other act done in violation of the foregoing provisions of this section shall be void. No conveyance, assignment or transfer of any property of a corporation formed under or subject to the banking law, exceeding in value one thousand dollars, shall be made by such corporation, or by any officer or director thereof, unless authorized by previous resolution of its board of directors, except promissory notes or other evidences of debt issued or received by the officers of the corporation in the transaction of its ordinary business and except payments in specie or other current money or in bank bills made by such officers. No such conveyance, assignment or transfer shall be void in the hands of a purchaser for a valuable consideration without notice. Every director or officer of a corporation who shall violate or be concerned in violating any provisions of this section, shall be personally liable to the creditors and stockholders of the corporation of which he shall be director or an officer to the full extent of any loss they may respectively sustain by such violation.

Thus amended by chap. 354, Laws of 1901.
See section 5 of the amendatory act as to its effect.
See section 54, Stock Corporation Law, section 30 Railroad Law, chap. 392, Laws of 1875, section 8, Labor Law, chaps. 418 and 419, Laws of 1897, *post.*

Section 49 repealed by chap. 354, Laws of 1901.

Application to court to order issue of new in place of lost certificate of stock.

§ 50. The owner of a lost or destroyed certificate of stock, if the corporation shall refuse to issue a new certificate in place thereof, may apply to the supreme court, at any special term held in the district where he resides, or in which the principal business office of the corporation is located, for an order requiring the corporation to show cause why it should not be required to issue a new certificate in place of the one lost or destroyed. The application shall be by petition, duly verified by the owner, stating the name of the corporation, the number and date of the certificate, if known, or if it can be ascertained by the petitioner; the number of shares named therein, to whom issued, and as particular a statement of the circumstances attending such loss or destruction as the petitioner can give. Upon the presentation of the petition the court shall make an order requiring the corporation to show cause, at a time and place therein mentioned, why it should not issue a new certificate of stock in place of the one described in the petition. A copy of the petition and order shall be served on the president or other head of the corporation, or on the secretary or treasurer thereof, personally, at least ten days before the time for showing cause.

Order of court upon such application.

§ 51. Upon the return of the order, with proof of due service thereof, the court shall, in a summary manner, and in such mode as it may deem advisable, inquire into the truth of the facts stated in the petition, and hear the proofs and allegations of the parties in regard thereto, and if satisfied that the petitioner is the lawful owner of the number of shares, or any part thereof, described in the petition, and that the certificate therefor has been lost or destroyed, and cannot after due diligence be found, and that no sufficient cause has been shown why a new certificate should not be issued, it shall make an order requiring the corporation, within such time as shall be therein designated, to issue and deliver to the petitioner a new certificate for the number of shares specified in the order, upon depositing such security, or filing a bond in such form and with such sureties as to the court shall appear sufficient to indemnify any person other than the petitioner who shall thereafter be found to be the lawful owner of the certificate lost or destroyed; but such provision requiring security to be deposited or bond filed is to be construed as excluding an application made by a domestic municipal corporation or by a public officer in behalf of such corporation; and the court may direct the publication of such notice, either before or after making such order as it shall deem proper. Any person claiming any rights under the certificates alleged to have been lost or destroyed shall have recourse to such indemnity, but in any application under the provisions of this act in which a domestic municipal corporation or a public officer in behalf of such corporation, shall be by the foregoing provisions of this section, excused from depositing security or filing a bond, such municipal corporation shall be liable for all damages that may be sustained by any person, in the same case and to the same extent as sureties to a bond or undertaking would have been, if such a bond or undertaking had been filed; and the corporation issuing such certificate, shall be discharged from all liability to such person upon compliance with such order; and obedience to the order máy be enforced by attachment against the officer or officers of the corporation on proof of his or their refusal to comply with it.

Thus amended by chap. 35, Laws of 1905.

Financial statement to stockholders.

§ 52. Stockholders owning five per centum of the capital stock of any corporation other than a monied corporation, not exceeding one hundred thousand dollars, or three per centum where it exceeds one hundred thousand dollars, may make a written request to the treasurer or chief fiscal officer thereof, for a statement of its affairs, under oath, embracing a particular account of all its assets and liabilities, and the treasurer shall make such statement and deliver it to the person presenting the request within thirty days thereafter, and keep on file for twelve months thereafter a copy of such statement, which shall at all times during business hours be exhibited to any stockholder demanding an examination thereof; but the treasurer or such chief fiscal officer shall not be required to deliver more than one such statement in any one year. The supreme court, or any justice thereof, may upon application, for good cause shown, extend the time for making and delivering such certificate. For every neglect or refusal of the treasurer or other chief fiscal officer thereof to comply with the provisions of this section he shall forfeit and pay to the person making such request the sum of fifty dollars, and the further sum of ten dollars for every twenty-four hours thereafter until such statement shall be furnished.

Stock books of foreign corporations.

§ 53. Every foreign stock corporation having an office for the transaction of business in this state, except moneyed and railroad corporations, shall keep therein a book - to be known as a stock book, containing the names, alphabetically arranged, of all persons who are stockholders of the corporation, showing their places of residence, the number of shares of stock held by them respectively, the time when they respectively became the owners thereof, and the amount paid thereon. Such stock book shall be open daily, during business hours, for the inspection of its stockholders and judgment creditors, and any officer of the state authorized by law to investigate the affairs of any such corporation. If any such foreign stock corporation has in this state a transfer agent, whether such agent shall be a corporation or a natural person, such stock book may be deposited in the office of such agent and shall be open to inspection at all times during the usual hours of transacting business, to any stockholder, judgment creditor or officer of the state authorized by law to investigate the affairs of such corporation. For any refusal to allow such book to be inspected, such corporation and the officer or agent so refusing shall each forfeit the sum of two hundred and fifty dollars to be recovered by the person to whom such refusal was made.

Thus amended by chap. 384, Laws of 1897.
See chap. 690, Laws of 1899, *post*.

Liabilities of stockholders.

§ 54. Every holder of capital stock not fully paid, in any stock corporation, shall be personally liable to its creditors, to an amount equal to the amount unpaid on the stock held by him for debts of the corporation contracted while such stock was held by him. As to existing corporations the liability imposed by this section shall be in lieu of the liability imposed upon stockholders of any existing corporation, under any general or special law, (excepting laws relating to moneyed corporations, and corporations and associations for banking purposes,) on account of any indebtedness hereafter contracted or any stock hereafter issued; but nothing in this section contained shall create or increase any liability of stockholders of any existing corporation under any general or special law. The stockholders of every stock corporation shall jointly and severally be personally liable for all debts due and owing to any of its laborers, servants or employes other than contractors, for services performed by them for such corporation. Before such laborer, servant or employe shall charge such stockholder for such services, he shall give him notice in writing,

within thirty days after the termination of such services, that he
intends to hold him liable, and shall commence an action therefor
within thirty days after the return of an execution unsatisfied
against the corporation upon a judgment recovered against it for
services. No person holding stock in any corporation as collateral
security, or as executor, administrator, guardian or trustee,
unless he shall have voluntarily invested the trust funds in such
stock, shall be personally subject to liability as a stockholder;
but the person pledging such stock shall be considered the holder
thereof and shall be liable as stockholder, and the estates and
funds in the hands of such executor, administrator, guardian or
trustee shall be liable in the like manner and to the same extent
as the testator or intestate, or the ward or person interested in
such trust fund would have been, if he had been living and competent to act and held the same stock in his own name, unless
it appears that such executor, administrator, guardian or trustee
voluntarily invested the trust funds in such stocks, in which case
he shall be personally liable as a stockholder.

Thus amended by chap. 354, Laws of 1901.
See section 5 of the amendatory act as to its effect.
See chap. 392, Laws of 1875, *post;* chaps. 418 and 419, Laws of 1897;
section 62, Stock Corporation Law; section 8, Labor Law, *post;* section 30,
Railroad Law, *post;* see next section.

Limitation of stockholder's liability.

§ 55. No action shall be brought against a stockholder for
any debt of the corporation until judgment therefor has been
recovered against the corporation, and an execution thereon has
been returned unsatisfied in whole or in part, and the amount
due on such execution shall be the amount recoverable, with costs
against the stockholder. No stockholder shall be personally liable
for any debt of the corporation not payable within two years from
the time it is contracted, nor unless an action for its collection
shall be brought against the corporation within two years after
the debt becomes due; and no action shall be brought against a
stockholder after he shall have ceased to be a stockholder, for
any debt of the corporation, unless brought within two years from
the time he shall have ceased to be a stockholder.

Increase or reduction of number of shares.

§ 56. The number of shares into which the capital stock of any stock corporation is divided may be increased or reduced by a two-thirds vote of all stock duly represented at a meeting held and conducted in like manner, and upon filing a like certificate, as required for the increase or reduction of its capital stock. If such increase or reduction of the number of shares be so authorized, the corporation shall issue to each stockholder certificates, for as many shares of the new stock as equal in par value the shares of the old stock held by him, upon surrender and cancellation of such old stock. This section does not authorize the increase or reduction of the capital stock of such corporation.

Thus amended by chap. 354, Laws of 1901.
See section 5 of the amendatory act as to its effect.

Voluntary dissolution.

§ 57. Any stock corporation, except a moneyed or a railroad corporation, may be dissolved before the expiration of the time limited in its certificate of incorporation or in its charter as follows: The board of directors of any such corporation may at a meeting called for that purpose upon, at least, three days' notice to each director, by a vote of a majority of the whole board, adopt a resolution that it is in their opinion advisable to dissolve such corporation forthwith, and thereupon shall call a meeting of the stockholders for the purpose of voting upon a proposition that such corporation be forthwith dissolved. Such meeting of the stockholders shall be held, not less than thirty nor more than sixty days after the adoption of such resolution, and the notice of the time and place of such meeting so called by the directors shall be published in one or more newspapers published and circulating in the county wherein such corporation has its principal office, at least once a week for three weeks successively next preceding the time appointed for holding such meeting, and on or before the day of the first publication of such notice, a copy thereof shall be served personally on each stockholder, or mailed to him at his last known post-office address. Such meeting shall be held in the city, town or village in which the last preceding annual meeting of the corporation was held, and said meeting may, on the day so appointed, by the consent of a majority in interest of the stockholders present, be adjourned from time to time, and notice of such adjournment shall be published in the newspapers in which the notice of the meeting is published. If at any such meeting the holders of two-thirds in amount of the stock of the corporation, then outstanding, shall, in person or by attorney, consent that such dissolution shall take place and signify such consent, in writing, then, such corporation shall file such consent, attested by its secretary or treasurer, and its president or vice president, together with the powers of attorney signed by such stockholders executing such consent by attorney, with a statement of the names and residences of the then existing board of directors of said corporation, and the names and residences of its officers duly verified by the secretary or treasurer or president of said corporation, in the office of the secretary of state. The secretary of state shall thereupon issue to such corporation, in duplicate, a certificate of the filing of such papers and that it appears therefrom that such corporation has complied with this section in order to be dissolved, and one of such duplicate certificates shall be filed by such corporation in the office of the clerk of the county in which such corporation has its principal office; and thereupon such corporation shall be dissolved and shall cease to carry on business, except for the purpose of adjusting and winding up its business. The board of directors shall cause a copy of such certificate to be published at least once a week for two weeks in one or more newspapers published and circulating in the county in which the principal office of such corporation is located, and at the expiration of such publication, the said corporation by its board of directors shall proceed to adjust and wind up its business and affairs with power to carry out its contracts and to sell its assets at public or private sale, and to apply the same in discharge of debts and obligations of such corporation, and, after paying and adequately providing for the payment of such debts and obligations, to distribute the bal-

ance of assets among the stockholders of said corporation, according to their respective rights and interest. Said corporation shall
nevertheless continue in existence for the purpose of paying, satisfying and discharging any existing debts or obligations, collecting and distributing its assets and doing all other acts required in
order to adjust and wind up its business and affairs, and may sue
and be sued for the purpose of enforcing such debts or obligations,
until its business and affairs are fully adjusted and wound up.
After paying or adequately providing for the debts and obligations of the corporation the directors may, with the written consent of the holders of two-thirds in amount of the capital stock,
sell the remaining assets or any part thereof to a corporation
organized under the laws of this state or any other state, and engaged in a business of the same general character, and take in payment therefor the stock or bonds or both of such corporation and
distribute them among the stockholders, in lieu of money, in proportion to their interest therein, but no such sale shall be valid
as against any stockholder, who, within sixty days after the mall-
ing of notice to him of such sale shall apply to the supreme court in
the manner provided by section thirty-three of this act, for an appraisal of the value of his interest in the assets so sold; unless
within thirty days after such appraisal the stockholders consenting to such sale, or some of them, shall pay to such objecting stockholder or deposit for his account, in the manner directed by the
court, the amount of such appraisal and upon such payment or
deposit the interest of such objecting stockholder shall vest in the
person or persons making such payment or deposit.

Thus amended by chap. 760, Laws of 1900.
See provisions of the Code of Civil Procedure.
See section 30, General Corporation Law, *ante;* section 61, Stock Corpora-
tion Law, chap. 310, Laws of 1886, *post.*

Merger.

§ 58. Any domestic stock corporation and any foreign stock
corporation authorized to do business in this state lawfully owning all the stock of any other stock corporation organized for, or
engaged in business similar or incidental to that of the possessor
corporation may file in the office of the secretary of state, under

its common seal, a certificate of such ownership, and of the resolution of its board of directors to merge such other corporation, and thereupon it shall acquire and become, and be possessed of all the estate, property, rights, privileges and franchises of such other corporation, and they shall vest in and be held and enjoyed by it as fully and entirely and without change or diminution as the same were before held and enjoyed by such other corporation, and be managed and controlled by the board of directors of such possessor corporation, and in its name, but without prejudice to any liabilities of such other corporation or the rights of any creditors thereof. Any bridge corporation may be merged under this section with any railroad corporation which shall have acquired the right by contract to run its cars over the bridge of such bridge corporation.

Thus amended by chap. 98, Laws of 1902.

Change of place of business.

§ 59. Any stock corporation now existing or hereafter organized under the laws of this state, except moneyed corporations, may at any time change its principal office and place of business from the city, town or county named in its certificate of incorporation, or to which it may have been changed under the provisions of this section, to any other city, town or county in this state, in which it may desire to actually transact and carry on its regular business from day to day, provided, and* such change has been authorized, either by unanimous consent of the stockholders expressed in writing and duly acknowledged and filed in the office of the secretary of state, or by a vote of the stockholders of said corporation at a special meeting of stockholders called' for that purpose. When such change shall be authorized by the stockholders as herein provided, the president and secretary and a majority of the directors of such corporation shall sign a certificate stating the name of said corporation, the city, town and county where its principal office and place of business was originally located, and to which it may have been subsequently changed, and the city, town

*So in the original.

and county to which it is desired to change its said principal office and place of business, and that it is the purpose of said corporation to actually transact and carry on its regular business from day to day at such place, and that such change has been authorized as herein provided, and the names of the directors of said corporation and their respective places of residence, which certificate shall be verified by the oaths of all the persons signing the same, and when so signed and verified, shall be filed in the office of the secretary of state and a duplicate thereof in the office of the clerk of the county from which said principal office and place of business is about to be removed or changed, and another in the office of the clerk of the county to which said removal or change is to be made, and thereupon the principal office and place of, business of such corporation shall be changed as stated in said certificate.

Thus amended by chap. 489, Laws of 1905.

Liabilities of officers, directors and stockholders of foreign corporations.

§ 60. Except as otherwise provided in this chapter the officers, directors and stockholders of a foreign stock corporation transacting business in this state, except moneyed and railroad corporations, shall be liable under the provisions of this chapter, in the same manner and to the same extent as the officers, directors and stockholders of a domestic corporation, for:

1. The making of unauthorized dividends;

2. The creation of unauthorized and excessive indebtedness;

3. Unlawful loans to stockholders;

4. Making false certificates, reports or public notices;

5. An illegal transfer of the stock and property of such corporation, when it is insolvent or its insolvency is threatened;

6. The failure to file an annual report.

Such liabilities may be enforced in the courts of this state, in the same manner as similar liabilities imposed by law upon the officers, directors and stockholders of domestic corporations.

This section added by chap. 384, Laws of 1897.
See chap. 690, Laws of 1899, *post.*
See sections of Penal Code as to certain penalties, *post.*

Dissolution by incorporators.

§ 61. The incorporators named in any certificate of incorpora·
tion filed for the purpose of creating a domestic stock corpora·
tion, other than a moneyed or transportation corporation, may,
before the payment of any part of the capital, and before be·
ginning business, surrender all corporate rights and franchises,
by signing, verifying and filing in the office of the secretary of
state and the clerk of the county where the certificate of incor·
poration is filed, a certificate setting forth that no part of the
capital has been paid, that there are no liabilities, that such
business has not been begun, and surrendering all rights and fran·
chises; and proof of the facts set forth in such certificate to
the satisfaction of the secretary of state; and thereupon the said
corporation shall be dissolved, and its corporate existence and
powers shall cease.

This section added by chap. 296, Laws of 1904.
See provisions of the Code of Civil Procedure.
See section 30, General Corporation Law; section 57, Stock Corporation Law,
ante; chap. 310, Laws of 1886, *post.*

Partly paid stock.

§ 62. The original or the amended certificate of incorporation
of any stock corporation may contain a provision expressly
authorizing the issue of the whole or of any part of the capital
stock as partly paid stock, subject to calls thereon until the
whole thereof shall have been paid in. In such case, if in or
upon the certificate issued to represent such stock, the amount
paid thereon shall be specified, the holder thereof shall not be
subject to any liability except for the payment to the corpora·
tion of the amount remaining unpaid upon such stock, and for
the payment of indebtedness to employes pursuant to sections
fifty-four and fifty-five of this chapter; and in any such case, the
corporation may declare and may pay dividends upon the basis
of the amount actually paid upon the respective shares of stock
instead of upon the par value thereof.

This section added by chap. 354, Laws of 1901.
See section 5 of the amendatory act as to its effect.
See section 54, Stock Corporation Law, *ante,* and statutes cited there-
under.

THE RAILROAD LAW.

CHAP. 565, LAWS OF 1890.

AN ACT in relation to railroads, constituting chapter thirty-nine
of the general laws.

(As amended to and including the session of the Legislature of 1906.)

[SEE SECTIONS OF CODE OF CRIMINAL PROCEDURE AND PENAL CODE,
THIS VOLUME.]

CHAPTER XXXIX OF THE GENERAL LAWS.

THE RAILROAD LAW.

ARTICLE I.

ORGANIZATION, GENERAL POWERS, LOCATION.

Short title.

SECTION 1. This chapter shall be known as the railroad law.

Incorporation.

*§ 2. Fifteen or more persons may become a corporation, for the purpose (1) of buiding, maintaining and operating a railroad, or (2) of maintaining and operating a railroad already built, not owned by a railroad corporation, or for both purposes, or (3) of building, maintaining and operating a railroad for use by way of extension or branch or cut-off of any railroad then existing, or for shortening or straightening or improving the line or grade of such railroad or of any part thereof, by executing, acknowledging and filing a certificate, in which shall be stated:

1. The name of the corporation.
2. The number of years it is to continue.
3. The kind of road to be built or operated.
4. Its length and termini.

*The first paragraph of section 2 thus amended by chap. 727, Laws of 1905.

5.   The name of each county in which any part of it is to be located.

6.   The amount of capital stock, which shall not be less than ten thousand dollars for every mile of road built, or proposed to be built, except a narrow-gauge road, when it shall not be less than three thousand dollars for every such mile.

7.   The number of shares into which the capital stock is to be divided.

8.   If the capital stock is to consist of common and preferred stock, the amount of each class and the rights and privileges of the latter over the former.

9.   The names and post-office addresses of the directors of the corporation, not less than nine, who shall manage its affairs for the first year.

10.   The place where its principal office is to be located.

11.   If a street surface railroad, the names and description of the streets, avenues and highways in which the road is to be constructed.

12.   If it is to be a railway corporation, specified in article five of this chapter, the statements required by that article to be inserted in the certificate of incorporation.

13.   The name and post-office address of each subscriber to the certificate and the number of shares of stock he agrees to take.

Such certificate shall have indorsed thereon, or annexed thereto, to be taken as a part thereof, an affidavit of at least three of such directors, that at least ten per cent of the minimum amount of capital stock authorized by law has been subscribed thereto, and paid in good faith and in cash to the directors named in the certificate, and that it is intended in good faith to build, maintain and operate the road mentioned therein. In case of a railway corporation specified in article five of this chapter, the affidavit of the directors shall show that the full amount of such capital stock has been in good faith subscribed, and there shall be annexed to the certificate of incorporation and as a part thereof the certificate of the railroad commissioners showing the organization of the corporation for the purposes mentioned in the certificate.

The filing of every certificate, where the amount of stock required by this section has not been in good faith subscribed and paid in cash, shall be void.

Thus amended by chap. 676, Laws of 1892.
See section 7, General Corporation Law, *ante*, section 3 Railroad Law, *post*, chap. 238, Laws of 1893, *post*.

Supplemental certificate.

§ 3. If the names and places of residence of the directors of the corporation have been omitted from the certificate, when executed and acknowledged, and thereafter the requisite number of directors has been chosen at a meeting of the subscribers to the certificate, a supplemental certificate, containing their names and places of residence, may be filed with such certificate with the same force and effect as if the names and places of residence of the directors had been originally inserted therein.

See section 7, General Corporation Law, section 2, Railroad Law, *ante;* chap. 238, Laws of 1893, *post*.

Additional powers conferred.

§ 4. Subject to the limitations and requirements of this chapter, every railroad corporation, in addition to the powers given by the general and stock corporation laws, shall have power.

Entry upon lands for purposes of survey.

1. To cause the necessary examination and survey for its proposed railroad to be made for the selection of the most advantageous route; and for such purpose, by its officers, agents or servants, to enter upon any lands or waters subject to liability to the owner for all damages done.

Acquisition of real property.

2. To take and hold such voluntary grants of real estate and other property as shall be made to it to aid in the construction, maintenance and accommodation of its railroad; and to acquire by condemnation such real estate and property as may be neces.

sary for such construction, maintenance and accommodation in the manner provided by law, but the real property acquired by condemnation shall be held and used only for the purposes of the corporation during the continuance of the corporate existence.

Construction of road.

3. To lay out its road not exceeding six rods in width, and to construct the same; and, for the purpose of cuttings and embankments, to take such additional lands as may be necessary for the proper construction and security of the road; and to cut down any standing trees that may be in danger of falling on the road, upon making compensation therefor.

Intersection of streams, highways, plank-roads, turnpikes and canals.

4. To construct its road across, along or upon any stream, water-course, highway, plank-road, turnpike, or across any of the canals of the state, which the route of its road shall intersect or touch.

Intersection of other railroads.

5. To cross, intersect, join, or unite its railroad with any other railroad before constructed, at any point on its route and upon the ground of such other railroad corporation, with the necessary turnouts, sidings, switches, and other conveniences in furtherance of the objects of its connections.

See section 12' Railroad Law, post.

Buildings and stations.

6. To erect and maintain all necessary and convenient buildings, stations, fixtures and machinery for the accommodation and use of its passengers, freight and business.

Transportation of persons and property.

7. To take and convey persons and property on its railroad by the power or force of steam or of animals, or by any mechani-

cal power, except where such power is specially prescribed in this chapter and to receive compensation therefor.

Time and manner of transportation.

8. To regulate the time and manner in which passengers and property shall be transported, and the compensation to be paid therefor.

Purchase of lands and stock in other states.

9. To acquire and dispose of any real property in any other state through which any part of its railroad is operated, and stock in any foreign corporation owning lands in another state for the purpose of securing for such railroad corporation in this state a permanent supply of fuel for its use, and stock of corporations in this state, formed for the purpose of erecting union railway depots.

Creation of Mortgage.

10. From time to time to borrow such sums of money as may be necessary for completing and finishing or operating or improving its railroad, or for any other of its lawful purposes and to issue and dispose of its bonds for any amount so borrowed, and to mortgage its property and franchises to secure the payment of any debts contracted by the company for the purposes aforesaid, notwithstanding any limitation on such power contained in any general or special law. But no mortgage, except purchase-money mortgages, shall be issued by any railroad corporation under this or any other law without the consent of the board of railroad commissioners, and the consent of the stockholders owning at least two-thirds of the stock of the corporation, which consent shall be in writing, and shall be given and certified and be filed and recorded in the office of the clerk or register of the county where it has its principal place of business, as provided in section two of the stock corporation law; or else the consent of the board of railroad commissioners and the consent by their votes of stockholders owning at least two-thirds of the stock of the corporation which is represented and voted upon in person or by proxy at a meeting called for that purpose upon a notice

stating the time, place and object of the meeting, served at least three weeks previously upon each stockholder personally, or mailed to him at his post-office address, and also published at least once a week for three weeks successively in some newspaper printed in the city, town or county where such corporation has its principal office, and a certificate of the vote at such meeting shall be signed and sworn to and shall be filed and recorded as provided by section two of the stock corporation law. When authorized by the stockholders consent to any bonds made or issued under this section, the directors, under such regulations as they may adopt, may confer on the holder of any such bonds the right to convert the principal thereof, after two and not more than twelve years from the date of the bond, into stock of the corporation at a price fixed by the board of directors, which may be either par or a price not less than the market value thereof at the date of such consent to such bonds; and if the capital stock shall not be sufficient to meet the conversion when made, the board of directors shall authorize an increase of capital stock sufficient for that purpose.

Subdivision 10 thus amended by chap. 504, Laws of 1902.
See sections 2 and 8, Stock Corporation Law, *ante*.

When corporate powers to cease.

§ 5. If any domestic railroad corporation shall not, within five years after its certificate of incorporation is filed, begin the construction of its road and expend thereon ten per centum of the amount of its capital, or shall not finish its road and put it in operation in ten years from the time of filing such certificate, its corporate existence and powers shall cease. But if any such steam railroad corporation whose certificate of incorporation was filed since the year eighteen hundred and eighty, and whose road as designated in such certificate is wholly within one county and not more than ten miles in length, has acquired the real property necessary for its road-bed by purchase, its corporate existence and powers shall not be deemed to have ceased because of its failure to comply with the provisions of this article; and the time for beginning the construction of its road and expend-

ing thereon ten per centum of its capital, is extended until thirteen years from the date of the filing of such certificate and
the time for finishing its road and putting it in operation, is extended until eighteen years from the date of such filing. This
section shall not apply to any street surface railroad company
incorporated prior to July first, eighteen hundred and ninety-
five, which has obtained or become the owner of the consents of
the local authorities, of any city of the first or second class, given
under article four of the railroad law to the use of public streets,
avenues or highways for the construction and operation of the
railroad thereon.

Thus amended by chap. 508, Laws of 1901.
See other laws as to expiration of time to construct, *post*.
See 106 App. Div. 240; 185 N. Y. 171.
See section 99, Railroad Law, *post*.

Location of route.

§ 6. Every railroad corporation, except a street surface railroad corporation and an elevated railway corporation, before constructing any part of its road in any county named in its certificate of incorporation, or instituting any proceedings for the
condemnation of real property therein, shall make a map and
profile of the route adopted by it in such county, certified by
the president and engineer of the corporation, or a majority of
the directors, and file it in the office of the clerk of the county
in which the road is to be made. The corporation shall give
written notice to all actual occupants of the lands over which
the route of the road is so designated, and which has not been
purchased by or given to it, of the time and place such map
or profile were filed, and that such route passes over the lands
of such occupants. Any such occupant or the owner of the land
aggrieved by the proposed location, may, within fifteen days after
receiving such notice, give ten days' written notice to such corporation and to the owners or occupants of lands to be affected
by any proposed alteration, of the time and place of an application
to a justice of the supreme court, in the judicial district where the
lands are situated, by petition duly verified, for the appointment
of commissioners to examine the route.

The petition shall state the objections to the route designated, shall designate the route to which it is proposed to alter the same, and shall be accompanied with a survey, map and profile of the route designated by the corporation, and of the proposed alteration thereof, and copies thereof shall be served upon the corporation and such owners or occupants with the notice of the application. The justice may, upon the hearing of the application, appoint three disinterested persons, one of whom must be a practical civil engineer, commissioners to examine the route proposed by the corporation, and the route to which it is proposed to alter the same, and after hearing the parties, to affirm the route originally designated, or adopt the proposed alteration thereof, as may be consistent with the just rights of all parties and the public, including the owners or occupants of lands upon the proposed alterations; but no alteration of the route shall be made except by the concurrence of the commissioner who is a practical civil engineer, nor which will cause greater damage or injury to lands or materially greater length of road than the route designated by the corporation, nor which shall substantially change the general line adopted by the corporation.

The commissioners shall, within thirty days after their appointment, make and certify their written determination, which with the petition, map, survey and profile, and any testimony taken before them shall be immediately filed in the office of the county clerk of the county. Within twenty days after such filing, any party may, by written notice to the other, appeal to the general term of the supreme court from the decision of the commissioners, which appeal shall be heard and decided at the next term held in the department in which the lands of the petitioners or any of them are situated, for which the same can be noticed, according to the rules and practice of the court. On the hearing of such appeal, the court may affirm the route proposed by the corporation or may adopt that proposed by the petitioner.

The commissioners shall each be entitled to six dollars per day for their services, and to their reasonable and necessary expenses, to be paid by the persons who applied for their ap-

pointment. If the route of the road, as designated by the corporation, is altered by the commissioners, or by the order of the
court, the corporation shall refund to the petitioner the amount
so paid, unless the decision of the commissioners is reversed upon
appeal taken by the corporation. No such corporation shall institute any proceedings for the condemnation of real property in
any county until after the expiration of fifteen days from the
service by it of the notice required by this section. Every such
corporation shall transmit to the board of railroad commissioners
the following maps, profiles and drawings exhibiting the character-
istics of their road, to wit:

A map or maps showing the length and direction of each straight
line; the length and radius of each curve; the point of crossing
of each town and county line, and the length of line of each town
and county accurately determined by measurements to be taken
after the completion of the road.

Whenever any part of the road is completed and used, such
maps and profiles of such completed part shall be filed with such
board within three months after the completion of any such portion and the commencement of its operation; and when any additional portion of the road shall be completed and used, other
maps shall be filed within the same period of time, showing the additional parts so completed. If the route, as located upon the
map and profile filed in the office of any county clerk, shall have
been changed, it shall also cause a copy of the map and profile
filed in the office of the railroad commissioners, so far as it may relate to the location in such county, to be filed in the office of the
county clerk.

Thus amended by chap. 676, Laws of 1892.

Acquisition of title to real property; additions, betterments and
    facilities.

*§ 7. All real property, required by any railroad corporation for
the purpose of its incorporation or for any purpose stated in
the railroad law, shall be deemed to be required for a public
use, and may be acquired by such corporation. If the corpora-

tion is unable to agree for the purchase of any such real property, or of any right, interest or easement therein, required for any such purpose, or if the owner thereof shall be incapable of selling the same, or if after diligent search and inquiry the name and residence of any such owner cannot be ascertained, it shall have the right to acquire title thereto by condemnation. Every railroad corporation shall have the power from time to time to make and use upon or in connection with any railroad either owned or operated by it, such additions, betterments and facilities as may be necessary or convenient for the better management, maintenance or operation of any such railroad, and shall have the right by purchase or by condemnation, to acquire any real property required therefor, and it shall also have the right of condemnation in the following additional cases:

1. Where title to real property has been acquired, or attempted to be acquired, and has been found to be invalid or defective.

2. Where its railroad shall be lawfully in possession of a lessee, mortgagee, trustee or receiver, and additional real property shall be required for the purpose of running or operating such railroad.

*3. Where it shall require for any railroad owned or operated by it any further rights to lands or the use of lands for additional main tracks or for branches, sidings, switches, or turnouts or for connections or for cut-offs or for shortening or straightening or improving the line or grade of its road or any part thereof. Also where it shall require any further rights to lands or the use of lands for filling any structures of its road, or for constructing, widening or completing any of its embankments or roadbeds, by means of which greater safety or permanency may be secured, and such lands shall be contiguous to such railroad and reasonably accessible.

4. Where it shall require any further right to lands or to the use of lands for the flow of water occasioned by railroad embankments or structures now in use, or hereafter rendered necessary, or for any other purpose necessary for the operation

of such railroad, or for any right to take and convey water from any spring, pond, creek or river to such railroad, for the uses and purposes thereof, together with the right to build or lay aqueducts or pipes for the purpose of conveying such water, and to take up, relay and repair the same, or for any right of way required for carrying away or diverting any water, stream or floods from such railroad for the purpose of protecting its road or for the purpose of preventing any embankment, excavation or structure of such railroad from injuring the property of any person who may be rendered liable to injury thereby.

Waters commonly used for domestic, agricultural or manufacturing purposes, shall not be taken by condemnation to such an extent as to injuriously interfere with such use in future. No railroad corporation shall have the right to acquire by condemnation any right or easement in or to any real property owned or occupied by any other railroad corporation, except the right to intersect or cross the tracks and lands owned or held for right of way by such other corporation, without appropriating or affecting any lands owned or held for depots or gravel-beds.

Thus amended by chap. 676, Laws of 1892, and chap. 727, Laws of 1905.
*The first paragraph and subdivision 3 of section 7 thus amended by chap. 727, Laws of 1905.
See section 4 of this law.
As to condemnation by street railroads, see section 90 and section 4, and this section of this law.
As to condemning railroad property, see section 3370, Condemnation Law, *ante.*

Railroads through public lands.

§ 8. The commissioners of the land office may grant to any domestic railroad corporation land belonging to the people of the state, except the reservation at Niagara and the Concourse lands on Coney Island, which may be required for the purpose of its road on such terms as may be agreed upon by them; or such corporation may acquire title thereto by condemnation; and the county or town officers having charge of any land belonging to any county or town, required for such corporation for the purposes of its road, may grant such land to the corporation for such compensation as may be agreed upon. In case the land or any right, interest or easement therein, required by such railroad corporation is used for prison purposes the commissioners of the land office may grant such land, or any right, interest or easement therein, provided the plans of such railroad corporation for the use of such prison lands, or such right, interest or easement therein, have the approval of the superintendent of state prisons.

Thus amended by chap. 313, Laws of 1904.

Railroads through Indian lands.

§ 9. Any railroad corporation may contract with the chiefs of any nation of Indians, over whose lands it may be necessary to construct its railroad, for the right to make such road upon such lands, but such contract shall not vest in the corporation the fee to the land, nor the right to occupy the same for any purposes other than may be necessary for the construction, occupancy and maintenance of such railroad, and such contract shall not be valid or effectual until it shall be ratified by the county court of the county where the land shall be situated.

Railroads through Chautauqua assembly grounds.

§ 10. No railroad corporation shall build, construct or operate any railroad in, upon, over or through the grounds, lands or premises owned by the Chautauqua assembly corporation in the town and county of Chautauqua, without the written consent of a majority of the board of trustees of such assembly corporation.

Intersection of highways additional lands for.

§ 11. No railroad corporation shall erect any bridge or other obstruction across, in or over any stream or lake, navigated by steam or sail boats at the place where it may be proposed to be erected, nor shall it construct its road in, upon or across any street of any city without the assent of the corporation of such city, nor across, upon or along any highway in any town or street in any incorporated village, without the order of the supreme court of the district in which such highway or street is situated,

8

made at a special term thereof, after at least ten days written
notice of the intention to make application for such order shall
have been given to the commissioners of highways of such town,
or board of trustees of the village in which such highway or
street is situated. Every railroad corporation which shall build
its road along, across or upon any stream, watercourse, street,
highway, plankroad or turnpike, which the route of its road shall
intersect or touch, shall restore the stream or watercourse, street,
highway, plankroad and turnpike, thus intersected or touched, to
its former state, or to such state as not to have unnecessarily impaired its usefulness, and any such highway, turnpike or plank-
road may be carried by it, under or over its track, as may be found
most expedient. Where an embankment or cutting shall make a
change in the line of such highway, turnpike or plankroad desirable, with a view to a more easy ascent or descent, it may construct
such highway, turnpike or plankroad, on such new line as its directors may select, and may take additional lands therefor by condemnation if necessary. Such lands so taken shall become part of
such intersecting highway, turnpike or plankroad, and shall be
held in the same manner and by the same tenure as the adjacent
parts of the highway, turnpike or plankroad are held for highway
purposes. Every railroad corporation shall pay all damages sustained by any turnpike or plankroad corporation in consequence
of its crossing or occupation of any turnpike or plankroad, and
in case of inability to agree upon the amount of such damages
it may acquire the right to such crossing or occupation by condemnation.

See chap. 300, Laws of 1835; also section 60 Railroad Law.
See 177 N. Y. 337.

Intersection of other railroads.

§ 12. Every railroad corporation, whose road is or shall be
intersected by any new railroad, shall unite with the corporation owning such new railroad in forming the necessary intersections and connections, and grant the requisite facilities therefor. If the two corporations cannot agree upon the amount of
compensation to be made therefor or upon the line or lines,
grade or grades, points or manner of such intersections and con-

nections, the same shall be ascertained and determined by com. missioners, one of whom must be a practical civil engineer and surveyor, to be appointed by the court, as is provided in the condemnation law. Such commissioners may determine whether the crossing or crossings of any railroad before constructed shall be beneath, at, or above the existing grade of such railroad, and upon the route designated upon the map of the corporation seek. ing the crossing or otherwise. All railroad corporations whose roads are or shall hereafter be so crossed, intersected or joined, shall receive from each other and forward to their destination all goods, merchandise and other property intended for points on their respective roads, with the same dispatch as, and at a rate of freight not exceeding the local tariff rate charged for similar goods, merchandise and other property, received at or forwarded from the same point for individuals and other cor- porations.

Thus amended by chap. 676, Laws of 1892.

See subdivision 5, section 4, Railroad Law, *ante;* sections 35 and **68,** Railroad Law, and chap. 239, Laws of 1893, *post.*

See 171 N. Y., 589; 75 App. Div. 412; 175 N. Y. Mem. 468; 106 App. Div. 375.

Change of route, grade or terminus.

§ 13. Every railroad corporation, except elevated railway cor- porations, may, by a vote of two-thirds of all its directors, alter or change the route or any part of the route of its road or its termini, or locate such route, or any part thereof, or its termini, in a county adjoining any county named in its certificate of incor- poration, if it shall appear to them that the line can be improved thereby, upon making and filing in the clerk's office of the proper county a survey, map and certificate of such alteration or change. If the same is made after the corporation has commenced grading the original route, compensation shall be made to all persons for injury done by such grading to any lands donated to the corpora- tion. But neither terminus can be changed, under this section, to any other county than one adjoining that in which it was pre- viously located; nor can the route or terminus of any railroad be so changed in any town, county or municipal corporation, which has issued bonds and taken any stock or bonds in aid of the construction of such railroad without the written consent of a majority of the taxpayers appearing upon the last assessment roll of such town, county or municipal corporation, unless such terminus, after the change, will remain in the same village or city as theretofore. No alteration of the route of any railroad after its construction shall be made, or new line or route of road laid out or established, as provided in this section, in any city or village, unless approved by a vote of two-thirds of the common council of the city or trustees of the village. Any railroad corporation whose road as located terminates at any railroad previously constructed or located, whereby communication might be had with any incorporated city of the state, may amend its certificate of incorporation so as to terminate its road at the point of its intersection with any railroad subsequently located to intersect it, and thereby, by itself or its connection, afford communication with such city, with the consent of the stockholders owning two-thirds of the stock of the corporation. Any railroad corporation may, by a vote of its directors, change the grade of any part of its road, except that in the city of Buffalo such change must conform to the general plan heretofore adopted and filed by the grade crossing commissioners of said city, or any modification thereof, within the territory covered by said general plan, in such manner as it may deem necessary to avoid accidents and facilitate the use of such road; and it may by such vote alter the grade of its road, for such distance and in such manner as it may deem necessary, on each or either side of the place where the grade of its road has been changed by direction of the superintendent of public works, at any point where its road crosses any canal or canal feeder, except that in the city of Buffalo such change must conform to the general plan heretofore adopted and filed by the grade crossing commissioners of said city, or any modification thereof, within the territory covered by said general plan. The superin-tendent of public works shall have a general and supervisory power over that part of any railroad which passes over, or ap-

proaches within ten rods of any canal or canal feeder belong
ing to the state so far as may be necessary to preserve the free
and perfect use of such canals or feeders, or to make any repairs,
improvements or alterations, in the same. Any railroad cor
poration whose tracks cross any of the canals of the state, and
the grade of which may be raised by direction of the superin
tendent of public works, with the assent of such superintendent,
may lay out a new line of road to cross such canal at a more
favorable grade, and may extend such new line and connect the
same with any other line of road owned by such corporation
upon making and filing in the clerk's office of the proper county
a survey map and certificate of such new or altered line. No
portion of the track of any railroad, as described in its certificate
of incorporation, shall be abandoned under this section.

Thus amended by chap. 235, Laws of 1897.
See chap. 338, Laws of 1894. See chap. 340, Laws of 1902, *post.* See 172
N. Y., 462, 177 N. Y., 337.

Cor··ruction of part of line in another state.

§ 14. Any railroad corporation, whose proposed railroad is to
be built between any two points in this state, may, by a vote of
two-thirds of all its directors, locate and construct a part of its
road in an adjoining state; and the sections of its road within
this state shall be deemed a connected line, according to the
certificate of incorporation, and the directors may reduce the
capital stock of the corporation to such amount as may be
deemed proper, but not less than ten thousand dollars per mile
for the number of miles of road to be actually constructed in
this state.

Two roads having the same location.

§ 15. If two railroad corporations for a portion of their re
spective lines embrace the same location of line, or if their lines
connect, or are tributary to each other, such corporations may by
agreement provide for the construction by one of them of so
much of such line as is common to both, or connects with
its own line, and for the manner and terms upon which

the business thereon shall be performed, and the corporation that is not to construct the part of the line which is common to both, may amend its certificate of incorporation, and terminate its line at the point of intersection, and may reduce its capital to a sum not less than ten thousand dollars for each mile of road proposed to be constructed in such amended certificate.

Tunnel railroads.

§ 16. When, according to the route and plan for the building of its road, adopted by any railroad corporation, including corporations organized under chapter one hundred and forty of the laws of eighteen hundred and fifty, and the acts amendatory thereof, and supplementary thereto, it shall be necessary or proper to build it or any part of it underground, or to tunnel or bridge any river or waters, such corporation may enter upon, acquire title to and use such lands under water and uplands, except on or along any canals of the state, as shall be necessary for the purpose herein mentioned, and may construct, erect and secure the necessary foundations and other structures which may be required for operating and maintaining such road, or connecting the same with another, and to acquire, in the manner provided by law, such land or rights or easements in lands along its route, upon, over or beneath the surface thereof as may be necessary for the construction of its road and making such connections. Where such road runs underneath the ground, at such depth as to enable the corporation to tunnel the same, such tunnel shall be so built and at all times kept in such condition as to make the surface of the ground above the same and in the neighborhood thereof firm and safe for buildings and other erections thereon, and if surface excavations are made the surface shall be restored to its former condition as soon as can be done, except so far as may be actually required for ventilation of the tunnel beneath the same or access thereto. Such road or any part of it may be built within the limits of any city or incorporated village of this state, and run by means of a tunnel underneath any of the streets, roads or public places thereof, provided such corporation shall before constructing the same underneath any such street, road or public place, have obtained the consent of the owners of one-half in value of the property bounded on the line of such street, road or public place, and the consent of the board of trustees of the village, by a resolution adopted at a regular meeting and entered on the records of the board, or of the proper authorities of the city having control of such streets, roads or public places. If the consent of such property owners can not be obtained, the general term of the supreme court in the district in which said city or village or any part thereof is situated, may upon application appoint three commissioners, who shall determine, after a hearing of all parties interested, whether such railroad ought to be built underneath such streets, roads or public places, or any of them, and in what manner the same may be so built with the least damage to the surface and to the use of the surface by the public and the determination of the commissioners confirmed by the court may be taken in lieu of the consent of the property owners. All railroad corporations constructing their road under this section shall be subject to all the provisions of this chapter applicable thereto. Any other railroad corporation may connect its road therewith, at such points or places as it may elect, and where such connections shall be made by connecting roads, the railroad corporations owning such roads shall build, at their joint expense, and for their joint use, such passenger and freight depots, and other accommodations for handling passengers and freight, as may be required for the convenience of the public. All railroad corporations, constructing any tunnel under this section shall be liable to any person or corporation for all damages which may be sustained by reason of the construction of such tunnel. Whenever it shall be necessary in constructing any railroad authorized by this section through any city or incorporated village, to alter the position or course of any sewer, or water or gas pipes, it shall be done at the expense of the railroad corporation under the direction of the department or corporation having charge thereof, so as not to interfere with such work. In all cases the uses of streets, docks and lands beneath which such railroad is constructed, and on the route thereof and the right of way beneath the same, for the purpose of such railroad shall be considered, and is hereby declared, a public use, consistent with and one of the uses for which streets and docks are publicly held. No public park or square in any city or village of this state shall be used or occupied by any corporation for any of the purposes of this section, and every road constructed hereunder in or through any such street or public place shall be wholly underground and constructed in a tunnel and not otherwise, but nothing in this section shall operate to revive any charter or franchise heretofore granted by or in the city of Brooklyn. This act does not authorize the construction of any bridge over or across the East or North Rivers.

Thus amended by chap. 316, Laws of 1893.

Railroads in other countries.

§ 17. A railroad corporation may be formed under this chapter for the purpose of constructing, maintaining and operating in any foreign country a railroad for public use in the transportation of persons and property, or for the purpose of maintaining and operating therein any railroad already constructed, in whole or in part, for the like public use, and of constructing, mantaining and operating, in connection therewith, telegraph lines and lines of steamboats or sailing vessels. Any corporation formed for the construction and operation of a railroad by stationary power, may construct, operate and maintain a railroad in any other state or country, if not in conflict with the laws thereof, but the assent of the inventors or patentees of the method of propulsion used must be first obtained in the same manner and to the same extent as would be necessary within the United States. The term "foreign" in this and the next two sections of this law shall include Porto Rico.

Thus amended by chap. 225, Laws of 1902.

Additional corporate powers of such road.

§ 18. The corporation specified in the preceding section shall have the following additional powers:

1. To expend money in making preliminary examinations and surveys for its proposed railroad, telegraph lines, and lines of steamboats and sailing vessels, and in acquiring from foreign countries, nations or governments, the grants, concessions and privileges herein authorized.

2. To take and receive from foreign countries, nations and governments, such grants, concessions or privileges, for the construction, acquisition, maintenance and operation of railroads, telegraph lines and vessels, as may be consistent with the purposes of the corporation, and as may be granted and conceded to it, and to hold the same under such restrictions and with such duties and liabilities as may be fixed by the laws of such foreign country, nation or government, or as may be annexed to such grants or concessions.

3. To construct, acquire, maintain and operate the lines of railroad, telegraph and shipping provided for by its certificate of incorporation, and to take and hold by purchase or by voluntary grant such real estate and other property in foreign countries as may be necessary and convenient for the construction, maintenance and accommodation of such lines, and to sell, convey, mortgage or lease such real estate or other property; and to acquire by purchase or otherwise any railroad or lines of telegraph constructed or in process of construction in any foreign country, and any grants, concessions, franchises, rights, privileges and immunities relating thereto, and to issue therefor the capital stock of the company or any part thereof at such valuation or valuations and on such terms as may be agreed upon, and to mortgage or sell and convey such railroad or lines of telegraph constructed or in process of construction in any foreign country, and any grants, concessions, franchises, rights, privileges and immunities relating thereto, or any part of its property to any person or corporation created by this or any other state or foreign government, subject to the laws of the country

or countries where such property may be, and the power of sale
hereby granted shall be exercised only by a majority of the entire
board of directors of the corporation, with the written concurrence of the holders of two-thirds in amount of its capital stock.

4.   To take and convey persons and property on its transportation lines by the power or force of steam or of animals, or
by mechanical or other power, and receive compensation therefor subject to the laws of the place or country where the same
are situated.

5.   To acquire and use such real estate and other property in
this state as may be necessary in the conduct of its business,
but the value of such real estate held at any one time shall not
exceed the sum of one million dollars.

Thus amended by chap. 504, Laws of 1897.

Location of principal office of such road.

§ 19.   Every such corporation shall maintain its principal
office within this state and shall have during business hours, an
officer or agent upon whom service of process may be made, and
shall hold in this state at least one meeting of the stockholders
in each year for the choice of directors, which shall be known
as the annual meeting and be held at the time and place fixed
by the by-laws of the corporation.

Thus amended by chap. 676, Laws of 1892.

Individual, joint stock association, or other corporation may lay down and maintain railroad tracks in certain cases.

§ 20.   Any individual, joint stock association or corporation,
engaged in any lawful business in this state, may, except in any
city of the state, lay down and maintain such railroad tracks on
or across any street or highway, not exceeding three miles in
length, as shall be necessary for the transaction of its business,
and to connect any place of business owned by them with the
track of any railroad corporation, and render such place of business more accessible to the public, upon obtaining the written
consent of the owners of all the lands bounded on and of the
local authorities having control of that portion of the street or

highway, upon which it is proposed to construct or operate such railroad. If the consent of such property owners cannot be obtained, the general term of the supreme court of the department in which such railroad is to be constructed, may upon application, appoint three commissioners, who shall determine, after a hearing of all parties interested, whether such railroad ought to be constructed or operated, and the amount of damages, if any, to be paid to such property owners, and their determination confirmed by the court may be taken in lieu of the consent of the property owners. But no such railroad shall be so located, graded, built or operated as to interfere with or obstruct the traveled part of any highway, or its use as a highway, or the use of any street or highway intersecting the same. See chap. 300, Laws of 1835.

Powers of electric light and power corporations.

§ 21. Whenever all of the stockholders of any domestic electric light and power company, incorporated under a general or special law, having not less than five stockholders, and actually engaged in carrying on business in this state, shall execute and file, in the offices in which its original certificates of incorporation are filed, an amended certificate of incorporation, complying in every other respect than as to the number of signers and directors, who shall not be less than five, with the provisions of the railroad law, and in which certificate the corporate name of such corporation shall be amended by adding before the word "company," in its corporate name, the words, "and railroad," or the words, "railroad and land," such corporation shall have the right to build, maintain and operate by electricity as a motive power, a railroad or railroads, not exceeding twenty-five miles in length, and within that distance from the power station, and shall also have the right to acquire the property and franchises of a railroad company or companies owning such a railroad or railroads, already constructed, and so operated, and to maintain and operate the same, provided that the directors of such railroad company or companies and all of its or their stockholders shall first have assented in writing to the transfer of the property and franchises of such railroad company or companies, to such corporation; in which event and by the filing of such assent of directors and stockholders in the offices where the certificates of incorporation of the railroad company or companies were required to be filed, the rights, property and franchises of such railroad company or companies shall be transferred to, and shall vest in such corporation, and such corporation so acquiring such railroad or railroads shall be subject to all the provisions of chapter thirty-nine of the general laws with respect to the railroad property or properties and franchises, and shall have all the powers. rights and privileges conferred by said chapter upon railroad corporations; provided that no such corporation shall construct any railroad which is in whole or in part a street surface railroad without complying with the provisions of article four of the railroad law. Upon filing such certificate, such corporation shall also have the right to acquire by gift or by voluntary purchase and sale land not exceeding two thousand acres along the line of, or contiguous to, said railroad, and to hold, improve, lease or sell same. Whenever any such corporation shall furnish power to any water-works corporation carrying on its business in the county, or in a county adjoining that in which the operations of such corporation are carried on, it may acquire the shares of the capital stock of said water-works corporation, and, if such corporation shall become the owner of all the stock of said water-works corporation, it may, on executing and filing a certificate in accordance with the requirements of section fifty-eight of the stock corporations law, become possessed of all the estate, rights, property, privileges and franchises of such water-works corporation, with the effect provided in said section fifty-eight. This section shall not confer any powers upon any corporation located in, or authorize the construction, maintenance or operation of a railroad in a city of the first or second class, except in that part of any city of the first class which is or may be situate in a county of less than one hundred thousand inhabitants, according to the last preceding enumeration for the national census.

Thus amended by chap. 731, Laws of 1901.

*§ 21. Any corporation, whose railroad is or shall be not 'longer than sixteen miles and is or shall be in large part intended for or used in summer travel or the convenience of summer sojourners need not operate its road beyond the months of June, July, August and September, inclusive. The motive power may be electricity. If the road be not longer than ten miles, such corporation may fix and collect fare for transporting each passenger, together with ordinary baggage, if any, not to exceed fifteen cents for each mile and fraction thereof.

This section added by chap. 700, Laws of 1892.
See sections 37 and 55, Railroad Law, *post*.

Substituted lines in cases of eminent domain.

§ 22. Where a portion of a steam surface railroad or branch thereof, shall be specifically authorized by statute to be taken for any other public use, and such portion lies wholly outside of any city, any corporation owning or operating such portion may locate, as provided in section six of this article, and may construct and operate, in substitution for such portion, and with proper connections with the former line, a new line of steam surface railroad, wholly or partly in the 'same or any adjoining county, and wholly outside of any city, and not exceeding twenty-five miles in length, in the manner, with the powers and subject to the limitations and requirements provided in this chapter with respect to steam surface railroads.

This section added by chap. 656, Laws of 1898.

§ 23. Section twenty-four of the stock corporation law does not apply to a railroad corporation.

This section added by chap. 80, Laws of 1898.
Section 24, Stock Corporation Law, repealed by chap. 354, Laws of 1901.

---

*So in the original.

ARTICLE II.

Construction, Operation and Management.

Liability of corporation to employes of contractor.

§ 30. An action may be maintained against any railroad corporation by any laborer for the amount due him from any contractor for the construction of any part of its road, for ninety or any less number of days' labor performed by him in constructing such road, if within twenty days thereafter a written notice shall have been served upon the corporation, and the action shall have been commenced after the expiration of ten days and within six months after the service of such notice, which shall contain a statement of the month and particular days upon which the labor was performed and for which it was unpaid, the price per day, the amount due, the name of the contractor from whom due, and the section upon which performed, and shall be signed by the laborer or his attorney and verified by him to the effect that of his own knowledge the statements contained in it are true. The notice shall be served by delivering the same to an engineer, agent or superintendent having charge of the section of the road, upon which the labor was performed, personally, or by leaving it at his office or usual place of business with some person of suitable age or discretion; and if the corporation has no such agent, engineer or superintendent, or in case he cannot be found and has no place of business open, service may in like manner be made on any officer or director of the corporation.

See chap. 392, Laws of 1875, *post;* see sections 48, 54 and 62, Stock Corporation Law, *ante;* see section 8, Labor Law, chaps. 418 and 419, Laws of 1897, *post.*

Weight of rail.

§ 31. The rail used in the construction or the relaying of the track of every railroad hereafter built or relaid in whole or in part shall be of iron or steel, weighing not less than twenty-five pounds to the lineal yard on narrow gauge roads, and on all other roads not less than fifty-six pounds to the lineal yard on grades of one hundred and ten feet to the mile or under, and not less than seventy pounds to the lineal yard on grades of over one hundred and ten feet to the mile, except for turnouts, sidings and switches.

Fences, farm-crossings and cattle-guards.

§ 32. Every railroad corporation, and any lessee or other person in possession of its road, shall, before the lines of its road · are opened for use, and so soon as it has acquired the right of way for its roadway erect and thereafter maintain fences on the sides of its road of height and strength sufficient to prevent cattle, horses, sheep and hogs from going upon its road from the adjacent lands with farm crossings and openings with gates therein at such farm crossings whenever and wherever reasonably necessary for the use of the owners and occupants of the adjoining lands, and shall construct where not already done, and hereafter maintain, cattle-guards at all road crossings, suitable and sufficient to prevent cattle, horses, sheep and hogs from going upon its railroad. So long as such fences are not made, or are not in good repair, the corporation, its lessee or other person in possession of its road, shall be liable for all damages done by their agents or engines or cars to any domestic animals thereon. When made and in good repair, they shall not be liable for any such damages, unless negligently or willfully done. A sufficient post and wire fence of requisite height shall be deemed a lawful fence within the provisions of this section, but barbed wire shall not be used in its construction.

No railroad need be fenced, when not necessary to prevent horses, cattle, sheep and hogs from going upon its track from the adjoining lands. Every adjoining land owner, who, or whose grantor, has received compensation for fencing the line of land taken for a railroad, and has agreed to build and maintain a lawful fence along such line, shall build and main.

tain such fence. If such owner, his heir or assign shall not
build such fence, or if built, shall neglect to maintain the
same during the period of thirty days after he has been notified
so to do by the railroad corporation, such corporation shall thereafter build and maintain such fence, and may recover of the
person neglecting to build and maintain it the expense thereof.
And when such railroad shall cross timbered or forest lands,
the company shall construct and maintain suitable and sufficient
crossings, whenever and wherever reasonably necessary to enable
the respective owners of said lands, to transport logs, timber and
lumber for manufacture or sale, or for banking on any stream, to
be floated or driven down the same. In case of any neglect or
dispute the supreme court may by mandamus or other appropriate proceedings, compel the same, and also fix the point or location of any such crossing.

Thus amended by chap. 676, Laws of 1892.
See 44 Misc. 111, 345.

Sign boards and flagmen or gates at crossings.

§ 33. Every railroad corporation shall cause a sign board to
be placed, well supported and constantly maintained, at every
crossing where its road is crossed by a public highway at grade.
Such sign board shall be of a shape and design to be approved
by the board of railroad commissioners, and shall have suitable
words painted thereon to warn travelers of the existence of such
grade crossing. The board of railroad commissioners shall have
power to prescribe the location and elevation of such sign and
the words of warning thereon. The commission may dispense
with the use of such sign boards at such crossings as they may
designate in cities and villages. At any point where a railroad
crosses a street, highway, turnpike, plank-road, or traveled way
at grade, or where a steam railroad crosses a horse railroad at
grade, and the corporation owning or operating such railroad,
refuses, upon request of the local authorities, to station a flagman or erect gates, to be opened and closed when an engine or
train passes, the supreme court or the county court, may, upon

9

the application of the local authorities and upon ten days' notice
to the corporation, order that a flagman be stationed at such
point, or that gates shall be erected thereat, and that a person be
stationed to open and close them when an engine or train passes,
or may make such other order respecting the same as it deems
proper. Whenever the crossing by a railroad at grade of the
streets, highways, turnpike, plank-roads, or traveled ways of any
village or city, having a population by the last state or federal
enumeration of less than fifty thousand, shall be protected by
gates with persons to open and close the same, when an engine
or train passes, the local authorities of the city or village shall
not impose any limitation, less than forty miles an hour, on the
rate of speed at which such engine or train shall be run, or
enforce any existing limitation upon such rate of speed, less than
forty miles an hour.

Thus amended by chap. 301' Laws of 1901.
See sections 36 and 68, Railroad Law.

Notice of starting trains; no preferences.

§ 34. Every railroad corporation shall start and run its cars
for the transportation of passengers and property at regular
times, to be fixed by public notice, and shall furnish sufficient
accommodations for the transportation of all passengers and
property which shall be offered for transportation at the place
of starting, within a reasonable time previously thereto, and at
the junctions of other railroads, and at the usual stopping places
established for receiving and discharging way passengers and
freight for that train; and shall take, transport and discharge
such passengers and property at, from and to, such places, on
the due payment of the fare or freight legally authorized therefor. No station established by any railroad corporation for the
reception or delivery of passengers or property, or both, shall
be discontinued without the consent of the board of railroad
commissioners first had and obtained. No preference for the
transaction of the business of a common carrier upon its cars,
or in its depots or buildings, or upon its grounds, shall be granted

by any railroad corporation to any one of two or more persons, associations or corporations competing in the same business, or in the business of transporting property for themselves or others. Any such station in an incorporated village shall have the same name as the village; if any road shall have more than one such station in any such village the station nearest the geographical center thereof shall have such name.

Thus amended by chap. 676, Laws of 1892.
See 92 App. Div. 584; 181 N. Y. Mem. 533.

Accommodation of connecting roads.

§ 35. Every railroad corporation whose road, at or near the same place, connects with or is intersected by two or more railroads competing for its business, shall fairly and impartially afford to each of such connecting or intersecting roads equal terms of accommodation, privileges and facilities in the transportation of cars, passengers, baggage and freight over and upon its roads and over and upon their roads, and equal facilities in the interchange and use of passenger, baggage, freight and other cars required to accommodate the business of each road, and in furnishing passage tickets to passengers who may desire to make a continuous trip over any part of its roads and either of such connecting roads. The board of railroad commissioners may, upon application of the corporation owning or operating either of the connecting or intersecting roads, and upon fourteen days' notice to the corporation owning or operating the other road, prescribe such regulations as will secure, in their judgment, the enjoyment of equal privileges, accommodations and facilities to such connecting or intersecting roads as may be required to accommodate the business of each road, and the terms and conditions upon which the same shall be afforded to each road. The decision of the commissioners shall be binding on the parties for two years, and the supreme court shall have power to compel the performance thereof by attachment, mandamus, or otherwise.

See section 12, Railroad Law. *ante.*
See 171 N. Y., 589; 75 App. Div. 412; 175 N. Y. Mem. 468.

Locomotives must stop at grade crossings; interlocking devices at street and steam railroad grade crossings.

§ 36. All trains and locomotives on railroads crossing each other at grade shall come to a full stop before crossing, not less than two hundred or more than eight hundred feet from the crossing, and shall then cross only when the way is clear and upon a signal from a watchman stationed at the crossing. If the corporations can not agree as to the expense of the watch-man, it shall be determined by the supreme court, upon motion thereto by either of them. If the corporations disagree as to the precedence of trains, the board of railroad commissioners may, after hearing, upon the application of either corporation, prescribe rules in relation thereto. The full stop and crossing on signal may be discontinued if the board of railroad commis-sioners shall decide it to be impracticable, or if, with the approval of the commissioners, an interlocking switch and signal apparatus is adopted and put in operation as * such a crossing. The full stop and crossing on signal shall not be required in depot yards, or the approaches thereto, if the crossing roads are under lease or subject to the same management or control in the use of tracks. An engineer, violating the foregoing provisions of this section, or any such rule of the railroad commissioners, shall be liable to a penalty of one hundred dollars; and any corporation or person operating the railroad, violating any of such provisions or rules shall be liable to a penalty of five hundred dollars. The board of railroad commissioners may, whenever in its judgment the public safety requires the erection of interlocking switch and signal devices at points where steam and street surface railroads inter-sect at grade, direct the erection of such devices and apportion the expense of construction, operation and maintenance thereof between the companies affected thereby. No railroad corpora-tion, or any officer, agent or employe thereof, shall stop its cars, horses, or locomotives upon a grade crossing of a rail-road of another corporation, for the purpose of receiving or deliv-

---

*So in the original.

ering passengers or freight, or other purpose, and any person or corporation violating this provision, shall be liable to a penalty of two hundred and fifty dollars.

Thus amended by chap. 466, Laws of 1898.
See sections 33 and 68, Railroad Law.

Rates of fare.

§ 37. Every railway corporation may fix and collect the following rates of fare as compensation to be paid for transporting any passenger and his baggage, not exceeding one hundred and fifty pounds in weight, for each mile or fraction of a mile.

1. Where the motive power is rope or cable, propelled by stationary power, five cents, with right to a minimum fare of ten cents; but if the railroad is less than two miles in length, and overcomes an elevation of five hundred feet or more to the mile, five cents for each one hundred feet of elevation so overcome, and the same rates of fare if the motive power is locomotives, furnished with cogs working into cogs on the railway, and the length of road does not exceed four miles.

2. If a road, not incorporated prior to May 15, 1879, and not located in the counties of New York and Kings, or within the limits of any incorporated city, and not more than twenty-five miles in length, five cents; if over twenty-five and not more than forty miles, four cents; and if over forty miles, three cents. Where by the laying down of a third rail upon a railroad of the ordinary gauge, a narrow-gauge track is created and used for the transportation of passengers, and the length of road does not exceed six miles, including any connecting road of the same gauge, such railroad, for the purpose of fare, shall be deemed a narrow gauge road.

3. If its railroad overcomes an elevation of two hundred feet to the mile, for at least two consecutive miles, and does not exceed twenty miles in length, ten cents; if it overcomes an elevation exceeding three hundred feet to the mile, within a distance of two miles, five cents for each one hundred feet of elevation; and where it overcomes an elevation of more than one thousand feet, within a distance of two miles, seven cents for each one hundred feet of elevation in a mile.

4. If the line of its road does not exceed fifteen miles in length, and does not enter or traverse the limits of any incorporated city, and the distance traveled thereon by the passenger does not exceed one mile, five cents.

5. In all other cases, three cents for every such mile or fraction thereof, with a right to a minimum single fare of not less than five cents.

This chapter shall not be construed to allow any rate of fare for way passengers greater than two cents per mile to be charged or taken over the track or tracks of the railroad known as the New York Central Railroad Company, and the rate of fare for way passengers over the track or tracks of such company shall continue to be two cents per mile and no more, wherever it is restricted to that rate of fare, nor shall any consolidated railroad corporation charge a higher rate of fare per passenger per mile, upon any part or portion of the consolidated line than was allowed by law to be charged by each existing corporation thereon previously to such consolidation.

* Thus amended by chap. 676, Laws of 1892.

As to rate of fare for emigrants, see chap. 474, Laws of 1855, and § 626, Penal Code, *post*. See, also, chap. 228, Laws of 1857, and chap. 38, Laws of 1889, *post*. See, also § 21, Railroad Law, *ante*.

See also chap. 1027, Laws of 1895, *post*.

Legislature may alter or reduce fare; anti-ticket scalping act.

§ 38. The legislature may, when any such railroad shall be opened for use, from time to time, alter or reduce the rate of freight, fare or other profits upon such road; but the same shall not, without the consent of the corporation, be so reduced as to produce with such profits less than ten per centum per annum on the capital actually expended; nor unless on an examination of the amounts received and expended, to be made by the board of railroad commissioners they shall ascertain that the net income derived by the corporation from all sources, for the year then last past, shall have exceeded an annual income of ten per centum upon the capital of the corporation actually expended. No person shall issue or sell, or offer to sell any passage ticket or instrument giving or purporting to give any right, either absolute

or upon any condition or contingency to a passage or conveyance upon any vessel or railway train, or for a berth or state-
room in any vessel unless he is an authorized agent of the owners
or consignees of such vessel or of the company running such
trains, excepting as allowed by sections six hundred and twenty-
two and six hundred and twenty-three of the penal code; and
no person is deemed an authorized agent of such owners, consignees or company unless he has received a certificate of
authority in writing therefor, specifying the name of the company, line, vessel or railway for which he is authorized to act as
agent, and the city, town or village, together with the street and
street number in which his office is kept for the sale of tickets;
and no general passenger agent or other officer of a common carrier whose duty it may be to supply tickets to the agents of said
common carrier for sale to the public shall supply tickets for sale
to any persons other than such regularly authorized agents or
persons specified in sections six hundred and twenty-two and
six hundred and twenty-three of the penal code.

Thus amended by chap. 639, Laws of 1901.
As to unconstitutionality of chap. 639, see 168 N. Y., p. 671.
See sections 615, et seq., Penal Code, post.

Penalty for excessive fare.

§ 39. Any railroad corporation, which shall **ask** or receive
more than the lawful rate of fare, unless such overcharge was
made through inadvertence or mistake, not amounting to gross
negligence, shall forfeit fifty dollars, to be recovered with the
excess so received by the party paying the same; but no action
can be maintained therefor, unless commenced within one year
after the cause of action accrued.

Passenger refusing to pay fare may be ejected.

§ 40. If any passenger shall refuse to pay his fare the conductor of the train, and the servants of the corporation, may put
him and his baggage out of the cars, using no unnecessary force,

on stopping the train, at any usual stopping place, or near any dwelling house, as the conductor may elect.

Sleeping and parlor cars.

§ 41. Any railroad corporation may contract with any person, association or corporation for the hauling by the special or regular trains of said railroad corporation, the parlor, drawing-room or sleeping car or cars of such person, association or corporation, in which extra accommodations shall be furnished, for which said person, association or corporation furnishing such parlor, drawing-room or sleeping car or cars, may charge for the carriage and transportation of persons and property therein, a reasonable compensation for such extra accommodation, in addition to the fare and charges now allowed by law for the carriage and transportation of passengers and property in the ordinary cars of said railroad corporation. But said railroad corporation so contracting shall be liable in the same way and to the same extent as if the said car or cars were owned by it, and shall furnish sufficient ordinary cars for the reasonable accommodation of the traveling public.

Thus amended by chap. 676, Laws of 1892.

Persons employed as drivers, conductors, motormen or gripmen.

§ 42. Any railroad corporation may employ any inhabitant of the State, of the age of twenty-one years, not addicted to the use of intoxicating liquors, as a car driver, conductor, motorman or gripman, or in any other capacity, if fit and competent therefor. All applicants for positions as motormen or gripmen on any street surface railroad in this State shall be subjected to a thorough examination by the officers of the corporation as to their habits, physical ability and intelligence. If this examination is satisfactory, the applicant shall be placed in the shop or power house where he can be made familiar with the power and machinery he is about to control. He shall then be placed on a car with an instructor, and when the latter is satisfied as to the applicant's capability for the position of motorman or gripman, he shall so certify to the officers of the company, and, if appointed, the applicant shall first serve on the lines of least travel. Any violation of the provisions of this section shall be a misdemeanor.

Thus amended by chap. 513, Laws of 1895.

See section 420, Penal Code, *post;* also section 41, chap. 112, Laws of 1896, *post;* also chap. 415, Laws of 1897, *post;* also section 56, Code of Criminal Procedure, and section 29, Rapid Transit Act, *post.*

Employers' liability.

§ 42-a. In all actions against a railroad corporation, foreign or domestic, doing business in this state, or against a receiver thereof, for personal injury to, or death resulting from personal injury of any person, while in the employment of such corporation, or receiver, arising from the negligence of such corporation or receiver or of any of its or his officers or employees, every employee, or his legal representatives, shall have the same rights and remedies for an injury, or for death, suffered by him, from the act or omission of such corporation or receiver or of its or his officers or employees, as are now allowed by law, and, in addition to the liability now existing by law, it shall be held in such actions that persons engaged in the service of any railroad corporation, foreign or domestic, doing business in this state, or in the service of a receiver thereof, who are entrusted by such corporation or receiver, with the authority of superintendence, control or command of other persons in the employment of such corporation or receiver, or with the authority to direct or control any other employee in the performance of the duty of such employee, or who have, as a part of their duty, for the time being, physical control or direction of the movement of a signal, switch, locomotive engine, car, train or telegraph office, are vice-principals of such corporation or receiver, and are not fellow-servants of such injured or deceased employee. If an employee, engaged in the service of any such railroad corporation, or of a receiver thereof, shall receive any injury by reason of any defect in the condition of the ways, works, machinery, plant, tools or implements, or of any car, train, locomotive or attachment thereto belonging, owned or operated, or being run and operated by such corporation or receiver, when such defect could have been discovered by such corporation or receiver, by reasonable and proper care, tests or inspection, such corporation or receiver, shall be deemed to have had knowledge of such defect before and at the time such injury is sustained; and when the fact of such defect shall be proved upon the trial of any action in the courts of this state, brought by such employee or his legal representatives, against any such railroad corporation or receiver, on account of such injuries so received, the same shall be prima facie evidence of negligence on the part of such corporation or receiver. This section shall not affect actions or causes of action now existing; and no contract, receipt, rule or regulation, between an employee and a railroad corporation or receiver, shall exempt or limit the liability of such corporation or receiver from the provisions of this section.

Added by chap. 657, Laws of 1906.
See chap. 600, Laws of 1902, *post;* see 87 App. Div. 631; 178 N. Y. 147; 90 App. Div. 577; 181 N. Y. 519; see provisions of Interstate Commerce Brakes and Couplers' Act, *post.*

Conductors and employes must wear badges.

§ 43. Every conductor and employe of a railroad corporation employed in a passenger train, or at stations for passengers, shall wear upon his hat or cap a badge, which shall indicate his office or employment, and the initial letters of the corporation employing him. No conductor or collector without such badge shall demand or receive from any passenger any fare or ticket or exercise any of the powers of his employment. No officer or employe without such badge shall meddle or interfere with any passenger, his baggage or property.

Thus amended by chap. 676, Laws of 1892.
See section 425, Penal Code, *post.*

Checks for baggage.

§ 44. A check, made of some proper substance of convenient size and form, plainly stamped with numbers, and furnished with a convenient strap or other appendage for attaching to baggage, shall be affixed to every piece or parcel of baggage when taken for transportation for a passenger by the agent or employee of such corporation, if there is a handle, loop or fixture therefor upon the piece or parcel of baggage, and a duplicate thereof given to the passenger or person delivering the same to him. If such check be refused on demand the corporation shall pay to the passenger the sum of ten dollars, and no fare shall be collected or received from him; and if he shall have paid his fare it shall be refunded to him by the conductor in charge of the train. Such baggage shall be delivered, without unnecessary delay, to the passenger or any person acting in his behalf, at the place to which it was to be transported, where the cars usually stop, or at any other regular intermediate stopping place upon notice to the baggage-master in charge of baggage on the train of not less than thirty minutes, upon presentation of such duplicate check to the officer or agent of the railroad corporation, or of any corporation, over any portion of whose road it was transported. Bicycles are hereby declared to be and be deemed baggage for the purposes of this article and shall be transported as baggage for passengers by railroad corporations and subject to the same liabilities, and no such passenger shall be required to crate, cover or otherwise protect any such bicycle; provided, however, that a railroad corporation shall not be required to transport, under the provisions of this act, more than one bicycle for a single person.

Thus amended by chap. 388, Laws of 1902.

Penalties for injuries to baggage.

§ 45. Any person, whose duty it is for or on behalf of the common carrier to handle, remove, or care for the baggage of passengers, who shall recklessly or willfully injure or destroy any trunk, valise, box, bag, package or parcel, while loading, unloading, transporting, delivering or storing the same, or any railroad corporation, which shall knowingly keep in its employment any such willful or reckless person, or which shall permit any injury or destruction of such property, through failure to provide sufficient help and facilities for the handling thereof, shall pay to the party injured thereby the sum of fifty dollars, in addition to such damages.

Unclaimed freight and baggage.

§ 46. Every railroad or other transportation corporation, doing business in this state, which shall have unclaimed freight or baggage, not live stock or perishable, in its possession for the period of sixty days, may deliver the same to any warehouse company, or person or persons engaged in the warehouse business, within this state, and take a warehouse receipt for the storage thereof. Upon such delivery and upon taking such warehouse receipt, every such railroad or other transportation corporation shall be discharged of all liability in respect to any such unclaimed freight or baggage from and after such delivery. At any time within two years after such delivery, such railroad or other transportation corporation shall surrender and transfer such warehouse receipt to the owner of any such unclaimed freight or baggage upon demand, and upon payment of all charges and expenses for transportation and storage then due, if any, to any such railroad or other transportation corporation. In case any such railroad or other transportation company shall have had unclaimed freight or baggage, not live stock or perishable, in its possession for a period of one year and shall not have delivered the same to a warehouse company or person or persons engaged in the warehouse business as above provided, then such railroad or other transportation company may proceed to sell the same at public auction, and out of the proceeds may retain the charges of transportation, handling and storage of such unclaimed freight or baggage, and the expenses of advertising and sale thereof; but no such sale shall be made until the expiration of four weeks from the first publication of notice of such sale, to be published weekly in a newspaper published in or nearest the town or city to which such unclaimed freight or baggage was consigned, or at which it was directed to be left, and also at the town or city where such sale is to take place; and said notice shall contain a general description of such unclaimed freight or baggage, the name of the shipper thereof, if known, and a statement of the consignment thereof, whether to a designated consignee or to order, if known, or the place, at which the same was to be left, as near as may be; and the expenses incurred for advertising shall be a lien upon such unclaimed freight or baggage in a ratable proportion, according to the value of each article, package or parcel, if more than one. Such railroad or other transportation company shall make an entry of the balance of the proceeds of the sale, if any, of the unclaimed freight or baggage consigned to the same consignee or covered by each consignment, as near as can be ascertained, and at any time within five years thereafter, shall refund any surplus so retained to the owners of such unclaimed freight or baggage, his personal representatives or assigns, on satisfactory proof of such ownership. In case such balance shall not be claimed by the rightful owner within five years after the sale as above specified, then it shall be paid to the county treasurer, for the use of the county poor of the county where the sale is made.

Unclaimed live stock and perishable freight or baggage may be sold by any such railroad or other transportation corporation without notice, as soon as it can be, upon the best terms that can be obtained. All moneys arising from the sale of any such unclaimed live stock, perishable freight or baggage, after deducting therefrom all charges and expenses for transportation, storage, keeping, commissions for selling the property, and any amount previously paid for its loss or non-delivery, shall be deposited by the corporation making such sale with a report thereof, and proof that the property was live stock or perishable freight, with the comptroller for the benefit of the general fund of the state, and shall be held by him in trust for reclamation by the person or persons entitled to receive the same.

Thus amended by chap. 582, Laws of 1899.
See chap. 488, Laws of 1899 and chap. 313, Laws of 1901, *post.*

Tickets and checks for connecting steamboats.

§ 47. The proprietors of any line of steamboats, terminating or stopping for passengers at any place where a railroad corporation has a depot or station, may furnish tickets and baggage

checks to such corporation for the use of passengers, traveling
over its road, who desire to connect with such line of boats at
any such place, and the railroad corporation shall sell such
tickets and deliver a duplicate of one of such checks to any
such passenger applying therefor, and shall account for and pay
over to the proprietor of such line of boats all moneys received
by it for the sale of such tickets; and any such railroad corporation may furnish tickets and checks for baggage to the proprie
tors of any such line of steamboats for the use of passengers
traveling over any part of such line of boats, who desire to con
nect with the railroad of any such corporation at any such place,
and such proprietors shall sell such tickets and deliver a duplicate of one of such checks to any such passenger applying
therefor, and shall account for and pay over to such corporation
all moneys received by them for the sale of such tickets. No
greater rate of fare shall be charged by any railroad corporation
to any such passenger for the distance traveled over its road than
is charged to travelers for the same distance whose trip ends
at the place where connection is made with any such line of
boats, and no greater rate of fare shall be charged by the proprietors of any such steamboat line to any such passenger for
the distance traveled over its line, than is charged to travelers
for the same distance whose trip ends at the place where connection is made with any such railroad. Any additional cost of
transfer of a passenger or his baggage from railroad depot or
station to steamboat landing, or from steamboat landing to depot
or station, shall be borne by the passenger or the proprietors of
the steamboat line or the railroad corporation at whose instance
or for whose benefit such tranfer is made. Every railroad cor.
poration and the proprietors of any line of steamboats, their
agents or servants, who shall neglect or refuse to sell tickets or
furnish a check to any passenger applying for the same, when
the same shall have been furnished to them, shall pay to such
passenger the sum of ten dollars, and no fare or toll shall be col.
lected from him for riding over such road or upon such boats, as
the case may be; and in addition thereto any railroad corporation

so neglecting or refusing, shall pay the proprietors of such line of boats two hundred and fifty dollars for each day it shall so neglect or refuse; and the proprietors of any such line of boats so neglecting or refusing, shall pay to such railroad corporation a like sum for each day they shall so neglect or refuse.

Every such railroad corporation shall also receive any freight which shall be delivered at any station on the line of its road, marked to go by way of boat or any particular line of boats from any station on its road at which such boat or line of boats termi nates or stops for freight, and shall transport such freight with all convenient speed to such station, and on its arrival there cause the proprietors of the steamboat line by which it is directed to be sent, or their agent, to be notified of such arrival, and shall deliver such freight to such proprietors or their agent with the bill of charges thereon due such railroad corporation, for the payment of which charges the proprietor or proprietors of such steamboat line shall be responsible, and shall account for and pay the same to such railroad corporation on demand. The railroad corporation shall not charge for the transportation of such freight over its road any greater sum pro rata than it charges for carrying the same kind of freight the same distance over its road, if it was to be transported by such corporation by rail to its final destination, or to the terminus of the road of such corporation in case it terminates before such final destina tion is reached. Any freight delivered by the proprietors of any steamboat or steamboat line, or their authorized agent, at any station, at a place where such steamboat or steamboats have a landing, to any such railroad corporation, for transportation over its road or any part thereof, shall be transported by such corpora tion to its place of destination for the same price pro rata which would be charged for the same kind of freight the same distance over its road, if the same had been taken on at the point of first shipment by boat, or at the terminus of the road of such corpora tion, in case it does not extend to the point of first shipment.

Rights and liabilities as common carriers.

§ 48. Every railroad corporation doing business in this state shall be a common carrier. Any one of two or more corporations owning or operating connecting roads, within this state, or partly within and partly without the state, shall be liable as a common carrier, for the transportation of passengers or delivery of freight received by it to be transported by it to any place on the line of a connecting road; and if it shall become liable to pay any sum by reason of neglect or misconduct of any other corporation it may collect the same of the corporation by reason of whose neg- lect or misconduct it became liable.

Thus amended by chap. 676, Laws of 1892.
See section 12, Railroad Law, *ante;* sections 381 and 383, Penal Code, *post.*

Switches; warning signals; automatic couplers; automatic or other safety brake; tools in passenger car; water.

§ 49. It shall be the duty of every railroad corporation oper-ating its road by steam:

1. To lay, in the construction of new and in the renewal of existing switches, upon freight or passenger main line tracks, switches on the principle of either the so-called Tyler, Wharton, Lorenze, or split-point switch, or some other kind of safety switch, which shall prevent the derailment of a train, when such switch is misplaced or a switch interlocked with dis. tant signals.

2. To erect and thereafter maintain such suitable warning signals at every road, bridge, or structure which crosses the railroad above the tracks, where such warning signals may be necessary, for the protection of employes on top of cars from injury.

Subdivision 3, relating to guard posts, repealed by chap. 740, Laws of 1900, but see section 424, Penal Code, *post.*

4. To use upon every new freight car, built or purchased for use, couplers which can be coupled and uncoupled automatically, without the necessity of having a person guide the link, lift the pin by hand, or go between the ends of the cars.

5. To attach to every car used for passenger transportation an automatic air-brake or other form of safety-power brake, applied from the locomotive, excepting cars attached to freight trains, the schedule rate of speed of which does not exceed twenty miles an hour.

6. To provide each closed car in use in every passenger train owned or regularly used upon a railroad, with one set of tools, consisting of an axe, sledge hammer, crowbar and hand saw and such other or additional tools as the board of railroad commissioners may require, to be placed where directed by the board of railroad commissioners.

Subdivision 6 thus amended by chap. 521, Laws of 1898.

7. To provide, in each passenger car, where the line of road shall exceed forty continuous miles in length, a suitable receptacle for water, with a cup or drinking utensil attached upon or near such receptacle, and to keep such receptacle, while the car is in use, constantly supplied with cool water.

Every corporation, person or persons, operating such railroad, and violating any of the provisions of this section, except subdivision seven, shall be liable to a penalty of one hundred dollars for each offense, and the further penalty of ten dollars for each day that it shall omit or neglect to comply with any of such provisions. For every violation of the provisions of the seventh subdivision of this section every such corporation shall be liable to a penalty of twenty-five dollars for each offense.

As to automatic brakes and couplers, see, also, chaps. 543 and 544, Laws 1893, *post*. See section 424, Penal Code, *post*.

Inspection of locomotive boilers.

§ 49-a. It shall be the duty of every railroad corporation operated by steam power, within this state, and of the directors, managers or superintendents of such railroad to cause thorough inspections to be made of the boilers of all the locomotives which shall be used by such corporation or corporations, on said railroads. Said inspections shall be made, at least once every three months, by competent and qualified inspectors of boilers,

10

under the direction and superintendence of said corporation or
corporations, or the directors, managers or superintendents
thereof. The person or persons who shall make said inspections, shall make and subscribe his name to a written or printed
certificate which shall contain the number of each boiler inspected,
the date of its inspection, the condition of the boiler inspected,
and shall cause said certificate or certificates to be filed in the
office of the railroad commissioners, within ten days after each
inspection shall be made, and also with the officer or employee
of such railroad having immediate charge of the operation of
such locomotive. If it shall be ascertained by such inspection
and test, or otherwise, that any locomotive boiler is unsafe for
use, the same shall not again be used until it shall be repaired,
and made safe. A certificate of a boiler inspector to the effect
that the same is in a safe condition for use shall be made and
filed in the office of the railroad commissioners. Every corporation, director, manager or superintendent operating such railroad and violating any of the provisions of this section shall be
liable to a penalty, to be paid to the people of the state of
New York, of one hundred dollars for each offense, and the
further penalty of one hundred dollars for each day it or they
shall omit or neglect to comply with said provisions, and the
making or filing of a false certificate shall be a misdemeanor.
Any person, upon application to the secretary of said board of
railroad commissioners and on the payment of such reasonable
fee as said board may by rule fix, shall be furnished with a copy
of any such certificate.

Added by chap. 611, Laws of 1905.
See sections 199 and 362, Penal Code, *post*.

State inspector of locomotive boilers.

*§ 2. § 49-b. Within twenty days after this section takes effect,
the state railroad commission shall appoint a competent person
as inspector of locomotive boilers, who shall receive a compensation to be fixed by the commission, not exceeding three thous.
and dollars per year. Such inspector shall, under the direction

*So in original.

of the commission, inspect boilers or* locomotives used by railroad corporations operating steam railroads within the state, and may cause the same to be tested by hydrostatic test and shall perform such other duties in connection with the inspection and test of locomotive boilers as the commission shall direct. But this section shall not relieve any railroad corporation from the duties imposed by the preceding section.

Added by chap. 611, Laws of 1905.

Railroad commissioners may approve other safeguards.

§ 50. The board of railroad commissioners may, on the application of any railroad corporation, authorize it to use any other safeguard or device approved by the board, in place of any safeguard or device required by this article, which shall thereafter be used in lieu thereof, and the same penalties for neglect or refusal to use the same shall be incurred and imposed as for a failure to use the safeguard or device hereinbefore required, in lieu of which the same is to be used.

Use of stoves or furnaces prohibited.

§ 51. It shall not be lawful for any railroad corporation, operating a steam railroad in this state, of the length of fifty miles or more, excepting foreign railroad corporations, incorporated without the jurisdiction of the United States, running cars upon tracks in this state for a distance of less than thirty miles, to heat its passenger cars, on other than mixed trains, excepting dining-room cars, by any stove or furnace kept inside the car, or suspended therefrom, unless in case of accident or other emergency, when it may temporarily use such stove or furnace with necessary fuel, in cars which have been equipped with apparatus to heat by steam, hot water or hot air from the locomotive, or from a special car, the present stove may be retained to be used only when the car is standing still, and no stove or furnace shall be used in a dining-room car, except for cooking purposes, and of pattern and kind to be approved by the railroad commissioners. This section shall not be held to affect or interfere with the use by the commissioners of fisheries of this

---

* So in original.

or other states, or of the United States, of stoves for heating or cooking or boilers for hatching operations in their fish car or cars. Any person or corporation, violating any of the provisions of this section, shall be liable to a penalty of one thousand dol lars, and to the further penalty of one hundred dollars for each and every day during which such violation shall continue.

Thus amended by chap. 299, Laws of 1896.
See section 423, Penal Code, *post*.

Canada thistles to be cut.

§ 52. Every railroad corporation doing business within this state, shall cause all Canada thistles, white and yellow daisies and other noxious weeds growing on any lands owned or occu- pied by it, to be cut down twice in each and every year, once between the fifteenth day of June and the twenty-fifth day of June, and once between the fifteenth day of August and the twenty-fifth day of August. If any such corporation shall neglect to cause the same to be só cut down, any person may cut the same, between the twenty-fifth day of June and the fifth day of July inclusive, and between the twenty-fifth day of August and the fifth day of September inclusive in each year, at the expense of the corporation on whose lands the same shall be so cut, at the rate of three dollars per day for the time occupied in cutting.

Riding on platform; walking along track.

§ 53. No railroad corporation shall be liable for any injury to any passenger while on the platform of a car, or in any baggage, wood or freight car, in violation of the printed regulations of the corporation, posted up at the time in a conspicuous place inside of the passenger cars, then in the train, if there shall be at the time sufficient room for the proper accommodation of the passenger inside such passenger cars. No person other than those connected with or employed upon the railroad shall walk upon or along its track or tracks, except where the same shall be laid across or along streets or highways, in which case he shall not walk upon the track unless necessary to cross the same.

Any person riding, leading or driving any horse or other animal upon any railroad, or within the fences and guards thereof, other than at a farm or street or forest crossing, without the consent of the corporation, shall forfeit to the people of the state the sum of ten dollars, and pay all damages sustained thereby to the party aggrieved.

Thus amended by chap. 676, Laws of 1892.

Corporations may establish ferries.

§ 54. Any steam railroad corporation, incorporated under the laws of this state, with a terminus in the harbor of New York, may purchase or lease boats propelled by steam or otherwise, and operate the same as a ferry or otherwise, over the waters of the harbor of New York; but this section shall not be construed to affect the rights of the cities of New York and Brooklyn.

Thus amended by chap. 676, Laws of 1892.

Certain railroads may cease operation in winter.

§ 55. The directors of any railroad corporation operating a railroad, constructed and used principally for transporting lumber or ores, during the summer months, or for summer travel, may, by a resolution duly passed at a meeting thereof, apply to the board of railroad commissioners for permission to cease the operation of their road during the winter season, for a period, not exceeding seven months in any one year, specifying the date of such suspension, and the date of the reopening thereof; and such board may, in their discretion, make an order granting the application wholly or in part, and thereupon such railroad corporation shall be relieved of the duty of operating its road during the period specified in the order. A copy of such order shall be posted in all the depots and at the termini of such railroad, and published in every newspaper in each town in any part of which such road shall be constructed at least four weeks prior to the date of such suspension.

See section 21, Railroad Law, ante.

Mails.

§ 56. Any railroad corporation shall, when applied to by the postmaster-general, convey the mails of the United States on its road, and in case such corporation and the postmaster-general shall not agree as to the rate of transportation therefor, and as to the time, rate of speed, manner and condition of carrying the same, the board of railroad commissioners shall fix the prices, terms and conditions therefor, after giving the corporation a reasonable opportunity to be heard. Such price shall not be less for carrying such mails in the regular passenger trains than the amount which such corporation would receive as freight on a like weight of merchandise transported in their merchandise trains, and a fair compensation for the post-office car. If the postmaster-general shall require the mail to be carried at other hours, or at higher speed than the passenger trains are run, the corporation shall furnish an extra train for the mail, and be allowed an extra compensation for the expenses and wear and tear thereof, and for the service to be fixed as herein provided.

Every railroad corporation refusing or neglecting to comply with any provision of this section shall forfeit to the people of the state one hundred dollars for every day such neglect or refusal continues.

Thus amended by chap. 676, Laws of 1892.

Corporations must make annual and quarterly and further reports.

§ 57. Every person or corporation owning, leasing, operating or in possession of a railroad, wholly or partly, in this state, shall make an annual report to the board of railroad commissioners of its operations for the year ending with June thirtieth, and of its condition on that day which shall be verified by the oaths of the president, or treasurer, and the general manager, or acting superintendent, and shall be filed in the office of such board on or before September first in each year. Every such person or corporation shall make quarterly and further reports to such board in the form and within the time prescribed by it. Such board may in its discretion change the date of the annual report and of filing the same, but the length of time between the date of the annual report and the filing of the same shall not be less than herein prescribed. Any person or railroad corporation which shall neglect to make any such report, or which shall fail to correct any such report within ten days after notice by the board of railroad commissioners, shall be liable to a penalty of two hundred and fifty dollars, and an additional penalty of twenty-five dollars for each day after September first on which it shall neglect to file the same, to be sued for in the name of the people of the state of New York, for their use.

The board of railroad commissioners may extend the time herein limited for cause shown.

Thus amended by chap. 676, Laws of 1892.

See section 158, Railroad Law, *post;* also sections 101a, 416, 602 and 611, Penal Code, *post.*

Policemen.

§ 58. The governor may appoint any conductor or brakeman on any train conveying passengers on any steam railroad in this state, a policeman, with all the powers of a policeman in cities and villages, for the preservation of order and of the public peace, and the arrest of all persons committing offenses upon the land or property of the corporation owning or operating such railroad; and he may also appoint, on the application of any such corporation, or of any steamboat company, such additional policemen, designated by it, as he may deem proper, who shall have the same powers. Every such policeman shall within fifteen days after receiving his commission, and before entering upon the duties of his office, take and subscribe the constitutional oath of office, and file it with his commission in the office of the secretary of state. Every such policeman shall when on duty wear a metallic shield, with the words "railroad police" or "steamboat police" as the case may be, and the name of the corporation for which appointed inscribed thereon, which shall always be worn in plain view, except when employed as a detective. The compensation of every such policeman shall be such as may be agreed upon between him and the corporation for which he is appointed, and shall be paid by the corporation. When any corporation shall no longer require the services of any such policeman they may file notice to that effect in the office in which notice of his appointment was originally filed, and thereupon such appointment shall cease and be at an end.

Thus amended by chap. 380, Laws of 1906.
See section 119, Penal Code, *post*.

Requisites to exercise of powers of future railroad corporations.

§ 59.   No railroad corporation hereafter formed under the laws of this state shall exercise the powers conferred by law upon such corporations or begin the construction of its road until the directors shall cause a copy of the articles of association to be published in one or more newspapers in each county in which the road is proposed to be located, at least once a week for three successive weeks, and shall file satisfactory proof thereof with the board of railroad commissioners; nor until the board of railroad commissioners shall certify that the foregoing conditions have been complied with, and also that public convenience and a necessity require the construction of said railroad as proposed in said articles of association.   The foregoing certificate shall be applied for within six months after the completion of the three weeks' publication hereinbefore provided for.   If certificate is refused no further proceedings shall be had before said board, but the application may be renewed after one year from the date of such refusal.   Prior to granting or refusing said certificate the board shall have a right to permit errors, omissions or defects to be supplied and corrected.   After a refusal to grant such certificate the board shall certify a copy of all maps and papers on file in its office and of the findings of the board when so requested by the directors aforesaid.   Such directors may thereupon present the same to a general term of the supreme court of the department within which said road is proposed in whole or in part to be constructed, and said general term shall have power, in its discretion, to order said board, for reasons stated, to issue said certificate, and it shall be issued accordingly.   Such certificate shall be filed in the office of the secretary of state, and a copy thereof, certified to be a copy by the secretary of state, or his deputy, shall be evidence of the fact therein stated. Nothing in this section shall prevent any such railroad corporation from causing such examinations and sur-veys for its proposed railroad to be made as may be necessary to the selection of the most advantageous route; and for such purpose by its officers or agents and servants, to enter upon the lands or water of any person, but subject to the responsibility for all damages which shall be done thereto.

Thus amended by chap. 545, Laws of 1895.

See chap. 597, Laws of 1903, *post;* also chap. 649, Laws of 1896, *post;* also latter part of section 180, Tax Law, *post.*

See 96 Appellate Division p. 471, 178 N. Y., 75; 105 App. Div., 273; 103 App. Div. 123; 184 N. Y. Mem. 59; 101 App. Div. 251; 184 N. Y. Mem. 47; 113 App. Div. Mem. 8.

See other decisions of courts under this section since 1892.

Railroad commissioners may certify part of the route of a street surface railroad; power to revoke certificates; street surface railroad extension.

§ 59-a. Whenever application is made by a street surface rail-road company for a certificate of public convenience and a neces-sity as required by the provisions of the foregoing section, and it shall appear to the board of railroad commissioners, after exami-nation of the proposed route of the applicant company that public convenience and a necessity do not require the construc-tion of said railroad as proposed in its articles of association but do require the construction of a part of the said railroad, the board of railroad commissioners may issue its certificate for the construction of such part of the said railroad as seems to it to be required by public convenience and a necessity. In case any rail-road company which shall hereafter obtain the certificate of the board of railroad commissioners that public convenience and a necessity require the construction of the whole or a part of the said railroad shall fail to begin such construction within two years from the date of the issuing of said certificate, the board of railroad commissioners may inquire into the reason for such failure and the said board may revoke said certificate if it shall appear to it to be in the public interest so to do. Any street sur-face railroad company which proposes to extend its road beyond the limits of any city or incorporated village by a route which will be practically parallel with a street surface railroad already constructed and in operation shall first obtain the certificate of the board of railroad commissioners that public convenience and a necessity require the construction of such extension as provided in the case of a railroad corporation newly formed. Before making application for such certificate the corporation shall cause to be advertised the route of the proposed extension in one or more newspapers in each county in which such extension is to be constructed, at least once a week for three successive weeks. and shall file satisfactory proof of such publication with the board of railroad commissioners. Nothing in this section shall prevent street railroad companies. from making extensions within the limits of cities or incorporated villages upon compliance with the provisions of law now applicable thereto.

Added by chap. 643, Laws of 1898, and thus amended by chap. 226, Laws of 1902. See statutes in this volume as to extension and limitation of time in which to construct railroads.

See 96 Appellate Division, p. 471, 178 N. Y. 75, and decisions cited under immediately preceding section.

Revocation of certificate under certain circumstances.

§ 59-b. Whenever it shall be made to appear to the board of railroad commissioners that any steam railroad corporation, which has obtained from it a certificate under section fifty-nine of the railroad law since eighteen hundred and ninety-four and whose road is less than ten miles in length, and was to be built in the counties of Saratoga and Washington, shall not have completed its construction and put it in operation within three years after obtaining such certificates,* the said board, on notice to such corporation, shall have the power to revoke the said certificate and consent and thereupon the corporate existence and power of such railroad corporation shall cease and determine.

Added by chap. 597, Laws of 1899.

Grade crossing law, sections 60-69.

§ 60. All steam surface railroads, hereafter built except additional switches and sidings, must be so constructed as to avoid

---

* So in original.

all public crossings at grade, whenever practicable so to do. Whenever application is made to the board of railroad commissioners, under section fifty-nine of the railroad law, there shall be filed with said board a map showing the streets, avenues and highways proposed to be crossed by the new construction, and the said board shall determine whether such crossing shall be under or over the proposed railroad, except where said board shall determine such method of crossing to be impracticable. Whenever an application is made under this section to determine the manner of crossing, the said board shall designate a time and place when and where a hearing will be given to such railroad company, and shall notify the municipal corporation having jurisdiction over such streets, avenues or highways proposed to be crossed by the new railroad. The said board shall also give public notice of such hearing in at least two newspapers, published in the locality affected by the application, and all persons owning land in the vicinity of the proposed crossings shall have the right to be heard. The decision of the said board rendered in any proceedings under this section shall be communicated, within twenty days after final hearing, to all parties to whom notice of the hearing in said proceedings was given, or who appeared at said hearing by counsel or in person.

Added by chap. 754, Laws of 1897.
See section 96, Railroad Law, *post.*
See 88 App. Div. 387; 179 N. Y.

§ 61. When a new street, avenue or highway, or new portion of a street, avenue or highway shall hereafter be constructed across a steam surface railroad, other than pursuant to the provisions of section sixty-two of this act, such street, avenue or highway or portion of such street, avenue or highway, shall pass over or under such railroad or at grade as the board of railroad commissioners shall direct. Notice of intention to lay out such street, avenue or highway, or new portion of a street, avenue or highway, across a steam surface railroad, shall be given to such railroad company by the municipal corporation at least fifteen days prior to the making of the order laying out such street, avenue or highway by service personally on the president or vice-president of the railroad corporation, or any general officer thereof. Such notice shall designate the time and place and when and where a hearing will be given to such railroad company, and such railroad company shall have the right to be heard before the authorities of such municipal corporation upon the question of the necessity of such street, avenue or highway. If the municipal corporation determines such street, avenue or highway to be necessary, it shall then apply to the board of railroad commissioners before any further proceedings are taken, to determine whether such street, avenue or highway shall pass over or under such railroad, or at grade, whereupon the said board of railroad commissioners shall appoint a time and place for hearing such application, and shall give such notice thereof, as they judge reasonable, not, however, less than ten days, to the railroad company whose railroad is to be crossed by such new street, avenue or highway, or new portion of a street, avenue or highway, to the municipal corporation and to the owners of land adjoining the railroad and that part of the street, avenue or highway to be opened or extended. The said board of railroad commissioners shall determine whether such street, avenue or highway, or new portion of a street, avenue or highway, shall be constructed over or under such railroad or at grade; and if said board determine that such street, avenue or highway shall be carried across such railroad above grade, then said board shall determine the height, the length and the material of the bridge or structure by means of which such street, avenue or highway shall be carried across such railroad, and the length, character and grades of the approaches thereto; and if said board shall determine that such street, avenue or highway shall be constructed or extended below the grade, said board shall determine the manner and method in which the same shall be so carried under, and the grade or grades thereof, and if said board shall determine that said street, avenue or highway shall be constructed or extended at grade, said board shall determine the manner and method in which the same shall be carried over said railroad at grade and what safeguards shall be maintained. The decision of the said board as to the manner and method of carrying such new street, avenue or highway, or new portion of a street, avenue or highway, across such railroad, shall be final, subject, however, to the right of appeal hereinafter given. The decision of said board rendered in any proceeding under this section shall be communicated within twenty days after final hearing to all parties to whom notice of the hearing in such proceeding was given or who appeared at such hearing by counsel or in person.

Thus amended by chap. 520, Laws of 1898.
See chap. 462, Laws of 1903, *post.*
See section 96, Railroad Law, *post.*
See decisions of courts under this section, including 167 N. Y. 256.

§ 62. The mayor and common council of any city, the president and trustees of any village, the town board of any town within which a street, avenue or highway crosses or is crossed by a steam surface railroad at grade, or any steam surface railroad company, whose road crosses or is crossed by a street, avenue or highway at grade, may bring their petition, in writing, to the board of railroad commissioners, therein alleging that public safety requires an alteration in the manner of such crossing, its approaches, the method of crossing, the location of the highway or crossing, the closing and discontinuance of a highway crossing and the diversion of the travel thereon to another highway or crossing, or if not practicable to change such crossing from grade or to close and discontinue the same, the opening of an additional crossing for the partial diversion of travel from the grade crossing, and praying that the same may be ordered; whereupon the said board of railroad commissioners shall appoint a time and place for hearing the petition, and shall give such personal notice thereof as they shall judge reasonable, of not less than ten days, however, to said petitioner, the railroad company, the municipality in which such crossing is situated, and to the owners of the lands adjoining such crossing and adjoining that part of the highway to be changed in grade or location, or the land to be opened for a new crossing, and shall cause notice of said hearing to be advertised in at least two newspapers published in the locality affected by the application; and after such notice of hearing the said board of railroad commissioners shall determine what alterations or changes, if any, shall be made. The decision of said board of railroad commissioners rendered in any proceeding under this section, shall be communicated within twenty days after final hearing to all parties to whom notice of the hearing in said proceeding was given, or who appeared at said hearing by counsel or in person. Any person aggrieved by such decision, or by a decision made pursuant to sections sixty and sixty-one hereof, and who was a party to said proceeding, may within sixty days appeal therefrom to the appellate division of the supreme court in the department in which such grade crossing is situated and to the court of appeals, in the same manner and with like effect as is provided in the case of appeals from an order of the supreme court.

Thus amended by chap. 359, Laws of 1899.
See chap. 164, Laws of 1902, *post.*
See 176 N. Y., 324; 177 N. Y., 337; 179 N. Y., 393; 181 N. Y., 132.
See section 96, Railroad Law, *post.*
See chap. 115, Laws of 1898, *post.*

§ 63. The municipal corporation in which the highway crossing is located, may, with the approval of the railroad company, acquire by purchase any lands, rights or easements necessary or required for the purpose of carrying out the provisions of sections sixty, sixty-one and sixty-two of this act, but if unable to do so shall acquire such lands, rights or easements by condemnation either under the condemnation law, or under the provisions of the charter of such municipal corporation. The railroad company shall have notice of any such proceedings and the right to be heard therein.

Thus amended by chap. 226, Laws of 1899.

§ 64. When a highway crosses a railroad by an overhead bridge, the frame work of the bridge and its abutments, shall be maintained and kept in repair by the railroad company, and the roadway thereover and the approaches thereto shall be maintained and kept in repair by the municipality in which the same are situated; except that in the case of an overhead bridge constructed prior to the enactment of sections sixty-one and sixty-two of this act, the roadway over and the approaches to which the railroad company was under obligation to maintain and repair, such obligations shall continue, provided the railroad company shall have at least ten days' notice of any defect in the roadway thereover and the approaches thereto, which notice must be given in writing by the commissioner of highways or other duly constituted authorities, and the railroad company shall not be liable by reason of any such defect unless it shall have failed to make repairs within ten days after the service of such notice upon it. When a highway passes under a railroad, the bridge and its abutments shall be maintained and kept in repair by the railroad company, and the subway and its approaches shall be maintained and kept in repair by the municipality in which the same are situated.

Thus amended by chap. 140, Laws of 1902.
See chap. 164, Laws of 1902, *post*.

§ 65. Whenever, under the provisions of section sixty of this act, new railroads are constructed across existing highways, the expense of crossing above or below the grade of the highway shall be paid entirely by the railroad corporations. Whenever under the provisions of section sixty-one of this act a new street, avenue or highway is constructed across an existing railroad, the railroad corporation shall pay one-half and the municipal corporation wherein such street, avenue or highway is located, shall pay the remaining one-half of the expense of making such crossing above or below grade; and whenever a change is made as to an existing crossing in accordance with the provisions of section sixty-two of this act, fifty per centum of the expense thereof shall be borne by the railroad corporation, twenty-five per centum by the municipal corporation, and twenty-five per centum by the state. Whenever, in carrying out the provisions of sections sixty-one or sixty-two of this act, two or more lines of steam surface railroad, owned and operated by different corporations, cross a highway at a point where a change in grade is made, each corporation shall pay such proportion of fifty per centum of the expense thereof as shall be determined by the board of rail road commissioners. In carrying out the provisions of sections sixty, sixty-one and sixty-two of this act the work shall be done by the railroad corporation or corporations affected thereby, subject to the supervision of and approval of the board of rail road commissioners, and in all cases, except where the entire expense is paid by the railroad corporation, the expense of construction shall be paid primarily by the railroad company, and the expense of acquiring additional lands, rights or easements, shall be paid primarily by the municipal corporation wherein such highway crossings are located. Plans and specifications of all changes proposed under sections sixty-one and sixty-two of this act, and an estimate of the expense thereof shall be submitted to the board of railroad commissioners for their approval before the letting of any contract. In case the work is done by contract the proposals of contractors shall be submitted to the board of railroad commissioners, and if the board shall determine that the bids are excessive it shall have the power to require the submission of new proposals. The board of rail road commissioners may employ temporarily such experts and engineers as may be necessary to properly supervise any work that may be undertaken under sections sixty, sixty-one or sixty-two of this act, the expense thereof to be paid by the comptroller upon the requisition and certificate of the said board, said expense to be included in the cost of the particular change in grade on account of which it is incurred and finally apportioned

in the manner provided in this section. Upon the completion
of the work and its approval by the board of railroad commissioners an accounting shall be had between the railroad corporation and the municipal corporation, of the amounts expended by
each with interest, and if it shall appear that the railroad corporation or the municipal corporation have expended more than
their proportion of the expense of the crossing as herein provided, a settlement shall be forthwith made in accordance with
the provisions of this section. All items of expenditure shall be
verified under oath, and, in case of a dispute between the railroad corporation and the municipal corporation as to the amount
expended, any judge of the supreme court in the judicial district
in which the municipality is situated, may appoint a referee to
take testimony as to the amount expended, and the confirmation
of the report of the referee shall be final. In the event of the
failure or refusal of the railroad corporation to pay its proportion of the expense, the same, with interest from the date of
such accounting, may be levied and assessed upon the railroad
corporation and collected in the same manner that taxes and
assessments are now collected by the municipal corporation within
which the work is done; and in the event of the failure or refusal
of the municipal corporation to pay its proportion of the expense,
suit may be instituted by the railroad corporation for the collection of the same with interest from the date of such accounting,
or the railroad corporation may offset such amount with interest
against any taxes levied or assessed against it or its property by
such municipal corporation. The legislature shall annually appropriate out of any moneys not otherwise appropriated the sum of
one hundred thousand dollars for the purpose of paying the
state's proportion of the expense of a change in an existing grade
crossing. If, in any year, any less sum than one hundred thousand
dollars is expended by the state for the purpose aforesaid the
balance remaining unexpended shall be applied to reduce the
amount appropriated by the state in the next succeeding year,

11

except that no such deduction shall be made in case there are outstanding and unadjusted obligations on account of a change in an existing grade crossing for a proportion of which the state is liable under the provisions of this section. In the event of the appropriation made by the state in any one year being insufficient to pay the state's proportion of the expense of any change that may be ordered the first payment from the appropriation of the succeeding year shall be on account of said change, and no payment shall be made on account of any subsequent change that may be ordered, nor shall any subsequent change be ordered until the obligation of the state on account of the first named change in grade has been fully discharged, unless the same shall be provided for by an additional appropriation to be made by the legislature. The state's proportion of the expense of changing any existing grade crossing shall be paid by the state treasurer on the warrant of the comptroller, to which shall be appended the certificate of the board of railroad commissioners to the effect that the work has been properly performed and a statement showing the situation of the crossing that has been changed, the total cost and the proportionate expense thereof, and the money shall be paid in whole or in part to the railroad corporation or to the municipal corporation as the board of railroad commissioners may direct, subject, however, to the rights of the respective parties as they appear from the accounting to be had as hereinbefore provided for. No claim for damages to property on account of the change or abolishment of any crossing under the provisions of this act shall be allowed unless notice of such claim is filed with the board of railroad commissioners within six months after completion of the work necessary for such change or abolishment.

Thus amended by chap. 517, Laws of 1900.

§ 66. The railroad commissioners may, in the absence of any application therefor, when, in their opinion, public safety requires

an alteration in an existing grade crossing, institute proceedings on their own motion for an alteration in such grade crossing, upon such notice as they shall deem reasonable, of not less
than ten days, however, to the railroad company, the municipal
corporation and the person or persons interested, and proceedings shall be conducted as provided in section sixty-two of this
act. The changes in existing grade crossings authorized or
required by the board of railroad commissioners in any one year
shall be so distributed and apportioned over and among the
railroads and the municipalities of the state as to produce such
equality of burden upon them for their proportionate part of
the expenses as herein provided for as the nature and circumstances of the cases before them will permit.

Added by chap. 754, Laws of 1897.
See 189 N. Y., Mem., 11.

§ 67. It shall be the duty of the corporation, municipality or
person or persons to whom the decisions or recommendations of
the board of railroad commissioners are directed, as provided
in sections sixty, sixty-one, sixty-two and sixty-six of this act to
comply with such decisions and recommendations, and in case
of their failure so to do, the board shall present the facts in the
case to the attorney-general, who shall thereupon take proceedings to compel obedience to the decisions and recommendations
of the board of railroad commissioners. The supreme court at
a special term shall have the power in all cases of such decisions
and recommendations by the board of railroad commissioners to
compel compliance therewith by mandamus, subject to appeal to
the appellate division of the supreme court and the court of
appeals, in the same manner, and with like effect, as is provided
in case of appeals from any order of the supreme court.

Added by chap. 754, Laws of 1897.

§ 67-a. Whenever in carrying out any of the provisions of sections sixty, sixty-one, sixty-two, sixty-three, sixty-four, sixty-five,
sixty-six, or sixty-seven of this act, any municipality shall incur

any expense or become liable for the payment of any moneys, it shall be lawful for such municipality to temporarily borrow such moneys on the notes or certificates of such municipality, and to include the amount of outstanding notes or certificates, or any part thereof, in its next annual tax levy for municipal purposes, or in the discretion of the common council in case of a city, the board of trustees in case of a village or the town board in case of a town, to borrow the same, or any part thereof, on the credit of the municipality, and to issue bonds therefor, which bonds shall be signed by the mayor and clerk in case of a city, the president and clerk in case of a village and the town board in case of a town, and shall be in such form and for such sums and be payable at such times and places with interest not exceeding four per centum per annum, as the common council in case of a city, the board of trustees in case of a village, and the town board in case of a town, shall direct.

Thus amended by chap. 198, Laws of 1902.

§ 68. All steam railroads hereafter constructed across the tracks of any other railroad and any street surface railroad hereafter constructed across a steam railroad shall be above, below, or at grade of such existing railroad as the board of railroad commissioners shall determine, and such board shall in such determination fix the proportion of expense of such crossing to be paid by each railroad.

Thus amended by chap. 739, Laws of 1900.

See sections 12, 33, 35 and 36, Railroad Law, *ante*, and chap. 239, Laws of 1893, *post*.

See 75 Appellate Division, p. 412, 175 N. Y. Mem. 468.

§ 69. The provisions of this act shall also apply to all existing or future steam surface railroads, on which, after the passage of this act, electricity or some other agency than steam shall be substituted as a motive power.

Added by chap. 754, Laws of 1897.

CHAP. 754, LAWS OF 1897.

AN ACT to amend railroad law, and the act amendatory thereof, relative to grade crossings.

Section 1. Article two of chapter five hundred and sixty-five of the laws of eighteen hundred and ninety, entitled "An act in relation to railroads, constituting chapter thirty-nine of the general laws," known as the railroad law, as amended by chapter six hundred and seventy-six of the laws of eighteen hundred and ninety-two, is hereby amended by adding thereto the following sections:

See sections 60–69 of Railroad Law, above.

§ 2. None of the provisions of this act shall apply to crossings in the city of Buffalo under the jurisdiction of the grade crossing commissioners of that city, nor shall they apply to the University avenue or Brown street crossing, in the city of Rochester.

§ 3. All acts and parts of acts inconsistent with this act are hereby repealed.

§ 4. This act shall take effect the first day of July, eighteen hundred and ninety-seven.

ARTICLE III.

CONSOLIDATION, LEASE, SALE, AND REORGANIZATION.

Consolidation of corporations owning continuous lines.

§ 70. Any railroad or other corporation, organized under the laws of this state, or of this state and any other state, and owning or operating a railroad, bridge or tunnel, either wholly within or partly within and partly without the state, or whose lines or routes of road have been located but not constructed, may merge and consolidate its capital stock, franchises, and property with the capital stock, franchises and property of any other railroad, tunnel or bridge corporation or corporations organized under the laws of this state or of this state and any other state, or under the laws of any other state or states, whenever the two or more railroads of the companies or corporations so to be consolidated, tunnels, bridges or branches or any part thereof, or the line or routes of their road, if not constructed, shall or may form a continuous or connected line of railroad with each other or by means of any intervening railroad bridge, tunnel or ferry and any such consolidated corporation may thereupon construct or finish the construction of such continuous line of railroad, if not previously constructed, and operate the same, subject to all provisions of law applicable to such railroad corporations. Where the road to be operated is in whole or in part a tunnel or sub-surface road, authorized by section 16 of this chapter, its consolidation with another road or roads under the provisions of this section shall not prevent any connecting railroad from having equal rights of transit for its passengers and freight through or over the tunnel or bridge of any such road, upon the same equitable terms, nor shall such consolidation be made where such tunnel or subsurface road exceeds five miles in length.

Thus amended by chap. 676, Laws of 1892.
See chap. 193, Laws of 1897, chap. 201, Laws of 1899, and chap. 30, Laws of 1903, *post.*

Conditions.

§ 71. Such consolidation shall be made in the following manner:

Joint agreement; amount of capital stock.

1. The directors of the corporations proposing to consolidate may enter into a joint agreement, under the corporate seal of each corporation, for the consolidation of such corporations, and pre-

scribing the terms and conditions thereof, the mode of carrying the same into effect, the name of the new corporation, the number and names of the directors and other officers thereof, and who shall be the first directors and officers and their places of residence, the number of shares of the capital stock, the amount or par value of each share, and the manner of converting the capital stock of each corporation into that of the new corporation, and how and when the directors and officers shall be chosen, with such other details as they shall deem necessary to perfect such new organization and the consolidation of such corporations. But in no case shall the capital stock of the corporation formed by such consolidation exceed the sum of the capital stock of the corporations so consolidated, at the par value thereof. Nor shall any bonds or other evidences of debt be issued as a consideration for, or in connection with, such consolidation. If either of the corporations so to be consolidated is a corporation organized under the laws of any other state the joint agreement herein provided for may fix the location of the principal office of the new corporation in either state.

Subdivision 1 thus amended by chap. 228, Laws of 1904.

Agreement to be submitted to meeting of stockholders.

2. If stockholders owning two-thirds of all the stock of each of such corporations shall by a consent in writing, acknowledged as are deeds entitled to be recorded and endorsed upon said lease or agreement, signify their assent thereto, it shall be deemed and taken as the adoption of such agreement by and on behalf of such corporation, and the original or a certified copy thereof shall be filed as hereinafter provided. If such agreement shall not be consented to in writing by holders of two-thirds of the stock of either of such corporations as hereinbefore provided, such agreement shall be submitted to the stockholders of each of such corporations at a meeting thereof called separately for the purpose of taking the same into consideration. Due notice of the time and place of holding such meeting, and the object thereof, shall be given by each corporation to its stockholders

by written or printed notices addressed to each of the persons
in whose names the capital stock of such corporation stands on
the books thereof, and delivered to such persons respectively, or
sent to them by mail, when their post-office address is known to
the corporation, at least thirty days before the time of holding
such meeting, and also by a general notice published at least
once a week for four weeks successively in some newspaper
printed in the city, town or county where such corporation has
its principal office or place of business. At such meeting of
stockholders such agreement shall be considered, and a vote by
ballot taken for the adoption or rejection of the same, and if the
votes of the stockholders owning at least two-thirds of the stock
of each corporation present and voting in person or by proxy
shall be for the adoption of such agreement, then that fact shall
be certified thereon by the secretaries of the respective corporations, under the seal thereof, and the agreement so adopted, or
a certified copy thereof, shall be filed in the office of the secretary
of state, and in the office of the clerk of the county where the
new corporation is to have its principal place of business, and
shall from thence be deemed and taken to be the agreement and
act of consolidation of such corporations, and thereafter such
corporations, parties thereto, shall be one corporation by the
name provided in such agreement, but such act of consolidation
shall not release such new corporation from any of the restrictions, liabilities or duties of the several corporations so consolidated.

Thus amended by chap. 676, Laws of 1892.

New Corporation.

§ 72. Upon the consummation of such act of consolidation all
the rights, privileges, exemptions and franchises of each of the
corporations, parties to the same, and all the property, real, personal and mixed, and all the debts due on whatever account to
either of them, as well as all stock subscriptions and other things
in action belonging to either of them shall be taken and deemed
to be transferred to and vested in such new corporation, with-

out further act or deed; and all claims, demands, property, rights of way, and every other interest shall be as effectually the property of the new corporation as they were of the former corporations, parties to such agreement and act; and the title to all real estate, taken by deed or otherwise, under the laws of this state, vested in either of such corporations, parties to such agreement and act, shall not be deemed to revert or be in any way impaired by reason of this act, or anything done by virtue thereof, but shall be vested in the new corporation by virtue of such act of consolidation. And it shall be lawful for any railroad company or corporation, now or hereafter formed by the consolidation of one or more railroad companies or corporations organized under the laws of this state, or under the laws of this state and other states, with one or more railroad companies or corporations organized under the laws of any other state, or of the laws of this state and other states, to issue its bonds for the purpose of paying or retiring any bonds theretofore issued by either of said companies or corporations so consolidated, or for any purpose and to the amount authorized by the laws of the state under which either of said companies or corporations so consolidated was organized, and secure the same by a mortgage upon its real or personal property, franchises, rights and privileges, whether within or without this state, and subject to the remedies for the enforcement of the same under the laws of either of said states. Nothing in this act contained shall authorize the execution of any such mortgage without the consent of the stockholders as now required by the laws of this state, nor compel any bondholder to accept payment in whole or in part of any bond or bonds held by him or to surrender the same before they shall become due.

Thus amended by chap. 362, Laws of 1891.

Creditors' rights not to be impaired.

§ 73. The rights of all creditors of, and all liens upon the property of, either of such corporations, parties to such agreement and act, shall be preserved unimpaired, and the respective corporations shall be deemed to continue in existence to pre-

serve the same, and all debts and liabilities incurred by either
of such corporations shall thenceforth attach to such new corporation, and be enforced against it and its property to the same
extent as if incurred or contracted by it. No actions or proceedings in which either of such corporations is a party shall abate
or be discontinued by such agreement and act of consolidation,
but may be conducted to final judgment in the names of such
corporations, or such new corporation may be, by order of the
court, on motion substituted as a party.

Assessment of property of new corporation.

§ 74. The real estate of such new corporations, situate within
this state, shall be assessed and taxed in the several towns and
cities where the same shall be situated in like manner as the
real estate of other railroad corporations is or may be taxed and
assessed, and such proportion of the capital stock and personal
property of such new corporation shall in like manner be assessed
and taxed in this state, as the number of miles of its railroad
situate in this state bears to the number of miles of its railroad
situate in the other state or states.

Stocks of municipal corporations, how represented.

§ 75. At any meeting of the stockholders of any railroad corporation to consider any agreement or proposition to consolidate
or lease, the commissioners or other officers of any municipal
corporation holding or having charge of any of the capital stock
of such railroad corporation shall represent such municipal corporation, and may act and vote in person or by proxy on all
matters relating to such consolidation or lease in the same manner
as individual stockholders.

Thus amended by chap. 546, Laws of 1893.
See section 6, Stock Corporation Law, *ante;* town bonding acts, *post.*

Foreclosure of mortgages made by (consolidated) railroads partly
in the state.

§ 76. Whenever a railroad corporation of this or of any other
state or states whose line of road lies partly in this state and
partly in another state or states, shall have executed a mortgage upon its entire line of railroad, and a sale of the entire line

of road under such mortgage shall have been or may hereafter be ordered, adjudged and decreed by a court of competent jurisdiction of the state or states, or by a court of the United States sitting within the state or states in which the greater part of such line of railroad may be situated, upon the confirmation of such judgment or decree, and of the sale made thereunder, by the supreme court of this state or by the circuit court of the United States in the judicial district in which some part of such line of road is situated, such sale shall operate to pass title to the purchaser, of that part of the line of railroad lying in this state, together with its appurtenances and franchises, with the same force and effect as if the judgment or decree under which such sale is had, had been made by a court of competent jurisdiction of this state. Such judgment or decree and sale may be so ordered, adjudged, decreed or confirmed in any action or proceeding heretofore or hereafter brought in the supreme court, or in a court of the United States sitting in this state, for the foreclosure of such mortgage, or in aid of an action for that purpose in such other state or states, if it shall appear that such confirmation is for the interest of the public and of the parties, due and lawful provision being made for and in respect of any liens upon that part of the line of road or other property sold situate in this state, and for such costs, expenses, and charges which may appear to be just and lawful. If a receiver of the entire line of such railroad shall have been, or may hereafter be appointed by such court of competent jurisdiction of the state in which the greater part of the line of railroad is situated, or by a court of the United States sitting in such other state, such receiver may perform, within this state, the duties of his office not inconsistent with the laws of this state, and may sue and be sued in the courts of this state.

Thus amended by chap. 356, Laws of 1896; see section 3 of said act, printed after section 77 of this act.

Powers of corporations organized to acquire and operate railroads partly in the state.

§ 77. A railroad corporation created under the laws of the state or states in which the greater part of the line of its rail-

road may be situated, or a railroad corporation created under
the railroad law, or under article one of the stock corporation
law in this state, for the purpose of taking title to, and operating, the line of road as so sold, under a judgment or decree of a
court of this state, or of a court of the United States sitting in
this state, for the foreclosure of a mortgage, with its franchises
and appurtenances, may hold, possess and operate not only those
parts of the railroad lying in other states, but also that part of
the line of such railroad lying in this state, and shall be subject
to the duties and liabilities to which such corporation was, by
the laws of this state, subject, and to such further or other duties
and liabilities as are now or may hereafter be imposed by law
upon railroad corporations of this state, and the provisions of
the stock corporation law concerning reorganization of corporations shall apply to, and in respect of, every such successor railroad corporation. An exemplified copy of the certificate or certificates of incorporation, under and by virtue of which any such
corporation is created in any other state; and a certified copy of
the judgment or decree of any court sitting in any other state,
under which said railroad shall have been sold, and a certified
copy of the order or judgment or decree of confirmation and
approval required by the preceding section, or of the order, judgment or decree of the court of this state, or of the United States
in this state, which decreed the sale, confirming the same, shall
be filed in the office of the secretary of state for this state, and
in the office of the courty* clerk of the county where its principal
business office in this state is or shall be located.

    Thus amended by chap. 356, Laws of 1896.

    § 3 of chap. 356, Laws of 1896: This act shall take effect immediately,
and shall apply in respect of decrees, foreclosures, sales, confirmations,
reorganizations and incorporations, whether heretofore or hereafter made,
provided, however, that nothing in this act shall affect any action or proceeding pending in any court, on or before the first day of April, eighteen
hundred and ninety-six, to establish the invalidity of any foreclosure or
reorganization theretofore had, or to enforce any judgment or claim arising
before such foreclosure or reorganization.

Lease of road.

    § 78. Any railroad corporation or any corporation owning or
operating any railroad or railroad route within this state may

---

* So in original.

contract with any other such corporation for the use of their respective roads or routes, or any part thereof, and thereafter use the same in such manner and for such time as may be prescribed in such contract. Such contract may provide for the exchange or guaranty of the stock and bonds of either of such corporations by the other and shall be executed by the contracting corporations under the corporate seal of each corporation, and if such contract shall be a lease of any such road and for a longer period than one year, such contract shall not be binding or valid unless approved by the votes of stockholders owning at least two-thirds of the stock of each corporation which is represented and voted upon in person or by proxy at an annual meeting of the stockholders for the purpose of electing directors, called in the manner prescribed by law, provided that the notice of such meeting shall state that one of the purposes thereof will be the approval of such lease, or at a meeting, called separately for that purpose upon a notice stating the time, place and object of the meeting, served at least thirty days previously upon each stockholder personally, or mailed to him at his post office address and also published at least once a week, for four weeks successively, in some newspaper printed in the city, town or county where such corporation has its principal office, and there shall be indorsed upon the contract the certificate of the secretaries of the respective corporations under the seals thereof, to the effect that the same has been approved by such votes of the stockholders, and the contract shall be executed in duplicate and filed in the offices where the certificates of incorporation of the contracting corporations are filed. The road of a corporation cannot be used under any such contract in a manner inconsistent with the provisions of law applicable to its use by the corporation owning the same at the time of the execution of the contract. Such contracts shall be executed by the corporations, parties thereto, and proved and acknowledged in such manner as to entitle the same to be recorded in the office of the clerk or register of each county through or into which the road so to be used shall run. If any contract so recorded shall be or has been terminated by the contracting corporations in pursuance of resolutions of their respective boards of directors prior to the time specified in such contract for the termination thereof, then the contracting corporations shall execute, acknowledge and procure to be recorded in each office where such contract is recorded a certificate to the effect that such contract has been terminated, stating the date of the termination thereof, and said certificates so recorded shall be presumptive evidence of the termination of such contract accordingly. Nothing in this section shall apply to any lease in existence prior to May first, eighteen hundred and ninety-one.

Thus amended by chap. 695, Laws of 1905.

Lessees of railroad may acquire stock therein.

§ 79. Any railroad corporation created by the laws of this state, or its successors, being the lessee of the road of any other railroad corporation, may take a surrender or transfer of the capital stock of the stockholders, or any of them in the corporation whose road is held under lease, and issue in exchange therefor the like additional amount of its own capital stock at par, or on such other terms and conditions as may be agreed upon between the two corporations; and whenever the greater part of the capital stock of any such corporation shall have been so surrendered or transferred, the directors of the corporation taking such surrender or transfer shall thereafter, on a resolution electing so to do, to be entered on their minutes, become ex-officio the directors of the corporation whose road is so held under lease, and shall manage and conduct the affairs thereof, as provided by law; and whenever the whole of such capital stock shall have been so surrendered or transferred, and a certificate thereof filed in the office of the secretary of state, under the common seal of the corporation to whom such surrender or transfer shall have been made, the estate, property, rights, privileges and franchises of the corporation whose stock shall have been so surrendered or transferred, shall thereupon vest in and be held and enjoyed by the corporation, to whom such surrender or transfer shall have been made, as fully and entirely, and without change or diminution, as the same were before held and enjoyed, and be managed and controlled by the board of directors of the corporation, to whom such surrender or transfer of such stock shall have been made, and in the corporate name of such corporation. Where stock shall have been so surrendered or transferred, the existing liabilities of the corporation, and the rights of the creditors and of any stockholder not surrendering or transferring his stock, shall not be affected thereby.

Consolidation and lease of parallel lines prohibited.

§ 80. No railroad corporation or corporations owning or operating railroads whose roads run on parallel or competing lines, except street surface railroad corporations, shall merge or consolidate, or enter into any contract for the use of their respective roads, or lease the same, the one to the other, unless the board of railroad commissioners of the state or a majority of such board shall consent thereto.
Thus amended by chap. 676, Laws of 1892.

Mortgagee may purchase at foreclosure sale.

§ 81. Any mortgagee of the property and franchises of any railroad corporation may become the purchaser of the same at any sale thereof under the mortgage, upon foreclosure by advertisement, or under a judgment, or decree, or otherwise, and hold and use the same, with all the rights and privileges belonging thereto or connected therewith for the period of six months, and convey the same to any railroad corporation.

Certificates of stock, may be issued after foreclosure in certain cases.

§ 82. If any person or corporation shall be entitled to certificates of stock subscribed to and paid for in any railroad corporation whose property and franchises have been sold under mortgage foreclosure, and such certificates have not been issued before foreclosure, the officers of the corporation shall, at any time within six months after the foreclosure sale issue and deliver to the person or corporation entitled thereto, upon demand, such certificates of stock, which shall have all the force and effect and confer upon the holder all the rights which he would have had if such certificates of stock had been issued at the time of the payment of the subscription thereto.

Liabilities of reorganized railroad corporations.

§ 83. A railroad corporation, reorganized under the provisions of law, relating to the formation of new or reorganized corporations upon the sale of their property or franchise, shall not be compelled or required to extend its road beyond the portion thereof constructed, at the time the new or reorganized corporation acquired title to such railroad property and franchise, provided the board of railroad commissioners of the state shall certify that in their opinion the public interests under all the circumstances do not require such extension. If such board shall so certify and shall file in their office such certificate, which certificate shall be irreversible by such board, such corporation shall not be deemed to have incurred any obligation so to extend its road and such certificate shall be a bar to any proceedings to compel it to make such extension or to annul its existence for failure so to do, and shall be final and conclusive in all courts and proceedings whatever. This section shall not authorize the abandonment of any portion of a railroad which has been constructed and operated, or apply to Kings county.

As to other states and foreign countries.

§ 84. All the provisions contained in the several sections of this act shall extend, apply to and cover the consolidation, lease, sale or reorganization of any railroad or other corporation heretofore or hereafter organized, under the laws of this State, and any other State or country, to build, lease, buy, sell, maintain or operate any of the lines or routes of railroads, tunnels, bridges, ferries or branches or any part thereof mentioned in this article, and any similar lines or routes of railroad, tunnels, bridges, ferries or any part thereof, constructed or to be located and constructed in any foreign country.

This section added by chap. 921, Laws of 1895.

ARTICLE IV.

STREET SURFACE RAILROADS.

Street surface railroads; general provisions.

§ 90. The provisions of this article shall apply to every corporation which, under the provisions thereof, or of any other law, has constructed or shall construct or operate, or has been or shall be organized to construct or operate, a street surface

---

*So in original.

railroad, or any extension or extensions, branch or branches thereof, for public use in the conveyance of persons and property for compensation, upon and along any street, avenue, road, highway, or private property, in any city, town or village, or in any two or more civil divisions of the State, and every such corporation must comply with the provisions of this article. Any street surface railroad corporation, at any time proposing to extend its road or to construct branches thereof, may, from time to time, make and file in each of the .offices in which its certificate of incorporation is filed, a statement of the names and description of the streets, roads, avenues, highways and private property in or upon which it is proposed to construct, maintain or operate such extensions or branches. Upon filing any such statement and upon complying with the conditions set forth in section ninety-one of the railroad law, every such corporation shall have the power and privilege to construct, extend, operate and maintain such road, extensions or branches, upon and along the streets, avenues, roads, highways and private property named and described in its certificate of incorporation or in such statement. Every such corporation, before constructing any part of its road upon or through any private property described in its articles of association or certificate of incorporation or statement, and before instituting any proceeding for the condemnation of any real property, shall make a map and profile of the route adopted by it upon or through any private property, which map and profile shall be certified by the president and engineer of the company, or a majority of its directors, and shall be filed in the office of the clerk of the county in which the road is to be constructed, and all provisions of section six of the act hereby amended so far as applicable shall apply to the route so located. If any such street surface railroad company is unable to agree for the purchase of any such real property, or of any right or easement therein required for the purpose of its railroad, or if the owner thereof shall be incapable of selling the same, or if, after diligent search and inquiry, the name and residence of such owner can not be ascertained, it shall have the right to acquire title thereto by condemnation in the manner and by the proceedings provided by. the condemnation law. Nothing in this section shall be deemed to authorize a street railroad corporation to acquire real property within a city by condemnation.

Thus amended by chap. 933, Laws of 1895.
See, also, chap. 604, Laws of 1892, and chap. 679, Laws of 1893, *post.*
See 96 App. Div., 471, 178 N. Y., 75.
See 88 App. Div., p. 201.

Consent of property owners and local authorities.

§ 91. A street surface railroad, or extensions or branches thereof, shall not be built, extended or operated unless the consent in writing acknowledged or proved as are deeds entitled.to be recorded, of the owners in cities and villages, of one-half in value, and in towns, not within the corporate limits of a city or village, of the owners of two-thirds in value, of the property bounded on and also the consent of the local authorities having control of that portion of a street or highway upon which it is proposed to build or operate such railroad, extension or branch shall have been first obtained. Such consents of property owners in the county of Kings which shall be hereafter executed, may be forfeited unless within sixty days after the execution thereof, the same shall be recorded in the office of the register of such county. Such register is hereby directed upon the payment of the proper fees to record all consents left with him for that purpose in books to be provided by him and paid for out of the funds provided to meet the expenses of said office. Such books shall be indexed according to the names of the consenting property owners and also according to the names of the streets, roads or other highways upon which the property to which the consent relates shall be bounded on. In case the recording of such consents shall be hindered, delayed or prevented by legal proceedings in any court or from any other or different cause not within the control of the corporation upon which such requirement is imposed, the time for the performance of such act is hereby and shall be deemed to be extended for the period covered by such hindrance, delay or prevention. The consents of property

owners in one city, village or town, or in any other civil division of
the state, shall not be of any effect in any other city, village or
town or other civil divisions of the state. Consents of property
owners heretofore obtained to the building, extending, operating or
change of motor power shall be effectual for the purposes therein
mentioned and may be deemed to be sufficiently proved and shall
be entitled to be recorded, wherever such consents shall have
been signed, executed or acknowledged before an officer authorized
by law to take acknowledgments of deeds, or before or in the
presence of a subscribing witness, and without regard to whether
or not the subscribing witness shall have affixed his signature in
the presence of the subscriber, provided that the proof of such
signing, execution or acknowledgment shall have been made by
such subscribing witness in the manner prescribed by chapter
three, part two of the revised statutes. In cities the common
council, acting subject to the power now possessed by the mayor
to veto ordinances; in villages the board of trustees, and in towns
the commissioner or commissioners of highways shall be the local
authorities referred to; except that in villages where the control
of the streets is vested in any other board or authorities, such
other board or authorities shall be the local authorities referred
to, and the consent of such other board or authorities hereafter
or heretofore obtained shall be sufficient; if in any city or county
the exclusive control of any street, avenue or other property,
which is to be used or occupied by any such railroad, extension
or branch, is vested in any other authority, the consent of such
authority shall also be first obtained. The value of the property
above specified shall be ascertained and determined by the assessment roll of the city, village or town in which it is situated,
completed last before the local authorities shall have given their
consent, except property owned by such city, village or town, or
by the state of New York, or the United States of America, the
value of which shall be ascertained and determined by making
the value thereof to be the same as is shown by such assessment
roll to be the value of the equivalent in size and frontage of the
adjacent property on the same street or highway; and the consent

of the local authorities shall operate as the consent of such city, village or town as the owners of such property. Whenever heretofore or hereafter a railroad has been or shall be constructed and put in operation for one year or the motive power thereon has been or shall be changed and put in operation for a similar length of time, such facts shall be presumptive evidence that the requisite consents of local authorities, property owners and other authority to the construction, maintenance and operation of such railroad or change of motive power have been duly obtained. No consent of local authorities heretofore given shall be deemed invalid because of any portion of the road or route consented to not being connected with an existing road or route of the corporation obtaining or acquiring such consent and all statements of extension filed under section ninety of this article in reference to the route or part thereof described in any consent of local authorities are hereby ratified and confirmed, whether the same were filed before or after the obtaining or acquiring of such consents, provided, however, that nothing herein contained shall be construed to affect any portion of a street surface railroad which is now in or upon any portion of a street which is under the jurisdiction of a park department in any city containing a population of over twelve hundred thousand inhabitants.

Thus amended by chap. 650, Laws of 1905.
See chap. 379, Laws of 1902, *post*.
See 48 Misc. 162.
See provisions of Greater New York Charter, Cities of the Second Class Charter, and Village Law, printed hereinafter.

Consent of local authorities; how procured.

§ 92. The application for the consent of the local authorities shall be in writing and before acting thereon such authorities shall give public notice thereof and of the time and place when it will first be considered, which notice shall be published daily in any city for at least fourteen days in two of its daily newspapers if there be two, if not, in one, to be designated by the mayor, and in any village or town for at least fourteen days in a newspaper published therein, if any there shall be, and if none, then daily in two daily newspapers if there be two, if not, one

published in the city nearest such village or town. Such consent must be upon the expressed condition that the provisions
of this article pertinent thereto shall be complied with, and shall
be filed in the office of the clerk of the county in which such
railroad is located. Whenever the consent of the common council of a city is applied for, the first consideration, of which
notice is hereby required, may be by committee of such common
council. Any such notice, publication or consideration heretofore or hereafter given, made or had in substantial conformity
with the requirements of this section, is and shall be sufficient
notice, publication and consideration for all the purposes hereof
notwithstanding any conflicting provision of any local or special
act or charter.

Thus amended by chap. 434, Laws of 1893.

Condition upon which consent shall be given; sale of franchise at public auction.

§ 93. The consent of the local authorities in cities containing
twelve hundred and fifty thousand inhabitants or more, according to the last federal census or state enumeration, must contain
the condition that the right, franchise and privilege of using any
street, road, highway, avenue, park or public place shall be sold
at public auction to the bidder who will agree to give the city
the largest percentage per annum of the gross receipts of such
corporation, with a bond or undertaking in such form and
amount and with such conditions and sureties as may be
required and approved by the comptroller or other chief fiscal
officer of the city, for the fulfillment of such agreement and for
the commencement and completion of its railroad within the
time designated by law and for the performance of such additional conditions as the local authorities in their discretion may
prescribe. Whenever such consent shall provide for the sale
at public auction of the right to construct and operate a branch
or extension of an existing railroad, such consent shall provide
that but one fare shall be exacted for passage over such branch
or extension and over the line of road which shall have applied

therefor; and further, that if such right shall be purchased by
any corporation other than the applicant, that the gross receipts
from joint business shall be divided in the proportion that the
length of such extension or branch so sold shall bear to the
entire length of the road whether owned or leased which shall
have applied therefor and of such branch or extension, and that
if such right shall be purchased by the applicant, the percentage
to be paid shall be calculated on such portion of its gross receipts
as shall bear the same proportion to the whole value thereof
as the length of such extension or branch shall bear to the entire
length of its road, whether owned or leased. The bidder to
whom such right, franchise and privilege may be sold must be
a duly incorporated railroad corporation of this state, organized
to construct, maintain and operate a street railroad in the
city for which such consent may be given; but no such corporation shall be entitled to bid at such sale unless at least five
days prior to the day fixed for such sale, or five days prior to
the day to which such sale shall have been duly adjourned, the
corporation shall have filed with the comptroller or other chief
fiscal officer of the city, a bond in writing and under seal, with
sufficient sureties, to be approved by such comptroller or officer,
conditioned that if such right, franchise and privilege shall be
sold to such corporation, to pay to the city where such railroad
is situated the sum of fifty thousand dollars as liquidated damages and not by way of penalty in the event of the failure of
such bidder to fulfill the terms of sale, comply with the provisions of this article pertinent thereto, and complete and
operate its railroad according to the plan or plans and upon the
route or routes fixed for its construction within the time hereinafter designated for the construction and completion of its
railroad, and also conditioned to pay to the corporation first
applying for the consent, if it shall not be the successful bidder,
the necessary expenses incurred by such corporation prior to
the sale pursuant to the requirements and direction of the local
authorities, within twenty days after such sale and upon the
certificate of the comptroller or other officer conducting the

same as to the sum or amount to be paid. Notice of the time
and place and terms of sale, and of the route or routes to be
sold, and of the conditions upon which the consent of the local
authorities to the construction, operation and extension of such
street railroad will be given, must be published by such authorities for at least three successive weeks, and in any city having
two or more daily newspapers, at least three times a week in
two of such papers to be designated by the mayor, and in any
city where two daily papers are not published, at least once a
week in a newspaper published therein to be designated by the
mayor. The comptroller or other chief fiscal officer of the city
shall attend and conduct such sale and may adjourn the same,
but not more than four weeks in all, unless further adjournments should, in his discretion, be necessary by reason of the
pendency of legal proceedings, and shall cancel any bid if in
excess of the gross receipts, leaving in force the highest bid not
in excess, or if the bidder shall not have furnished adequate
security entitling such bidder to bid, or shall otherwise fail to
comply with the terms and conditions of sale, and shall resell
the consent and license in the same manner as hereinbefore provided for the first sale. The bidder who may build and operate
such railroad shall at all times keep accurate books of account
of the business and earnings of such railroad, which books shall
at all times be subject to the inspection of the local authorities.
In the event of the failure or refusal of the corporation operating
or using such railroad to pay the rental or percentages of gross
earnings agreed upon, and after notice of not less than sixty
days to pay the same, the local authorities interested therein
may apply to any court having jurisdiction upon at least twenty
days notice to such corporation, and after it shall have had an
opportunity to be heard in its defense, for judgment declaring
the consent and right to operate and use such railroad forfeited
and authorizing the sale again of the same in the manner hereinbefore prescribed, provided, however, that no such resale of
any such consent and right heretofore granted shall be authorized except upon the condition that the same shall be subject

to all liens and incumbrances existing on said railroads at the time such forfeiture may have been declared. All consents hereafter given by the local authorities, unless it be otherwise provided in such consent or in some renewal thereof may be forfeited at the expiration of two years thereafter, and every consent by the local authorities of any city of the first class or of any city, town or village now embraced within the corporate limits of any city of the first class heretofore given to or acquired or owned by any street surface railroad corporation, since January first, eighteen hundred and ninety, is hereby ratified and confirmed, and shall be deemed to be in full force and effect, and shall continue until and including December thirty-first, nineteen hundred and three when it may be forfeited unless prior thereto the required consent of property owners, or determinations by the appellate division of the supreme court, in lieu thereof, shall have been first obtained. The board of sinking fund commissioners of any city shall have power to reduce, compromise or release any obligation or liability to the mayor, aldermen and commonalty of such city under the provisions of chapter six hundred and forty-two of the laws of eighteen hundred and eighty-six, or of this chapter whenever, in the opinion of such board, such release or compromise shall be just or equitable, or for the public interest, the reason for any such release or compromise to be stated in the recorded proceedings of such board. No lease by any company organized under section two of the railroad law and owning a right, privilege or franchise of using any street, avenue, highway or public place for railroad purposes, which has heretofore been sold under the provisions of this section, hereafter made to any street surface railroad company which is not subject to the payment of any percentage pursuant to this section, and which is not organized for the purpose of operating a railroad in a city of the first class, shall be valid until the leased company shall have filed in the office of the secretary of state and in the office of the clerk of the county where its certificate of incorporation is filed, its acceptance in writing and under its corporate seal of the provisions of this section as now amended; and upon such acceptance being filed, the total percentage amount thereafter to be paid annually under this section and under section ninety-five of this act, shall be at the rate of five per centum of the gross receipts derived from the operation of the roads of the lessor and lessee companies considered as one system. The lessee company, at the time of filing its acceptance aforesaid, shall also file in the same offices a bond to the people of the state, executed in duplicate by it and a surety company authorized by law to act as surety on bonds and undertakings, in the penal sum of fifty thousand dollars, and conditioned for the faithful payment annually of the total percentage aforesaid, and such bond shall be deemed to be a full compliance with the condition for a bond or undertaking required by this section to be provided for in the conditions of the consent of the local authorities and shall supersede any such bond or undertaking theretofore given. Whenever it shall be desired to unite two street surface railroad routes at some point not over one-half mile from such respective lines or routes, and establish by the construction of such connection a new route for public travel, and the corporation or corporations owning or using such railroads shall consent to operate such connection as a part of a continuous route for one fare, and it shall appear to the local authorities that such connection cannot be operated as an independent railroad without inconvenience to the public, but that it is to the public advantage that the same should be operated as a continuous line or route with existing railroads, or whenever for the purpose of connecting with any ferry or railroad depot, it shall be desired to construct an extension or branch not more than one-half mile in length, of any street surface railroad corporation, no sale of such franchise shall be made as provided in this section, but any consent of the local authorities for the construction and operation of such connection, extension or branch shall provide that the corporation or corporations operating such connection, extension or branch shall pay into the treasury of said city annually the percentage provided for extensions or branches in section ninety-five of this chapter, for the purposes, at the times, in the manner and upon the conditions set forth in such section. The provisions of this section as now amended shall apply to all cities of the first class, but nothing herein contained shall be construed as superseding, repealing or modifying any provision of the charter of any city, village or town, nor as modifying or affecting the terms of a certain contract bearing date January first, eighteen hundred and ninety-two, entered into by and between the city of Buffalo and the various street surface railroad corporations therein named in such contract, except that the provisions of this act as amended, which continue and confirm the consents of local authorities shall apply to street surface railroads in the city of Buffalo, as well as in other cities of the first-class. This section shall not modify or affect any contract heretofore entered into between a street surface railroad corporation and any city of the third class, town or village regulating the payment of percentages or paving of streets, and any city of the third class, town or village, is hereby authorized to enter into any such form of contract with any street surface railroad corporation, and any such contract heretofore entered into is hereby ratified and confirmed. The local authorities may, in their discretion, make their consent to depend upon any further conditions respecting other or further security, or deposit, suitable to secure the construction, completion and operation of the railroad within any time not exceeding the period prescribed in this article and respecting the character, quality or motive power of the road to be completed and respecting the grouping of streets, avenues and highways into one route, or into several routes, for the purpose of a single sale of the franchise, right or privilege for all the routes collectively, or of the separate sale for each route or street, as said local authorities may think expedient and respecting the payment of the percentage agreed to be paid at the sale upon all the lines operated by the successful bidder within the city and respecting any matter involved in or affecting the computation of percentage payments and respecting the use of the railroads to be constructed under the consent by any other company and respecting the interchange of traffic and division of fares between the company operating such railroads and any other company, and respecting the application of any provision herein contained as to carriage of passengers for single fare and the division of gross receipts and the payment of percentages to the line leased or operated under contract by the applicant for an extension, and also respecting any other matter concerning which, in their judgment, further conditions would be for the public interest. Any and all consents, sales and proceedings heretofore granted, made or taken in substantial compliance with the provisions of this section, as now last amended, are hereby approved, ratified and confirmed, and any purchaser or successor to or transferee of the rights of the purchaser of any right or privilege heretofore sold substantially in accordance with the provisions of this section as now amended, is authorized to acquire the requisite consents of property owners, or, in lieu thereof, determinations by the appellate division of the supreme court, and to proceed with the construction of its road, at any time within three years hereafter.

Thus amended by chap. 494, Laws of 1901.

See section 77, Greater New York Charter; cities of the second class act; section 112, Railroad Law, *post*.

Proceedings if property owners do not consent.

§ 94. If the consent of property owners required by any provision of this article can not be obtained, the corporation failing to obtain such consents may apply to any general term of the supreme court held in the department in which it is proposed to construct its road for the appointment of three commissioners to determine whether such railroad ought to be constructed and operated. Notice of such application must, at least ten days prior thereto, be served, personally, upon each non-consenting property owner by delivering the same to the person to whom such property is assessed upon such assessment-roll or by duly mailing the same, properly folded and directed, to such property owner at his post-office address with the postage prepaid thereon. If the person upon whom service is to be made is unknown, or

his residence and post-office address are unknown and cannot by reasonable diligence be ascertained, service of such notice may be made by publishing the same in such newspaper of the county as the court may direct, at least once a week for two successive weeks. Upon due proof of service of such notice the court to which the application is made shall appoint three disinterested persons, who shall act as commissioners, and who shall, within ten days after their appointment, cause public notice to be given of their first meeting in the manner directed by the court, and may adjourn from time to time, until all their business is completed. Vacancies may be filled by the court after such notice to parties interested as it may deem proper to be given; and the evidence taken before as well as after the happening of the vacancy shall be deemed to be properly before such commissioners. After a public hearing of all parties interested, the commissioners shall determine whether such railroad ought to be constructed and operated, and shall make a report thereon, together with the evidence taken, to the general term, within sixty days after appointment, unless the court, or a judge thereof, for good cause shown, shall extend such time; and their determination that such road ought to be constructed and operated, confirmed by such court, shall be taken in lieu of the consent of the property owners hereinbefore required. The commissioners shall each receive ten dollars for each day spent in the performance of their duties and their necessary expenses and disbursements, which shall be paid by the corporation applying for their appointment.
Thus amended by chap. 676, Laws of 1892.

Percentage of gross receipts to be paid in cities or villages; report of officers.

§ 95. Every corporation building or operating a railroad or branch or extension thereof, under the provisions of this article, or of chapter 252 of the laws of 1884, within any city of the state having a population of 1,200,000 or more, shall, for and during the first five years after the commencement of the operation of any portion of its railroad annually, on November first, pay into the treasury of the city in which its road is located, to the credit of the sinking fund thereof, three per cent of its gross receipts for and during the year ending September thirtieth next preceding; and after the expiration of such five years, make a like annual payment into the treasury of the city to the credit of the same fund, of five per cent of its gross receipts. If a street surface railroad corporation existing and operating any such railroad in any such city on May 6, 1884, shall have thereafter extended its tracks or constructed branches therefrom, and shall operate such branches or extensions under the provisions of chapter 252 of the laws of 1884, of of this article, such corpora- tion shall pay such percentages only upon such portion of its gross receipts as shall bear the same proportion to its whole gross receipts as the length of such extension or branches shall bear to the entire length, of its line. In any other incorporated city or village the local authorities shall have the right to require, as a condition to their consent to the construction, operation or extension of a railroad under the provisions of this article, the payment annually of such percentage of gross receipts, not exceeding three per cent, into the treasury of the city or village as they may deem proper. In case of extension the amount to be paid shall be ascertained in the manner hereto- fore provided. The corporation failing to pay such percentage of its gross earnings shall, after November first, pay in addition thereto five per cent a month on such percentage until paid. The president and treasurer of any corporation required by the pro- visions of this article to make a payment annually upon its gross receipts shall, on or before November first in each year make a verified report to the comptroller or chief fiscal officer of the city of the gross amount of its receipts for the year ending Sep- tember thirtieth, next preceding, and the books of such corpora- tion shall be open to inspection and examination by such comp- troller or officer, or his duly appointed agent, for the purpose of ascertaining the correctness of its report as to its gross receipts. The corporate rights, privileges and franchises acquired under this article or such chapter by any corporation, which shall fail to comply with all the provisions of this section, shall be forfeited to the people of the state, and upon judgment of forfeiture rendered in an action brought in the name of the people by the attorney-general, shall cease and determine.

Thus amended by chap. 676, Laws of 1892.

See Greater New York Charter; cities of the second class act; chap. 637, Laws of 1901, *post*.

Extension of route over rivers; terminus in other counties; when property owners withhold consent; supreme court may appoint Commissioners.

§ 96. Any street railroad in operation in this state, which shall, by a two-thirds vote of its directors, decide to extend the route of its road, so as to cross a river over and by any bridge now or hereafter constructed under the provisions of any law of this state, may so extend their route over and across such bridge upon such terms as may be mutually agreed upon between it and such bridge company, and may locate the terminus of their road in the county adjoining the one in which their road is now located and in operation, upon first obtaining the consent of such bridge company or its lessees, and the consent of the owners of one-half in value of the property bounded on, and the consent also of the local authorities having the control of that portion of a street or highway upon which it is proposed to construct or operate such railroad, or in case the consent of such property owners cannot be obtained the appellate division of the supreme court in the district in which it is proposed to be constructed may, upon application, appoint three commissioners, who shall determine after a hearing of all parties interested, whether such railroad ought to be constructed, or operated, and their determination, confirmed by the court, may be taken in lieu of the consent of the property owners. Whenever a terminus of any public viaduct, bridge or bridges, or public viaduct connected with any bridge or bridges, heretofore or hereafter constructed in and owned and maintained by any city of the first class, or town adjoining the same, is or shall be located at or adjacent to or within one-half mile of the route of any existing street surface railroad, the corporation owning or operating such railroad may, irrespective of any provisions otherwise applicable thereto contained in any general or local act, upon obtaining the consent of the local authorities and property owners as above provided, and upon complying with the provisions of the railroad law applicable thereto, extend its road or route and construct and operate its railroad, to, upon and across such viaduct, bridge or bridges and approaches thereto for the purpose of connecting with another railroad route not more than one-half mile distant from such bridge or viaduct so as to afford a continuous ride for one fare, subject to the provisions of the railroad law, or for the purpose of reaching the depot, station or terminus of another railroad not more than one-half mile distant from such bridge or viaduct. This section shall not apply to any bridge over the Hudson or East rivers in the counties of New York and Kings, nor to any bridge or viaduct constructed under the provisions of any so-called grade crossing law.

Thus amended by chap. 419, Laws of 1901.
See sections 60, 61 and 62, Railroad Law, *ante*.

Use of tracks of other roads.

§ 97. Any railroad corporation in this state, whose cars are run and operated by horses or other motive power, authorized by this article, upon the surface of the street, excepting in the city and county of New York, may, for the purpose of enabling it to connect with and run and operate its cars between its tracks, and a depot or car-house owned by it, run upon, intersect, and use, for not exceeding five hundred feet, the tracks of any other railroad corporation, the cars of which are run and operated in like manner with the necessary connections and switches for the proper working and accommodation of the cars upon such tracks, and in connection with such depot or car-house, upon paying therefor such compensation as it may agree upon with the corporation owning the tracks to be so run upon, intersected, and used; and in case such corporations cannot agree upon the amount of such compensation, the same shall be ascertained and determined in the manner prescribed in the condemnation law.

Repair of streets; rate of speed; removal of ice and snow.

§ 98. Every street surface railroad corporation so long as it shall continue to use any of its tracks in any street, avenue or public place in any city or village shall have and keep in permanent repair that portion of such street, avenue or public place between its tracks, the rails of its tracks, and two feet in width outside of its tracks, under the supervision of the proper local authorities, and whenever required by them to do so, and in such manner as they may prescribe. In case of the neglect of any corporation to make pavements or repairs after the expiration of thirty days notice to do so, the local authorities may make the same at the expense of such corporation, and such authorities may make such reasonable regulations and ordinances as to the rate of speed, mode of use of tracks, and removal of ice and snow, as the interests or convenience of the public may require. A corporation whose agents or servants willfully or negligently violate such an ordinance or regulation, shall be liable to such city or village for a penalty not exceeding five hundred dollars to be specified in such ordinance or regulation.

Thus amended by chap. 676, Laws of 1892.
See chap. 182, Laws of 1898, *post.*
See 182 N. Y., 99.
See 112 App. Div. 581; 186 N. Y. Mem. 4.

Within what time road to be built.

§ 99. In case any such corporation shall not commence the construction of its road, or of any extension or branch thereof, within one year after the consent of the local authorities and property owners or the determination of the appellate division of the supreme court as herein required, shall have been given or renewed, and shall not complete the same within three years after such consents, or determination shall have been obtained, its rights, privileges and franchises in respect of such railroad or extension or branch, as the case may be, may be forfeited. If the performance of any act required by the railroad law or any prior acts within the times therein prescribed, is hindered, delayed or prevented by legal proceedings in any court, such court may also extend such time for such period as the court shall deem proper or if the performance of any act required by said article within the times therein prescribed is hindered, delayed or prevented by works of public improvement, or from any other or different cause, not within the control of the corpora‑ tion upon which such requirement is imposed, the time for the performance of such act is hereby and shall be deemed to be extended for the period covered by such hindrance, delay or pre‑ vention. The time for compliance with any requirement in this or any former act, by a street surface railroad corporation incor‑ porated for the purpose of constructing a street surface railroad and which has prior to the passage of this act obtained or shall prior to June thirtieth, nineteen hundred and three obtain such consents or determination is hereby extended until June thir‑ tieth, nineteen hundred and four.

Thus amended by chap. 209, Laws of 1902.
See 106 App. Div. 240; 185 N. Y. 171.
See section 5, Railroad Law, ante.

Motive power.

§ 100. Any street surface railroad may operate any portion of its road by animal or horse power, or by cable, electricity, or any power other than locomotive steam power, which said loco‑ motive steam power is primarily generated by the locomotive propelling the cars, and in the use of which either escaping steam or smoke is visible, which may be approved by the state board of railroad commissioners, and consented to by the owners of one-half of the property bounded on that portion of the rail‑ road, with respect to which a change of motive power is pro‑ posed; and if the consent of such property owners cannot be obtained, the determination of three disinterested commissioners, appointed by the appellate division of the supreme court of the department in which such railroad is located, in favor of such motive power, confirmed by the court, shall be taken in lieu of the consent of the property owners. The consent of the property owners shall be obtained and the proceedings for the appoint‑ ment and the determination of the commissioners and the con‑

firmation of their report shall be conducted in the manner prescribed in sections ninety-one and ninety-four of this article, so
far as the same can properly be made applicable thereto. Any
railroad corporation making a change in its motive power under
this section, may make any changes in the construction of its road
or roadbed or other property rendered necessary by the change
in its motive power. Where a street surface railroad in the
counties of Herkimer and Hamilton is located wholly outside
the limits of an incorporated city or village, such railroad may,
with the approval of the state board of railroad commissioners
be operated by locomotive steam power, provided that such
steam power is generated by oil from and including April fifteenth to and including November thirtieth, and by either oil or
coal from and including December first to and including April
fourteenth.

Thus amended by chap. 553, Laws of 1901.
See chap. 597, Laws of 1898, post.

Rate of fare.

§ 101. No corporation constructing and operating a railroad
under the provisions of this article, or of chapter two hundred
and fifty-two of the laws of eighteen hundred and eighty-four,
shall charge any passenger more than five cents for one continuous ride from any point on its road, or on any road, line or
branch operated by it, or under its control, to any other point
thereof, or any connecting branch thereof, within the limits of
any incorporated city or village. Not more than one fare shall
be charged within the limits of any such city or village, for passage over the main line of road and any branch or extension
thereof if the right to construct such branch or extension shall
have been acquired under the provisions of such chapter or of
this article; except that in any city of the third class, or incorporated village, it shall be lawful for such corporation to charge
and collect as a maximum rate of fare for each passenger, ten
cents, where such passenger is carried in a car which overcomes
an elevation of at least four hundred and fifty feet within a
distance of one and a half miles. This section shall not apply

to any part of any road constructed prior to May six, eighteen hundred and eighty-four, and then in operation, unless the corporation owning the same shall have acquired the right to extend such road, or to construct branches thereof under such chapter, or shall acquire such right under the provisions of this article, in which event its rate of fare shall not exceed its authorized rate prior to such extension. The legislature expressly reserves the right to regulate and reduce the rate of fare on any railroad constructed and operated wholly or in part under such chapter or under the provisions of this article.

Thus amended by chap. 688, Laws of 1897.
See 111 App. Div. 39; 187 N. Y. 48.

Construction of road in street where other road is built.

§ 102. No street surface railroad corporation shall construct, extend or operate its road or tracks in that portion of any street, avenue, road or highway, in which a street surface railroad is or shall be lawfully constructed, except for necessary crossings, or, in cities, villages and towns of less than one million two hundred and fifty thousand inhabitants over any bridges, without first obtaining the consent of the corporation owning and maintaining the same, except that any street surface railroad company may use the tracks of another street surface railroad company for a distance not exceeding one thousand feet, and if in a city having a population of less than thirty-five thousand inhabitants, except Long Island City, for a distance not exceeding fifteen hundred feet, and in cities, villages and towns of less than one million two hundred and fifty thousand inhabitants, shall have the right to lay its tracks upon, and run over and use any bridges used wholly or in part as a foot-bridge, whenever the court upon an application for commissioners shall be satisfied that such use is actually necessary to connect main portions of a line to be constructed or operated as an independent railroad, or to connect said railroad with a ferry, or with another existing railroad, and that the public convenience requires the same, in which event the right to use shall only be given for a compensation to an extent and in a manner to be ascertained and determined by commissioners to be appointed by the courts as is provided in the condemnation law, or by the board of railroad commissioners in cases where the corporations interested shall unite in a request for such board to act. Such commissioners in determining the compensation to be paid for the use by one corporation of the tracks of another shall consider and allow for the use of the tracks for all injury and damage to the corporation whose tracks may be so used. Any street surface railroad corporation may, in pursuance of a unanimous vote of the stockholders voting at a special meeting called for that purpose by notice in writing, signed by a majority of the directors of such corporation, stating the time, place and object of the meeting, and serving upon each stockholder appearing as such upon the books of the corporation, personally or by mail, at his last known post-office address, at least sixty days prior to such meeting, guarantee the bonds of any other street surface railroad corporation whose road is fully or partly in the same city or town or adjacent cities or towns.

Thus amended by chap. 693, Laws of 1894.

Abandonment of part of route.

§ 103. Any street surface railroad corporation may declare any portion of its route which it may deem no longer necessary for the successful operation of its road and convenience of the public to be relinquished or abandoned. Such declaration of abandonment must be adopted by the board of directors of the corporation under its seal, which shall be submitted to the stockholders thereof at a meeting called and conducted in the same manner as required by law for meetings of stockholders for the approval of leases by railroad corporations for the use of their respective roads. If the stockholders shall, at such meeting, ratify and adopt such declaration of abandonment, the secretary of the company shall so certify under the seal of the corporation, upon such declaration. Such declaration shall then be submitted to the board of railroad commissioners for its approval, and if approved by such board, such approval shall be indorsed *therein or annexed thereto and the declaration so certified and indorsed shall be filed and recorded in the office of the secretary of state, and from the time of such filing, such portion of the route designated in the declaration shall be deemed to be abandoned.

Thus amended by chap. 478, Laws of 1900.

Contracting corporations to carry for one fare; penalty.

§ 104. Every such corporation entering into such contract shall carry or permit any other party thereto to carry between any two points on the railroads or portions thereof embraced in such contract any passenger desiring to make one continuous trip between such points for one single fare, not higher than the fare lawfully chargeable by either of such corporations for an adult passenger. Every such corporation shall upon demand, and without extra charge, give to each passenger paying one single fare a transfer, entitling such passenger to one continuous trip to any point or portion of any railroad embraced in such contract, to the end that the public convenience may be promoted by the operation of the railroads embraced in such contract substantially as a single railroad with a single rate of fare. For every refusal to comply with the requirements of this section the corporation so refusing shall forfeit fifty dollars to the aggrieved party. The provisions of this section shall only apply to railroads wholly within the limits of any one incorporated city or village.

Thus amended by chap. 676, Laws of 1892.

See 179 N. Y., 450, and other decisions of courts on this section, 187 N. Y. 48.

Effect of dissolution of charter as to consents.

§ 105. Whenever any street surface railroad corporation shall have been dissolved or annulled, or its charter repealed by an act of the legislature, the consent of owners of property bounded on, and the consent of the local authorities having the control of that portion of a street or highway upon which the railroad of such corporation shall have been theretofore constructed and

*So in the original.

operated, and the order of the general term confirming the report
of any commissioner that such railroad ought to be constructed
or operated, shall not, nor shall either thereof, be deemed to be
in any way impaired, revoked, terminated or otherwise affected
by such act of dissolution, annulment or repeal, but the same
and each thereof shall continue in full force, efficacy and being.
The right to the further enjoyment and to the use thereof, subsequent to such act of dissolution, annulment or repeal, and of
all the powers, privileges and benefits therein or thereby created,
shall be sold at public auction by the local authorities within
whose jurisdiction such railroad shall be, in the same manner as
is provided in section ninety-three of this article. When such
sale shall have been so made, the purchaser thereat shall have
the right to the further enjoyment and use of such consents and
orders, and of each thereof, and of all the powers, privileges and
benefits therein or thereby created, in like manner as if such
purchaser had been originally named in such consents, reports
and orders; if such purchaser shall be otherwise authorized by
law to construct, maintain and operate a street surface railroad
within the municipality within which such railroad shall be. ·
Thus amended by chap. 676, Laws of 1892.

Corporate rights saved in case of failure to complete road; right
to operate branches; conditions; former consents ratified;
limitations.

§ 106. The corporate existence of and powers of every street
surface railroad corporation, which has completed a railroad
upon the greater portion of the route designated in its certificate of incorporation, within ten years from the date of filing
such certificate in the office of the secretary of state,. and which
has operated such completed portion of its railroad continuously
for a period of five years last past, and is now operating the same,
shall continue with like force and effect, as though it had in all
respects complied with the provisions of law with reference to
the time when it should have fully completed its road. Every
such corporation shall have the right to operate any extensions
and branches of its railroad, now constructed and operated by it,
which have been so constructed and operated by it, for a period

of ten years last past, with like force and effect, as though the route of such extensions and branches were designated in its certificate of incorporation. But every such street railroad corporation is authorized to operate such railroad and any extensions or branches thereof, upon condition that it has heretofore, or shall hereafter, obtain the consent of the local authorities having the control of that portion of the streets, avenues or highways included in such railroad, or any extension or branch thereof, to the construction and operation of the same, and also upon the condition that it has heretofore or shall hereafter first obtain the consent of the owners of one-half in value of the property bounded on the portion of the streets, avenues or highways included in the route of such railroad, or any extensions or branches thereof, to the construction and operation of the same, or in case the consent of such property owners cannot be obtained, the appellate division of the supreme court of the department in which such railroad or any extension or branch thereof is located, may, upon application, appoint three commissioners who shall determine, after a hearing of all the parties interested, whether such railroad ought to be constructed or operated, and their determination, confirmed by the court, may be taken in lieu of the consent of the property owners. If any street surface railroad corporation shall have made and filed a statement or statements of proposed extensions or branches embracing a line from the boundary of a city or village to the boundary of another city or village generally parallel with the route specified in its certificate of incorporation and generally distant not more than one-half mile therefrom, and shall have made and filed an agreement of consolidation with some other street surface railroad corporation formed to build a street railroad upon a route continuous or connecting with one or more of the routes described in such statement or statements of proposed extensions or branches, and thereafter there shall have been constructed and operated for a period of four years a street surface railroad from such city or village to such other city or village upon a line embraced in any such proposed extensions or branches, such consolidated corporation may relinquish and abandon any unconstructed route or unconstructed portions of route specified in the certificate of incorporation or in any statements of proposed extensions or branches of such first-mentioned corporation by filing in the office of the secretary of state a copy of a resolution of the board of directors of such consolidated corporation certified by its president and secretary, declaring such unconstructed route or unconstructed portions of route relinquished and abandoned, and thereupon the corporate rights, powers and franchises of such consolidated corporation shall be and continue the same as though the certificate of incorporation of such constituent corporation had specified the constructed and not the unconstructed portions of such route and proposed extensions and branches. All consents heretofore given, or grants made by local authorities having the control of the portion of any street, avenue, or highway included in the route of such railroad, or any extensions or branches thereof, to any such street surface railroad corporation, are hereby ratified and confirmed and declared valid. This section shall be applicable to any corporations whose lines are wholly within any towns, cities or villages having less than twenty thousand inhabitants. This section shall not apply to or affect any railroad corporation in the city of New York; nor any special grant made to or authority conferred upon any street surface railroad corporation by any law of this state; nor any pending litigation; nor shall it impair existing rights, privileges or franchises of any street surface railroad corporation.

Thus amended by chap. 198, Laws of 1900.
See chap. 604, Laws of 1892; also, chap. 679, Laws of 1893, *post.*

When sand and salt may be used on tracks.

§ 107. The owner or operator of any street surface railroad in cities of this state, may place upon the space between the rails, and upon the rails of such road sand in sufficient quantities to prevent the horses traveling thereon from slipping, and to enable cars operated by mechanical, or electrical appliances to be safely and properly operated. The owner or operator of any street surface railroad in cities of this state may use salt in necessary quantities, upon the rails of all the switches, curves, turnouts and crossovers, between the first day of November of each year and the first day of May following, for the removal of snow and ice therefrom and to prevent the same from freezing. The quantity of salt to be used and the manner of applying salt to the rails, to be under the direction of the city officials having charge of the streets of said cities.

Thus amended by chap. 491, Laws of 1899.
See Greater New York Charter.

Road not to be constructed upon ground occupied by public buildings or in public parks.

§ 108. No street surface railroad shall be constructed or ex-tended upon ground occupied by buildings belonging to any town, city, county or to the state, or to the United States, or in public parks, except in tunnels to be approved by the local authorities having control of such parks. Provided however that the commissioners of the state reservation at Niagara, by and with the consent of the commissioners of the land office, may construct. without expense to the state, street railroad tracks upon and along that part of the riverway, so called, between Falls and Niagara streets, in the city of Niagara Falls, and in their discretion may grant revocable licenses to street surface railroad companies to use such tracks upon such terms as said commissioners may prescribe.

Thus amended by chap. 710, Laws of 1899.

Center-bearing rails prohibited.

§ 109. No street surface railroad corporation shall hereafter lay down in the streets of any incorporated city or village of this state what are known as " center-bearing " rails; but in all cases, whether in laying new track or in replacing old rails, shall lay down " grooved " or some other kind of rail not " center-bearing " approved by the local authorities. Such grooved or other rail shall be of such shape and so laid as to permit the paving-stones to come in close contact with the projection which serves to guide the flange to the car wheel. Where in any city, the duty of repairing and repaving streets, as distinguished from the authorization of such paving, repairing and repaving, is by law vested in any local authority other than the common council of such city, such other local authority shall be the local authority referred to in this section.

Thus amended by chap. 676, Laws of 1892.

Right to cross bridge substituted for a bridge crossed for five years.

§ 110. Should any street surface railroad company have crossed any bridge as a part of its route for a period of more than five years and should any other bridge be substituted there for at any time, such company shall have the right to cross such substituted bridge and to lay and use railway tracks thereon for the transit of its cars and to make all changes and extensions of its route subject to all the provisions of this act, as the convenient operation of its cars and public convenience may require.

Added by chap. 676, Laws of 1892.

Protection of employees.

§ 111. Every corporation operating a street surface railroad in this state, except such as operate a railroad or railroads either in the borough of Manhattan or Brooklyn, in the city of New York; shall cause the front and rear platforms of every passenger car propelled by electricity, cable or compressed air, operated on any division of such railroad which extends in or between towns or outside of city limits, during the months of December, January, February and March, except cars attached to the rear of other cars, to be enclosed from the fronts of the platforms to the fronts of the hoods, so as to afford protection to any person stationed by such corporation on such platforms to perform duties in connection with the operation of such cars. Every corporation or person using and operating a car in violation of this section shall be liable to a penalty of twenty-five dollars per day for each car so used and operated, to be collected in an action brought by the attorney-general and to be paid to the treasurer of the state of New York, or in a suit by the attorney of the municipality in which the violation of the provision of this act occurs, to be paid in the treasury of such municipality.

Added by chap. 325, Laws of 1903; see chap. 325, following.

CHAP. 325, LAWS ÓF 1903.

AN ACT to amend the railroad law, in relation to the protection of certain employees of street railroads. .

SECTION 1. Article four of chapter five hundred and sixty-five of the laws of eighteen hundred and ninety, entitled " An act in relation to railroads, constituting chapter thirty-nine of the general laws," is hereby amended by adding thereto a new section to be section one hundred and eleven, and to read as follows :

*   *   *   *   *   *   *   *   *

See section 111 of Railroad Law, above.

§ 2. All street surface railroad passenger cars hereafter purchased, built or rebuilt and operated in the state of New York on and after the passage of this act, except those owned by any company operating either in the borough of Manhattan or Brooklyn, in the city of New York shall be constructed in accordance with the provisions of section one of this act.

§ 3. This act shall take effect December first, nineteen hundred and four. Except that where the cars of any corporation affected by section one of this act are operated wholly in cities other than the boroughs of Manhattan or Brooklyn in the city of New York, the cars belonging to the corporations so operated shall be equipped with the enclosures provided for in section one of this act as follows, viz.: One-third thereof before December first, nineteen hundred and four, one-third thereof after December first, nineteen hundred and four and before December first, nineteen hundred and five, and the remaining one-third thereof after December first, nineteen hundred and five, and before December first, nineteen hundred and six.

Protection to employes.

§ 111a. Every corporation operating a street surface railroad in the counties of Albany and Rensselaer shall cause the front and rear platforms of every car propelled by electricity, cable or compressed air, during the months of December, January, February and March, except cars attached to the rear of other cars, to be enclosed from the front and at least one side of the platform to the hood, so as to afford protection to any person stationed by such corporation or person on such platforms to perform duties in connection with the operation of such cars. Platforms on cars on such street surface railroads used more than one mile outside the limits of a city shall be completely enclosed from platform to hood. Every corporation using and operating a car in violation of this section shall be liable to a penalty of twenty-five dollars per day for each car so used and operated to be collected by the people to the use of the poor of the county in which such corporation has its principal office, in an action brought by the attorney-general or the district attorney of such county. The supreme court may, on the application of a citizen, direct the district attorney to bring such action.

Added by chap. 426, Laws of 1903, taking effect Sept. 1, 1904.

Protection of employees in the counties of Kings and Queens.

*§ 112. Every corporation operating a street surface railroad in the counties of Kings or Queens, shall cause the front and rear platforms of every passenger car propelled by electricity, cable or compressed air, operated on any division of such railroad during the months of December, January, February and March, except cars attached to the rear of other cars, to be enclosed from the fronts of the platforms to the fronts of the hoods so as to afford protection to any person stationed by such corporation on such platforms to perform duties connected with the operation of such cars. Every corporation or person using and operating a car in violation of such section shall be liable to a penalty of twenty-five dollars per day for each car used and operated, to be collected in an action brought by the attorney-general and to be paid to the treasurer of the city of New York, or in a suit by the district attorney of the counties of Kings or Queens to be paid into the treasury of the city of New York. One-third of the cars operated by any corporation in either of the above named counties shall be equipped with the enclosures provided for in section one of this act on or before December first, nineteen hundred and five, one-third thereof after December first, nineteen hundred and five, and before December first, nineteen hundred and six, and the remaining one-third thereof after December first, nineteen hundred and six, and before December first, nineteen hundred and seven.

Added by chap. 453, Laws of 1905.

As to payments to cities of the first class.

*§ 112. The board of estimate and apportionment, or if such board do not exist, the local authorities which have power to make appropriation of moneys to be raised by taxation, in any city of the first class, shall have the power in their discretion, to

*So in original.

enter into a contract or contracts on behalf of the city with any
railroad corporation or corporations owning or operating street
surface railroads or other railroads in such city, for the purpose
of adjusting any or all differences now existing between such
corporation or corporations and such city with respect to car
license fees, percentages upon gross earnings, rentals and any
other payments, other than taxes upon real and personal property and capital stock, payable or claimed to be payable to the
city under existing acts of the legislature, municipal ordinances,
grants by, or contracts with, the municipal authorities or otherwise; and any such contract may provide for the payment of an
annual amount to be ascertained as in such contract provided in
lieu of any or all payments of any of the classes hereinbefore
mentioned, other than taxes. Any such contract which shall be
with a corporation operating lines of railroad by lease may
provide for an annual payment, to be ascertained as in such
contract provided, which shall be in lieu of any or all of the
payments of any or all of said classes, other than taxes upon
real and personal property and capital stock, which would otherwise be payable in respect of the leased lines so long as the lease
or leases thereof shall continue. The annual payments provided
for in any contract made under the authority of this act shall,
so long as such contract is in force, supersede the payments
which would otherwise be payable by the corporation or corporations making such contract and in lieu of which the annual
payments provided for in such contract are substituted. Any
contract made hereunder may, with the approval of the municipal authorities by whom the contract was made or their successors in office, be modified from time to time by the parties
thereto for the purpose of meeting changed conditions. No
contract shall be made or modified hereunder without the written consent and approval of the mayor and of the comptroller or
other chief financial officer of the city.

Added by chap. 651, Laws of 1905.

See sections 93 and 95, Railroad Law, *ante;* chap. 637, Laws 1901, *post.*

ARTICLE V.

*OTHER RAILROADS IN CITIES AND COUNTIES.

Application for railway; commissioners.

§ 120. Upon the application of at least fifty reputable householders and taxpayers of any county or city, verified upon oath before a justice of the supreme court, that there is need in said county or city of a steam railway in the streets, avenues and public places thereof for the transportation of passengers, mails or freight, the board of supervisors of such county may, within thirty days thereafter by resolution, approve of the application, and authorize its presentation to the supreme court, and if the railway is to be built wholly within the limits of a city, upon the application of a like number of householders and taxpayers

*See Rapid Transit Act, also chap. 294, Laws of 1891, *post.*

of the city to the mayor thereof, such mayor may, within thirty
days thereafter, indorse upon the application his approval and
direction that it may be presented to the supreme court, and if
the railway is to be built, partly within the limits of a city and
partly without, such application shall be approved, both by the
mayor of the city and the board of supervisors of the county, and
its presentation to the supreme court authorized by them, and
upon the presentation of such application so approved and
authorized to a special term of the supreme court, held in the
district where such railway is to be built, or some part thereof,
the court may appoint five commissioners, residents of the city
if the railway is to be built wholly within the city, and of the
county, if it is to be built wholly or partly outside of the limits
of a city, to determine the necessity of such railroad, the route
thereof, the time within which and the conditions upon which it
shall be constructed, the damages to the property owners along
the line thereof and all the matters lawfully submitted to them,
and discharge the duties imposed upon them by law.

Oath and bond of commissioners.

§ 121. Within ten days after his appointment and before entering upon the discharge of any of the duties of his office, each
commissioner shall take and subscribe the constitutional oath of
office, which shall be filed in the office of the clerk of the county
and shall execute a bond to the people of the state in the penal
sum of twenty-five thousand dollars, with two or more sureties,
to be approved by a justice of the supreme court of the department in which the railway is to be built and conditioned for the
faithful performance of the duties of the office, which bond shall
be filed in the office of the clerk of the county.

First meeting of commissioners.

§ 122. Within fifteen days after their appointment, the commissioners shall meet in some convenient place in the county or
city and organize themselves as a board with appropriate officers.

Determination of necessity of railroad and route.

§ 123. The commissioners shall, within thirty days after such organization, determine upon the necessity of such steam railroad, and if they find it to be necessary, they shall, within sixty days after such organization, fix and determine the route therefor, and shall have the exclusive power to locate such route, over, under, through or across the streets, avenues, places or lands in such county or city, and to provide for the connection or junction with any other railway or bridge, if the consent of the owners of one-half in value of the property bounded on and the consent of the local authorities having control of that portion of a street or highway, upon which it is proposed to construct or operate such railway have been first obtained. If the consent of such property owners can not be obtained, the determination of three commissioners appointed by the general term of the supreme court of the department where the railroad is to be constructed, made after due hearing of all parties interested, and confirmed by the court, that such railway ought to be constructed and operated, may be taken in lieu of the consent of such property owners. No such railway shall be located in or upon such portion of any street, avenue, place or lands in such county as are now occupied by an elevated or underground railway or in which such a railway has already been authorized by law to be so located and constructed, or which are contained in public parks, or occupied by buildings belonging to the county or the state or United States, or in or upon the following streets, avenues and public places, viz.: Broadway, Fifth avenue, Fourth avenue above Forty-second street, in the city of New York; Debevoise place, Irving place, Lefferts place, those portions of Grand, Classon and Franklin avenues and Dowling street lying between the southerly line of Lexington avenue and the northerly line of Atlantic avenue, that portion of Classon avenue lying between the northerly line of Lexington avenue and the southerly line of Park avenue, and that portion of Washington avenue lying between Park and Atlantic avenues in the city of Brooklyn; and that portion of the city of Buffalo lying between Michigan and Main streets, but such railway may be located and constructed across such excepted streets, avenues and places at their intersection only with other streets, avenues and places.

Thus amended by chap. 676, Laws of 1892.

Adoption of plans, and terms upon which road shall be built.

§ 124. The commissioners by such public notice, and under such conditions, and with such inducements as they may pre-scribe, shall invite a submission of plans for the construction and operation of such railway, and shall meet at a time and place in such notice named, not more than ninety days after their organization, and decide upon the plans for the construction thereof, with the necessary supports, turnouts, switches, sidings, connections, landing-places, stations, buildings, platforms, stair-ways, elevators, telegraph and signal devices, or other requisite appliances, upon the route or location determined upon by them. They shall, upon notice to the local authorities, and after hear-ing all parties interested, fix and determine what compensation. if any, in a gross sum, or in a certain percentage of receipts, shall annually be paid to the local authorities by the corporation formed for the purpose of constructing, maintaining and operat-ing such railway for public use in the conveyance of persons and property, for the use and occupation by the corporation of the streets, avenues and highways in and upon which its railway is to be constructed, and the time when such railway, or a portion thereof, shall be constructed and ready for operation, and the maximum rates to be paid for transportation and conveyance thereon, and the hours during which special cars or trains shall be run at reduced rates of fare; and the amount of the capital stock of such corporation, and the number of shares into which it shall be divided, and the percentage thereof to be paid in cash on subscribing for such shares.

The commissioners may select two or more routes, upon one of which such railway may be constructed and operated; and the local authorities may consent to the construction and opera-tion of such railway upon one or more of such routes, or parts thereof; and the commissioners shall have power to change and readopt routes and plans for the construction and operation of such railway, after they have been submitted to the local authorities, in cases where such authorities may recommend such changes, or may not be willing to consent to the construction or operation of the railway, upon the routes and plans adopted, unless such changes are made therein.

Thus amended by chap. 676, Laws of 1892. See statutes published herein as to abandonment of route and extension and limitation of time in which to build railroads.

Appraisal of damages and deposit of money as security.

§ 125. The commissioners shall, within one hundred and ten days after their organization, ascertain and determine the aggregate pecuniary damage arising from the diminution in the value of the property bounded on that portion of such street or streets, highway or highways, upon which it is proposed to construct and operate such railway to be caused by the construction and operation thereof. For that purpose they shall view the several parcels of real property so bounded, and shall appraise separately the pecuniary damages arising from such diminution in value of each parcel thereof, and for the purposes of such appraisal they shall give notice of the time and place, when and where they will meet to hear the owners, or persons interested in such real property, which notice shall be published for at least ten days consecutively in at least two newspapers in the county where such railway is to be constructed, and shall take such material testimony upon the probable diminution in value of any or all such parcels to be so caused as may be offered by or in behalf of any person or party interested therein, and the aggregate sum of the amounts so appraised and determined by them shall be the aggregate pecuniary damage required to be ascertained and determined as above provided. No corporation which shall hereafter be organized under this article shall enter upon any street, highway or lane therein, until it shall first have deposited with some trust company, to be designated by the mayor of the city within which it is proposed to construct the railway or any part thereof, and by the board of supervisors,

when the road does not lie wholly within a city, a sum of money
equal to the amount so ascertained and determined by the commissioners to be the aggregate pecuniary damage to such property within the city, or within the county outside of any city, or
shall have secured the payment of such amount by depositing
with such trust company negotiable securities, equivalent at
their par and actual value to such aggregate amount, and
approved by the mayor of the city in which such road is wholly
or in part located, and by the county treasurer of the county if
the road is located wholly or in part outside of the limits of
such city. The court may accept in lieu of the deposit of money
or securities herein required the bond of the corporation, with
two or more sureties, to be approved by the court, to the effect
that the corporation before constructing or operating its railway
in front of any premises, shall pay to the owner of the real property all the damages sustained, or which will be sustained by
him, as fixed and determined by such commissioners, and the
costs allowed, if any. Such bond shall be in a sum double the
amount of such damages, and the sureties shall justify in the
aggregate to an amount equal to the amount of such bond. Such
corporation shall also, at the same time, deposit with such trust
company or with the county treasurer, as the commissioners may
direct, the sum of five thousand dollars in cash, for the payment
of the expense of apportioning and distributing such fund.
Unless such moneys or securities shall be deposited by such corporation within one year after it shall have obtained the consent
of the local authorities, and of the property owners, or the confirmation by the general term of the supreme court, of the determination of three commissioners in lieu thereof, and in the case
of a corporation heretofore organized within one year after it
shall have obtained the confirmation by the general term of the
supreme court of the report of three commissioners in lieu of
the consent of property owners, or within one year after the
commissioners appointed to ascertain and determine the aggregate pecuniary damages as provided in this article, shall have
made their report, then such corporation shall be deemed not

to have accepted the franchises granted. Where the commissioners shall fix and determine different periods of time within which different sections of such railway shall be constructed and ready for operation, they shall ascertain, determine, and report separately the aggregate pecuniary damage to property bounded upon that portion of such street or streets upon which each of such sections is located. Upon the deposit by the corporation as above provided of moneys or securities equivalent to the aggregate pecuniary damage to be sustained by any one of such sections, or of any bond given in lieu thereof, it shall immediately be vested with the right and privilege to construct its railway through such section.

Thus amended by chap. 676, Laws of 1892.

Shall prepare certificate of incorporation; proviso as to forfeiture.

§ 126. The commissioners shall prepare an appropriate certificate of incorporation for the corporation in the last section mentioned in which shall be set forth and embodied, as component parts thereof, the several conditions, requirements and particulars by such commissioners determined pursuant to the provisions of this article, and which shall also provide for the release and forfeiture to the supervisors of the county, or if the road is to be constructed wholly or partly within a city, to such city, of all rights and franchises acquired by such corporation in case such railway or railways shall not be completed within the time and upon the conditions therein provided; and the commissioners shall thereupon and within one hundred and twenty days after their organization cause a suitable book of subscription to the capital stock of such corporation, to be opened pursuant to due public notice at a banking office in such county or city. A failure by any corporation heretofore or hereafter organized under this article to complete its railway within the time limited in and by its certificate of incorporation shall only work a forfeiture of the franchises of such corporation with respect to that portion of its route which such corporation shall have failed to complete, and shall not affect the rights and franchises of

such corporation to construct and operate such part of its railway which it shall have completed within the term prescribed
by its certificate of incorporation, or as to which the time for
completion shall not have expired, notwithstanding anything to
the contrary in its certificate of incorporation.

Organization.

§ 127. Whenever the whole capital stock of such corporation
or an amount of such capital stock proportioned to the part of
such railway directed by the commissioners to be constructed,
shall have been subscribed by not less than fifteen persons, and
the fixed percentage of such subscriptions shall have been paid,
in cash, the commissioners shall, by written or printed notice
of ten days, served personally or by mail, call a meeting of such
subscribers for organization, and appoint the inspectors of election to serve thereat. At such meeting, or at any subsequent
one to which the same may be adjourned, a majority in number
and amount of such subscribers may elect persons, of a number
to be theretofore determined by the commissioners not less than
nine, who shall be directors for one year of the corporation
formed for the purposes of constructing and operating such
railway.

Commissioners to deliver certificate; affidavit of directors.

§ 128. Within ten days after the election of such directors
the commissioners shall deliver to them a certificate in duplicate,
verified by the oath of three commissioners, before a justice of
the supreme court, setting forth the certificate of incorporation
and the organization of the corporation for the purposes therein
mentioned, and within five days after the reception by them of
such certificates, three of the directors so elected shall make
affidavit in duplicate that the full amount of stock has been subscribed in good faith to construct, maintain and operate the
railway or railways in such certificate of incorporation mentioned, and such directors shall file such affidavits and certificate
in the office of the secretary of state, and a duplicate of the same

in the office of the clerk of the county wherein such railway shall be located; and thereupon the persons who have so subscribed such certificate of incorporation and all persons who shall become stockholders in such corporation shall be a corporation by the name specified in such certificate, and be subject to the duties, liabilities and restrictions of such corporations.

Powers.

§ 129. Every such corporation shall have power, in addition to the powers conferred by the general and stock corporation laws and by subdivisions two, five and seven of section eight* of this chapter:

1. To take and convey persons and property on their railroad by the power or force of steam or by any motor other than animal power, and to receive compensation therefor.

2. To enter upon and underneath the several streets, avenues and public places and lands designated by the commissioners, and enter into and upon the soil of the same, to construct, maintain, operate and use in accordance with the plan adopted by the commissioners, a railway upon the route or routes and to the points decided upon and to secure the necessary foundations and erect the columns, piers and other structures which may be required to secure safety and stability in the construction and maintenance of the railways constructed upon such plan and for operating the same; and to make such excavations and openings along the route through which such railways shall be constructed as shall be necessary from time to time. In all cases the surface of the streets around such foundations, piers and columns shall be restored to the condition in which they were before such excavations were made, as near as may be, and any interference with or change in the water mains, or in the sewers or lamp posts, except such changes as may be made with the concurrence of the proper department or authority shall be avoided; and the use of the streets, avenues, places and lands designated by the commissioners and the right of way through

---

*So in the original.

the same for the purpose of a railway, as herein authorized, shall be considered and is hereby declared to be a public use, con-sistent with the uses for which the roads, streets, avenues and public places are publicly held. No such corporation shall have the right to acquire the use or occupancy of public parks or squares in any such city or county, or the use or occupancy of any of the streets or avenues, except such as may have been designated for the route or routes of such railway, and except such temporary privileges as the proper authorities may grant to such corporations to facilitate such construction, and no such railway shall be constructed across the track of any steam rail-way now in actual operation at the grade thereof, nor shall any piers or supports for any elevated railway be erected upon a railway track now actually in use in any street or avenue; and no such corporation shall construct a street surface railroad to run in whole or in part upon the surface of any street or high-way under the provisions of this article.

Crossing of horse railroad track.

§ 130. Whenever the route selected by the commissioners for the construction of such railway shall intersect, cross or coin-cide with any horse railway track occupying the surface of the street or avenues, such railway corporation is hereby authorized to remove, for the purpose of constructing its road, the tracks of such horse railway; but the same shall be done in such man-ner as to interfere as little as possible with their practical opera-tion or working, and upon the construction of such railway, where such removals or changes have been made, the same shall be restored as near as may be to the condition in which they were previous to the construction of such railroad. All such removals and restorations shall be made at the proper cost and charges of such corporation, but no authority is herein given to any such corporation to use the tracks of any horse railway.

Where route coincides with another route.

§ 131. Whenever the route or routes determined upon by the commissioners coincide with the route or routes covered by the charter of an existing corporation, formed for the purpose of constructing and operating such a railway, and it has not forfeited its charter or failed to comply with the provisions thereof, requiring the construction of a road or roads within the time therein prescribed, such corporation shall have the like power to construct and operate such railway upon the fulfillment of the like requirements and conditions imposed by the commissioners as a corporation specially formed under this article, and the commissioners may fix and determine the route or routes by which any elevated steam railway now in actual operation may connect with other steam railways or the depots thereof, or with steam ferries, upon making compensation therefor, and in case such corporations can not agree with the owners of such steam railways, depots or ferries upon the amount of such compensation, and such owners may be entitled to compensation therefor, the amount of such compensation shall be ascertained and paid in the manner prescribed in the condemnation law, and upon fulfillment by such elevated railway corporation, so far as it relates to such connection, of the requirements and conditions imposed by this article, it shall possess all the powers conferred by section 129 of this article, and when any connecting route or routes shall be so designated, such elevated railway corporation may construct such connection with all the rights and with like effect as though the same had been part of the original route of such railway.

Thus amended by chap. 676, Laws of 1892.

Commissioners to transfer plans, etc.

§ 182. Within one month after such corporation shall have been formed and organized in the manner hereinbefore provided, the commissioners shall transfer and deliver to the corporation all plans, specifications, drawings, maps, books and papers in their possession, and they shall, within the like period of one month after the organization of such corporation, cause to be paid to the treasurer thereof all money collected under the provisions of this article, after deducting therefrom the necessary expenses incurred by the commissioners and the amounts due to them for their salaries.

Commissioners to file report; confirmation thereof.

§ 133. The commissioners shall within one hundred and forty days after their appointment, make a report to a special term of the supreme court of the department in which such railway may be located, of the amount of the pecuniary damage arising from the diminution of value of each parcel of property bounded on that portion of the street or streets, highway or highways, upon which it is proposed to construct such railway or railways, which will be caused by the construction, maintenance and operation thereof. The name and place of residence of the owner or owners of each parcel shall be stated if the same are known, or can be ascertained, and if not known the name of the person or persons appearing by the certificate of the clerk or register of the county, to have the title thereto from the records in his office, and a specific description of each parcel of property with reasonable certainty. The testimony, if any, taken by the commissioners as to the amount of such damage, shall accompany their report. Within thirty days after filing and recording its certificate of incorporation, the corporation authorized to construct and operate such railway or railways shall move to confirm such report by giving notice of such motion to the property owners in the manner in which notice of the time and place of hearing before the commissioners is required by section 125 to be given, and if the corporation fails to so move, any property owner may make the motion; and thereafter the proceedings shall be conducted in the manner prescribed in the condemnation law. Before constructing and operating its railway in front of any real property bounded upon any street, avenue or public place wherein the corporation is authorized by the certificate and report of the commissioners to construct and operate its road, such corporation shall pay to the owner of the real property the damages sustained or which will be sustained by him in conse. quence thereof, as finally fixed and ascertained, and the costs allowed him, if any, and the court may direct that such damages be paid out of the moneys deposited pursuant to the provisions of section 125, or in case negotiable securities shall have been deposited in lieu of money, that so much of such securities shall be sold as may be necessary to raise the amount required to be paid to such owner for damages and costs if any. If a bond shall have been executed in lieu of such deposit, the court may order the sureties in such bond to pay the damages so fixed and ascertained, and in default thereof may cause them to be proceeded against and punished as for a contempt of court.

Thus amended by chap. 676, Laws of 1892.

Pay of commissioners.

§ 134. Each of the commissioners shall be paid for his services at the rate of ten dollars per day for each day of actual service as such commissioner, and all expenses necessarily incurred by him in the discharge of his duties, to be paid by such corporation, but if a sufficient amount of capital stock shall not be subscribed within one year after the appointment of such commissioners to authorize the formation of such corporation, the commissioners shall receive no salary, and shall cause to be returned to the subscribers for such stock the amounts paid in by them, after deducting therefrom the necessary expenses incurred by the commissioners, but the time, if any, unavoidably consumed by the pendency of legal proceedings shall not be deemed a part of any period of time limited by this article.

Quorum; term of office; removal; vacancies in board of commissioners.

§ 135. A majority of the members of any board of commissioners appointed under this article shall be a quorum for the transaction of any business or the performance of any duty or function, or the exercise of any power, conferred or enjoined upon them. Any commissioner may be removed for cause at any time by the power appointing him, but no commissioner shall

be removed without due notice and an opportunity to be heard
in defense; and no commissioner thus removed is, or shall be
eligible to be again appointed to the office of commissioner. In
case of the death, resignation or removal from office of any commissioner the vacancy shall be filled by the power appointing
him, within thirty days after such removal, or within thirty days,
after notice in writing to such appointing power given by some
member of the board, or by the corporation hereinafter mentioned, of such death or resignation, and a certificate of every
such appointment shall be filed as hereinbefore required. Except
as otherwise provided by law, the terms of office of the commissioners shall determine and expire with the performance of their
functions as hereinabove prescribed.

Abandonment or change of route; new commissioners; their powers and proceedings.

§ 136. Any corporation heretofore organized or hereafter to
be organized under this article, its successor or assigns, which
shall have constructed or put in operation a railway upon a part
and not upon the whole of the route fixed, determined and
located for such railway by a board of commissioners, may at
any time apply for authority to abandon any portion of the
route upon which the railway shall not have been theretofore
constructed or shall not then be in operation, with or without a
change and relocation of such portion, and with or without
extension of the portion not abandoned, or of any part thereof.
Such application shall be made by petition in writing, addressed
by such corporation to the board of supervisors of the county
in which such portion of the route so desired to be changed or
abandoned shall be situated, which is not within the limits of
any city, or if such route, or any part thereof, shall be within
the limits of a city, to the mayor of the city, for the route or
portion thereof within such city. Five commissioners may be
appointed pursuant to such an application as hereinafter pro-

vided, who shall be residents of the county or city and who shall have full power as herein provided. When such application is made by a corporation heretofore organized such commissioners may be appointed within thirty days after presentation of the same by such board of supervisors, or, as the case may be, by such mayor. When such application is made by a corporation hereafter to be organized under this article, such board of supervisors, or, as the case may be, such mayor, may within thirty days after presentation of such application, indorse thereon their or his approval and direction that it may be presented to the supreme court in the manner provided in section 120 of this article, and such court may thereupon appoint such commissioners. Within ten days after his appointment each commissioner so appointed shall take, subscribe and file the oath and give and file the bond prescribed by section 121 of this article; and if any one so appointed shall not comply with this requirement, he shall be deemed to have declined to accept such appointment, and to have made a vacancy which the appointing power shall fill by another appointment as herin* provided. Within fifteen days after such appointments shall have been so made, the commissioners shall meet at some convenient place in such county and complete their organization as a board with appropriate officers. Such board shall have all the authority conferred by law upon commissioners appointed, or authorized to be appointed under this article. Before proceeding to hear the application of the corporation, the board shall give such public notice as it may deem most proper and effective of the time and place of the hearing. Within thirty days after completing their organization such board shall hear the application of the corporation, and all parties who may be interested therein, and within sixty days after their organization they shall determine whether any part of such route should be authorized to be abandoned, or should be changed and relocated with or without extension or extensions. If the board shall determine that no abandonment of any part of the route should be allowed, and that no change

---

*So in the original.

and relocation of any part thereof should be effected, and that no extension should be made, the board shall dismiss the application. If the board shall determine that an abandonment of any portion of the route should be allowed, or that any change in or extension thereof should be made, the board shall proceed to authorize and require the same upon such conditions as to the board shall seem proper, and with or without extension of the remainder of the route or of any part thereof, by fixing, determining and locating the route or routes of the extension or extensions, if any, and by directing the abandonment of the part of the route theretofore located, but by the board allowed to be abandoned, if any, and by fixing, determining and relocating the part of the route theretofore located, but by the board changed, if any; and the board shall cause to be made in duplicate a survey and map of the route as so changed and fixed, determined and located. Neither such corporation nor any assign or successor thereof shall thereafter have any authority, by reason of anything done under this article to operate or construct any railway upon any portion of the route by the board so required to be abandoned. The board shall also fix and determine the time within which the railway by it authorized and required upon any portion of the route so changed, shall be reconstructed and ready for operation. If the railway on any portion of the route not by the board changed or allowed to be abandoned, shall not have been theretofore constructed and made ready for operation, the board may extend, and fix and determine anew the time within which such railway shall be completed, but such extension of time shall not be for a longer period than that originally allowed by law for the completion thereof. If the board shall have determined that any portion of the route there-tofore located should be allowed to be abandoned, with or with-out a change or relocation thereof or any part thereof, and with or without extension, or if the board shall have extended the time within which such railway shall be completed, the board shall make a report in writing in accordance with the determina-tion so made, describing the portion of the route, if any there

be, as so fixed, determined and located anew, and the part, if
any there be, of the route allowed to be abandoned, and stating
the period of time, if any, by the board fixed and determined
within which such corporation shall construct and complete the
railway theretofore authorized or by it authorized to be constructed, and prescribing that a failure by the corporation, its
successors or assigns, to complete it within the time, if any so
limited, shall work a forfeiture to the supervisors of the county
if no part of the road is within a city, or in any city, to such city,
of the rights and franchises of such corporation with respect to
that portion of the route so fixed, determined and located anew,
and with respect to the then authorized extension or extensions,
if any there be of said route, upon which a railway shall not be
constructed within the time so limited; but the time, if any,
unavoidably consumed by the pendency of legal proceedings,
shall not be deemed a part of any period of time limited in this
article, and any recital of any forfeiture of any of the rights or
franchises prescribed by any commissioners heretofore appointed,
to be to the mayor, aldermen and commonalty of the city of New
York, shall be as effectual for any and all purposes as if such forfeiture had been in terms recited to be to the board of supervisors of the county of New York. Such report shall be signed
in duplicate by at least a majority of the then members of the
board, and there shall be thereto annexed the survey and map
as hereinabove directed, showing the line and location of each
and all the routes, with or without the extension or extensions,
as fixed, determined and located, and showing also the parts or
part, if any there shall be, of the route or routes as theretofore
fixed, determined and located, but by the board allowed to be
abandoned. Within ten days after so signing such report the
board shall cause the same to be filed in the office of the secretary of state, and the duplicate thereof in the office of the clerk
of the county wherein such railway shall be located; and thereupon the corporation making such application, its successors or
assigns, is and shall be authorized to construct, maintain and
operate a steam railway for the transportation of passengers,

mail and freight, upon the route or routes so fixed, determined and located, and in said report described, but the construction or operation of a railway upon any new location or selection of route is not and shall not be thus authorized except upon the condition that the consent of the owners of one-half in value of the property bounded on, and the consent also of the local author-ities having control of that portion of a street or highway upon which it is proposed to construct or operate such railway be first obtained, or in case the consent of such property owners can not be obtained, that the determination of three commission-ers, to be upon application appointed by the general term of the supreme court, in the district in which such railroad is proposed to be constructed, be given after a hearing of all parties inter-ested that such railway ought to be constructed or operated, which determination, confirmed by the court, may be taken in lieu of the consent of the property owners. Such corporation is and the successors and assigns thereof shall be authorized to maintain and operate all the railroads and the appurtenances thereof by it or them theretofore constructed upon any portion of a route or routes which shall have been located by commis-sioners under this article, and to complete within the time in and by such report so extended, fixed and determined anew, and thereafter to maintain and operate, the railway and the appur-tenances, upon so much of the route or routes theretofore fixed, determined and located as shall not have been so authorized and required to be abandoned, and with the same rights and effect, in all respects, as if such extended period of time had been orig-inally fixed and determined, and in the original certificate of incorporation of such corporation recited, for completing such railway and putting it in operation. The other terms and con-ditions in and by such certificate mentioned and prescribed, except as the same are hereinbefore modified or may be modified by the board as hereinabove authorized, shall apply to the rail-way herein authorized to be constructed and operated upon the route or routes as so changed, fixed, determined and located, with the same force and effect as if such route or routes, as

finally so changed and located, had been in and by such articles
or certificates themselves prescribed. If a new location or extension of routes shall be fixed and determined by commissioners
who shall have been appointed by the court pursuant to this
section, they shall also ascertain and determine the aggregate
pecuniary damages arising from the diminution of value of the
property bounded on that portion of the street or highway upon
the line of such new location or extension and of each parcel of
real property so bounded, and their proceedings thereupon shall
be conducted in the same manner and upon the like notice as
the proceedings for that purpose before the commissioners specified in section 125 and shall make to the supreme court the
report required by section 133, and thereupon the same proceedings shall be had as are provided for in such last named section.
Each commissioner shall be paid for his services at the rate of
ten dollars per day for each day of actual services as such commissioner, and all reasonable expenses incurred by him in or
about any of the matters referred to such board, to be paid by
the corporation making the application so heard and determined.
No corporation shall be authorized under this section to extend,
abandon or change the location of its route, or any part thereof,
where the greater portion of the route or routes is or shall be in
that portion of the city of New York south or west of Harlem
river, or of any route or part thereof in the city of Brooklyn or
county of Kings, or to construct, extend, abandon or change the
location of any railway or route for a railway over, under,
through or across any street, avenues, place or lands south of
One Hundred and Twenty-eighth street or west of Third avenue
in that portion of the city of New York south or west of Harlem
river, or where a railway might not by law be constructed, or
was not by law authorized to be by a board of commissioners
located on the 5th day of June, 1888.

Thus amended by chap. 676, Laws of 1892.

Increased deposit, when and how required.

§ 137. In case any of the securities deposited in lieu of money
as provided in section one hundred and twenty-five, shall in the

15

opinion of the county treasurer or trust company with whom they may be deposited, fall below their actual value at the time of deposit, the county treasurer or trust company shall call upon such railway corporation to substitute therefor other securities equivalent at their par or market value to the amount in lieu of which the securities for which they are to be substituted were deposited, and in case such other securities shall not be furnished, the county treasurer or trust company shall call upon such corporation to furnish as a substitute, and it shall so furnish an amount of money equal to the amount in lieu of which the securities first above referred to were deposited.

Trains to come to full stop, etc.

§ 138. All trains upon elevated railroads shall come to a full stop before any passenger shall be permitted to leave such train; and no train on such railroad shall be permitted to start until every passenger desiring to depart therefrom shall have left the train, provided such passenger has manifested his or her intention to so depart by moving toward or upon the platform of any car; nor until every passenger upon the platform or station at which such train has stopped, and desiring to board or enter such cars, shall have actually boarded or entered the same, but no person shall be permitted to enter or board any train after due notice from an authorized employee of such corporation that such train is full and that no more passengers can be then received.

Gates or vestibule doors.

§ 139. Every car used for passengers upon elevated railroads shall have gates at the outer edge of its platforms so constructed that they shall, when opened, be caught and held open by such catch or spring as will prevent their swinging and obstructing passengers in their egress from or ingress to such cars, or vestibule doors so constructed as to slide into the body of the car; and every such gate or door shall be kept closed while the car is in motion; and when the car has stopped and a gate or door has been opened, the car shall not start until such gate or door is again firmly closed.

Thus amended by chap. 273, Laws of 1903.

Penalty for violation of this article.

§ 140. Any elevated railroad corporation that shall fail or neglect to comply with or enforce the provisions of this article, shall upon the petition of any citizen to any court of record, and upon due notice to such corporation, and proof of such failure or neglect, pay to the clerk of the court wherein such petition was made, a sum not less than two hundred and fifty nor more than one thousand dollars, as such court may direct by its order. The sum so ordered to be paid shall be paid by such clerk of the court to the county treasurer, and shall be distributed by such treasurer equally among the public hospitals of the county in which the proceeding is had, at such time, as the board of supervisors or board of aldermen in any such county shall direct. Nothing in this section shall relieve elevated railroad corporations from any liability under which they may now be held by existing laws for damages to persons or property.

Thus amended by chap. 676, Laws of 1892.

Sections to be printed and posted.

§ 141. The officers and board of directors of such railroad corporations shall cause copies of sections one hundred and thirty-eight, one hundred and thirty-nine and one hundred and forty to be printed conspicuously and posted in he* depots or stations and in each car belonging to them.

Extension of time.

§ 142. The time within which any act is required to be done under this article may be extended by the supreme court for good cause shown, for one year, and but one extension will be granted. Any company that has heretofore constructed or is now operating an elevated railroad shall be deemed to have been duly incorporated notwithstanding any failure on the

---

*So in the original.

part of commissioners to insert in its articles of association provisions complying with statutory requirements relative to such
articles.

Added by chap. 676, Laws of 1892.

ARTICLE VI.

THE BOARD OF RAILROAD COMMISSIONERS.

Members.

§ 150. There shall continue to be a board of railroad commissioners, consisting of five competent persons, one of whom
shall be experienced in railroad business, appointed by the
governor, by and with the advice and consent of the senate,
each of whom shall hold office for the term of five years, and
until his successor shall have been appointed and shall have
qualified. A commissioner shall in like manner be appointed
upon the expiration of the term of any commissioner; and
when any vacancy shall occur in the office of any commissioner,

a commissioner shall in like manner be appointed for the residue of the term. If the senate shall not be in session when the vacancy occurs, the governor shall appoint a commissioner to fill the vacancy, subject to the approval of the senate when convened.

Thus amended by chap. 728, Laws of 1905.

Suspension from office.

§ 151. Any commissioner may be suspended from office by the governor upon written charges preferred. The governor shall report such suspension and the reasons therefor to the senate at the beginning of the next ensuing session, and if a majority of the senate shall approve the action of the governor, such commissioner shall be removed from office and his office become vacant.

Secretary and marshal of board.

§ 152. The board shall have a secretary and a marshal who shall be appointed by it and serve during its pleasure. The secretary shall keep a full and faithful record of the proceedings of the board, and be the custodian of its records, and file and preserve at its general office all books, maps, documents and papers intrusted to his care, and be responsible to the board for the same. Under the direction of the board he shall be its chief executive officer, shall have general charge of its office, superintend its clerical business, conduct its correspondence, be the medium of its decisions, recommendations, orders and bequests*, prepare for service such papers and notices as may be required of him by the commissioners, and perform such other duties as the board may prescribe, and he shall have power to administer oaths in all cases pertaining to the duties of his office. He shall have the power to designate from time to time one of the clerks appointed by the board to act as assistant secretary during his absence from the county of Albany, and the clerk so designated for the time designated shall within the county of Albany only, possess the powers conferred by this section upon the secretary of the board.

Thus amended by chap. 534, Laws of 1892.

*So in the original.

Additional officers; their duties.

§ 153. The board may also appoint, to serve during its pleasure, the following officers or any of them: An accountant, who shall be thoroughly skilled in railroad accounting, and who shall, under the direction of the board, make examinations of the books and accounts of railroad and other corporations, and supervise the quarterly and annual reports made by the railroad corporations to the board, and collect and compile railroad statistics, and perform such other duties as the board may prescribe. An inspector, who shall be a civil engineer, skilled in railroad affairs; also, an inspector, who shall be an expert in electrical railroad affairs, each of whom shall make such inspections of railroads and other matters relating thereto, as directed by the board, and report to it. Such additional clerical force as may be necessary for the transaction of its business. The board may also employ engineers, accountants and other experts whose services they may deem to be of temporary importance in conducting any investigation authorized by law.

Thus amended by chap. 456, Laws of 1896.

Oath of office; eligibility of officers of board.

§ 154. Each Commissioner, and every person appointed to office by the board, shall, before entering upon the duties of his office, take and subscribe the constitutional oath of office. No person shall be appointed to or hold the office of commissioner or be appointed by the board to, or hold any office, place or position under it who holds any official relation to any railroad corporation, or owns stock or bonds therein, or who is in any manner pecuniarily interested in any firm or corporation having business relations with any such corporation.

Principal office and meetings of board.

§ 155. The principal office of the board shall be at the city of Albany, in rooms designated by the capitol commissioners, and it may have a branch office at the city of New York, and one at the city of Buffalo; and the board, or a quorum thereof, shall meet at least once a month during the year at the office in Albany.

The board shall have an official seal, to be prepared by the secretary of state in accordance with law, and its offices shall be supplied with necessary postage, stationery, office furniture and appliances, to be paid for as other expenses authorized by this article, and it shall have prepared for it by the state the necessary books, maps and statistics, incidentally necessary for the discharge of its duties.

Quorum.

§ 156. Three of the commissioners shall constitute a quorum for the transaction of any business, or the performance of any duty of the board and may hold meetings thereof at any time or place within the state. All examinations or investigations made by the board may be held and taken by and before any one of the commissioners or the secretary of the board, by the order of the board, and the proceedings and decisions of such single commissioner or secretary, shall be deemed to be the proceedings and decisions of the board, when approved and confirmed by it.
Thus amended by chap. 728, Laws of 1905.

General powers and duties of board.

§ 157. The board shall have power to administer oaths in all matters relating to its duties, so far as necessary to enable it to discharge such duties, shall have general supervision of all railroads and shall examine the same and keep informed as to their condition, and the manner in which they are operated for the security and accommodation of the public and their compliance with the provisions of their charters and of law. The commissioners or either of them in the performance of their official duties may enter and remain during business hours in the cars, offices and depots, and upon the railroads of any railroad corporation within the state, or doing business therein; and may examine the books and affairs of any such corporation and compel the production of books and papers or copies thereof, and the board may cause to be subpoenaed witnesses, and if a person duly subpoenaed fails to obey such subpoena without reasonable cause, or shall without such cause refuse to be examined, or to answer a legal or pertinent question, or to produce a book or paper which he is directed by subpoena to bring, or to subscribe his deposition after it has been correctly reduced to writing, the board may take such proceedings as are authorized by the Code of Civil Procedure upon the like failure or refusal of a witness subpoenaed to attend the trial of a civil action before a court of record or a referee appointed by such court. The board shall also take testimony upon, and have a hearing for and against any proposed change of the law relating to any railroad, or of the general railroad law, if requested to do so by the legislature, or by the committee on railroads of the senate or the assembly, or by the governor, and may take such testimony and have such a hearing when requested to do so by any railroad corporation, or incorporated organization representing agricultural or commercial interests in the state, and shall report their conclusions in writing to the legislature, committee, governor, corporation or organization making such request; and shall recommend and draft such bills as will in its judgment protect the people's interest in and upon the railroads of this state.

Form of report by railroad corporations.

§ 158. The board shall prescribe the form of the report required by the railroad law to be made by railroad corporations, and may from time to time make such changes and additions in such form, giving to the corporation six months' notice before the expiration of any fiscal year, of any changes or additions which would require any alteration in the method or form of keeping their accounts, and on or before June thirtieth in each year, shall furnish a blank form for such report. When the report of any corporation is defective, or believed to be erroneous, the board shall notify the corporation to amend the same within thirty days. The originals of the reports, subscribed and sworn to as prescribed by law, shall be preserved in the office of the board.

Thus amended by chap. 158, Laws of 1904.

See section 57, Railroad Law, *ante;* also sections 101a, 416, 602 and 611, Penal Code, *post.*

Investigation of accidents.

§ 159. The board shall investigate the cause of any accident on any railroad resulting in loss of life or injury to persons, which in their judgment shall require investigation, and include the result thereof in their annual report to the legislature. Before making any such examination or investigation, or any investigation or examination under this article, reasonable notice shall be given to the corporation, person or persons conducting and managing such railroad of the time and place of commencing the same. The general superintendent or manager of every railroad shall inform the board of any such accident immediately after its occurrence. If the examination of the books and affairs of the corporation, or of witnesses in its employ, shall be necessary in the course of any examination or investigation into its affairs, the board, or a commissioner thereof, shall sit for such purpose in the city or town of this state where the principal business office of the corporation is situated if requested so to do by the corporation; but the board may require copies of books and papers, or abstracts thereof, to be sent to them to any part of this state.

Recommendations of board, where law has been violated.

§ 160. If, in the judgment of the board, it shall appear that any railroad corporation has violated any constitutional provision or law, or neglects in any respect to comply with the terms of the law by which it was created, or unjustly discriminates in its charges for services, or usurps any authority not granted by law, or refuses to comply with the provisions of any law, or with any recommendation of the board, it shall give notice thereof in writing to the corporation, and if the violation, neglect or refusal is continued after such notice, the board may forthwith present the matter to the attorney-general, who shall take such proceedings thereon as may be necessary for the protection of the public interests.

See decisions of courts as to powers of the board.

Recommendations of board, when repairs or other changes are
    necessary.

§ 161. If in the judgment of the board, after a careful personal examination of the same, it shall appear that repairs are
necessary upon any railroad in the state, or that any addition
to the rolling stock, or any addition to or change of a station
or station houses, or that additional terminal facilities shall be
afforded, or that any change of the rates of fare for transporting
freight or passengers or in the mode of operating the road or
conducting its business, is reasonable and expedient in order to
promote the security, convenience and accommodation of the
public, the board shall give notice and information in writing
to the corporation of the improvements and changes which they
deem to be proper, and shall give such corporation an opportunity for a full hearing thereof, and if the corporation refuses
or neglects to make such repairs, improvements and changes,
within a reasonable time after such information and hearing,
and fails to satisfy the board that no action is required to be
taken by it, the board shall fix the time within which the same
shall be made, which time it may extend. It shall be the duty
of the corporation, person or persons owning or operating the
railroad to comply with such decisions and recommendations of
the board as are just and reasonable. If it fails to do so the
board shall present the facts in the case to the attorney-general
for his consideration and action, and shall also report them in
its annual or in a special report to the legislature. Elevated
railroad corporations are included in the application of this
section.

Thus amended by chap. 373, Laws of 1902.
See decisions of courts as to powers of the board.

Legal effect of recommendations and action of the board.

§ 162. No examination, request or advice of the board, nor
any investigation or report made by it, shall have the effect to
impair in any manner or degree the legal rights, duties or obligations of any railroad corporation, or its legal liabilities for
the consequence of its acts, or of the neglect or mismanagement

of any of its agents or employes. The supreme court at special
term shall have power in its discretion in all cases of decisions
and recommendations by the board which are just and reasonable to compel compliance therewith by mandamus, subject to
appeal to the general term and the court of appeals, and upon
such appeal, the general term and the court of appeals may
review and reverse upon the facts as well as the law.

Thus amended by chap. 676, Laws of 1892.
See 89 App. Div., 325.

Corporations must furnish necessary information.

§ 163. Every railroad corporation shall, on request, furnish
the board any necessary information required by them concerning the rates of fare for transporting freight and passengers
upon its road and other roads with which its business is connected, and the condition, management and operation of its road,
and shall, on request, furnish to the board copies of all contracts
and agreements, leases or other engagements entered into by it
with any person or corporation. The commissioners shall not give
publicity to such information, contracts, agreements, leases or
other engagements, if, in their judgment, the public interests
do not require it, or the welfare and prosperity of railroad corporations of the state might be thereby injuriously affected.

See section 416, Penal Code, *post*.

Attendance of witnesses and their fees.

§ 164. All subpoenas shall be issued by the president of the
board, or by any two members thereof, and may be served by
any person of full age authorized by the board to serve the same.
The fees of witnesses before the board shall be two dollars for
each day's attendance, and five cents for every mile of travel by
the nearest generally traveled route in going to and returning
from the place where the attendance of the witness is required,
and the fees shall be audited and paid by the comptroller on the
certificate of the secretary of the commission.

Fees to be charged and collected by the board.

§ 165. The board shall charge and collect the following fees:
For copies of papers and records not required to be certified, or

otherwise authenticated by the board, ten cents for each folio of one hundred words; for certified copies of official documents filed in its office, fifteen cents for each folio, and one dollar for every certificate under seal affixed thereto; for each certified copy of the quarterly report made by a railroad corporation to the board, fifty cents; for each certified copy of the annual report of the board, one dollar and fifty cents; for certified copies of evidence and proceedings before the board, fifteen cents for each folio. No fees shall be charged or collected for copies of papers. records or official documents, furnished to public officers for use in their official capacity, or for the annual reports of the board in the ordinary course of distribution. All fees charged and col lected by the board belong to the people of the state, and shall be paid quarterly, accompanied with a detailed statement thereof into the treasury of the state to the credit of the general fund.

Annual report of board.

§ 166. The board shall make an annual report on or before the second Monday in January in each year, which shall contain:

1. A record of their meetings and an abstract of their pro ceedings during the preceding year.

2. The result of any examination or investigation conducted by them.

3. Such statements, facts and explanations as will disclose the actual workings of the system of railroad transportation in its bearing upon the business and prosperity of the state, and such suggestions as to the general railroad policy of the state, of the amendment of its laws, or the condition, affairs or con. duct of any railroad corporation, as may seem to them appro. priate.

4. Drafts of all bills submitted by them to the legislature and the reasons therefor.

5. Such tables and abstracts of all the reports of all the rail. road corporations as they may deem expedient.

6. A statement in detail of the traveling expenses and dis bursements of the commissioners, their clerks, marshal and experts.

Five hundred copies of the report with the reports of the rail-road corporations of the state, in addition to the regular number prescribed by law, shall be printed as a public document of the state, bound in cloth for the use of the commissioners, and to be distributed by them in their discretion to railroad corpora-tions and other persons interested therein.

See Section 9, Chap. 507, Laws of 1901.

Certified copies of papers filed to be evidence.

§ 167. Copies of all official documents filed or deposited according to law in the office of the board, certified by a member of the board or the secretary thereof to be true copies of the originals under the official seal of the board, shall be evidence in like manner as the originals.

Acts prohibited.

§ 168. No railroad commissioner shall, directly or indirectly, solicit or request from, or recommend to any railroad corpora-tion, or any officer, attorney or agent thereof, the appointment of any person to any place or position nor shall any railroad corporation, its attorney or agent, offer any place, appointment or position or other consideration to such commissioners, or either of them, nor to any clerk or employe of the commissioners or of the board; neither shall the commissioners or either of them, nor their secretary, clerks, agents, employes or experts, accept, receive or request any pass from any railroad in this state, for themselves or for any other person, or any present, gift or gratuity of any kind from any railroad corporation; and the request or acceptance by them, or either of them, of any such place or position, pass, presents, gifts or other gratuity shall work a forfeiture of the office of the commissioner or commis-sioners, secretary, clerk or clerks, agent or agents, employe or employes, expert or experts, requesting or accepting the same.

See section 417, Penal Code, *post;* also section 416, Penal Code, *post.*

Salaries; expenses; transportation.

§ 169. The annual salary of each commissioner shall be eight thousand dollars; of the secretary six thousand dollars; of the marshal fifteen hundred dollars, of the accountant and of the inspector such sum as the board may fix, not exceeding three thousand dollars each; of the clerical force such sums respectively as the board may fix. In the discharge of their official duties, the commissioners, their officers, clerks and all experts and agents whose services are deemed temporarily of importance, shall be transported over the railroads in this state free of charge upon passes signed by the secretary of state and the commissioners shall have reimbursed to them the necessary traveling expenses and disbursements of themselves, their officers, clerks and experts, not exceeding in the aggregate nine hundred dollars per month. All salaries and disbursements shall be audited and allowed by the comptroller and paid monthly by the state treasurer upon the order of the comptroller out of the funds provided therefor.

Thus amended by chap. 728, Laws of 1905.
See 11 Misc. 103.

Total annual expense.

§ 170. The total annual expense of the board authorized by law, excepting only rent of offices and the cost of printing and binding the annual reports of the board as provided by law, shall not exceed one hundred thousand dollars; and shall be borne by the several corporations owning or operating railroads according to their means, to be apportioned by the comptroller, who, on or before July first, in each year, shall assess upon each of such corporations its proportion of such expenses, one-half in proportion to its net income for the fiscal year next preceding that in which the assessment is. made, and one-half in proportion to the length of its main road and branches, except that each corporation whose line of road lies partly within and partly without the state, shall in respect of its net income be assessed on a part bearing the same proportion to its whole net income that the line of its road within the state bears to the whole length of road, and in respect of its main road and branches shall be assessed only on that part which lies within the state. Such assessment shall be collected in the manner provided by law for the collection of taxes upon corporations.

Thus amended by chap. 728, Laws of 1905.

Application of this article.

§ 171. The provisions of this article shall apply to all rail-roads within the state, and the corporations, receivers, trustees, directors or others, owning or operating the same or any of them, and to all sleeping and drawing-room car corporations, and to all other associations, partnerships or corporations engaged in transporting passengers or freight upon any such railroad as lessee or otherwise.

§ 172. The railroad commissioners may in their discretion act as judges to award prizes which may be offered by any responsible person for improvements in machinery or appliances for operating railroads.

This section added by chap. 452, Laws of 1894.

Sections 180 to 183, both inclusive, were repealed by chap. 676, Laws of 1892.

Sections of the Constitution of the State of New York Relating to Railroads.

(See town bonding acts, *post*.)

ARTICLE I.—SECTION 18. The right of action now existing to recover damages for injuries resulting in death, shall never be abrogated; and the amount recoverable shall not be subject to any statutory limitation.

ARTICLE III.—SECTION 18. The legislature shall not pass a private or local bill in any of the following cases:

 *   *   *   *   *   *   *   *   *   *

Granting to any corporation, association or individual the right to lay down railroad tracks.

Granting to any private corporation, association or individual any exclusive privilege, immunity or franchise whatever.

 *   *   *   *   *   *   *   *   *   *

The legislature shall pass general laws providing for the cases enumerated in this section, and for all other cases which in its judgment, may be provided for by general laws. But no law shall authorize the construction or operation of a street railroad except upon the condition that the consent of the owners of one-half in value of the property bounded on, and the consent also of the local authorities having the control of, that portion of a street or highway upon which it is proposed to construct or operate such railroad be first obtained, or in case the consent of such property owners cannot be obtained, the Appellate Division of the Supreme Court, in the department in which it is proposed to be constructed, may, upon application, appoint three commissioners who shall determine, after a hearing of all parties interested, whether such railroad ought to be constructed or operated, and their determination, confirmed by the court, may be taken in lieu of the consent of the property owners.

ARTICLE VII.—SECTION 7. The lands of the State, now owned or hereafter acquired, constituting the forest preserve as now fixed by law, shall be forever kept as wild forest lands. They shall not be leased, sold or exchanged. or be taken by any corporation, public or private, nor shall the timber thereon be sold, removed or destroyed.

Article VIII.—Section 1. Corporations may be formed under general laws; but shall not be created by special act, except for municipal purposes, and in cases where, in the judgment of the legislature, the objects of the corporation cannot be attained under general laws. All general laws and special acts passed pursuant to this section may be altered from time to time or repealed.

§ 2. Dues from corporations shall be secured by such individual liability of the corporators and other means as may be prescribed by law.

§ 3. The term corporations as used in this article shall be construed to include all associations and joint-stock companies having any of the powers or privileges of corporations not possessed by individuals or partnerships. And all corporations shall have the right to sue and shall be subject to be sued in all courts in like cases as natural persons.

Article XIII.—Section 5. No public officer, or person elected or appointed to a public office, under the laws of this State, shall directly or indirectly ask, demand, accept, receive or consent to receive for his own use or benefit, or for the use or benefit of another, any free pass, free transportation, franking privilege or discrimination in passenger, telegraph or telephone rates, from any person or corporation, or make use of the same himself or in conjunction with another. A person who violates any provision of this section, shall be deemed guilty of a misdemeanor, and shall forfeit his office at the suit of the Attorney-General. Any corporation, or officer or agent thereof, who shall offer or promise to a public officer, or person elected or appointed to a public office, any such free pass, free transportation, franking privilege or discrimination shall also be deemed guilty of a misdemeanor and liable to punishment except as herein provided. No person, or officer or agent of a corporation, giving any such free pass, free

16

transportation, franking privilege or discrimination hereby prohibited, shall be privileged from testifying in relation thereto, and
he shall not be liable to civil or criminal prosecution therefor if
he shall testify to the giving of the same.

Other General Acts Relating to Railroads.

CHAP. 133, LAWS OF 1847.

AN ACT authorizing the incorporation of rural cemetery associations.

§ 10. The cemetery lands and property of any association formed pursuant to this act, and any property held in trust by it for any of the purposes mentioned in section nine of this act, shall be exempt from all public taxes, rates and assessments, and shall not be liable to be sold on execution, or be applied in payment of debts due from any individual proprietor. But the proprietors of lots or plots in such cemeteries, their heirs or devisees, may hold the same exempt therefrom, so long as the same shall remain dedicated to the purposes of a cemetery, and during that time no street, road, avenue or public thoroughfare shall be laid out through such cemetery, or any part of the lands held by such association for the purposes aforesaid, without the consent of the trustees of such association, and of two-thirds of the lot owners thereof and then only by special permission of the legislature of the state.

Thus amended by chap. 237, Laws of 1904.
All the rest of the act was repealed by the Membership Corporation Law
See section 91, Highway Law, *post*.

CHAP. 62, LAWS OF 1853.

AN ACT to regulate the construction of roads and streets across railroad tracks.

Laying out streets or highways across railroad tracks.

SECTION 1. It shall be lawful for the authorities of any city, village or town in this state, who are by law empowered to lay out streets and highways, to lay out any street or highway across the track of any railroad now laid or which may hereafter be laid, without compensation to the corporation owning such railroad; but no such street or highway shall be actually opened for use until thirty days after notice of such laying out has been served personally upon the president, vice-president, treasurer or a director of such corporation.

Railroad corporations to cause street laid out across their track to be taken across at most convenient place for public travel.

§ 2. It shall be the duty of any railroad corporation, across whose track a street or highway shall be laid out as aforesaid, immediately after the service of said notice, to cause the said street or highway to be taken across their track, as shall be most convenient and useful for public travel, and to cause all necessary embankments, excavation and other work to be done on their road for that purpose; and all the provisions of the act, passed April second, eighteen hundred and fifty, in relation to crossing streets and highways, already laid out, by railroads, and in relation to cattle, guards and other securities and facilities for crossing such roads, shall apply to streets and highways hereafter laid out.

Penalty for neglect or refusal.

§ 3. If any railroad corporation shall neglect or refuse, for thirty days after the service of the notice aforesaid, to cause the necessary work to be done and completed, and improvements made on such streets or highways across their road, they shall forfeit and pay the sum of twenty dollars for every subsequent day's neglect or refusal, to be recovered by the officers laying out such street or highway, to be expended on the same; but the time for doing said work may be extended, not to exceed thirty days, by the county judge of the county in which such street or high way, or any part thereof, may be situated, if, in his opinion the said work cannot be performed within the time limited by this act.

This act has been repealed by the provisions of the grade crossing law, sections 60-69 of the Railroad Law. (158 N. Y., 410.)

CHAP. 474, LAWS OF 1855.

AN ACT for the protection of immigrants, second class, steerage and deck passengers.

SECTION 1. It shall be the duty of all companies, associations, and persons, hereafter undertaking to transport or convey, or engaged in transporting or conveying, by railroad, steamboat, canal-boat or propeller, any immigrant, second class, steerage, or deck passenger, from the city, bay, or harbor of New-York, to any point or place, distant more than ten miles therefrom, or from the cities of Albany, Troy and Buffalo, the town or harbor of Dunkirk, or the Suspension Bridge, to any other place or places, to deliver to the mayors of the city of New-York, Albany, Troy, and Buffalo, on or before the first day of April in each and every year, a written or printed statement of the price, or rates of fare, to be charged by such company, association or person, for the conveyance of such immigrant, second class, steerage and deck passengers respectively, and the price per hundred pounds for the carriage of the luggage, and the weight of luggage to be carried free of such passengers from and to each and every place, from and to which any such company, association, or person, shall undertake to transport and convey such passengers; and such prices or rates shall not exceed the prices and rates charged by the company, association or person, after the time of delivering such statement to the said mayors; and such statement shall also contain a particular description of the mode and route by which such passengers are to be transported and conveyed, specifying whether it is to be by railroad, steamboat, canal-boat or propeller, and what part of the route is by each, and also the class of passage, whether by immigrant trains, second class, steerage or deck passage. In case such companies, association, or person, shall desire thereafter to make any change or alteration in the rates or prices of such transportation and conveyance, they shall deliver to the said mayors respectively a similar statement of the prices and rates as altered and changed by them; but the rates and prices so changed and altered, shall not be charged or received until five days after the delivery of the statement thereof to the said mayors respectively.

§ 2. Every ticket, receipt or certificate which shall be made or issued by any company, association or person, for the conveyance of any immigrant, second class, steerage or deck passengers, or as evidence of their having paid for a passage, or being enti-

tled to be conveyed from either or any of the points or places
in the first section of this act mentioned to any other place or
places, shall contain or have endorsed thereon a printed state‑
ment of the names of the particular railroad or railroads, and of
the line or lines of steamboats, canal boats and propellers, or of
the particular boats or propellers, as the case may be, which are
to be used in the transportation and conveyance of such passen‑
gers, and also the price or rate of fare charged or received for
the transportation and conveyance of any such passenger or pas‑
sengers with his or their luggage.

§ 3. It shall not be lawful for any person or persons to
demand or receive, or bargain for the receipt of any greater or
higher price or rate of fare for the transportation and convey‑
ance of any such immigrant, second class, steerage or deck pas‑
sengers with their luggage, or either, from either or any of the
points or places in the first section of this act mentioned, to any
other point or place, than the prices or rates contained in the
statements which shall be delivered to the mayors of the cities
of New-York, Albany, Troy and Buffalo, and said commissioners,
respectively, as in the said first section provided for, or the price
or rates which shall be established and fixed for the transporta‑
tion and conveyance of such passengers and their luggage, or
either, by the proprietors or agents of the line or lines, or means
of conveyance, by which such passenger or passengers and their
luggage are to be transported or conveyed. In all cases each
immigrant over four years of age conveyed by railroad shall be
furnished with a seat with permanent back to the same, and
when conveyed by steamboat, propeller or canal boat, shall be
allowed at least two and one half feet square in the clear on
deck. Such deck shall be covered and made water tight over‑
head, and shall be properly protected at the outsides, either by
curtains or partitions, and shall be properly ventilated.

§ 4. Any company, association, person or persons, violating
or neglecting to comply with any of the provisions of the first
or second sections of this act, shall be liable to a penalty of
two hundred and fifty dollars for each and every offense,

to be sued for and recovered in the name of the people of this state;

*   *   *   *   *   *   *   *   *   *

See section 626, Penal Code, *post*.

CHAP. 228, LAWS OF 1857.

AN ACT in relation to the payment of fare upon the New-York Central railroad.

SECTION 1. The New-York Central railroad company, at every station on its road, where a ticket office is now or may hereafter be established, shall keep the same open for the sale of tickets at least one hour prior to the departure of each passenger train from such station; but nothing herein contained shall require said company to keep such office open between nine o'clock P. M. and five o'clock A. M., except at Albany, Schenectady, Utica, Syracuse, Rochester, Buffalo, and Suspension Bridge, which shall be kept open as hereinbefore required between five o'clock A. M. and eleven o'clock P. M.

§ 2. If any person shall, at any station, where a ticket office is established and open, enter the cars of said company, as a passenger thereon, without having first purchased a ticket for that purpose, it shall be lawful for the said company to demand and receive from such person a sum not exceeding five cents, in addition to the usual rate of fare for the distance such person may desire to be transported.

See section 37 Railroad Law, *ante;* chap. 38, Laws of 1889, *post*.

CHAP. 10, LAWS OF 1860.

*AN ACT relative to railroads in the city of New York.

SECTION 1. It shall not be lawful hereafter to lay, construct or operate any railroad in, upon or along any or either of the streets or avenues of the city of New York, wherever such railroad may commence or end, except under the authority and subject to the regulations and restrictions which the legislature may hereafter grant and provide. This section shall not

---

*While this is not a general act, it is deemed of sufficient importance to be printed here.

be deemed to affect the operation, as far as laid, of any railroad now constructed and duly authorized. Nor shall it be held to impair, in any manner, any valid grant for or relating to any railroad, in said city, existing on the first day of January, eighteen hundred and sixty.

§ 2. All acts and parts of acts inconsistent with this act are hereby repealed.

§ 3. This act shall take effect immediately.

CHAP. 590, LAWS OF 1872.

AN ACT to regulate processions and parades in the cities of the state of New York.

No procession or parade to interfere with free passage of cars upon railways.

Section 1. No procession or parade shall use any street upon the surface of which is a railway track or tracks by marching upon the said track or tracks, and a free passage of cars upon railway tracks shall not be interfered with by the formation, halt or march of any such procession or parade, or of the persons composing it. Whenever any procession shall find it necessary to march across a railway track, the portion of said procession which in so marching is likety* to stop the passage of any car or cars upon said track shall come to a halt in order to permit said car to proceed.

*　　*　　*　　*　　*　　*　　*　　*　　*　　*

Penalty.

§ 4. Every person willfully violating any provision of this act shall be guilty of a misdemeanor, punishable with a fine not exceeding twenty dollars, or imprisonment not exceeding ten days, or both at the discretion of the court.

See section 426, Penal Code, post.

---

*So in the original.

CHAP. 392, LAWS OF 1875.

AN ACT for the better security of railroad employees for labor performed.

* * * * * * * * * *

Personal liability of stockholders; notice; time for commencing action.

§ 8. Each and all the stockholders of such corporation shall be jointly and severally liable for the debts due or owing to any of its laborers or servants, other than contractors for personal service for ninety days' service, or less than ninety days' service, performed for such corporation, but shall not be liable to an action therefor, before an execution shall be returned unsatisfied in whole or in part against the corporation, and the amount due on such execution shall be the amount recoverable with costs against such stockholders, before such laborer or servant shall charge such stockholders for such ninety days' service or less than ninety days' service, he shall give notice in writing, within twenty days after the performance of such service, that he intends to so hold him liable, and shall commence such action therefor within thirty days after the return of such execution unsatisfied, as above mentioned; and every such stockholder against whom any such recovery by such laborer or servant, shall have been had, shall have a right to recover the same of the other stockholders in such corporation in ratable proportion to the amount of the stock they shall respectively hold with himself.

See sections 48, 54 and 55, Stock Corporation Law, and section 30, Railroad Law, *ante;* and section 8, Labor Law, and chaps. 418 and 419, Laws of 1897, *post.*

CHAP. 317, LAWS OF 1881.

AN ACT to authorize a change, in certain cases, of the time for holding elections in railroad companies.

Companies may change time for holding elections.

SECTION 1. Any railroad company, the time for the annual election of directors in which is now fixed for any day in the month of June, may by a vote of a majority of the stock, either in person or by proxy, thereof to that effect, and filing in the office of the secretary of state a copy of such proceedings, certified by the secretary of the company under its corporate scal, change the time for holding such annual election to any day in the month of April; provided, however, that the first election held under such resolution shall be held in the month of April which shall precede the time at which such election would otherwise have been held.

See section 20, Stock Corporation Law, *ante*.

CHAP. 452, LAWS OF 1881.

AN ACT to authorize corporations owning canals to construct and operate railroads alongside of or in lieu thereof.

Corporation owning canal may construct railroad.

SECTION 1. It shall be lawful for any corporation of this state owning and operating a canal to construct and operate along or in lieu of such canal a railroad and the exercise of the authority hereby conferred shall not be deemed to forfeit or impair its corporate rights under its charter or act of incorporation.

Corporate powers.

§ 2. Such company in the construction and maintenance of any such railroad under the authority of this act shall have, possess and enjoy all the powers and privileges contained in an act entitled "An act to authorize the formation of railroad corporations and to regulate the same," passed April second, eighteen hundred and fifty, and the several acts amending the same. and be subject to all the duties, liabilities and provisions so far as relates to any powers or privileges by this act upon said company conferred and hereafter exercised.

Not authorized to construct railroad in any other locality.

§ 3. Nothing in this act contained shall authorize the construction of any railroad except upon or along such canal owned and operated by any such company, and not in any other locality.

See chap. 469, Laws of 1899.

CHAP. 378, LAWS OF 1883.

AN ACT in relation to receivers of corporations.

Application for appointment of receiver, where made.

SECTION 1. Every application hereafter made for the appointment of a receiver of a corporation, other than applications made
by the attorney-general on behalf of the people of the state, shall
be made at a special term of the supreme court, held in and
for the judicial district in which the principal business office
of the corporation is located; and all such applications made
by the attorney-general shall be made in the judicial district in
which the action in which the appointment is sought is triable;
and any action or proceeding hereafter brought by the attorney-
general on behalf of the people of the state against any corporation for the purpose of procuring its dissolution, the appointment
of a receiver, or the sequestration of its property, may be brought
in any county of the state, to be designated by the attorney-
general.

Thus amended by chap. 282, Laws of 1896.

Compensation.

§ 2. A receiver of a corporation, except a receiver appointed in
proceedings for its voluntary dissolution, is entitled, in addition
to his necessary expenses, to such commissions, not exceeding
two and one-half per centum upon the sums received and disbursed by him, as the court by which or the judge by whom he is
appointed allows, but except upon a final accounting such a receiver shall not receive on account of his services for any one
year a greater amount than twelve thousand dollars, nor for any
period less than a year more than at that rate. Upon final
accounting, the court may make an additional allowance to such
receiver, not exceeding two and one-half per centum upon the
sums received and disbursed by him, if the court is satisfied that
he has performed services that fairly entitle him to such additional allowance. Where more than one receiver shall be appointed, the compensation herein . provided shall be divided
between said receivers.

Thus amended by chap. 349, Laws of 1906.

§ 2-a. If the receiver of a corporation employs counsel he shall within three months after he has qualified as receiver enter into a written contract fixing the compensation of such counsel at not exceeding a certain amount or a certain percentage of the sums received and disbursed by him, which contract must be approved by the supreme court, on at least eight days' notice to the attorney-general. A payment by such receiver to his counsel on account of services shall only be made, pursuant to an order of the court, on notice to the attorney-general and subject to review on the final accounting. A contract with counsel shall not be made for a longer period than eighteen months, but may be renewed from time to time for periods of not more than one year, if approved by the supreme court on at least eight days' notice to the attorney-general.

Added by chap. 349, Laws of 1906, which act repealed section 76 of title 4 of chap. 8 of part 3 of the Revised Statutes, entitled, " Powers and duties of permanent receivers," and also provided that acts inconsistent with itself are repealed.

Order appointing receiver to designate place of deposit.

§ 3. All orders appointing receivers of corporations shall designate therein one or more places of deposit, wherein all funds of the corporation not needed for immediate disbursement shall be deposited, and no deposits or investments of such trust funds shall be made elsewhere, except upon the order of the court upon due notice given to the attorney-general.

Duties of receiver.

§ 4. It shall be the duty of every receiver of an insurance, banking or railroad corporation, or trust company, to present every six months to the special term of the supreme court, held in the judicial district wherein the place of trial or venue of the action or special proceeding in which he was appointed may then be, on the first day of its first sitting, after the expiration of such six months, and to file a copy of the same, if a receiver of a bank or trust company, with the bank superintendent; if a receiver of an insurance company, with the superintendent of insurance; and in each case with the attorney-general, an account

exhibiting in detail the receipts of his trust, and the expenses
paid and incurred therein during the preceding six months; and
it shall be unlawful for any receiver of the character specified in
this section to pay to any attorney or counsel any costs, fees or
allowances until the amounts thereof shall have been stated to
the special term in this manner, as expenses incurred, and shall
have been approved by that court, by an order of the court duly
entered; and any such order shall be the subject of review by
the appellate division and the court of appeals on an appeal
taken therefrom by any party aggrieved thereby. Of the intention to present such account, as aforesaid, the attorney-general,
and also the surety or sureties on the official bond of such
receiver, shall be given eight days' notice in writing; and the
attorney-general shall examine the books and accounts of such
receiver at least once every twelve months.
Thus amended by chap. 139, Laws of 1896.

**Intervenor to pay his own legal expenses; no allowance to be
made for costs to attorneys.**

§ 5. In case of the intervention of any policy-holder or depositor, by permission of the court, such policy-holder or depositor
shall defray the legal expenses thereof, and no allowance shall
be made for costs or fees to any attorney of such policy-holder
or depositor.

Receiver to close up affairs within one year.

§ 6. The affairs of every insolvent corporation now in the
hands of any receiver shall be fully closed up by the receiver
thereof within one year from the passage of this act, unless
the court, upon application by said receiver and upon due notice
to the attorney-general, shall give additional time for that
purpose.

Attorney-general may apply to have receiver removed; appeal.

§ 7. The attorney-general may, at any time he deems that the
interests of the stockholders, creditors, policy-holders, depositors
or other beneficiaries interested in the proper and speedy dis-

tribution of the assets of any insolvent corporation will be sub‑
served thereby, make a motion in the supreme court at a special
term thereof, in any judicial district, for an order removing the
receiver of any insolvent corporation and appointing a receiver
thereof in his stead, or to compel him to account. or for such
other and additional order or orders as to him may seem proper
to facilitate the closing up of the affairs of such receivership, and
any appeal from any order made upon any motion under this
section shall be to the general term of said court of the depart‑
ment in which such motion is made.

Copies of all papers to be served on attorney-general.

§ 8. A copy of all motions and all motion papers, and a copy
of any other application to the court, together with a copy of
the order or judgment to be proposed thereon to the court, in
every action or proceeding now pending for the dissolution of
a corporation or a distribution of its assets, or which shall here‑
after be commenced for such purpose, shall, in all cases, be
served on the attorney-general, in the same manner as provided
by law for the service of papers on attorneys who have appeared
in actions, whether the applications but for this law would be
ex parte or upon notice, and no order or judgment granted shall
vary in any material respect from the relief specified in such
copy or order, unless the attorney-general shall appear on the
return day and have been heard in relation thereto; and any
order or judgment granted in any action or proceeding aforesaid,
without such service of such papers upon the attorney-general,
shall be void, and no receiver of any such corporation shall pay
to any person any money directed to be paid by any order or
judgment made in any such action or proceeding, until the expi‑
ration of eight days after a certified copy of such order or judg‑
ment shall have been served as aforesaid upon the attorney‑
general.

Applications under this act; where to be made; venue changed.

§ 9. All applications to the court, contemplated by this act,
shall be made in the judicial district where the principal office

of the corporation against which proceedings are taken is located, excepting such applications as are made in actions brought by the attorney-general on behalf of the people of the state, and all such applications shall be made in the judicial district in which the action is triable.

Thus amended by chap. 282, Laws of 1896.

Preference on calendar.

§ 10.   All actions or other legal proceedings and appeals therefrom or therein brought by or against a receiver of any of the insolvent corporations referred to in this act, shall have a preference upon the calendars of all courts next in order to actions or proceedings brought by the people of the state of New York.

Repeal.

§ 11.   All acts or parts of acts inconsistent herewith are hereby repealed.

See chap. 285, Laws of 1884; chap. 310, Laws of 1886; section 8, Labor Law; chaps. 522 and 534, Laws of 1898, and chap. 404, Laws of 1902, *post.*
See section 5, Stock Corporation Law; section 76, Railroad Law, *ante.*
See provisions of the Code of Civil Procedure as to receivers.

CHAP. 285, LAWS OF 1884.

AN ACT to provide for the transfer of securities and property by bankrupt corporations to the receivers of such corporations and for the transfer by the superintendent of the insurance department to receivers of insolvent life insurance and annuity companies of funds and securities deposited with such superintendent by such companies for the security of policyholders.

Where receivers have or shall be appointed for any corporation other than an insurance company on application by attorneygeneral, property to vest in receiver; proviso.

SECTION 1.   In all cases where receivers have been or shall be appointed for any corporation of this state other than an insurance company on application by the attorney-general, all property, real and personal, and all securities of every kind and nature belonging to such corporation, no matter where located or by whom held, shall be transferred to, vested in and held by such receiver; provided, however, that such transfer shall only be made when directed by an order of the supreme court, due notice of the application for such order having been made on the attorney-general and the custodian of the funds, securities or property.

*   *   *   *   *   *   *   *   *   *

See chap. 310, Laws of 1886; chaps. 522 and 534, Laws of 1898, and chap. 404, Laws of 1902, *post*. See chap. 378, Laws of 1883, *ante*.

CHAP. 490, LAWS OF 1885.

AN ACT concerning tramps.

*   *   *   *   *   *   *   *   *   *

Penalty for entering building without consent.

§ 4. Any tramp who shall enter any building against the will of the owner or occupant thereof, under such circumstances as shall not amount to burglary, or willfully or maliciously injure the person or property of another, which injury under existing law does not amount to a felony, or shall be found carrying any firearms or other dangerous weapon, or burglar's tools, or shall threaten to do any injury to any person or to the real or personal property of another, when such offense is not now punishable by imprisonment in the state prison, shall be deemed guilty of felony, and on conviction, shall be punished by imprisonment in the state prison at hard labor for not more than three years.

*   *   *   *   *   *   *   *   *   *

See sections 887a and 889, Code of Criminal Procedure, *post*.

CHAP. 310, LAWS OF 1886.

AN ACT to provide for the winding up of corporations which have been annulled and dissolved by legislative enactment.

Duty of attorney-general.

SECTION 1. Whenever any corporation organized under the laws of this State shall be annulled and dissolved by an act of the Legislature, it shall be the duty of the Attorney-General immediately thereafter to bring a suit to wind up and finally settle and adjust the affairs of such annulled and dissolved corporation.

Suit, where to be brought.

§ 2.   Such suit shall be brought in the supreme court in the name of the people of the State, in any county which the attorney-general may select.   The president, or vice-president, or secretary, or treasurer of such dissolved corporation, who may have been in office at the time of the dissolution thereof, shall be named, as such officer, as defendant in such suit, and the summons and complaint therein shall be served upon him.   If, at the time of such annulment and dissolution, there shall not be one of the above designated officers of such corporation, then such suit shall be brought against and the summons and complaint therein served upon any one of the persons who were last acting as directors of such corporation.

Court to appoint receiver.

§ 3.   It shall be the duty of the special term of the supreme court in the county designated in such summons and complaint, or of any judge of said court who resides in the judicial department in which such county is situated, upon the presentation of a certified copy of the act of the Legislature annulling and dissolving a corporation, and of the summons and complaint founded thereon, immediately to appoint a receiver of the assets and property of such dissolved corporation; and the person so appointed shall be both the temporary and permanent receiver thereof, and shall give a bond with sureties to be approved by said court or such judge thereof, to the people of the State in the penalty of not less than ten thousand dollars, conditioned for the faithful discharge of his duties as such receiver, and for his due accounting for, and paying over all moneys and property which may come to his hands as such receiver.   No one of the officers, directors or stockholders of such corporation shall be appointed such receiver thereof.

17

Receiver to make inventory.

§ 4. Such receiver shall, immediately after his appointment and the approval of his bond, cause an inventory of all the property of such dissolved corporation to be taken and filed in the office of the clerk of the county in which such action is pending, and for the purpose of ascertaining the nature, extent and location of such property, the said receiver shall have power to compel the attendance of witnesses, as hereinafter provided, and all evidence taken by or before said receiver in relation to such property shall be filed by him in the office of such county clerk.

Notice to creditors; powers and duties of receivers; creditors to present claims.

§ 5. The said receiver shall, immediately after his appointment, publish in two newspapers to be designated by said court, or such judge thereof, daily for one week, and for such longer time, not exceeding one month, as the said court or such judge thereof may by order designate, a notice to all creditors of such dissolved corporation to present their claims and demands against, and all evidences of indebtedness of, such dissolved corporation, to such receiver at a time and place to be designated in such notice. Such receiver is hereby authorized to examine on oath any of such creditors, or claimants, or other witnesses, as to any and all matters pertaining to any claim or demand or evidence of indebtedness so presented. At the expiration of ten days from the date specified in such notice, or within such further time as may be allowed by said court or such judge thereof, the said receiver shall make a list of all the claims presented to or proved before him, in which list he shall specify the amount, origin and true consideration of each claim so presented to or proved before him, and the name of the person in whose behalf the same is presented or proved, and the date when such claimant became the true owner thereof. Such list when so completed shall be verified by such receiver, and shall thereupon be filed, together with such evidence as may have been taken by him, in the office of the said county clerk. The said receiver shall, immediately after such filing, publish a notice daily for fourteen days in two newspapers to be designated by said court, or such judge thereof, stating that such list will be presented to such court, or to a judge thereof, residing in such county, on a day and at a place to be designated in such notice, and the said court or such judge thereof will then and there be asked for an order directing the sale at public auction of all the property specified in such inventory. Any creditor or stockholder may appear· and be heard at such time and place. It shall be the duty of said court, or of such judge thereof, to whom such list shall be presented, to examine the same together with such evidence as the receiver shall have taken, and to reject all claims, demands and evidences of indebtedness which were not legally incurred or created by said corporation, or which were in excess of its powers, or which are for any reason shown to be illegal; and no claim or demands shall be allowed for any greater amount than the money value of the consideration therefor, unless the said court or judge shall find and decide from the evidence taken by and before the receiver, that the person professing to own such claim does in truth own the same by reason of having taken a negotiable instrument or paper before the act dissolving and annulling the corporation alleged to be bound by such instrument or paper, and also before such instrument or paper was by its terms due, and that the same was taken for value paid and parted with in good faith before said act of dissolution and without knowledge or notice of any defect, want or deficiency of previous consideration, or other equity, offset, or defense originally attaching to such instrument or paper, or to the claim or demand upon which the same are founded. Such examination and rejection shall be made by such court or such judge thereof, and not by any referee.

When claim of creditor is debarred; right of creditor to appeal; sale of property; allowance to receiver; distribution of assets.

§ 6. All creditors whose claims shall not have been presented as above provided shall be debarred from participating in the avails of the sale of the property described in said inventory. Any creditor whose claim may have been rejected, and who shall have appealed, may apply to said court or such judge thereof for an order that a pro rata amount of the avails of such sale which would have appertained to the claim of such creditor, had not the same been rejected, may be retained in court to abide the result of his appeal, and said court, or such judge thereof, shall have discretion to grant the same. Any claimant feeling aggrieved by such rejection may appeal therefrom to the general term and to the Court of Appeals, in the manner now provided by law for such appeals from orders in civil actions, but neither of such appeals shall stay the proceedings of such receiver, or court, or judge thereof, or a sale of such property as herein provided for. The amount of all claims and demands so rejected by said court or such judge shall be deducted from the total amount of claims and demands so filed by the said receiver, and an entry of such rejection shall be made upon said list by said court or such judge, and thereupon the said court or such judge shall by order, reciting the proceedings direct the immediate sale by said receiver, at public auction, at a time and place and in the manner, and after such notice as may be provided in said order, of all the property in said inventory specified, to such person, firm or corporation as shall bid the highest sum or amount therefor. The receiver shall report to said court or such judge thereof, the name of the highest bidder, the amount bid, and thereupon said court or such judge thereof shall by order forthwith direct the said receiver by proper written instrument to convey and transfer all of the property described in said inventory, and offered for sale at said auction, to said highest bidder, who on receiving the same shall pay to the receiver the sum bid. The said court or such judge thereof, shall allow to the receiver two per cent upon the whole amount received by him from the sale of the property described in said inventory for his compensation as such receiver, and also his disbursements, including witness' fees, and the service of subpoenas, and to the Attorney-General, and to such other counsel as the receiver may find it necessary to employ, a reasonable counsel fee. The residue of the amount in the hands of the receiver shall be by him distributed among the owners of the claims in said list, which have been allowed subject to the deductions above provided for in case of an appeal, pro rata, or in full if such residue shall be sufficient therefor, and the receipts of such owners therefor shall be taken upon such list of claims. The balance of such residue, if any shall be distributed among the lawful stockholders of such corporation in proportion to their interest therein.

Proceedings not to be stayed.

§ 7. No issue raised by answer, or demurrer, or otherwise to the complaint hereinbefore provided for shall stay the proceedings of the receiver, or court or a judge thereof.

Discharge of receiver.

§ 8. The said receiver after such payment may apply to said court, or a judge thereof, for his final discharge, and if it shall appear that the said receiver has in all things fulfilled his duty in the premises, the said court or judge shall grant such final discharge, and said receiver, until so discharged, may as such receiver sue for and collect all debts due, and demands owing to such corporation.

Subpoenas, by whom issued; receiver may administer oaths; false swearing, perjury.

§ 9. It shall be the duty of the clerk of the county in which such suit is brought, to issue, upon the request of the receiver, subpoenas to compel the attendance of witnesses to enable him to ascertain the nature, extent and location of the property of said corporation, and to give evidence concerning any claim which may be presented by any creditor against the estate of such corporation, which subpoenas shall be served in like manner as in civil actions, and the fees of the witness shall be the same as are now established by law in such actions. The receiver shall have full power and authority to administer oaths to all such witnesses and to any creditor of such dissolved corporation, and to examine them concerning the property of such dissolved corporation, and as to the claims presented against it. Disobedience to such subpoenas shall be a contempt of court, and shall be punished in like manner as other contempts of court are now punishable. Willful false swearing by any witness or creditor in any such examination shall be deemed perjury, and shall be punishable as such in like manner as if committed by a witness on a trial of a civil action.

Leave to sue receiver, how and where obtainable.

§ 10. All applications for leave to sue such receiver and all applications for injunctions to restrain his proceedings shall be made only to the supreme court in the county in which such action was brought, and shall not be made to any other court, or to the supreme court in any other county, and shall not be granted except upon eight days' notice to the Attorney-General of the time and place of making such application. In any action hereafter brought or now pending by the Attorney-General, to close up, determine or settle the affairs of any corporation dissolved by legislative enactment, the judgment or determination of the supreme court at general term may be reviewed upon appeal to the Court of Appeals, as now provided by law, whether the judgment rendered in the case be interlocutory or final.

Thus amended by chap. 601, Laws of 1887.

Repeal, etc.

§ 11. This act shall take effect immediately, and all acts and parts of acts inconsistent therewith are hereby repealed.

See section 5, Stock Corporation Law; section 76, Railroad Law; chap. 378, Laws of 1883; chap. 285, Laws of 1884, *ante;* chaps. 522 and 534, Laws of 1898, chap. 404, Laws of 1902, and section 31, Rapid Transit Act, *post.*

See section 30, General Corporation Law; sections 57 and 61, Stock Corporation Law, *ante;* also provisions Code of Civil Procedure.

CHAP. 38, LAWS OF 1889.

AN ACT to regulate the payment of fares upon railroads.

Extra fare may be exacted when no ticket is purchased; rebate ticket to be issued therefor.

SECTION 1. It shall be lawful for any company owning or operating a steam railroad in this State, to demand and collect an excess charge of ten cents over the regular or established rate of fare, from any passenger who pays fare in the car in which he or she may have taken passage, except where such passage is wholly within the limits of any incorporated city in this State, provided, however, that it shall be the duty of such company to give to any passenger paying such excess, a receipt or other evidence of such payment, and which shall legibly state that it entitles the holder thereof to have such excess charge refunded, upon the delivery of the same at any ticket office of said company, upon the line of their railroad, and said company shall refund the same upon demand; and provided further that this act shall not apply to any passenger taking passage from a station or stopping place when tickets cannot be purchased during half an hour previous to the schedule time for the departure of said train, on which such passenger takes passage.

See section 37 Railroad Law, *ante;* chap. 228, Laws of 1857, *ante.*

CHAP. 555, LAWS OF 1890.

AN ACT to provide for the improvement and maintenance of the public roads in certain counties as county roads.

*　　*　　*　　*　　*　　*　　*　　*　　*　　*

Construction of horse, electric or other railways.

§ 7. No horse railway or electric or other railway shall be laid, constructed or operated on said county roads, unless, in addition to the requirements of existing laws, the same shall be authorized by a two-third vote of the board of supervisors and unless the same shall be constructed with a flat or grooved rail, and in case of horse railways, paved between the tracks in the manner prescribed by the board of supervisors in the resolution authorizing the same and the same constantly maintained in good order and condition by said railroad company, and the railroad or corporation constructing the same shall agree thereto, and it shall be the duty of the said board of supervisors to require from said railroad or corporation, or other person, a bond with sufficient sureties as a guarantee, and conditioned for the performance of their agreement, and the board of supervisors may, from time to time, require such bond to be renewed in case the sureties, or any of them, in its judgment, shall become insufficient.

* * * * * * * * * *

See special acts as to railroads on certain of these highways.

CHAP. 566, LAWS OF 1890.

AN ACT in relation to transportation corporations, excepting railroads, constituting chapter forty of the general laws.

* * * * * * * * * *

Existing routes and extensions.

§ 23. Any corporation incorporated under any law of this state heretofore enacted which owns and operates a lawfully established stage route which has been continuously operated by such company or its predecessors in title to such route for five years last past in any city of the first-class, is hereby authorized and empowered to extend its existing routes at any time or times and to operate the same as extended with stages and omnibuses propelled by electricity or any other motive power, in and upon any streets and highways of such city, without further or other authority, proceeding, or consent required under any act, general, public, private or local; provided, however, that such extensions shall not become valid until they shall have been first approved by the state board of railroad commissioners, who, on giving their approval, shall make a certificate of such extension or extensions of route as approved, which certificate shall be filed in the office of the secretary of state, and in the office of the clerk of the county in which such extension is located.

Such company, on filing in said offices an acceptance of the exten
sions specified in such certificate and on operating such exten
sions, shall have the right to charge a fare not exceeding ten
cents per passenger for a continuous ride over the whole or any
part of the routes owned or operated by it, and shall pay a
license fee to the city in which it operates equal to the charge
now in force for licensing similar stages and omnibuses, and
shall also pay to the comptroller or other chief fiscal officer of
said city five per centum per annum of its gross receipts from
the operation of said routes.

Added by chap. 657, Laws of 1900.
See provisions of Greater New York Charter, *post*.
See section 163, Highway Law, chap. 538, Laws of 1904; section 666, Penal
Code, *post*.

* * * * * * * * * *

Crossings.

§ 33. Whenever any tramway, constructed by any such corporation, shall cross a railroad, highway, turnpike, plank-road
or canal, such tramway shall be so constructed as not to interfere with the free use of such railroad, highway, turnpike, plank-
road or canal for the purposes for which they were intended.

* * * * ' ** * * * *

Railroad, turnpike, plank-road and highway crossings.

§ 43. Whenever any line of pipe of any such corporation shall
necessarily cross any railroad, highway. turnpike or plank-road,
such line of pipe shall be made to cross under such railroad,
highway, turnpike or plank-road and with the least injury thereto
practicable, and unless the right to cross the same shall
be acquired by agreement, compensation shall be ascertained and
made to the owners thereof, or to the public in case of highways, in the manner prescribed in the condemnation law, but
no exclusive title or use shall be so acquired as against
any rail-road, turnpike or plank-road corporation, nor as against
the rights of the people of this state in any public highway, but
the rights acquired shall be a common use of the lands in such
manner as to be of the least practical injury to such railroad,

turnpike or plank-road, consistent with the use thereof by such pipe-line corporation, nor shall any such corporation take or use any lands, fixtures or erections of any railroad corpora tion, or have the right to acquire by condemnation the title or use, or right to run along or upon the lands of any such corpora tion, except for the purpose of directly crossing the same when necessary.

*   *   *   *   *   *   *   *   *   *

CHAP. 568, LAWS OF 1890.

AN ACT in relation to highways, constituting chapter nineteen of the general laws.

*   *   *   *   *   *   *   *   *   *

General powers of commissioner.

SECTION 4. The commissioners of highways in the several towns, shall have the care and superintendence of the highways and bridges therein, except as otherwise specially provided in relation to incorporated villages, cities and other localities; and they shall

1. Cause such highways and bridges to be kept in repair, and give the necessary directions therefor, and shall inspect the highways and bridges in each highway district between the first and fifteenth day of September in each year, or at such other time as the board of supervisors by resolution may pre scribe. If it appears to him upon such inspection that the labor assessed in any highway district has not been entirely performed therein, he shall transmit a statement to the supervisor of his town containing the number of days' labor which in his opinion have not been performed in such district, and a list of all per sons and corporations owning property therein, and the number of days of labor still to be performed by such persons and cor porations. A notice of the transmission of such statement and of the day and place where the persons assessed for highway labor in such district may be heard before such supervisor, shall be posted in at least three conspicuous places in the road dis trict affected by such statement. On the day and at the place specified in such notice, the supervisor shall hear all persons

interested in the performance of labor on the highways in such
district. After such hearing, the supervisor shall correct such
list in accordance with the testimony and facts as they appear
to him and shall make a return thereof to the board of supervisors in the same manner as unpaid taxes and unperformed
labor are returned by the town board to the board of supervisors. The board of supervisors at its annual meeting in each
year, shall cause the amount of the arrearages for highway
labor contained in such lists, estimating each day's labor at one
dollar and fifty cents a day, to be collected from the property of
the person or corporation specified in such list, in the same manner as arrearages for unperformed labor.

Subdivision 1, thus amended by chap. 75, Laws of 1902.

*   *   *   *   *   *   *   *   *   *

4. Assign to each of the highway districts such of the inhabitants and corporations liable to work on highways, or who are
assessed for highway taxes thereon, as they shall think proper,
having regard to proximity of residence as much as may be.

Subdivision 4, thus amended by chap. 611, Laws of 1904.

*   *   *   *   *   *   *   *   *   *

Subdivision 8. Have power to enter upon the lands of any person adjoining any of the rivers, streams or creeks of the state,
drive spiles, throw up embankments and perform such other labor
as may be necessary upon the banks of such rivers, streams or
creeks for the purpose of keeping them or any of them within
their proper channels and preventing their encroachment upon
any of the highways of the state; to enter upon any lands adjoining any highway and which lands during the spring freshets or
any time of high water are subject to overflow from such rivers,
streams or creeks, and to remove or change the position of any
fence or other obstruction which prevents the free flow
of water under or through any highway, bridge or culvert
whenever the same may be necessary for the protection of any
highway; to protect such highways and the property of the
town from damages by reason of such rivers, streams or creeks
washing away their embankments, or changing the location of

the channels: to enter upon any lands adjacent to any of the highways of the town and with the approval of the town board to remove any fence or other obstruction which causes snow to drift in and upon said highway, and erect snow fences or other devices upon such lands to prevent the drifting of snow in or upon any such highway; and to agree with the owner of any such lands upon the amount of damages, if any, sustained by him in consequence of such entry upon his lands and the performance of the work herein authorized, and the amount of the damages so agreed upon shall be a town charge, and shall be audited and paid in the same manner as other town charges. If the commissioners are unable to agree with such owner upon the amount of damages thus sustained, the amount thereof shall be ascertained and determined and paid in the same manner as damages for the laying out and opening of highways are required by law to be ascertained, determined and paid, where the commissioners and land owner are unable to agree upon the amount thereof.

Subdivision 8, thus amended by chap. 478, Laws of 1904.

*   *   *   *   *   *   *   *   *

General duties of overseers.

§ 20. Each overseer of highways in every town, shall

1. Repair and keep in order the highways within his district.

2. Warn all persons and corporations assessed to work on the highways in his district, to come and work thereon.

3. Cause the noxious weeds within the bounds of the highway within his district, to be cut down or destroyed twice in each year, once before the first day of July, and again before the first day of September; and the requisite labor therefor shall be considered highway work.

4. Collect all fines and commutation money, and execute all lawful orders of the commissioners.

5. Cause all loose stone lying in the beaten track of every highway within his district, to be removed once in every month, from the first day of April until the first day of December, in each year. Stones so removed shall not be thrown into the gut.

ter, nor into the grass adjoining such highway, but they shall be conveyed to some place, from which they shall not work back or be brought back into the track by the use of road machines or other implements used in repairing such highways. Any person who shall violate the provisions hereof or who shall deposit or throw loose stones in the gutter or grass adjoining a highway or shall deposit or throw upon a highway ashes, papers, stones, sticks, or other rubbish, to the detriment or injury of the public use of, or travel upon such highway, shall be liable to a penalty of ten dollars, to be sued for and recovered by the commissioner or commissioners of highways, or in case of his or their refusal or neglect to act, by any taxpayer of the town in the name of the town in which the offence shall be committed, and when recovered, one-half of the amount shall be applied by them in improving the highways and bridges in such town. The other half shall be paid to the person upon whose written information the action was brought. Any commissioner of highways who shall neglect to prosecute for or join in an action with the other commissioners of highways to recover such penalty, knowing the same to have been incurred, or within twenty days after a sworn statement has been laid before them showing that a party is liable to such penalty, shall be guilty of a misdemeanor.

Subdivision 5, thus amended by chap. 106, Laws of 1902.

6. Cause the monuments erected or to be erected, as the boundaries of highways, to be kept up and renewed, so that the extent of such highway boundaries may be publicly known.

Opening obstructed highways.

§ 21. Whenever the labor in any district has been worked out, commuted for, or returned to the supervisor in a town under the labor system of taxation for working its highways, or in those towns that have adopted the money system of taxation for working the highways, and the town has not been divided into highway districts, the moneys voted at the town meeting for the removal of obstructions caused by snow and the prevention of such obstructions has been expended and the highways are

obstructed by snow, and notice has been given to the overseer
or highway commissioner in writing, by any two or more inhabitants of the town, liable to the payment of highway tax, requesting the removal of such obstruction, the overseer of highways in
such district or the highway commissioner of the town shall
immediately call upon all persons, corporations and occupants of
lands owned by non-residents liable to highway tax therein or in
the locality where such obstruction exists, to assist in removing
such obstruction and such labor so called for by the overseer or
highway commissioner, shall be assessed upon those liable to
perform the same or in the locality where such obstruction exists,
in proportion to their original assessments. Whenever in a town
that has adopted the money system of taxation for working the
highways, and has been divided into highway districts, the
moneys, if any, voted at the town meeting for the removal of
obstructions caused by snow and the prevention of such obstructions has been expended, or in which no money was voted at the
town meeting for such purpose, and the highways in any district
are obstructed by snow, the overseer of highways of such district shall immediately call upon the persons and corporations
in such district assessed for highway labor in pursuance of subdivision six of section thirty-three of this chapter to assist in
removing such obstruction, and shall credit such persons or corporations with the days' labor so performed. Should any persons,
corporations or occupants of lands owned by non-residents so
called out neglect or refuse to appear at the place designated by
the overseer or the commissioner of highways, or to commute at a
dollar a day within twenty-four hours after due notice, the overseer or commissioner of highways shall cause the obstruction to
be immediately removed and on or before September first of each
year, or at such other time as the board of supervisors may by
resolution prescribe, make out a list of all persons, corporations
or occupants of lands owned by non-residents who shall fail to
work out such labor or commute therefor, with the number of
days not worked or commuted for by each, charging for each
day in such list at the rate of one dollar and fifty cents per

day, verified to the effect that such persons, corporations or occupants of lands owned by non-residents have been notified to appear
and perform such labor or commute therefor, and that the same
has not been performed or commuted; said list shall be certified
by the commissioner of highways of such town to the town board
and by said town board to the board of supervisors, and the
amount of such arrearages shall be levied by such board of supervisors against and collected from the real or personal estate of
such persons and corporations and from the real estate owned by
non-residents specified in such list in the manner now provided by
law for the return, assessment and collection of arrearages for
unperformed highway labor. Each overseer of highways and highway commissioner neglecting to perform such duty shall be liable
to a penalty of five dollars per day, for every day he neglects,
without good and sufficient reasons, to have such highway opened
after receiving such written notice, and for each day after
September first or the day so fixed, he neglects to make out,
verify and deliver such list, the penalty to be collected in justices's*
court, by the supervisor in the name of the town, and paid over
to the highway fund of the town. No persons or corporations
shall be allowed any sum for highway labor performed in removing obstructions caused by snow unless authorized or directed by
the overseer or commissioner of highways to perform such labor.
No moneys collected or received under section fifty-three shall be
appropriated for removing obstructions caused by snow or preventing such obstructions.

Thus amended by chap. 672, Laws of 1905.

* H * * * * * * * *

§ 33. Subdivision 6. In a town which has adopted the money
system of taxation for working its highways, and which has
been divided into highway districts, and in which the money, if
any, voted at the town meeting is deemed by the commissioner
of highways insufficient for the removal of obstructions caused
by snow and the prevention of such obstructions, or in which
no money is voted at the town meeting for such purpose, the

*So in the original.

commissioner of highways shall annually on or before November fifteenth make an estimate of the probable number of days' labor needed during the following year for the removal of obstructions caused by snow in the highways and for the prevention of such obstructions, and shall assess such days' labor as provided by this subdivision. Every person liable to assessment under subdivision two of this section shall be assessed one day. The balance of such estimated number of days shall, in the same manner as is provided by subdivision three of this section for the assessment of highway labor in towns under the labor system, be assessed upon the estates, real and personal, of persons liable to assessment under such subdivision. Copies of the lists of persons and corporations assessed shall be prepared by the commissioner and delivered to the several overseers in the town in the manner provided by section thirty-four of this chapter.

Subdivision 6 added by chap. 672, Laws of 1905.

*   *   *   *   *   *   *   *   *   *

Commutations.

§ 62. Every person and corporation shall work the whole number of days for which he or it shall have been assessed, except such days as shall be commuted for, at the rate of one dollar per day and such commutation money shall be paid to the overseers of highways of the district in which the labor shall be assessed, within at least twenty-four hours before the time, when the person or corporation is required to appear and work on the highways; but any corporation must pay its commutation money on or before the first day of June in each year to the commissioner or commissioners of highways of the town in which the labor shall be assessed, and such commutation money shall be expended by the commissioner or commissioners of highways upon the roads and bridges of the town as may be directed by the town board except that in the counties of Albany, Dutchess, Fulton, Hamilton, Greene, Herkimer, Lewis, Montgomery, Putnam, Richmond, Rockland, Schoharie, Suffolk, Tompkins, Ulster, Westchester and Yates, the commissioner or commissioners shall pay the same to the overseers of the districts, respectively, in which the labor commuted for was assessed.

Thus amended by chap. 495, Laws of 1904.

*　　*　　*　　*　　H　　*　　*　　*　　*　　*

Penalties for neglect to work or commute.

§ 65. Every person or corporation assessed highway labor, who shall not commute, and who shall not appear and work when duly notified, shall be liable to a penalty of one dollar and fifty cents for every day he shall so fail to appear and work; and for wholly omitting to comply with any requisition to furnish a team, cart, wagon, implements and man, he shall be liable to a penalty of five dollars for each day's omission, and for omitting to furnish either a cart, wagon, plow, team or man to manage the team, he shall be liable to a penalty of one dollar and fifty cents for each day's omission; and if any person shall after appearing, remain idle, or not work faithfully, or hinder others from working, he shall be liable to a penalty at the rate of one dollar and fifty cents a day, for each hour. In those towns in which the money system of taxation has been adopted, any person who is taxed a poll tax for highway purposes as provided in section fifty-three of this chapter, and who does not pay such tax in the manner and at the time, prescribed by law, shall be liable to a penalty of five dollars. The penalties herein imposed, may be recovered by action by the overseer of highways as such, or by the highway commissioner in those towns having no such overseers, and, when collected, shall be expended and disposed of by the overseer or commissioner in the same manner as commutation moneys. The penalties, when recovered, shall be applied in satisfaction of the labor assessed, for omission to perform which, the penalties were respectively imposed. The overseer of highways may excuse any omission to perform labor when required, if a satisfactory reason shall be given therefor; but the acceptance of any such excuse shall not exempt the person excused from commuting for, or working the whole number of days for which he shall have been assessed during the year.

Thus amended by chap. 242, Laws of 1902.

18

Assessment for unperformed labor.

§ 66. Every overseer of highways shall on or before September first of each year, or at such other time as the board of supervisors may by resolution prescribe, make out and deliver to the commissioner of highways of his town, a list of all persons and corporations who have not worked out, or commuted for their highway assessment, with the number of days not worked or commuted for by each, charging for each day in such a list, at the rate of one dollar and fifty cents per day; and also a list of all the lands of nonresidents and persons unknown, which were assessed on his warrant by the commissioners of highways, or added by him, on which the labor assessed has not been performed or commuted for, and the number of days' labor unpaid by each, charging for the same at the rate of one dollar and fifty cents per day, which list shall be accompanied by the affidavit of the overseer, that he has given the notice required, to appear and work, and that the labor specified in the list returned has not been performed or commuted, and it shall be the duty of the commissioner of highways to collect and present such lists to the town board of his town at the meeting held on the Thursday next preceding the annual meeting of the board of supervisors. The town board shall certify the amount of unpaid taxes so returned to them by the commissioner of highways to the board of supervisors.

Thus amended by chap. 75, Laws of 1902.

*   *   *   *   *   *   *   *   *   *

Noxious weeds in highway.

§ 70. Every person or corporation, owning or occupying, under a lease for one or more years, any lands, abutting upon any highway, shall cause all noxious weeds, briers and brush growing upon such lands within the bounds of the highway, to be cut or destroyed between the fifteenth day of June and the first day of July, and between the fifteenth day of August and the first

day of September, in each and every year; but boards of supervisors may fix a different period or periods, for such cutting or
destruction in their respective counties. No person shall place
or cause to be placed, any noxious weeds, or the seeds of such
weeds, within the bounds of any public highway. Any willful
violation of this section, shall subject the person or corporation
so offending to a penalty of ten dollars for each offense. ·
Thus amended by chap. 681, Laws of 1899.

*   *   *   *   *   *   *   *   *   *

Limitations upon laying out highways.

§ 90. No highways shall be laid out less than three rods in
width, nor through an orchard of the growth of four years or
more, or any garden cultivated as such for four years or more,
or grape vineyards of one or more years' growth, and used in good
faith for vineyard purposes, or buildings or any fixtures or
erections for the purposes of trade or manufactures, or any yard
or inclosure necessary to the use and enjoyment thereof, without
the consent of the owner or owners thereof, unless so ordered by
the county court of the county in which the proposed highway
is situated; such order shall be made on the certificate of the
commissioners of highways of the town or towns in which the
proposed highway is situated, showing that the public interest
will be greatly promoted by the laying out and opening of such
highway, and that commissioners appointed by the court have
certified that it is necessary; a copy of the certificate with eight
days' notice of the time and place of the hearing before the county
court shall be served on the owners of the land, or if they are not
residents of the county upon the occupants; the county court
upon such certificates, and the proofs and other proceedings
therein, may order the highway to be laid out and opened, if it
deems it necessary and proper. The commissioners of highways
shall then present the order of the county court, with the certificate and proofs upon which it was granted, certified by such
court to the general term of the supreme court in the judicial

department in which the land is situated upon the usual notice of motion, served upon the owner or occupant, or the attorney who appeared for them in the county court. If such general term of the supreme court shall confirm the order of the county court, the commissioners of highways shall then lay out and open such highway as in other cases. The provisions of this section shall not apply to vineyards planted or to buildings, fixtures, erections, yards, or inclosures, made or placed on such land after an application for the laying out and opening the highway shall have been made. In case the highway to be laid out shall constitute an extension or continuation of a public highway already in use, and shall not, as to such new portion, exceed half a mile in length, the commissioners may lay out such extension or continuation of a width of less than three rods, provided however, that it be not less than the widest part of the highway of which it is an extension or continuation. In such case the commissioners shall specify in their certificate the precise width of the new portion of such highway, and shall certify that such width is as great at least as the widest part of the highway of which it is a continuation or extension. No highway shall be laid out which shall be identical or substantially so with a highway previously discontinued or abandoned 'for public purposes within seven years of such discontinuance or abandonment, in counties adjoining cities with upward of one million inhabitants.

Thus amended by chap. 265, Laws of 1906.

Laying out highways through burying-grounds.

§ 91. No private road or highway shall be laid out or constructed upon or through any burying-ground, unless the remains therein contained are first carefully removed, and properly reinterred in some other burying-ground, at the expense of the persons desiring such road or highway, and pursuant to an order of the county court of the county in which the same is situated, obtained upon notice to such persons as the court may direct.

See chap. 133, Laws of 1847, *ante.*

Highways abandoned.

§ 99. Every highway that shall not have been opened and
worked within six years from the time it shall have been dedicated to the use of the public, or laid out, shall cease to be a
highway; but the period during which any action or proceeding
shall have been, or shall be pending in regard to any such highway, shall form no part of such six years; and every highway
that shall not have been travelled or used as a highway for six
years, shall cease to be a highway, and every public right of way
that shall not have been used for said period shall be deemed
abandoned as a right of way. The commissioners of highways
shall file, and cause to be recorded in the town clerk's office of
the town, written description, signed by them, of each highway
and public right of way so abandoned, and the same shall thereupon be discontinued.

Thus amended by chap. 622, Laws of 1899.

* * * * * * * * * *

Entitled to free use of highways.

§ 163. The commissioners, trustees, or other authorities having
charge or control of any highway, public street, park, parkway,
driveway or place, shall have no power or authority to pass,
enforce or maintain any ordinance, rule or regulation, by
which any person using a bicycle or tricycle shall be
excluded or prohibited from the free use of any highway, public street, avenue, roadway, driveway, park, parkway or place, at any time when the same is open to
the free use of persons having and using other pleasure carriages,
except upon such driveway, speedway or road as has been or may
be expressly set apart by law for the exclusive use of horses and
light carriages. But nothing herein shall prevent the passage,
enforcement or maintenance of any regulation, ordinance or rule,
regulating the use of bicycles or tricycles in highways, public
streets, driveways, parks, parkways and places, or the regulation
of the speed of carriages, vehicles, or engines, in public parks

and upon parkways and driveways in the city of New York.
under the exclusive jurisdiction and control of the department
of parks of said city nor prevent any such commissioners, trustees, or other authorities in any other city from regulating the
speed of any vehicles herein described in such manner as to limit
and determine the proper rate of speed with which such vehicles
may be propelled, nor in such manner as to require, direct or prohibit the use of bells, lamps and other appurtenances nor to pro
hibit the use of any vehicle upon that part of the highway, street.
park, or parkway, commonly known as the footpath or sidewalk.

Thus amended by chap. 540, Laws of 1904. See section 23, Transportation
Corporation Law, *ante;* Greater New York Charter; chap. 538, Laws of 1904;
section 666, Penal Code, *post.*

*   *   *   *   *   *   *   *   *   *

When schedules to be posted.

§ 174. Every person licensed to operate or control any ferry
in this state, or between this state and any other state, operating from or to a city of fifty thousand inhabitants or over, shall
post in a conspicuous and accessible position outside and adjacent to each entrance to such ferry, and in at least four accessible places, in plain view of the passengers upon each of the
boats used on such ferry, a schedule plainly printed in the English language, of the rates of ferriage charged thereon, and authorized by law to be charged for ferriage over such ferry. If any
such person shall fail to comply with the provisions of this section, or shall post a false schedule, he shall be guilty of a misdemeanor.

Thus amended by chap. 313, Laws of 1900.

*   *   *   *   *   *   H   *   *   *

CHAP. 267, LAWS OF 1891.

AN ACT to authorize change of gauge on railroads and to provide
for an increase of floating and bonded indebtedness.

SECTION 1. Any railroad company incorporated under chapter one hundred and forty of the laws of eighteen hundred and

fifty, entitled "An act to authorize the formation of railroad corporations and to regulate the same," and acts amendatory thereof and supplementary thereto, may change the gauge of its road on consent of the board of railroad commissioners and approval of the stockholders of said railroad company owning three-fourths in amount of the capital stock, said approval of said stockholders to be made at a special meeting of the stockholders of said company called for that purpose; and upon like consent of said board of railroad commissioners, and upon like approval of the stockholders of said railroad company owning three-fourths in amount of the said capital stock of said company, the floating and bonded indebtedness of said railroad company may be increased to an amount necessary to make such change of gauge and to provide for the operating expenses of said railroad, notwithstanding restrictions or limitations contained in the original certificate of incorporation of said railroad -company.

CHAP. 294, LAWS OF 1891.

AN ACT in relation to elevated railways in cities.

When elevated road may abandon part of its route; proceedings in such case.

SECTION 1. Any company operating an elevated railway or railways in any city of this state for the transportation of passengers, mails or freight, and which, prior to the passage of this act shall have built and operated six-tenths of its route as set forth and embodied in its articles of incorporation, may declare relinqiushed* and abandoned any portion of its said route, which it may deem no longer necessary for the successful operation of its road and the convenience of the public. Such declaration of abandonment to be valid, shall be adopted by the board of directors, under the seal of such company, and shall be submitted to the stockholders thereof at a meeting called for the purpose of taking the same into consideration. Due notice of the time and

---

*So in the original.

place of holding said meeting, and stating the object thereof shall be given by the company to its stockholders by written or printed notices addressed to each of the persons in whose name the capital stock of the company stands on the books thereof, at the address of such persons as stated on the books, or as known to the secretary of the company, and delivered or mailed to such persons, or the legal representatives of such persons, respectively, at least thirty days before the time of holding the meeting of such company, and also by a general notice published daily for at least four weeks in some newspaper last designated for the publication of the session laws or of judicial proceedings and legal notices in the county where the route of such company is located; and at the said meeting of stockholders the declaration of the said directors shall be considered and a vote by ballot taken for the adoption or rejection of the same, each share entitling the holder thereof to one vote, and said ballots shall be cast in person or by proxy, and if two-thirds of all the votes of the stock-holders cast in person or by proxy at said meeting shall be for the adoption of said declaration of abandonment, then that fact shall be certified thereon by the secretary of the company under the seal thereof, and the declaration so adopted shall be sub-mitted for approval to the state board of railroad commissioners, and if approved by them, such approval shall be indorsed thereon, and the said declaration so certified and indorsed shall be filed and recorded in the office of the secretary of state, and from the time of such filing such portion of said route designated, in such declaration of such company shall be deemed to be abandoned. A copy of such declaration of abandonment, duly certified by the secretary of state, under his official seal, shall be presumptive evidence in all courts and places of the facts which it recites, and of the regularity of the proceedings resulting in such abandon-ment.

See Article V, Railroad Law, *ante.*

CHAP. 360, LAWS OF 1891.

AN ACT to confer upon the board of railroad commissioners of the state of New York authority to compel the lighting and ventilation of all tunnels within this state which are used by steam railroads.

SECTION 1. The board of railroad commissioners of the state of New York are hereby authorized, empowered and given full and complete authority to require and compel all tunnels used or to be used by railroads operated by steam in this state to be properly ventilated, in such manner and by such means and mechanical appliances as said board of railroad commissioners, or a majority of the same, may direct.

§ 2. The board of railroad commissioners of this state are also hereby authorized, empowered and given full and complete authority to require and compel all tunnels used, or to be used by railroads operated by steam in this state, to be properly lighted by electricity or otherwise, or by such means or in such manner as said board of railroad commissioners, or a majority of the same, may direct.

§ 3. Whenever said board of railroad commissioners of this state, or a majority thereof, shall cause to be personally served upon any railroad corporation controlling any tunnel, or part of a tunnel, in this state for the purpose of operating a railroad or moving, hauling or propelling cars therein by steam by delivering a copy personally to the president, general manager or any director of said corporation of a notice or order, signed by a majority of said board of railroad commissioners, stating and specifying the structures to be erected, the manner, means, mechanical appliance and apparatus to be used in lighting or ventilating any tunnel or tunnels used by said corporation for the purpose of moving, hauling or propelling cars by steam therein as aforesaid, said corporation shall, within thirty days from and after the service of said notice or order as aforesaid, cause said tunnel or tunnels so used by it as aforesaid to be lighted or ventilated, or both, in the manner and by the means and use of the mechanical apparatus and appliances specified and pointed out in said notice or order.

§ 4. After the expiration of thirty days from the service of said order or notice specified in the preceding section, as therein directed, if said corporation shall not have fully complied with the provisions and requirements of said notice or order as aforesaid and as therein directed and required, said board of railroad commissioners, or a majority of said board, may apply to the supreme court of this state for a writ of mandamus to compel said corporation or corporations so neglecting or refusing to obey and comply with the provisions of said order or notice to comply with and obey the provisions and requirements of said notice or order, and said court shall have full power and authority to hear and determine said matter, and, after giving the corporation or corporations proceeded against an opportunity to be heard in its or their defense, to compel said corporation or corporations so proceeded against to obey said order or notice, and forthwith comply with and carry out the provisions and requirements therein contained.

§ 5. Every corporation violating any of the provisions of this act shall be guilty of a misdemeanor, and may be indicted therefor, and may be compelled to appear and plead to an indictment therefor in the person of its president, secretary, treasurer or any director thereof, and a bench warrant may issue out of any competent court to compel such attendance and pleading, and upon conviction thereof, punished by a fine of one thousand dollars, and an additional fine of five hundred dollars a day for each and every day or part of a day after thirty days from the due service of said notice or order that said corporation shall refuse or neglect to obey and carry out the requirements and provisions of the same, and duly sentenced to pay the same.

§ 6. It shall be the duty of the district attorney prosecuting any corporation for a violation of any of the provisions of this act, that shall be convicted thereof and sentenced to pay a fine therefor, to cause a judgment-roll to be made up, consisting of the indictment orders and sentence of the court and a formal judgment, to be prepared by him, which judgment shall be duly signed by the clerk of the county in which said trial took place; said judgment-roll shall be filed by said county clerk and said judgment shall be duly recorded in the book of judgments in said county and duly entered and docketed by said county clerk in said county the same as if said judgment had been obtained in a civil action, and said judgment so duly entered and docketed shall become and be a lien upon all of the real estate of said corporation against which the same is obtained, and the collection thereof may be enforced by execution to be issued and signed by the district attorney of the county where the trial of said indictment took place, in the same manner and to the same extent as executions are collected in civil action.

§ 7. In cities in this state having a population of one million inhabitants or over, where tunnels are or may hereafter be operated or controlled by any railroad corporation such portions of any mechanical or other devices or appliances as may be required under the provisions of this act to be constructed on or above the surface of any streets, avenues or other places under which such tunnels may be built, shall be subject as to form, material and construction, to the approval of the local authorities of such cities, except that in the city of New York such approval shall be by a majority vote of the mayor, the comptroller, the commissioner of public works and the president of the department of public parks of said city.

CHAP. 425, LAWS OF 1892.

AN ACT to authorize the state engineer and surveyor to file certain reports with the board of railroad commissioners.

SECTION 1. The state engineer and surveyor is hereby authorized and directed, within ten days after the passage of this act, to file with the board of railroad commissioners all original reports from railroad corporations now in his custody and filed in his office in pursuance of section thirty-one of chapter one hundred and forty of the laws of eighteen hundred and fifty.

CHAP. 604, LAWS OF 1892.

AN ACT for the relief of street surface railroad companies organized under chapter two hundred and fifty-two of the laws of eighteen hundred and eighty-four.

Section 1. Any street railroad company now organized under chapter two hundred and fifty-two of the laws of eighteen hundred and eighty-four, which shall have heretofore constructed and is now operating any extension or branch of its railroad along any streets or highways or portion thereof within any county named in its articles of association, in a city not exceeding in population fifty thousand inhabitants, and shall heretofore have obtained the consent of the owners of one-half in value of the property bounded on and the consent also of the local authorities having control of that portion of a street or highway upon which it has constructed or operated such railroad, is hereby authorized to operate and maintain the same respectively in like manner and as fully as if the said streets and highways, or portions thereof, were fully named and described in its articles of association, and upon filing in the office of the secretary of state a certificate signed by its board of directors, which certificate shall contain a statement of the names of cities, towns, villages and counties, and the names or descriptions of the streets, avenues and highways in which such extension or branch has been constructed the places from and to which the same has been constructed and is to be maintained and operated, and the length thereof, as near as may be; thereupon the said extensions and branches shall be deemed and considered a part of the lines of railway of such corporation from the date of the filing thereof, with the same force and effect as if the same were fully named and described in its original articles of association, and all corporate action relating to the construction, maintenance and operation of such extensions or creating liens upon the same by the said corporation, are hereby validated and confirmed.

§ 2. Nothing in this act contained shall affect or impair any vested right or any pending litigation.

See sections 90 and 106, Railroad Law, *ante;* chap. 679, Laws of 1893, *post.*

CHAP. 711, LAWS OF 1892.

AN ACT to provide for and limit the hours of service on railroads.

*   *   *   *   *   *   *   *   *   *

§ 4. Any railroad company or corporation, or any officer, agent or employe of any such company or corporation, violating or permitting the violation of any of the provisions of this act, shall be guilty of a misdemeanor, and on conviction shall be punished by a fine of five hundred dollars for each offense.

See decision of Court of Appeals under this act, 130 N. Y., 554.
See, also, subdivision 4, section 384-h, Penal Code, *post.*
See section 7, Labor Law, *post.*

CHAP. 238, LAWS OF 1893.

AN ACT in relation to filing amended affidavits to certificates of incorporation of railroad companies.

SECTION 1. Where it does not appear by the affidavit endorsed on or annexed to any certificate of incorporation, or articles of association of any railroad company, filed under the laws of this state, that the amount of capital stock required by the provisions of said laws to be paid in good faith and in cash to the directors named in such certificate has been so paid, or where the affidavit required by law is omitted and where such payment has been made to the directors named in said certificate or articles, or any of them, for the use of the company prior to the passage of this act, an affidavit of at least three of the directors named in said certificate, stating that at least the amount of capital stock of such corporation required by the law in force at the time of filing said certificate or articles to be subscribed thereto, has been heretofore subscribed for in good faith and that the amount required by the law in force at the time of filing said certificate to be paid on subscriptions in good faith and in cash to the directors named in the certificate of incorporation has been paid heretofore in cash and in good faith to the directors named in said articles of association, or any of them, for the use of said corporation and that it is intended in good faith to build, construct, maintain and operate the road mentioned in said certificate may be filed in the office of the secretary of state, which affidavit shall be annexed to said certificate of incorporation and upon such filing said certificate, or articles shall for all purposes have the same force and effect as if an affidavit in all respects regular and in conformity with law had been annexed to said certificate or articles when said certificate was filed and as if a subscription and payment in all respects sufficient and in conformity with law had been made to the directors named in the articles of association or certificate, prior to the original filing of said articles or certificate, and said certificate of incorporation and the original filing thereof shall be and be deemed valid from the time of such original filing and such corporation shall be and be deemed a valid corporation from said time of original filing and shall now and hereafter have all the rights, privileges, powers and franchises to which if a valid corporation it would have been entitled by law at the time of such original filing together with such other rights, privileges, powers and franchises as have been since or may hereafter be granted by law to such valid corporations, provided that nothing herein contained shall affect or impair any vested right; and provided that the word " heretofore " and the words " prior to the passage of this act " shall be taken to refer to the time of passage of the amendatory act under which this section as herein framed is enacted. A copy of said certificate or articles of association with a copy of said affidavit hereinabove authorized, certified to be a copy by the secretary of state or his deputy shall in all courts and places and for all purposes be presumptive evidence of the incorporation of such corporation and of the facts stated in said certificate and affidavit. This act as here amended shall not apply to nor affect any street surface railroad company the route of which in whole or in part lies within any city of the first or second class in this state, and shall not apply to nor affect any railroad corporation incorporated under any private or local bill or act.

Thus amended by chap. 627, Laws of 1903.

See section 2 and section 3, Railroad Law, and section 7, General Corporation Law, *ante*.

CHAP. 239, LAWS OF 1893.

AN ACT in relation to the intersections and crossings of the tracks and roadbeds of certain railroads laid in, across or upon the highways, streets, avenues or roads of the cities, towns and villages of the state.

SECTION 1. Whenever the railroad or route of any street surface railroad corporation shall intersect and cross, or shall cross the tracks and roadbed of any railroad, operated by locomotive, steam or other power, which are laid in, across or upon the surface of any street, avenue, road or highway in any city, town or village of the state, having less than five hundred thousand inhabitants, and such street surface railroad corporation having been unable to agree with the corporation owning the tracks and roadbed so intersected or to be intersected and crossed, as to the line or lines, grade or grades, points or manner of such intersection and crossing, or upon the compensation to be made therefor, shall have applied to the court by petition to appoint commissioners to determine the same, the court shall upon application made by such street surface railroad corporation, at, or after, the time of the appointment of such commissioners, or, if an answer to the petition of such street surface railroad corporation has been interposed, at any time thereafter, direct that such street surface railroad corporation, be permitted to lay its tracks across and to intersect, upon the surface of the street, avenue, road or highway, the tracks and roadbed of such railroad operated by locomotive, steam, or other power, provided, such street surface railroad corporation shall at the time of obtaining such order make and file with the clerk of said court, its bond or undertaking in writing, in an amount and with surety or sureties to be approved by the court, conditioned for the full and faithful performance by such street surface railroad corporation of any and all conditions and requirements which may be imposed by said commissioners and be affirmed by the court, in determining the line or lines, grade or grades, points or manner of such intersection and crossing and as to the amount of compensation to be paid therefor, and also conditioned to conform such crossing and intersection made by virtue of such order of the court to the requirements made by said commissioners as affirmed by the court.

§ 2.   No street surface railroad shall, be, allowed to lay its tracks at grade across the tracks or roadbed of any railroad operated by locomotive steam power at any point where there are three or more tracks of the steam road proposed to be crossed, which tracks have been constructed and in operation at least two years, unless the written consent of the state railroad commissioners be first obtained for such crossing at grade. But this section shall not affect the operation of section one of this act in any suit or proceeding now pending nor any renewals of said pending suit or proceeding brought for any cause.

See sections 12, 35 and 08, Railroad Law, *ante.*
See 75 App. Div., 412; 175 N. Y., mem. 6.

CHAP. 338, LAWS OF 1893.

AN ACT in relation to agriculture, constituting articles one, two, three, four, and five of chapter thirty-three of the general laws.

*   *   *   *   *   *   *   *   *   *

Suppression of infectious and contagious disease.

§ 60. Whenever any infectious or contagious disease, affecting domestic animals shall exist, be brought into or break out in this state the commissioner of agriculture shall take measures to promptly suppress the same, and to prevent such disease from spreading. The local boards of health shall notify the commissioners of the existence of infectious or contagious disease affecting domestic animals in the districts subject to their jurisdiction. Any person or persons importing or bringing into this state neat cattle for dairy or breeding purposes shall report immediately upon bringing such cattle into the state to the commissioner of agriculture in writing, giving a statement of the number of cattle thus brought in, the place where they were procured, the lines over which they were brought and their point of destination within the state, stating when they will arrive at such point of destination, and upon the filing with the commissioner of agriculture at the time of making the said report, a certificate issued by duly authorized veterinary practitioner, to the effect that he has duly examined said animal or animals and that said animals are free from any infectious or contagious disease, the commissioner of agriculture may issue a permit to said person or persons to remove said cattle immediately. Otherwise, said person or persons shall hold or detain such animals at least forty-eight hours at such point of destination for inspection and examination, provided they are not sooner examined or inspected, by the commissioner of agriculture or his duly authorized agent or agents. Each animal brought into the state in violation of the above provisions shall constitute a separate and distinct violation of the agricultural law. The provisions of this section, relating to the importation of neat cattle for dairy or breeding purposes, shall not apply to cattle imported into this state at a point where there is federal inspection.

Thus amended by chap. 214, Laws of 1903, taking effect July 1, 1903.

✻ ✻ ✻ ✻ ✻ ✻ ✻ ✻ ✻ ✻

19

Detention and destruction of animals.

§ 63. The commissioner or an assistant commissioner, may order all or any animals coming into the state to be detained at any place or places for the purpose of inspection and examination. He may prescribe regulations for the destruction of animals affected with infections or contagious disease, and for the proper disposal of their hides and carcasses, and ot all objects which might carry infection and contagion. Whenever, in his judgment necessary, for the more speedy and economical suppression or prevention of the spread of any such disease, he may cause to be slaughtered, and to be afterwards disposed of, in such manner as he may deem expedient, any animal or animals, which, by contact or association with diseased animals, or by other exposure to infection or contagion, may be considered or suspected to be liable to contract or communicate the disease sought to be suppressed or prevented. The commissioner may direct that an animal shall be condemned, quarantined or slaughtered as tuberculous, under the provisions of this article, if it shall be found to be tuberculous by a physical examination. If the owner of animals suspected of being tuberculous desires to have such animals tested with tuberculin and enters into a written agreement with the state in the manner prescribed by the commissioner of agriculture, before such test is made, to the effect that he will disinfect his premises and either consent to the slaughter of the animals responding to such test, or hold them and their products in strict quarantine, pursuant to the directions of the commissioner of agriculture, such test shall be made by a medical or veterinary practitioner designated by the commissioner. The commissioner may also in his discretion order such tuberculin test to be made, and if the animal responds to such test, he may cause such animal to be slaughtered or held in strict quarantine.

Thus amended by chap. 321, Laws of 1901.

Regulations and the enforcement thereof.

§ 65. The commissioner may prescribe such regulations as in his judgment may be thought suited for the suppression or prevention of the spread of any such disease, and for the disinfection of all premises, buildings, railway cars, vessels, and other objects from or by means of which infection or contagion may take place or be conveyed. He may alter or modify, from time to time, as he may deem expedient, the terms of all notices, orders and regulations issued or made by him, and may at any time cancel or withdraw the same. He may call upon the sheriff or deputy sheriff, to carry out and enforce the provisions of any notice, order or regulation which he may make, and all such sheriffs and deputy sheriffs shall obey and observe all orders and instructions which they may receive from him in the premises. If the commissioner shall quarantine any particular district or territory for the purpose of stopping or preventing the spread of the disease known as rabies, and if any dog be found loose within the said quarantine district in violation of said quarantine or regulation, any person may kill or cause to be killed such dog and shall not be held liable for damages for such killing.

Thus amended by chap. 321, Laws of 1901.

*   *   *   *   *   *   *   *   *   *

Federal regulations.

§ 70-c. The commissioner of agriculture may accept, in behalf of the state, the rules and regulations prepared and adopted by the commissioner of agriculture or the secretary or department of agriculture of the United States, under any act of congress for the establishment of a bureau of animal industry or to prevent the exportation of diseased cattle or to provide means for the extirpation and suppression of pleuro-pneumonia and other contagious diseases among domestic animals and shall co-operate with the authorities of the United States in the enforcement of the provisions of any such act.

Thus amended by chap. 321, Laws of 1901.

Rights of federal inspectors.

§ 70-d. The inspectors of the bureau of animal industry of the United States shall have the right of inspection, quarantine and condemnation of animals affected with any contagious, infectious or communicable disease, or suspected to be so affected or that may have been exposed to any such disease, and for such purposes they may enter upon any ground or premises; they may call the sheriffs, constables and peace officers to assist them in discharge of their duties in carrying out the provisions of any such act; and all sheriffs, constables and peace officers shall assist such inspectors when so requested, and such inspectors shall have the same powers and protection as peace officers, while engaged in the discharge of their duties. All animals entering the state, which pass inspection by the federal authorities, shall be permitted to proceed to place of destination without further inspection under this act. This state shall not be liable for any damages or expenses caused or made by such inspectors.
Thus amended by chap. 321, Laws of 1901.

*   *   *   *   *   *   *   *   *   *

§ 70-e. No person shall slaughter or expose for sale, or sell any calf or carcass of the same or any part thereof, unless it is in good healthy condition. No person shall sell or expose for sale any such calf or carcass of the same or any part thereof, except the hide unless it was, if killed at least four weeks of age at the time of killing. No person or persons shall bring or cause to be brought into any city, town or village any calf or carcass of the same or any part thereof for the purposes of selling, offering or exposing the same for sale, unless it is in a good healthy condition and no person or persons shall bring any such calf or carcass of the same or any part thereof except the hide into any city, town or village for the purpose of selling, offering or exposing the same for sale, unless the calf is four weeks of age or, if killed, was four weeks of age at the time of killing, provided however that the provisions of this statute shall not apply to any calf or carcass of the same or any part thereof, which is slaughtered, sold, offered or exposed for sale, for any other purpose than for food. Any person or persons exposing for sale, selling or shipping any calf or carcass of the same will be presumed to be so exposing, selling or shipping the said calf or carcass of the same for food. Any person or persons shipping any calf for the purpose of being raised, if the said calf is under four weeks of age, shall ship it in a crate, unless said calf is accompanied by its dam. Any person shipping calves under four weeks of age for fertilizer purposes must slaughter the said calves before so shipping. Any person or persons duly authorized by the commissioner of agriculture to examine any calf or veal offered or exposed for sale or kept with any stock of goods apparently exposed for sale and if such calf is under four weeks of age, or the veal is from a calf killed under four weeks of age, or from a calf in an unhealthy condition when killed, he may seize the same and cause it to be destroyed and disposed of in such manner as to make it impossible to be thereafter used for food.

Thus amended by chap. 372, Laws of 1906.

Shipping veal.

§ 70-f. On and after the passage of this act it shall be unlawful for any corporation, partnership, person or persons to ship to or from any part of this state any carcass or carcasses of a calf or calves or any part of such carcass except the hide, unless they shall attach to every carcass or part thereof so shipped in a conspicuous place a tag, that shall stay thereon during such transportation, stating the name or names of the person or persons who raised the calf, the name of the shipper, the points of shipping and the destination and the age of the calf.

Receiving veal for shipment by common carriers.

§ 70-g. On and after the passage of this act, no railroad company, express company, steamboat company, or other common carrier, shall carry or receive for transportation any carcass or

carcasses of calves, or any part of the same except the hide,
unless the said carcass or carcasses or parts thereof shall be
tagged as herein provided.

Sections 70-e, 70-f and 70-g, added by chapter 30, Laws 1902.
See chapter 491, Laws 1898, *post*.

*   *   *   *   *   *   *   *   *   *

**The prevention of disease in fruit trees and the extirpation of
insect pests that infest the same.**

§ 82. No person shall knowingly or wilfully keep any peach,
almond, apricot or nectarine trees affected with the contagious
disease known as yellows. Nor shall any person knowingly or
wilfully keep any plum, cherry or other trees affected with the
contagious disease or fungus known as black knot, nor any tree,
shrub or plant infested with or by San José scale or other
insect pest dangerously injurious to or destructive of the trees,
shrubs or other plants; every such tree, shrub or plant shall be a
public nuisance and as such shall be abated and no damage
shall be awarded for entering upon premises upon which there
are trees, shrubs or plants infected with yellows or black knot
or infested with San Jose scale, for the purpose of legally
inspecting the same nor shall any damage be awarded for the
destruction by the commissioner of agriculture, or his duly
authorized agents or representatives of such trees, shrubs or
plants, or altogether destroying such tree if necessary to suppress such disease, if done in accordance with the provisions
of this article, except as otherwise herein provided. Every person, when he becomes aware of the existence of such disease or
insect pest in any tree owned by him, shall forthwith report
the same to the commissioner of agriculture at Albany, New
York, and the said commissioner shall take such action as the
law provides. If in the judgment of said commissioner of agriculture or the person or persons representing him the trees,
shrubs or other plants so infected, infested or diseased should
be destroyed, then such destruction shall be carried on and com-

pleted under the supervision of the commissioner of agriculture or the person or persons duly appointed by him and
authorized so to do, without unnecessary delay, but the owner
of the trees, shrubs or plants shall be notified immediately upon
its being determined that such trees, shrubs or plants
should be destroyed by a notice in writing signed by said commissioner or the person or persons representing him, which said
notice in writing shall be delivered in person to the
owner of such trees, shrubs or plants, or left at the usual place of
residence of such owner, or if such owner be not a resident
of the town, by leaving such notice with the person in charge
of the premises, trees, shrubs or plants or in whose possession they may be; such notice shall contain a brief statement
of the facts found to exist whereby it is deemed necessary to
destroy such trees, shrubs. or plants, and shall call attention
to the law under which it is proposed to destroy them, and
the owner shall within ten days from the date upon which
such notice shall have been received, remove and burn all such
diseased or infested trees, shrubs or plants. If however, in
the judgment of the commissioner of agriculture, any trees, shrubs
or plants infected with any disease or infested with dangerously injurious insects can be treated with sufficient
remedies, he may direct such treatment to be carried out by
the owner under the direction of the commissioner's agent or
agents. In cases of objections to the findings of the inspector
or agent of the commissioner of agriculture an appeal may be
made to the commissioner of agriculture whose decision shall be
final. An appeal must be taken within three days from service
of said notice, and shall act as a stay of proceedings until it is
heard and decided. When the commissioner of agriculture, or
the person or persons appointed by him, shall determine that any
tree or trees, shrubs or other plants must be treated or destroyed
forthwith, he may employ all necessary assistance for that purpose, and such person or persons, agent or agents, employee or

employees, may enter upon any or all premises in any city or
town necessary for the purposes of such treatment, removal
or destruction.

Thus amended by chap. 519, Laws of 1902. This section was also amended
by chap. 27, Laws of 1902, taking effect immediately. Chap. 27 was superseded by chap. 519.

Appointment and duties of the agent of the commissioner of agriculture.

§ 83. When the commissioner of agriculture knows or has
reason to believe that any such contagious disease exists, or
that there is good reason to believe that it exists, or danger is
justly apprehended of its introduction in any town or city in
the state, or that any dangerously injurious insect pest exists
within this state, and has reason to believe that danger may be
justly apprehended from its existence, he shall forthwith send
some competent person and such agent. or agents as he may
deem necessary to assist extirpating said pest or pests, disease
or diseases, and the said commissioner of agriculture is hereby
authorized and empowered to take such steps and do whatever
may be deemed necessary to so control or prevent the spread or
extirpate said pest or pests, disease or diseases, and he shall
cause an examination to be made at least once each year, prior to
September first, of each and every nursery or other place where
trees, shrubs or plants, commonly known as nursery stock, are
grown for sale, for the purpose of ascertaining whether the trees,
shrubs or plants therein kept or propagated for sale are infected
with any such contagious disease or diseases, or infested with
such pest or pests. If after such examination it is found that the
said trees, shrubs or other plants so examined are free in all
respects from any such contagious or infectious disease or diseases, dangerously injurious pest or pests, the said commissioner
or his duly authorized agent or other person designated to make
such examination, shall thereupon issue to the owner or pro.
prietor of the said stock thus examined a certificate setting forth

the fact that the stock so examined is apparently **free from** any and all such disease or diseases, pest or pests. Should any nurseryman, agent or dealer or broker send out or deliver within the state, trees, vines, shrubs, plants, buds or cuttings, commonly known as nursery stock, and which are subject to the attacks **of** insects and diseases above provided for, unless he has in his possession a copy of said certificate, dated within a year thereof, deface or destroy such certificate, or wrongfully be in possession of such certificate, he shall be guilty of a misdemeanor. All nursery stock consigned for shipment, or shipped by freight, express or other means of transportation, shall be accompanied by a copy of said certificate attached to each car, box, bale, bundle or package. Any person consigning for shipment or shipping nursery stock as above without such certificate attached shall be guilty of a misdemeanor. All transportation companies, within this state receiving or carrying nursery stock from any point without the state to any point within the state shall immediately, upon receiving such consignments, notify the commissioner of agriculture of the fact that such consignment is in their possession, giving the name of the consignor and consignee, and the point of destination of such consignment. All trees, plants, shrubs, buds or cuttings, commonly called nursery stock, grown in any nursery in this state, in which San Jose scale has been found within two years of the date of the dissemination of said nursery stock or grown in said nursery within one-half a mile of where said scale was found, and also all nursery stock from outside of this state, disseminated or planted in this state, after the first day of July nineteen hundred and two, must be fumigated with hydrocyanic gas, in such manner as may be directed by the commissioner of agriculture of this state. Such fumigation must be done by the grower, consignor or consignee of such stock before planting, dissemination or reshipment, except such trees, shrubs, plants, buds or cuttings grown in this state as are planted **by the grower** or propagator for himself, or **such as from** its nature or state of growth would be exempt; in such cases the said commissioner shall declare such trees, shrubs, plants, buds or cuttings free from such treatment. All nursery stock brought into this state from outside of this state must be accompanied by a certificate from the consignor that it has been fumigated as aforesaid. Should any such stock arrive without such certificate, the transportation company delivering it shall at once notify the said commissioner to that effect. The consignee shall also at once notify him of that fact, and shall proceed to fumigate said stock, as directed by the commissioner of agriculture without delay. Should any nursery stock purchased within one year be found infested with San Jose scale on the premises of any nurseryman, it shall not be considered such an infestation as to require the fumigation of other stock not so purchased. The words "nursery stock" wherever used in this article shall apply to and include all trees, shrubs, plants, buds, willow grown for nursery, baskets, or other commercial purposes or cuttings, whether grown in a nursery or elsewhere so far as it relates to fumigation. The provisions of this and the preceding section shall not apply to florists green house plants, flowers or cuttings commonly known as green house stock, and no certificate shall be required for shipment of native stock collected in the United States, not grown in nurseries, nor to stock so shipped into the state that its sale and shipment become either inter-state commerce traffic or commerce with foreign nations.

Thus amended by chap. 519, Laws of 1902.

*   *   *   *   *   *   *   *   *   *

Statements to be attached to packages; contents; analysis.

§ 121. No manufacturer, firm, association, corporation or person shall sell, offer or expose for sale or for distribution in this state any concentrated commercial feeding stuff used for feeding live stock, unless each car or other amount shipped in bulk shall have affixed to it or be accompanied by a plainly printed statement clearly and truly certifying the name or trade-mark under

.which the article is sold, the name of the manufacturer, the place of manufacture, the shipper and the place of business and a statement of the constituents of such concentrated feeding stuff as shown by a chemical analysis. Such statement to show the percentage it contains of crude protein and of crude fat. If such concentrated feeding stuff is in packages such statement shall be affixed to the package, and shall also state the number of pounds in such package. · Whenever any feeding stuff is sold at retail in bulk or in packages belonging to the purchaser, the agent or dealer, upon request of the purchaser shall furnish to him the certified statement named in this section.

Thus amended by chap. 558, Laws of 1904.

CHAP. 543, LAWS OF 1893.

AN ACT to promote the safety of railway employes by compelling the equipment of freight cars with continuous power or air brakes, and locomotives with driving-wheel brakes.

SECTION 1. That from and after the first day of January, eighteen hundred and ninety-five, it shall be unlawful for any railroad company to use within the state on its line or lines any locomotive engine not equipped with a power driving wheel brake and appliances for operating the train brake system.

§ 2. That on and after the first day of January, eighteen hundred and ninety-eight, the use of cars known and designated as "coal jimmies" in any form shall be unlawful within the state, except upon any railroad whose main line is less than fifteen miles in length and whose average grade exceeds two hundred feet to the mile, under a penalty of one hundred dollars for each offense, said penalty to be recovered in an action to be brought by the attorney-general in the name of the people and in the judicial district where the principal office of the company within the state is located. This section shall not be construed to authorize the interchange of such "coal jimmies" with, and the use thereof upon, railroads of more than fifteen miles in length or whose average grade is less than two hundred feet to the mile.

Thus amended by chap. 549, Laws of 1900.

§ 3. That on and after the first day of January, nineteen hundred and one, it shall be unlawful for any railroad or other company to haul or permit to be hauled or used on its line or lines within this state any freight train that has not a sufficient number of cars in it so equipped with continuous power or air brakes that the engineer on the locomotive drawing such train can control its speed without requiring brakemen to use the common hand brake for that purpose.

Thus amended by chap. 549, Laws of 1900.

§ 4. That within sixty days from the passage of this act every railroad or other company operating a line of railroad within the state shall file with the board of railroad commissioners at its office in Albany a verified statement of the total number of freight cars owned or operated by it, the number of such cars equipped with such continuous power or air brakes and the number unequipped, and shall thereafter annually and in the month of January, for the ensuing ten years, file with said board a verified report of the number of cars so equipped in each year and the number of cars, if any, remaining unequipped.

§ 5. That on and after January first, nineteen hundred and one any railroad or other company hauling or permitting to be hauled on its line or lines any freight train in violation of any of the provisions of this act, shall be liable to a penalty of one hundred dollars for each and every violation, to be recovered in any action to be brought by the attorney-general in the name of the people and in the judicial district wherein the principal office of the company within the state is located, and it shall be the duty of the board of railroad commissioners of the state to notify the attorney-general of all such violations coming to its notice.

Thus amended by chap. 549, Laws of 1900.

§ 6. That the board of railroad commissioners may, from time to time, after full hearing given and for good cause shown, extend the time within which any company shall comply with the requirement of this act, not exceeding, however, four years from the first day of January, eighteen hundred and ninety-eight.

Thus amended by chap. 549, Laws of 1900.

§ 7. All acts or parts of acts inconsistent with the provisions of this act are hereby repealed.

Section 5 of chapter 549, Laws of 1900, provides that "all acts or parts of acts inconsistent with the provisions of this act are hereby repealed."

CHAP. 544, LAWS OF 1893.

AN ACT to promote the safety of railway employes by compelling the equipment of freight cars with automatic couplers.

SECTION 1. That from and after the passage of this act, every new freight car which is to be used in this state shall be equipped with couplers of the master car builders' type, which can be coupled automatically by impact, and which may, except in cases of accident, be uncoupled without the necessity of a person going between the cars.

§ 2. That from and after the passage of this act, in addition to such new freight cars, there shall be equipped each year with such couplers, by every company operating a line or lines of railroad within the state, at least twenty per centum of all freight cars owned or operated by such companies, and used within the state, which are not so equipped, except certain cars known and designated as "coal jimmies," and that on and after the first day of January, eighteen hundred and ninety-eight, the use of said "coal jimmies" in any form shall be unlawful within this state, except upon any railroad whose main line is less than fifteen miles in length and whose average grade exceeds two hundred feet to the mile, under penalty of one hundred dollars for each offense, said penalty to be recovered in an action to be brought by the attorney-general, in the name of the people, and in the judicial district where the principal office of the company within the state is located. This section shall not be construed to authorize the interchange of such "coal jimmies" with, and the

use therefor* upon, railroads of more than fifteen miles in length
or whose average grade is less than two hundred feet to the
mile.

Thus amended by chap. 485, Laws of 1896.

§ 3. That on and after the first day of January, eighteen
hundred and ninety-eight, it shall be unlawful for any railroad or
other company to haul, or permit to be hauled or used, on its
line or lines within the state, any freight car not equipped with
couplers of the master car builders' type, and coupling automatically by impact, and which can be uncoupled, except in cases
of accident, without the necessity of men going between the
ends of the cars.

§ 4. That within sixty days from the passage of this act,
every railroad or other company operating a line of railroad
within the state, shall file with the board of railroad commissioners, at its office in Albany, a verified statement of the total
number of freight cars owned or operated by it, the number of
such cars equipped with the automatic couplers, and the number
unequipped; and shall thereafter annually, and in the month of
Jannary, for the ensuing five years, file with said board a verified
report of the number of cars so equipped in each year, and the
number of cars, if any, remaining unequipped.

§ 5. That on and after January first, eighteen hundred and
ninety-eight, any railroad or other company using, or permitting
to be used, on its line or lines, any freight car not equipped with
couplers as provided for in this act, shall be liable to a penalty of
one hundred dollars for each and every violation, to be recovered
in an action to be brought by the attorney-general, in the name
of the people, and in the judicial district wherein the principal
office of the company within the state is located; and it shall be
the duty of the board of railroad commissioners of the state to
notify the attorney-general of all such violations coming to its
notice.

*So in the original.

§ 6. That the board of railroad commissioners may, from time to time, after full hearing given and for good cause shown, exempt any company from the provisions of this act, as to the equipment of twenty per cent of its cars in any particular year or years, and may extend the time within which any company shall comply with the requirements of this act, not exceeding however, five years from the first day of January, eighteen hundred and ninety-eight.

§ 7. All acts or parts of acts inconsistent with the provisions of this act are hereby repealed.

CHAP. 661, LAWS OF 1893.

AN ACT in relation to the public health, constituting chapter twenty-five of the general laws.

*   *   *   *   *   *   *   *   *   *

Local boards of health.

§ 20. There shall continue to be local boards of health and health officers in the several cities, villages and towns of the state. In the cities, except cities of the first and second class, the board shall consist of the mayor of the city who shall be its president, and, at least six other persons, one of whom shall be a competent physician, who shall be appointed by the common council, upon the nomination of the mayor, and shall hold office for three years. Appointments of members of such boards shall be made for such shorter terms as at any time may be necessary, in order that the terms of two appointed members shall expire annually. In the cities, except cities of the first and second class, and such other cities whose charters otherwise provide the board shall appoint a competent physician, not one of its members, to be the health officer of the city and shall fill any vacancy that now exists or may hereafter exist from expiration of term or otherwise in the office of health officer of the city. In villages the board shall consist of not less than three nor more than seven persons, not trustees of the village, who shall be appointed

by the board of trustees at the first meeting of the board of trustees of such village, after the next annual election of the village;
the members of said board of health shall at their first meeting
divide themselves by lot into three classes, whose terms of office
shall expire respectively in one, two and three years, from the
annual election held prior to their appointment; and in case of
an increase in the membership of such board, as hereinafter provided, there shall be a like apportionment by lot, of the added
members, in respect to their terms of office, at the first meeting
of said board after such increase occurs, whereby the whole number of terms expiring annually shall be as nearly equal as possible. From and after the appointment of said board as above
provided, the appointment of the successors of said members shall
be made immediately after the annual elections of said village
and shall continue in office until their successors are appointed
unless removed therefrom; provided, however, that upon failure
to appoint such board of health at such first meeting such appointment may be made at any subsequent meeting, in the event
of no appointment having been made by the proper authorities
as hereinafter provided. The board of trustees of such village
may, in its discretion, at the first meeting of such board held
after any annual election of the village, increase the number of
members of the board of health of such village, and appoint such
additional members and thereafter appoint their successors, providing the number of members of such board of health, as increased, shall not exceed seven. Every such village board shall
elect a president and secretary the president to be elected from
among the members of said board. In towns the board of health
shall consist of the town board and another citizen of the town of
full age biennially appointed by the town board at a meeting
thereof after each biennial town meeting for the term of two
years from and after such town meeting and until his successor
is appointed. The state commissioner of health shall appoint for
each municipality except in the cities of the state on the nomi-

nation of the local board of health, a competent physician, not a
member of the local board of health, to be the health officer of
the municipality. The term of office of the health officer shall be
four years and he shall hold office until the appointment of his
successor. If a local board of health fails to nominate a physician for appointment to the position of heath officer within
thirty days after the expiration of the term of office of the health
officer, or if a vacancy in the office is not filled within thirty days,
the state commissioner of health shall appoint a competent
physician to the position, or, should a local board of health
nominate a physician for appointment to the position of health
officer, who, in the judgment of the state commissioner of health
is not properly qualified for appointment to the position, the state
commissioner of health shall notify the local board of health of
such fact, and thereupon such local board of health shall within
thirty days from the date of such notice present to the state
commissioner of health the name of another physician for appointment to the position of health officer, failing in which, the
state commissioner of health shall appoint a physician to the
position. He may be removed for just cause by the local board
of health after a hearing, such removal must be approved by the
state commissioner of health. The health officer need not reside
within the village or town for which he shall be chosen, but
unless he shall, he must reside in an adjoining town. If the
proper authorities shall not fill any vacancies occurring in the
membership of any local board within thirty days after the
happening of such vacancy, the mayor of the city, president of
the village, or supervisor of the town, shall appoint a competent
person to fill the vacancy for the unexpired term, which appointment shall be immediately filed in the office of the county clerk,
and a duplicate thereof filed with the clerk of the municipality
for which such appointment is made. Notice of the membership
and organization of every local board of health shall be forth-

20

with given by such board to the state department of health. The term municipality, when used in this article, means the city, village or town for which any such local board may be or is appointed. The provisions herein contained for the appointment and number of members of boards of health, and for the appointment of health officers, shall apply to all towns and villages, whether such villages are organized under general or special laws.

Thus amended by chap. 253, Laws of 1906

General powers and duties of local boards of health.

§ 21. Every such local board of health shall meet at stated intervals to be fixed by it, in the municipality. The presiding officer of every such board may call special meetings thereof where in his judgment the protection of the public health of the municipality requires it, and he shall call such meeting upon the petition of at least twenty-five residents thereof, of full age, setting forth the necessity of such meeting. Every such local board shall prescribe the duties and powers of the local health officer, who shall be its chief executive officer, and direct him in the performance of his duties, and fix his compensation. In addition to his compensation so fixed, the board of health may allow the reasonable expenses of said health officer in going to, attending and returning from, the annual sanitary conference of health officers, or equivalent meeting, held yearly within the state, and may also in its judgment whenever the services rendered by its health officer during any year are extraordinary, or extra hazardous, by reason of epidemic, or otherwise, allow to him such further sum in addition to said fixed compensation as shall be audited by the town board of a town or by the board of trustees of a village which said expenses and said additional compensation shall be a charge upon and paid by the municipality as provided in section thirty of this act. Every such local board shall make and publish from time to time all such orders and regulations as they may deem necessary and proper for the

preservation of life and health, and the execution and enforcement of the public health law in the municipality. It shall make
without publication thereof, such orders and regulations for the
suppression of nuisances, and concerning all other matters in its
judgment detrimental to the public health in special or individual cases, not of general application, and serve copies thereof
upon the owner or occupant of any premises whereon such
nuisances of other matters may exist, or upon which may exist
the cause of other nuisances to other premises, or cause the same
to be conspicuously posted thereon. It may employ such persons
as shall be necessary to enable it to carry into effect its orders
and regulations, and fix their compensation. It may issue
subpoenas, compel the attendance of witnesses, administer oaths
to witnesses and compel them to testify, and for such purposes
it shall have the same powers as a justice of the peace of the state
in a civil action of which he has jurisdiction. It may designate
by resolution one of its members to sign and issue such subpoenas. No subpoenas shall be served outside the jurisdiction
of the board issuing it, and no witness shall be interrogated or
compelled to testify upon matters not related to the public health.
It may issue warrants to any constable or policeman of the
municipality to apprehend and remove such persons as can not
otherwise be subjected to its orders or regulations, and a warrant
to the sheriff of the county to bring to its aid the power of the
county whenever it shall be necessary to do so. Every warrant
shall be forthwith executed by the officer to whom directed, who
shall have the same powers and be subject to the same duties in
the execution thereof, as if it had been duly issued out of a court
of record of the state. Every such local board may prescribe and
impose penalties for the violation of or failure to comply with
any of its orders or regulations, not exceeding one hundred dollars for a single violation or failure, to be sued for and recovered
by it in the name and for the benefit of the municipality; and to

maintain actions in any court of competent jurisdiction to restrain by injunction such violations, or otherwise to enforce such
orders and regulations. Whenever such local board of health in
any incorporated village shall deem the sewers of such village
insufficient to properly and safely sewer such village, and protect
the public health, it shall certify such fact in writing to the board
of trustees of such village, stating and recommending what additions or alterations should in the judgment of such board of
health be made with its reasons therefor, and thereupon such
board of trustees shall immediately convene and consider such
recommendations, and if approved by such board of trustees, the .
same shall be certified to the state commissioner of health for
his approval, and if such recommendations shall be approved by
the state commissioner of health, it shall be the duty of the board
of trustees or other board of such village having jurisdiction of
the construction of sewers therein, if there be such a board,
whether sufficient funds shall be on hand for such purpose or not
to forthwith make such additions to or alterations in the sewers
of such village and execute such recommendations, and the expenses thereof shall be paid for wholly by said village in the
same manner as other village expenses are paid or by an assessment of the whole amount against the property benefited, or
partly by the village and partly by an assessment against the
property benefited, as the board of trustees of such village shall
by resolution determine. If the board of trustees shall determine
that such expenses shall be paid partly by the village and partly
by an assessment against the property benefited, as authorized
by this section, it shall in the resolution making such determination fix the proportion of such expense to be borne by each, and
the proportion thereof to be raised by an assessment against the
property benefited shall be assessed and collected in the manner
provided by the village law for the assessment and collection of
sewer assessments. Said village is hereby authorized to raise
such sum as may be necessary for the payment of the expenses

incurred, which are a village charge, if any, as herein provided. in addition to the amount such village is now authorized to raise by law for corporation purposes, and such board shall have the right to acquire such lands, rights of way, or other easements, by gift, or purchase, or in case the same can not be acquired by purchase may acquire the same by condemnation in the manner provided by law.

Thus amended by chap. 39, Laws of 1906.

Burial and burial permits.

§ 23. Every such local board shall prescribe sanitary regulations for the burial and removal of corpses, and shall designate the persons who shall grant permits for such burial, and permits for the transportation of any corpse which is to be carried for burial beyond the county where the death occurred. Every undertaker, sexton or other person having charge of any corpse, shall procure a certificate of the death and the probable cause duly certified by the physician in attendance upon the deceased during his last illness, or by the coroner where an inquisition is required by law, and if no physician was in attendance, and no inquest has been held or required by law, an affidavit stating the circumstances, time and cause of death, and sworn to by some credible person known to the officer granting the permit, and there shall be no burial or removal of a corpse until such certificate or affidavit has been presented to the local board or to the person designated by it, and thereupon a permit for such burial or removal has been obtained. When application is made for a permit to transport a corpse over any railroad or upon any passenger steamboat within the state, the board of health, or the officers to whom such application is made, shall require such corpse to be inclosed in a hermetically sealed casket of metal or other indestructible material, if the cause of death shall have been from a contagious or infectious disease.

*   *   *   *   *   *   *   *   *   *

Nuisances.

§ 25. Every such board shall receive and examine into all complaints made by any inhabitant concerning nuisances, or causes of danger or injury to life and health within the municipality, and may enter upon or within any place or premises where nuisances or conditions dangerous to life and health or which are the cause or nuisances existing elsewhere are known or believed to exist, and by its members or other persons designated for that purpose, inspect and examine the same. The owners, agents and occupants of any such premises shall permit such sanitary examinations to be made, and the board shall furnish such owners, agents and occupants with a written statement of the results and conclusions of any such examination. Every such local board shall order the suppression and removal of all nuisances and conditions detrimental to life and health found to exist within the municipality. Whenever the state department of health shall by notice to the presiding officer of any local board of health, direct him to convene such local board to take certain definite proceedings concerning which the state department of health shall be satisfied that the action recommended by them is necessary for the public good, and is within the jurisdiction of such board of health, such presiding officer shall convene such local board, which shall take the action directed.

Thus amended by chap. 383, Laws of 1903.

Removal of nuisances.

§ 26. If the owner or occupant of any premises whereon any nuisance or condition deemed to be detrimental to the public health exist or the cause of the existence elsewhere, fails to comply with any order or regulation of any such local board for the suppression and removal of any such nuisance or other matter, in the judgment of the board detrimental to the public health, made, served or posted as required in this article, such boards or their servants or employes may enter upon the premises to which such order or regulation relates, and suppress or remove such nuisance or other matter. The expense of such suppression or removal shall be paid by the owner or occupant of such premises, or by the person who caused or maintained such nuisance or other matters, and the board may maintain an action in the name of the municipality to recover such expense, and the same when recovered shall be paid to the treasurer of the municipality, or if it has no treasurer to its chief fiscal officer, to be held and used as the funds of the municipality. Whenever the suppression or removal of such nuisance or conditions detrimental to health demand the immediate expenditure of money, every such local board of health shall be authorized to use for such purpose any money in the hands of the board, or may call on the city council, village trustees or town board for such money or it may borrow the same on the credit of the municipality. All such moneys so expended or borrowed shall be immediately repaid to the fund or source whence they were received on the recovery of the same by action or otherwise from the persons responsible for the expenses of suppression or removal.

Thus amended by chap. 383, Laws of 1903.

* * * * * * * * * *

Jurisdiction of town and village boards.

§ 29. A town board of health shall not have jurisdiction over any city or incorporated village or part of such city or village in such town if such city or village has an organized board of health. The boards of health of any town and the incorporated villages therein, or any two or more towns and the incorporated villages therein, may unite, with the written approval of the state department of health, in a combined sanitary and registration district, and appoint for such district one health officer and registering officer, whose authority in all matters of general application shall be derived from the boards of health appointing him; and in special cases not of general application

arising within the jurisdiction of but one board shall be derived from such board alone. When one or more towns and the incorporated villages therein unite in one registration district, the registrar of vital statistics of such combined district will be required to make separate returns to the state department of health of village and town certificates of births, marriages and deaths.
Thus amended by chap. 383, Laws of 1903.

*   *   *   *   *   *   *   *   *   *

Mandamus.

§ 31. The performance of any duty or the doing of any act enjoined, prescribed or required by this article, may be enforced by mandamus at the instance of the state department of health or its president or secretary, or of the local board of health, or of any citizen of full age resident of the municipality where the duty should be performed or the act done.
Thus amended by chap. 383, Laws of 1903.

*   *   *   *   *   *   *   *   *   *

CHAP. 679, LAWS OF 1893.

AN ACT for the relief of street surface railroad companies.

SECTION 1. Any street surface railroad corporation which shall have heretofore constructed and is now operating any extension or branch of its railroad along any streets or highways or portion thereof in a city having less than fifty thousand inhabitants, or in any town adjoining such city, and which shall heretofore have obtained consent of the owners of one-half in value of the property bounded on, and the consents also of the local authorities having control of that portion of the streets, roads or highways upon which such extension or branch is constructed and is being operated to the construction and operation of the same, is hereby authorized to operate and maintain any such branch or extension, upon filing in the office of the secretary of state a certificate, signed by its board of directors, which certificate shall contain a statement of the names of the cities, towns, villages and counties, and the names or description of the streets, avenues and highways in which such extensions or branches have been constructed, the places from and to which the same have been constructed and are to be maintained and operated and the length thereof as near as may be; thereupon said extensions and branches shall be deemed and considered a part of the lines of said railway from the date of the filing thereof, and all corporate action relating to the construction, maintenance and operation of such extensions or branches, or creating liens upon the same by said corporation are hereby validated and confirmed.

§ 2. Nothing in this act contained shall affect or impair any vested right or any pending litigation, nor shall any corporation which shall avail itself of the provisions of this act be deemed thereby to have waived any rights which it theretofore had to maintain and operate any branch or extension named in any certificate filed by it hereunder.

See sections 90 and 106, Railroad Law, chap. 604, Laws of 1892, *ante.*

*CHAP. 743, LAWS OF 1894.

AN ACT to facilitate travel upon elevated railroads in the city of New York.

SECTION 1. Any passenger upon the Manhattan elevated railway who has paid the fare required for passage from any point on said railway east of Broadway, between the Battery and One Hundred and Twenty-ninth street, not exceeding five cents, shall be entitled to a continuous passage, without change of cars, on the suburban rapid transit railway or on any railway owned or operated by the Manhattan railway company, within the city of New York, in connection with said Manhattan elevated railway from One Hundred and Twenty-ninth street, or other termini of the lines of said Manhattan elevated railway south of the Harlem river, to any station on the route of said suburban rapid transit

*While this is not a general act it is considered of enough importance to be printed here.

railroad, or such other elevated railroad as may be operated by the Manhattan railway company north of the Harlem river, without the payment of additional fare; and any passenger on the suburban rapid transit railroad, or any elevated railway owned or operated by the Manhattan railway company in connection with the Manhattan elevated railroad, within the city of New York, running southward to One Hundred and Twenty-ninth street, or other termini of the Manhattan railroad, who has paid the fare required on said suburban rapid transit railroad to One Hundred and Twenty-ninth street in the city of New York, not exceeding five cents, shall be entitled to a continuous passage, without change of cars, over the Manhattan elevated railway to any station on its route east of Broadway, between One Hundred and Twenty-ninth street and the Battery, without the payment of additional fare.

CHAP. 240, LAWS OF 1895.

AN ACT to provide for licensing foreign stock corporations.

SECTION 1. Every foreign corporation except banking, fire, marine, casualty and life insurance companies, and corporations wholly engaged in carrying on manufactures in this state, co-operative fraternal insurance companies, endowment orders and building and loan associations, now authorized to do business in this state, under the provisions of chapter six hundred and eighty-seven of the laws of eighteen hundred and ninety-two, entitled "An act to amend the general corporation law," shall pay to the state treasurer for the use of the state, a license fee of one-eighth of one per centum for the privilege of exercising its corporate franchises or carrying on its business in such corporate or organized capacity in this state, on the first day of December, eighteen hundred and ninety-five, to be computed upon the basis of the amount of capital stock employed by it within this state during the year preceding that date, and every such foreign cor. poration which shall hereafter be authorized to do business in this state shall pay a like license fee for the privilege, to be computed upon the basis of the capital stock employed by it within this state for its business during the first year of carrying on its business in this state. The amount of capital upon which such taxes shall be paid shall be fixed by the comptroller, who shall have the same authority to examine the books and records in this state of such foreign corporations, and the employees thereof, and the same power to issue his warrant for the collection of such taxes, as he now has with regard to domestic corporations. Every such foreign corporation hereafter authorized to do business in this state shall, before receiving the certificate of authority provided by law, pay to the state treasurer, for the use of the state, the tax hereinbefore provided for. No action shall be maintained or recovery had in any of the courts of this state by such foreign corporation doing business in this state, without obtaining the certificate of authority prescribed by law, and a receipt for the license fee hereby imposed.

See section 181, Tax Law, *post*.

CHAP. 417, LAWS OF 1895.

AN ACT to regulate the exercise of their franchises by certain public corporations, by requiring them to afford facilities for the transaction of the public business, to certain public officers and employes.

SECTION 1. The mayor of each city of this State and the president of each incorporated village may issue, under the seal of his office, to each policeman and fireman appointed by the duly-constituted authorities of such city or village, a certificate of the appointment and qualification of such policeman or fireman as such, and specifying the duration of his term of office; and it shall thereupon be the duty of every street surface and elevated railroad company carrying on business within such city or village, to transport every such policeman or fireman free of charge while he is traveling in the course of the performance of the duties of his office. Every telegraph or telephone company engaged in business within such city or village, shall afford to such police-man or fireman the use of its telegraph lines or telephones for the purpose of making and receiving reports and communications in the course of the performance of his official duties.

§ 2. Every policeman or fireman who shall permit any other person to use the certificate issued to him as provided by this act, or to present or make use of the same, except while acting in the course of the performance of his official duties, or who shall use such certificate after the expiration of his term of office or his resignation or removal therefrom, shall be deemed guilty of a misdemeanor.

Unconstitutional; see Wilson v. United Traction Company, 72 App. Div., p. 233.

See chap. 683, Laws of 1897, *post.*

CHAP. 1027, LAWS OF 1895.

AN ACT in relation to the issue of mileage books by railroad corporations.

SECTION 1. Every railroad corporation operating a railroad in this state, the line or lines of which are more than one hundred miles in length, and which is authorized by law to charge a maximum fare of more than two cents per mile, and not more than three cents per mile, and which does charge a maximum fare of more than two cents per mile, shall issue mileage books having either five hundred or one thousand coupons attached thereto, entitling the holder thereof, upon complying with the conditions hereof, to travel either five hundred or one thousand miles on the line or lines of such railroad, for which the corporation may charge a sum not to exceed two cents per mile. Such mileage books shall be kept for sale by such corporation at every ticket office of such corporation in an incorporated village or city, and any of such books shall be issued immediately upon application therefor. Upon presentation of such mileage book to a con-ductor on any train on any line of railroad owned or operated by said railroad corporation, the holder thereof, or any member of his family or firm, or any salesman of his firm, shall be entitled to travel for a number of miles equal to the number of coupons detached by such conductor. Such mileage book shall entitle the holder thereof to the same rights and privileges in respect to the transportation of person and property to which the highest class ticket issued by such corporation would entitle him. Such mileage books shall be good until all coupons attached thereto have been used. Any railroad corporation which shall refuse to issue a mileage book, as provided by this section, or in violation hereof, to accept such mileage book for transportation, shall forfeit fifty dollars, to be recovered by the party to whom such refusal is made; but no action can be maintained therefor unless commenced within one year after the cause of action accrues.

Thus amended by chap. 577, Laws of 1898.

Unconstitutional as to companies existing prior to its passage (162 N. Y. 230). See, also, 162 N. Y., 42, 171 N. Y., 566, as to companies formed since its passage. See, also, 86 App. Div., 379, and 179 N. Y., 589. See also subdivision 3, section 3, Stock Corporation Law.

CHAP. 112, LAWS OF 1896.

AN ACT in relation to the traffic in liquors, and for the taxation and regulation of the same, and to provide for local option, constituting chapter twenty-nine of the general laws.

CHAPTER XXIX OF THE GENERAL LAWS.

The Liquor Tax Law.

Note.—Many sections of the Liquor Tax Law apply to railroad companies which receive liquor tax certificates. Having in mind the purposes sought to be fulfilled by this compilation of railroad laws it is thought best to publish here only certain portions.

*   *   *   *   *   *   *   *   *   *

Excise taxes upon the business of trafficking in liquors; enumeration.

§ 11, subdivision 4. Upon the business of trafficking in liquors upon any car, steamboat or vessel within this state, to be drunk on such car or on any car connected therewith, or on such steamboat or vessel, or upon any boat or barge attached thereto, or connected therewith there is assessed an excise tax, to be paid by every corporation, association, copartnership or person engaged in such traffic, and for each car, steamboat or vessel, boat or barge, upon which such traffic is carried on, the sum of three hundred dollars.

Subdivision 4, thus amended by chap. 115, Laws of 1903.

* , * * * · * * * * * *

§ 23, subdivision 2. No corporation or association incorporated or organized under the laws of another state or country; provided, however, that if such corporation or association be acting as a common carrier or be operating dining, buffet, parlor or sleeping cars in this state, it may be granted a liquor tax certificate under subdivision four of section eleven of this act. And in case any car for which a liquor tax certificate is held shall be withdrawn from the service for repairs, or leave the state, such certificate may be temporarily transferred to a substitute car, in accordance with such rules and regulations as the state commissioner of excise shall prescribe, without payment of any transfer fee.

Subdivision 2, thus amended by chap. 367, Laws of 1900.
See chap. 80, Laws of 1900, not printed herein.

*_ * * * · * * * * * *

Employment of persons addicted to intoxication by common carriers.

§ 41. Any person or officer of an association or corporation engaged in the business of conveying passengers or property for hire, who shall employ in the conduct of such business, as an engineer, fireman, conductor, switch-tender, train dispatcher, telegrapher, commander, pilot, mate, fireman or in other like capacity, so that by his neglect of duty the safety and security of life, person or property so conveyed might be imperiled, any person who habitually indulges in the intemperate use of liquors, after notice that such person has been intoxicated, while in the active service of such person, association or corporation, shall be guilty of a misdemeanor.

See Section 420, Penal Code, and section 56, Code of Criminal Procedure, section 29, Rapid Transit Act, *post;* also section 42, Railroad Law, *ante.*

* * * * * * * * * *

CHAP. 376, LAWS OF 1896.

AN ACT relating to domestic commerce law, constituting chapter thirty-four of the general laws.

*   *   *   *   *   *   *   *   *   *

Standard and storage of illuminating oils.

§ 24.   *   *   *   *   *   *

No such oil or fluid which will ignite at a temperature below three hundred degrees Fahrenheit shall be burned or be carried as freight in any passenger or baggage car or passenger boat moved by steam or electric power in this state, or in any stage or street car, however propelled, except that coal oil, petroleum and its products may be carried, when securely packed in barrels or metallic packages, in passenger boats propelled by steam when there are no other public means of transportation. * * * The state board of health * * * shall adopt such measures to enforce the provisions of this section * * * as to them may seem necessary. * * * This section shall not apply to the city of New York, and shall not supersede but shall be in addition to the ordinances or regulations of any city or village made pursuant to law for the inspection or control of combustible materials therein.

*   *   *   *   *   *   *   *   *   *

Unlawful detention of milk cans.

§ 29. No person shall, without the consent of the owner or shipper, or his agent, use, sell, dispose of, buy or traffic in any can, irrespective of its condition, or the use to which it may have been applied, belonging to any dealer in or shipper of milk or cream in this state, or which may be shipped to any town, village or city in the state which can has the name or initials of such owner, dealer or shipper stamped, marked or fastened thereupon, or wilfully mar, erase or change by remarking or otherwise such name or initials. If any person without the consent of such owner, dealer or shipper, or his agent, uses, sells, disposes of, buys, traffics in, or, has in his possession or under his control any such can, it shall be presumptive evidence that such use, sale, disposal, purchase, traffic or possession, is unlawful. Any such owner, dealer or shipper, or his agent, may take possession of any can used in violation of this section wherever found, and if filled or partly filled with milk or cream, and the person in whose possession it is found does not when requested immediately empty the same, such owner, dealer or shipper, or his agent, may empty the same into the street or elsewhere, and shall not be liable for damages for any act done pursuant to the provisions of this section. Any person violating any provision of this section shall forfeit to such owner, or dealer, or shipper, or his agent, the sum of fifty dollars for every such violation, and an action may be brought therefor in the name of any such agent without joining the real party in interest that he represents, and in any such action brought for any such violation different persons may be joined as plaintiffs, whether jointly or severally interested therein, and different persons may be joined as defendants therein who have severally violated any such provisions, and a recovery may be had in favor of one or more of such plaintiffs against one or more of such defendants. Such action may be brought in a court of record having jurisdiction thereof, and the place of trial thereof may be laid in the county where such owner, dealer or shipper, resides at the time of the commencement thereof; or it may be brought in a justice's court, or other court not of record having similar jurisdiction in the city or county where a violation of this section is committed; the district courts of the city of New York shall have jurisdiction of such action irrespective of the residence of any party or the location of the subject matter. If at the time of the issue of the summons in a court not of record, the plaintiff or his agent make affidavit that he has reason to believe and does believe that any defendant has any such can or cans secreted upon his premises, the justice or other magistrate or court issuing the summons, must without requiring an undertaking grant an order for the arrest of the defendant, which order shall also contain a direction to the officer to whom the same is issued, immediately search the place or premises mentioned in said affidavit, and if any such can, or cans are there found to bring the same together with the defendant or other persons in whose possession said can or cans are found, before such justice, magistrate or court. The proceedings may be amended at any time by adding parties or otherwise as justice may require; and the judgment may provide for the disposition of the can, or cans so found. If upon the issue of any such process, the constable, or other officer, shall be unable to find the person, or persons therein named, but shall find any can or cans, as therein set forth, he shall bring such can or cans before such justice or magistrate who shall thereupon proceed to determine the right of such complainant thereto, and if upon such hearing had thereon he shall be satisfied that such can or cans rightfully belong to such complainant, or that he is entitled to the possession thereof, he shall forthwith deliver the same into his possession or the possession of his agent. The several superintendents of the railroad companies, and the branches and connections thereof, and steamboat lines operating their roads or lines, or any portion thereof in this state shall have power to collect, gather and take into possession from any person or whenever found thereupon, any cans belonging to such owner, dealer or shipper, and return the same to such owner, dealer, or shipper and may appoint an agent for that purpose, and such superintendent and such agent appointed by him shall have the same power and authority under this section as an agent of such owner, dealer or shipper. The certificate of such superintendent appointing such agent duly acknowledged shall be presumptive evidence of the appointment and authority of such agent. Any person authorized by this section to seize and take into his possession any such

21

cans may, in case of resistance, call to his aid any police officer
or constable of the town, village or city, who shall when so called
on assist him in seizing or taking possession of such cans.

Thus amended by chap. 482, Laws of 1902.
See section 56 Code of Criminal Procedure, and section 427a Penal Code, *post.*
Also chapter 977, Laws of 1896, *post.*
See chap. 168, Laws of 1904, not printed herein.

*   *   *   *   *   *   *   *   *   *

Fees and charges for elevators and warehouses.

§ 32. The maximum charge for elevating, receiving, weighing
and discharging grain by means of floating and stationary elevators and warehouses in any city having a population of one hundred and thirty thousand or over, shall not exceed five-eighths
of one cent a bushel. In the process of handling grain by means
of floating and stationary elevators, the lake vessels or propellers, the ocean vessels or steamships and canal boats shall
only be required to pay the charge of trimming or shoveling to
the leg of the elevator when unloading, and trimming cargo when
loading; and in any case the fee charged for the use of a shovel
operated by steam or any other mechanical power, in connection
with any floating or stationary elevator, shall not exceed the
sum of one dollar and fifty cents for each one thousand bushels
elevated. For every violation of any provision of this article,
the person committing such violation shall forfeit to the people
of the state the sum of two hundred and fifty dollars. A person
injured by a violation of this section, may recover any damages
sustained from the person violating the same.

Thus amended by chap. 366, Laws of 1903.

*   *   *   *   *   *   *   *   *   *

CHAP. 388, LAWS OF 1896.

AN ACT to provide for a better system of lighting passenger
cars on elevated railroads in cities of over twelve hundred
thousand inhabitants.

SECTION 1. Within one year from the passage of this act every
corporation operating an elevated railroad in any city of over
twelve hundred thousand inhabitants in this state computed
according to the last census, shall equip two-fifths of all cars

used for the transportation of passengers with the most approved system of lighting passenger cars now in use upon railroads, either by electricity or gas of not less than eighteen candle power, and shall likewise equip an additional two-fifths of all such cars within two years from the passage of this act, and shall likewise equip all remaining such cars within three years from the passage of this act, and every such corporation is hereby prohibited from using after one year from the passage of this act, kerosene or coal oils as a means of lighting more than three-fifths in number of all such cars, and after two years from the passage of this act, no more than one-fifth in number of all such cars, and after three years from the passage of this act such corporation is prohibited from using kerosene or coal oils as a means of lighting any of its passenger cars.

§ 2. Any violation of the provisions of this act shall render any such corporation liable to pay a fine or penalty of fifty dollars for each and every day, for each and every passenger car run over its railroad which is not equipped and lighted as provided in the first section of this act; and such fine may be recovered by any passenger on such railroad who may sue therefor; and any violation of the provisions of this act on the part of any such railroad corporation shall also be a misdemeanor.

CHAP. 649, LAWS OF 1896.

AN ACT to validate and confirm certain consents heretofore given by the local authorities of cities of the first and second class in the construction, operation and maintenance of street surface railroads therein.

SECTION 1. All consents given since December first, eighteen hundred and ninety-five, and prior to February first, eighteen hundred and ninety-six, by the local authorities of any city of the first or second class, to the construction, operation and maintenance of a street surface railroad in any such city by a railroad corporation which has not complied with the provisions of section tifty-nine of the railroad law or has failed to obtain the certificate therein provided for, are hereby validated and confirmed, and any such corporation may construct, operate and maintain a street surface railroad over, along and upon the streets, avenues, highways and public places described in such consent upon obtaining the consent of the owners of property bounded on such streets, avenues, highways or public places as provided by law.

See section 59, Railroad Law, *ante*.

CHAP. 962, LAWS OF 1896.

AN ACT to amend section nineteen hundred and forty-eight of the code of civil procedure, by adding at the end thereof a new subdivision, relating to actions against foreign corporations.

SECTION 1. Section nineteen hundred and forty-eight of the code of civil procedure is hereby amended by adding a new subdivision thereto, as subdivision four, as follows:

4. Against a foreign corporation which exercises within the state any corporate rights, privileges or franchises, not granted to it by the law of this state; or which within the state, has violated any provision of law, or, contrary to law, has done or omitted any act, or has exercised a privilege or franchise, not conferred upon it by the law of this state, where, in a similar case, a domestic corporation would, in accordance with section seventeen hundred and ninety-eight of this act, be liable to an action to vacate its charter and to annul its existence; or which exercises within the state any corporate rights, privileges or franchises in a manner contrary to the public policy of the state.

See sections 15, *et seq.*, General Corporation Law, *ante;* section 7, Stock Corporation Law, *ante;* chap. 690, Laws 1899, *post*.

CHAP. 977, LAWS OF 1896.

AN ACT to amend chapter four hundred and one of the laws of eighteen hundred and eighty-seven, entitled "An act in relation to milk cans," as amended by chapter twenty-five of the laws of eighteen hundred and ninety.

SECTION 1. Chapter four hundred and one of the laws of eighteen hundred and eighty-seven, entitled "An act in relation to milk cans," as amended by chapter twenty-five of the laws of eighteen hundred and ninety, is hereby amended so as to read as follows:

*   *   *   *   *   *   *   *   *   *

§ 10. The owner or owners, dealer or dealers, shipper or shippers, and the several superintendents of the various railroad companies and the branches and connections thereof, and the steamboat lines operating their lines, or any portion thereof, in the state of New York, or elsewhere, shall have power to collect, gather and take into his possession, from any person or persons within the state of New York, or wherever found in this state, any such milk or cream can or cans, and shall have power to appoint an agent therefor.

§ 11. The certificate of any superintendent of any of the railroad companies or steamboat lines mentioned in this act, or any person or persons authorized thereto, in this act, appointing an agent to collect such can or cans, duly acknowledged before a notary public, shall be presumptive evidence of the authority of such agent.

§ 12. Such agent shall have full power to collect, gather and take into his possession from any person or persons, or corporation, or wherever found, any such milk or cream can or cans, and in case of resistance may call to his aid the assistance of any constable or police officer who shall assist him to take possession of such can or cans.

§ 13. All acts or parts of acts inconsistent with the provisions of this act are hereby repealed.

See section 29, chap. 376, Laws of 1896, *ante.*

NOTE.—Other provisions of this act than those printed here may apply to railroad companies.

CHAP. 193, LAWS OF 1897.

AN ACT in relation to the consolidation of domestic and foreign railroad corporations.

SECTION 1. The consolidation heretofore effected of a domestic railroad corporation with a foreign railroad corporation, shall not be deemed invalid because such roads at the time of the consolidation did not form a connected and continuous line, if, when the consolidation was effected, an intermediate line, by purchase or by a lease, of not less than ninety-nine years became, with the consolidated roads, a continuous and connecting line of railroad, and such consolidation is hereby ratified and confirmed.

See section 70 *et seq.*, Railroad Law, *ante;* chap. 201, Laws of 1899, chap. 30, Laws 1903, *post.*

CHAP. 286, LAWS OF 1897.

AN ACT to provide for the widening and improving of highways in towns having a total population of eight thousand or more inhabitants and containing an incorporated village having a total population of not less than eight thousand and not more than fifteen thousand inhabitants.

*　　*　　*　　*　　*　　*　　*　　*　　*　　*

§ 10. No surface railway shall be constructed on any said highway so widened, except within eleven feet on each side of the center line of said highway, and no such railway shall be operated by horse or horses. A distance of not less than twenty feet on each side of such twenty-two feet so reserved for railroad purposes shall be improved for highway purposes and not less than sixteen feet of said twenty feet shall be of macadam. Sidewalks shall be graded on each side of said highway to a width of not less than fifteen feet each.

*　　*　　*　　*　　*　　*　　*　　*　　*　　*

CHAP. 378, LAWS OF 1897—GREATER NEW YORK CHARTER.

§ 17. The legislative power of The City of New York, except as otherwise herein provided, shall be vested in one house to be known and styled as "the board of aldermen of The City of New York."

Thus amended by chap. 629, Laws of 1905.

*   *   *   *   *   *   *   *   *   *

§ 28. The board of aldermen shall, whenever a vacancy occurs in the office of the city clerk, appoint a clerk, who shall perform such duties as may be prescribed for him. The clerk so appointed shall also be the city clerk and the clerk of the board of aldermen, and shall hold his office for six years, and until his successor shall be appointed and has qualified, unless removed for cause. The city clerk shall have charge of all the papers and documents of the city, except such as are by law committed to the keeping of the several departments or of other officers, and except as provided in section one hundred and thirty-six of this act as amended. He shall keep the record of the proceedings of the board of aldermen. He shall also keep a separate record of all the ordinances of the board of aldermen in a book to be provided for that purpose, with proper indices, which book shall be deemed a public record of such ordinances, and each ordinance shall be attested by said clerk. He shall also keep a separate and public record which shall be known as the "street franchise book". In such record he shall forthwith transcribe verbatim from copies duly certified by or under the authority of the board granting, making or adopting the same, every grant, franchise, contract or resolution in the nature of a franchise affecting any of the streets, avenues, highways, boulevards, concourses, driveways, bridges, tunnels, parks, parkways, waterways, docks, wharves, bulkheads, piers or public grounds or waters within or belonging to the city which shall hereafter be granted, made or adopted by the board of estimate and apportionment or the board of rapid transit railroad commissioners of the city, together with copies of all formalities of the execution or verification thereof, and shall forthwith, after so transcribing the same, make and transmit to the board which shall have made, granted or adopted such grant, franchise, contract or resolution a copy of such record, with a minute of the date, volume and page thereof, duly certified by him. Copies of all papers duly filed in his office, and transcripts thereof, and of the records of proceedings of the board of aldermen, and copies of the laws and ordinances of said city, certified by him under the corporate seal, shall be admissible in evidence in all courts and places in the same manner and for the same purposes as papers or documents similarly authenticated by the clerk of a county. Said city clerk may be removed on charges by a two-thirds vote of all the members of the board of aldermen, subject, however, to judicial review on certiorari. He shall collect the following fees: For a copy of any book, account, record or other paper filed in his office, five cents for each folio; for a certification of any book, account, record or other paper filed in his office, twenty-five cents, and five cents in addition for each folio in excess of five; for each bond filed in his office, twelve cents; for filing all other papers, required by law to be filed in his office, six cents; for a certificate of appointment of a commissioner of deeds, twenty-five cents.

Thus amended by chap. 629, Laws of 1905.

*   *   *   *   *   *   *   *   *   *

§ 41. The ordinances which on December thirty-first, eighteen hundred and ninety-seven, were in force respectively in The City of New York, the city of Brooklyn, Long Island City, and the other municipal and public corporations and parts thereof consolidated with The City of New York, except so far as the same have since been modified, amended, or repealed by the municipal assembly of The City of New York, and all ordinances which on January first, nineteen hundred and two, are in force in The

City of New York, are, so far as the same are not inconsistent with this act, hereby continued in full force and effect within the former limits of said respective cities and municipal and public corporations, or parts thereof, subject to modification, amendment or repeal by the board of aldermen of The City of New York. Such ordinances may be enforced by and in the name of "The City of New York". But all such ordinances affecting or relating to grants, franchises or contracts, or resolutions in the nature of a franchise heretofore made, granted or adopted, or to be hereafter made, granted or adopted, or rights now or hereafter existing, involving the occupation or use of any street, avenue, highway, boulevard, concourse, driveway, bridge, tunnel, park, parkway, waterway, dock, wharf, bulkhead, pier or public grounds or waters which are within or belong to the city, shall hereafter be subject to modification, amendment or repeal by the board of estimate and apportionment in like manner in which and within the same limits within which they have heretofore been subject to modification, amendment or repeal by the said board of aldermen, Provided, however, that this section shall not apply to or affect any franchise, grant, contract or right authorized by the board of rapid transit railroad commissioners of the city.

Thus amended by chap. 629, Laws of 1905.

* * * * * * * * * *

§ 43. The board of aldermen shall have power to make, establish, alter, modify, amend and repeal all ordinances, rules, and police, health, park, fire and building regulations, not contrary to the laws of the state, or the United States, as they may deem necessary to carry into effect the powers conferred upon The City of New York by this act, or by any other law of the state, or by grant; and such as they may deem necessary and proper for the good government, order and protection of persons and property, and for the preservation of the public health, peace and prosperity of said city, and its inhabitants, except so far as power is conferred by this act upon presidents of boroughs, the police, health, park and fire departments respectively to make rules for the government of the persons employed in and by said departments. Nothing in this section contained shall be construed to impair the powers conferred by this act upon the department of education; and except so far as the legislative power respecting the health, police, park, fire and building departments shall be conferred upon said departments respectively by the provisions of this act, and except that any modification of the existing rules, regulations and ordinances affecting any of the departments and all ordinances to be passed to govern the board of public improvements or any of the departments thereof, must originate with the department concerned, or with said board, and must be adopted or rejected by the board of aldermen without amendment. But nothing in this section or this act contained shall be construed to impair the power or control conferred by this act upon the board of estimate and apportionment with respect to the streets, avenues, highways, boulevards, concourses, driveways, bridges, tunnels, parks, parkways, waterways, docks, bulkheads, wharves, piers and all public grounds and waters which are within or belong to the city.

Thus amended by chap. 629, Laws of 1905.

§ 44. No enumeration of powers in this act shall be held to limit the legislative power of the board of aldermen except as in this act specifically provided and the board of aldermen in addition to all enumerated powers may exercise all of the powers vested in The City of New York by this act, or otherwise, by proper ordinances, rules, regulations and by-laws not inconsistent with the provisions of this act, or with the constitution or laws of the United States or of this state; and, subject to such limitations, may from time to time ordain and pass all such ordinances, rules, regulations and by-laws, applicable throughout the whole of said city or applicable only to specified portions thereof, as to the said board of aldermen may seem meet for the good rule and government of the city, and to carry out the purposes and provisions of this act or of other laws relating to the said city, and may provide for the enforcement

of the same by such fines, penalties, forfeitures and imprisonment as may by ordinance or by law be prescribed.
Thus amended by chap. 629, Laws of 1905.

§ **45.** Nothing in this act contained shall repeal or affect
in any manner the provisions of the rapid transit acts
applicable to the corporation heretofore known as the
mayor, aldermen and commonalty of The City of New
York, or any municipality united therewith or territory
embraced therein, or to repeal or affect the existing general laws
of the state in respect to street surface railroads. The consent
or approval of the board of aldermen to or for the issue of corporate stock of The City of New York, as provided by section
one hundred and sixty-nine shall not be necessary to authorize
the comptroller to issue such stock for the purposes prescribed
in chapter four of the laws of eighteen hundred and ninety-one as
amended. The board of estimate and apportionment and the
comptroller of The City of New York shall, anything herein contained to the contrary notwithstanding, be subject to all the
duties and obligations prescribed in said chapter four of the laws
of eighteen hundred and ninety-one as amended for the board of
estimate and apportionment and comptroller therein mentioned.
Upon the execution of any contract made pursuant to chapter four
of the laws of eighteen hundred and ninety-one as amended, the
board of rapid transit railroad commissioners may, in its discretion, make request upon the board of estimate and apportionment for the authorization of such corporate stock, either for
such amounts from time to time as they shall deem the progress
of the work to require, or for the full amount sufficient to pay
the entire estimated expense of executing such contract. In case
they shall make requisition for the entire amount, the comptroller shall endorse on the contract his certificate that funds are
available for the entire contract whenever such stock shall have
been authorized to be issued by said board of estimate and apportionment; and in such case such stock may be issued from time
to time thereafter in such amounts as may be necessary to meet

the requirements of such contract. The certificate of the comptroller, mentioned in section one hundred and forty-nine of this
act, shall not be necessary to make such contract binding on The
City of New York.

Thus amended by chap. 629, Laws of 1905.
See Rapid Transit Act, *post*.

*   *   *   *   *   *   *   *   *   *

§ 47. The board of aldermen shall have power to provide by
ordinance for the acquisition, construction, or establishment of
markets; for the acquisition and construction of parks, parkways, playgrounds, boulevards and driveways; for the building
of bridges over, and of tunnels under any stream or waterway
within or adjoining the limits of the city; for the building of
docks, wharves, or piers, and for acquiring land by purchase or
condemnation, for said purposes; for acquiring, constructing, improving, permanently bettering and equipping public buildings,
including school houses and sites therefor for the use of the
city; for the repaving of streets; for building, repairing and
equipping boats and vessels or other floating craft of any kind
that may be needed for the use and purposes of the city; for
the establishing, building and equipping of telegraph or other
systems of communication for the use and purposes of the police
department and other departments of the city government; for
the construction and equipment of public comfort stations; for
the making and completing of maps of all the territory embraced
within each of the boroughs of said city; and for any of the
foregoing purposes, may create loans and authorize the issue of
bonds, or other evidences of indebtedness, to pay for the same,
payable at such times, and in such manner, and at such rates
of interest as it may by ordinance prescribe; but no bonds or
other evidences of indebtedness shall be issued under the authority
of this section, unless the proposition for creating such debt,
shall first be approved by a majority vote of the whole board
of estimate and apportionment, entered on the minutes of record
of such board. In addition to the specific purposes hereinbefore
set forth, the board of aldermen may also create loans and author.

ize the issue of bonds for any other purpose connected with the exercise of the various powers conferred by this act upon The City of New York or any department or official thereof; provided, however, that no bonds or other evidences of indebtedness shall be issued for such additional purposes unless first approved by a unanimous vote of the board of estimate and apportionment, entered upon the minutes of record of said board; Provided, however, that all the powers in this section or elsewhere in this act granted to the board of aldermen shall be subject to the control of the board of estimate and apportionment over all the streets, avenues, highways, boulevards, concourses, driveways, bridges, tunnels, parks, parkways, waterways, docks, bulkheads, wharves, piers and all public grounds and waters which are within or belong to the city as provided in this act.

Thus amended by chap. 629, Laws of 1905.

§ 48. After any proposition for creating a debt by the issue of bonds for any of the purposes specified in section forty-seven of this act as amended, has been approved by a resolution or vote of the board of estimate and apportionment, it shall be the duty of the board of aldermen upon receiving a copy of such resolution or vote to appoint a day not less than one week nor more than two weeks after receipt thereof for the consideration of the subject matter. The board of aldermen shall, on the day so fixed, proceed with the consideration thereof, and may continue and adjourn such consideration from time to time until a final vote shall be taken thereon as hereinafter provided. Within six weeks after the copy of such resolution or vote of the board of estimate and apportionment shall have been first received by the board of aldermen, a final vote shall be taken thereon by ayes and noes. Provided, however, that the said board of aldermen may by unanimous vote approve any such proposition for the issue of bonds forthwith and without appointing a day for the consideration thereof, and any such proposition so approved heretofore or hereafter shall be valid.

If a majority of all the members of the board of aldermen shall vote against such proposition it shall be deemed to be rejected. If a majority of all the members of the board of aldermen shall not vote against such proposition within the six weeks above limited, then it shall be deemed at the expiration of said period to have been passed by the requisite vote of the board of aldermen. The action of the board of aldermen in passing any such proposition whether by an affirmative vote, or by a failure of a majority of all the members of the board of aldermen to vote against the same, shall be subject to the approval of the mayor and to the action of the board of aldermen in case of a veto, as provided in this act.

Thus amended by chap. 636, Laws of 1906.

*   *   *   *   *   *   *   *   *   *

§ 50. Subject to the constitution and laws of the state, the board of aldermen shall have power to regulate the use of streets and sidewalks by foot passengers, animals or vehicles; to regulate the speed at which vehicles shall be driven or ridden and at which vehicles shall be propelled in the streets; to regulate processions or parades occupying or marching upon any street; to prevent encroachments upon and obstructions to the streets and to authorize and require their removal by the proper officers; to regulate the opening of street surfaces for purposes authorized by law; to regulate the numbering of houses and lots in the streets and the naming of streets, except that it shall not be lawful to number or renumber any houses or to change the name of any street save between the first day of December in any year and the first day of May next ensuing; to regulate and prevent the throwing or depositing of ashes, garbage or other filth or rubbish of any kind upon the streets; to regulate the use of the streets for signs, signposts, awnings, awning posts, horsetroughs, urinals, posts for telegraph or other electric wires, and other purposes; to regulate street pavements, crosswalks, curbstones, gutter-stones and sidewalks; to provide for regulating, grading, flagging, curbing, guttering and lighting the streets; to regulate public cries, advertising noises, steam whistles, and ringing bells

in the streets; to regulate the exhibiting of banners, placards
or flags in or across the streets or from houses or other buildings; to regulate the exhibition of advertisements or handbills
along the streets; and to make all such regulations in reference
to the running of stages, omnibuses, trucks and cars as may
be necessary for the convenient use and the accommodation of
the streets, piers, wharves or stations. Whenever the, word
"street" or the plural thereof occurs in this section it shall be
deemed to include all that is included by the terms "street, avenue, road, alley, lane, highway, boulevard, concourse, public
square and public place", or the plurals thereof respectively.
Wherever the word "vehicle" or the plural thereof occurs in
this section it shall be deemed to include wagons, trucks, carts,
cabs, carriages, stages, omnibuses, motors, automobiles, locomo-
biles, locomotives, bicycles, tricycles, sleighs or other conveyances for persons or property. The board of aldermen shall not
have power to authorize the placing or continuing of any encroachment or obstruction upon any street or sidewalk, except
the temporary occupation thereof during the erection or repairing of a building on a lot opposite the same, nor shall they permit the erection of booths and stands within stoop lines, except
for the sale of newspapers, periodicals, fruits and sodawater, and
with the consent. in such cases of the owner of the premises.
The board of aldermen shall not. pass any special ordinance in
relation to any of the matters mentioned in this section. All
ordinances in relation thereto shall be general ordinances which
may either apply throughout the whole city or throughout specified portions thereof, and shall provide for the enforcement
thereof as specified in section forty-four of this act as amended.
Nothing herein contained shall be construed to prevent the
board of aldermen from providing by special ordinance for the
erection or maintenance on the streets or waters within The City
of New York of fountains, public comfort stations, urinals, public baths, or other like structures maintained by the public

authorities; for the establishment of which the said board is hereby empowered to provide. All general ordinances relating to authorized structures, encroachments or obstructions in or upon the streets or sidewalks by persons other than the authorities of The City of New York, or other public authorities, shall fix a definite license fee for every such authorized structure, encroachment or obstruction, according to the character, extent and duration thereof, and shall provide for the issuing of revocable licenses therefor, which shall be according to an established form and shall be regularly numbered and duly registered as shall be prescribed by the board of aldermen. But no ordinance hereafter adopted or power hereafter exercised by the board of aldermen shall limit, apply to or affect any franchise, grant, contract or resolution in the nature of a franchise hereafter made, approved or authorized by the board of estimate and apportionment as in this act provided, or by the board of rapid transit railroad commissioners of The City of New York.

Thus amended by chap. 629, Laws of 1905.

*　　*　　*　　*　　*　　*　　*　　*　　*　　*

Inalienable rights of the city to its properties.

§ 71. The rights of the city in and to its water front, ferries, wharf property, land under water, public landings, wharves, docks, streets, avenues, parks, and all other public places are hereby declared to be inalienable.

Re-enacted by chap. 466, Laws of 1901.

§ 72. Every grant of or relating to a franchise of any character to any person or corporation must, unless otherwise provided in this act, be by ordinance of the board of aldermen or by resolution of the board of estimate and apportionment or a contract executed by or under the authority of the said board of estimate and apportionment, provided that every such ordinance, resolution or contract shall be subject to the provisions of this act with respect to approval by the mayor. But this section shall not apply to any franchise, right or contract authorized by the board of rapid transit railroad commissioners of The City of New York.

Thus amended by chap. 629, Laws of 1905.

§ 73. After the approval of this act no franchise or right to use the streets, avenues, waters, rivers, parkways or highways of the city shall be granted by any board or officer of The City of New York under the authority of this act to any person or corporation for a longer period than twenty-five years, except as herein provided, but such grant may, at the option of the city, provide for giving to the grantee the right on a fair revaluation or revaluations to renewals not exceeding in the aggregate twenty-five years. Nothing in the foregoing provisions of this section contained shall apply to consents granted to tunnel railroad corporations, nor shall anything in this section or in this title contained apply to grants made pursuant to the rapid transit act, chapter four of the laws of eighteen hundred and ninety-one or the acts amendatory thereof. The board of estimate and apportionment is hereby authorized, in its discretion to grant a franchise or right to any railroad corporation to use any of said streets, avenues, waters, rivers, parkways or highways in The City of New York for the construction and operation of a tunnel railroad underneath the surface thereof for any period not exceeding fifty years, and any such grant may at the option of the city provide for giving to the grantee the right, on a fair revaluation or revaluations, to renewals not exceeding in the aggregate twenty-five years, provided, however, that any grant to construct a tunnel railroad or renewal thereof, shall only be made after an agreement has been entered into by such a tunnel corporation to pay to The City of New York at least three per centum, of the net profits derived from the use of any tunnel which it shall construct, after there shall have first been retained by such company from such net profits a sum equal to five per centum upon the sum expended

22

to construct such tunnel. At the termination of any franchise or right granted by the board of estimate and apportionment all the rights or property of the grantee in the streets, avenues, waters, rivers, parkways and highways shall cease without compensation. Every such grant of a franchise and every contract made by the city in pursuance thereof may provide that upon the termination of the franchise or right granted by the board of estimate and apportionment the plant of the grantee with its appurtenances, shall thereupon be and become the property of the city without further or other compensation to the grantee; or such grant and contract may provide that upon such termination there shall be a fair valuation of the plant which shall be and become the property of the city on the termination of the contract on paying the grantee such valuation. If by virtue of the grant or contract the plant is to become the city's without money payment therefor, the city shall have the option either to take and operate the said property on its own account, or to lease the same for a term not exceeding twenty years. If the original grant shall provide that the city shall make payment for the plant and property, such payment shall be at a fair valuation of the same as property, excluding any value derived from the franchise; and if the city shall make payment for such plant it shall in that event have the option either to operate the plant and property on its own account or to lease the said plant and property and the right to the use of streets and public places in connection therewith for limited periods, in the same or similar manner as it leases the ferries and docks. Every grant shall make adequate provision by way of forfeiture of the grant, or otherwise, to secure efficiency of public service at reasonable rates and the maintenance of the property in good condition throughout the full term of the grant. The grant or contract shall also specify the mode of determining the valuation and revaluations therein provided for.

Thus amended by chap. 629, Laws of 1905.

§ 74. Before any grant of the franchise or right to use any
street, avenue, waterway, parkway, park, bridge, dock, wharf
highway or public ground or water within or belonging to the
city shall be made by the board of estimate and apportionment,
the proposed specific grant embodied in the form of a contract
with all of the terms and conditions, including the provisions as
to rates, fares and charges, and together with the form of the
resolution or resolutions for the granting of the same, shall be
entered in the minutes of the board of estimate and apportionment and after such entry shall be published at least twenty
days in the City Record and at least twice in two daily newspapers published in the city to be designated by the mayor at
the expense of the proposed grantee. The board of estimate
and apportionment shall, before authorizing any such contract
or adopting any such resolution, set a date or dates for a public
hearing thereon at which citizens shall be entitled to appear
and be heard. No such hearing shall be held however until
notice thereof shall have been published for at least ten days
immediately prior thereto in the City Record and at least twice
in two daily newspapers published in the city to be designated
by the mayor, at the expense of the proposed grantee, and the
said board of estimate and apportionment before authorizing
any such contract or adopting any such resolution shall make
inquiry as to the money value of the franchise or right proposed to be granted and the adequacy of the compensation proposed to be paid therefor, and publish the results of such inquiry
at least ten days in the City Record and at least twice in the
daily newspapers in which such form of contract shall be published. Every such contract or resolution shall be entered on
the minutes or record of such board of estimate and apportionment, and every contract or resolution containing or making
such grant shall require the concurrence of members of the
board of estimate and apportionment entitled as provided by
law to three-fourths of the total number of votes to which all

the members of the said board shall be entitled, and the votes shall be shown by the ayes and noes as recorded in the minutes of the board. Thirty days at least shall intervene between the introduction and final passage of any such resolution or authorization of such contract. The separate and additional approval of the mayor shall be necessary to the validity of every such contract or resolution. This act shall apply to any renewal or extension of the grant or leasing of the property to the same grantee or to others. Within five days after the adoption of any such resolution or any such authorization, a copy thereof, including the full text of the franchise, grant or contract, and duly attested by the clerk of the board of estimate and apportionment, shall be transmitted to each of the following: The comptroller, the corporation counsel, the city clerk and the board of rapid transit railroad commissioners of The City of New York, to be preserved by them among the archives of their departments or office. All such certified copies shall be deemed to be public records.

Thus amended by chap. 630, Laws of 1905, which provides that "All acts or parts of acts inconsistent with this act are hereby repealed." See chap. 629, Laws of 1905, amending this section.

§ 75. The board of aldermen may, from time to time, with respect to any grant which that board shall, under the authority of this act, have the exclusive power to make, pass appropriate ordinances, not inconsistent with the constitution and laws of the state, to carry the provisions of this title into effect, but shall not part with the right and duty at all times to exercise in the interest of the public, full municipal superintendence, regulation and control in respect of all matters connected with such grant, and not inconsistent with the terms thereof.

Thus amended by chap. 629, Laws of 1905.

City may dispose of buildings not required for public use.

§ 76. Nothing in this title contained shall prevent the city from disposing of any building or parcel of land no longer needed for public use, provided such disposition shall be approved by the sinking fund commissioners, and shall be at public sale, and be provided for by ordinance.

Re-enacted by chap. 466, Laws of 1901.

Acts not applicable to grants under this title.

§ 77. Section ninety-three of chapter five hundred and sixty-five of the laws of eighteen hundred and ninety and any acts amendatory thereof or supplemental thereto, shall have no application to grants made under and pursuant to this title.

Thus amended by chap. 466, Laws of 1901.

*   *   *   *   *   *   *   *   *   *

§ 242. The board of estimate and apportionment shall have power over the following subjects:

(1) To appropriate, from time to time, for the maintenance, improvement and extension of the system of water supply of the borough of Brooklyn, the moneys received from water rents in the said borough, subject, however, to the charges now imposed by law upon said revenues.

(2) To appropriate, from time to time, for the maintenance of the New York and Brooklyn bridge the moneys received from the revenues of said bridge.

The board of estimate and apportionment shall have also (3) the control of all the streets, avenues, highways, boulevards, concourses, driveways, bridges, tunnels, parks, parkways, waterways, docks, bulkheads, wharves, piers and all other public grounds and waters within or belonging to the city; except as in this act otherwise provided. The powers by this act granted to the board of aldermen with respect to the streets, avenues, highways, boulevards, concourses, driveways, bridges, tunnels, parks, parkways, docks, waterways, bulkheads, wharves, piers and public grounds and waters which are within or belong to the city shall be subject to such control of the board of estimate and apportionment. If and when the board of estimate and apportionment shall deem it proper in the case of any application or matter affecting any street, avenue, highway, boulevard, concourse, driveway, bridge, tunnel, park, parkway, waterway, dock, wharf, pier or public ground or water within or belonging to the city, whether the board of aldermen or any other department or officer shall have acted or omitted to act, the board of estimate and apportionment may itself originally act or may, by amendment, revision or repeal of any resolution, ordinance, grant or other action adopted or had by the board of aldermen or any other department or officer, exercise its said power of control; and if and when the board of estimate and apportionment shall so act or exercise such control, such action or control shall be fully and finally operative, notwithstanding any resolution, ordinance, grant or other action adopted or had by the board of aldermen or any other department or officer of the city or any omission to act on the part of the board of aldermen or other department or officer. The board of estimate and apportionment shall hereafter, except in the cases where franchises, rights or contracts shall be granted or authorized pursuant to the rapid transit act, chapter four of the laws of eighteen hundred and ninety-one, and the amendments thereof, have the exclusive power in behalf of the city to grant to persons or corporations franchises or rights or make contracts providing for or involving the occupatiou or use of any of the streets, avenues, highways, boulevards, concourses, driveways, bridges, tunnels, parks, parkways, waterways, docks, bulkheads, wharves, piers or public grounds or waters within or belonging to the city, whether on, under or over the surface thereof, for railroads, pipe or other conduits or ways or otherwise for the transportation of persons or property or the transmission of gas, electricity, steam, light, heat or power, provided, however, that no such exercise of power by the board of estimate and apportionment shall be operative until the same shall be in writing approved by the mayor separately from and after the action of the board of estimate and apportionment; and provided, further, that this section shall not prevent the exercise by the board of aldermen of the powers expressly granted it by sections forty-nine, fifty, fifty-one and fifty-two of this act; but such exercise of powers by the board of aldermen shall in every case be subject to the control by this act granted to the board of estimate and apportionment over all the streets, avenues, highways, boulevards, concourses, driveways, bridges, tunnels, parks, parkways, waterways, docks, bulkheads, wharves, piers and all public grounds and waters which are within or belong to the city. If and when the board of rapid transit railroad commissioners for The City of New York shall, under any of the provisions of chapter four of the laws of eighteen hundred and ninety-one, or of any of the acts amending the same, conclude or determine upon the construction of any rapid transit railway or railways or adopt any route or routes, plans or specifications therefor, or if and when the said board of rapid transit railroad commissioners shall grant any right or rights, franchise or franchises or enter into any contract or contracts under any of the provisions of the said chapter four of the said laws of eighteen hundred and ninety-one or any of the said amendments thereof, the said board shall transmit to the board of estimate and apportionment a copy of any and every such determination or conclusion, grant or contract, and in case any such determination, conclusion, route, plan, specification, right, franchise, or contract, shall require or involve the use of any street, avenue, highway, boulevard, concourse, driveway, bridge, tunnel, park, parkway, waterway, dock, bulkhead, wharf, pier or any public ground or water which is within or belongs to the city, the said board of estimate and apportionment shall within sixty days after the receipt by it of such copy of such determination, conclusion, grant or contract determine whether or not it will, as the local authority having the control of such street, avenue, highway, boulevard, concourse, driveway, bridge, tunnel, park, parkway, dock, waterway, bulkhead, wharf, pier or other public ground or water which is within or belongs to the city, consent or refuse to consent to such route, determination, conclusion, plan, specification, right, franchise or contract, and shall within such sixty days transmit in writing to the said board of rapid transit railroad commissioners its said determination whether of consent or refusal. Provided, however, that the said board of estimate and apportionment and the said board of rapid transit railroad commissioners may by resolution adopted by each of them extend such period of sixty days. Hereafter no consent or approval of any such determination, conclusion, route, plan, specification, right, franchise or contract by the board of aldermen or any department or officer of the city shall be necessary.

Thus amended by chap. 629, Laws of 1905; section 15 of said chapter is as follows:

(Chapter 629, Laws of 1905.) § 15. This act and all the amendments hereby made to the sections thereof hereby amended shall be applicable to every grant, franchise or contract heretofore made, authorized or issued by the said board of rapid transit railroad commissioners, but not yet consented to by the common council or board of aldermen of the city, as well as to all grants, franchises or contracts hereafter made, authorized or issued by the said board of rapid transit railroad commissioners.

* * * * * * * * * *

Stages and omnibuses; consents of property owners necessary before franchise granted.

§ 1458. No stage or omnibus route, or authority to run stages or omnibuses in The City of New York, shall hereafter be granted by the board of aldermen, unless a majority of the owners of property upon the streets, in or upon which any such route or privilege is to be operated, shall before the board of aldermen act on the subject, first consent in writing thereto.

Thus amended by chap. 466, Laws of 1901.

Application to mayor, etc.; before route established.

§ 1459. Before any route for the running of omnibuses or stages shall be established or allowed to be operated in said city, except as provided in this act, the application therefor shall be made in writing to the mayor of said city, specifying the route proposed to be established and the number of stages or omnibuses proposed to be run thereon; and unless the said mayor shall communicate such application to the board of aldermen with his approval thereof, and said board of aldermen after receiving such communication and approval shall vote in favor thereof by a three-fourths vote of all the members, no such route shall be established or operated; and upon such favorable action such route may be established and operated accordingly and the owner. ship thereof may be transferred.

Thus amended by chap. 466, Laws of 1901.

Stage route to be disposed of like other franchises.

§ 1460. Any stage route or privilege hereafter granted by the board of aldermen shall be disposed of in the manner provided by law for the disposition of the franchises of said city.
Thus amended by chap. 466, Laws of 1901.

Not to be run except in conformity with preceding sections or as hereinafter provided.

§ 1461. It shall not be lawful to run stages or omnibuses in The City of New York, as constituted by this act, except in con- formity with the preceding sections, and no stage route shall after April first, nineteen hundred and one, be established or operated upon that portion of any street, avenue, road or high- way in which a street surface railway or stage route is or shall be lawfully established, and in operation for a distance greater than one thousand feet, without first obtaining the consent of the corporation owning such railway or stage route, but nothing in this act shall be construed to affect the right possessed by any company to operate stage routes or extensions then established and in lawful operation, nor to affect any authority conferred upon any such company to acquire rights and privileges under chapter six hundred and fifty-seven of the laws of nineteen hun- dred, nor to affect any acts heretofore done thereunder.
Thus amended by chap. 466, Laws of 1901.
See section 163 Highway Law, section 23 Transportation Corporations Law, *ante;* chap. 538, Laws 1904, section 666 Penal Code, *post.*
See section 49 as to licensing of street cars, etc.; section 315 as to police at railroad stations; section 749 as to hose bridges over railway tracks during fires; subdivision 7, section 1069 as amended by chap. 542, Laws of 1904, as to contracts for transportation of school children; section 1456, until changed by board of aldermen, allows salt or saltpetre to be used upon curves, cross- ings or switches of railroad tracks for the purpose of dissolving snow or ice. See also other provisions of the act which apply to railroads.

CHAP. 411, LAWS OF 1897.

AN ACT to amend the executive law, relating to the fees to be paid for filing certain certificates of incorporation.

SECTION 1. Subdivision twelve of section twenty-six of chapter six hundred and eighty-three of the laws of eighteen hundred and ninety-two, entitled " An act in relation to executive officers, constituting chapter nine of the general laws," is hereby amended to read as follows:

12. For filing and recording the original certificate of incorporation of a railroad corporation for the construction of a railroad in a foreign country, fifty dollars; for filing the original certificates of every other railroad corporation, twenty-five dollars; for filing the original certificate of any other stock corporation, ten dollars; for filing any original certificate of incorporation drawn under article two of the membership corporations law ten dollars.

CHAP. 414, LAWS OF 1897.

AN ACT in relation to villages, constituting chapter twenty-one
of the general laws.

Short title.

SECTION 1. This chapter shall be known as the village law.

*   *   *   *   *   *   *   *   *   *

Franchises; filing; duty of clerk.

§ 82-a. Duplicate originals of every resolution, certificate or other instrument whereby a village, or any board or officer thereof, grants a franchise, including a privilege or consent of any kind, to a public service corporation shall be executed and deposited with the village clerk; and such franchise shall not be operative for any purpose until so executed and deposited. The village clerk, upon receiving the same, shall file one such duplicate in his office with the records and papers of the village and shall immediately cause the other to be filed in the office of the clerk of the county in which the village is situated.

Added by chap. 397, Laws of 1906.

*   *   *   *   *   *   *   *   *   *

Village ordinances.

§ 89. The board of trustees has power to enact, amend and repeal ordinances for the following purposes:

*   *   *   *   *   *   *   *   *   *

Blowing of steam.

7. To regulate or prevent the blowing of steam into, upon or over the streets.

*   *   *   *   *   *   *   *   *   *

Poles and wires; granting franchises.

9. To regulate the erection of telegraph, telephone or electric-light poles, or the stringing of wires in, over or upon the streets or public grounds, or upon, over or in front of any building or buildings; but after this section takes effect no franchise, or right, to erect or construct any line of poles or wires to furnish light or power within such village or to build, construct, erect or maintain any additional line of sewer, water or gas pipes, over, along, across, or under any of the streets, avenues, lanes or public grounds of such village shall be granted to any individual, firm, association, copartnership or corporation when such village owns and uses an electric-light plant or water-works; until the question of granting such right or franchise shall have been duly submitted to the qualified electors of such village, at an annual election, or at a special election duly called and held for that purpose, and adopted by a majority of the votes of duly qualified voters cast at such election.

Subdivision 9 thus amended by chap. 577, Laws of 1906.

Railroad crossings; speed.

10. To regulate the time during which cars, engines or trains may stand upon the street crossings of railroads; to regulate the speed of locomotives and cars, subject to the provisions of the railroad law, and by a two-thirds vote of all the members of the board, to require railroad companies to erect gates at cross-ings, to employ competent men to attend the same, and to employ competent flagmen at such crossings.

*   *   *   *   *   *   *   *   *   *

Improper noises.

18. To regulate or prevent the ringing of bells, blowing of horns and steam whistles, and the making of other improper noises in the village.

*   *   *   *   *   *   *   *   *   *

Collection of taxes by collector.

§ 115. Upon receiving the assessment-roll and warrant the collector shall cause a notice to be published at least once in the official paper, if any, and also in each other newspaper published in the village, and posted conspicuously in five public places in the village, stating that on six days specified therein, not less than nine nor more than twenty days after the publication and posting thereof, he will attend at a convenient place in the village, specified in the notice, for the purpose of receiving taxes. At least seven days before the first date fixed in such notice, the collector shall serve a copy thereof upon each corporation named in or subject to taxation upon the assessment-roll, and whose principal office is not in the village, by delivering such copy to a person designated by the corporation for that purpose by a written designation filed with the village clerk, or to any person in the village acting as the agent or representative in any capacity of such corporation. If there is no such designated person or agent in the village, service of such notice upon the corporation shall not be required. Any person or corporation paying taxes within twenty days from the date of the notice, shall be charged with one per centum thereon, and thereafter with five per centum, for the fees of the collector. If a notice is not served upon a corporation as herein required, the collector shall only be entitled to one per centum as his fees upon the taxes assessed against it. After the expiration of such twenty days the collector shall proceed to collect the taxes remaining unpaid, and for that purpose he possesses all the powers of a town collector. The laws relating to town collectors shall also, so far as consistent with this chapter, apply to the collection of village taxes.

*   *   *   *   *   *   *   *   *   *

Effect of determination.

§ 148. The determination by the board has the following effect:

1. If the petition for the laying out, alteration or widening of a street be granted, the board of trustees may acquire the land for such improvement by purchase or by proceedings under this article. But no street shall be laid out through a building or any fixtures or erections for the purposes of trade or manufacture, or any yard or enclosure necessary to be used for the enjoy-

ment thereof, without the consent of the owner, except upon the order of a justice of the supreme court residing in the judicial district in which the village or a part thereof is situated, to be granted upon an application by the board of trustees on a notice to the owner of not less than ten days.

* * * * * * * * * *

CHAP. 415, LAWS OF 1897.

AN ACT in relation to labor, constituting chapter thirty-two of the general laws.

ARTICLE I.

Short title.

SECTION 1. This chapter shall be known as the labor law.

Definitions.

§ 2. The term employee, when used in this chapter, means a mechanic, workingman or laborer who works for another for hire.

The person, employing any such mechanic, workingman or laborer, whether the owner, proprietor, agent, superintendent, foreman or other subordinate, is designated in this chapter as an employer. * * Whenever, in this chapter, authority is conferred upon the commissioner of labor, it shall also be deemed to include his assistant or a deputy acting under his direction.

Thus amended by chap. 550, Laws of 1904.

* * * * * * * * * *

Hours of labor on street surface and elevated railroads.

§ 5.. Ten consecutive hours' labor, including one-half hour for dinner shall constitute a day's labor in the operation of all street surface and elevated railroads, of whatever motive power, owned or operated by corporations in this state, whose main line of travel or whose routes lie principally within the corporate limits of cities of more than one hundred thousand inhabitants. No employe of any such corporation shall be permitted or allowed to work more than ten consecutive hours, including one-half hour for dinner, in any one day of twenty-four hours.

In cases of accident or unavoidable delay, extra labor may be performed for extra compensation.

*   *   *   *   *   *   *   *   *   *

Regulation of hours of labor on steam surface and elevated railroads.

§ 7. Ten hours labor, performed within twelve consecutive hours, shall constitute a legal day's labor in the operation of steam surface and elevated railroads owned and operated within this state, except where the mileage system of running trains is in operation. But this section does not apply to the performance of extra hours of labor by conductors, engineers, firemen and trainmen in case of accident or delay resulting therefrom. For each hour of labor performed in any one day in excess of such ten hours, by any such employe, he shall be paid in addition at least one-tenth of his daily compensation.

No person or corporation operating a line of railroad of thirty miles in length or over, in whole or in part within this state, shall permit or require a conductor, engineer, fireman or trainman, who has worked in any capacity for twenty-four consecutive hours, to go again on duty or perform any kind of work, until he has had at least eight hours' rest.

See chap. 711, Laws of 1892, *ante.*

Payment of wages by receivers.

§ 8. Upon the appointment of a receiver of a partnership or of a corporation organized under the laws of this state and doing business therein, other than a moneyed corporation, the wages of the employes of such partnership or corporation shall be preferred to every other debt or claim.

See section 5, Stock Corporation Law, section 30, Railroad Law, *ante,* and statutes cited.

Cash payment of wages.

§ 9. Every manufacturing, mining, quarrying, mercantile, railroad, street railway, canal, steamboat, telegraph and telephone company, every express company, and every water company, not municipal, and every person, firm or corporation, engaged in or upon any public work for the state or any municipal corporation thereof, either as a contractor or a subcontractor therewith, shall pay to each employee engaged in his, their or its business the wages earned by such employee in cash. No such company, person, firm or corporation shall hereafter pay such employees in script, commonly known as store money-orders. No person, firm or corporation engaged in carrying on public work under contract with the state or with any municipal corporation of the state, either as a contractor or subcontractor therewith, shall, directly or indirectly, conduct or carry on what is commonly known as a company store, if there shall, at the time be any store selling supplies, within two miles of the place where such contract is being executed. Any person, firm or corporation violating the provisions of this section shall be guilty of a misdemeanor.

Thus amended by chap. 316, Laws of 1906.

When wages are to be paid.

§ 10. Every corporation or joint stock association, or person carrying on the business thereof by lease or otherwise, shall pay weekly to each employe the wages earned by him to a day not more than six days prior to the date of such payment.

But every person or corporation operating a steam surface railroad shall, on or before the twentieth day of each month, pay the employes thereof the wages earned by them during the preceding calendar month.

Penalty for violation of preceding sections.

§ 11. If a corporation or joint stock association, its lessee or other person carrying on the business thereof, shall fail to pay the wages of an employe as provided in this article, it shall forfeit to the people of the state the sum of fifty dollars for each such failure, to be recovered by the factory inspector in his name of office in a civil action; but an action shall not be maintained therefor, unless the factory inspector shall have given to the employer at least ten days' written notice, that such an action will be brought if the wages due are not sooner paid as provided in this article.

On the trial of such action, such corporation or association shall not be allowed to set up any defense, other than a valid assignment of such wages, a valid set-off against the same, or the absence of such employe from his regular place of labor at the time of payment, or an actual tender to such employe at the time of the payment of the wages so earned by him, or a breach of contract by such employe or a denial of the employment.

Assignment of future wages.

§ 12. No assignment of future wages, payable weekly, or monthly in case of a steam surface railroad corporation, shall be valid if made to the corporation or association from which such wages are to become due, or to any person on its behalf, or if made or procured to be made to any person for the purpose of relieving such corporation or association from the obligation to pay weekly, or monthly in case of a steam surface railroad cor poration. Charges for groceries, provisions or clothing shall not be a valid off-set for wages in behalf of any such corporation or association.

No such corporation or association shall require any agree ment from any employe to accept wages at other periods than as provided in this article as a condition of employment.

*　　*　　*　　*　　*　　*　　*　　*　　*　　*

ARTICLE X.

STATE BOARD OF MEDIATION AND ARBITRATION.

Arbitration by the board.

§ 142. A grievance or dispute between an employer and his employes may be submitted to the board of arbitration and mediation for their determination and settlement. Such sub-

*Repealed by implication, see chap. 9, Laws of 1901, *post.*

mission shall be in writing, and contain a statement in detail of the grievance or dispute and the cause thereof, and also an agreement to abide the determination of the board, and during the investigation to continue in business or at work, without a lock-out or strike.

Upon such submission, the board shall examine the matter in controvery. For the purpose of such inquiry they may subpoena witnesses, compel their attendance and take and hear testimony. Witnesses shall be allowed the same fees as in courts of record. The decision of the board must be rendered within ten days after the completion of the investigation.

Mediation in case of strike or lock-out.

§ 143. Whenever a strike or lock-out occurs or is seriously threatened, the board shall proceed as soon as practicable to the locality thereof, and endeavor by mediation to effect an amicable settlement of the controversy. It may inquire into the cause thereof, and for that purpose has the same power as in the case of a controversy submitted to it for arbitration.

Decisions of board.

§ 144. Within ten days after the completion of every examination or investigation authorized by this article, the board or a majority thereof shall render a decision, stating such details as will clearly show the nature of the controversy and the points disposed of by them, and make a written report of their findings of fact and of their recommendations to each party to the controversy.

Every decision and report shall be filed in the office of the board and a copy thereof served upon each party to the controversy, and in case of a submission to arbitration, a copy shall be filed in the office of the clerk of the county or counties where the controversy arose.

Annual report.

§ 145. The board shall make an annual report to the legislature, and shall include therein such statements and explanations as will disclose the actual work of the board, the facts relating to each controversy considered by them and the decision thereon together with such suggestions as to legislation as may seem to them conducive to harmony in the relations of employers and employes.

Submission of controversies to local arbitrators.

§ 146. A grievance or dispute between an employer and his employes may be submitted to a board of arbitrators, consisting of three persóns, for hearing and settlement. When the employes concerned are members in good standing of a labor organization, which is represented by one or more delegates in a central body, one arbitrator may be appointed by such central body and one by the employer. The two so designated shall appoint a third, who shall be chairman of the board.

If the employes concerned in such grievance or dispute are members of good standing of a labor organization which is not represented in a central body, the organization of which they are members may select and designate one arbitrator. If such employes are not members of a labor organization, a majority thereof at a meeting duly called for that purpose, may designate one arbitrator for such board.

Consent; oath; powers of arbitrators.

§ 147. Before entering upon his duties, each arbitrator so selected shall sign a consent to act and take and subscribe an oath to faithfully and impartially discharge his duties as such arbitrator, which consent and oath shall be filed in the clerk's office of the county or counties where the controversy arose. When such board is ready for the transaction of business, it shall select one of its members to act as secretary, and notice of the time and place of hearing shall be given to the parties to the controversy.

The board may, through its chairman subpoena witnesses, compel their attendance and take and hear testimony.

The board may make and enforce rules for its government and the transaction of the business before it, and fix its sessions and adjournments.

Decision of arbitrators.

§ 148. The board shall, within ten days after the close of the hearing, render a written decision signed by them giving such details as clearly show the nature of the controversy and the questions decided by them. Such decision shall be a settlement of the matter submitted to such arbitrators, unless within ten days thereafter an appeal is taken therefrom to the state board of mediation and arbitration.

One copy of the decision shall be filed in the office of the clerk of the county or counties where the controversy arose and one copy shall be transmitted to the secretary of the state board of mediation and arbitration.

Appeals.

§ 149. The state board of mediation and arbitration shall hear, consider and investigate every appeal to it from any such board of local arbitrators and its decisions shall be in writing and a copy thereof filed in the clerk's office of the county or counties where the controversy arose and duplicate copies served upon each party to the controversy. Such decision shall be final and conclusive upon all parties to the arbitration.

*   *   *   *   *   *   *   *   *   H

See sections of the Penal Code, *post.*

CHAP. 418, LAWS OF 1897.

AN ACT in relation to liens, constituting chapter forty-nine of the general laws.

*   *   *   *   *   *   *   *   *   *

Liens for labor on railroads.

§ 6. Any person who shall hereafter perform any labor for a railroad corporation shall have a lien for the value of such labor upon the railroad track, rolling-stock and appurtenances of such railroad corporation and upon the land upon which such railroad track and appurtenances are situated, by filing a notice of such lien in the office of the clerk of any county wherein any part of such railroad is situated, to the extent of the right, title and interest of such corporation in such property, existing at the time of such filing. The provisions of this article relating to the contents, filing and entry of a notice of a mechanic's lien, and the priority and duration thereof, shall apply to such liens. A copy of the notice of such lien shall be personally served upon such corporation within ten days after the filing thereof in the manner prescribed by the code of civil procedure for the service of summons in actions in justices' courts against domestic railroad corporations.

*   *   *   *   *   *   *   *   *   *

Conditional sale of railroad equipment and rolling stock.

§ 111. Whenever any railroad equipment and rolling stock is sold, leased or loaned under a contract which provides that the title to such property, notwithstanding the use and possession thereof by the vendee, lessee or bailee, shall remain in the vendor, lessor or bailor, until the terms of the contract as to the payment of installments, amounts or rentals payable, or the performance of other obligations thereunder, are fully complied with and that title to such property shall pass to the vendee, lessee or other bailee on full payment therefor, such contract shall be invalid as to any subsequent judgment creditor of or purchaser from such vendee, lessee or bailee for a valuable consideration, without notice, unless

1. Such contract is in writing, duly acknowledged and recorded in the book in which real estate mortgages are recorded in the office of the county clerk or register of the county in which is located the principal office or place of business of such vendee, lessee or bailee; and unless

2. Each locomotive or car so sold, leased or loaned, has the name of the vendor, lessor or bailor, or of the assignee of such vendor, lessor or bailor, plainly marked upon both sides thereof, followed by the word owner, lessor, bailor or assignee, as the case may be.

See sections 48, 54 and 55, Stock Corporation Law; section 30, Railroad Law; chap. 392, Laws of 1875, section 8, Labor Law, *ante;* chap. 419, Laws of 1897, *post.*

Other provisions of the Lien Law apply to railroads. See sections 3398, 3441 of the Code of Civil Procedure, relating to the enforcement of mechanics' liens and liens on vessels; it is deemed advisable to publish but one of them here, as follows:

CHAP. 419, LAWS OF 1897.

AN ACT to amend the code of civil procedure, relating to the enforcement of mechanics' liens on real property and liens on vessels.

*   *   *   *   *   *   *   *   *   *

Judgment in actions to foreclose a mechanic's lien on property of a railroad corporation.

§ 3419. If the lien is for labor done or materials furnished for a railroad corporation, upon its land, or upon or for its track, rolling stock or the appurtenances of its railroad, the judgment shall not direct the sale of any of the real property described in the notice of the lien, but when in such case, a judgment is entered and docketed with the county clerk of the county where the notice of lien is filed, or a transcript thereof is filed and docketed in any other county, it shall be a lien upon the real property of the railroad corporation, against which it is obtained, to the same extent, and enforcible in like manner as other judgments of courts of record against such corporation.

*   *   *   *   *   *   *   *   *   *

See sections 48, 54 and 55, Stock Corporation Law; section 30, Railroad Law; chap. 392, Laws of 1875; section 8, Labor Law; chap. 418, Laws of 1897, *ante.*

CHAP. 592, LAWS OF 1897.

AN ACT in relation to navigation, constituting chapter thirty of the general laws.

*   *   *   *   *   *   *   *   *   *

Lights upon swing-bridges.

§ 40. Every corporation, company or individual, owning, maintaining or operating a swing-bridge across the Hudson river shall, during the season of navigation between sundown and sunrise keep and maintain the following lights: Upon every swing-bridge with water on each side of pivot pier, eight lights, located as follows: One red light on or over the north and one on or over the south end of the east rest piers; one red light on or over the north and one on or over the south end of the west

rest pier, and a green light on each corner of the bridge when
open. If there is a waterway on only one side of the pivot pier,
five lights, located as follows: One red light on or over the
north and one on or over the south end of the rest pier nearest
the channel, and a green light upon each end of the bridge when
open upon the corners nearest the channel. Such lights shall
be of the usual brilliancy of lights used for such purposes and
known as signal lanterns.

See section 433a, Penal Code, *post*.

CHAP. 612, LAWS OF 1897.
NEGOTIABLE INSTRUMENT LAW.

(This act contains general provisions affecting railroads, but it is not
thought necessary to print portions of it here.)

*CHAP. 663, LAWS OF 1897.

AN ACT providing for and regulating the carriage of passen
gers across the New York and Brooklyn bridge and affecting
the rates of fare therefor.

SECTION 1. The trustees of the New York and Brooklyn bridge
are hereby authorized and empowered to abolish all fares upon
the railroadways of the said bridge, save and except as herein
after provided.

§ 2. The said trustees may continue to maintain and to operate the present railroad on said bridge and to charge such fares
for the carriage of passengers thereon as they may deem fit, but
not, however, in excess of the present rate.

§ 3. And the said trustees are hereby authorized and empowered to contract with any street surface or elevated railroad corporation or corporations, operating its or their roads in either
the city of New York or the city of Brooklyn, respectively permitting its or their carriage of passengers across the said bridge,
but each and every contract therefor must provide that said
corporation will not charge any fare in excess of, or additional
to, the fare exacted by it from any passenger for one continuous
ride upon any of its routes in either of the cities of New York

---

*While this is not a general act, it is deemed of enough importance to
print here.

or Brooklyn, as the case may be, so that the said route of said corporation or corporations operated across said bridge under said contract, so far as the exaction of a fare is concerned, shall be taken and deemed to be a part of the continuous route or one of the continuous routes of said railroad corporation or corporations whereon one fare is exacted, so that no extra or additional fare shall be exacted by any such street surface or elevated railroad corporation from any passenger carried to or from the bridge and across the bridge in addition to the fare exacted from such passenger for carriage to and from the bridge only, but nothing in this act shall be construed as preventing the said trustees from making a proper charge to any railroad corporation for each car crossing said bridge.

§ 4. Within sixty days after the passage of this act, the said trustees shall prepare plans and specifications regulating the operation over said bridge of the cars of such corporation or corporations with whom it may contract, as such trustees shall deem best adapted to promote the public comfort and convenience and to subserve the purposes for which said bridge was constructed, and, except as otherwise provided by said trustees, such plans and specifications shall be in substantial conformity with the plans recommended to the said trustees by Virgil G. Bogue, George H. Thompson and Leffert L. Buck, expert engineers, by their report bearing date February eighth, eighteen hundred and ninety-seven. And said trustees shall also prepare such form of contracts and specifications thereunder as they shall deem best fitted for the public interests, regulating the operation of the said cars of the said corporation or corporations and the establishment of its route or their route upon said bridge, and shall have power to exact such bond or obligation as they may deem proper for the faithful performance of any contract or contracts made with any and all of said corporations, as aforesaid.

§ 5. All acts and parts of acts inconsistent with this act are hereby repealed.

See chap. 712, Laws of 1901, *post.*

*CHAP. 683, LAWS OF 1897.

AN ACT to regulate the exercise of their franchises by certain public corporations by requiring them to afford facilities for the transaction of the public business to certain public officers and employes of the city of New York.

SECTION 1. The mayor of the city of New York may issue under the seal of his office to each policeman and fireman appointed by the duly constituted authorities of said city a certificate of the appointment and qualification of such police man or fireman as such, and specifying the duration of his term of office; and it shall be thereupon the duty of every street sur face, elevated railroad or railroad company operating cars by steam or electricity and carrying on business within said city to transport every such policeman or fireman free of charge while he is traveling in the course of the performance of the duties of his office within said city limits. Every telegraphic or telephone company engaged in business within such city or† vil lage, shall afford to such policeman or fireman the use of its telegraph lines or telephones for the purpose of making and receiving reports and communications in the course of the per formance of his official duty.

§ 2. Every policeman or fireman who shall permit any other person to use the certificate issued to him as provided by this act, or to present or make use of the same, except while acting in the course of the performance of his official duties, or who shall use such certificate after the expiration of his term of office or his resignation or removal therefrom, shall be deemed guilty of a misdemeanor.

See chap. 417, Laws of 1895, *ante.*
See Wilson v. United Traction Company, 72 Appellate Division, p. 233.

CHAP. 115, LAWS OF 1898.

AN ACT to provide for the improvement of the public highways.

*　　*　　*　　*　　*　　*　　*　　*　　*　　*

§ 4. If he shall approve such resolution, such state engineer shall cause the highway or section thereof therein described to

---

*While this is not a general act, it is deemed of enough importance to print here.
†So in original.

be mapped both in outline and profile. He shall indicate how much of such highway or section thereof may be improved by deviation from the existing lines whenever it shall be deemed of advantage to obtain a shorter or more direct road without lessening its usefulness or wherever such deviation is of advantage by reason of lessened gradients. And if the boundaries of the proposed improved highway shall deviate from the existing highway the board of supervisors must make provision for securing the requisite right of way as provided by law and the cost and expenses of procuring such right of way shall be taken into consideration and paid for by the comptroller as a part of the cost of such improvement. Whenever practicable the state engineer shall provide for the abolition of railroad grade crossings of an improved highway under and pursuant to the provisions of sections sixty to sixty-nine of the railroad law; he may provide for the widening of an existing highway; and he may include as a part of the work necessary culverts, drains, ditches, waterways, embankments and retaining walls, and whenever in the construction of any such improved highway it may be necessary as an incident to the proper construction and maintenance thereof to open or maintain ditches or drains upon adjacent lands for the purpose of properly draining such highway the owner of adjacent lands shall be compensated for the amount of damages, if any, sustained by said owner in consequence of the entry upon his lands and construction of the drains hereby authorized as provided in the highway law and the amount of such damages shall be taken into consideration and paid by the comptroller as part of the cost of such improvement; and said state engineer shall have the power within the boundary of the highways to remove or to plant trees for the preservation of said highways and to erect suitable signboards. He shall also cause plans and specifications of such highway or section thereof to be thus improved to be made for telford, macadam or gravel roadway or other suitable construction, taking into consideration climate, soil and materials to be had in the vicinity thereof and the extent and nature of the traffic likely to be upon such highway, specifying in his judgment the kind of road a wise economy demands. The improved or permanent roadway of all highways so improved shall not be less than eight feet nor more than sixteen feet in width unless for special reasons to be stated by such state engineer it is required that it shall be of greater width.

Thus amended by chap. 468, Laws of 1906.

*　　*　　*　　*　　*　　*　　*　　*　　*　　*

§ 19. No street surface railroad shall be constructed upon a portion of a highway, which portion has been or may be hereafter improved under the provisions of this act and the acts amendatory thereof and supplemental thereto, except upon the consent of, and under such conditions and regulations as may be prescribed by the state engineer and surveyor.

Added by chap. 379, Laws of 1902.
See sections 60-69, and section 91, Railroad Law, *ante;* chap. 164, Laws of 1902, *post.*

CHAP. 182, LAWS OF 1898.

AN ACT for the government of cities of the second class.

*　　*　　*　　*　　*　　*　　*　　*　　*　　*

§ 19. No ordinance shall be passed by the common council on the same day in which it is introduced, except by unanimous consent, and no appropriation of money shall be made for any purpose, except by an ordinance, passed by a majority of all the members, specifying by items the amount thereof and the department or specific purpose for which the appropriation is made; and no ordinance shall be passed making or authorizing a sale or lease of city real estate or of any franchise belonging to or under the control of the city, except by a vote of three-fourths of all the members of the common council; and in case of the proposed sale of real estate or the proposed sale or proposed lease of a franchise, except as hereinafter provided, the ordinance must provide for a disposition, under proper regulations for the protection of the city, at public auction, after public notice for at least three weeks, to the highest bidder; and a proposed sale or proposed lease thus originated shall not be valid nor take effect, unless the aforesaid notice shall have been given and the aforesaid disposition, namely, a sale at public auction to the highest bidder shall have been had, and unless subsequently approved by a resolution of the board of estimate and apportionment. No such franchise shall be granted or be operated for a period longer than fifty years. The common council may, however, grant to the owner or lessees of an existing franchise, under which operations are being actually carried on, such additional rights or extensions, in the street or streets in which the said franchise now exists, upon such terms as the interests of the city may require, with or without sale and advertisement, as said common council may determine; provided, however, that no such grant shall be operative unless subsequently approved by resolution of the board of estimate and apportionment, and also by the mayor.

Thus amended by chap. 52, Laws of 1906:

*   *   *   *   *   *   *   *   *   *

§ 150. When a street has once been established, graded, paved, flagged and curbed at the expense of the owners of property deemed to be benefited thereby, every expense thereafter of keeping the street between the sidewalks in repair and clean shall be borne wholly by the city, except that it shall be the duty of all railroad companies to cause that part of the streets throughout the city upon which their tracks are laid, lying between the outer rails of the tracks and for two feet on either side thereof, to be kept in repair under the direction of the commissioner of public works.

*   *   *   *   *   *   *   *   *   *

Other provisions of this act apply to railroad companies. See sections 91, 93 and 98, Railroad Law, *ante.*

See chap. 473, Laws of 1906, *post.*

CHAP. 217, LAWS OF 1898.

AN ACT to carry into effect the provisions of chapter seven hundred and fifty-four of the laws of eighteen hundred and ninety-seven, entitled "An act to amend the railroad law and the acts amendatory thereof, relative to grade crossings," and making an appropriation therefor.

SECTION 1. The sum of one hundred thousand dollars is hereby appropriated out of any moneys in the treasury not otherwise appropriated to carry into effect the provisions of chapter seven hundred and fifty-four of the laws of eighteen

hundred and ninety-seven, entitled "An act to amend the railroad law and the acts amendatory thereof, relative to grade
crossings."

§ 2. The board of railroad commissioners is hereby authorized and empowered to expend an amount not exceeding ten
thousand dollars in the employment of expert and clerical service necessary to supervise the work performed under the said
chapter seven hundred and fifty-four of the laws of eighteen
hundred and ninety-seven, and to prepare plans, maps and specifications therefor; said ten thousand dollars to be paid by the
treasurer upon the warrant of the comptroller, as directed by
the said board of railroad commissioners, from the money appropriated by this act.

CHAP. 263, LAWS OF 1898.

AN ACT for the relief of certain railroad corporations.

SECTION 1. Any railroad corporation that was duly incorporated after the year eighteen hundred and eighty-five, under
the provisions of chapter one hundred and forty, of the laws of
eighteen hundred and fifty, and the acts amendatory thereof,
and that within two years after its certificate of incorporation
was filed, began the construction of its road and expended five
hundred thousand dollars thereon, but failed to finish its road
and put it in operation within ten years from the time of filing
such certificate, shall be entitled to, and have all the rights and
be subject to all the obligations intended or provided by the
next section of this act.

§ 2. Any such company or corporation may finish its road
and put it in operation; and the rights, powers, privileges, franchises, obligations, duties, restrictions and limitations of any
such corporation shall be as though the time heretofore provided by law to finish its road and put it in operation, had been
fifteen years from the date of filing its certificate of incorporation; and all rights or franchises acquired by any such corporation to construct its road in, upon, along or across any street or
highway, and all proceedings to locate or extend its route or
change its termini, or acquire any franchise, and all liens or
obligations against any such corporation are hereby expressly
conferred, imposed and continued to the same effect as though

the time for finishing its road had been fifteen years as aforesaid. This act shall not apply to any street railroad, whether
surface, elevated or depressed, nor to any railroad more than
twenty miles in length.

See chap. 495, Laws of 1898, and chapters 597 and 626, Laws of 1903,
post; section 5 and other provisions of the Railroad Law, ante;

CHAP. 491, LAWS OF 1898.

AN ACT to amend chapter three hundred and thirty-eight, laws
of eighteen hundred and ninety-three, entitled " An act in relation to agriculture, constituting articles one, two, three, four
and five of chapter thirty-three of the general laws," in relation
to sale and transportation of calves.

SECTION 1.   Chapter three hundred and thirty-eight, laws of
eighteen hundred and ninety-three, entitled " An act in relation
to agriculture, constituting articles one, two, three, four, five,
six and seven of chapter thirty-three of the general laws," is
hereby amended by adding the following sections, to be known
as section seventy-one, seventy-two and seventy-three.

§ 71.   No person shall slaughter, for the purpose of selling the
same for food, or expose for sale or sell within this state, or
bring or cause to be brought into any city, town or village within
this state for food any calf or carcass of the same, or any part
thereof except the hide, unless it is in good, healthy condition,
and was at least four weeks of age at the time of killing.   Any
person or persons duly authorized by the commissioner of agriculture, may examine any calf or veal found within this state
offered or exposed for sale, or kept with intent to sell as food,
and if, such calf is under four weeks of age, or the veal is from
a calf killed under four weeks of age, or from a calf in an
unhealthy condition when so killed, he may seize the same and
cause it to be destroyed or disposed of in such manner as to make
it impossible to be thereafter used as food.

§ 72.   On and after the passage of this act it shall be unlawful
for any corporation, partnership, person or persons to ship to or
from any part of this state any carcass or carcasses of a calf or
calves or any part of such carcass except the hide, unless they
shall attach to every carcass or part thereof so shipped in a
conspicuous place a tag, that shall stay thereon during such

transportation, stating the name or names of the person or persons who raised the calf, the name of the shipper, the points of shipping and the destination and the age of the calf.

§ 73. On and after the passage of this act, no railroad company, express company, steamboat company, or other common carrier, shall carry or receive for transportation any carcass or carcasses of calves, or any part of the same except the hide, unless the said carcass or carcasses or parts thereof shall be tagged as herein provided.

See sections 70-e, 70-f and 70-g, Agricultural Law, *ante*.

CHAP. 495, LAWS OF 1898.

AN ACT to extend the time for the commencement of construction or the completion of railroads that have been placed in the hands of receivers by the supreme court.

SECTION 1. All railroad corporations that have been organized under the laws of this state, and have been placed in the hands of a receiver or receivers by the supreme court of this state, and that are now in the hands of such receiver or receivers, are hereby granted five years from and after the passage of this act within which to complete their said roads, and the charter or charters of such companies shall not be deemed or taken as forfeited by their failure to complete their said roads within the time originally limited in the general laws of this state for the completion of such roads. And the said companies are hereby authorized to proceed and build their said roads and complete the same within five years after the passage of this act, and the corporate powers and rights shall not be deemed or held to have ceased by reason of lapse of time or by reason of the appointment of such a receiver or receivers.

See chap. 203, Laws of 1898, section 5 and other provisions of the Railroad Law, *ante*, and chapters 597 and 626, Laws of 1903, *post*.

CHAP. 522, LAWS OF 1898.

AN ACT to authorize and empower receivers of corporations appointed by a judgment or order in an action or special proceeding to sell the property of the corporation at private sale.

SECTION 1. A receiver duly appointed in this state by and pursuant to a judgment in an action, or by and pursuant to an order in a special proceeding, may, upon application to the court by which such judgment was rendered, or such order was made, and upon notice to such parties as may be entitled to notice of applications made in such action or special proceedings, be authorized by the said court to sell or convey the property, whether real or personal, of the corporation of which he is the receiver, at private sale, upon such terms and conditions as the court may direct.

§ 2.   All sales of the property of a corporation heretofore made at private sale by such a receiver, and conveyances thereof, where such sales or conveyances have been authorized or directed by the court having jurisdiction of the action or special proceeding in which such receiver was appointed, are hereby ratified and confirmed in so far as the legal capacity and statutory power of the receiver to make the same are concerned.

See chap. 378, Laws of 1883; chap. 285, Laws of 1884; chap. 310, Laws of 1886, and sections 5, Stock Corporation Law and 76, Railroad Law, *ante;* and chap. 534, Laws of 1898, and chap. 404, Laws of 1902, *post.*

CHAP. 534, LAWS OF 1898.

AN ACT to facilitate the collection and recovery of the assets of corporations for which receivers have been appointed.

Section 1.   Whenever any receiver of a domestic corporation, or of the property within this state of any foreign corporation, shall have been appointed and qualified, as provided in title two of chapter fifteen, or title eleven of chapter seventeen, of the code of civil procedure, either before, upon, or after final judgment or order in the action or special proceeding in which such appointment was made, shall, by his own verified petition, affidavit or other competent proof, show to the supreme court, at a special term thereof, held within the judicial district wherein such appointment was made, that he has good reason to believe that any officer, stockholder, agent or employe of such corporation, or any other person whomsoever, has embezzled or concealed, or withholds or has in his possession. or under his control, or has wrongfully disposed of, any property of such corporation which of right ought to be surrendered to the receiver thereof; or that any person can testify concerning the embezzlement, concealment, withholding, possession, control or wrongful disposition of any such property, the court shall make an order, with or without notice, commanding such person or persons to appear at a time and place to be designated in the order, before the court or before a referee named by the court for that purpose, and to submit to an examination concerning such embezzlement, concealment, withholding, possession, control or wrongful disposition of such property; and at the time of making such order or at any time thereafter, the court may, in its discretion, enjoin and restrain the person or persons so ordered to appear and be examined from in any manner disposing of any property of such corporation which may be in the possession or under the control of the person so ordered to be examined, until the further order of the court in relation thereto. No person so ordered to appear and be examined shall be excused from answering any question on the ground that his answer might tend to convict him of a criminal offense; but his testimony taken upon such examination shall not be used against him in any criminal action or proceeding.

§ 2. Any person so ordered to appear and be examined shall be entitled to the same fees and mileage, to be paid at the time of serving the order, as are allowed by law to witnesses subpoenaed to attend and testify in an action in the supreme court, and shall be subject to the same penalties upon failure to appear and testify in obedience to such an order as are provided by law in the case of witnesses who fail to obey a subpoena to appear and testify in an action.

§ 3. Any person appearing for examination in obedience to such order shall be sworn by the court or referee to tell the truth, and shall be entitled to be represented on such examination by counsel, and may be cross-examined, or may make any voluntary statement in his own behalf concerning the subject of his examination which may seem to him desirable or pertinent thereto.

§ 4. The court before which such examination is taken, as well as the referee, if one be appointed for that purpose, shall have power to adjourn such examination from time to time, and may rule upon any question or objection arising in the course of such examination, to the same extent that might be done if the person so examined were testifying as a witness in the trial of an action.

§ 5. When the examination of any person under such order shall be concluded, the testimony shall be signed and sworn to by the person so examined, and shall be filed in the office of the clerk of the county where the action is pending, or was tried, in which the receiver was appointed; and if from such testimony it shall appear to the satisfaction of the court that any person so examined is wrongfully concealing or withholding, or has in his possession or under his control, any property which of right belongs to such receiver, the court may make an order commanding the person so examined forthwith to deliver the same to such receiver, who shall hold the same subject to the further order of the court in relation thereto; and otherwise, the court may, at the conclusion of any such examination, make such final order in the premises as the interests of justice require.

See chap. 378, Laws of 1883; chap. 285, Laws of 1884; chap. 310, Laws of 1886; chap. 522, Laws of 1898; and sections 5, Stock Corporation Law, and 76, Railroad Law, *ante;* and chap. 404, Laws of 1902, *post.*

CHAP. 574, LAWS OF 1898.

AN ACT to amend the code of civil procedure, section one hundred and ninety-one, relative to appeals to the court of appeals.

SECTION 1. Section one hundred and ninety-one of the code of civil procedure is hereby amended so as to read as follows:
Limitations, exceptions and conditions.

§ 191. The jurisdiction conferred by the last section is subject to the following limitations, exceptions and conditions:

1. No appeal shall be taken to said court, in any civil action or proceeding commenced in any court other than the supreme court, court of claims, county court, or a surrogate's court, unless

24

the appellate division of the supreme court allows the appeal by an order made at the term which rendered the deter mination, or at the next term after judgment is entered there upon and shall certify that in its opinion a question of law is involved which ought to be reviewed by the court of appeals.

2. No appeal shall be taken to said court from a judgment of affirmance hereafter rendered in an action to recover damages for a personal injury, or to recover damages for injuries resulting in death, or in an action to set aside a judgment, sale, transfer, conveyance, assignment or written instrument, as in fraud of the rights of creditors, or in an action to recover wages, salary or compensation for services, including expenses incidental thereto, or damages for breach of any contract therefor, or in an action upon an individual bond or individual undertaking on appeal, when the decision of the appellate division of the supreme court is unanimous, unless such appellate division shall certify that in its opinion a question of law is involved which ought to be reviewed by the court of appeals, or unless in case of its refusal to so certify, an appeal is allowed by a judge of the court of appeals.

Subdivision 2 thus amended by chap. 592, Laws of 1900, taking effect September 1, 1900.

3. The jurisdiction of the court is limited to a review of questions of law.

4. No unanimous decision of the appellate division of the supreme court that there is evidence supporting or tending to sus· tain a finding of fact or a verdict not directed by the court, shall be reviewed by the court of appeals.

CHAP. 597, LAWS OF 1898.

AN ACT to provide for a change of motive power in the opera· tion of certain railways in and near public parks in the cities of the state of New York.

Section 1. Any railroad company having the right to use any railway now constructed in any public tunnel, road or way depressed below the surface of and wholly within any public park

in any city within the state of New York having a population
of one million five hundred thousand or upwards, may change
the motive power and operate any such railway by cable power,
underground current of electricity, compressed air, or any other
motive power other than locomotive steam power, that may be
consented to by the authorities having control of such park or
parks, and by the board of railroad commissioners of the state
of New York, and may make changes in the construction of the
road or roadbed or other property made necessary by the change
of motive power. Such reconstruction shall be at the sole cost
and expense of the railroad company making such change, and
when completed such improved railway shall be the property
of the municipal corporation having control of such public tunnel,
road or depressed way.

See section 100, Railroad Law, *ante.*

CHAP. 201, LAWS OF 1899.

AN ACT to facilitate the proving of the incorporation of new
   corporations formed by the consolidation of two or more corporations.

SECTION 1. Where two or more corporations have been or shall
hereafter be, consolidated and merged into a new corporation,
a certificate of the secretary of state under his official seal concisely stating the names of the respective corporations consolidated, the dates of the filing of the certificates respectively of
the incorporation of such corporations in his office, the object
for which they were formed, including the nature and locality
of their business as set forth in their respective incorporation
papers on file in his office, the date of the filing of the consolidation agreement and other proceedings in his office, the name of
the new corporation formed by such consolidation and merger,
the term of its incorporate existence, the place where its principal office is situated and the amount of its capital stock, shall
be presumptive and prima facie evidence in all actions and
special proceedings for all purposes of the incorporation of the
corporations so consolidated, the incorporation of the new cor-

poration by such consolidation and merger from the date of filing of said consolidation agreement and proceedings, and of the other facts so certified by him.

See section 70 *et seq.*, Railroad Law, and chap. 193, Laws of 1897, *ante;* chap. 30, Laws of 1903, *post.*

CHAP. 320, LAWS OF 1899.

AN ACT to amend section three hundred and forty-one of the code of civil procedure, relating to jurisdiction of county courts.

SECTION 1. Section three hundred and forty-one of the code of civil procedure is hereby amended so as to read as follows:

§ 341. For the purpose of determining the jurisdiction of a county court, in either of the cases specified in the last section, a domestic corporation or joint-stock association, whose principal place of business is established, by or pursuant to a statute, or by its articles of association, or is actually located within the county, or in case of a railroad corporation where any portion of the road operated by it is within the county, it is deemed a resident of the county; and personal service of a summons, made within the county, as prescribed in this act, or personal service of a mandate, whereby a special proceeding is commenced, made within the county, as prescribed in this act for personal service of a summons, is sufficient service thereof upon a domestic corporation wherever it is located.

§ 2. This act shall take effect September first, eighteen hundred and ninety-nine.

CHAP. 488, LAWS OF 1899.

AN ACT authorizing the sale of property left in street surface railroad cars, and the disposition of the proceeds thereof.

SECTION 1. It shall be the duty of every street surface railway corporation doing business in this state, which shall have unclaimed property left in its cars, to ascertain if possible, the owner or owners of such property, and to notify such owner or owners of the fact by mail as soon as possible, after such property comes into its possession. Every such corporation which shall have such property not perishable, in its possession for the period of three months, may sell the same at public auction, after giving notice to that effect, by one publication, at least ten days prior to the sale, in a daily newspaper published in the city or village in which such sale is to take place, of the time and place at which such sale will be held, and such sale may be adjourned from time to time until all the articles offered for sale are sold. All perishable property so left, may be sold by any such street surface railroad corporation without notice, as soon as it can be, upon the best terms that can be obtained.

§ 2. All moneys arising from the sale of any such unclaimed property, after deducting charges for storage and expenses of sale, shall be paid by any such corporation to the treasurer of any association, composed of the employees of such street railroad corporation, having for its object the pecuniary assistance of its members in case of disability caused by sickness or accident, for the use and benefit of such association and its members; and where no such association of the employees of any such street railroad corporation is in existence at the time of any such sale, such moneys shall be paid over to the county treasurer of the county in which such sale took place for the benefit of such county.

See section 46, Railroad Law, *ante;* chap. 313, Laws of 1901, *post.*

CHAP. 497, LAWS OF 1899.

AN ACT to regulate the use of lands forming part of the right of way of any railroad company, the road of which has been removed from the surface in, or adjacent to, streets and highways in all cities of the first class in this state.

SECTION 1. Whenever the right of way, grade or tracks of any steam railroad company in or adjacent to any street or highway in any city of the first class are required by law to be changed or altered by elevating or depressing the same for the purpose of discontinuing the use of steam power upon the surface of such highway or street, such alteration or change of grade shall not be deemed to curtail or affect any right which such railroad company or its lessees or assigns may have to main tain and operate a surface passenger railway within the limits of the right of way so depressed or elevated, and over and under the railroad tracks so depressed or elevated, with all turnouts, sidings and tracks necessary to secure the continuous connection and operation of such surface railroad.

§ 2. In the event that any such turnouts, sidings or tracks shall extend beyond the lines of the right of way of such railroad corporations so depressed or elevated, in or upon any of the streets or highways aforesaid, such turnouts, sidings or tracks so extending beyond the lines of such right of way shall only be constructed upon condition that the consent of the owners of one-half in value of the property bounded on, and the consent also of the local authorities having the control of that portion of such street or highway upon which it is proposed to construct or operate such turnouts, sidings or tracks, shall be first obtained; or, in case the consent of such property owners cannot be obtained, the appellate division of the supreme court in the department where such construction is proposed, may upon application appoint three commissioners who shall determine, after a hearing of all parties interested, whether such turnouts, sidings and tracks so extending beyond the limits of such right of way and on said highway ought to be constructed or operated; and their determination, confirmed by the court, may be taken in lieu of the consent of the property owners.

§ 3. Any such surface railroad shall be operated by some power other than steam locomotives, and shall not be used except for passenger traffic.

CHAP. 690, LAWS OF 1899.

AN ACT to prevent monopolies in articles or commodities of common use, and to prohibit restraints of trade and commerce, providing penalties for violations of the provisions of this act, and procedure to enable the attorney-general to secure testimony in relation thereto.

SECTION 1. Every contract, agreement, arrangement or combination whereby a monopoly in the manufacture, production or sale in this state of any article or commodity of common use is or may be created, established or maintained, or whereby com. petition in this state in the supply or price of any such article or commodity is or may be restrained or prevented, or whereby for the purpose of creating, establishing or maintaining a monopoly within this state of the manufacture, production or sale of any such article or commodity, the free pursuit in this state of any lawful business, trade or occupation is or may be restricted or prevented, is hereby declared to be against public policy, illegal and void.

§ 2. Every person or corporation, or any officer or agent thereof, who shall make or attempt to make or enter into any such contract, agreement, arrangement or combination, or who within this state shall do any act pursuant thereto, or in, toward or for the consummation thereof, wherever the same may have been made, is guilty of a misdemeanor, and on conviction thereof shall, if a natural person, be punished by a fine not exceeding five thousand dollars, or by imprisonment for not longer than one year, or by both such fine and imprisonment; and if a corporation, by a fine of not exceeding five thousand dollars.

§ 3. The attorney-general may bring an action in the name and in behalf of the people of the state against any person, trustee, director, manager or other officer or agent of a corporation, or against a corporation, foreign or domestic, to restrain and prevent the doing in this state of any act herein declared to be illegal, or any act, in, toward or for the making or consummation of any contract, agreement, arrangement or combination herein prohibited, wherever the same may have been made.

§ 4. Whenever the attorney-general has determined to commence an action or proceeding under this chapter, he may present to any justice of the supreme court, before beginning such action or proceeding under this chapter, an application in writing, for an order directing the persons mentioned in the application to appear before a justice of the supreme court, or a referee designated in such order, and answer such questions as may be put to them or to any of them, and produce such papers, documents and books concerning any alleged illegal contract, arrangement, agreement or combination in violation of this chapter; and it shall be the duty of the justice of the supreme court, to whom such application for the order is made, to grant such application. The application for such order made by the attorney-general may simply show, upon his information and belief that the testimony of such person or persons is material and necessary. The provisions of article one, of title three, of chapter nine of the code of civil procedure, relating to the application for an order for the examination of witnesses before the commencement of an action and the method of proceeding on such examinations shall not apply except as herein prescribed. The order shall be granted by the justice of the supreme court to whom the application has been made, with such preliminary injunction or stay as may appear to such justice to be proper and expedient, and shall specify the time when and place where the witnesses are required to appear, and such examination shall be held either in the city of Albany, or in the judicial district in which the witness resides, or in which the principal office, within this state, of the corporation affected, is located. The justice or referee may adjourn such examination from time to time and witnesses must attend accordingly. The testimony of each witness must be subscribed by him, and all must be filed in the office of the clerk of the county in which such order for examination is filed.

§ 5. The order for such examination must be signed by the justice making it, and the service of a copy thereof, with an endorsement by the attorney-general, signed by him, to the effect that the person named therein is required to appear and be examined at the time and place, and before the justice or referee specified in such indorsement, shall be sufficient notice for the attendance of witnesses. Such endorsement may contain a clause requiring such person to produce on such examination all books, papers and documents in his possession, or under his control, relating to the subject of such examination. The order shall be served upon the person named in the indorsement aforesaid, by howing him the original order, and delivering to and leaving with him, at the same time, a copy thereof indorsed as above provided, and by paying or tendering to him the fee allowed by law to witnesses subpoenaed to attend trials of civil actions in a court of record in this state.

§ 6. No person shall be excused from answering any questions that may be put to him, or from producing any books, papers or documents, on the ground that the testimony or evidence, documentary or otherwise, required of him may tend to incriminate him, but no person shall be prosecuted in any criminal action or proceedings, or subjected to any penalty or forfeiture, for or on account of any transaction, matter or thing concerning which he may testify, or produce evidence, documentary or otherwise, before said justice or referee appointed in the order for his examination, or in obedience to the subpoena of the court, or referee acting under such order, or either of them or in any such case or proceeding.

§ 7. A referee appointed as provided in this act possesses all the powers and is subject to all the duties of a referee appointed under section ten hundred and eighteen of the code of civil procedure, so far as practicable, and may punish for contempt a witness duly served as prescribed in this act for non-attendance or refusal to be sworn or to testify, or to produce books, papers and documents according to the direction of the indorsement aforesaid, in the same manner, and to the same extent as a referee appointed to hear, try and determine an issue of fact or of law.

§ 8. Chapter three hundred and eighty-three of the laws of eighteen hundred and ninety-seven is hereby repealed.

See sections 7, 30, 53 and 60, Stock Corporation Law, *ante*. See 155 N· Y., p. 441; also other decisions.

CHAP. 20, LAWS OF 1900.

AN ACT for the protection of the forests, fish and game of the state, constituting chapter thirty-one of the general laws.

ARTICLE I.

*   *   *   *   *   *   *   *   *   *

Transportation.

§ 8. Deer or venison killed in this state shall not be transported from or through any county, or possessed for that purpose, except as follows: One carcass or a part thereof may be transported from the county where killed when accompanied by the owner. No person shall transport or accompany more than two deer in any year under this section. Deer or venison killed in this state shall not be accepted by a common carrier for transportation from November nineteenth to September thirtieth, both inclusive, but if possession is obtained for transportation after September thirtieth and before midnight of November eighteenth, it may when accompanied by the owner lawfully remain in the possession of such common carrier the additional time necessary to deliver the same to its destination. Possession of deer or venison by a common carrier, or by any person in its employ while engaged in the business of such common carrier, unaccompanied by the owner shall constitute a violation of this section by such common carrier. This section does not apply to the head, feet or skin of deer if carried separately.

Thus amended by chap. 478, Laws of 1906.

*   *   *   *   *   *   *   *   *   *

Wild moose, elk, caribou and antelope.

§ 11. There shall be no open season for wild moose, elk, caribou or antelope, but they may be brought into the state for breeding purposes. The flesh or any portion of any such animal shall not be possessed, sold or transported during the close season for deer or during the open season for deer unless the animal was killed without the state or by the owner thereof in a private park within the state during the open season for deer. Possession thereof during such open season shall be presumptive evidence that it was unlawfully taken by the possessor. The forest, fish and game commission may acquire by gift, purchase or capture, a sufficient number of wild moose and elk to stock the Adirondack region, and may care for, herd and yard the same temporarily, and liberate them in such region, at such times and places as it deems most conducive to their probable subsistence and increase.

Thus amended by chap. 587, Laws of 1904.

*   *   *   *   *   *   *   *   *   *

Penalties.

§ 16. A person who violates any provision of this article is guilty of a misdemeanor, and in addition thereto, is liable as follows: For each violation of sections one to eleven, both inclusive, to a penalty of one hundred dollars, and for each deer, elk, caribou, antelope, or part of any such animal taken or possessed in violation of any provision of any of said sections, an additional penalty of one hundred dollars; for each wild moose or part of such animal taken or possessed in violation of any provision of said sections, an additional penalty of two hundred and fifty dollars; for each wild black bear taken or possessed in violation of section eleven-a, a penalty of fifty dollars; for each violation of section twelve, to a penalty of twenty-five dollars, and for each squirrel or part thereof taken or possessed in violation of said section, an additional penalty of ten dollars; for each violation of section thirteen, a penalty of twenty-five dollars, and for each rabbit taken or possessed in violation of such section, an additional penalty of ten dollars; for each beaver taken in violation of section fourteen to a penalty of one hundred dollars; for each violation of section fifteen, to a penalty of twenty-five dollars; and for each violation of section fifteen-a to a penalty of ten dollars. A person failing to file a report with the forest, fish and game commission of killing or taken* of a wild black bear under provision of section eleven-a shall be liable to a penalty of twenty-five dollars. A person convicted of a misdemeanor for a violation of section eleven of this article shall be punished by imprisonment for a term of not less than three months nor more than one year.

Thus amended by chap. 319, Laws of 1905.

ARTICLE II.

*   *   *   *   *   *   *   *   *   *

Woodcock, grouse and quail, not to be transported.

§ 29. Woodcock, grouse and quail shall not be transported within this state or into the state from a point without the state

*So in original.

less than twenty-five miles from the state line, unless accompanied by the actual owner thereof, and no person shall transport or accompany more than thirty-six grouse or thirty-six woodcock in any calendar year, or more than twelve of either kind at one time. Possession thereof by a common carrier, or employee thereof, at the time actually engaged in the business of such common carrier, unaccompanied by the actual owner thereof, shall constitute a violation of this section by such employee and common carrier. No common carrier or person in its employ shall transport such birds as owner.

*   *   *   *   *   *   *   *   *   *

Taking game in Westchester county.

§ 37. Game shall not be taken in a public highway, or on the lands of a railway or lands purchased or condemned for the Croton aqueduct within the county of Westchester.

Birds and game not transported.

§ 38. Birds or quadrupeds or parts thereof, game, except fish taken in this state, shall not except as herein provided be transported without the state; nor shall the same be taken or possessed with intent to transport the same without the state. Any person doing any act with reference to such birds or game in aid of such taking or transportation with knowledge of the intention to so transport the same shall be deemed to have violated this section. This section does not apply to the head, feet or skin of deer when severed from the carcass, or to quadrupeds named in section fifteen of this act.

Thus amended by chap. 580, Laws of 1904.

Penalties.

§ 39. A person who violates any provision of this article is guilty of a misdemeanor, and is liable to a penalty of sixty dollars and to an additional penalty of twenty-five dollars for each bird, or quadruped or part of bird or quadruped bought, sold, offered for sale, taken, possessed, transported or had in possession for transportation in violation thereof.

Thus amended by chapter 318, Laws of 1905.

*   *   *   *   *   *   *   *   *   *

ARTICLE III.

*   *   *   *   *   *   *   *   *   *

Certain fish not to be transported.

§ 60. Lake trout taken in inland waters and trout shall not be transported in this state except when accompanied by the actual owner. No person shall transport or accompany at any one time more than twelve pounds of trout. Possession of lake trout or trout by a common carrier or employee thereof, while actually engaged in the business of such common carrier, unaccompanied by the actual owner, shall constitute a violation of this section by such employee and common carrier.

*   *   *   *   *   *   *   *   *   *

Penalties.

§ 69. A person who violates any of the provisions of this article is guilty of a misdemeanor and in addition thereto is liable as follows: For each violation of section forty-three in relation to waters inhabited by trout, of sections fifty-two and fifty-three in relation to polluting streams, section fifty-four relating to drawing off water, section fifty-six in relation to explosives, section sixty in relation to transportation of fish, section sixty-three in relation to the use of net and angling, section sixty-six in relation to thumping, and section sixty-seven relative to carp in Conesus and Hemlock lakes in the county of Livingston, a penalty of sixty dollars, for all other violations of said article, a penalty of twenty-five dollars and an additional penalty of ten dollars for each fish taken or possessed in violation thereof.

Thus amended by chap. 583, Laws of 1904.

*   *   *   *   *   *   *   *   *   *

ARTICLE VII.

Definitions.

§ 140. The following words and phrases used in this act are defined as follows:

1. " Grouse " includes ruffed grouse, partridge and every member of the grouse family.

2. " Trout " includes speckled trout, brown trout, rainbow trout, red throat trout and brook trout.

3. " Lake trout " for the purposes of this act includes landlocked salmon and ouananische.

4. " Black bass " includes Oswego bass.

5. " Pike " for the purposes of this act includes wall-eyed pike.

6. " Angling " means taking fish by book and line in hand or rod in hand; or if from a boat not exceeding two lines with or without rod to one person.

7. It is unlawful to take fish or game during time described as " close season." Fish and game for which close seasons are established may be hunted and caught in a lawful manner during that part of the year which is not included in such close seasons respectively. The " open season " is that part of the year when they may be taken in a lawful manner.

Subdivision 7 thus amended by chap. 593, Laws of 1900.

8. " Taking " includes pursuing, shooting, hunting, killing, capturing, trapping, snaring and netting fish and game, and all lesser acts such as disturbing, harrying or worrying, or placing, setting, drawing, or using any net or other device commonly used to take fish and game, whether they result in taking or not; and includes every attempt to take and every act of assistance to every other person in taking or attempting to take fish or game. A person who counsels, aids or assists in a violation of any of the provisions of the forest, fish and game law, or knowingly shares in any of the proceeds of said violation by receiving or possessing either fish, birds, game or timber, shall be deemed to have incurred the penalties provided in this act against the person guilty

of such violation. Whenever taking is allowed by law, reference
is had to taking by lawful means and in lawful manner.

Subdivision 8 thus amended by chap 580, Laws of 1904.

9. " Person " includes a co-partnership, joint stock company
or corporation.

10. Where lands are referred to as " inclosed," the boundary
may be indicated by wire, ditch, hedge, fence, road, highway,
water or in any visible or distinctive manner which indicates a
separation from the surrounding or contiguous territory.

11. Gender and number shall be disregarded in construing
this act whenever it is necessary to carry out the spirit thereof.

12. Commission, commissioners and board of commissioners
are synonymous with commission of forest, fish, and game. `

*   *   *   *   *   *   *   *   *   *

Construction.

§ 142. This act is intended to be a restatement of existing
law with such changes as clearly appear. The terms, of office
of the present commissioners are not affected thereby. References in laws not repealed to provisions in acts incorporated in
this act and repealed, shall be construed as applying to such
provisions in this act. Nothing in this act shall be construed
as amending or repealing any provision of the criminal or penal
code.

*   *   *   *   *   *   *   *   *   *

ARTICLE IX.

*   *   *   *   *   *   *   *   *   *

Powers of game protectors.

§ 173. Game protectors shall enforce all laws relating to fish
and game; all laws of boards of supervisors relating to the same;
and shall have power to execute all warrants and search warrants
issued for a violation of the forest, fish and game law; to serve
a summons issuing from justices' court; to serve subpoenas
issued for the examination and investigation or trial of offenses

against any of said laws; to make search where they have cause
to believe that fish or game is possessed in violation of law, and
without search warrant to examine the contents of any boat, car,
box, locker, basket, creel, crate, gamebag, or other package, and
the contents of any building other than a dwelling house, to
ascertain whether any of the provisions of this act or of any law
for the protection of fish, shellfish, and game have been violated,
and to use such force as may be necessary for the purpose of
such examination and inspection; and with a search warrant to
search and examine the contents of any building or dwelling
house; to arrest without warrant any person committing a misdemeanor under the provisions of this act in their presence, and
take such person immediately before a magistrate having jurisdiction for trial.

Thus amended by chap. 285, Laws of 1905.

*   *   *   *   *   *   *   *   *   *

ARTICLE X.

Actions for penalties by the people.

§ 185. Actions for penalties for a violation of the forest, fish
and game provisions of this act shall be in the name of the people
of the state of New York; and must be brought on the order of
the commissioner. The forest, fish and game commissioner may
employ necessary counsel in the office of the forest, fish and game
commission, and may likewise designate and appoint an attorney
or attorneys to represent the department in the prosecution or
defense of any action or proceeding brought under the provisions
of the forest, fish and game law. They shall be paid by the state
treasurer on the warrant of the comptroller such compensation
as shall be agreed upon by the forest, fish and game commissioner. Such actions may be discontinued by order of the court
on the application of the commissioner upon such terms as the
court may direct. Such actions if in justices' courts, may be
brought in any town of the county in which the penalty is incurred or of the county in which the defendant resides.

Thus amended by chap. 199, Laws of 1906.

*   *   *   *   *   *   *   *   *   *

Search warrants; when issued.

§ 191. Any justice of the peace, police justice, county judge, judge of a city court or magistrate having criminal jurisdiction, shall if it appear probable that fish or game taken or possessed contrary to the provisions of this act, is concealed, issue a search warrant for the discovery thereof, according to the practice provided in sections seven hundred and ninety-four to seven hundred and ninety-seven inclusive of the code of criminal procedure.

* * * * * * * * * *

ARTICLE XIII.

* * * * * * * * * *

Chief fire warden and foresters.

§ 224-a. The commissioner shall appoint a chief fire warden who shall receive an annual salary of eighteen hundred dollars and his necessary traveling expenses and who shall have supervision of town fire wardens, visit and instruct them in their duties and enforce the law as to fire districts in towns and under the authority of the commissioner commence prosecution for violations of laws to prevent forest fires; and may from time to time employ expert foresters and a foreman of laborers all of whom shall hold office during the pleasure of the commissioner and perform such duties for the preservation of forests as the commissioner shall prescribe. The commissioner may also appoint five inspectors at least four of whom may during seasons of the year when forest fires occur, serve along lines of steam railroads in the forest preserve counties of the Adirondacks. They shall inspect such railroads and the engines thereon reporting to the commissioner the condition thereof for the purposes of fire prevention, and perform such other duties in preventing forest fires and protecting the forest and reforestation as the superintendent of forests or the commissioner shall direct. They shall also have the powers of game protectors, and shall each receive an annual salary of nine hundred dollars and an allowance for expenses not exceeding four hundred and fifty dollars.

Thus amended by chap. 519, Laws of 1906.

25

Fire patrol.

§ 224-b. Whenever in the judgment of the commissioner it is
necessary to protect the forests from fire, he shall organize and
as long as necessary maintain a fire patrol along the lines of
railroads in forests in counties containing parts of the forest preserve, and at such other places in such counties as the public
interest requires. Such patrol shall be organized and maintained under the chief fire warden and inspectors who shall
themselves be placed in charge of sections of the exposed areas
as fire patrols. Game protectors may so far as the public interest
will permit, be detailed as additional assistant fire wardens for
such patrol under the chief fire warden. The commissioner may
also in case of immediate peril from fire with the consent of the
governor, employ temporarily such additional assistants to maintain an efficient fire patrol as the public interest requires. The
chief fire warden and inspectors when engaged in inspection of railroad lines and engines or on fire patrol duty
on railroad lines, as herein provided, shall be transported without charge from point to point as their duties shall require, by
the railroad companies on whose lines such fire patrol and inspection are maintained. The commissioner shall keep account of
the cost of maintaining any such fire patrol and system of inspection along the line of a railroad in the forest preserve, including
therein the salaries, expenses and wages of public officers or
employees directly engaged in maintaining such patrol for the
time that the said patrol and inspection are maintained, and one-
half the cost thereof during the preceding year shall be paid by
the railroad company on the first day of December of each year
to the commissioner. The commissioner may also organize in
any town in the forest preserve a fire patrol during the season
when fires occur. One-half the expense thereof shall be a town
charge, and one-half shall be paid by the state unless according
to the last assessment roll of such town more than one-half of
the landed property therein in value, is the property of the state
in which case the state shall pay such a proportion of the cost
of such patrol as the value of the lands held by the state bears

to the entire assessed valuation of such town, and the remainder shall be a town charge. If the state pay the whole amount the commissioner may collect the amount payable by any town of such town.

Thus amended by chap. 285, Laws of 1905.

Fire wardens and fire districts.

§ 225. The commission may from time to time in every town having lands which are part of the forest preserve, and may in every town having lands which would become part of the forest preserve if acquired by the state, appoint a fire warden who shall act during the pleasure of the commission. When required by the commission, such fire warden shall, and any such fire warden may establish two or more fire districts in his town. He may also by a written appointment filed in the town clerk's office, from time to time appoint a resident citizen in each district as district fire warden who shall act during the pleasure of the fire warden. In every other town the supervisor shall be fire warden by virtue of his office. If the supervisor be absent when fire occurs, or fails to act, any justice of the peace in the town may act as fire warden. If in a town situated in a county containing lands of the forest preserve, the commission is unable to find a suitable person who will accept the position of fire warden, then the supervisor of that town shall act as fire warden and discharge all the duties devolving on that office by law, and shall promptly make to the chief fire warden a report of each forest fire that occurs in his town.

Thus amended by chap. 590, Laws of 1904.

Duties of fire wardens.

§ 226. Under the commission a fire warden is charged with preventing and extinguishing forest fires in his town. During a season of drought a fire warden may with the approval of the commissioner, establish a fire patrol in his town. In case of fire in or threatening forest or woodland, the district fire warden, if any, or if none, the fire warden shall attend forthwith and use all necessary means to confine and extinguish the same. The

fire warden may destroy fences or plow land, or in an emergency,
set backfires to check fire. Either the fire warden or a district
fire warden may summon any resident of his town to assist in
putting out fires. Any person summoned who is physically able
and refuses to assist, shall be liable to a penalty of ten dollars.
An action for trespass shall not be against persons crossing or
working upon lands of another to extinguish fire. In case a
forest fire burn over more than an acre of land, the fire warden
of the town in which it occurs shall make a report thereof to
the commission, giving the area burned over, the quantity of
timber, wood, logs, bark or other forest products, and of fences,
bridges and buildings destroyed with an estimate of the value
thereof. He shall also report the cause of such fire and the means
used in putting it out.

Thus amended by chap. 590, Laws of 1904.

*   *   *   *   *   *   *   *   *   *

Railroads in forest lands.

§ 228. Every railroad company shall on such part of its road
as passes through forest lands or lands subject to fires from any
cause, cut and remove from its right of way along such lands
at least twice a year, all grass, brush and other inflammable
materials. Where the railroad runs through forest lands in
counties containing part of the forest preserve, it shall so cut
and remove the same from its right of way whenever required
by the commissioner; employ in seasons of drought and before
vegetation has revived in the spring, sufficient trackmen to
promptly put out fires on its right of way; provide locomotives
thereon with netting of steel or iron wire so constructed as to
give the best practicable protection against the escape of fire
and sparks from the smoke stacks thereof and adequate devices
to prevent the escape of fire from ash pans and furnaces which
shall be used on such locomotives. The railroad commission
must upon the request of the forest, fish and game commissioner,
and on notice to the railroad company or companies affected,
require any railroad company having a railroad running through
forest lands in counties containing parts of the forest preserve,

to adopt such devices and precautions against setting fire upon its line in such forest lands as the public interest requires. No railroad company or employee thereof shall deposit fire coals or ashes on its track or right of way near such lands. In case of fire on its own or neighboring lands, the railroad company shall use all practicable means to put it out. Engineers, conductors or trainmen discovering or knowing of fires in fences or other material along or near the right of way of the railroad in such lands, shall report the same at the first station to the station agent, and such station agent shall forthwith notify the nearest fire warden or game protector thereof, and use all necessary means to extinguish the same. Any railroad company failing or neglecting to comply with any of the provisions of this section, or any order of the railroad commission made pursuant to the provisions of this section, shall be liable to a penalty of one hundred dollars for each day that it continues a violation thereof. and any officer or employee of a railroad company violating any provision of this section or neglecting to comply with any requirement of the railroad commission duly ordered, shall be liable to a penalty of one hundred dollars for every such violation. The supreme court may on notice to the persons or corporations affected enforce compliance with any such order of the railroad commission.

Thus amended by chap. 590, Laws of 1904.

Fires to clear land.

§ 229. Fallows, stumps, logs, brush, dry grass or fallen timber, shall not be burned in the territory hereinafter described from April first to May thirty-first both inclusive, or from September sixteenth to November tenth both inclusive. From June first to September fifteenth both inclusive, such fires may be set therein if written permission of the fire warden or district fire warden of the town or district in which the fire is set has been first obtained. If in a locality near forest or woodland, the fire warden or district fire warden shall be personally present when the fire is started. Such fires shall not be started during a heavy

wind or without sufficient help present to control the same, and
the same shall be watched by the person setting the fire until
put out. Any person violating any provision of this section is
guilty of a misdemeanor, and in addition thereto is liable to a
penalty of three hundred dollars. This section applies to Hamilton county; to the towns of Minerva, Newcomb, North Hudson,
Schroon, Keene, Jay, Lewis, North Elba, Saint Armond, and Wil-
mingtou, Essex county; the towns of Waverly, Harrietstown,
Brandon, Santa Clara, Brighton, Belmont, Franklin, Duane and
Altamont, Franklin county; the towns of Hopkinton, Colton.
Clifton, Fine, Edwards, Pitcairn, Clare, Russell, Piercefield and
Parishville of St. Lawrence county; the towns of Diana, Crog-
han, Watson, Greig, and Lyonsdale of Lewis county; to the
towns of Webb, Wilmurt, Ohio, Salisbury and Russia, Herkimer
county; the towns of Forestport and Remsen, Oneida county;
the towns of Stratford, Caroga, Bleecker, and Mayfield, Fulton
county; the towns of Day, Edinburg, Hadley and Corinth, Saratoga county; the towns of Johnsburgh, Thurman and Stony Creek.
Warren county; the towns of Putnam, Dresden, and Fort Ann.
Washington county; the towns of Altona, Dannemora, Ellen-
burgh, Saranac and Black Brook, Clinton county; the towns of
Denning, Hardenburgh, Shandaken, Olive, Rochester, Wawar-
sing and Woodstock, Ulster county; the towns of Neversink and
Rockland, Sullivan county; the towns of Andes, Colchester, Han-
cock and Middletown, Delaware county; the towns of Hunter,
Jewett, Lexington and Windham, Greene county.

Thus amended by chap. 186, Laws of 1903.

Forest fires prohibited.

§ 230. A person who wilfully or negligently sets fire to waste
or forest lands of the state or of a private person, or who suffers
a fire on his own lands to extend therefrom or to state lands
is guilty of a misdemeanor and may be imprisoned not more than
one year and be liable to pay a fine of not more than two hundred
and fifty dollars or both. He shall also be liable to the state
or any person for the damages caused by such wrongful act. If

state lands in the forest preserve are or have been damaged
wilfully or negligently as aforesaid, an action to recover the
damages shall be maintained in the name of the people of the
state on the order of the commissioner by counsel designated
by him, and recovery shall be had therefor. The fact that such
fire may have extended to state lands by crossing one or more
tracts of land intermediate the place of setting fire and the state
lands, shall not bar recovery by the state when the damage
done is within five miles of the place where the fire was set.
This act shall not be construed to limit the recovery in cases
where there are no such intervening tracts of land.

Thus amended by chap. 590, Laws of 1904.

Proceeds of actions for forest fires.

§ 231. Moneys received in the name of the people for violations of sections two hundred and four, two hundred and twenty-
eight, two hundred and twenty-nine, and two hundred and thirty
of this act, shall be paid to the commission who shall apply so
much thereof as may be necessary to the payment of the expenses
of collections and shall pay one-half of the balance, not exceeding in any one case fifty dollars, to the firewarden or district
firewarden upon whose information the action was brought. The
balance of such receipts shall be available for enforcing the various
provisions of law for the protection of forests against fire.

Added by chap. 491, Laws of 1901.

CHAP. 135, LAWS OF 1900.

AN ACT to amend section six of the code of civil procedure, in
relation to a court transacting business on Sunday.

SECTION 1. Section six of the code of civil procedure is hereby
amended so as to read as follows:

Courts not to sit on Sunday, except in special cases.

§ 6. A court shall not be opened, or transact any business on
Sunday, except to receive a verdict or discharge a jury. An
adjournment of a court on Saturday, unless made after a cause
has been committed to a jury, must be to some other day than

Sunday. But this section does not prevent the exercise of the jurisdiction of a magistrate, where it is necessary to preserve the peace, or, in a criminal case, to arrest, commit or discharge a person charged with an offense, or the granting of an injunction order by a justice of the supreme court when in his judgment it is necessary to prevent irremediable injury or the service of a summons with or without a complaint if accompanied by an injunction order and an order of such justice permitting service on that day.

CHAP. 9, LAWS OF 1901.

AN ACT to create a department of labor and the office of commissioner of labor, and abolishing the offices of commissioner of labor statistics and factory inspector, and the state board of mediation and arbitration.

Department of labor and office of commissioner of labor created.

SECTION 1. A department of labor and the office of commissioner of labor are hereby created. Within twenty days after this act takes effect, the governor, by and with the advice and consent of the senate, shall appoint a commissioner of labor, who shall hold his office until January first, nineteen hundred and five. A successor to such commissioner shall be appointed in like manner and shall hold his office for a term of four years, beginning on the first day of January of the year in which he is appointed. Such commissioner shall be the head of such department and receive an annual salary of three thousand five hundred dollars.

Offices abolished; powers of *commissioners of labor.

§ 2. The offices of commissioner of labor statistics and factory inspector, and the state board of mediation and arbitration, shall be abolished upon the appointment and qualification of such commissioner of labor. The commissioner of labor shall have the powers conferred and perform the duties imposed by law upon the commissioner of labor statistics and the factory inspector.

*So in original.

Deputy commissioners.

§ 3. The commissioner of labor shall forthwith upon entering upon the duties of his office appoint and may at pleasure remove, two deputy commissioners of labor to be designated respectively as the first and second deputy commissioners of labor, each of whom shall receive an annual salary of two thousand five hundred dollars. Upon the appointment of such deputies the offices of the assistant factory inspector, deputy commissioner of labor statistics, and chief clerk of the commissioner of labor statistics are abolished.

Bureaus of department.

§ 4. The department of labor shall be divided by the commissioner of labor into three bureaus as follows: factory inspection, labor statistics and mediation and arbitration. The bureau of factory inspection shall be under the special charge of the first deputy commissioner of labor, who, under the supervision and direction of the commissioner of labor shall have such of the powers conferred, and perform such of the duties imposed, by law upon the factory inspector, as shall be designated by the commissioner of labor. The bureau of labor statistics shall be under the special charge of the second deputy commissioner of labor, who, subject to the supervision and direction of the commissioner of labor shall have such of the powers conferred and perform such of the duties imposed by law upon the commissioner of labor statistics, as shall be designated by the commissioner of labor. The bureau of mediation and arbitration shall be under the special charge and supervision of the commissioner of labor, who, together with the first and second deputy commissioners of labor shall constitute a board, which shall have the powers conferred, and perform the duties imposed, by law on the state board of mediation and arbitration. The powers hereby conferred upon the first and second deputy commissioners shall not include the appointment of officers, clerks or other employes in any of the bureaus of the department of labor.

Officers and employes.

§ 5. Except as provided by this act, the deputies, officers and employes in the office of or appointed by the factory inspector, the commissioner of labor statistics, and the state board of mediation and arbitration are continued in office until removed pursuant to law.

Construction.

§ 6. Wherever the terms commissioner of labor statistics, or factory inspector, occur in any law, they shall be deemed to refer to the commissioner of labor, and wherever the term state board of mediation and arbitration occurs in any law, it shall be deemed to refer to the board created by this act.
Pending actions and proceedings.

§ 7. This act shall not affect pending actions or proceedings, civil or criminal, brought by or against the commissioner of labor statistics or factory inspector. All proceedings and matters pending before the state board of mediation and arbitration when this act takes effect shall be continued and completed before the board hereby created; and where a grievance or dispute has been submitted to the state board of mediation and arbitration, prior to the taking effect of this act, the board hereby created may make such further investigation in relation thereto as it deems necessary.
Repeal.

§ 8. All acts and parts of acts inconsistent with this act are hereby repealed.

See article 10, Labor Law, chap. 415, Laws of 1897, *ante.*

CHAP. 313, LAWS OF 1901.

AN ACT in relation to the sale of unclaimed articles of baggage in hotels, and to amend section one of chapter three hundred of the laws of eighteen hundred and thirty-seven, entitled " An act relative to unclaimed trunks and baggage."

SECTION 1. Every hotel, inn or tavern keeper within this state who shall have any unclaimed article, goods, or thing in his possession for a period of one year, at least, whether a receipt or check for the same may, or may not, have been given to the person or persons who left the same, may proceed to sell the same at public auction and out of the proceeds may retain the expenses of advertising the sale thereof; but, no such sale shall be made unless, in case the name and residence of the owner shall be known or ascertained, notice of such sale be sent to the owner by mail; nor shall any such sale be made until the expiration of four weeks from the publication of a notice of such sale in a newspaper published at or nearest the place at which such article, goods or thing was left and where such sale is to take place; and said notice shall contain a description of such article, goods or thing and the time and place of sale; and the expenses incurred for advertising shall be a lien upon such article, goods or thing in a ratable proportion, according to the value of each article, package or parcel, if more than one.

§ 2. Such hotel, inn or tavern keeper shall make an entry of the balance of the proceeds of the sale, if any, of each article, goods or thing left by the same person, as near as the same can be ascertained, and at any time within five years thereafter shall refund any surplus so retained to the owner of such article, goods or thing, his heirs or assigns, on satisfactory proof of such ownership.

§ 3. In case such balance shall not be claimed by the rightful owner within five years after the sale as above specified then it shall be paid to the county treasurer for the use of the county poor of said county.

§ 4. Section one of chapter three hundred of the laws of eighteen hundred and thirty-seven, entitled "An act relative to unclaimed trunks and baggage" is hereby amended to read as follows:

§ 1. The proprietor or proprietors of the several lines of stages and the proprietors of the several canal boat lines, and the proprietors of the several steamboats, and the several incorporated railroad companies, who shall have any unclaimed trunks, boxes or baggage within his, their, or either of their custody, shall im-

mediately enter the time the same was left, with a proper description thereof, in a book to be by them provided and kept for that
purpose. In case the name and residence of the owner shall
be ascertained it shall be the duty of such person who shall
have any such property as above specified, to immediately notify
the owner thereof by mail.

See section 46, Railroad Law, and chap. 488, Laws of 1899, *ante.*

CHAP. 406, LAWS OF 1901.

AN ACT to amend the banking law with reference to the loaning
  of the available fund of a savings bank for current expenses.

Section 1. Section one hundred and eighteen of the banking
law is hereby amended so as to read as follows:
Available fund for current expenses; how loaned.

§ 118. The trustees of every such corporation shall as soon as
practicable invest the moneys deposited with them in the securities authorized by this article; but for the purpose of meeting
current payments and expenses in excess of the receipts, there
may be kept an available fund not exceeding ten per centum of
the whole amount of deposits with such corporation, on hand or
deposit in any bank in this state organized under any law of this
state or of the United States, or with any trust company incorporated by any law of the state; but the sum so deposited in any
one bank or trust company shall not exceed twenty-five per
centum of the paid-up capital and surplus of any such bank or
company; or such available fund, or any part thereof, may be
loaned upon pledge of the securities or any of them named in
subdivisions one, two, three, four and five of the preceding section but one, or upon the first mortgage bonds, or any of them,
of the railroads mentioned and described in subdivision six of
said preceding section but one, but not in excess of ninety per
centum of the cash market value of such securities so pledged.
Should any of the securities so held in pledge depreciate in value,
after making any loan thereon, the trustees shall require the
immediate payment of such loan or of a part thereof, or addi-

tional security therefor, so that the amount loaned shall at no time exceed ninety per centum of the market value of the securities pledged for the same.

See chap. 295. Laws of 1902, and chap. 401, Laws of 1905, *post.*

CHAP. 637, LAWS OF 1901.

AN ACT relating to the payment of a percentage of the gross receipts due to a city or village from a corporation building or operating a street surface railroad, or a branch or extension thereof.

SECTION 1. Every corporation building or operating a street surface railroad, or a branch or extension thereof, under the provisions of article four of the railroad law, or chapter two hundred and fifty-two of the laws of eighteen hundred and eighty-four, which, at any time during the period of six years prior to January first, nineteen hundred and one, became liable to pay any percentage based upon the gross receipts of said corporation, under the provisions of section ninety-five of the railroad law, and which heretofore has paid or hereafter shall pay, separately or together, the amount of such percentage and, in addition thereto, interest thereon at the rate of seven percentum per annum, computed from the time such percentage became due by such section ninety-five up to the time such percentage was or shall be paid, by virtue of such payment or payments, shall be discharged of liability with the same force and effect as if the amount of such percentage had been paid upon the date when it first became due under the provisions of the said section of the said railroad law.

§ 2. All acts and parts of acts inconsistent herewith are hereby repealed.

See sections 95 and 112, Railroad Law, *ante.*

*CHAP. 712, LAWS OF 1901.

AN ACT to relieve the congestion and facilitate the traffic on
the New York and Brooklyn bridge, and to improve and extend
the footpaths, roadways, railway tracks and other facilities for
the use of pedestrians, vehicles and railway passengers at the
westerly or Manhattan terminal of said bridge.

SECTION 1. The commissioner of bridges of the city of New
York is hereby authorized to prepare or to cause to be prepared
and to submit to the board of estimate and apportionment of
such city, and with the approval of said board by a majority vote
thereof to adopt plans and specifications for the reconstruction of
the westerly or Manhattan terminal of the New York and Brooklyn bridge, or for the construction of an extension thereof by a
loop system or otherwise, or for both such construction and reconstruction, for the better accommodation of pedestrians, vehicles
and railroad passengers using said bridge or terminal, which
plans and specifications may also provide for the construction,
maintenance and operation of railroad tracks in and upon such
terminal or extension, or any part thereof, and may also provide
for the location of such extension through, over or under any
such streets, highways, avenues, private or public property, buildings, parks or places as said commissioner, with such approval
of said board, shall determine to be the most feasible location
therefor. Provided, however, that if any such extension, construction or reconstruction shall involve the appropriation or
occupation of the sub-surface of any street, park or public place,
or if any such extension, construction or reconstruction
shall involve construction of any railroad elevated above
the surface of any such street, park or public place, or any
other construction, and such railroad or other construction shall
in any way interfere with any rapid transit structure authorized by the board of rapid transit railroad commissioners, then
in either such case the plans and specifications for any such
extension, construction or reconstruction, so far as the same

*While this is not a general act, it is considered of enough importance to
print here.

shall or may interfere with any rapid transit structure, shall require the approval also of the board of rapid transit railroad commissioners for the said city. The said commissioner is also authorized, with the approval of said board of estimate and apportionment by a majority vote thereof, to select and specify such real estate, tenements, hereditaments, corporeal or incorporeal rights in the same as such commissioner with such approval of said board shall determine to be necessary for such construction or reconstruction purposes, which are hereby declared to be public uses and purposes, and the city of New York is hereby authorized to acquire title thereto by condemnation. The said commissioner is also authorized to employ and consult with expert engineers in the preparation of and determination upon such plans, specifications and location, and to pay said engineers a reasonable compensation for such employment and consultation in the same manner as other persons employed by the said commissioner are paid.

§ 2. Upon the adoption, with the approval of said board of estimate and apportionment as aforesaid, of such plans, specifications and location, the said commissioner of bridges is hereby authorized with the approval of the said board of estimate and apportionment, by a majority vote thereof, to enter into one or more contracts in the name and on behalf of such city for the construction of any such extension or reconstruction of such terminal in accordance with such plans and specifications, and upon the location so approved and adopted. Such contracts may be made with any person or persons, corporation or corporations who or which are competent to enter into such contracts on their part, or may be made with any of the railroad corporations which have or shall have the right to operate cars across said bridge or connecting with said terminal. The said commissioner of bridges with the approval of said board of estimate and apportionment by a majority vote thereof, may also in the name and on behalf of said city enter into one or more contracts with one or more of such railroad corporations, for the operation of railroad tracks in or upon said terminal and extension and across said bridge or any part of either thereof, upon such terms and conditions and for such periods of time as shall be provided in such contracts. Any contract hereby authorized may provide either that the expense of all construction and reconstruction authorized by this act shall be borne by the person or persons, corporation or corporations with whom or which the contract shall be made for such operation; or may, with the approval of said board of estimate and apportionment, by a majority vote thereof, provide for the payment of the whole or any part of the cost of such construction and reconstruction and the cost of any land that may be acquired therefor, by the city of New York, from the proceeds of its bonds issued for that purpose. No such contract shall grant any right to any such person or persons, corporation or corporations for a period greater than twenty-five years from and after the completion of the structure or other property for which such contract shall be made, except that there may be a provision for a renewal of the contract for a further term of twenty-five years upon the payment by the person or persons, corporation or corporations with whom or which the contract shall be made of an annual rental not less than the maximum annual rental paid during any portion of the original term of twenty-five years; nor shall any such contract be made unless it shall be therein provided that the person or persons, corporation or corporations with whom or which the contract shall be made shall annually pay to the city for the use of the extension, structure, or other property provided by the city an annual rental not less than the original amount of the interest payable by the city upon its bonds issued to provide the cost thereof, and in addition thereto an amount not less than one per centum on such cost. No such contract which authorizes or may authorize the construction of any railroad under any street, park or public place, or which authorizes or may authorize any railroad elevated above the surface of any street, park or public place which will or may interfere with any rapid transit structure already authorized by the said board of rapid transit railroad commissioners shall be so valid or binding without the approval of said board.

§ 3. All structures and construction work of every nature erected or constructed under or in pursuance of this act shall immediately upon the erection or construction of the same, or any part thereof, be and become the property of the city of New York, and together with all property acquired for the purposes of such construction or reconstruction under or in pursuance of this act shall be a part of the New York and Brooklyn bridge.

§ 4. The city of New York is hereby authorized to acquire title by deed or voluntary grant, or by condemnation, to any and all real estate, tenements, hereditaments, or corporeal or incorporeal rights in the same which the said commissioner shall from time to time with the approval of the said board of estimate and apportionment by a majority vote thereof select and determine to be necessary for such construction or reconstruction purposes, and on the determination of said commissioner, with the approval of said board of estimate and apportionment by a majority vote thereof, to take proceedings for the acquisition of the same, or any part thereof, by condemnation, the corporation counsel shall take and conduct the proceedings for acquiring such title by condemnation in the name and on behalf of the city of New York in the manner prescribed in the Greater New York charter.

§ 5. In case such construction, reconstruction, or any portion thereof, shall be made, or any such real estate, tenements, hereditaments, corporeal or incorporeal rights in the same shall be acquired, at the public expense, then and in such case, for the purpose of providing the necessary means therefor, the board of estimate and apportionment in said city, shall by a majority vote thereof, from time to time and as the same shall be necessary, and upon the requisition of the said commissioner, direct the comptroller of said city, and it shall thereupon become his duty, to issue the bonds of said city for a term not exceeding fifty years at such a rate of interest, not exceeding three and one-half per centum per annum, as said board of estimate and apportionment by a majority vote may prescribe. Said bonds shall

26

not be sold for less than the par value thereof, and the proceeds of the same shall be paid out and expended for the purposes for which the same are issued, upon vouchers certified by said commissioner. Said bonds shall be free from all taxation for city and county purposes, and shall be payable at maturity so far as may be out of a sinking fund to be established and created out of the payments therefor, as hereinbefore provided, or otherwise as shall be determined by said board of estimate and apportionment by a majority vote thereof. But this provision that the said bonds shall be payable out of such sinking fund or otherwise, shall not diminish or affect the obligation of said city as a debtor upon said bonds, or any other right or remedy of any holder or owner of any such bonds, to collect the principal or interest thereof.

§ 6. No street railroad shall be constructed or operated under and by virtue of this act unless the consent of the local authorities having the control of that portion of a street or highway upon which it is proposed to construct or operate such railroad be first obtained, and unless there be also obtained the consent of the owners of one-half in value of the property bounded on such portion of such street or highway, or unless in case the consent of such property owners cannot be obtained, the appellate division of the supreme court in the first judicial department shall upon application appoint three commissioners to determine whether such railroad ought to be constructed and operated, and they shall determine, after a hearing of all parties interested, that such railroad ought to be constructed and operated, and their determination shall be confirmed by the court, which determination shall be taken in lieu of the consent of the property owners. If any part of such extension of such terminal, in accordance with such plans and specifications and upon the location so approved and adopted and authorized to be constructed and operated under and by virtue of this act, shall be a street railroad, then such portion of such extension constituting such a street railroad shall be the property of the city and a part of the New York and Brooklyn bridge and may be constructed and operated, provided, however, and upon the condition that the consent of the local authorities having the control of, that portion of the street or highway upon which it is proposed to construct or operate any portion of such extension constituting a street railroad be first obtained, and that there be also obtained the consent in writing, acknowledged or proved as are deeds entitled to be recorded, of the owners of one-half in value of the property bounded on such portion of such street or highway; or in case the consent of such property owners cannot be obtained, the appellate division of the supreme court, in the first judicial department, shall upon application appoint three commissioners to determine whether such railroad ought to be constructed and operated, and they shall determine, after a hearing of all parties interested, that such railroad ought to be constructed and operated, and their determination shall be confirmed by the court, which determination shall be taken in lieu of the consent of the property owners. The value of such property bounded on such portion of such street or highway shall be ascertained and determined by the assessment roll of said city, completed last before such local authorities shall have given such consent, except property owned by such city, the value of which shall be ascertained or determined by making the value thereof to be the same as is shown by such assessment roll to be the value of the equivalent in size and frontage of the opposite property on the same street; and the said consent of the said local authorities shall operate as the consent of such city as the owner of such property. Every such consent of such local authorities expressed by resolution adopted in accordance with the ordinary and regular procedure of said local authorities shall be their complete and sufficient consent without the necessity of complying with any other conditions or requirements of any other general or special law. If the consent of property owners required by this section cannot be obtained, the said commissioner of bridges may apply to the appellate division of the supreme court in the first judicial department for the appointment of three commissioners to determine whether the portion of such extension for which such consent is by this section required, ought to be constructed and operated. Notice of such application must, at least ten days prior thereto, be served upon each non-consenting property owner, by delivering the same to the person to whom such property is assessed upon such assessment roll, or by duly mailing the same, properly folded and directed, to such property owner at his post-office address, with the postage prepaid thereon. If the person upon whom service is to be made is unknown, or his residence and post-office address are unknown and cannot by reasonable diligence be ascertained, service of such notice may be made by publishing the same in such newspaper of the county as the court may direct, at least once a week for four successive weeks. Upon due proof of service of such notice the court to which the application is made shall appoint three disinterested persons, who shall act as commissioners, and who shall, within ten days after their appointment, cause public notice to be given of their first meeting in the manner directed by the court, and may adjourn from time to time, until all their business is completed. Vacancies may be filled by the court after such notice to parties interested as it may deem proper to be given, and the evidence taken before as well as after the happening of the vacancy shall be deemed to be properly before such commissioners. After a public hearing of all parties interested, the commissioners so appointed shall determine whether such portion of such extension ought to be constructed and operated, and shall make a report thereon, together with the evidence taken, to the appellate division, within sixty days after their appointment, unless the court, or a judge thereof, for good cause shown, shall extend such time; and the determination of said commissioners so appointed, that such portion of such extension ought to be constructed and operated, confirmed by such court, shall be taken in lieu of the consent of the property owners hereinbefore required. The commissioners shall each, receive ten dollars for each day spent in the performance of their duties and their necessary expenses and disbursements, which shall be paid by the city. .

§ 7. All acts and parts of acts inconsistent with this act, so far as inconsistent herewith, are hereby repealed.

See chap. 663, Laws 1897, *ante.*

*CHAP. 164, LAWS OF 1902.

AN ACT to amend chapter eighty-three of the laws of nineteen hundred and one, entitled " An act to provide for the improvement of the public highways in the county of Orange," in relation to railroad crossings and the use of such public highways after construction.

SECTION 1. Section five of chapter eighty-three of the laws of nineteen hundred and one, entitled "An act to provide for the improvement of the public highways in the county of Orange," is hereby amended to read as follows:

§ 5. Any highway or section thereof constructed or improved under this act shall be maintained by the county, and the expense thereof shall be a county charge. The supervisor of each town in which any such highway or section thereof is located, shall annually pay to the county treasurer all highway taxes collected in his town on account of property abutting on such highway or section thereof. The money so paid to the county treasurer by the supervisor of the several towns in pursuance of this section, and any additional money appropriated by the board of supervisors for such purpose shall constitute a fund for the maintenance of the highways in such county constructed under the provisions of this act and of chapter one hundred and fifteen of the laws of eighteen hundred and ninety-eight. No street surface railroad shall be constructed upon any part of the highway in the county of Orange improved under this act, and chapter one hundred and fifteen of the laws of eighteen hundred and ninety-eight, and the acts amendatory thereof and supplemental thereto. If any telegraph, telephone or electric light poles are erected along such highway in such county, they shall be located in all cases at least twenty feet from the centre of the highway.

Thus amended by chap. 334, Laws of 1904.

*While this is not a general act, it is considered of enough importance to print here.

§ 2. Section six of such act is hereby amended to read as follows:

§ 6. Whenever a public highway in the county of Orange improved under this act and chapter one hundred and fifteen of the laws of eighteen hundred and ninety-eight, and .the acts amendatory thereof and supplemental thereto, crosses a railroad and a change is made in the manner of such crossing from grade to overhead or under grade crossing, or the elimination of a crossing, the board of supervisors or the sub-contractor for such improvement, may agree with the railroad corporation owning or operating such railroad upon the cost of such change and the making thereof, in which case the railroad corporation shall pay one-half thereof to the county treasurer of the county of Orange, who shall pay one-half of the amount received from such railroad corporation to the state engineer and surveyor, to be expended by him for highway improvement under the provisions of chapter one hundred and fifteen of the laws of eighteen hundred and ninety-eight, and the acts amendatory thereof and supplemental thereto; and the county treasurer shall credit the remaining one-half or any part thereof to the sinking fund authorized to be established by this act or to the general fund of the county, as the board of supervisors shall direct. When a highway improved under this act and chapter one hundred and fifteen of the laws of eighteen hundred and ninety-eight and the acts amendatory thereof and supplemental thereto, crosses a street surface railroad by an overhead bridge, the frame work of the bridge and its abutments shall be maintained and kept in repair by the railroad company, and the roadway thereover and the approaches thereto, shall be maintained and kept in repair by the municipality in which the same are situated. When such a highway passes under a street surface railroad, the bridge and its abutments shall be maintained and kept in repair by the railroad company, and the subway and its approaches shall be maintained and kept in repair by the municipality in which the same are situated.

See section 62 et seq., Railroad Law, ante; chap. 379, Laws of 1902, post.

CHAP. 295, LAWS OF 1902.

AN ACT to amend the personal property law, relative to investment of trust funds.

SECTION 1. Section nine of chapter four hundred and seventeen of the laws of eighteen hundred and ninety-seven, entitled
" An act in relation to personal property, constituting chapter
forty-seven of the general laws " is hereby amended to read as
follows:

Investment of trust funds.

§ 9. An executor, administrator, guardian, trustee or other
person holding trust funds for investment may invest the same
in the same kind of securities as those in which savings banks of
this state are by law authorized to invest the money deposited
therein, and the income derived therefrom, and in bonds and
mortgages on unincumbered real property in this state worth
fifty per centum more than the amount loaned thereon.

See chap. 406, Laws of 1901, *ante;* chap. 401, Laws of 1905, *post.*

CHAP. 340, LAWS OF 1902.

AN ACT to amend the canal law, relative to street railways
crossing canals.

SECTION 1. Section twenty-five of chapter three hundred and
thirty-eight of the laws of eighteen hundred and ninety-four,
entitled " An act relating to canals, constituting chapter thirteen of the general laws," is hereby amended to read as
follows:

Powers with reference to railroad near the canals.

§ 25. The superintendent of public works shall have a general
supervisory power over so much of any railroad as passes over
any canal or feeder belonging to the state, or approaches within
ten rods thereof, so far as may be necessary to preserve the
free and perfect use of such canals or feeders, or for making any
repairs, improvements or alterations thereupon. No railroad
corporation shall construct its railroad over or at any place
within ten rods of any canal or feeder belonging to the state,
unless it submits to the superintendent of public works a map,

plan and profile of such canal or feeder and of the route designated for its railroad, exhibiting distinctly and accurately the
relation of each to the other at all the places within the limits of
ten rods thereof, and obtain the written permission of the superintendent of public works and of the canal board for the construction of such railroad, with such conditions, directions and instructions as in his judgment the free and perfect use of any such
canal or feeder may require. Whenever any street railway shall
cross over any bridge spanning a canal, or canal feeder, the company owning, maintaining and operating the same shall be deemed
liable for and shall pay all damages that may occur or arise, either
to the state or to individuals, by reason of its laying and maintaining its tracks or rails over, upon and across any such bridge,
or by reason of the operation of its cars over the same; and any
such company shall upon demand of the superintendent of public
works, make any repairs to such structure to insure the continued safety thereof as shall have been rendered necessary by
reason of such use of said structure by said company. Any company so maintaining or operating a street railroad over, upon and
across any such bridge shall indemnify the state against any and
all loss, damages or claims for damage, for injuries to person or
property of passengers which shall be incurred by or made against
such state by reason of the operation of such railway over any
such bridge, and the superintendent of public works may, in his
discretion, require any company so maintaining or operating a
street railway to furnish a bond, with sureties to be approved by
him, to indemnify the state from all such loss, damage or claims.
All such permits heretofore or hereafter granted shall be revocable
whenever the free and perfect use of any such canal or feeder may
so require, or if such railway company shall fail to make any
such repairs when required by the superintendent of public works
and the railroad company using or occupying any bridge over the
same shall, within a reasonable time after the service upon it of
written notice of such revocation, or to make such repairs by the
superintendent of public works, remove at its own cost and expense its railroad from such bridge and from the limits of ten
rods of said canal or feeder.

See section 13, Railroad Law.

CHAP. 404, LAWS OF 1902.

AN ACT to amend section three thousand three hundred and twenty of the code of civil procedure, relative to receiver's commissions.

SECTION 1. Section thirty-three hundred and twenty of the code of civil procedure is hereby amended so as to read as follows: Receiver's commissions; cost of bonds; trustee's commissions.

§ 3320. A receiver, except as otherwise specially prescribed by statute, is entitled, in addition to his necessary expenses, to such commissions, not exceeding five per centum upon the sums received and disbursed by him, as the court by which, or the judge by whom, he is appointed allows. But if in any case the commissions of a temporary or permanent receiver, so computed, shall not amount to one hundred dollars, said court or judge may, in its or his discretion, allow said receiver such a sum, not exceeding one hundred dollars, for his commissions as shall be commensurate with the services rendered by said receiver. Any receiver, assignee, guardian, trustee, committee, executor, administrator or person appointed under section ninety-one of the real property law or under section eight of the personal property law required by law to give a bond as such may include as a part of his necessary expenses, such reasonable sum, not exceeding one per centum per annum upon the amount of such bond paid his surety thereon, as such court or judge allows. A trustee of an express trust is entitled, and two or more trustees of such a trust are entitled, to be apportioned between or among them according to the services rendered by them respectively, as compensation for services as such, over and above expenses, to commissions as follows: For receiving and paying out all sums of principal not exceeding one thousand dollars, at the rate of five per centum. For receiving and paying out any additional sums of principal not exceeding ten thousand dollars, at the rate of two and one-half per centum. For receiving and paying out all sums of principal above eleven thousand dollars, at the rate of one per centum. And for receiving and paying out income in each year, at the like rates. In all

cases a just and reasonable allowance must be made for the necessary expenses actually paid by such trustee or trustees. If the
value of the principal of the trust estate or fund equals or exceeds
one hundred thousand dollars, each such trustee is entitled to the
full commission on principal, and on income for each year, to
which a sole trustee is entitled, unless the trustees are more than
three, in which case three full commissions at the rates aforesaid
must be apportioned between or among them according to the
services rendered by them respectively. If the instrument creating
the trust provides specific compensation for the services of the
trustee or trustees, no other compensation for such services shall
be allowed unless the trustee or trustees shall, before receiving
any compensation for such services, by a written instrument duly
acknowledged, renounce such specific compensation.

Thus amended by chap. 755, Laws of 1904, taking effect Sept. 1, 1904.
See chap. 378, Laws 1883; chap. 285, Laws 1884; chap. 310, Laws 1886;
chap. 522, Laws 1898; chap. 534, Laws 1898, and sections 5, Stock Corporation Law, and 76, Railroad Law, *ante*.

CHAP. 600, LAWS OF 1902.

AN ACT to extend and regulate the liability of employers to
make compensation for personal injuries suffered by employees.

SECTION 1. Where, after this act takes effect, personal injury
is caused to an employee who is himself in the exercise of due
care and diligence at the time:

1. By reason of any defect in the condition of the ways, works
or machinery connected with or used in the business of the
employer which arose from or had not been discovered or reme-
died owing to the negligence of the employer or of any person
in the service of the employer and entrusted by him with the
duty of seeing that the ways, works or machinery were in proper
condition;

2. By reason of the negligence of any person in the service
of the employer entrusted with and exercising superintendence
whose sole or principal duty is that of superintendence, or in
the absence of such superintendent, of any person acting as

superintendent with the authority or consent of such employer; the employee, or in case the injury results in death, the executor or administrator of a deceased employee who has left him surviving a husband, wife or next of kin, shall have the same right of compensation and remedies against the employer as if the employee had not been an employee of nor in the service of the employer nor engaged in his work. The provisions of law relating to actions for causing death by negligence, so far as the same are consistent with this act, shall apply to an action brought by an executor or administrator of a deceased employee suing under the provisions of this act.

§ 2. No action for recovery of compensation for injury or death under this act shall be maintained unless notice of the time, place and cause of the injury is given to the employer within one hundred and twenty days and the action is commenced within one year after the occurrence of the accident causing the injury or death. The notice required by this section shall be in writing and signed by the person injured or by some one in his behalf, but if from physical or mental incapacity it is impossible for the person injured to give notice within the time provided in said section, he may give the same within ten days after such incapacity is removed. In case of his death without having given such notice, his executor or administrator may give such notice within sixty days after his appointment, but no notice under the provisions of this section shall be deemed to be invalid or insufficient solely by reason of any inaccuracy in stating the time, place or cause of the injury if it be shown that there was no intention to mislead and that the party entitled to notice was not in fact misled thereby. The notice required by this section shall be served on the employer or if there is more than one employer, upon one of such employers, and may be served by delivering the same to or at the residence or place of business of the person on whom it is to be served. The notice may be served by post by letter addressed to the person on whom it is to be served, at his last known place of residence or place of business and if served by post shall be deemed to have been served at the time when the letter containing the same would be delivered in the ordinary course of the post. When the employer is a corporation, notice shall be served by delivering the same or by sending it by post addressed to the office or principal place of business of such corporation.

§ 3. An employee by entering upon or continuing in the service of the employer shall be presumed to have assented to the necessary risks of the occupation or employment and no others. The necessary risks of the occupation or employment shall, in all cases arising after this act takes effect be considered as including those risks, and those only, inherent in the nature of the business which remain after the employer has exercised due care in providing for the safety of his employees, and has complied with the laws affecting or regulating such business or occupation for the greater safety of such employees. In an action maintained for the recovery of damages for personal injuries to an employee received after this act takes effect, owing to any cause for which the employer would otherwise be liable, the fact that the employee continued in the service of the employer in the same place and course of employment after the discovery by such employee, or after he had been informed of, the danger of personal injury therefrom, shall not, as a matter of law, be considered as an assent by such employee to the existence or continuance of such risks of personal injury therefrom, or as negligence contributing to such injury. The question whether the employee understood and assumed the risk of such injury, or was guilty of contributory negligence, by his continuance in the same place and course of employment with knowledge of the risk of injury shall be one of fact, subject to the usual powers of the court in a proper case to set aside a verdict rendered contrary to the evidence. An employee, or his legal representative, shall not be entitled under this act to any right of compensation or remedy against the employer in any case where such employee knew of the defect or negligence which caused the injury and failed, within a reasonable time, to give, or cause to be given, information thereof to the employer, or to some person superior to himself in the service of the employer who had intrusted to him some general superintendence, unless it shall appear on the trial that such defect or negligence was known to such employer, or superior person, prior to such injuries to the employee.

§ 4. An employer who shall have contributed to an insurance fund created and maintained for the mutual purpose of indemnifying an employee for personal injuries, for which compensation may be recovered under this act, or to any relief society or benefit fund created under the laws of this state, may prove in mitigation of damages recoverable by an employee under this act such proportion of the pecuniary benefit which has been received by such employee from such fund or society on account of such contribution of employer, as the contribution of such employer to such fund or society bears to the whole contribution thereto.

§ 5. Every existing right of action for negligence or to recover damages for injuries resulting in death is continued and nothing in this act contained shall be construed as limiting any such right of action, nor shall the failure to give the notice provided for in section two of this act be a bar to the maintenance of a suit upon any such existing right of action.

See section 42a, Railroad Law, *ante*.
See 87 App. Div. 631; 178 N. Y. 147; 90 App. Div. 577; 181 N. Y. 519.
See provisions of Interstate Commerce Brakes and Couplers' Act, *post.*

CHAP. 30, LAWS OF 1903.

AN ACT in relation to the consolidation of domestic and foreign railroad corporations.

SECTION 1. The consolidation heretofore effected of a domestic railroad corporation with a foreign railroad corporation, shall not be deemed invalid because such roads at the time of the consolidation did not form a connected and continuous line, if, when the consolidation was effected, or thereafter, an intermediate line, by purchase or by a lease, of not less than ninety-nine years became, with the consolidated roads, a continuous and connecting line of railroad.

See section 70, *et seq.*, Railroad Law, chap. 193, Laws of 1897, and chap. 201, Laws of 1899, *ante.*

CHAP. 175, LAWS OF 1903.

AN ACT to amend subdivision nineteen of section fourteen of title seven of the consolidated school law as amended by section five of chapter two hundred and sixty-four of the laws of eighteen hundred and ninety-six relating to the conveying of school children.

SECTION 1. Subdivision nineteen of section fourteen of title seven of the consolidated school law as amended by section five of chapter two hundred sixty-four of the laws of eighteen hundred ninety-six is hereby amended to read as follows:

19. Whenever any district shall have contracted with the school authorities of any city, village or other school district for the education therein of the pupils residing in such school district, or whenever in any school district children of school age shall reside so remote from the schoolhouse therein that they are practically deprived of school advantages during any portion of the school year, the inhabitants thereof entitled to vote are authorized to provide, by tax or otherwise, for the conveyance of any or all pupils residing therein to the schools of such city, village or district with which such contract shall have been made, or to the school maintained in said district, and the trustees thereof may contract for such conveyance when so authorized in accordance with such rules and regulations as they may establish, and for the purpose of defraying any expense incurred in carrying out the provisions of this act, they may if necessary use any portion of the public money apportioned to such district as a district quota.

CHAP. 308, LAWS OF 1903.

AN ACT to regulate the junk business, and to require a person engaging in such business to procure a license.

SECTION 1. On and after July first, nineteen hundred and three, it shall be unlawful for any person, association, copartnership or corporation to engage or continue in the business of buying or sell-ing old metal, which business is herein designated junk business, and which person, association, copartnership or corporation is herein designated junk dealer, unless such junk dealer shall have complied with the provisions of this act and obtained a license so to do from the mayor of the city, if the principal place of business of such junk dealer is in a city, or the president of the village if such place of business is in an incorporated village, otherwise from the supervisor of the town in which such place of business is located; for which license shall be paid such mayor, president or supervisor for the use of such city, village or town, the sum of five dollars, which license shall expire on June thirtieth of each year.

§ 2. No person, association, copartnership or corporation shall be entitled to nor receive such license who or which, and in case of a copartnership or association any member of which, has been since January first, nineteen hundred and three, or who or which shall hereafter be convicted of larceny or knowingly receiving stolen property, or of a violation of this act.

§ 3. On purchasing any pig or pigs of metal, copper wire or brass car journals, such junk dealer shall cause to be subscribed by the person from whom purchased a statement as to when, where and from whom he obtained such property, also his age, residence by city, village or town, and the street and number thereof, if any, and otherwise such description as will reasonably locate the same, his occupation and name of his employer and place of employment or business, which statement the junk dealer shall forthwith file in the office of the chief of police of the city or village in which the purchase was made, if made in a city or incorporated village, and otherwise in the office of the sheriff of the county in which made.

§ 4. Every junk dealer shall on purchasing any of the property described in the last section place and keep each separate purchase in a separate and distinct pile, bundle or package, in the usual place of business of such junk dealer, without removing, melting, cutting or destroying any article thereof, for a period of five days immediately succeeding such purchase, on which pack

age, bundle or pile shall be placed and kept by such dealer a tag
bearing the name and residence of the seller, with the date, hour
and place of purchase, and the weight thereof.

§ 5.	Each violation of this act, either by the junk dealer, the
agent or servant thereof, and each false statement made in or on
any statement or tag above mentioned shall be a misdemeanor
and the person convicted shall, in addition to other penalties im-
posed, forfeit his license to do business.	But nothing herein con-
tained shall apply to cities of the first class.

Thus amended by chap. 528, Laws of 1906.
See section 56, Code of Criminal Procedure; sections 290, 550 of Penal
Code, *post*.

*CHAP. 462. LAWS OF 1903.

AN ACT to except certain street opening proceedings in the
county of Kings from the provisions of the railroad law, relating to grade crossings, and to legalize the appointment of commissioners in said proceedings.

Section 1.	The proceedings now pending in the county of
Kings in which commissioners of estimate and assessment have
already been appointed for the purpose of acquiring title for street
purposes to the lands and premises required for the opening of
Eleventh avenue from Fifty-ninth street to Eighty-third street,
East Fortieth street from Avenue H to Flatlands avenue, Eighth
avenue from Fiftieth street to Seventh avenue, East Nineteenth
street from Avenue M to Foster avenue, Ninth avenue from
Thirty-seventh street to Bay Ridge avenue, Sixth avenue from
Sixtieth street to Fort Hamilton avenue, Sixty-second street
from Tenth avenue to Sixth avenue, Seventeenth avenue the from
Flatbush line to Bath avenue, Tenth avenue from Thirty-eighth
street to Fifty-third street, and from Seventh avenue to Fort
Hamilton avenue, Dumont avenue from East Ninety-eighth
street to New Lots avenue, Forty-ninth street from the former
city line to West street, Sixteenth avenue from Flatbush avenue

* While this is not a general act, it is printed here as it refers to section 61, Railroad Law.

to Eighty-fourth street,. Foster avenue from Flatbush avenue to Coney Island avenue, Eighty-fifth street from Narrows avenue to Stillwell avenue, Forty-fifth street from the old city line to West street, Fifty-second street from the old city line to the old road leading to New Utrecht, Fifty-third street from the old city line to West street, and Sixty-second street from Tenth avenue to Sixth avenue, are hereby excepted from the provisions of sections sixty-one and sixty-nine of chapter five hundred and sixty-five of the laws of eighteen hundred and ninety, as amended by chapter seven hundred and fifty-four of the laws of eighteen hundred and ninety-seven relating to railroad crossings; and the appointment of commissioners of estimate and assessment in such proceedings is hereby legalized, ratified and confirmed; provided, however, that no crossing shall be actually established or constructed over any railroad crossed by any street or avenue opened in any such proceeding, until a crossing shall be allowed and established by the railroad commissioners as provided by section sixty-one of the railroad law.

See section 61, Railroad Law, *ante.*

CHAP. 597, LAWS OF 1903.

AN ACT to amend chapter seven hundred of the laws of eighteen hundred and ninety-five, entitled "An act to extend the time of commencement or construction or completion of railroads other than street surface railroads," in relation to the extension of time for such commencement or completion.

SECTION 1.   Chapter seven hundred of the laws of eighteen hundred and ninety-five, entitled "An act to extend the time for commencement or construction or completion of railroads, other than street surface railroads," as amended by chapter six hundred and forty-seven of the laws of eighteen hundred and ninety-nine, and as further amended by chapter six hundred and seventeen of the laws of nineteen hundred and one, and as further amended by chapter four hundred and eighty-seven of the laws

27.

of nineteen hundred and two, is hereby amended to read as follows:

§ 1. The time or times prescribed for the commencement of the construction or the completion of its raliroads,* or any other portions thereof, by any railroad company existing at the time herein mentioned, which has at said time acquired at least one-third of its right of way or begun the construction of any portion of its railroads, or shall have heretofore obtained a certificate from the board of railroad commissioners that public convenience required the construction of said railroads, is hereby extended three years from the first day of January, nineteen hundred and four.

See chap. 263, and chap. 495, Laws of 1898, and sections 5, 59, 59-a, 59-b, 99, 106, 124, Railroad Law, *ante,* and acts which this act amends; also chap. 626, Laws of 1903, *post.*

CHAP. 626, LAWS OF 1903.

AN ACT to suspend the limitation of time for commencement of construction or the completion of railroads while in the hands of receivers.

SECTION 1. In every case where a receiver of the property or franchises of a domestic railroad corporation has been heretofore appointed by a court of this state or by a court of the United States having jurisdiction within the limits of this state, the time intervening between the entry of the order, judgment or decree appointing a receiver in the first instance and the entry of the order, judgment or decree finally terminating the receivership, shall not be nor be taken to be part of the time limited by law for beginning the construction of its road by such railroad corporation, or for the expenditure by it of ten per centum on the amount of its capital stock on such construction, or for finishing its road or putting it in operation, and the expiration heretofore or hereafter during such receivership of the time so limited shall not be taken to have terminated or in any way to have affected the existence, franchises, rights or privileges of

---

*So in original.

said corporation; but such corporation shall have all rights, privileges, powers and franchises to which if a valid corporation it would have been entitled by law at the time of filing its certificate of incorporation, together with such rights, privileges, powers and franchises as have since been or may hereafter be granted by law to such corporations; provided that nothing herein contained shall in any way alter, affect or impair any vested right or interest. And such corporation, or in case of a sale of its franchise by the court, then the successor corporation acquiring the franchise, shall be entitled to the same period of time for the performance of said acts and things after the termination of receivership, as remained to said corporation at the time of entry of the order, judgment or decree appointing the receiver in the first instance. This act as here amended shall not apply to nor affect any street surface railroad company the route of which in whole or in part lies within any city of the first or second class in this state, and shall not apply to nor affect any railroad corporation incorporated under any private or local bill or act.

See chap. 263, and chap. 495, Laws of 1898, sections 5, 59, 59-a, 59-b, 99, 106, 124, Railroad Law; also chap. 597, Laws of 1903, *ante.*

CHAP. 232' LAWS OF 1904.

AN ACT relating to commissioners of jurors for each county of the state having a certain population and regulating and prescribing his duties and also providing in what manner juries shall be made up and jurors drawn in courts of record in such counties; how they may be exempted or excused and the length of service of such jurors.

SECTION 1. The selection and summoning of grand and trial jurors in the counties of this state having a population of over one hundred and eighty thousand, according to the last preceding United States enumeration of inhabitants shall be performed by a person to be appointed by a board which shall consist of the county judge, sheriff, district attorney and county treasurer of such county, who shall be known as the commissioner of jurors of such county and who shall hold his office for four years from the second Monday of May in the year of his appointment. But in case this act shall in the future apply to any county not now affected by the United States enumeration, determining that it has the requisite population, it shall not affect the term of the office of the commissioner of jurors, in a county wherein a commissioner of jurors has been appointed under the provisions of this act.

*   *   *   *   *   *   *   *   *   *

§ 10.

*   *   *   *   *   *   *   *   *   *

Either of the following persons, although qualified are entitled to an exemption from service as a grand or trial juror upon his claiming an exemption.

*   *   *   *   *   *   *   *   *   *

9. A superintendent, conductor or engineer employed by a railroad company other than a street railway company or a telegraph operator employed by a telegraph company who is actually doing duty in an office or along the railroad or telegraph line of the company by which he is employed.

*   *   *   *   *   *   *   *   *   *

§ 36. Nothing in this act contained shall affect any legal action or proceeding now pending.

§ 37. The counties of Albany, Erie, Kings, Monroe and New York are hereby excepted from the operation of this act.

§ 38. All acts and parts of acts inconsistent with this act are hereby repealed.

See other statutes, not printed herein, as to exemption of railroad employees from jury duty.

CHAP. 538, LAWS OF 1904.

AN ACT in relation to the registration and identification of motor vehicles and the use of the public highways by such vehicles.

Short title.

SECTION 1. Subdivision 1. The short title of this act shall be the "motor vehicle law." Except as otherwise herein pro.

vided, it shall be controlling, (1) upon the registration and numbering of motor vehicles and chauffeurs, (2) on their use of the
public highways, and (3) on the penalties for the violation of any
of the provisions of this act.

Definitions.

Subdivision 2. The words and phrases used in this act shall,
for the purposes of this act, unless the same be contrary to
or inconsistent with the context, be construed as follows: (1)
"motor vehicle" shall include all vehicles propelled by any
power other than muscular power, excepting such motor vehicles
as run only upon rails or tracks, provided that nothing herein
contained shall, except as provided by subdivision four of section three of this act, apply to motor cycles, motor bicycles,
traction engines or road rollers; (2) "public highways" shall include any highway, county road, state road, public street, avenue, alley, park, parkway, driveway or public place in any city,
village or town; (3) "closely built up" shall mean, (a) the terri
tory of a city, village or town contiguous to a public high
way which is at that point built up with structures devoted to
business, (b) the territory of a city, village or town contiguous
to a public highway not devoted to business, where for not less
than one-quarter of a mile the dwelling houses on such highway
average less than one hundred feet apart, and also (c) the territory outside of a city or village contiguous to a public highway
within a distance of one-half mile from any postoffice, provided
that for a distance of at least one-quarter of a mile within such
limits the dwelling houses on such highway average less than
one hundred feet apart, and provided further that the
local authorities having charge of such highway shall have
placed conspicuously thereon signs of sufficient size to be easily
readable by a person using the highway, bearing the words
"Slow down to ten miles," and also an arrow pointing in the
direction where the speed is to be reduced; (4) "local authori-

ties " shall include all officers of counties, boroughs, cities, villages or towns, as well as all boards, committees and other
public officials of such counties, boroughs, cities, villages or
towns; (5) " chauffeur " shall mean any person operating a motor
vehicle as mechanic, employee or for hire.

Filing statement.

§ 2. Subdivision 1. Every person hereafter acquiring a motor
vehicle shall, for every vehicle owned by him, file in
the office of the secretary of, state a statement of his
name and address, with a brief description of the vehicle to be
registered, including the name of the maker, factory number,
style of vehicle and motor power, on a blank to be prepared and
furnished by such secretary for that purpose; the filing fee shall
be two dollars.

Registration and record.

Subdivision 2. The secretary of state shall thereupon file
such statement in his office, register such motor vehicle in a book
or index to.be kept for that purpose, and assign it a distinctive
number.

Registration seal.

Subdivision 3. The secretary of state shall forthwith on such
registration, and without other fee, issue and deliver to the
owner of such motor vehicle a seal of aluminum or other
suitable metal, which shall be circular in form, approxi-
mately two inches in diameter, and have stamped thereon the
words "Registered motor vehicle, No. ——, New York motor
vehicle law," with the registration number inserted therein;
which seal shall thereafter at all times be conspicuously displayed on the motor vehicle, to which such number has been
assigned.

Owners previously registered.

Subdivision 4. If the vehicle has been previously registered, the certificate issued thereon shall be returned to the secretary of state and in lieu thereof such secretary shall issue to said owner a registration seal containing the number of such previous registration, upon payment of a fee of one dollar. Upon the sale of a motor vehicle, the vendor, except a manufacturer or dealer, shall, within ten days, return to the secretary of state the registration seal affixed to such vehicle.

Display of registration number.

Subdivision 5. Every motor vehicle shall also at all times have the number assigned to it by the secretary of state displayed on the back of such vehicle in such manner as to be plainly visible, the numbers to be in Arabic numerals, black on white ground, each not less than three inches in height, and each stroke to be of a width not less than half an inch, and also as a part of such number the initial letters of the state in black on white ground, such letters to be not less than one inch in height.

Registration by manufacturers or dealers.

Subdivision 6. A manufacturer of or dealer in motor vehicles shall register one vehicle of each style or type manufactured or dealt in by him, and be entitled to as many duplicate registration seals for each type or style so manufactured or dealt in as he may desire on payment of an additional fee of fifty cents for each duplicate seal. If a registration seal and the corresponding number shall thereafter be affixed to and displayed on every vehicle of such type or style as in this section provided, while such vehicle is being operated on the public highways, it shall be deemed a sufficient compliance with subdivisions one, three, five and eight of this section, until such vehicle shall be sold or let for hire.

Nothing in this subdivision shall be construed to apply to a motor vehicle employed by a manufacturer or dealer for private use or for hire.

Fictitious seal or number.

Subdivision 7. No motor vehicle shall be used or operated upon the public highways after thirty days after this act takes effect which shall display thereon a registration seal or number belonging to any other vehicle, or a fictitious registration seal or number.

Unregistered vehicle not to be operated.

Subdivision 8. No motor vehicle shall be used or operated upon the public highways after thirty days after this act takes effect, unless the owner shall have complied in all respects with this section, except that any person purchasing a motor vehicle from a manufacturer, dealer or other person after this act goes into effect shall be allowed to operate such motor vehicle upon the public highways for a period of five days after the purchase and delivery thereof, provided that during such period such motor vehicle shall bear the registration number and seal of the previous owner under which it was operated or might have been operated by him.

Exemption of nonresident owners.

Subdivision 9. The provisions of this section shall not apply to motor vehicles owned by nonresidents of this state, provided the owners thereof have complied with any law requiring the registration of owners of motor vehicles in force in the state, territory or federal district of their residence, and the registration number showing the initial of such state, territory or federal district shall be displayed on such vehicle substantially as in this section provided.

Speed permitted.

§ 3. Subdivision 1. No person shall operate a motor vehicle on a public highway at a rate of speed greater than is reasonable and proper, having regard to the traffic and use of the highway, or so as to endanger the life or limb of any person, or the safety of any property; or in any event on any public highway where the territory contiguous thereto is closely built up, at a greater rate than one mile in six minutes, or elsewhere in a city or village at a greater rate than one mile in four minutes, or elsewhere outside of a city or village at a greater rate than one mile in three minutes; subject, however, to the other provisions of this act.

Speed at crossings, et cetera.

Subdivision 2. Upon approaching a bridge, dam, sharp curve, or steep descent, and also in traversing such bridge, dam, curve or descent, a person operating a motor vehicle shall have it under control and operate it at a rate of speed not exceeding one mile in fifteen minutes, and upon approaching a crossing of intersecting highways at a speed not greater than is reasonable and proper, having regard to the traffic then on such highway and the safety of the public.

Meeting horses, et cetera.

Subdivision 3. Upon approaching a person walking in the roadway of a public highway, or a horse or horses, or other draft animals, being ridden, led or driven thereon, a person operating a motor vehicle shall give reasonable warning of its approach, and use every reasonable precaution to ensure the safety of such person or animal, and, in the case of horses or other draft animals, to prevent frightening the same.

Stopping on signal.

Subdivision 4. A person operating a motor vehicle or motor cycle or motor bicycle shall, at request or on signal by putting up the hand, from a person riding, leading or driving a restive horse or horses or other draft animals, bring such motor vehicle, cycle or bicycle immediately to a stop, and, if traveling in the opposite direction, remain stationary so long as may be reasonable to allow such horse or animal to pass, and, if traveling in the same direction, use reasonable caution in thereafter passing such horse or animal; provided that, in case such horse or animal appears badly frightened or the person operating such motor vehicle is requested so to do, such person shall cause the motor of such vehicle, cycle or bicycle to cease running so long as shall be reasonably necessary to prevent accident and insure the safety of others.

Giving name and address.

Subdivision 5. In case of accident to a person or property on the public highways, due to the operation thereon of a motor vehicle, the person operating such vehicle, shall stop, and, upon request of a person injured, or any person present, give such person his name and address, and, if not the owner, the name and address of such owner.

Speed tests and races.

Subdivision 6. Local authorities may, notwithstanding the other provisions of this section, set aside for a given time a specified public highway for speed tests or races, to be conducted under proper restrictions for the safety of the public.

Rules of the road.

§ 4. Subdivision 1. Whenever a person operating a motor vehicle shall meet on a public highway any other person riding or driving a horse or horses or other draft animals, or any other vehicle, the person so operating such motor vehicle shall seasonably turn the same to the right of the center of such highway so as to pass without interference. Any such person so operating a motor vehicle shall, on overtaking any such horse, draft animal or other vehicle, pass on the left side thereof, and the rider or driver of such horse, draft animal or other vehicle shall, as soon as practicable, turn to the right so as to allow free passage on the left. Any such person so operating a motor vehicle shall at the intersection of public highways, keep to the right of the intersection of the centers of such highways when turning to the right and pass to the right of such intersection when turning to the left. Nothing in this subdivision shall, however, be construed as limiting the meaning or effect of the provisions of section three of this act.

Brakes, lamps, horn, et cetera.

Subdivision 2. Every motor vehicle while in use on a public highway shall be provided with good and efficient brakes, and also with a suitable bell, horn or other signal and be so constructed as to exhibit, during the period from one hour after sunset to one hour before sunrise, two lamps showing white lights visible within a reasonable distance in the direction toward which such vehicle is proceeding, showing the registered number of the vehicle in separate Arabic numerals, not less than one inch in height and each stroke to be not less than one-quarter of an inch in width, and also a red light visible in the reverse direction.

Local ordinances prohibited.

Subdivision 3. Subject to the provisions of this act, local authorities shall have no power to pass, enforce or maintain any ordinance, rule or regulation requiring of any owner or operator of a motor vehicle any license or permit to use the public highways, or excluding or prohibiting any motor vehicle whose owner has complied with section two of this act from the free use of such highways, except such driveway, speedway or road as has been or may be expressly set apart by law for the exclusive use of horses and light carriages, or except as herein provided, in any way affecting the registration or numbering of motor vehicles or prescribing a slower rate of speed than herein specified at which such vehicles may be operated, or the use of the public highways, contrary to or inconsistent with the provisions of this act; and all such ordinances, rules or regulations now in force are hereby declared to be of no validity or effect; provided, however, that the local authorities of cities and incorporated villages may limit by ordinance, rule or regulation hereafter adopted the speed of motor vehicles on the public highways, on condition that such ordinance, rule or regulation shall also fix the same speed limitation for all other vehicles, such speed limitation not to be in any case less than one mile in six minutes in incorporated villages, and on further condition that such city or village shall also have placed conspicuously on each main public highway where the city or village line crosses the same and on every main highway where the rate of speed changes, signs of sufficient size to be easily readable by a person using the highway, bearing the words "Slow down to — miles" (the rate being inserted) and also an arrow pointing in the direction where the speed is to be reduced or changed, and also on further condition that such ordinance, rule or regulation shall fix the penalties for violation thereof similar to and no greater than those fixed by such local authorities for violations of speed limitation by any other vehicles than motor vehicles, which penalties shall during the existence of the ordinance, rule or regulation supersede those specified in section six of this act, and provided further, that nothing in this act contained shall be construed as limiting the power of local authorities to make, enforce and maintain, further ordinances, rules or regulations, affecting motor vehicles which are offered to the public for hire.

Parks, parkways and cemeteries excepted.

Subdivision 4. Local authorities may, notwithstanding the provisions of this act, make, enforce and maintain such reasonable ordinances, rules or regulations concerning the speed at which motor vehicles may be operated in any parks or parkways within a city but, in that event, must, by signs at each entrance of such park and along such parkway, conspicuously indicate the rate of speed permitted or required, and may exclude motor vehicles from any cemetery or grounds used for the burial of the dead.

No effect on right to damages.

Subdivision 5. Nothing in this act shall be construed to curtail or abridge the right of any person to prosecute a civil action for damages by reason of injuries to person or property resulting from the negligent use of the highways by a motor vehicle or its owner or his employee or agent.

Filing chauffeur's statement.

§ 5. Subdivision 1. Every person hereafter desiring to operate a motor vehicle as a chauffeur shall file in the office of the secretary of state, on a blank to be supplied by such secretary, a statement which shall include his name and address and the trade name and motive power of the motor vehicle or vehicles he is able to operate; and shall pay a registration fee of two dollars.

Chauffeur's registration and record.

Subdivision 2. The secretary of state shall thereupon file such statement in his office, register such chauffeur in a book or index to be kept for that purpose, and assign him a number.

Chauffeur's badge.

Subdivision 3. The secretary of state shall forthwith, upon such registration and without other fee, issue and deliver to such chauffeur a badge of aluminum or other suitable metal, which shall be oval in form, and the greater diameter of which shall not be more than two inches, and such badge shall have stamped thereon the words: " Registered chauffeur, No. ——, New York motor vehicle law," with the registration number inserted therein; which badge shall thereafter be worn by such chauffeur pinned upon his clothing in a conspicuous place at all times while he is operating a motor vehicle upon the public highways. If the operator or chauffeur has previously been registered in the office of the secretary of state, the certificate heretofore issued to him, shall be returned to such secretary, who shall issue to said operator or chauffeur, in lieu thereof, a chauffeur's badge upon the payment of a fee of one dollar.

Fictitious badge.

Subdivision 4. No chauffeur, having registered as hereinabove provided, shall voluntarily permit any other person to wear his badge, nor shall any person while operating a motor vehicle wear any badge belonging to another person, or a fictitious badge.

Unregistered chauffeur cannot operate.

Subdivision 5. No person shall operate a motor vehicle as a chauffeur upon the public highways after thirty days after this act takes effect, unless such person shall have complied in all respects with the requirements of this section.

Penalties for excessive speed, et cetera.

§ 6. Subdivision 1. The violation of any of the provisions of subdivision five of section two, or of subdivision seven of section two, or of section three, or of section five of this act, or of any ordinance, rule or regulation adopted by local authorities in pursuance of subdivision four of section four of this act, shall be deemed a misdemeanor, punishable by a fine not exceeding one hundred dollars for the first offense, and punishable by a fine of not less than fifty dollars nor more than one hundred dollars, or imprisonment not exceeding thirty days, or both, for a second offense, and punishable by a fine of not less than one hundred

dollars nor more than two hundred and fifty dollars and imprisonment not exceeding thirty days for a third or subsequent offense.

Penalties for other violations.

Subdivision 2. The violation of any other provision of this act
shall be punished by a fine not exceeding twenty-five dollars for
the first offense, a fine not less than twenty-five dollars nor more
than fifty dollars for a second offense, and a fine not less than
fifty dollars nor more than one hundred dollars, or imprisonment
not exceeding ten days, or both, for a third or subsequent offense.

Release from custody, bail, et cetera.

Subdivision 3. In case the owner of a motor vehicle shall be
taken into custody because of a violation of any provision of this
act, he shall be forthwith taken before an accessible captain or
a sergeant or acting sergeant of police in any city or village,
or any justice of the peace or magistrate, and be entitled to an
immediate hearing; and if such hearing cannot then be had be
released from custody on giving a bond or undertaking executed
by a fidelity or surety company organized under the laws of this
state and having a deposit of at least two hundred thousand
dollars with the superintendent of insurance of this state, said
bond or undertaking to be in an amount not exceeding the
maximum fine for the offense with which the owner is charged
and to be conditioned for the owner's appearance in answer for
such violation at such time and place as shall then be indicated;
or on giving his personal undertaking to appear in answer for
such violation, at such time and place as shall then be indicated,
secured by the deposit of a sum equal to the maximum fine for
the offense with which he is charged, or in lieu thereof, by leaving
the motor vehicle, being operated by such person with such
officer; or in case such officer is not accessible, be forthwith released from custody on giving his name and address to the
officer making such arrest, and depositing with such officer a sum
equal to the maximum fine for the offense for which such arrest

is made, or in lieu thereof, by leaving the motor vehicle, being operated by such person, with such officer, provided, that in such case the officer making such arrest shall give a receipt in writing for such sum or vehicle and notify such person to appear before the most accessible magistrate, naming him, on that or the following day, specifying the place and hour. In case security shall be deposited, as in this subdivision provided, it shall be returned to the person depositing, forthwith on such person giving a bond or undertaking of a fidelity or surety company, as in this section provided, or on such person being admitted to bail as provided in section five hundred and fifty-four of the code of criminal procedure, and the return of any receipt or other voucher given at the time of such deposit. In case such undertaking of a fidelity or surety company be not given, or such personal undertaking with security or such deposit shall not be made by an owner so taken into custody, the provisions of section five hundred and fifty-four of the code of criminal procedure, shall apply.

Subdivision 3 thus amended by Chap. 128, Laws of 1906.

Acts repealed.

§ 7. All acts and parts of acts inconsistent herewith or contrary hereto are, so far as they are inconsistent or contrary, hereby repealed.

When this act takes effect.

§ 8. This act shall take effect immediately, except that no penalty shall be asserted or imposed for the violation of any of the provisions of section two or section five hereof committed prior to thirty days after this act takes effect.

See sections 1458-1461, Greater New York Charter, section 23 Transportation Corporations Law, section 163 Highway Law, *ante;* section 666 Penal Code, *post.*

CHAP. 734, LAWS OF 1904.

AN ACT to establish a permanent commission for the regulation of the flow of water courses in this state in aid of the public health and safety, to be known as the river improvement commission.

SECTION 1. After the passage of this act the state engineer and surveyor, the attorney-general, the superintendent of public works, the forest, fish and game commissioner, and one commissioner who shall be a civil engineer, to be appointed by the governor by and with the advice and consent of the senate, shall constitute a commission to be known as the river improvement commission.

§ 2. Any county, city, town or village located upon any river or water course, or any person or persons possessing riparian rights thereon, may present to the commission, a petition duly verified, setting forth the facts showing that the restricted or unrestricted flow thereof is a menace to the public health and safety and that it is necessary to the preservation of the public health and safety to regulate the same, and praying that the flow of water in such river or water course shall be regulated under the provisions of this act, so far as necessary for that purpose. Such petition may be made on behalf of any county by the board of supervisors thereof, on behalf of any town by the supervisor thereof, on behalf of any city by the mayor or board of aldermen thereof, on behalf of any village by the president or board of trustees thereof.

§ 3. Such commission on receipt of any such petition shall forthwith determine whether the regulation of the flow of any such river or water course is of sufficient importance to the public health or safety to warrant the interference of the state under the provisions of this act, and shall certify its determination thereupon. If it shall determine that the relief prayed for should be granted, such commission shall at once make or cause

28

to be made such preliminary surveys and investigations as may
be proper to determine the causes of the excessive, restricted
or irregular flow in such river or water course, the available
means to correct the same for the preservation of the public
health and safety, and if relief therefrom is in the opinion of
the commission practicable, to take such other and further action
with reference to relieving the same as is hereinafter provided
for.

§ 4. If such commission shall determine that a more beneficial
flow of water in such river or water course can be had by construction of dykes, clearing out or changing the channel, the
erection of a dam or dams or other public works thereon, or upon
any tributary thereof, it shall cause to be made preliminary plans
and specifications of such proposed improvements, together with
a survey of the lands upon which such improvements are to be
located, giving the location thereof, and of all lands to be taken,
flowed or damaged thereby, with a description by survey or otherwise, of all rights affected thereby, and estimates of the total
cost thereof. The commission shall also cause a map to be made
showing all such lands, the number of acres in each separate
tract and the names of the owners and occupants thereof so far
as the said commission can ascertain the same. The commission
or the members thereof may enter upon such lands as the commission shall deem necessary for the purpose of doing such work,
either by themselves or by their engineers, agents or servants
employed by them for that purpose. The commission shall also
prepare a statement or list of the counties, towns, cities, villages
and individual properties which in its judgment will be benefited
thereby, together with a statement of the proportional share of
said total cost which should be borne by the said counties, towns,
cities and villages respectively, and by the individual owners of
property benefited collectively, expressed in decimals; and in
case any part or proportion of the cost of such improvement is

not properly assessable upon the counties, towns, cities, villages or individual properties, or any of them, as not in the nature of a local improvement, such part or proportion of the expense shall be deducted from the total cost before apportioning the same upon the counties, towns, cities, villages and individual properties as aforesaid, and shall be certified by the said commission to the legislature as a state charge. Said preliminary maps, plans, specifications, estimates and statements shall thereupon be filed in the office of the county clerk of any county benefited and of each county in which any of the aforesaid towns, cities, villages or individual properties benefited are situated. Upon the completion and filing of such preliminary maps, plans, specifications, estimates and statements, the commission shall give notice of the filing thereof, and of the time and place where said commission will give a hearing to persons interested therein, by advertising for five weeks in two newspapers published in each county where such improvement is proposed to be made, and in the state paper published at Albany, at which time and place any person interested may appear, and make any objection to or suggest any modifications in said plans and specifications, and said commission shall have power to adjourn said hearing from time to time as justice may require. Thereupon said commission shall determine whether such proposed improvement shall be abandoned or proceeded with, and what, if any, modifications should be made in said plans, specifications, estimates and statements. If said commission shall determine that said maps and plans should be modified so as to include territory to be benefited or otherwise, not included in the maps, plans and statements already filed, then they shall cause modified maps, plans, specifications, estimates and statements to be prepared and filed as hereinbefore provided, for said preliminary maps, plans, specifications, estimates and statements, and shall give notice of their completion and filing and of a hearing thereupon, in the manner hereinbefore prescribed for a hearing upon said preliminary maps, plans, specifications, estimates and statements. If said commission shall finally determine that the proposed improvement be made, it shall thereupon make a final ·order directing the same to ·be made, and shall cause to be prepared a final map, detailed plans, specifications and estimates of the total cost thereof. The commission shall cause the said final order, map, plans, specifications and estimates, or duplicates thereof, certified by them, to be filed in the office of the county clerk of each county in which lands affected or benefited thereby are located. No such improvement shall be undertaken under this act pursuant to any such final order, or any other proceedings had thereon except as hereinbefore provided, until after the said final order shall·have been approved by a subsequent act of the legislature which act shall authorize and specifically designate the improvement singly directed by such final order to be made. If so approved, the said final order shall become effectual and not otherwise.

§ 5. When any such final order shall have been made and approved by an act of the legislature as hereinbefore provided, such commission shall advertise two successive weeks in the state paper and in two newspapers published in the county wherein such work is to be performed, and if in more than one county, then in each of such counties, and in such other newspaper as shall be deemed of advantage, for bids or proposals for said work to be made in writing for the construction of such dam or dams, dykes or other works according to such plans and specifications. Upon the receipt of the proposals, such commission may enter into a contract or contracts with the lowest responsible bidders for the work to be done, or may reject any or all bids and again advertise for further bids. Before entering into any such contract, a bond with sufficient sureties shall be required, con. ditioned that the contractor will perform all work within the time prescribed in accordance with the plans and specifications, and will indemnify the state and said commission of and from all liability for damages occasioned or suffered by reason of the negligence or willful fault of such contractor, his employees or any subcontractor or his employees in doing such work. Partial payments for work actually done may be provided for in the contracts and paid in the manner hereinafter provided to an amount not to exceed ninety per centum of the contract price. The payments due on account of any such contracts or for any necessary expense or work in connection therewith in pursuance of this act shall be paid from the river improvement fund as hereinafter provided for.

§ 6. The commission may enter upon any land, structures and waters which in its judgment shall be necessary to enter upon for the purposes of this act. If the owner of any property to be taken shall agree with said commission upon the sum to be paid therefor, or for any damages sustained, such sum shall be paid as hereinafter provided as part of the necessary expense incurred in carrying out any improvement under the provisions of this act.

§ 7. If the commission cannot agree with the owners upon the compensation and damages to be paid for the property to be so taken and appropriated the commission shall thereupon serve upon such persons a notice that the lands and property described therein have been appropriated by the state for the purposes of this act, and shall proceed to acquire title thereto under the provisions of title one of chapter twenty-three of the code of civil procedure, known as the condemnation law.

§ 8. When proceedings are taken under the condemnation law the commission shall file in the comptroller's office a certified copy of the final order provided for in section thirty-three hundred and seventy-one of the code of civil procedure, and a certified copy of the judgment therein rendered pursuant to section thirty-three hundred and seventy-three of said code, together with a certificate of the attorney-general that no appeal from such final order and judgment has been or will be taken by the state, or if an appeal has been taken, a certified copy of the final judgment of the appellate court affirming in whole or in part said final judgment. The comptroller shall issue to the said commission or such officer thereof, as it shall direct, his warrant for the payment of the amount due upon such final order and judgment with interest from the date of the judgment until the thirtieth day after the entry of such final order and judgment, and the same shall be paid out of the river improvement fund hereinafter provided for. Such warrant shall be payable to and shall be delivered by the commission or its officers to the owner or owners of said judgment according to the terms thereof.

§ 9. As soon as the total cost of such improvements, including compensation for lands, property, property rights and all damages whatsoever suffered by reason thereof, and all expenses of the commission necessarily incurred or to be incurred in connection therewith, less the amount thereof chargeable to the state, can be determined, said commission shall make a complete and detailed verified statement thereof. They shall apportion the same between the respective counties, towns, cities, villages and individual properties which according to their determination* made as hereinbefore provided, are benefited by said improvements. Said apportionment shall be in writing, and shall specify the proportion thereof to be paid by each of said counties, towns, cities and villages as a whole for public benefits which each as a whole will receive therefrom, and it shall specify the benefits of individual properties, whether in such counties, cities, towns and villages aforesaid or not. The commission shall express such proportions in decimals according to the benefits received therefrom, and shall determine whether the same shall be paid in one assessment or in

*So in the original.

annual assessments not exceeding twenty in all. If the commission determine that the sum so apportioned shall be paid in annual installments, it shall add to each apportionment an amount sufficient to pay all necessary interest money, specifying the amount of each installment. Upon completion of such apportionment, the commission shall cause a true copy thereof to be served upon the chairman of the board of supervisors of each county, the mayor of each city, the supervisor of a town, the president of a village named in said apportionment, or if service cannot be had upon such mayor, supervisor, or president, then upon the board of aldermen of the city, the town board of the town, or the board of trustees of the village, by delivering the same openly. to one of them while in session. A copy thereof shall also be served upon each individual owner of property assessed, either by delivery to such owner or by posting the same upon the said property, and by duly publishing a copy thereof for three weeks in two newspapers published in the county where such property is situated. With such apportionment and as a part thereof, shall be served a notice specifying a time and place where such commission shall meet to hear any county, town, city, village or person interested or aggrieved thereby. Said apportionment and notice shall be served at least fifteen days before such meeting if the service is personal, and at least three weeks before said meeting, if the same is by publication. The affidavit of the person serving or publishing such notice shall be evidence thereof. The commission shall meet at the time and place specified and hear all persons interested in or aggrieved by said apportionment. After such hearing the commission may modify or amend such apportionment in which .case it shall serve a true copy thereof and notice of a hearing thereon in the same manner upon the same conditions and with the same force and effect as the first apportionment and notices. Any county, city, town or village, or any person deeming itself aggrieved may review the determination of the commission in the same manner as a review is had of the determination of a board of assessors in making an assessment. Whenever it shall be determined by the commission that any portion of the total cost of such improvement shall be borne by the individual properties benefited, it shall proceed to apportion that part among such individual properties in the fol·lowing manner. A committee of three of its members shall be appointed who shall have power to apportion and assess such cost upon the individual properties benefited in proportion to the benefit received. Said committee shall prepare or cause to be prepared a list showing each parcel benefited together with the name of the owner thereof so far as the same can be ascertained. The said committee shall view the premises and determine the proportion of benefit received by each parcel. They shall thereupon cause to be prepared a statement of their determination showing the parcels benefited with the proportion of benefit received expressed in decimals. They shall cause a copy of such statement to be served upon the owner or owners of each parcel assessed together with notice of a time and place not less than two weeks at which a hearing will be given thereon, at which any person deeming himself aggrieved shall be heard. Such notice shall be served personally, and in case personal service cannot be made, by publication thereof for two weeks in two newspapers published in the county where said property is situated. Upon said hearing the committee may confirm, modify or alter their determination, and shall thereupon make a final decision assess·ing that portion of the cost of such improvement to be borne by the individual properties benefited, upon the said properties in proportion to the benefit received expressed in decimals, and determining whether the same shall be paid in one sum or in annual installments not exceeding twenty in all, and shall cause a copy thereof to be served upon the owner or owners of each parcel assessed. The determination of such committee may be reviewed in the same manner as a review is had of a determination of the board of assessors in making an assessment. The said committee shall report such final determination and assessment, with their proceedings thereon to the commission and upon the adoption and confirmation thereof by said commission the same shall be and become operative as an apportionment and assessment of the costs and expenses to be borne by the individual properties benefited by such improvement.

§ 10. The commission shall then make a final statement of the total cost and expense of such improvement, and of the apportionment and assessment thereof and file the same as hereinafter provided. Said statement shall contain a statement of the total amount of said costs and expenses, and a statement of the respective counties, cities, towns and villages benefited thereby with the proportion of benefit received by each county, city, town or village expressed in decimals. It shall also contain a statement of the amount of such costs and expenses which is to be paid by the individual properties benefited, with a description of each parcel, the name of the owner or owners, so far as known, the city, town or village where situated and the proportion of benefit received expressed in decimals. It shall also contain a statement whether the amount so assessed upon any county, city, town, village or individual is to be paid in one sum or in annual installments as hereinbefore provided and the amount of each annual installment in case the same is to be so paid. A copy of such statement duly verified under the seal of the commission shall be filed with the clerk of each county, town, city or village containing any lands herein stated to be benefited. The clerk of such county, city, town or village, shall make and deliver to the board of supervisors of such county, the common council of such city, the board of trustees of such village, and the assessors of such town, city or village, a copy of such statement. The board of supervisors of each such county shall levy and assess upon the county and upon each town specified in such statement the amount of such benefit which in such statement is certified to be the proportion which should be borne by the county or by such town as a whole. The common council of each city and the board of trustees of each village shall in like manner levy and assess upon such cities and villages respectively the amount stated in such statement which should be paid by each of such cities and villages respectively. The assessors of each town, city or village containing individual properties upon which a portion of such cost is assessed shall enter on a separate page in their assess- ment roll a statement of the total amount to be so paid by such individual properties, a description of each parcel and the pro- portion of benefit received expressed in decimals, as contained in the statement filed with them. And the board of supervisors of each county where such property is situated shall levy and assess against each such parcel so much of the amount to be raised as shall correspond with the amount of benefit received as indicated by the decimal set down after the description thereof as hereinbefore provided and shall by their warrant direct the collection thereof in the same manner and by the same procedure as general taxes are collected, except that no personal property of the owner of the parcel shall be seized or sold to pay the tax, and that the particular tax assessed on account of such improve- ment, shall be satisfied only by a sale and conveyance of the parcel benefited. And in case it is determined that the amount required is to be paid in annual installments, the board of supervisors or the assessors of the city, town or village, as the case may be, shall annually assess the annual installment to be paid by such county, city, town, village or individual, in the manner provided by this section, until the whole shall be paid. Upon the assessment by the commission of the benefits as provided in this section, the amounts apportioned shall be and remain charges against the several municipalities and liens upon the several parcels of property charged therewith, until paid or otherwise removed, superior in force and effect to all other liens except unpaid general taxes. All moneys collected under and by virtue of the provisions of this act shall be paid to the county treasurer of the county benefited or of the county in which the town, city, village or property is located, who shall pay the same on or before the first day of June in each year to the comptroller of the state, who shall deposit the same in a depository bank to the credit of the river improvement fund as herein provided for. Provided, however, that any county, city, village or individual who may elect to pay the whole of their apportionment, or the portion thereof at any time remaining unpaid, instead of in installments as hereinbefore provided, may pay the same to the county treasurer, and be discharged therefrom.

§ 11. The commission may from time to time make and issue bonds to pay the cost of improvements under this act. Separate issues of bonds shall be made for each separate work of improvement, and no issue shall exceed the aggregate assessment made for the improvement on which such issue of bonds is made. Such bonds shall show upon their face that the payment thereof is secured by an assessment for an improvement as provided in this act, and the proceeds of the assessment for the improvement on which such bonds are issued, shall be pledged for the payment of such issue of bonds. They shall by their terms become due and payable as determined by the commission not exceeding twenty years from the date of issue, and bearing interest not exceeding four per centum per annum, payable semiannually. Before issue such bonds must be approved as to amount, and countersigned by the comptroller. They shall also be signed by the president of the commission, and have the seal of the commission attached thereto. Such bonds shall be exempt from taxation in this state. They shall be sold by the comptroller at not less than par and accrued interest, and the proceeds thereof

deposited in a national or state bank either at Albany or in one
of the counties in which such improvement is made, to be approved
by said comptroller and the president of the commission. But
before any such deposit is made, the comptroller shall require
from such bank a bond as security for repayment of the same,
to be approved by him as to form, conditions and sufficiency
of sureties which shall provide for the repayment to such commission upon demand of the moneys so deposited. Moneys received under the provisions of this act shall constitute a fund
to be known as the river improvement fund and all requisitions of the commission for payments for the purposes of this
act shall be made by the commission or the officer of the commission authorized by it so to do and countersigned by the comptroller, upon that part of the river improvement fund applicable
to the improvement for which such requisition is made.

§ 12. To temporarily provide for the expenditures which must
necessarily be made before the proceeds from the sale of the bonds
herein authorized become available, the commission is hereby
authorized to issue certificates of indebtedness bearing interest
at five per centum per annum which may be used only for the
payment of liabilities incurred under this act in anticipation of
the sale of bonds therefor. A separate issue of such certificates
may be made for each separate work of improvement, the amounts
to be approved by the comptroller, not to exceed the aggregate
estimated cost for such improvement made as in pursuance of
section four of this act. These certificates shall be issued in the
name of the commission and shall be styled " river improvement
certificates." They shall be signed by the president of said commission, countersigned by the comptroller, shall have the seal of
the commission attached, be attested by its secretary and be payable principal and interest from the river improvement fund
created by this act in like manner and effect as requisitions by
the commission are herein provided to be paid.

§ 13. The commission shall have an official seal. The term of the member of the commission not holding a state office other than member of the commission, shall be five years. The commission shall organize under this act by the selection of one of its members as president who shall preside at its meetings, and perform such other duties as are provided by law, or directed by the commission. The member of the commission not holding a state office, other than as a member of the commission, shall not receive a salary, but shall be paid his necessary and reasonable expenses actually incurred in the prosecution of his duties, and may also receive a just and reasonable per diem compensation to be fixed by his associate members of the commission, subject to the approval of the governor, for time actually employed by him in the work of the commission. Three members of the commission shall constitute a quorum at any hearing by the commission but a majority of the commission must concur in any determination of the commission and at least four members must concur in any determination for an improvement under this act. The commission is hereby authorized and empowered to employ a secretary and such engineers, stenographers, clerks and other subordinates as the duties imposed upon them by this act may require, and to fix and pay the reasonable salaries and expenses of such officers, and of all other subordinates for the purpose of proceedings by them under this act. The commission shall have power to charge to each improvement undertaken by it such portion of the expenses so incurred as it shall determine ratably and equitably is chargeable thereto and to include the same in the apportionment or assessment of the cost and expenses of such improvement.

§ 14. The care, control, operation and maintenance of improvements provided for in this act shall devolve upon the commission, and the expenses thereof shall be a charge upon the various municipalities and properties according to the benefits derived therefrom respectively, to be collected in the same manner that the original cost and expense of the improvement was collected. Any person who shall open or close or cause to be opened or closed a gate or gates in any dam constructed under this act without the consent of the commission, or an officer thereof, shall be guilty of a misdemeanor.

§ 15. The commission shall annually on or before the first Monday in February in each year submit a written report to the legislature. This report shall contain

1. An exhibit of the personnel of the commission and of all engineers and other persons connected with the commission.

2. A financial statement showing fully and clearly the condition of the finances of the commission, the amounts and dates of maturity of all bonds and certificates of indebtedness, the amounts of money received and their sources; the amounts of money paid and the purposes for which the same was paid.

3. A statement of the several petitions received by the commission and the action taken thereon.

4. A descriptive statement of each work of improvement on which work has been done during the previous year.

5. A statement of the conditions of improvements previously completed and the results secured by the work of improvement in each case.

In addition to the details as outlined above, the commission shall report to the legislature such other matters as it shall deem proper.

§ 16. The sum of ten thousand dollars or so much thereof as may be necessary is hereby appropriated out of any moneys in the treasury not otherwise appropriated to enable the commission to commence proceedings under this act. The provisions of this act, or the proceedings had or the work done in accordance therewith, shall not be construed as annulling or affecting any power of eminent domain, right, privilege or franchise heretofore created or conferred by law or acquired thereunder nor to permit the actual construction of any dam upon lands which now constitute a private park under and pursuant to article eleven of chapter twenty of the laws of nineteen hundred or pursuant to law, without the consent of the owner of such lands.

See chap. 418, Laws of 1906, *post*, which act transfers the powers and duties of the River Improvement Commission to the State Water Supply Commission, and see chap. 723, Laws of 1905, *post*.

CHAP. 401, LAWS OF 1905.

AN ACT to amend the banking law, relative to securities in which deposits in savings banks may be invested.

SECTION 1. Subdivision five of section one hundred and sixteen of chapter six hundred and eighty-nine of the laws of eighteen hundred and ninety-two, entitled "An act in relation to banking corporations," as amended by chapter four hundred and forty of the laws of eighteen hundred and ninety-three, chapter eight hundred and thirteen of the laws of eighteen hundred and ninety-five, chapter four hundred and fifty-four of the laws of eighteen hundred and ninety-six, chapter three hundred and eighty-six of the laws of eighteen hundred and ninety-seven, and chapter five hundred and ninety-eight of the laws of nineteen hundred and two, is hereby amended to read as follows:

5. In the stocks or bonds of any incorporated city situated in one of the states of the United States which was admitted to statehood prior to January first, eighteen hundred and ninety-six, and which, since January first, eighteen hundred and sixty-one, has not repudiated or defaulted in the payment of any part of the principal or interest of any debt authorized by the legislature of any such state to be contracted, provided said city has a population, as shown by the federal census next preceding said investment, of not less than forty-five thousand inhabitants, and was incorporated as a city at least twenty-five years prior to the making of said investment, and has not, since January first, eighteen hundred and seventy-eight, defaulted for more than ninety days in the payment of any part either of principal or interest of any bond, note or other evidence of indebtedness, or effected any compromise of any kind with the holders thereof. But if, after such default on the part of any such state or city,

the debt or security, in the payment of the principal or interest of which such default occurred, has been fully paid, refunded or compromised by the issue of new securities, then the date of the first failure to pay principal or interest, when due, upon such debt or security, shall be taken to be the date of such default, within the provisions of this subdivision, and subsequent failures to pay instalments of principal or interest upon such debt or security, prior to the refunding or final payment of the same, shall not be held to continue said default or to fix the time thereof, within the meaning of this subdivision, at a date later than the date of said first failure in payment. If at any time the indebtedness of any such city, together with the indebtedness of any district, or other municipal corporation or subdivision except a county, which is wholly or in part included within the bounds or limits of said city, less its water debt and sinking funds shall exceed seven per centum of the valuation of said city for purposes of taxation, its bonds and stocks shall thereafter, and until such indebtedness shall be reduced to seven per centum of the valuation for the purposes of taxation, cease to be an authorized investment for the moneys of savings banks, but the superintendent of the banking department may, in his discretion, require any savings bank to sell such bonds or stock of said city as may have been purchased prior to said increase of debt.

Subdivision 5 thus amended by chap. 581, Laws of 1906.

§ 2. Subdivision six of section one hundred and sixteen of said chapter, as amended by chapter eight hundred and thirteen of the laws of eighteen hundred and ninety-five, chapter two hundred and thirty-six of the laws of eighteen hundred and ninety-eight, chapter three hundred and eighty-six of the laws of eighteen hundred and ninety-nine, chapter forty-two of the laws of nineteen hundred, chapter four hundred and forty of the laws of nineteen hundred and two, and chapter six hundred and forty of the laws of nineteen hundred and three, is hereby amended to read as follows:

6. In bonds and mortgages on unincumbered real property situated in this state, to the extent of sixty per centum of the value

thereof. Not more than sixty-five per centum of the whole amount of deposits shall be so loaned or invested. If the loan is on unimproved and unproductive real property, the amount loaned thereon shall not be more than forty per centum of its actual value. No investment in any bonds and mortgages shall be made by any savings bank except upon the report of a committee of its trustees charged with the duty of investigating the same, who shall certify to the value of the premises mortgaged or to be mortgaged, according to their best judgment, and such report shall be filed and preserved among the records of the corporation. Also in the following securities:

(a) The first mortgage bonds of any railroad corporation of this state, the principal part of whose railroad is located within this state, or of any railroad corporation of this or any other state or states connecting with and controlled and operated as a part of the system of any such railroad corporation of this state, and of which connecting railroad at least a majority of its capital stock is owned by such a railroad corporation of this state or in the mortgage bonds of any such railroad corporation of an issue to retire all prior mortgage debt of such railroad companies respectively; provided that at no time within five years next preceding the date of any such investment shall such railroad corporation of this state or such connecting railroad corporation respectively have failed regularly and punctually to pay the matured principal and interest of all its mortgage indebtedness, and in addition thereto regularly and punctually to have paid in dividends to its stockholders during each of said five years an amount at least equal to four per centum upon all its outstanding capital stock; and provided, further, that at the date of every such dividend the outstanding capital stock of such railroad corporation, or such connecting railroad company respectively shall have been equal to at least one-third of the total mortgage indebtedness of such railroad corporations respectively, including all bonds issued or to be issued under any mortgage securing any bonds in which such investment shall be made.

29

(b) The mortgage bonds of the following railroad corpora-
tions: The Chicago and Northwestern railroad company, Chicago,
Burlington and Quincy railroad company, Michigan Central railroad company, Illinois Central railroad company, Pennsylvania
railroad company, Delaware and Hudson company, Delaware,
Lackawanna and Western railroad company, New York, New
Haven and Hartford railroad company, Boston and Maine railroad company, Maine Central railroad company, the Chicago and
Alton railroad company, Morris and Essex railroad company,
Central railroad of New Jersey, United New Jersey railroad and
canal company, also in the mortgage bonds of railroad companies whose lines are leased or operated or controlled by any
railroad company specified in this paragraph if said bonds be
guaranteed both as to principal and interest by the railroad company to which said lines are leased or by which they are operated
or controlled.   Provided that at the time of making investment
authorized by this paragraph the said railroad corporations issuing such bonds shall have earned and paid regular dividends of
not less than four per centum per annum in cash on all their
issues of capital stock for the ten years next preceding such
investment, and provided the capital stock of any said railroad
corporations shall equal or exceed in amount one-third of the par
value of all its bonded indebtedness; and further provided that
all bonds authorized for investment by this subdivision shall be
secured by a mortgage which is a first mortgage on either the
whole or some part of the railroad and railroad property of the
company issuing such bonds, or that such bonds shall be mortgage bonds of an issue to retire all prior mortgage debts of such
railroad company; provided, further, that the mortgage which
secures the bonds authorized by this subdivision is dated,
executed and recorded prior to January first, nineteen hundred
and five.

(c) The mortgage bonds of the Chicago, Milwaukee and Saint
Paul railway company, and the Chicago, Rock Island and Pacific
railway company, so long as they shall continue to earn and pay
at least four per centum dividends per annum on their outstanding capital stock, and provided their capital stock shall equal

or exceed in amount one-third of the par value of all their bonded indebtedness, and further provided that all bonds of either of said companies hereby authorized for investment shall be secured by a mortgage which is a first mortgage on either the whole or some part of the railroad or railroad property actually in the possession of and operated by said company, or that such bonds shall be mortgage bonds of an issue to retire all prior debts of said railroad company; provided, further, that the mortgage which secures the bonds authorized by this subdivision is dated, executed and recorded prior to January first, nineteen hundred and five.

(d) The first mortgage bonds of the Fonda, Johnstown and Gloversville railroad company, or in the mortgage bonds of said railroad company of an issue to retire all prior mortgage debts of said railroad company, and provided the capital stock of said railroad company shall equal or exceed in amount one-third of the par value of all its bonded indebtedness and provided also that such railroad be of standard gauge of four feet eight and one-half inches, and in the mortgage bonds of the Buffalo Creek railroad company of an issue to retire all prior mortgage debts of said railroad company, provided that the bonds authorized by this subdivision are secured by a mortgage dated, executed and recorded prior to January first, nineteen hundred and five.

(e) The mortgage bonds of any railroad corporation incorporated under the laws of any of the United States, which actually owns in fee not less than five hundred miles of standard gauge railway exclusive of sidings, within the United States, provided that at no time within five years next preceding the date of any such investment shall such railroad corporation have failed regularly and punctually to pay the matured principal and interest of all its mortgage indebtedness and in addition thereto regularly and punctually to have paid in dividends to its stockholders during each of said five years an amount at least equal to four per centum upon all its outstanding capital stock; and provided further that during said five years the gross earnings in each year from the

operations of said company, including therein the gross earnings of all railroads leased and operated or controlled and operated by said company, and also including in said earnings the
amount received directly or indirectly by said company from the
sale of coal from mines owned or controlled by it, shall not
have been less in amount than five times the amount necessary
to pay the interest payable during that year upon its entire outstanding indebtedness, and the rentals for said year of all leased
lines, and further provided that all bonds authorized for investment by this subdivision shall be secured by a mortgage which is
at the time of making said investment or was at the date of the
execution of said mortgage (1) a first mortgage upon not less
than seventy-five per centum of the railway owned in fee by the
company issuing said bonds exclusive of sidings at the date of
said mortgage or (2) a refunding mortgage issued to retire all
prior lien mortgage debts of said company outstanding at the
time of said investment and covering at least seventy-five per
centum of the railway owned in fee by said company at the date
of said mortgage. But no one of the bonds so secured shall be
a legal investment in case the mortgage securing the same shall
authorize a total issue of bonds which together with all outstanding prior debts of said company, after deducting therefrom in case of a refunding mortgage, the bonds reserved under
the provisions of said mortgage to retire prior debts at maturity, shall exceed three times the outstanding capital stock of
said company at the time of making said investment. And no
mortgage is to be regarded as a refunding mortgage, under the
provisions of this act, unless the bonds which it secures mature
at a later date than any bond which it is given to refund, nor
unless it covers a mileage at least twenty-five per centum greater
than is covered by any one of the prior mortgages so to be
refunded.

(f) Any railway mortgage bonds which would be a legal investment under the provisions of subdivision (e) of this section,
except for the fact that the railroad corporation issuing said
bonds actually owns in fee less than five hundred miles of road,
provided that during five years next preceding the date of any

such investment the gross earnings in each year from the operations of said corporation, including the gross earnings of all lines leased and operated or controlled and operated by it, shall not have been less than ten million dollars.

(g) The mortgage bonds of a railroad corporation described in the foregoing subdivisions (e) or (f) or the mortgage bond of a railroad owned by such corporation, assumed or guaranteed by it by endorsement on said bonds, provided said bonds are prior to and are to be refunded by a general mortgage of said corporation the bonds secured by which are made a legal investment under the provisions of said subdivisions (e) or (f) ; and provided, further, that said general mortgage covers all the real property upon which the mortgage securing said underlying bonds is a lien.

(h) Any railway mortgage bonds which would be a legal investment under the provisions of subdivisions (e) or (g) of this section, except for the fact that the railroad corporation issuing said bonds actually owns in fee less than five hundred miles of road, provided the payment of principal and interest of said bonds is guaranteed by endorsement thereon by, or provided said bonds have been assumed by a corporation whose first mortgage, or refunding mortgage bonds, are a legal investment under the provisions of subdivision (e) or (f) of this section. But no one of the bonds so guaranteed or assumed shall be a legal investment in case the mortgage securing the same shall authorize a total issue of bonds which, together with all the outstanding prior debts of the corporation making said guarantee or so assuming said bonds, including therein the authorized amount of all previously guaranteed or assumed bond issues, shall exceed three times the capital stock of said corporation, at the time of making said investment.

(i)   The first mortgage bonds of a railroad the entire capital stock of which, except shares necessary to qualify directors, is owned by, and which is operated by a railroad whose last issued refunding bonds are a legal investment under the provisions of subdivisions (a), (e), or (f) of this section, provided the payment of principal and interest of said bonds is guaranteed by indorsement thereon by the company so owning and operating said road, and further provided the mortgage securing said bonds does not authorize an issue of more than twenty thousand dollars in bonds for each mile of road covered thereby. But no one of the bonds so guaranteed shall be a legal investment in case the mortgage securing the same shall authorize a total issue of bonds which together with all the outstanding prior debts of the company making said guarantee, including therein the authorized amount of all previously guaranteed bond issues, shall exceed three times the capital stock of said company, at the time of making said investment. Bonds which have been or shall become legal investments for savings banks under any of the provisions of this act shall not be rendered illegal as investments, though the property upon which they are secured has been or shall be conveyed to another corporation, and though the railroad corporation which issued or assumed said bond has been or shall be consolidated with another railroad corporation, if the consolidated or purchasing corporation shall assume the payment of said bonds and shall continue to pay regularly interest or dividend or both upon the securities issued against, in exchange for or to acquire the stock of the company consolidated or the property purchased or upon securities subsequently issued in exchange or substitution therefor, to an amount at least equal to four per centum per annum upon the capital stock outstanding at the time of such consolidation or purchase of said corporation which has issued or assumed said bonds. Not more than twenty-five per centum of the assets of any bank shall be loaned or invested in railroad bonds, and not more than ten per centum of the assets of any bank shall be invested in the bonds of any one railroad corporation described in paragraph a of this subdivision, and not more than five per centum of such assets in the bonds of any other railroad corporation. In determining the amount of the assets of any bank under the provisions of this subdivision its securities shall be estimated in the manner prescribed for determining the per centum of surplus by section one hundred and twenty-four of this act. Street railroad corporations shall not be considered railroad corporations within the meaning of this subdivision.

Paragraph (i) thus amended by chap. 581, Laws of 1906.
See chap. 406, Laws of 1901, and chap. 295, Laws of 1902, *ante;* and acts which this act amends.

CHAP. 723, LAWS OF 1905.

AN ACT to establish a state water commission, to define its powers and duties, and making an appropriation therefor.

SECTION 1. The governor, by and with the advice and consent of the senate, shall within fifteen days after this act takes effect, appoint five citizens of the state, one of whom shall be designated as president to constitute a commission to be known as the state water supply commission. Any three of said commissioners shall constitute a quorum for the transaction of business. The commission shall make necessary rules and regulations for the proceedings hereunder.

§ 2. No municipal corporation or other civil division of the state, and no board, commission or other body of or for any such municipal corporation or other civil division of the state shall, nor shall any person or water-works corporation engaged in supplying or proposing to supply the inhabitants of any municipal corporation with water, after this act takes effect, have any power to acquire, take, or condemn lands for any new or additional sources of water supply, until such person, corporation or civil division, has first submitted the maps and profiles therefor to said commission, as hereinafter provided, and until said commission shall have approved the same.

Thus amended by chap. 415, Laws of 1906.

§ 3. Any municipal corporation or other civil division of the state, or any person or water-works corporation, may make application by petition in writing to the said commission for the approval of its maps and profiles of such new or additional source or sources of water supply. Such application shall be accompanied by an exhibit of maps of the lands to be acquired and profiles thereof showing the sites and areas of the proposed reservoirs and other works, the profiles of the aqueduct lines and

the flow lines of the water when impounded, plans and surveys
and abstract of official reports relating to the same, showing the
need for a particular source or sources of supply and the reasons
therefor, and shall be accompanied by a plan or scheme to determine and provide for the payment of the proper compensation
for any and all damages to persons or property, whether direct
or indirect, which will result from the acquiring of said lands
and the execution of said plans. Such petition shall also be
accompanied by such proof as to the character and purity of the
water supply proposed to be acquired as the state water supply
commission shall require. If such petition is made by a person
or water-works corporation, it shall be accompanied by an undertaking in such amount and with such sureties as the state water
supply commission shall determine, that such person or water-
works corporation will pay the expenses of the hearing and determination as hereinafter provided. Said commission shall thereupon cause public notice to be given that on a day therein named
the commission will meet at its office in the city of Albany, or
at such other place as it may particularly specify in said notice,
for the purpose of hearing all persons, municipal corporations
or other civil divisions of the state that may be affected thereby.
Such notice shall be published in such newspapers and for such
length of time, not exceeding four weeks, as the commission shall
determine. At any time prior to the day specified in such notice
any person or municipal corporation or the proper authorities
of any civil division of the state may file in the office of the commission at Albany objections to the project proposed by such
application. Every objection so filed shall particularly specify
the ground thereof. Said commission shall, upon the day specified in said notice, or upon such subsequent day or days to which
it may adjourn the hearing, proceed to examine the said maps
and profiles and to hear the proofs and arguments submitted
in support and in opposition to the proposed project, but no person, municipal corporation or local authorities shall be heard in
opposition thereto except on objections filed as authorized by this
section. The commission shall determine whether the plans

proposed are justified by public necessity, and whether such plans are just and equitable to the other municipalities and civil divisions of the state affected thereby and to the inhabitants thereof, particular consideration being given to their present and future necessities for sources of water supply, and whether said plans make fair and equitable provisions for the determination and payment of any and all damages to persons and property, both direct and indirect which will result from the execution of said plans. Said commission shall within ninety days after the final hearing and with all convenient speed, either approve such application as presented or with such modifications in the plans submitted as it may deem necessary to protect the water supply and the interest of any other municipal corporation, or other civil division of the state, or the inhabitants thereof, or to bring into cooperation all municipal corporations, or other civil divisions of the state, which may be affected thereby. Or it may reject the application entirely or permit another to be filed in lieu thereof, but it shall, however, make a reasonable effort to meet the needs of the applicant, with due regard to the actual or prospective needs and interests of all other municipal corporations and civil divisions of the state affected thereby and the inhabitants thereof. Whenever the commission shall make a decision on any application submitted to it it shall state the same in writing and sign the same and cause its official seal to be affixed thereto and file the same, together with all plans, maps, surveys and other papers or records relating thereto in its office. The decision of the commission and its action on any application may be reviewed by certiorari proceedings. The expense of any such hearing and determination by the commission shall be certified by said commission to the person, water-works corporation, municipal corporation or other civil division of the state making such application and shall be paid by said applicant within thirty days thereafter upon the certificate of the commission to the persons entitled thereto.

Thus amended by chap. 415, Laws of 1906.

§ 4. Said commission shall have power to subpœna and require the attendance in this state of witnesses and the production by them of books and papers pertinent to the investigation and in quiries which it is authorized to make by this act, and to examine them and such public records as it shall require in relation thereto. And for the purposes of the examinations authorized by this act, the commission shall possess all the powers conferred by the legislative law upon a committee of the legislature or by the code of civil procedure upon a board or committee, and may invoke the power of any court of record in the state to compel the attendance and testifying of witnesses and the production by them of books and papers as aforesaid.

Thus amended by chap. 415, Laws of 1906.

§ 5. The commission shall have an official seal. The term of each member of the commission shall be five years, except that the members of said commission first appointed shall hold office respectively one for one year, one for two years, one for three years, one for four years and one for five years, and as the term of each commissioner expires or otherwise becomes vacant his successor shall be appointed in the manner hereinbefore provided for the appointment of the original commissioners. The members of the commission shall receive an annual salary of five thousand dollars each and be paid their necessary and reasonable expenses actually incurred in the prosecution of their duties, payable monthly. The commission is hereby authorized and empowered to employ a secretary and such engineers, stenographers, clerks and other subordinates as the duties imposed upon them by this act may require, and to fix and pay the reasonable salaries and expenses of such officers, and of all other subordinates for the purpose of proceedings by them under this act, subject to the approval of the governor.

Thus amended by chap. 415, Laws of 1906.

§ 6. In addition to the powers and duties heretofore conferred upon it, said commission shall immediately after its appointment proceed to make an investigation and report to the legislature as part of its first annual report hereinafter provided for, concerning the available sources of water supply in this state, the respective purity and quantity of each source of supply and the availability of each to be used for localities other than those im.

mediately adjacent thereto. Said commission shall also investigate and report at said time the present water supply of each municipal corporation and other civil divisions of the state to ascertain the present and future needs of each of said municipal corporations and other civil divisions of the state, and the supply therefor, and the purity of each of said supplies. Said commission shall also report the present dispositions of sewerage of each municipal corporation and other civil division of the state, and, if necessary, of adjoining states, with special reference to said disposition affecting the various municipal corporations and other civil divisions of the state in relation to the water supply of this state. Said commission shall also report the advisability of, the time required for and the expenses incident to, the construction of a state system of water supply and for a state system for the disposition of sewerage, if necessary, for all or any of the municipal corporations and other civil divisions of this state, and make such recommendations connected with the subjects of said investigations herein provided for as said commission shall determine. In said investigation concerning either the water supply or disposition of sewerage, said commission shall, so far as possible, make use of all reports and surveys in regard thereto which have heretofore been made. For the purposes of such investigations as are provided for in this section said commission shall have all the powers and authority conferred by section four hereof.

§ 7. The commission shall annually, on or before the first day of February in each year, submit a written report of its proceedings during the preceding year to the legislature.

§ 8. Nothing herein contained shall in any way affect the acquiring of lands by the aqueduct commissioners of The City of New York under the provisions of chapter four hundred and ninety of the laws of eighteen hundred and eighty-three as heretofore amended.

§ 9. The sum of forty thousand dollars or so much thereof as may be necessary is hereby appropriated out of any moneys in the treasury, not otherwise appropriated, to be paid by the state treasurer upon the warrant of the comptroller for the purposes of this act.

§ 10. All other acts and parts of acts inconsistent with this act are hereby repealed.

See River Improvement Commission Acts, chap. 734, Laws of 1904, *ante*, and chap. 418, Laws of 1906, *post*.

CHAP. 260, LAWS OF 1906.

AN ACT creating a commission to confer with the governor and legislature of the state of New Jersey for the purpose of developing a system of transit between the city of New York and the state of New Jersey.

SECTION 1. Within twenty days after this takes effect, the governor may in his discretion appoint a commission of three members to confer with the governor and the legislature of the state of New Jersey, or the duly designated representatives thereof, during the present session of such legislature or thereafter, for the purpose of securing the passage of an act by the legislature of that state providing for the appointment of a joint commission, under proper legislation of both states, to purchase the necessary land or water rights, and to secure the necessary federal consent to the construction of one or more bridges over the Hudson river from the city of New York to the state of New Jersey at the joint expense of the two states. The commissioners appointed in pursuance of this act shall receive no compensation for their services, but shall be entitled to their actual and necessary traveling and other expenses.

§ 2. The sum of one thousand dollars, or so much thereof as may be needed, is hereby appropriated out of any money in the treasury, not otherwise appropriated, for the purpose of paying the expenses of the commissioners appointed pursuant to this act, payable by the treasurer on the warrant of the comptroller, on itemized vouchers certified to by the chairman of the commission.

* While this is not a general act it is deemed of sufficient importance to print here.

CHAP. 321, LAWS OF 1906.

AN ACT to amend the legislative law relative to services in legislative matters.

SECTION 1. Chapter six hundred and eighty-two of the laws of eighteen hundred and ninety-two, being chapter eight of the general laws and known as the legislative law, is hereby amended by adding to article three a section designated as section sixty-six to read as follows:

§ 66. Every person retained or employed for compensation as counsel or agent by any person, firm, corporation or association to promote or oppose directly or indirectly the passage of bills or resolutions by either house or to promote or oppose executice approval of such bills or resolutions, shall, in each and every year, before any service is entered upon in promoting or opposing such legislation, file in the office of the secretary of state a writing subscribed by such counsel or agent stating the name or names of the person or persons, firm or firms, corporation or corporations, association or associations, by whom or on whose behalf he is retained or employed, together with a brief description of the legislation in reference to which such service is to be rendered. No notice so filed shall be valid for more than thirty days after the adjournment of the session of the legislature held in the year in which the same is filed. It shall be the duty of the secretary of state to provide a docket to be known as the docket of legislative appearances, with appropriate blanks and indices, and to forthwith enter therein the names of the counsel and agents so retained or employed and of the persons, firms, corporations or associations retaining or employing them, together with a brief description of the legislation in reference to which the service is to be rendered, which docket shall be open to public inspection. Upon the termination of such employment the fact of such termination, with the date thereof, may be entered by direction of either such counsel or agent or of the employer. No person, firm, corporation or association shall retain or employ any person to promote or oppose legislation for compensation contingent in whole or in part upon the passage or defeat of any legislative measure or measures. No person shall for compensation engage in promoting or opposing legislation except upon appearance entered in accordance with the foregoing provisions of this section. And no person shall accept any such employment or render any such service for compensation contingent upon the passage or defeat of any legislative measure or measures. It shall be the duty of every person, firm, corporation or association within two months after the adjournment of the legislature to file in the office of the secretary of state an itemized statement verified by the oath of such person, or in case of a firm of a member thereof, or in case of a domestic corporation or association of an officer thereof, or in case of a foreign corporation or association of an officer or agent thereof, showing in detail all expenses paid, incurred or promised directly or indirectly in connection with legislation pending at the last previous session, with the names of the payees and the amount paid to each, including all disbursements paid, incurred or promised to counsel or agents, and also specifying the nature of said legislation and the interest of the person, firm, corporation or association therein. The provisions, however, of this section requiring docket entries shall not apply to duly accredited counsel or agents of counties, cities, towns, villages, public boards and public institutions. And the provisions hereof shall not be construed as affecting professional services in drafting bills or in advising clients and in rendering opinions as to the construction and effect of proposed or pending legislation where such professional service is not otherwise connected with legislative action. Every person, every member of any firm, and every association or corporation violating any provision of this section and every person causing or participating in a violation thereof shall be guilty of a misdemeanor and, in case of an individual, shall be punishable by imprisonment in a penitentiary or county jail for not more than one year or by a fine of not more than one thousand dollars or by both, and, in case of an association or corporation, by a fine of not more than one thousand dollars. And in addition to the penalties hereinbefore imposed any corporation or association failing to file the statement of legislative expenses within the time required shall forfeit to the people of the state the sum of one hundred dollars per day for each day after the expiration of the two months within which such statement is required to be filed, to be recovered in an action to be brought by the attorney-general.

CHAP. 418, LAWS OF 1906.

AN ACT to transfer and confer the powers and impose and devolve the duties of the river improvement commission, as created and established by chapter seven hundred and thirty-four of the laws of nineteen hundred and four; upon the state water supply commission, as created and established by chapter seven hundred and twenty-three of the laws of nineteen hundred and five.

Transfer of powers of river improvement commission, to the state water supply commission.

SECTION 1. Thirty days after the passage of this act, all of the powers and duties, of the river improvement commission as created and established by chapter seven hundred and thirty-four of the laws of nineteen hundred and four, shall be and hereby are transferred to, devolved upon and shall be exercised and performed by the state water supply commission, as created and established by chapter seven hundred and twenty-three of the laws or nineteen hundred and five. The state water supply commission shall have power and authority to establish rules and regulations to carry into effect chapter seven hundred and thirty-four of the laws of nineteen hundred and four, and subject to the provisions and limitations of this act, shall possess and exercise all powers conferred by said law upon the river improvement commission.

Services of certain commissioners to cease; exception.

§ 2. The term of office of the civil engineer member of the river improvement commission, shall continue under his original appointment, but he shall thereafter be known and be a member of the state water supply commission and his services, duties and compensation shall be the same as the other members of the state water supply commission after the passage of this act, and no' services thereafter shall be required from or performed by the state engineer and. surveyor, the attorney-general, the superintendent of public works, or the forest, fish and game commissioner as a member of the river improvement commission.

§ 3. Nothing in this act shall be construed to nullify, discontinue, change, modify or affect any proceedings commenced by and pending before the river improvement commission, but all such proceedings may be continued, completed and finished by the state water supply commission.

§ 4. All appropriations heretofore made to the river improvement commission and now unexpended amounting in the aggregate to three thousand seven hundred and sixty-three dollars and seventy-five cents, are hereby transferred and appropriated to the state water supply commission for its use.

See River Improvement Commission Act, chap. 734, Laws of 1904, and State Water Commission Act, chap. 723, Laws of 1905, *ante*.

CHAP. 473, LAWS OF 1906.

AN ACT to provide for the government of cities of the second class.

*   *   *   *   *   *   *   *   *   *

Disposition of real estate; franchises.

§ 37. No ordinance shall be passed making or authorizing a sale or lease of city real estate or of any franchise belonging to or under the control of the city except by vote of three-fourths of all the members of the common council. In case of a proposed sale or lease of real estate or of a franchise, the ordinance must provide for a disposition of the same at public auction to the highest bidder, under proper regulations as to the giving of security and after public notice to be published once each week for three weeks in the official paper or papers. A sale or lease of real estate or a franchise shall not be valid or take effect unless made as aforesaid and subsequently approved by a resolution of the board of estimate and apportionment. No franchise shall be granted or be operated for a period longer than fifty years. The common council may, however, grant to the owner or lessees of an existing franchise, under which operations are being actually carried on, such additional rights or extensions in the street or streets in which the said franchise exists, upon such terms as the interests of the city may require, with or without an advertisement, as the common council may determine; provided, however, that no such grant shall be operative unless approved by the board of estimate and apportionment, and also by the mayor.

❋　　❋　　❋　　❋　　❋　　❋　　❋　　❋　　❋　　н

When to take effect.

§ 231.　This act shall take effect on the first day of January, nineteen hundred and eight, except that in a city which became a city of the second class under the state enumeration had in nineteen hundred and five, the elective officers provided in this act or otherwise by law for such city shall be elected at the city election to be held on the Tuesday succeeding the first Monday in November, nineteen hundred and seven.

See chap. 182, Laws of 1898, *ante*.
Other provisions of this act apply to railroad companies. See sections 91, 93 and 98, Railroad Law, *ante*.

30

TAX LAWS RELATING TO RAILROADS.

CHAP. 675, LAWS OF 1881.

AN ACT to facilitate the payment of school taxes by railroad companies.

Duty of school collector to deliver to county treasurer certain statement; duty of county treasurer in the premises.

SECTION 1. It shall be the duty of the school collector in each school district in this state, except in the counties of New York, Kings and Cattaraugus, within five days after the receipt by such collector of any and every tax or assessment-roll of his district, to prepare and deliver to the county treasurer of the county in which such district, or the greater part thereof, is situated, a statement showing the name of each railroad company appearing in said roll, the assessment against each of said companies for real and personal property respectively, and the tax against each of said companies. It shall thereupon be the duty of such county treasurer, immediately after the receipt by him of such statement from such school collector, to notify the ticket agent of any such railroad company assessed for taxes at the station nearest to the office of such county treasurer, personally or by mail, of the fact that such statement has been filed with him by such collector, at the same time specifying the amount of tax to be paid by such railroad company.

Thus amended, Laws of 1885, chap. 533.

Time in which tax may be paid with one per cent. fees.

§ 2. Any railroad company heretofore organized, or which may hereafter be organized, under the laws of this state, may within thirty days after the receipt of such statement by such county treasurer, pay the amount of tax so levied or assessed against it in such district and in such statement mentioned and contained with one per centum fees thereon, to such county treasurer, who is hereby authorized and directed to receive such amount and to give proper receipt therefor.

[466]

If tax not paid within thirty days, duty of collector to collect; limitation.

§ 3.   In case any railroad company shall fail to pay such tax within said thirty days, it shall be the duty of such county treasurer to notify the collector of the school district in which such delinquent railroad company is assessed, of its failure to pay said tax, and upon receipt of such notice it shall be the duty of such collector to collect such unpaid tax in the manner now provided by law, together with five per centum fees thereon; but no school collector shall collect by distress and sale any tax levied or assessed in his district upon the property of any railroad company until the receipt by him of such notice from the county treasurer.

Tax to be placed to credit of school district, paid to collector on demand, fees to go to collector on demand.

§ 4.   The several amounts of tax received by any county treasurer in this state, under the provisions of this act, of and from railroad companies shall be by such county treasurer placed to the credit of the school district for or on account of which the same was levied or assessed, and on demand paid over to the school collector thereof, and the one per centum fees received therewith shall be placed to the credit of, and on demand paid to, the school collector of such school district.

Tax may be paid to collector direct.

§ 5.   Nothing in this act contained shall be construed to hinder, prevent or prohibit any railroad company from paying its school tax to the school collector direct, as now provided by law.

CHAP. 686, LAWS OF 1892.

AN ACT in relation to counties, constituting chapter eighteen of the general laws.

*   *   *   *   *   *   *   *   *   *

Statement of railroad, telegraph, telephone and electric-light taxes.

§ 53. The clerk shall, within five days after the making out, or issuing of the annual tax-warrant by the board of supervisors, prepare and deliver to the county treasurer of his county, a statement showing the title of all railroad corporations and telegraph, telephone and electric-light lines in such county, as appear on the last assessment-roll of the towns or cities therein, the valuation of the property, real and personal, of such corporation and line in each town or city, and the amount of tax assessed or levied on such valuation in each town or city in his county.

CHAP. 908, LAWS OF 1896.

AN ACT in relation to taxation, constituting chapter twenty-four of the general laws.

CHAPTER XXIV OF THE GENERAL LAWS.

ARTICLE I.

Short title.

SECTION 1. This chapter shall be known as the tax law.

Definitions.

§ 2. 1. "Tax district" as used in this chapter, means a political subdivision of the state having a board of assessors authorized to assess property therein for state and county taxes.

2. "County treasurer" includes any officer performing the duties devolving upon such office under whatever name.

3. The terms "land," "real estate," and "real property," as used in this chapter, include the land itself above and under water, all buildings and other articles and structures, substructures and superstructures, erected upon, under or above, or affixed to the same; all wharves and piers, including the value of the right to collect wharfage, cranage or dockage thereon; all bridges, all telegraph lines, wires, poles and appurtenances; all supports and inclosures for electrical conductors and other appurtenances upon, above and under ground; all surface, under ground or elevated railroads, including the value of all franchises, rights or permission to construct, maintain or operate the same in, under, above, on or through, streets, highways, or public places; all railroad structures, substructures and superstructures, tracks and the iron thereon; branches, switches and other fixtures permitted or authorized to be made, laid or placed in, upon, above or under any public or private road, street or ground; all mains, pipes and tanks laid or placed in, upon, above or under any public or private street or place for conducting steam, heat, water, oil, electricity or any property, substance or product capable of transportation or conveyance therein or that is protected thereby, including the value of all franchises, rights, authority or permission to construct, maintain or operate, in, under, above, upon, or through, any streets, highways, or public places, any mains, pipes, tanks, conduits, or wires, with their appurtenances, for conducting water, steam, heat, light, power, gas, oil, or other substance, or electricity for telegraphic, telephonic or other purposes; all trees and underwood growing upon land, and all mines, minerals, quarries and fossils in and under the same, except mines belonging to the state. A franchise, right, authority or permission specified in this subdivision shall for the purpose of taxation be known as a "special franchise." A special franchise shall be deemed to include the value of the tangible property of a person, copartnership, association or corporation situated in, upon, under or above any street, highway, public place or public waters in connection with the special fran-chise. The tangible property so included shall be taxed as a part of the special franchise. No property of a municipal corporation shall be subject to a special franchise tax.

Subdivision 3 thus amended by chap. 712, Laws of 1899, taking effect October 1, 1899.

4. The term special franchise shall not be deemed to include the crossing of a street, highway or public place where such crossing is not at the intersection of another street or highway, unless such crossing shall be at other than right angles for a distance of not less than two hundred and fifty feet, in which case the whole of such crossing shall be deemed a special fran-chise. This subdivision shall not apply to any elevated rail-road.

Subdivision 4 added by chap. 490, Laws of 1901.

5. The terms "personal estate," and "personal property," as used in this chapter, include chattels, money, things in action, debts due from solvent debtors, whether on account, contract, note, bond or mortgage; debts and obligations for the payment of money due or owing to persons residing within this state, how-ever secured or wherever such securities shall be held; debts due by inhabitants of this state to persons not residing within the United States for the purchase of any real estate; public stocks, stocks in monyed* corporations, and such portion of the capital of incorporated companies, liable to taxation on their capital, as shall not be invested in real estate.

Made subdivision 5 by chap. 490, Laws of 1901.

Property liable to taxation.

§ 3. All real property within this state, and all personal prop-erty situated or owned within this state, is taxable unless exempt from taxation by law.

---

*So in original.

§ 4. Subdivision 16. The owner or holder of stock in an incorporated company liable to taxation on its capital, shall not be taxed as an individual for such stock.

See section 243 of this act (not printed herein), as to exemptions not applying to taxable transfers.

* * * * * * * * * *

When property of nonresidents is taxable.

§ 7. Subdivision 1. Nonresidents of the state doing business in the state, either as principals or partners, shall be taxed on the capital invested in such business, as personal property, at the place where such business is carried on, to the same extent as if they were residents of the state.

Subdivision 2. The personal property of nonresidents of the state having an actual situs in the state, and not forming a part of capital invested in business in the state, shall be assessed in the name of the owner thereof for the purpose of identification and taxed in the tax district where such property is situated, unless exempt by law. This subdivision shall not apply to money, or negotiable collateral securities, deposited by, or debts owing to, such nonresidents nor shall it be construed as in any manner modifying or changing the law imposing a tax on real estate mortgage securities.

Thus amended by chap. 248, Laws of 1906.

* * * * * * * * * *

Place of taxation of property of corporations.

§ 11. The real estate of all incorporated companies liable to taxation, shall be assessed in the tax district in which the same shall lie, in the same manner as the real estate of individuals. All the personal estate of every incorporated company liable to taxation on its capital shall be assessed in the tax district where the principal office or place for transacting the financial concerns of the company shall be, or if such company have no principal office, or place for transacting its financial concerns, then in the tax district where the operations of such company shall be carried on. In the case of toll bridges, the company owning such bridge shall be assessed in the tax district in which the tolls are collected; and where the tolls of any bridge, turnpike, or canal company are collected in several tax districts, the company shall be assessed in the tax district in which the treasurer or other officer authorized to pay the last preceding dividend resides.

Taxation of corporate stock.

§ 12. The capital stock of every company liable to taxation. except such part of it as shall have been excepted in the assess ment-roll or shall be exempt by law, together with its surplus profits or reserve funds exceeding ten per centum of its capital. after deducting the assessed value of its real estate, and all shares of stock in other corporations actually owned by such company which are taxable upon their capital stock under the laws of this state, shall be assessed at its actual value.

*   *   *   *   *   *   *   *   *   *

ARTICLE II.
Mode of Assessment.

Preparation of assessment roll.

§ 21. They shall prepare an assessment roll containing six separate columns and shall, according to the best information in their power, set down:

1. In the first column the names of all the taxable persons in the tax district.

2. In the second column the quantity of real property taxable to each person with a statement thereof in such form as the com missioners of taxes shall prescribe.

3. In the third column the full value of such real property

4. In the fourth column the full value of all the taxable per. sonal property owned by each person respectively after deducting the just debts owing by him.

5. In the fifth column the value of taxable rents reserved and chargeable upon lands within the tax district, estimated at a

principal sum, the interest of which, at the legal rate per annum, shall produce a sum equal to such annual rents and if payable in any other thing except money the value of the rents in money to be ascertained by them and the value of each rent assessed separately, and if the name of the person entitled to receive the rent assessed can not be ascertained by the assessors, it shall be assessed against the tenant in possession of the real property upon which the rents are chargeable.

6. In the sixth column the value of the special franchise as fixed by the state board of tax commissioners.

Thus amended by chap. 712, Laws of 1899, taking effect October 1, 1899.

7. Such assessment roll shall contain two additional columns in one of which shall be inserted the amount of the tax levied against each person named therein, and in the other the date of the payment of such tax.

Subdivision 7 added by chap. 159, Laws of 1901.

*   *   *   *   *   *   *   *   *   *

Reports of corporations.

§ 27. The president or other proper officer of every moneyed or stock corporation deriving an income or profit from its capital or otherwise shall, on or before June fifteenth, deliver to one of the assessors of the tax district in which the company is liable to be taxed and, if such tax district is in a county embracing a portion of the forest preserve, to the comptroller of the state, a written statement specifying: •

1. The real property, if any, owned by such company, the tax district in which the same is situated and, unless a railroad corporation, the sums actually paid therefor.

2. The capital stock actually paid in and secured to be paid in excepting therefrom the sums paid for real property and the amount of such capital stock held by the state and by any incorporated literary or charitable institution, and

3. The tax district in which the principal office of the company is situated or in case it has no principal office, the tax district in which its operations are carried on.

Such statement shall be verified by the officer making the same to the effect that it is in all respects just and true. If such statement is not made within twenty days after the fifteenth day of June, or is insufficient, evasive or defective, the assessors may compel the corporation to make a proper statement by mandamus.

Penalty for omission to make statement.

§ 28. In case of neglect to furnish such statements within thirty days after the time above provided, the company so neglecting shall forfeit to.the people of this state for each statement so omitted to be furnished, the sum of two hundred and fifty dollars, and it shall be the duty of the attorney-general to prosecute for such penalty upon information which shall be furnished him by the comptroller. Upon such statement being furnished and the costs of the suit being paid, the comptroller, if he shall be satisfied that such omission was not willful, may, in his discretion, discontinue such suit.

County clerks to furnish data respecting corporations.

§ 28-a. Between the first and fifteenth days of June in the year nineteen hundred and six, the county clerk in each county of the state, excepting counties containing a city of the second class and counties wholly situate within the corporate limits of a city, shall prepare from the records in his office.and mail to each of the town clerks in his said county, a certified statement containing the names of every stock corporation, incorporated within the five years next preceding the first day of June, nineteen hundred and six, whose principal business office or chief place of business is designated in its certificate of incorporation as being in such town or in any village or hamlet therein, together with the fact of such designation and the names and addresses of the directors of each such corporation so far as said county clerk can discover the same from the certificate of incorporation or from the latest certificate of election of directors of such corporation filed in his office. Annually thereafter, between the first and fifteenth days of June, said county clerk shall furnish to such town clerks the several statements aforesaid containing the above facts with reference to stock corporations whose certificates of incorporation have been filed with him since his last preceding annual state-ments to said several town clerks. Each town clerk receiving such statement shall forthwith file the same in his office and mail a notice of such filing to each of the assessors of his town.

Added by chap. 425, Laws of 1906.

*   *   *   *   *   *   *   *   *   *

Corporations, how assessed.

§ 31. The assessors shall assess corporations liable to taxa-tion in their respective tax districts upon their assessment rolls in the following manner:

1. In the first column the name of each corporation, and under its name the amount of its capital stock paid in and secured to be paid in; the amount paid by it for real property then owned by it wherever situated; the amount of all surplus profits or reserve funds exceeding ten per centum of their capital, after deducting therefrom the amount of said real property and the amount of its stock, if any, belonging to the state and to incorporated literary and charitable institutions.

2. In the second column the quantity of real property except special franchises owned by such corporation and situated within their tax district.

3. In the third column the actual value of such real property, except special franchises.

4. In the fourth column the amount of the capital stock paid in and secured to be paid in, and of all of such surplus profits or reserve funds as aforesaid, after deducting the sums paid out for all the real estate of the company, wherever the same may be situated. and then belonging to it, and the amount of stock,

if any, belonging to the people of the state and to incorporated literary and charitable institutions.

5. In the fifth column the value of any special franchise owned by it as fixed by the state board of tax commissioners.

Thus amended by chap. 712, Laws of 1899, taking effect October 1, 1899.

*   *   *   *   *   *   *   *   *   *

Notice of completion of assessment roll.

§ 35. The assessors shall complete the assessment roll on or before the first day of August, and make out a copy thereof, to be left with one of their number, and forthwith cause a notice to be conspicuously posted in three or more public places in the tax district, stating that they have completed the assessment roll, and that a copy thereof has been left with one of their number at a specified place, where it may be seen and examined by any person until the third Tuesday of August next following, and that on that day they will meet at a time and place specified in the notice to review their assessments. Upon application by a nonresident owner of real estate, having real estate in more than one tax district, the assessors may fix a time subsequent to the third Tuesday in August, but not later than the thirty-first day of August, for a hearing and to review their assessment. In any city the notice shall conform to the requirements of the law regulating the time, place and manner of revising assessments in such city. During the time specified in the notice the assessor with whom the roll is left shall submit to the inspection of every person applying for that purpose.

Thus amended by chap. 385, Laws of 1904.

*   *   *   *   *   *   *   *   *   *

§ 37. When the assessors or a majority of them shall have completed their roll, they shall severally appear before any officer of their county authorized by law to administer oaths and shall severally make and subscribe before such officer an oath in the following form: "We, the undersigned, do severally depose and swear that we have set down in the foregoing assessment roll all the real estate situated in the tax district in which we are assessors, according to our best information; and that, with the exception of those cases in which the value of the said real estate has been changed by reason of proof produced before us, and with the exception of those cases in which the value of any special franchise has been fixed by the state board of tax com. missioners, we have estimated the value of the said real estate at the sums which a majority of the assessors have decided to be the full value thereof; and, also, that the said assessment roll contains a true statement of the aggregate amount of the taxable personal estate of each and every person named in such roll over and above the amount of debts due from such persons, respect: ively, and excluding such stocks as are otherwise taxable, and such other property as is exempt by law from taxation, at the full value thereof, according to our best judgment and belief," which oath shall be written or printed on said roll, signed by the assessors and certified by the officer.

Thus amended by chap. 712, Laws of 1899, taking effect October 1, 1899.

*   *   *   *   *   *   *   *   *   H

Assessors to apportion valuation of railroad, telegraph, telephone, or pipe line companies between school districts.

§ 39. The assessors of each town in which a railroad, telegraph, telephone or pipe line company is assessed upon property lying in more than one school district therein, shall, within fifteen days after the final completion of the roll, apportion the assessed valuation of the property of each of such corporations among such school districts. Such apportionment shall be signed by the assessors or a majority of them, and be filed with the town clerk within five days thereafter, and thereupon the valuation so fixed shall become the valuation of such property in such school district for the purpose of taxation. In case of failure of the assessors to act, the supervisor of the town shall make such apportionment on request of either the trustees of any school district or of the corporation assesed.* The town clerk shall furnish the trustees a certified statement of the valuations apportioned to their respective districts. In case of any alteration in any school district affecting the valuation of such property, the officer making the same shall fix and determine the valuations in the districts affected for the current year.

*   *   *   *   *   *   *   *   *   *

Assessment of special franchises.

§ 42. The state board of tax commissioners shall annually fix and determine the valuation of each special franchise subject to assessment in each city, town, or tax district. After the time fixed for hearing complaints the tax commissioners shall finally determine the valuation of the special franchises, and shall file with the clerk of the city or town in which said special franchise is assessed a written statement duly certified by the secretary of the board of the valuation of each special franchise assessed therein as finally fixed and determined by said board; such statement of valuation shall be filed with the town clerk of the respective towns within thirty days next preceding the first day of July in each year; and with the clerks of cities of the state within thirty days before the date set opposite the name of each city in the following schedule. In the city of New York such statement shall be filed with the department of taxes and assessments.

SCHEDULE OF DATES FOR FILING OF ASSESSMENTS OF SPECIAL FRANCHISES.

Name of city.	Date.
Rochester	April first.
Jamestown	April first.
Ithaca	April first.
Gloversville	April first.

* So in original.

Name of city.	Date.
New York city	April first.
Auburn	May first.
Schenectady	June first.
Corning	June first.
Hornellsville	June first.
Oswego	June first.
North Tonawanda	July first.
Olean	July first.
Syracuse	July first.
Cohoes	July first.
Ogdensburg	July first.
Dunkirk	July first.
Troy	July first.
Rome	July first.
Watertown	July first.
Elmira	July first.
Lockport	July first.
Utica	July first.
Poughkeepsie	July first.
Little Falls	July first.
Watervliet	July first.
Niagara Falls	July first.
Kingston	July first.
Newburgh	July first.
Hudson	July first.
Amsterdam	July first.
Binghamton	July first.
Geneva	July first.
Middletown	July first.
Johnstown	July first.
Fulton	July first.
Plattsburgh	July first.
Tonawanda	July first.

Name of city.	Date.
Rensselaer	July first.
Oneida	July first.
Cortland	July first.
Yonkers	October first.
New Rochelle	October first.
Albany	October first.
Mount Vernon	October first.
Buffalo	December first.

Each city or town clerk shall, within five days after the receipt by him of the statement of assessment of a special franchise by the state board, deliver a copy of such statement certified by him to the assessors or other officers charged with the duty of making local assessments in each tax district in said city or town and to the assessors of villages and commissioners of highways within their respective towns and villages. The valuations of every special franchise as so fixed by the state board shall be entered by the assessors or other officers in the proper column of the assessment roll before the final revision and certification of such roll by them, and become part thereof with the same force and effect as if such assessment had been originally made by such assessor or other officer. If a special franchise assessed in a town is wholly within a village, the valuation fixed by the state board for the town shall also be the valuation for the village. If a part only of such special franchise is in a village, or is in a village situated in more than one tax district, it shall be the duty of the village assessors to ascertain and determine what portion of the valuation of such franchise, as the same has been fixed by the state board, shall be placed upon the tax roll for village purposes. The valuation apportioned to the town shall be the assessed valuation for highway purposes, and in case part of such special franchise shall be assessed in a village and part thereof in a town outside a village, the commissioner of highways of the town and village shall meet on the third Tuesday in August in each year and apportion the valuation of such special franchises between

such town outside the village and such village for highway purposes. In case of disagreement between them the decision of the
supervisor of the town shall be final. The town assessors shall
make an apportionment among school districts at the time and
in the manner required by section thirty-nine of this chapter. The
valuation so fixed by the state board shall be the assessed valuation on which all taxes based on such special franchise in the
. city, town or village for state, municipal, school or highway
purposes shall be levied during the next ensuing year. It shall
not be necessary for the state board of tax commissioners to give
notice to any person, copartnership, association or corporation
of the valuation of a special franchise located in any village for
village purposes except in a case where such valuation is required
to be made for such village purposes by the state board of tax
commissioners. The assessors or other taxing officer, or other
local officer in any city, town or village, or any state or county
officer, shall on demand furnish to the state board of tax commissioners any information required by such board for the purpose
of determining the value of a special franchise.

Thus amended by chap. 382, Laws of 1904; sections 2 and 3 chap. 382, Laws
of 1904 are as follows:

§ 2. This act shall not relate to the assessment of special franchises in the
city of Buffalo made or to be made by the state board of tax commissioners
in the year nineteen hundred and four for the purpose of raising the annual
taxes of said city of Buffalo for the fiscal year beginning July first, nineteen
hundred and four.

§ 3. Except as provided in section two hereof, this act shall take effect
immediately.

Report to state board of tax commissioners.

§ 43. Every person, co-partnership, association or corporation
subject to taxation on a special franchise, shall, within thirty
days after this section takes effect, or within thirty days after
such special franchise is acquired, make a written report to the
state board of tax commissioners containing a full description of
every special franchise possessed or enjoyed by such person, co-
partnership, association or corporation, a copy of the special law,

grant, ordinance, or contract under which the same is held, or
if possessed or enjoyed under a general law, a reference to such
law, a statement of any condition, obligation or burden imposed
upon such special franchise, or under which the same is enjoyed,
together with any other information relating to the value of
such special franchise, required by the state board. The state
board of tax commissioners may from time to time require a
further or supplemental report from any such person, co-partnership, association or corporation, containing information and
data upon such matters as it may specify. Every report required
by this section shall have annexed thereto the affidavit of the
president, vice-president, secretary or treasurer of the association
or corporation, or one of the persons or one of the members of
the co-partnership making the same, to the effect that the statements contained therein are true. Such board may prepare blanks
to be used in making the reports required by this section. Every
person, co-partnership, association or corporation failing to make
the report required by this section, or failing to make any special
report required by the state board of tax commissioners within
a reasonable time specified by it, shall forfeit to the people of
the state the sum of one hundred dollars for every such failure
and the additional sum of ten dollars for each day that· such
failure continues, and shall not be entitled to review the assessment by certiorari, as provided by section forty-five of this chapter.
Added by chap. 712, Laws of 1899, taking effect October 1, 1899.

Hearing on special franchise assessment.

§ 44. On making an assessment of a special franchise, the
state board of tax commissioners shall immediately give notice in
writing to the person, copartnership, association or corporation
affected, and to each city or town in which such special franchise
is subject to assessment, stating in substance that such assessment has been made, the total valuation of such special franchise,
and the valuation thereof in each city, town or tax district; and

that the board will meet at its office in the city of Albany on a day specified in such notice, which must not be less than twenty nor more than thirty days from the date of the notice, to hear and determine any complaint concerning such assessment. But no notice need be given any such town unless the supervisor thereof shall at least fifteen days prior to the time fixed for such hearing file with said board a request in writing for notice thereof. Such notice must be served at least ten days before the day fixed for the hearing; and it may be served on a copartnership, association or corporation, by mailing a copy thereof to it at its principal office or place of business and on a person, either personally or by mailing it to him at his place of business or last known place of residence; and on a city or town by mailing it to the mayor of such city or the supervisor of such town at the address specified in such request. A city or town entitled to notice under this section, shall have the right to be heard and to file affidavits and other proofs in respect to the valuation of such special franchise. Section thirty-six of this chapter applies so far as practicable to a hearing by the state board of tax commissioners under this section.

Thus amended by chap. 458, Laws of 1906.

Certiorari to review assessment.

§ 45. An assessment of a special franchise by the state board of tax commissioners may be reviewed in the manner prescribed by article eleven of this chapter, and that article applies so far as practicable to such an assessment, in the same manner and with the same force and effect as if the assessment had been made by local assessors; a petition for a writ of certiorari to review the assessment must be presented within fifteen days after the completion and filing of the assessment roll, and the first posting or publication of the notice thereof as required by law. Such writ must run to and be answered by said state board of tax commissioners and no writ of certiorari to renew* any assessment of a special franchise shall run to any other board or

---

*So in original.

officer unless otherwise directed by the court or judge granting the writ. An adjudication made in the proceeding instituted by such writ of certiorari shall be binding upon the local assessors and any ministerial officer who performs any duty in the collection of said assessment in the same manner as though said local assessors or officers had been parties to the proceeding. The state board of tax commissioners on filing with the city, town or village clerk a statement of the valuation of a special franchise, shall give to the person, co-partnership, association or corporation affected written notice that such statement has been filed, and such notice may be served on a co-partnership, association or corporation by mailing a copy thereof to it at its principal office or place of business, and on a person either personally or by mailing it to him at his place of business or last known place of residence.

Thus amended by chap. 254, Laws of 1900.

§ 45-a. In any proceeding for the review of an assessment of a special franchise made by the state board of tax commissioners, said state board of tax commissioners is authorized to appear by counsel to be designated by the attorney-general. The compensation of such counsel and the necessary and proper expenses and disbursements, including the expense of procuring the evidence of experts, incurred or made by him in the defense of such proceeding, and upon any appeals therein, shall when audited and allowed as are other charges against such tax district, be a charge upon the tax district upon whose rolls appears the assessment sought to be reviewed. Where, in one proceeding, there is reviewed the assessment of a special franchise in more than one tax district, separate accounts shall be rendered for said costs, expenses and disbursements to the proper officer of each of said tax districts and audited and allowed by him as aforesaid. For the purposes of this section, the city of New York shall be deemed one tax district.

Added by chap. 155, Laws of 1906.

Deduction from special franchise tax for local purposes.

§ 46. If, when the tax assessed on any special franchise is due and payable under the provisions of law applicable to the city, town or village in which the tangible property is located, it shall appear that the person, co-partnership, association or corporation affected has paid to such city, town or village for its exclusive use within the next preceding year, under any agreement therefor, or under any statute requiring the same, any sum based upon a percentage of gross earnings, or any other income, or any license fee, or any sum of money on account of such special franchise, granted to or possessed by such person, co-partnership, association, or corporation, which payment was in the nature of a tax, all amounts so paid for the exclusive use of such city, town or village except money paid or expended for paving or repairing of pavement of any street, highway or public place, shall be deducted from any tax based on the assessment made by the state board of tax commissioners for city, town or village purposes, but not otherwise; and the remainder shall be the tax on such special franchise payable for city, town or village purposes. The chamberlain or treasurer of a city, the treasurer of a village, the supervisor of a town, or other officer to whom any sum is paid for which a person, co-partnership, association, or corporation is entitled to credit as provided in this section, shall, not less than five nor more than twenty days before a tax on a special franchise is payable, make and deliver to the collector or receiver of taxes or other officer authorized to receive taxes for such city, town or village, his certificate showing the several amounts which have been paid during the year ending on the day of the date of the certificate. On the receipt of such certificate the collector, receiver or other officer shall immediately credit on the tax roll to the person, copartnership, association or corporation affected the amount stated in such

certificate, on any tax levied against such person, copartnership, association or corporation on an assessment of a special
franchise for city, town or village purposes only, but no credit
shall be given on account of such payment or certificate in any
other year, nor for a greater sum than the amount of the special
franchise tax for city, town or village purposes, for the current
year; and he shall collect and receive the balance, if any, of
such tax as required by law.

Added by chap. 712, Laws of 1899, taking effect October 1, 1899.

Special franchise tax not to affect other tax.

§ 47. The imposition or payment of a special franchise tax as
provided in this chapter shall not relieve any association, copartnership or corporation from the payment of any organization
tax or franchise tax or any other tax otherwise imposed by article nine of this chapter, or by any other provision of law; but
tangible property subject to a special franchise tax situated in,
upon, under or above any street, highway, public place or public
waters, as described in subdivision three of section two shall not
be taxable except upon the assessment made as herein provided
by the state board of tax commissioners.

Added by chap. 712, Laws of 1899, taking effect October 1, 1899.

*   *   *   *   *   *   *   *   *   *   *

ARTICLE III.
Equalization of Assessment and Levy of Tax.

*   *   *   *   *   *   *   *   *   *   *

**Statement of taxes upon certain corporations by clerk of super-
visors.**

§ 57. The clerk of each board of supervisors shall, within five
days after the tax warrant is completed, deliver to the county
treasurer, a statement showing the names, valuation of property and the amount of tax of every railroad corporation and
telegraph, telephone and electric-light line in each tax district
in the county, and on refusal or neglect so to do, shall forfeit to

the county the sum of one hundred dollars, to be sued for by the district attorney in the name of the county.

* * * * * * * * * *

ARTICLE IV.
Collection of Taxes.

* * * * * * * * * * *

Notice to non-residents.

§ 70a. A person who is the owner of, or liable to assessment for, an interest in real property situated and liable to assessment and taxation in a town in which he is not actually a resident may file with the town clerk of such town a notice stating his name, residence and post-office address, a description of the premises sufficient to identify the same, and if situated in a village or school district, the name of such village and number and designation of such school district. The town clerk shall, within five days after the delivery of the warrants for the collection of taxes in such tax districts, furnish to the collectors of the town, and the collector of each village and school district in which such real property is situated, and such collectors shall within such time apply for, a transcript of all notices so filed, and such collectors shall within five days after the receipt of such transcripts mail to each person filing such notice, at the post-office address stated therein, a statement of the amount of taxes due on said property. Upon the filing of such notice the town clerk shall be entitled to receive a fee of one dollar from the person offering such notice, which shall be in full for all services rendered hereunder.

Added by chap. 338, Laws of 1903.

* * * * * * * * * *

Payment of taxes by railroad and certain other corporations.

§ 73. Any railroad, telegraph, telephone or electric-light company may, within thirty days after receipt of notice by the county treasurer from the clerk of the board of supervisors, pay its tax. with one per centum fees, to the county treasurer, who shall credit the same with such fees to the collector of the tax district, unless otherwise required by law. If not so paid the county treasurer shall notify the collector of the tax district where it is due, and he shall then proceed to collect under his warrant. Until such notice from the treasurer the collector shall not enforce payment of such taxes, but may receive the same, with the fees allowed by law, at any time.

*   *   *   *   *   *   *   *   ▪   *

ARTICLE IX.

Corporation Tax.

*   ▼   ▼   *   *   *   *   *   ▼   ▼   *

Organization tax.

§ 180. Every stock corporation incorporated under any law of this state shall pay to the state treasurer a tax of one-twentieth of one per centum upon the amount of capital stock which the corporation is authorized to have, and a like tax upon any subsequent increase. Provided, that in no case shall such tax be less than one dollar. Such tax shall be due and payable upon the incorporation of such corporation or upon the increase of its capital stock. Except in the case of a railroad corporation neither the secretary of state nor county clerk shall file any certificate of incorporation or article of association, or give any certificate to any such corporation or association until he is furnished a receipt for such tax from the state treasurer, and no stock corporation shall have or exercise any corporate franchise or powers, or carry on business in this state until such tax shall have been paid. And in case of a decrease of capital stock, upon which the tax required by law has been paid, and a subsequent increase thereof, a tax shall be paid only upon so much of such increase as exceeds the amount of capital stock upon which a tax has been before paid. In case of the consolidation of existing

corporations into a corporation, such new corporation shall be required to pay the tax hereinbefore provided for only upon the
amount of its capital stock in excess of the aggregate amount of
capital stock of said corporations. This section shall not apply
to state and national banks or to building, mutual loan, accumu-
lating fund and cooperative associations. A railroad corporation
need not pay such tax at the time of filing its certificate of incorporation, but shall pay the same before the railroad commissioners shall grant a certificate, as required by the railroad law,
authorizing the construction of the road as proposed in its
articles of association, and such certificate shall not be granted
by the board of railroad commissioners until it is furnished with
a receipt for such tax from the state treasurer.

Thus amended by chap. 524, Laws of 1906.
See section 59, Railroad Law, *ante*.

License tax on foreign corporations.

§ 181. Every foreign corporation, except banking corporations, fire, marine, casualty and life insurance companies, co-
operative fraternal insurance companies, and building and loan
associations, authorized to do business under the general corporation law, shall pay to the state treasurer, for the use of the state,
a license fee of one-eighth of one per centum for the privilege of
exercising its corporate franchises or carrying on its business in
such corporate or organized capacity in this state, to be computed upon the basis of the capital stock employed by it within
this state, during the first year of carrying on its business in this
state; and if any year thereafter any such corporation shall
employ an increased amount of its capital stock within this state,
the same license fee shall be due and payable upon any such
increase. The measure of the amount of capital stock employed
in this state shall be such a portion of the issued capital stock
as the gross assets employed in any business within this state
bear to the gross assets wherever employed in business. For
purposes of taxation, the capital of a corporation invested in the
stock of another corporation shall be deemed to be assets located

where the physical property represented by such stock is located. No action shall be maintained or recovery had in any of the courts in this state by such foreign corporation without obtaining a receipt for the license fee hereby imposed within thirteen months after beginning such business within the state, or if at the time this section takes effect such a corporation has been engaged in business within this state for more than twelve months, without obtaining such receipt within thirty days after such tax is due.

Thus amended by chap. 474, Laws of 1906, taking effect October 31, 1906. See chap. 240, Laws of 1895, *ante.*

Franchise tax on corporations.

§ 182. For the privilege of doing business or exercising its corporate franchises in this state every corporation, joint-stock company or association, doing business in this state, shall pay to the state treasurer annually, in advance, an annual tax to be computed upon the basis of the amount of its capital stock, employed during the preceding year within this state, and upon each dollar of such amount. The measure of the amount of capital stock employed in this state shall be such a portion of the issued capital stock as the gross assets employed in any business within this state bear to the gross assets wherever employed in business. For purposes of taxation, the capital of a corporation invested in the stock of another corporation shall be deemed to be assets located where the physical property represented by such stock is located. If the dividends upon the capital stock amount to six, or more than six per centum upon the par value of the capital stock, during any year ending with the thirty-first day of October, the tax shall be at the rate of one-quarter of a mill for each one per centum of dividends made or declared upon the par value of the capital stock during said year. If such dividend or dividends amount to less than six per centum on the par value of the capital stock, and

(1) The assets do not exceed the liabilities, exclusive of capital stock, or

(2) The average price at which such stock sold during said year, did not equal or exceed its par value, or

(3) If no dividend was declared,

Then each dollar of the amount of capital stock employed in this state, determined as hereinbefore provided, shall be taxed at the rate of three-fourths of one mill. If such dividend or dividends amount to less than six per centum on the par value of the capital stock, and

(1) The assets exceed the liabilities, exclusive of capital stock, by an amount equal to or greater than the par value of the capital stock, or

(2) The average price at which such stock sold during said year is equal to or greater than the par value,

Then the amount of capital stock, determined as hereinbefore provided to be employed in this state, shall be taxed at the rate of one and one-half mills on each dollar of the valuation of the capital stock employed in this state, but such valuation shall not be less than

(1) The par value of such stock,

(2) The difference between the assets and liabilities, exclusive of capital stock,

(3) The average price at which such stock sold during said year.

If such corporation, joint-stock company or association shall have more than one kind of capital stock, and upon one of such kinds of stock a dividend or dividends amounting to six, or more than six per centum upon the par value thereof, has been made or declared, and upon the other no dividend has been made or declared, or the dividend or dividends made or declared thereon amount to less than six per centum upon the par value thereof, then the tax shall be at the rate of one-quarter of a mill for each one per centum of dividends made or declared upon the capital stock upon the par value of which the dividend or dividends made or declared amount to six or more than six per centum, and in addition thereto a tax shall be charged upon the capital stock

(1) Upon which no dividend was made or declared, or

(2) Upon which the dividend or dividends made or declared did not amount to six per centum on the par value,

At the rate as hereinbefore provided for the taxation of capital stock upon which no dividend was made or declared, or upon which the dividend or dividends made or declared did not amount to six per centum on the par value.

Thus amended by chap. 474, Laws of 1906, taking effect October 31, 1906.

Certain corporations exempt from tax on capital stock.

§ 183. Banks, savings banks, institutions for savings, title guaranty, insurance or surety corporations, every trust company incorporated, organized or formed, under, by or pursuant to a law of this state, and any company authorized to do a trust company business, solely or in connection with any other business, under a general or special law of this state, laundry corporations, manufacturing corporations to the extent only of the capital actually employed in this state in manufacturing, and in the sale of the product of such manufacturing, mining corporations wholly engaged in mining ores within this state, agricultural and horticultural societies or associations, and corporations, joint-stock companies or associations owning or operating elevated railroads or surface railroads not operated by steam, or formed for supplying water or gas for electric or steam heating, lighting or power purposes, and liable to a tax under sections one hundred and eighty-five and one hundred and eighty-six of this chapter, shall be exempt from the payment of the taxes prescribed by section one hundred and eighty-two of this chapter. But such a laundrying* manufacturing or mining corporation shall not be exempted from the payment of such tax, unless at least forty per centum of the capital stock of such corporation is invested in property in this state and used by it in its laundrying*, manu-facturing or mining business in this state.

Thus amended by chap. 474, Laws of 1906, taking effect October 31, 1906.

---

*So in original.

Additional franchise tax on transportation and transmission corporations and associations.

§ 184. Every corporation and joint-stock association formed for steam surface railroad, canal, steamboat, ferry, express, navigation, pipe-line, transfer, baggage express, telegraph, telephone, palace car or sleeping car purposes, and all other transportation corporations not liable to taxes under sections one hundred and eighty-five or one hundred and eighty-six of this chapter, shall pay for the privilege of exercising its corporate franchises or carrying on its business in such corporate or organized capacity in this state, an annual excise tax or license fee which shall be equal to five-tenths of one per centum upon its gross earnings within the state, which shall include its gross earnings from its transportation or transmission business originating and terminating within this state, but shall not include earnings derived from business of an interstate character. All settlemets* for such taxes heretofore based by the comptroller upon gross earnings excluding earnings from interstate business, have been ratified and confirmed, except that the accounts for taxation under section six of chapter three hundred and sixty-one of the laws of eighteen hundred and eighty-one, for the years eighteen hundred and ninety-two and eighteen hundred and ninety-three, shall be settled and adjusted by the comptroller by excluding the earnings of an interstate character as provided by this section.

Franchise tax on elevated railroads or surface railroads not operated by steam.

§ 185. Every corporation, joint-stock company or association owning or operating any elevated railroad or surface railroad not operated by steam shall pay to the state for the privilege of exercising its corporate franchise or carrying on its business in such corporate or organized capacity within this state, an annual tax which shall be one per centum upon its gross earnings from

---

*So .n original.

all sources within this state, and three per centum upon the
amount of dividends declared or paid in excess of four per centum
upon the actual amount of paid-up capital employed by such corporation, joint-stock company or association. Any such railroad
corporation whose property is leased to another railroad corporation shall only be required under this section to pay a tax
of three per centum upon the dividends declared and paid in
excess of four per centum upon the amount of its capital stock.
Thus amended by chap. 474, Laws of 1906, taking effect October 31, 1906.

* * * * * * * * * *

Reports of corporations.

§ 189. Corporations liable to pay a tax under this article shall
report as follows:

1. Corporations paying franchise tax.— Every corporation,
association or joint-stock company liable to pay a tax under
section one hundred and eighty-two of this chapter shall, on or
before November fifteenth in each year, make a written report
to the comptroller of its condition at the close of its business
on October thirty-first preceding, stating the amount of its
authorized capital stock, the amount of stock paid in, the date
and rate per centum of each dividend declared by it during the
year ending with such day, the entire amount of the capital of
such corporation, and the capital employed by it in this state
during such year.

2. Transportation and transmission corporations.—Every
transportation or transmission corporation, joint-stock company
or association liable to pay an additional tax under section one
hundred and eighty-four of this chapter, shall also, on or before
August first in each year, make a written report to the comptroller of its condition at the close of its business on June thirtieth preceding, stating the amount of its gross earnings from
all sources and the amount of its gross earnings from its transportation or transmission business originating and terminating
within this state.

3. Elevated and surface railroad corporations.—Every corporation, joint-stock company or association liable to pay a tax under section one hundred and eighty-five of this chapter, shall, on or before August first of each year, make a written report to the comptroller of its condition at the close of its business on June thirtieth preceding, stating the amount of its gross earnings from business done in this state, the amount of dividends of every nature declared or paid during the year ending June thirtieth, the authorized capital of the company and the amount of capital stock actually issued and outstanding.

* * * * * * * * * *

Value of stock to be appraised.

§ 190. If the dividend or dividends amount to less than six per centum on the par value of the capital stock, and

(1) The assets exceed the liabilities. exclusive of capital stock, by an amount equal to or greater than the par value of the capital stock, or

(2) The average price at which such stock sold during said year is equal to or greater than the par value of the capital stock,

Then the president, treasurer or secretary of the company liable to pay a tax under the provisions of section one hundred and eighty-two of this chapter, shall, under oath, between the first and fifteenth day of November in each year, estimate and appraise the capital stock of such company at a value which value shall not be less, however, than

(1) The average price at which such stock sold during said year,

(2) The difference between the assets and liabilities, exclusive of capital stock,

(3) The par value thereof,

And shall forward the same to the comptroller with the report provided for in the last section. If the comptroller is not satisfied with the valuation so made and returned he is authorized and empowered to make a valuation thereof, and settle an account upon the valuation so made by him, and the taxes, penalties and interest to be paid the state.

Thus amended by chap. 474, Laws of 1906, taking effect October 31, 1906.

Further requirements as to report of corporations.

§ 191. Every report required by this article shall have annexed thereto, the affidavit of the president, vice-president, secretary or treasurer of the corporation, association or joint-stock company or of the person or one of the persons, or the members of the partnership making the same, to the effect that the statements contained therein are true. Such reports shall contain any other data, information or matter which the comptroller may require to be included therein, and he may prescribe the form in which such reports shall be made and the form of oath thereto. When so prescribed such form shall be used in making the report. The comptroller may require at any time a further or supplemental report under this article, which shall contain information and data upon such matters as the comptroller may specify.

Powers of comptroller to examine into affairs of corporations.

§ 192. In case any report required by any of the preceding sections of this article shall be unsatisfactory to the comptroller or if any such report is not made as herein required, the comptroller is authorized to make an estimate of the dividen's paid by such corporation and the value of the capital stock employed by it, from any such report or from any other data, and to order and state an account according to the estimate and value so made by him for the taxes, percentage and interest due the state from such corporation, association, joint-stock company, person or partnership. The comptroller shall also have power to examine or cause to be examined in case of a failure to report or in case the report is unsatisfactory to him, the books and records of any such corporation, joint-stock asso.

ciation, company, foreign banker, person or partnership, and may hear testimony and take proofs material for his informa. tion, either personally or he may appoint a commissioner by a written appointment under his hand and official seal for that purpose. Every commissioner so appointed shall be authorized to make such examination and take such testimony and hear such proofs and report the proofs and testimony so taken and the result of his examination so made and the facts found by him to the comptroller. The comptroller shall, therefrom, or from any other data which shall be satisfactory to him, order and state an account for the tax due the state, together with the expenses of such examination and the taking of such testimony and proofs. Such expenses shall be fixed and adjusted by the comptroller.

Notice of statement of tax; interest.

§ 193. Upon auditing and stating every account for taxes or other charges under this article, the comptroller shall forthwith send notice thereof in writing to the person, partnership, com. pany, association or corporation against whom the same is made, which notice may be mailed to the post-office address of such person, partnership, association, company or corporation. All accounts so audited and stated shall bear interest upon the total amount found due thereon to the state, for taxes, percentage, interest and other charges, from the expiration of thirty days after sending such notice until payment thereof shall be made.

Payment of tax and penalty for failure.

§ 194. A tax imposed by section one hundred and eighty-two or one hundred and eighty-six of this chapter, shall be due and payable into the state treasury on or before the fifteenth day of January in each year. A tax imposed by section one hundred and eighty-four of this chapter on a transportation or transmis-

32

sion corporation, or by section one hundred and eighty-five, on elevated railroads or surface railroads not operated by steam shall be due and payable into the state treasury on or before the first day of August in each year. A tax imposed by section one hundred and eighty-seven of this chapter on an insurance corporation shall be due and payable into the state treasury on or before the first day of June in each year. A tax imposed by section one hundred and eighty-seven-a or one hundred and eighty-seven-b shall be due and payable into the state treasury on or before the first day of September in each year. A tax imposed by section one hundred and eighty-eight of this chapter on a foreign banker shall be due and payable into the state treasury on or before February first in each year. If such tax in any case is not paid within thirty days after the same becomes due, or if the report of any such corporation is not made within the time required by this article, the corporation, association, joint stock company, person or partnership, liable to pay the tax, shall pay into the state treasury in addition to the amount of such tax, a sum equal to five per centum thereof, and one per centum additional for each month the tax remains unpaid, which sum shall be added to the tax and paid or collected therewith. Every corporation, association, joint stock company, person or partnership failing to make the annual report required by this article, or failing to make any special report required by the comptroller, within any reasonable time to be specified by him, shall forfeit to the people of the state the sum of one hundred dollars for every such failure, and the additional sum of ten dollars for each day that such failure continues. Such tax shall be a lien upon and bind all the real and personal property of the corporation, joint stock company or association liable to pay the same from the time when it is payable until the same is paid in full.

Thus amended by chap. 558, Laws of 1901.

Revision and readjustment of accounts by comptroller.

§ 195. The comptroller may, at any time within one year from the time any such account shall have been audited and stated, and notice thereof sent to the person, partnership, company, association or corporation against whom it is stated, revise and readjust such account upon application therefor by the party against whom the account is stated or by the attorney-general, and if it shall be made to appear upon any such application by evidence submitted to him or otherwise, that any such account included taxes or other charges which could not have been lawfully demanded, or that payment has been legally made or exacted of any such account, he shall resettle the same according to law, and the facts and charge or credit, as the case may require, the difference if any, resulting from such revision or resettlement upon the accounts for taxes of or against any such person, partnership, company, association or corporation. Such credit, whether allowed before or after the passage of this act, may be, by the person, partnership, company, association or corporation in whose favor it is allowed, assigned to a person, partnership, company, association or corporation liable to pay taxes under article nine of this act and the assignee of the whole or any part of such credit on filing with the comptroller such assignment shall thereupon be entitled to credit on the books of the comptroller for the amount thereof on the current account for taxes of such assignee in the same way and with the same effect as though the credit had originally been allowed in favor of such assignee. The comptroller shall forthwith send written notice of his determination upon such application to the applicant, and to the attorney-general, which notice, may be sent by mail to his post-office address.

. Thus amended by chap. 642, Laws of 1903.

Review of determination of comptroller by certiorari.

§ 196. The determination of the comptroller upon any application made to him by any person, partnership, company, association or corporation for a revision and resettlement of any account, as prescribed in this article, may be reviewed both upon the law and the facts, upon certiorari by the supreme court at the instance of any person, partnership, company, association or corporation affected thereby, and in the name and on behalf of the people of the state. For the purpose of such review the comptroller shall return, on such certiorari, the accounts and all the evidence before him on such application. and all the papers and proofs upon the original statement of such account and all proceedings thereon. If the original or resettled accounts shall be found erroneous or illegal, either in point of law or of fact, by the supreme court, upon any such review, the accounts reviewed shall then be corrected and restated, and from any determination of the supreme court upon any such review, an appeal to the court of appeals may be taken by either party.

Regulations as to such writ of certiorari.

§ 197. No certiorari to review any audit and statement of an account or any determination by the comptroller under this article, shall be granted unless notice of application therefor is made within thirty days after the service of the notice of such determination. Eight days' notice shall be given to the comptroller of the application for such writ. The full amount of the taxes, percentage, interest and other charges, audited and stated in such account, must be deposited with the state treasurer before making the application and an undertaking filed with the comptroller in such amount and with such sureties as a justice of the supreme court shall approve, to the effect that if such writ is dismissed or the determination of the comptroller affirmed, the applicant for the writ will pay all costs and charges, which may accrue against him, or it in the prosecution of the writ, including costs of all appeals.

Warrant for the collection of taxes.

§ 198. After the expiration of thirty days from the sending by the comptroller of a notice of a statement of an account as provided in this article, unless the amount of such account shall have been paid or deposited with the state treasurer, if an appeal or other proceeding have been taken to review the same, and the undertaking given as provided in this article, the comptroller may issue a warrant under his hand and official seal, directed to the sheriff of any county of the state, commanding him to levy upon and sell the real and personal property of the person, partnership, company, association or corporation against which such account is stated, found within his county for the payment of the amount thereof with interest thereon and costs of executing the warrant, and to return such warrant to the comptroller and pay to the state treasurer the money collected by virtue thereof, by a time to be therein specified, not less than sixty days from the date of the warrant. Such warrant shall be a lien upon and shall bind the real and personal property of the person, partnership, company, association or corporation against which it is issued, from the time an actual levy shall be made by virtue thereof. The sheriff to whom any such warrant shall be directed shall proceed upon the same in all respects, with like effect, and in the same manner as prescribed by law in respect to executions issued against property upon judgments of a court of record, and shall be entitled to the same fees for his services in executing the warrant, to be collected in the same manner.

Information of delinquents.

§ 199. It shall be the duty of any person having knowledge of the evasion of taxation under this article by any corporation, association, joint-stock company, partnership or person liable to taxation thereunder, for any omission on their part to make the reports required by this article, to make a written report thereof

to the comptroller of the state, with such information as may
be in his possession as may lead to the recovery of any taxes
due the state therefrom. If, in his opinion, the interests of the
state require it, the comptroller may employ such person to
assist in the collection and preparation of evidence and in the
prosecution and trial of actions for such taxes, and so much of
the same, not exceeding ten per centum thereof, as may be collected from any such delinquent corporation, association, company, partnership or person, by reason of such report and such
services, as shall have been agreed upon between such person
and the comptroller or attorney-general as a compensation therefor, shall be paid to such person, and nothing shall be paid to
such person for such report or services unless there shall be a
recovery of taxes by reason thereof.

**Action for recovery of taxes; forfeiture of charter of delinquent
-   corporation.**

§ 200.   An action may be brought by the attorney-general, at
the instance of the comptroller, in the name of the state, to
recover the amount of any account audited and stated by the
comptroller under the provisions of this article. If any such
account shall remain unpaid at the expiration of one year after
notice of the statement thereof has been sent as required by
this article, and the comptroller is satisfied that the failure to
pay the same is intentional, he shall so report to the attorney-
general, who shall immediately bring an action, in the name
of the people of the state, for the forfeiture of the franchise of
any corporation, joint-stock company or association failing to
make such payment, and if it is found that such failure was
intentional, judgment shall be rendered in such action for the
forfeiture of its franchise and for its dissolution, and thereafter such franchise shall be annulled.

Reports to be made by the secretary of state.

§ 201. The secretary of state shall transmit on the first day of each month to the comptroller, a report of the stock corporations whose certificates of incorporation are filed, or of the foreign stock corporations to whom a certificate of authority has been issued to do business in this state, during the preceding month. Such report shall state the name of the corporation, its place of business, the amount of its capital stock, its purposes or objects, the names and places of residence of its directors, and, if a foreign corporation, its place of business within the state. The comptroller may prescribe the forms and furnish the blanks for such reports. The secretary of state shall make like reports to the comptroller whenever required by him relating to any such corporations whose certificates have been filed or to whom a certificate of authority has been issued prior to the time when this article takes effect, and during any period of time specified by the comptroller in his request for such report.

Exemptions from other state taxation.

§ 202. The personal property of every corporation, company, association or partnership, taxable under this article, other than for an organization tax, shall be exempt from assessment and taxation upon its personal property for state purposes, and the personal property of every corporation taxable under section one hundred and eighty-seven-a of this article, other than for an organization tax, and as provided in chapter thirty-seven of the general laws, shall be exempt from assessment and taxation for all other purposes, if all taxes due and payable under this article have been paid thereby. The personal property of a private or individual banker, actually employed in his business .as such banker, shall be exempt from taxation for state pur-poses, if such private or individual banker shall have paid all taxes due and payable under this article. Such corporation and

private or individual banker shall in no other respect be relieved
from assessment and taxation by reason of the provisions of
this article. The owner and holder of stock in an incorporated
trust company liable to taxation under the provisions of this
act shall not be taxed as an individual for such stock.

Thus amended by chap. 172, Laws of 1902.

Application of taxes.

§ 203. The taxes imposed by this article and the revenues
thereof shall be applicable to the general fund of the treasury
and to the payment of all claims and demands which are a lawful charge thereon.

*   *   *   *   *   *   *   *   *   *

ARTICLE XI.

Procedure.

Contents of petition.

§ 250. Any person assessed upon any assessment-roll, claiming to be aggrieved by any assessment for property therein, may
present to the supreme court a petition duly verified setting
forth that the assessment is illegal, specifying the grounds of
the alleged illegality, or if erroneous by reason of overvaluation,
stating the extent of such overvaluation, or if unequal in that
the assessment has been made at a higher proportionate valuation than the assessment of other property on the same roll by
the same officers, specifying the instances in which such inequality exists, and the extent thereof, and stating that he is or will
be injured thereby. Such petition must show that application
has been made in due time to the proper officers to correct such
assessment. Two or more persons assessed upon the same roll
who are affected in the same manner by the alleged illegality,
error or inequality, may unite in the same petition.

Allowance of writ of certiorari.

§ 251. Such petition must be presented to a justice of the
supreme court or at a special term of the supreme court in the

Allowance of writ of certiorari.

§ 251. Such petition must be presented to a justice of the
supreme court or at a special term of the supreme court in the
judicial district in which the assessment complained of was
made, within fifteen days after the completion and filing of the
assessment-roll and the first posting or publication of the notice
thereof as required by this chapter. Upon the presentation of
such petition, the justice or court may allow a writ of certiorari
to the officers making the assessment, to review such assessment, and shall prescribe therein the time within which a return
thereto must be made and served upon the relator's attorney,
which shall not be less than ten days, and may be extended by
the court or a justice thereof. Such writ shall be returnable to
a special term of the supreme court of the judicial district in
which the assessment complained of was made. The allowance
of the writ shall not stay the proceedings of the assessors or
other persons to whom it is directed or to whom the assessment
is delivered, to be acted upon according to law.

Return of writ.

§ 252. The officers making a return to such writ shall not be
required to return the original assessment-roll or other original
papers acted upon by them, but it shall be sufficient to return
certified or sworn copies of such roll or papers, or of such portions thereof as may be called for by such writ. The return
must concisely set forth such other facts as may be pertinent
and material to show the value of the property assessed on the
roll and the grounds for the valuation made by the assessing
officers and the return must be verified.

Proceedings upon return.

§ 253. If it shall appear upon the return to any such writ
that the assessment complained of is illegal or erroneous or unequal for any of the reasons alleged in the petition, the court
may order such assessment, if illegal, to be stricken from the
roll, or if erroneous or unequal, it may order a re-assessment of
the property of the petitioner, or the correction of his assess-

ment upon the roll, in whole or in part, in such manner as shall be in accordance with law, or as shall make it conform to the valuations and assessments of other property upon the same roll and secure equality of assessment. If upon the hearing it shall appear to the court, that testimony is necessary for the proper disposition of the matter, it may take evidence or may appoint a referee to take such evidence as it may direct, and report the same to the court, with his findings of fact and conclusions of law, which shall constitute a part of the proceedings upon which the determination of the court shall be made. A new assessment or correction of an assessment made by order of the court shall have the same force and effect as if it had been so made by the proper officers within the time prescribed by law for making such assessment.

Costs.

§ 254. Costs shall not be allowed against the officers whose proceedings may be reviewed under any such writ unless it shall appear to the court that they acted with gross negligence or in bad faith or with malice in making the assessment complained of. If the writ shall be quashed or the assessment confirmed, or if the assessment complained of shall be reduced by an amount less than half the reduction claimed before the assessing officers costs and disbursements shall be awarded against the petitioner. If the assessment shall be reduced by an amount greater than half the reduction claimed before the assessing officers, costs and disbursements shall be awarded against the tax district represented by the officers whose proceedings may be reviewed. The costs and disbursements shall not exceed those taxable in an action upon the trial of an issue of fact in the supreme court, except that if evidence shall be taken there shall be included in the taxable costs and disbursements the expense of furnishing to the court or to the referee a copy of the stenographer's minutes of the evidence taken.

Thus amended by chap. 281, Laws of 1905; sections 2 and 3 of said chapter being as follows:

§ 2. This amendment shall not apply to the proceedings under any writ granted prior to the first day of July, nineteen hundred and five.

§ 3. This act shall take effect July first, nineteen hundred and five.

Appeals.

§ 255. An appeal may be taken by either party from an order judgment or determination under this article as from an order and it shall be heard and determined in like manner as appeals in the supreme court from orders. All issues and appeals in any proceeding under this article shall have preference over all other civil actions and proceedings in all courts.

Refund of tax paid upon illegal, erroneous or unequal assessment.

§ 256. If in a final order in any such proceeding it shall be ordered or adjudged that the assessment complained of was illegal, erroneous or unequal, and such order shall not be made in time to enable the assessors or other officers to make a new or corrected assessment for the use of the board of supervisors, then at the first annual session of the board of supervisors after such correction there shall be audited and allowed to the petitioner and included in the tax levy of such town, village or city, made next after the entry of such order, and paid to the petitioner, the amount paid by him, in excess of what the tax would have been if the assessment had been made as determined by such order of the court, together with interest thereon from the date of payment. In case the amount deducted from such assessment by such order exceeds ten thousand dollars, so much thereof as shall be refunded by reason of such corrected assessment, other than the proportion or percentage thereof collected for such town, village or city purposes, shall be levied upon the county at large and paid to the petitioner without further audit. The board of supervisors shall audit and levy upon such town, village or city, the proportion or percentage of such excess of tax collected for such town, village or city purposes, which shall be collected and paid to the petitioner without other or further audit.

Supplementary proceedings to collect tax.

§ 259. If a tax exceeding ten dollars in amount levied against a person or corporation is returned by the proper collector uncollected for want of personal property out of which to collect the same, the supervisor of the town or ward, or the county treasurer or the president of the village, if it is a village tax, may, within one year thereafter, apply to the court for the institution of proceedings supplementary to execution, as upon a judgment docketed in such county, for the purpose of collecting such tax and fees, with interest thereon from the fifteenth day of February after the levy thereof. Such proceedings may be taken against a corporation, and the same proceedings may thereupon be had in all respects for the collection of such tax as for the collection of a judgment by proceedings supplementary to execution thereon against a natural person, and the same costs and disbursements may be allowed against the person or corporation examined as in such supplementary proceedings but none shall be allowed in his or its favor. The tax, if collected in such proceeding, shall be paid to the county treasurer or to the supervisor of the town, and if a village tax, to the treasurer of the village. The costs and disbursements collected shall belong to the party instituting the proceedings, and shall be applied to the payment of the expense of such proceeding. The president of a village and a county treasurer shall have no compensation for any such proceeding. A supervisor shall have no other compensation except his per diem pay for time necessarily spent in the proceeding.

Dismissal of suits or proceedings

§ 259-a. Where the person or corporation against whom a proceeding or suit is brought to collect a personal tax in arrears in any town or ward, village, county or city of this state is unable for want of property to pay the tax in whole or in part, or where for other reasons, upon the facts, it appears to the court just that said tax should not be paid, the court may dismiss such suit or proceeding on the payment of such part of the tax as may be just or on payment of costs.

Added by chap. 348, Laws of 1905.

* * * * * * * * * *

Attorney-general to bring action for sequestration.

§ 263. It shall be the duty of the attorney-general, on being informed by the comptroller or by the county treasurer of any county that any incorporated company refuses or neglects to pay the taxes imposed upon it, pursuant to articles one and two of this chapter, to bring an action in the supreme court for the sequestration of the property of such corporation and the court may so sequestrate the property of such corporation for the purpose of satisfying taxes in arrear,* with the costs of prosecution, and may, also, in its discretion, enjoin such corporation and further proceedings under its charter until such tax and the costs incurred in the action shall be paid. The attorney-general may recover such tax with costs from such delinquent corporation by action in any court of record.

* * * * * * * * * *

†ARTICLE XII.

Laws repealed; when to take effect.

LAWS REPEALED.

§ 280. Of the laws enumerated in the schedule hereto annexed, that portion specified in the last column is repealed.

When to take effect.

§ 281. This chapter shall take effect June fifteenth, eighteen hundred and ninety-six.

---

*So in original.
†See articles 14 and 15 (mortgage tax and stock transfer tax), following.

SCHEDULE OF LAWS REPEALED.

Revised Statutes.	Sections.
Part 1, ch. 13	All, except § 7 of tit. VI.
Part III, ch. 8, tit. XVII	§§ 28, 29, 30.

Laws of	Chapter.	Sections.
1835	11	All.
1836	461	All.
1841	341	All.
1842	154	All.
1842	318	All.
1845	180	29, 30, 31, 32.
1846	327	All.
1847	455	16.
1847	482	All.
1849	180	All.
1851	176	All.
1851	371	All.
1852	46	All.
1852	282	All.
1853	69	All.
1853	406	All.
1853	469	All.
1854	393	All.
1855	37	All.
1855	83	All.
1855	327	All.
1855	427	All.
1856	183	All.
1857	7	All.
1857	456	All.
1857	536	All.
1857	585	All.

LAWS OF	CHAPTER.	SECTIONS.
1858	110	All.
1858	357	All.
1859	312	All.
1860	209	All.
1862	194	All.
1862	285	1.
1865	453	All.
1866	136	All.
1866	528	All.
1866	820	All.
1867	361	All.
1867	694	All.
1868	575	All.
1869	859	All.
1870	280	All.
1870	325	All.
1870	492	Extract from § 2, authorizing comptroller to designate papers in which notice of sale of lands for non-payment of taxes shall be published.
1870	506	2, 3, 4, 5.
1871	110	All.
1873	327	All.
1873	809	All.
1874	351	All.
1875	331	All.
1875	466	All.
1875	474	All.
1876	49	All.

Laws of	Chapter.	Sections.
1876	96	All.
1876	101	All.
1878	152	All.
1879	492	All.
1880	80	All.
1880	91	All.
1880	269	All.
1880	327	All.
1880	448	All.
1880	542	All.
1880	552	All.
1881	8	All.
1881	166	All.
1881	293	All.
1881	361	All.
1881	402	5.
1881	433	All.
1881	640	All.
1882	151	All.
1882	409	312-327 inclusive.
1883	342	All.
1883	392	All.
1883	397	All.
1883	464	All.
1884	57	All.
1884	153	All.
1884	280	All.
1884	353	All.
1884	414	All.
1884	435	All.
1884	537	All.
1885	10	All.
1885	82	All.

Laws of	Chapter.	Sections.
1885	201	All.
1885	215	All.
1885	340	12.
1885	359	All.
1885	411	All.
1885	453	All.
1885	501	All.
1886	59	All.
1886	102	All
1886	143	All.
1886	206	All.
1886	315	All.
1886	659	1, 2, 3, 5, 6.
1886	679	All.
1887	284	All.
1887	342	All.
1888	110	All.
1889	191	All.
1889	193	All.
1889	353	All.
1889	462	All.
1889	463	All.
1889	469	All.
1889	563	All.
1890	145	All.
1890	174	All.
1890	206	All.
1890	497	All.
1890	522	All.
1890	553	All.
1890	556	All.
1891	163	All.
1891	211	All.

33

LAWS OF	CHAPTER.	SECTIONS.
1891	218	All.
1892	196	All.
1892	202	1.
1892	266	All.
1892	347	All.
1892	399	All.
1892	463	All.
1892	477	All.
1892	529	All.
1892	565	All.
1892	661	All.
1892	668	All.
1892	713	All.
1892	714	All.
1893	199	All.
1893	498	All.
1893	525	All.
1893	704	All.
1893	711	All.
1894	196	All.
1894	312	All.
1894	562	All.
1894	713	All.
1895	378	All.
1895	418	All.
1895	425	All.
1895	515	All.
1895	556	All.
1895	558	All.
1895	608	All.
1895	895	All.
Fisheries, Game and Forest Law		274.

*ARTICLE XIV.

Definitions.

§ 290. The words real property and real estate as used in this article, in addition to the definition thereof contained in section two of this chapter shall be understood to include everything a conveyance or mortgage of which can be recorded as a conveyance or mortgage of real property under the laws of the state. The words mortgage of real property as used in this article include every mortgage by which a lien is created over or imposed on real property or which affects the title to real property, notwithstanding that it may also be a lien on personal or other property or that personal or other property may form part of the security for the debt or debts secured by such mortgage. Executory contracts for the sale of real property under which the vendee has or is entitled to possession shall be deemed to be mortgages for the purposes of this article and shall be assessed at the amount unpaid on such contracts.

Exemption from local taxation.

§ 291. All mortgages of real property situated within the state which are taxed by this article and the debts and the obligations which they secure, together with the paper writings evidencing the same, shall be exempt from other taxation by the state, counties, cities, towns, villages, school districts and other local subdivisions of the state, except that such mortgage shall not be

* Article XIV is printed here as it was amended by chap. 532, Laws of 1906, taking effect July 1, 1906.

exempt from the taxes imposed by sections twenty four, one hundred and eighty-seven, one hundred and eighty-seven-a, one hundred and eighty-seven-b and article ten of the tax law; but the exemption conferred by this section shall not be construed to impair or in any manner affect the title of any purchaser of land or real estate which may be sold for nonpayment of taxes levied by any local authority.

Exemptions.

§ 292. No mortgage of real property situated within this state shall be exempt, and no person or corporation owning any debt or obligation secured by mortgage of real property situated within this state shall be exempt, from the taxes imposed by this article by reason of anything contained in any other statute, or by reason of any provision in any private act or charter which is subject to amendment or repeal by the legislature, or by reason of nonresidence within this state or for any other cause.

Recording tax.

§ 293. A tax of fifty cents for each one hundred dollars and each remaining major fraction thereof of principal debt or obligation which is, or under any contingency may be secured by mortgage of real property situated within the state recorded on or after the first day of July, nineteen hundred and six, is hereby imposed on each such mortgage, and shall be collected and paid as provided in this article.

Payment of taxes.

§ 294. The taxes imposed by this article shall be payable on the recording of each mortgage of real property subject to taxes thereunder. Such taxes shall be paid to the recording officer of any county in which the real property or any part thereof is situated. It shall be the duty of such recording officer to indorse upon each mortgage a receipt for the amount of the tax so paid. Any mortgage so indorsed may thereupon or thereafter be recorded by any recording officer and the receipt for such tax indorsed upon each mortgage shall be recorded therewith. The record of such receipt shall be conclusive proof that the amount of tax stated therein has been paid upon such mortgage.

Effect of nonpayment of taxes.

§ 295. No mortgage of real property shall be recorded by any county clerk, or register on or after the first day of July, nineteen hundred and six, unless there shall be paid the tax imposed by and as in this article provided. No mortgage of real property which is subject to the taxes imposed by this article shall be released, discharged of records* or received in evidence in any action or proceeding, nor shall any assignment of or agreement extending any such mortgage be recorded unless the taxes imposed thereon by this article shall have been paid as provided in this article. No judgment or final order in any action or proceeding shall be made for the foreclosure or enforcement of any mortgage which is subject to the taxes imposed by this article or of any debt or obligation secured by or which secures any such mortgage, unless the taxes imposed by this article shall have been paid as provided in this article.

Trust mortgages.

§ 296. In the case of mortgages made by corporations in trust to secure payment of bonds or obligations issued or to be issued thereafter, if the total amount of principal indebtedness which under any contingency may be advanced or accrue or which may become secured by any such mortgage which is subject to this article has not been advanced or accrued thereon or become secured thereby before such mortgage is recorded, it may contain at the end thereof a statement of the amount which at the time of the execution and delivery thereof has been advanced or accrued thereon, or which is then secured by such mortgage; thereupon the tax payable on recording of the mortgage shall be computed on the basis of the amount so stated to have been so advanced or accrued thereon or which is stated to be secured thereby. Such statement shall thereafter at all times be binding upon and con-

* So in the original.

clusive against the mortgagee, the holders of any bonds or obligations secured by such mortgage and all persons claiming through
the mortgagee any interest in the mortgage or in the mortgaged
premises. The tax for such sums of principal indebtedness as
may be advanced, accrue or become secured after the execution
and delivery of any such mortgage shall be payable at or before
the time when such sums are advanced, accrue or become secured.
Such additional tax shall be paid to the recording officer where
such mortgage has been or is first recorded and a receipt therefor
shall be indorsed upon the mortgage and payment therefor shall
be noted in the margin of the record of such mortgage and the
note of such payment or additional payment shall have the same
force and effect as the record of receipt of the tax which under
this article is payable at or before the recording of the mortgage.

Apportionment by state board of tax commissioners.

§ 297. When the real property covered by a mortgage is assessed in more than one county it shall be the duty of the state
board of tax commissioners to ascertain the assessed value of the
property in each county and to apportion the amount upon which
the tax shall be paid to the recording officer in each of the said
counties upon the basis of the relative assessments. Where the
mortgage is a first lien upon real property situate in one tax
district and a subsequent lien upon real property situate in
another tax district it shall be their duty to apportion the amount
of the tax properly to be credited to said tax districts by ascertaining the valuation of each parcel as appears from the last
preceding assessment-roll of the tax district in which such
parcel is located after deducting therefrom the taxable amount
of any prior lien. When the real property covered by a
mortgage is located partly within the state and partly without
the state it shall be the duty of the state board of tax commissioners to determine what proportion shall be taxable
under this article by determining the relative value of the
mortgaged property within this state as compared to the total
value of the entire mortgaged property, taking into consideration

in so doing the amount of all prior incumbrances upon such property or any portion thereof. If a mortgage covering property located partly within the state and partly without the state, is presented for record before such determination has been made, then there may be presented to the recording officer with such mortgage, a statement in duplicate verified by the mortgagor or an officer or duly authorized agent or attorney of the mortgagor, specifying the value of the property covered by the mortgage within the state and the property covered by the mortgage without the state, stated separately. One of such satements shall be filed by the recording officer and the other shall be transmitted by him to the state comptroller. The tax payable under this article before the determination by the state board of tax commissioners, shall be computed upon such proportion of the principal indebtedness secured by the mortgage as the value of the mortgaged property within the state shall bear to the total value of the entire mortgaged property as set forth in such statement. The state comptroller shall present the statement transmitted to him or a certified copy thereof to the state board of tax commissioners who shall thereupon on not less than ten days' notice, served personally or by mail upon the person making such statement, the mortgagee and upon the comptroller, proceed to determine what proportion of the principal indebtedness secured by the mortgage shall be used as the measure of taxation within the state under the provisions of this article. They may also determine at the same time the proportion of the tax which shall be paid by the recording officer who has received the same, to the several county treasurers of the respective counties in the state, in which parts of the mortgaged property are situated, and also the proportion of the tax to be distributed under the provisions of this article to be credited to each town or city within a county. The state board of tax commissioners shall report their determination to the state comptroller who shall file a certified copy of such determination with the recording officer of each county in which any part of the mortgaged property is situated.

The comptroller shall serve a copy of such certificate personally
or by mail upon the person making such statement and upon the
mortgagee together with a notice requiring the payment to the
proper recording officer within ten days thereafter, of the amount
of the tax on such mortgage, if any, which under the determination of said board remains unpaid. Such additional tax shall
become due and be deemed unpaid upon the expiration of such
period of ten days. The state board of tax commissioners shall
adopt rules to govern their procedure and the manner of taking
evidence in these matters and may require certified statements to
be furnished either by boards of assessors or recording officers of
the respective counties in relation thereto, and immediately upon
making their determination they shall file a certificate thereof
with the recording officer of each county within which a portion
of the mortgaged property is situated; and a minute of such
determination shall be entered in the margin of the record of the
said mortgage, and whenever the tax upon a mortgage secured by
real property assessed in two or more counties shall have been
paid, as provided by this article it shall also be the duty of the
state board of tax commissioners to equitably apportion between
the respective counties the amount upon which such tax is to be
computed and to file the certificate of their determination with
the recording officer, and thereupon said recording officer shall
pay over to the several county treasurers of the respective counties or to the chamberlain of the city of New York the sums
fixed by said certificate of determination.

Payment over and distribution of taxes.

§ 298. Upon the first day of each month the recording officer
of each county shall pay over to the county treasurer of said
county, and in the counties of New York, Kings, Queens and
Richmond to the chamberlain of the city of New York all moneys
received during the preceding month upon account of taxes paid
to him as herein described, after deducting the necessary expenses
of his office as provided in section two hundred and ninety-nine,
except taxes paid upon a mortgage which under the provisions

of section two hundred and ninety-seven is to be apportioned by
the state board of tax commissioners between several counties,
which taxes and money shall be paid over by him as provided by
the determination of said state board of tax commissioners within
five days after the filing of said determination in his office. The
county treasurer of each county and in the counties of New York,
Kings, Queens and Richmond the city chamberlain of the city of
New York shall on the first day of January, nineteen hundred
and seven, and quarterly thereafter, after having deducted the
necessary expenses of his office provided in section two hundred
and ninety-nine, transmit one-half of this net amount collected
under the provisions of this article to the state treasurer and
shall receive from the state treasurer a receipt therefor countersigned by the comptroller. And the remaining portion thereof
in the counties of New York, Kings, Queens and Richmond shall
be paid into the general fund of the city of New York and be
applied to the reduction of taxation, and in the other counties of
the state the remaining portion shall be held by the respective
county treasurers subject to the order of the board of supervisors
as hereinafter provided. Prior to the first day of December in
each year the county clerk shall cause to be prepared a list containing a description of all mortgages upon which taxes have been
paid by a reference to the date of each mortgage, the name of the
mortgagor and mortgagee, the amount of the principal debt upon
which the tax was paid together with the book and page where
said mortgage is recorded, together with the town, city or village
in which the mortgaged property is assessed, and if assessed in
two or more tax districts the amount apportioned to each tax
district by the state board of tax commissioners, and shall file the
statement in his office and shall furnish a copy thereof to the
clerk of the board of supervisors, and another copy thereof to the
county treasurer. The board of supervisors of the several counties shall, on or before the fifteenth day of December in each year,
ascertain from the statement filed with their clerk by the county
clerk the location of the mortgaged property with respect to the
several tax districts and the amount of tax properly to be credited

to each town, city and village and of the sum so credited to each
town which does not contain within its boundaries an incorporated village or portion thereof and to each city other than the
city of New York, one-half thereof shall be applicable to the payment of school taxes and one-half thereof shall be applicable to
the payment of state, county and city, or town expenses; where
the town contains within its limits a city, incorporated village,
or portion thereof, the supervisor shall apportion to the city, village or villages so much of the share credited to the said town
as the assessed value of said city, village or portion thereof bears
to twice the total assessed valuation of the town, and one-half
of the remaining balance shall be applicable to the payment of
state, county and town taxes, and one-half to the payment of
school taxes. The board of supervisors of each county, on or
before the fifteenth day of December each year shall determine
the respective sums applicable hereunder to each of the foregoing
purposes and shall issue their warrant for the payment to the
city or town collector of the amount payable to said city or town,
and their warrant for the payment to the village treasurer of the
sum of money to which the village shall be entitled, and for the
payment to the city official having authority to receive the other
moneys raised by tax for school purposes in said municipality,
and to the supervisor of each town of the amount to which the
town is entitled for the payment of school taxes; and it shall
be the duty of said supervisor of a town to apportion the sum
so paid to him for school purposes between the several school districts upon the basis of the aggregate days' attendance as appears
from the statement filed with him by the school commissioners
in March of each year and shall notify the trustee or trustees of
said school district of the amount standing to the district's credit
in his hands, which sum shall be deducted from the next annual
school levy of said district and shall be paid by the supervisor
to the collector of the school district as soon as the said collector
shall have received his warrant for the collection of the next
annual tax.

Expenses of officers.

§ 299. Recording officers and county treasurers and the chamberlain of the city of New York, shall severally be entitled to receive all their necessary expenses for the purposes of this act, including printing, hire of clerks and assistants, being first approved and allowed by the state board of tax commissioners, which shall be retained by them out of the moneys coming into their hands.

Supervisory power of state board of tax commissioners and state comptroller.

§ 300. The state board of tax commissioners shall have general supervisory power over all recording officers in respect of the duties imposed by this article and they may make such rules and regulations for the government of recording officers in respect to the matters provided for in this article as they may deem proper, provided that such rules and regulations shall not be inconsistent with this or any other statute. The state comptroller shall have general supervisory power over all county treasurers and the chamberlain of the city of New York in respect to the duties imposed upon them by this article, and may make such rules and regulations, not inconsistent with this or any other statute, for the government of said county treasurers and chamberlain as he deems necessary and appropriate to secure a due accounting for all taxes and moneys collected or received pursuant to any provision of this article. All recording officers and county treasurers, and the chamberlain of the city of New York, shall furnish such bond, conditioned for the faithful and diligent discharge of the duties required of them respectively by this article, to the people of the state, within such time, with such sureties and in such penal amount, not exceeding twenty-five thousand dollars, as the state comptroller may prescribe.

Tax on prior advance mortgages.

§ 301. A tax is imposed hereby on each mortgage of real property recorded prior to the first day of July, nineteen hundred and six, when any part of the amount of principal indebtedness which is or under any contingency may be secured by any such mortgage is advanced, after first day of July, nineteen hundred and six. The tax imposed by this section shall be at the rate of fifty cents for each one hundred dollars and each remaining major fraction thereof which is, or under any contingency may be secured by any mortgage taxed under this section, deducting therefrom however any tax paid on such mortgage under chapter seven hundred and twenty-nine of the laws of nineteen hundred and five. The tax imposed by this section shall be paid to the recording officer of the county in which the mortgage is first recorded and shall be paid when at any time any part of the said amount of principal indebtedness is advanced after the first day of July, nineteen hundred and six.

§ 23. *Chapter 532, Laws of 1906.* All taxes imposed by or which became due, payable or collectible on or before the thirtieth day of June, nineteen hundred and six, pursuant to chapter seven hundred and twenty-nine of the laws of nineteen hundred and five, and all taxes which under section two hundred and ninety-five of the said act are to become due and payable on the thirtieth day of July, nineteen hundred and six, and all other taxes, if any, which were imposed by chapter seven hundred and twenty-nine of the laws of nineteen hundred and five on any mortgage recorded prior to the first day of July, nineteen hundred and six, in respect to any period ending on or before the first day of July, nineteen hundred and six, shall be imposed, become due, be payable and collectible, and shall be paid over and distributed in the same manner, and with the same force and effect as if this act had not been enacted; and for the purpose of collecting, paying over, distributing and enforcing any such taxes, chapter seven hundred and twenty-nine of the laws of nineteen hundred and five shall be deemed to be in force, and the lien for such taxes shall attach and such taxes shall be levied and collected as provided in chapter seven hundred and twenty-nine of the laws of nineteen hundred and five, anything herein contained to the contrary notwithstanding.

*ARTICLE XV.

Tax on Transfers of Stock.

*Added by chap. 241, Laws of 1905.

Amount of tax.

§ 315. There is hereby imposed and there shall immediately accrue and be collected a tax as herein provided, on all sales, or agreements to sell, or memoranda of sales, or deliveries, or transfers, of shares or certificates of stock, in any domestic or foreign association, company or corporation, made after the first day of June, nineteen hundred and five, whether made upon or shown by the books of the association, company or corporation, or by any assignment in blank, or by any delivery, or by any paper or agreement or memorandum or other evidence of transfer or sale whether entitling the holder in any manner to the benefit of such stock, or to secure the future payment of money or the future transfer of any stock, on each share of one hundred dollars of face value or fraction thereof, two cents. It is not intended by this act to impose a tax upon an agreement evidencing the deposit of stock certificates as collateral security for money loaned thereon which stock certificates are not actually sold, nor upon such stock certificates so deposited. The payment of such tax shall be denoted by an adhesive stamp or stamps affixed as follows: In a case where the evidence of transfer is shown only by the books of the company the stamp shall be placed upon such books; and where the change of ownership is by transfer of a certificate the stamp shall be placed upon the certificate; and in cases of an agreement to sell or where the transfer is by delivery of the certificate assigned in blank there shall be made and delivered by the seller to the buyer a bill or memorandum of such sale to which the stamp provided for by this article shall be affixed; and every bill or memorandum of sale or agreement to sell before mentioned shall show the date thereof, the name of the seller, the amount of the sale, and the matter or thing to

which it refers, and no further tax is hereby imposed upon the delivery of the certificate of stock, or upon the actual issue of a new certificate when the original certificate of stock is accompanied by the duly stamped memorandum of sale. The comptroller may, upon satisfactory proof that stamps have been erroneously affixed and canceled in payment of the tax upon a transfer and to the loss of an innocent person, refund the amount thereof from appropriations made for necessary expenses under this act, provided the tax justly due is paid upon such transfer.
Thus amended by chap. 414, Laws of 1906.

§ 316. Stamps how prepared and sold.—Adhesive stamps for the purpose of paying the state tax provided for by this article shall be prepared by the state comptroller, in such form, and of such denominations and in such quantities as he may from time to time prescribe, and shall be sold by him to the person or persons desiring to purchase the same; he shall make provision for the sale of such stamps in such places and at such times as in his judgment he may deem necessary.

Penalty for failure to pay tax.

§ 317. Any person or persons who shall make any sale or transfer without paying the tax by this article imposed or who shall in pursuance of any sale or agreement deliver any stock, or evidence of the sale of or agreement to sell any stock or bill or memorandum thereof, without having the stamps provided for in this article affixed thereto, shall be deemed guilty of a misdemeanor, and upon conviction thereof shall pay a fine of not less than five hundred nor more than one thousand dollars, or be imprisoned not more than six months, or by both such fine and imprisonment at the discretion of the court.
Thus amended by chap. 414, Laws of 1906.

§ 318. Cancelling stamps; penalty for failure.—In every case where an adhesive stamp shall be used to denote the payment of the state tax provided by this article the person using or affixing the same shall write or stamp thereupon the initials of his name and the date upon which the same shall be attached or used, and shall cut or perforate the stamp in a substantial manner, so that such stamp cannot be again used; and if any person fraudulently makes use of an adhesive stamp to denote the state tax imposed by this article, without so effectually cancelling and obliterating such stamp such person shall be deemed guilty of a misdemeanor, and upon conviction thereof shall pay a fine of not less than two hundred nor more than five hundred dollars or be imprisoned for not less than six months, or both, at the discretion of the court.

§ 319. Contracts for dies; expenses how paid.—The state comptroller is hereby directed to make, enter into and execute for and in behalf of the state such contract or contracts for dies, plates and printing necessary for the manufacture of the stamps provided for by this article, and provide such stationery and clerk hire together with such books and blanks as in his discretion may be necessary for putting into operation the provisions of this article; he shall be the custodian of all stamps, dies, plates or other material or thing furnished by him and used in the manufacture of such state tax stamps, and all expenses incurred by him and under his direction in carrying out the provisions of this article shall be paid to him by the state treasurer from any moneys appropriated for such purpose.

§ 320. Illegal use of stamps; penalty.—Any person who shall wilfully remove or cause to be removed, alter or cause to be altered the cancelling or defacing marks of any adhesive stamp provided for by this article with intent to use the same, or to cause the use of the same after it shall have been once used, or shall knowingly or wilfully sell or buy any washed or restored stamp, or offer the same for sale, or give or expose the same to any person for use, or knowingly use the same or prepare the same with intent for the further use thereof; or shall wilfully use any counterfeit stamp or any forged stamp with intent to defraud the state of New York, shall be guilty of a misdemeanor and on conviction thereof shall be liable to a fine of not less than five hundred nor more than one thousand dollars, or be imprisoned for not more than six months, or by both such fine and imprisonment, at the discretion of the court.

Power of state comptroller.

§ 321. Every person, firm, company, association, or corporation, making a sale, agreement to sell, delivery, or transfer, of shares or certificates of stock shall keep a true record of such transaction and the date thereof. The state comptroller may at any time after transfers of stock which by the provisions of this article are subject to a state stamp tax, inquire into and ascertain whether the tax imposed by the provisions of this article has been paid. For the purpose of ascertaining such fact the comptroller shall have the right and it shall be his duty to examine the books and papers of any person, firm, company, association or corporation, and memoranda of transfers shall remain accessible for such inspection for three months from their respective dates. If from such examination the comptroller ascertains that the tax provided for in this article has not been paid he shall bring an action in any court of competent jurisdiction for the recovery of such tax and for any penalty incurred by any person under the provisions of this article.

Thus amended by chap. 414, Laws of 1906.

§ 322. Civil penalty; how recovered.—Any person who shall violate the provisions of this article shall in addition to the penalties herein provided forfeit to the people of the state a civil penalty of five hundred dollars for each violation. The state comptroller shall bring an action in his name as such comptroller in any court of competent jurisdiction for the recovery of any civil penalty and all moneys collected by him shall be paid into the state treasury.

§ 323. Effect of failure to pay tax.—No transfer of stock made after June first, nineteen hundred and five, on which a tax is imposed by this article, and which tax is not paid, at the time of such transfer shall be made the basis of any action or legal proceedings, nor shall proof thereof be offered or received in evidence in any court in this state.

§ 324. **Application of taxes.**—The taxes imposed under this article and the revenues thereof shall be paid by the state comptroller into the state treasury and be applicable to the general fund, and to the payment of all claims and demands which are a lawful charge thereon.

See § 517, Penal Code, *post.*

34

Bonding of Towns and Railroad Aid Debts.

(See section 6, Stock Corporation Law, section 75, Railroad Law, *ante*.)

ARTICLE VIII.—SECTION 10, CONSTITUTION OF THE STATE OF NEW YORK. No county, city, town or village shall hereafter give any money or property, or loan its money or credit to or in aid of any individual, association or corporation, or become directly or indirectly the owner of stock in, or bonds of, any association or corporation; nor shall any such county, city, town or village be allowed to incur any indebtedness except for county, city, town or village purposes. This section shall not prevent such county, city, town or village from making such provision for the aid or support of its poor as may be authorized by law. No county or city shall be allowed to become indebted for any pur pose or in any manner to an amount which, including existing indebtedness, shall exceed ten per centum of the assessed valua tion of the real estate of such county or city subject to taxation, as it appeared by the assessment-rolls of said county or city on the last assessment for state or county taxes prior to the incur ring of such indebtedness; and all indebtedness in excess of such limitation, except such as may now exist, shall be absolutely void, except as herein otherwise provided. No county or city, whose present indebtedness exceeds ten per centum of the assessed valuation of its real estate subject to taxation, shall be allowed to become indebted in any further amount until such indebted. ness shall be reduced within such limit. This section shall not be construed to prevent the issuing of certificates of indebted. ness or revenue bonds issued in anticipation of the collection of taxes for amounts actually contained, or to be contained in the taxes for the year when such certificates or revenue bonds are issued and payable out of such taxes. Nor shall this section be construed to prevent the issue of bonds to provide for the supply of water; but the term of the bonds issued to provide the supply of water shall not exceed twenty years and a sinking fund shall be created on the issuing of the said bonds for their redemption, by raising annually a sum which will produce an amount equal to the sum of the principal and interest of said bonds at their maturity. All certificates of indebtedness or revenue bonds issued in anticipation of the collection of taxes, which are not retired within five years after their date of issue, and bonds issued to provide for the supply of water, and any debt hereafter incurred by any portion or part of a city, if there shall be any such debt, shall be included in ascertaining the power of the city to become otherwise indebted. Whenever the boundaries of any city are the same as those of a county, or when any city shall include within its boundaries more than one county, the power of any county wholly included within such city to become indebted shall cease, but the debt of the county, heretofore existing shall not, for the purposes of this section, be reckoned as a part of the city debt. The amount hereafter to be raised by tax for county or city purposes, in any county containing a city of over one hundred thousand inhabitants, or any such city of this State, in addition to providing for the principal and interest of existing debt, shall not in the aggregate exceed in any one year two per centum of the assessed valuation of the real and personal estate of such county or city, to be ascertained as prescribed in this section in respect to county or city debt.

CHAP. 685, LAWS OF 1892.

AN ACT in relation to municipal corporations, constituting chapter seventeen of the general laws.

THE GENERAL MUNICIPAL LAW.

*   *   *   *   *   *   *   *   *   *

Funded and bonded debts.

§ 7. The bonded indebtedness of a municipal corporation, including interest due or unpaid, or any part thereof, may be

paid up or retired by the issue of the new substituted bonds for
like amounts by the board of supervisors or supervisor, board,
council or officers having in charge the payment of such bonds.
Such new bonds shall only be issued when the existing bonds
can be retired by the substitution of the new bonds therefor,
or can be paid up by money realized by the sale of such new
bonds. Where such bonded indebtedness shall become due within
two years from the issue of such new bonds, such new bonds may
be issued and sold to provide money in advance to pay up such
existing bonds when they shall become due. Such new bonds
shall contain a recital that they are issued pursuant to this section, which recital shall be conclusive evidence of their validity
and of the regularity of the issue; shall be made payable not
less than one or more than thirty years from their date; shall
bear date and draw interest from the date of the payment of
existing bonds, or the receipt of the money to pay the same, at
not exceeding the rate of five per centum per annum, payable
quarterly, semi-annually or annually; and an amount equal to
not less than two per centum of the whole amount of such new
bonds may be payable each year after the issue thereof. Such
new bonds shall be sold and negotiated at the best price obtainable, not less than their par value; shall be valid and binding on
the municipal corporation issuing them; and until payable shall
be exempt from taxation for town, county, municipal or state
purposes. All bonds and coupons retired or paid shall be immediately cancelled. A certificate shall be issued by the officer, board
or body issuing such new bonds, stating the amount of existing
bonds, and of the new bonds so issued, which shall be forthwith
filed in the office of the county clerk. Except as provided in this
section, new bonds shall not be issued in pursuance thereof, for
bonds of a municipal corporation adjudged invalid by the final
judgment of a competent court. A majority of the taxpayers of
a town, voting at a general town meeting, or special town meet-

ing duly called, may authorize the issue in pursuance of this section of new bonds for such invalid bonds, and each new bond so issued shall contain substantially the following recital: " The issue of this bond is duly authorized by a vote of the taxpayers of the said town," which shall be conclusive evidence of such fact. The payment, adjustment or compromise of a part of the bonded indebtedness of a municipal corporation shall not be deemed an admission of the validity or a recognition of any part of the bonded indebtedness of such municipal corporation not paid, adjusted or compromised.

Thus amended by chap. 333, Laws of 1901.

Municipal taxes of railroads payable to the county treasurer.

§ 12. If a town, village or city has outstanding unpaid bonds, issued or substituted for bonds issued, to aid in the construction of a railroad therein, so much of all taxes as shall be necessary to take up such bonds, except school districts and highway taxes, collected on the assessed valuation of such railroad in such municipal corporation, shall be paid over to the treasurer of the county in which the municipal corporation is located. Such treasurer shall purchase with such moneys of any town, village or city, such bonds, when they can be purchased at or below par, and shall immediately cancel them in the presence of the county judge. If such bonds cannot be purchased at or below par, such treasurer shall invest such moneys in the bonds of the United States, of the state of New York, or of any town or village or city of such state, issued pursuant to law; and shall hold such bonds as a sinking fund for the redemption and payment of such outstanding railroad aid bonds. If a county treasurer shall unreasonably neglect to comply with this section, any taxpayer of the town, village or city having so issued its bonds may apply to the county judge of the county in which such municipal corporation is situated, for an order compelling such treasurer to execute the provisions of this section. Upon application of the town board of any town, the board of supervisors of the county in which said town is situated may authorize payment by the county treasurer of all moneys thus paid to him in any year by the railroads mentioned in this section, to the supervisor of such town, for its use and benefit; to be applied either to the purchase of outstanding railroad aid bonds or the payment of interest thereon and any payment here-tofore made in good faith by the treasurer of any county to any town or to the supervisor thereof, of the taxes received, in any year by such treasurer, from railroad corporations in that town is hereby validated. The county treasurer of any county in which one or more towns therein shall have issued bonds for railroad purposes, shall when directed by the board of supervisors or county judge of the county, execute and file in the office of the clerk of the county an undertaking with not less than two sure-ties, approved by such board or judge, to the effect that he will faithfully perform his duties pursuant to this section. The annual report of a county treasurer shall fully state, under the head of "railroad sinking fund" the name and character of all such investments made by him or his predecessors, and the condi tion of such fund.

Thus amended by chap. 515, Laws of 1903.

Abolition of office of railroad commissioners.

§ 13. The board of supervisors of any county may, upon the application of the auditing board of any municipal corporation therein, by resolution, abolish the office of railroad commission-ers of such municipal corporation, and direct the manner of the transfer of their duties to the supervisor of the town, or the treasurer of the municipal corporation other than a town, and upon his compliance with such directions, such transferee shall be vested with all the powers conferred upon such railroad com missioners and subject to all the duties imposed upon them.

Appointment of railroad commissioners.

§ 14. The county judge of any county within which is a municipal corporation having or being entitled to have railroad commissioners, when this chapter shall take effect, and in which the duties imposed upon such commissioners are not fully performed, shall continue to appoint and commission, upon the application of twenty freeholders within such corporation, three persons, who shall be freeholders and resident taxpayers therein, commissioners for the purpose of performing the duties and completing the business required of them pursuant to this chapter or any law. Such commissioners shall hold their office for five years, and until others are appointed by the county judge, unless their duties shall be sooner performed, or the office shall be abolished, who shall also, in like manner, fill any vacancies that may exist therein. Such commissioners shall each receive the sum of three dollars per day for each day actually engaged in the discharge of their duties, and the necessary disbursements to be audited and paid by the usual auditing and disbursing officers of such municipal corporation. A majority of such commissioners, at a meeting of which all have notice, shall constitute a quorum.

Oath and undertaking of commissioners.

§ 15. Before entering upon their duties such commissioners shall take the constitutional oath of office, and make and file with the county clerk of their county, their joint and several undertaking, with two or more sureties to be approved by the county judge of their county, to the effect that they will faithfully discharge their duties as such commissioners, and truly keep, pay over and account for all moneys belonging to such corporation coming into their hands.

Exchange or sale of railroad stock and bonds.

§ 16. The commissioners or officers of a municipal corporation, having the lawful charge and control of any railroad stock or bonds, for or in payment of which the bonds of such municipal corporation have been lawfully issued in aid of such railroad corporation, may exchange the stock or bonds of such railroad corporation for and in payment of such bonds, or the new sub-stituted bonds of such municipal corporation, when such exchange can be made for not less than the par value of the stocks or bonds so held by them. If they can not make such exchange they may sell such stocks or bonds at not less than par; but they may, on the application and with the approval, of the governing board of the municipal corporation, owning such stock and bonds, exchange, sell or dispose of such stock or bonds, at the best price and upon the best terms obtainable, for the municipal corpora-tion they represent, and shall execute to the purchaser the neces-sary transfers therefor. All moneys received for any stock or bonds shall only be applied to the payment and extinguishment of the bonds of the municipal corporation, lawfully issued in aid of any such railroad, or substituted therefor; except that if the bonds so issued or substituted have all been paid, or the moneys so realized shall be more than sufficient to pay them in full, and all the costs and expenses of the sale, such proceeds or balance thereof shall be paid by the officers making the sale, to the super-visor of the town, or the treasurer of the municipal corporation, and applied to such lawful uses as the governing board of the municipal corporation, entitled to the same, may direct. The provisions of this section shall apply to all such commissioners or officers of a municipal corporation elected or appointed or acting under the provisions of any special act, and the authority hereby conferred shall not be limited by the provisions of any such special act.

Thus amended by chap. 490, Laws of 1893.

Annual report of commissioners and payment of bonds.

§ 17. The commissioners of a municipal corporation, having in charge the moneys received and collected, and who are respon-sible for the payment of the interest of the bonds lawfully issued by such municipal corporation, in aid of railroads, shall annually report to the governing board of the municipal corporation, the total amount of the municipal indebtedness of the municipal cor poration they represent, upon such bonds or such new bonds substituted therefor, the date of the bonds and when payable, the rate of interest thereon, the acts under which they were issued, the amount of principal and interest that will become due thereon before the next annual tax levy and collection of taxes for the next succeeding year, and the amount in their hands applicable to the payment of the principal or interest thereon. Each year such governing board shall levy and collect of the municipal corporation sufficient money to pay such principal and interest, as the same shall become due and payable. When collected, such moneys, with the unpaid sums on hand, shall be forthwith paid over to such commissioners, and applied by them to the pur poses for which collected or held. When paid, such bonds shall be presented by such commissioners to the governing board of the municipal corporation, at least five days before the annual town meeting, village or city election, or meeting of the board of super visors, next thereafter held, who shall cancel the same, and make and file a record thereof in the clerk's office of the municipal cor poration, whose bonds were so paid or canceled.

Thus amended by chapter 466, Laws of 1893.

Accounts and loans by commissioners.

§ 18. Such commissioners shall present to the auditing board of the municipal corporation they represent, at each annual meeting of such board, a written statement or report, showing all their receipts and expenditures, with vouchers. They shall also loan on proper security or collaterals, or deposit in some solvent bank, or banking institutions, at the best rate of interest they can obtain, or invest in the bonds of the municipal corpora tion they represent, or in bonds of the state, or of any town, village, city or county therein, issued pursuant to law, or in the bonds of the United States, all moneys that shall come into their

hands by virtue of their office, and not needed for current liabilities; and all earnings, profits or interest accruing from such
loans, deposits or investments, shall be credited to the municipal
corporation they represent, and accounted for in their annual
settlement with the governing board thereof.

Reissue of lost or destroyed bonds.

§ 19.   When any bonds lawfully issued by a municipal corporation in aid of any railroad, or in substitution for bonds so issued,
shall be lost or destroyed, such commissioners may issue new
bonds in the place of the ones so lost or destroyed, at the same
rate of interest, and to become payable at the same time, upon
the owner furnishing satisfactory proof, by affidavit, of such
ownership, and loss or destruction, and a written indemnity,
with at least two sureties, approved as to form and sufficiency
by the county judge of the county in which such municipal corporation is situated.   Every new bond so issued shall state upon
its face the number and denomination of the bond for which it
is issued, that it is issued in the place of such bond claimed to
have been lost or destroyed, that it is issued as a duplicate
thereof, and that but one is to be paid.   Such affidavit and indemnity, duly indorsed, shall be immediately filed in the county
clerk's office.

*   *   *   *   *   *   *   *   *   *

CHAP. 336, LAWS OF 1899.

AN ACT to confer jurisdiction upon the court of claims to hear.
audit and determine the alleged claims of the several counties
containing towns, villages or cities bonded to aid in the con
struction of any railroad passing through such town, village
or cities, on account of the payment to the state of the state
taxes collected from such railroads within such bonded towns.
villages or cities.

SECTION 1.   Any county of this state, containing one or more
towns, villages or cities which have heretofore issued bonds to

aid in the construction of any railroad passing through such towns, cities or villages, may present to the court of claims a claim for the amount of state taxes collected from or paid by any such railroad within the several towns, villages or cities of such county which were so bonded to aid in the construction of any such railroad, since the eighteenth day of May eighteen hundred and sixty-nine, and which said taxes were paid by the county treasurer of such county to the state treasurer. Jurisdiction is hereby conferred upon the court of claims to hear, audit and determine such claims and to make awards and render judgments therefor against the state and in favor of such claimants, without interest thereon.

§ 2. The amount which shall be awarded to any county as provided in section one of this act, shall be paid to the county treasurer of such county; and such county treasurer shall invest and apply the same in the manner and for the purposes provided by section four of chapter nine hundred and seven of the laws of eighteen hundred and sixty-nine, entitled "An act to amend an act entitled, 'An act to authorize the formation of railroad companies and to regulate the same,' passed April second, eighteen hundred and fifty, so as to permit municipal corporations to aid in the construction of such railroads," and the acts amendatory thereof; except that in case such county shall have heretofore paid to any such town, village or city, such state taxes or any portion thereof, or in case such county treasurer has heretofore set aside such state taxes or any portion thereof, for the benefit of such town, village or city, in the manner provided by said section four of chapter nine hundred and seven of the laws of eighteen hundred and sixty-nine and the acts amendatory thereof, then and in that case, such moneys or the portion thereof so paid or set aside as aforesaid, shall be used and applied by such county treasurer for the general purposes of the county.

§ 3. No award shall be made or judgment rendered herein against the state, unless the facts proved shall make out a case against the state, which would create a liability, were the same established in a court of law or equity against an individual or corporation or municipality; and in case such liability shall be satisfactorily established, then the court of claims shall award to and render judgment for the claimants for such sums as shall be just and equitable, notwithstanding the lapse of time since the accruing of said damages, provided any claim hereunder shall be filed with the court of claims within one year after the passage of this act.

See chap. 163, Laws of 1904; chap. 244, Laws of 1905, *post.*

CHAP. 163, LAWS OF 1904.

AN ACT to confer jurisdiction upon the court of claims to hear, audit and determine the alleged claims of the several counties containing towns, villages or cities bonded to aid in the construction of any railroad passing through such towns, villages or cities, on account of the payment to the state of the state taxes collected from such railroads within such bonded towns, villages or cities.

SECTION 1. Any county of this state, containing one or more towns, villages or cities which have heretofore issued bonds to aid in the construction of any railroad passing through such towns, cities or villages, may present to the court of claims a claim for the amount of state taxes collected from or paid by any such railroad within the several towns, villages or cities of such county which were so bonded to aid in the construction of any such railroad, since the eighteenth day of May, eighteen hundred and sixty-nine, and which said taxes were paid by the county treasurer of such county to the state treasurer. Jurisdiction is hereby conferred upon the court of claims to hear, audit and determine such claims and to make awards and render judgments therefor against the state and in favor of such claimants, without interest thereon.

§ 2. The amount which shall be awarded to any county as provided in section one of this act, shall be paid to the county treasurer of such county; and such county treasurer shall invest and apply the same in the manner and for the purpose provided by section four of chapter nine hundred and seven of the laws of eighteen hundred and sixty-nine, entitled "An act to amend an act entitled, 'An act to authorize the formation of railroad companies and to regulate the same,' passed April second, eighteen hundred and fifty, so as to permit municipal corporations to aid in the construction of such railroads," and the acts amendatory thereof; except that in case such county shall have heretofore paid to any such town, village or city, such state taxes or any portion thereof, or in case such county treasurer has heretofore set aside such state taxes or any portion thereof, for the benefit of such town, village or city, in the manner provided by said section four of chapter nine hundred and seven of the laws of eighteen hundred and sixty-nine and the acts amendatory thereof, then and in that case, such moneys or the portion thereof so paid or set aside as aforesaid, shall be used and applied by such county treasurer for the general purposes of the county.

§ 3. No award shall be made or judgment rendered herein against the state, unless the facts proved shall make out a case against the state, which would create a liability, were the same established in a court of law or equity against an individual or corporation or municipality; and in case such liability shall be satisfactorily established, then the court of claims shall award to and render judgment for the claimants for such sums as shall be just and equitable, notwithstanding the lapse of time since the accruing of said damages, provided any claim hereunder shall be filed with the court of claims within six months after the passage of this act.

See chap. 336, Laws of 1899, *ante;* chap. 244, Laws of 1905, *post.*

CHAP. 244, LAWS OF 1905.

AN ACT to amend the county law, in relation to the power of the board of supervisors of any county to sell, assign, transfer or set over a judgment obtained in the court of claims by such county against the state of New York.

SECTION 1. Section twelve of chapter six hundred and eighty-six of the laws of eighteen hundred and ninety-two, entitled "An act in relation to counties, constituting chapter eighteen of the general laws," as amended by chapter one hundred and thirty of the laws of nineteen hundred, and chapter two hundred and ninety-six of the laws of nineteen hundred, and chapter two hundred and fifty-five of the laws of nineteen hundred and one, and chapter four hundred and sixty-five of the laws of nineteen hundred and three, is hereby amended by adding at the end of such section, a new subdivision, to be known as subdivision nineteen, and to read as follows:

19. Whenever a judgment has been rendered in the court of claims in favor of any county against the state of New York, and the time to appeal therefrom has expired or the attorney-general has issued a certificate that there has been no appeal and that no appeal will be taken by the state from such judgment, the board of supervisors of such county may sell, assign, transfer or set over such judgment unto the comptroller, who may purchase the same as an investment for the various trust funds of the state or canal debt sinking fund, or unto any person, firm, association or corporation desiring to purchase such judgment, for a sum not less than the amount for which same was rendered with accrued interest but no judgment so acquired by the state shall be deemed merged or satisfied thereby. And such board of supervisors may designate and authorize its chairman and clerk, the treasurer of the county and the attorney of record procuring the entry of such judgment, or any or either of them to execute in the name of the county and deliver unto the party purchasing such judgment the necessary release, transfer or assignment required in law to complete such sale, setting over, transfer or assignment.

The Code of Criminal Procedure.

(As amended to and including the session of the Legislature of 1906).

Court of special sessions, jurisdiction of.

§ 56. Subject to the power of removal provided for in this chapter, courts of special sessions, except in the city and county of New York and the city of Albany, have in the first instance exclusive judisdiction to hear and determine charges of misdemeanors committed within their respective counties, as follows:

*   *   *   *   *   *   *   *   *   *

9. Intoxication of a person engaged in running any locomotive engine upon any railroad, or while acting as conductor of a car, or train of cars, on any such railroad, or a misdemeanor committed by any person on a railroad car or train.

*   *   *   *   *   *   *   *   *   *

23. Unlawfully frequenting or attending a steamboat landing, railroad depot, church, banking institution, broker's office, place of public amusement, auction room, store, auction sale at private residence, passenger car, hotel, restaurant, or at any other gathering of people.

*   *   *   *   *   *   *   *   *   *

35. For all violations of the provisions of the * * * * domestic commerce laws.

36. When a complaint is made to or a warrant is issued by a committing magistrate for a violation of the provisions of section six hundred and seventy-five of the penal code of the state of New York.

Subdivision 36 added by chap. 92, Laws of 1903, taking effect September 1, 1903.

*   *   *   *   *   *   *   *   *   *

39. All violations of the law regulating the junk business and requiring persons engaging in such business to procure a license.

Subdivision 39 added by chap. 497, Laws of 1906, taking effect September 1, 1906.

See section 42, Railroad Law, section 41, Liquor Tax Law, chap. 308, Laws of 1903, *ante;* sections 290, 420, 550, Penal Code, section 29, Rapid Transit Act, *post.*

Of crime committed in the state on board of any railway train, etc.

§ 137. When a crime is committed in this state, in or on board of any railway engine, train or car, making a passage or trip on or over any railway in this state, or in respect to any portion of the lading or freightage of any such railway train or engine car; the jurisdiction is in any county through which, or any part of which, the railway train or car passes, or has passed in the course of the same passage or trip, or in any county where such passage or trip terminates, or would terminate if completed.

Plea of guilty, how put in.

§ 335. A plea of guilty can only be put in by the defendant himself in open court, except upon an indictment against a corporation, in which case it may be put in by counsel.

Bail of certain railroad employes.

§ 554a. Whenever a person employed as an engineer, fireman, motorman, conductor, trainman or otherwise, on a train or car of a steam, elevated or street surface railroad, is arrested in any city on a criminal charge, arising from an accident in connection with the operation of such train or car, resulting in an injury or death to a person or injury to property, such engineer, fireman, motorman, conductor, trainman or other employe, shall be immediately taken before a magistrate, if one is accessible, and otherwise, before a captain or sergeant of police, or acting sergeant of police, in charge of a police station in such city, and be given an opportunity to be admitted to bail. Such bail shall be taken in the same manner, so far as practicable, as is provided by section five hundred and fifty-four of this code, for the taking of bail in case of misdemeanors by a captain or sergeant of police, or acting sergeant of police in a city or village, except that the amount of bail shall be fixed by such officer at not exceeding one thousand dollars, and except that the undertaking shall provide for the appearance of the defendant before the magistrate, coroner, or other officer, who, except for this section, would be authorized to take such bail. Such officer may however in his discretion, instead of exacting bail release such employe on his own recognizance, conditional for his appearance as above provided in case an undertaking is required.

Added by chap. 614, Laws of 1903, taking effect September 1, 1903.

§ 613. If chattels, books, papers or documents be required. a direction to the following effect must be contained in the subpoena: "And you are required also to bring with you the following," (describing intelligibly the chattels, books, papers or documents required).

Thus amended by chap. 547, Laws of 1897, taking effect September 1, 1897.

Summons upon an information or presentment against a corporation, by whom issued, and when returnable.

§ 675. Upon an information against a corporation, the magistrate must issue a summons, signed by him, with his name of office, requiring the corporation to appear before him, at a specified time and place, to answer the charge; the time to be not less than ten days after the issuing of the summons.

Form of the summons.

§ 676. The summons must be in substantially the following form:

"County of Albany, [or as the case may be.]

  "In the name of the people of the State of New York:

      "To the [naming the corporation.]

  "You are hereby summoned to appear before me, at [naming
  35

the place], on [specifying the day and hour], to answer a charge made against you, upon the information of A. B., for [designating the offense, generally.]

"Dated at the city, [or 'town,'] of   the   day of   , 18 ·

"G. H., Justice of the Peace."

[Or as the case may be.]

When and how served.

§ 677. The summons must be served at least five days before the day of appearance fixed therein, by delivering a copy thereof and showing the original to the president, or other head of the corporation, or to the secretary, cashier, or managing agent thereof.

Examination of the charge.

§ 678. At the time appointed in the summons, the magistrate must proceed to investigate the charge, in the same manner as in the case of a natural person brought before him, so far as those proceedings are applicable.

Cerificate of the magistrate, and return thereof with the depositions.

§ 679. After hearing the proofs, the magistrate must certify upon the depositions, either that there is or is not sufficient cause to believe the corporation guilty of the offense charged, and must return the depositions and certificate, in the manner prescribed in section 221.

Grand jury may proceed as in the case of a natural person.

§ 680. If the magistrate return a certificate that there is sufficient cause to believe the corporation guilty of the offense charged, the grand jury may proceed thereon as in the case of a natural person held to answer.

§ 681. When an indictment is filed against any corporation, such corporation must be arraigned thereon, and the court acquires jurisdiction over the corporation, in the manner following:

1. The clerk of the court wherein such indictment is found, or to which it is sent or removed, or the district attorney of the county, must issue a summons signed by him with his name of office, requiring such corporation to appear and answer the indictment by a demurrer or written plea to be verified in like manner as a pleading in a civil action, at a time and place to be specified in such summons, such time to be not less than five days after the issue thereof. The summons may be substantially in the following form:

Supreme court, county of , (state the proper county or court as the case may be)

The People of the State of New York

vs.

The A. B. Company.

You are hereby summoned to appear in this court and, by demurrer or plea in writing duly verified, answer an indictment filed against you by the grand jury of this county, on the day of , charging you with the crime of (designating the offense generally), at a term of the supreme court (or as the case may be) of this county, at (naming the place) on (stating the day and hour) and in case of your failure to so appear and answer, judgment will be pronounced against you.

Dated at the city (or town) of , the day of , 18

C. D.,

District Attorney.

(or by order of the court, E. F., Clerk, as the case may be.)

2. The summons must be served at least four days before the appearance fixed therein, in the same manner as is provided for the service of a summons upon a corporation in a civil action; and if the corporation does not appear in the manner and at the time and place specified in the summons, judgment must be pronounced against it.

3. Nothing contained in this section shall be construed as preventing the appearance of a corporation by counsel to answer an indictment, without the issuance or service of the summons as above provided. And when an indictment shall have been filed against a corporation it may voluntarily appear and answer the same by counsel duly authorized to so appear for it; in which case the court acquires full jurisdiction over the corporation in the same manner as if the summons had been issued and served.

§ 682. When a fine is imposed upon a corporation upon conviction, it may be collected in the same manner as a judgment in a civil action, and if an execution issued upon such judgment be returned unsatisfied, the district attorney of the county may thereupon bring an action in the name of the people of the state of New York, to procure a judgment sequestrating the property of the corporation, as provided by the Code of Civil Procedure.

Tramp defined.

§ 887a. A tramp is any person, not blind, over sixteen years of age, and who has not resided in the county in which he may be at any time for a period of six months prior thereto, who

1. Not having visible means to maintain himself, lives without employment; or

2. Wanders abroad and begs, or goes about from door to door, or places himself in the streets, highways, passages or public places to beg or receive alms; or

3. Wanders abroad and lodges in taverns, groceries, ale-houses, watch or station houses, outhouses, market places, sheds, stables, barns or uninhabited buildings, or in the open air, and does not give a good account of himself.

Section 887a added by chap. 664, Laws of 1898.

CHAP. 664, LAWS OF 1898.

§ 5. Sections two and six of chapter four hundred and ninety of the laws of eighteen hundred and eighty-five entitled "An act concerning tramps," are hereby repealed.

§ 6. This act shall not apply to cities of the first and second class.

See chap. 490, Laws of 1885, *ante.*

Examination as to residence.

§ 889.   When complaint is made to any magistrate by any citizen or peace officer against a person under sections one, five or six of section eight hundred and eighty-seven, the magistrate must, upon the examination of such person, cause testimony to be taken as to his residence, and if it appears that such person has not resided in the county for a period of six months prior to his arrest, such magistrate shall not commit such person as a vagrant, as provided by this article; but if he finds that such person is guilty of an offense charged in one of such subdivisions. and such person is not blind or under sixteen years of age, the magistrate shall adjudge him to be a tramp, and commit him to a penitentiary, as required by law.   On such examination the uncorroborated testimony of the defendant as to his place of residence shall not be deemed sufficient proof thereof.

Added by chap. 664, Laws of 1898.

The Penal Code.

(As amended to and including the session of the Legislature of 1906.)

Punishments, how determined.

§ 13. Whenever in this code, the punishment for crime is left
undetermined between certain limits, the punishment to be inflicted in a particular case must be determined by the court
authorized to pass sentence, within such limits as may be prescribed by this code. In all cases where a corporation is convicted of an offense for the commission of which a natural person
would be punishable with imprisonment, as for a felony, such
corporation is punishable by a fine of not more than five thousand dollars

Refusal to permit employes to attend election.

§ 41f. A person or corporation who refuses to an employe
entitled to a vote at an election or town meeting, the privilege
of attending thereat, as provided by the election law, or subjects
such employe to a penalty or reduction of wages because of the
exercise of such privilege, is guilty of a misdemeanor.

Duress and intimidation of voters.

§ 41s.   *   *   *   ⁎   *   *   *   *

3. Being an employer, pays his employes the salary or wages
due, in " pay envelopes," upon which there is written or printed
any political motto, device or argument containing threats,
express or implied, intended or calculated to influence the
political opinions or actions of such employes; or within ninety
days of a general election, puts or otherwise exhibits in the establishment or place where his employes are engaged in labor, any

hand-bill or placard containing any threat, notice or information that if any particular ticket or candidate is elected or defeated, work in his place or establishment will cease, in whole or in part, his establishment be closed up, or the wages of his employes reduced, or other threats, express or implied, intended or calculated to influence the political opinions or actions of his employes, is guilty of a misdemeanor, and if a corporation, in addition, forfeits its charter.

See, also, section 109, Election Law, not printed herein.

Contradictory statements under oath.

§ 101-a. In any prosecution for perjury the falsity of the testimony or statement set forth in the indictment shall be presumptively established by proof that the defendant has testified, declared, deposed or certified under oath to the contrary thereof in any other written testimony, declaration, deposition, certificate, affidavit or other writing by him subscribed.

Added by chap. 324, Laws of 1906, taking effect September 1, 1906.
See sections 57 and 158, Railroad Law, ante; and sections 416, 602, and 611, Penal Code, post.

Making arrests, etc., without lawful authority.

§ 119. No sheriff of a county, mayor of a city, or officials, or other person authorized by law to appoint special deputy sheriffs, special constables, marshals, policemen, or other peace officers in this state, to preserve the public peace or quell public disturbance, shall hereafter, at the instance of any agent, society, association or corporation, or otherwise, appoint as such special deputy, special constable, marshal, policemen, or other peace officer, any person who shall not be a citizen of the United States and a resident of the state of New York, and entitled to vote therein at the time of his appointment, and a resident of the same county as the mayor or sheriff or other official making such appointment; and no person shall assume or exercise the functions, powers, duties or privileges incident and belonging to the office of special deputy sheriff, special constables, marshal or policemen, or other peace officer, without having first received his appointment in writing from the authority lawfully appointing him. Any person or persons who shall, in this state, without due authority, exercise, or attempt to exercise the functions of, or hold himself out to any one as a deputy sheriff, marshal, or policeman, constable or peace officer, or any public officer, or person pretending to be a public officer, who, unlawfully, under the pretense or color of any process, arrests any person or detains him against his will, or seizes or levies upon any property, or dispossesses any one of any lands or tenements without a regular process therefor, or any person who knowingly violates any other provision of this section, is guilty of a misdemeanor. But nothing herein contained shall be deemed to effect, repeal or abridge the powers authorized to be exercised under sections one hundred and two, one hundred and four, one hundred and sixty-nine, one hundred and eighty-three, eight hundred and ninety-five, eight hundred and ninety-six and eight hundred and ninety-seven of the Code of Criminal Procedure; or under chapter three hundred and forty-six of the laws of eighteen hundred and sixty-three, as amended by chapter two hundred and fifty-nine of the laws of eighteen hundred and sixty-six, and chapter one hundred and ninety-three, of the laws of eighteen hundred and seventy-five; or under chapter two hundred and twenty-three of the laws of eighteen hundred and eighty; or under chapter five hundred and twenty-seven of the laws of eighteen hundred and seventy-three; or under chapter two hundred and five of the laws of eighteen hundred and seventy-five; but all places kept for summer resorts and the grounds of racing associations in the counties of New York, Kings and Westchester, are hereby exempted from the provisions of this act.

Thus amended by chap. 272, Laws of 1892.
* See section 58, Railroad Law, *ante*.

Compelling employes to agree not to join any labor organization a misdemeanor.

§ 171a. Any person or persons, employer or employers of labor, and any person or persons of any corporation or corpora.

tions on behalf of such corporation or corporations, who shall hereafter coerce or compel any person or persons, employe or employes, laborer or mechanic, to enter into an agreement, either written or verbal from such person, persons, employe, laborer or mechanic, not to join or become a member of any labor organization, as a condition of such person or persons securing employment, or continuing in the employment of any such person or persons, employer or employers, corporation or corporations, shall be deemed guilty of a misdemeanor. The penalty for such misdemeanor shall be imprisonment in a penal institution for not more than six months, or by a fine of not more than two hundred dollars, or by both such fine and imprisonment.

Murder in the first degree.

§ 183a. A person who wilfully, by loosening, removing or displacing a rail, or by any other interference, wrecks, destroys or so injures any car, tender, locomotive or railway train, or part thereof, while moving upon any railway in this state, whether operated by steam, electricity or other motive power, as to thereby cause the death of a human being, is guilty of murder in the first degree, and punishable accordingly.

Added by chap. 548, Laws of 1897.
See section 635, Penal Code, section 30, Rapid Transit Act, *post.*

Liability of persons in charge of steam engines.

§ 199. An engineer or other person having charge of a steam boiler, steam engine, or other apparatus for generating or applying steam, employed in a boat or railway, or in a manufactory, or in any mechanical works, who willfully, or from ignorance or gross neglect, creates, or allows to be created, such an undue quantity of steam as to burst the boiler, engine or apparatus, or to cause any other accident whereby the death of a human being is produced, is guilty of manslaughter in the second degree.

See section 49a Railroad Law, *ante;* section 362, Penal Code, *post.*

Use of force or violence, declared not unlawful, etc.

§ 223. To use or attempt, or offer to use, force or violence upon or toward the person of another, is not unlawful in the following cases:

*   *   *   *   *   *   *   *   *   *

5. When committed by a carrier of passengers, or the authorized agents or servants of such carrier, or by any person assisting them, at their request, in expelling from a carriage, railway car, vessel or other vehicle, a passenger who refuses to obey a lawful and reasonable regulation prescribed for the conduct of passengers, if such vehicle has first been stopped and the force or violence used is not more than sufficient to expel the offending passenger, with a reasonable regard to his personal safety.

*   *   *   *   *   *   *   *   *   *

Sunday labor.

§ 263. All labor on Sunday is prohibited, excepting the works of necessity or charity. In works of necessity or charity is included whatever is needful during the day for the good order, health or comfort of the community.

§ 290.

*   *   *   *   *   *   *   *   *   *

6. Or who, being the owner, keeper or proprietor of a junk shop, junk cart or other vehicle or boat or other vessel used for the collection of junk, or any collector of junk, receives or purchases any goods, chattels, wares or merchandise from any child under the age of sixteen years, is guilty of a misdemeanor.

Subdivision 6 added by chap. 309, Laws of 1903, taking effect September 1, 1903.

*   *   *   *   *   *   *   *   *   *

8. It shall be no defense to a prosecution for a violation of subdivisions three, four, five or six of this section, that in the transaction upon which the prosecution is based the child acted

as the agent or representative of another, or that the defendant dealt with such child as the agent or representative of another.

Subdivision 8 added by chap. 41, Laws of 1906, taking effect September 1, 1906.

See chap. 308, Laws of 1903, section 56, Code of Criminal Procedure, *ante;* section 550, Penal Code, *post.*

Mismanagement of steam boilers.

§ 362. An engineer or other person having charge of a steam boiler, steam engine, or other apparatus for generating or employing steam, employed in a railway, manufactory, or other mechanical works, who, willfully or from ignorance or gross neglect, creates or allows to be created such an undue quantity of steam as to burst the boiler, engine or apparatus, or cause any other accident whereby human life is endangered, is guilty of a misdemeanor.

See section 49a, Railroad Law, section 199, Penal Code, *ante.*

Innkeepers and carriers refusing to receive guests and passengers.

§ 381. A person who, either on his own account or as agent or officer of a corporation, carries on business as innkeeper or as common carrier of passengers, and refuses, without just cause or excuse, to receive and entertain any guests, or to receive and carry any passengers, is guilty of a misdemeanor.

Protecting civil and public rights.

§ 383. A person who:

1. Excludes a citizen of this state, by reason of race, color or previous condition of servitude, from the equal enjoyment of any accommodation, facility or privileges furnished by innkeepers or common carriers, or by owners, managers or lessees of theatres or other places of amusement, or by teachers and officers of the common schools and public instructions* of learning, or by cemetery associations; or

2. Denies or aids or incites another to deny to any other person because of race, creed or color, full enjoyment of any of

*So in the original.

the accommodations, advantages, facilities and privileges of any hotel, inn, tavern, restaurant, public conveyance on land or water, theatre or other place of public resort or amusement, is guilty of a misdemeanor, punishable by fine of not less than fifty dollars nor more than five hundred dollars.

Failure to furnish statistics to commissioner of labor statistics.

§ 384f. Any person who refuses, when requested by the commissioner of labor statistics,

1. To admit him or a person authorized by him to a mine, factory, workshop, warehouse, elevator, foundry, machine shop or other manufacturing establishment; or

2. To furnish him with information relative to his duties which may be in such person's possession or under his control; or,

3. To answer questions put by such commissioner in a circular or otherwise, or shall knowingly answer such questions untruthfully, is guilty of a misdemeanor, and on conviction therefor shall be punished by a fine of not less than fifty nor more than two hundred dollars.

Added by chap. 16, Laws of 1897.

Hours of labor to be required.

§ 384-h. Any person or corporation,

*   *   *   *   *   *   *   *   *   *

2. Who shall require more than ten hours labor, including one-half hour for dinner, to be performed within twelve consecutive hours, by the employes of a street surface and elevated railway owned or operated by corporations whose main line of travel or routes lie principally within the corporate limits of cities of more than one hundred thousand inhabitants; or,

*   *   *   *   *   *   *   *   *   *

4. Who shall require the employes of a corporation operating a line of railroad of thirty miles in length or over, in whole or in part within this state to work contrary to the requirements

of article one of the labor law, is guilty of a misdemeanor, and on conviction therefor shall be punished by a fine of not less than five hundred nor more than one thousand dollars for each offense. If any contractor with the state or a municipal corporation shall require more than eight hours for a days labor, upon conviction therefor in addition to such fine, the contract shall be forfeited at the option of the municipal corporation.

Added by chap. 416, Laws of 1897.
See 175 N. Y., 84; also 136 N. Y., 554.
See section 4, chap. 711, Laws of 1892, and Labor Law, chap. 415, Laws of 1897, *ante*.

Payment of wages.

§ 384-i. A corporation or joint stock association or a person carrying on the business thereof, by lease or otherwise, who does not pay the wages of its employes in cash, weekly or monthly as provided in article one of the labor law, is guilty of a misdemeanor, and upon conviction therefor, shall be fined not less than twenty-five nor more than fifty dollars for each offense.

Added by chap. 416, Laws of 1897.
See Labor Law, chap. 415, Laws of 1897, *ante*.

Keeping gunpowder unlawfully.

§ 389. A person who makes or keeps gunpowder, nitro-glycerine, or any other explosive or combustible material, within a city or village, or carries such materials through the streets thereof, in a quantity or manner prohibited by law or by ordinance of the city or village, is guilty of a misdemeanor. A person who manufactures gunpowder, dynamite, nitro-glycerine, liquid or compressed air or gases, except acetylene gas or other gases used for illuminating purposes, naphtha, gasoline, benzine or any explosive articles or compounds, or manufactures ammunition, fireworks or other articles of which such substances are component parts in a cellar, room or apartment of a tenement or dwelling house or any building occupied in whole or in part by persons or families for living purposes, is guilty of a misdemeanor. And a person who, by the careless, negligent, or unauthorized use or management of gunpowder or other explosive substances, injures or occasions the injury of the person or property of another, is punishable by imprisonment for not more than two years. Any person or persons who shall knowingly present, attempt to present, or cause to be presented or offered for shipment to any railroad, steamboat, steamship, express or other company engaged as common carrier of passengers or freight, dynamite, nitro-glycerine, powder or other explosives dangerous to life or limb, without revealing the true nature of said explosives or substance so offered or attempted to be offered to the company or carrier to which it shall be presented, shall be guilty of a felony, and upon conviction, shall be fiued in any sum not exceeding one thousand dollars and not less than three hundred dollars, or imprisonment in a state prison for not less than one nor more than five years, or be subject to both such fine and imprisonment. Nothing in this section contained shall be construed to prohibit or forbid the manufacture and sale of soda water, seltzer-water, ginger ale, carbonic or mineral water, or the charging with liquid carbonic acid gas of such waters or ordinary waters, or of beer, wines, ales or other malt and vinous beverages in such cellar, room or apartment of a tenement or dwelling house, or any building occupied in whole or in part by persons or families for living purposes.

Thus amended by chap. 486, Laws of 1902.

Unlawful acts of and neglect of duty by railroad officials.

§ 416. An officer, agent, attorney or employe of a railroad corporation, who:

1. Offers a place, appointment, position or any other consideration to a railroad commissioner or to a secretary, clerk, agent, employe or expert employed by the board of railroad commissioners; or

2. After due notice, neglects or refuses to make or furnish any statement or report lawfully required by the board of railroad commissioners or willfully hinders, delays or obstructs such commissioners in the discharge of their official duties,

Is guilty of a misdemeanor.

See article 6, Railroad Law, *ante*.
See sections 57 and 158, Railroad Law, section 101a, Penal Code, *ante;* sections 602 and 611, Penal Code, *post*.

Misconduct of railroad commissioners and of their employes.

§ 417. Any railroad commissioner, or any secretary, clerk, agent, expert or other person employed by the board of railroad commissioners, who:

1. Directly or indirectly solicits or requests from or recommends to any railroad corporation, or to any officer, attorney or agent thereof, the appointment of any person to any place or position; or,

2. Accepts, receives or requests, either for himself or for any other person, any pass, gift or gratuity from any railroad corporation; or,

3. Secretly reveals to any railroad corporation, or to any officer, member or employe thereof, any information gained by him from any other railroad corporation; is guilty of a misdemeanor.

See article 6, Railroad Law, *ante*.

Person unable to read not to act or be employed as engineer.

§ 418. Any person unable to read the time tables of a railroad and ordinary handwriting, who acts as an engineer or runs a locomotive or train on any railroad in this state; or any person who, in his own behalf, or in the behalf of any other person or corporation, knowingly employs a person so unable to read to act as such engineer or to run any such locomotive, is guilty of a misdemeanor; or who employs a person as a telegraph operator who is under the age of eighteen years, or who has less than one year's experience in telegraphing, to receive or transmit a telegraphic message or train order for the movement of trains, is guilty of a misdemeanor.

Misconduct of officials or employes on elevated railroads.

§ 419. Any conductor, brakeman, or other agent or employe of an elevated railroad, who:

1. Starts any train or car of such railroad, or gives any signal or order to any engineer or other person to start any such train or car, before every passenger therein who manifests an intention to depart therefrom by arising or moving toward the exit thereof, has departed therefrom; or before every passenger on the platform or station at which the train has stopped, who manifests a desire to enter the train, has actually boarded or entered the same, unless due notice is given by an authorized employe of such railroad that the train is full, and that no more passengers can then be received; or,

2. Obstructs the lawful ingress or egress of a passenger to or from any such car; or,

3. Opens a platform gate of any such car while the train is in motion, or starts such train before such gate is firmly closed; is guilty of a misdemeanor.

Intoxication or other misconduct of railroad or steamboat employes.

§ 420. 1. Any person who, being employed upon any railroad as engineer, conductor, baggagemaster, brakeman, switchtender, fireman, bridge-tender, flagman, signal man, or having charge of stations, starting, regulating or running trains upon a railroad, or, being employed as captain, engineer or other officer of a vessel propelled by steam, is intoxicated while engaged in the discharge of any such duties; or

2. An engineer, conductor, brakeman, switch-tender, or other officer, agent or employe of any railroad corporation, who willfully violates or omits his duty as such officer, agent or employe, by which human life or safety is endangered, the punish-

ment of which is not otherwise prescribed; is guilty of a misde meanor.

See section 41, Liquor Tax Law, *ante;* also section 42, Railroad Law, *ante;* also section 56, Code of Criminal Procedure, *ante;* section 29 Rapid Transit Act, *post.*

Failure to ring bell, etc.

§ 421. A person acting as engineer, driving a locomotive on any railway in this state, who fails to ring the bell, or sound the whistle, upon such locomotive, or cause the same to be rung or sounded, at least eighty rods from any place where such railway crosses a traveled road or street on the same level (except in cities), or to continue the ringing such bell or sounding such whistle at intervals, until such locomotive and the train to which the locomotive is attached shall have completely crossed such road or street or any officer or employe of a corporation in charge of a locomotive, train or car, who shall willfully obstruct, or cause to be obstructed, any farm or highway crossing with any locomotive, train or car for a longer period than five consecutive minutes, is guilty of a misdemeanor.

Thus amended by chap. 759, Laws of 1900, taking effect September 1, 1900.

Placing passenger car in front of merchandise or freight car.

§ 422. A person, being an officer or employe of a railway company, who knowingly places, directs or suffers a freight, lumber, merchandise, or oil car to be placed in rear of a car used for the conveyance of passengers in a railway train, is guilty of a misdemeanor.

Platforms and heating apparatus of passenger cars.

§ 423. A railroad corporation, or any officer or director thereof having charge of its railroad, or any person managing a railroad in this state, or any person or corporation running passenger cars upon a railroad into or through this state, who:

1. Fails to have the platforms or ends of the passenger cars run upon such railroad constructed in such manner as

36

will prevent passengers falling between the cars while in motion; or

2. Except temporarily, in case of accident or emergency, heats any passenger car, while in motion, on any such railroad more than fifty miles in length, except a narrow-gauge railroad which runs only mixed trains, between October fifteenth and May first, by any stove or furnace inside of or suspended from such car, except stoves of a pattern and kind approved by the board of railroad commissioners for cooking purposes in dining-room cars, and except within the extended time allowed by the railroad commissioners in pursuance of law for introducing other heating apparatus; is guilty of a misdemeanor.

Thus amended by chap. 692, Laws of 1892.
See section 51, Railroad Law, *ante*.

Guard posts; automatic couplers.

§ 424. All corporations and persons other than employes, operating any steam railroad in this state,

1. Failing to cause guard posts to be placed in prolongation of the line of bridge trusses upon such railroad, so that in case of derailment, the posts and not the trusses shall receive the blow of the derailed locomotive or car; or

2. Failing after November first, eighteen hundred and ninety-two, to equip all of their own freight cars, run and used in freight or other trains on such railroad, with automatic self couplers, or running or operating on such railroad any freight car belonging to any such person or corporation, without having the same equipped, except in case of accident or other emergency, with automatic self-couplers, and except within the extended time allowed by the board of railroad commissioners, in pursuance of law, for equipping such car with such couplers, is guilty of a misdemeanor, punishable by a fine of five hundred dollars for each offense.

Thus amended by chap. 664, Laws of 1896.
See, chap. 544, Laws of 1893, *ante*. Also section 49, Railroad Law, *ante*.

Advising or inducing employes not to wear uniform a misdemeanor.

§ 425. A person who,

1. Advises or induces any one, being an officer, agent or employe of a railway company, to leave the service of such company, because it requires a uniform to be worn by such officer, agent or employe, or to refuse to wear such uniform, or any part thereof; or,

2. Uses any inducement with a person employed by a railway company to go into the service or employment of any other railway company, because a uniform is required to be worn; or,

3. Wears the uniform designated by a railway company without authority;

Is guilty of a misdemeanor.
See section 43 Railroad Law, *ante.*

Riding on freight trains; getting on car or train while in motion; obstructing, etc., horse or street railroad cars; punishment.

§ 426. A person who,

1. Rides on any engine or any freight or wood car of any railway company, without authority or permission of the proper officers of the company or of the person in charge of the car or engine; or,

2. Who gets on any car or train while in motion (for the purpose of obtaining transportation thereon as passenger) or,

3. Who willfully obstructs, hinders or delays the passage of any car lawfully running upon any steam or horse or street railway;

Is guilty of a misdemeanor.
See chap. 590, Laws of 1872, *ante.*

Unauthorized manufacture, sale or use of illuminating oils.

§ 427a. A person who violates any provision of the domestic commerce law, relating to the standard, manufacture, sale, use or storage of any oil or burning fluid, wholly or partially composed of naphtha, coal oil, petroleum or products manufactured therefrom, or of other substance or materials which will flash at a temperature below one hundred degrees Fahrenheit, or relating to the burning or carriage of any such oil or fluid which will ignite at a temperature below three hundred degrees Fahrenheit, is guilty of a misdemeanor.

See chap. 376, Laws of 1896, *ante*.

Lights upon swing bridges.

§ 433a. A corporation, company or individual, owning, maintaining or operating a swing bridge across the Hudson river, who during the navigation season between sundown and sunrise, neglects to keep and maintain upon every such bridge the lights required by law, is guilty of a misdemeanor.

See chap. 592, Laws of 1897, *ante*.

Bribery of labor representatives.

§ 447-f. A person who gives or offers to give any money or other things of value to any duly appointed representative of a labor organization with intent to influence him in respect to any of his acts, decisions, or other duties as such representative, or to induce him to prevent or cause a strike by the employees of any person or corporation, is guilty of a misdemeanor; and no person shall be excused from attending and testifying, or producing any books, papers or other documents before any court or magistrate, upon any investigation, proceeding or trial, for a violation of this section, upon the ground or for the reason that the testimony or evidence, documentary or otherwise, required of him may tend to convict him of a crime or subject him to a penalty or forfeiture; but no person shall be prosecuted or subjected to any penalty or forfeiture for or on account of any transaction, matter or thing concerning which he may so testify or produce evidence, documentary or otherwise, and no testimony so given or produced shall be received against him upon any criminal investigation or proceeding.

Added by chap. 659, Laws of 1904, taking effect September 1, 1904.

Arson in first degree defined.

§ 486. A person who willfully burns, or sets on fire, in the night time, either

*   *   *   *   *   *   *   *   *   *

2. A car, vessel, or other vehicle, or a structure or building other than a dwelling-house, wherein, to the knowledge of the offender, there is at the time a human being;

Is guilty of arson in the first degree.

Arson in second degree.

§ 487. A person who,

*   H   *   *   *   *   *   *   *   *

4. Willfully burns, or sets on fire, in the night-time, a car, vessel, or other vehicle, or a structure or building, ordinarily occupied at night by a human being, although no person is within it at the time;

Is guilty of arson in the second degree.

Arson in third degree.

§ 488. A person who willfully burns, or sets on fire, either,

1. A vessel, car, or other vehicle, or a building, structure, or other erection, which is at the time insured against loss or damage by fire, with intent to prejudice the insurer thereof; or,

2. A vessel, car, or other vehicle, or a building, structure, or other erection under circumstances not amounting to arson in the first or second degree;

Is guilty of arson in the third degree.

Arson, how punished.

§ 489. Arson is punishable as follows:

1. In the first degree, by imprisonment for a term not exceeding forty years.

2. In the second degree, by imprisonment for a term not exceeding twenty-five years.

3. In the third degree, by imprisonment for a term not exceed
ing fifteen years.

Thus amended by chap. 549, Laws 1897, taking effect September 1, 1897.
(Chap. 549, Laws 1897.)
§ 2. The penalties above prescribed shall, however, only apply to offenses
committed after the taking effect of this act. Nothing herein contained shall
in any manner affect or impair any liability or punishment incurred prior to
the time this act takes effect, under or by virtue of the then existing provisions
of the section hereby amended, and all offenses of arson committed before that
time shall be punishable according to such previously existing provisions, as
fully, and in the same manner, as though this act had not been passed.

Burglary in third degree.

§ 498. A person who either,

1. With intent to commit a crime therein, breaks and enters
a building, or a room, or any part of a building; or,

2. Being in any building, commits a crime therein and breaks
out of the same;

Is guilty of burglary in the third degree.

"Building," defined.

§ 504. The term "building" as used in this chapter includes
a railway car, vessel, booth, tent, shop, enclosed ginseng garden.
or other erection or inclosure.

Thus amended by chap. 332, Laws of 1903, taking effect September 1, 1903.

Unlawfully entering building.

§ 505. A person who, under circumstances or in a manner
not amounting to burglary, enters a building, or any part thereof,
with intent to commit a felony or a larceny, or any malicious
mischief, is guilty of a misdemeanor.

Other cases of forgery in third degree.

§ 514. A person who either,

1. Being an officer or in the employment of a corporation,
association, partnership or individuals falsifies, or unlawfully
and corruptly alters, erases, obliterates or destroys any accounts,
books of accounts, records, or other writing, belonging to or

appertaining to the business of the corporation, association, or partnership or individuals;   *   *   *

Is guilty of forgery in the third degree.

Forging passage tickets.

§ 516. A person who, with intent to defraud, forges, counterfeits or falsely alters any ticket, cheque or other paper or writing, entitling or purporting to entitle the holder or proprietor thereof to a passage upon any railway or in any vessel or other public conveyance; and a person who, with like intent, sells, exchanges or delivers, or keeps or offers for sale, exchange or delivery, or receives upon any purchase, exchange or delivery, any such ticket, knowing the same to have been forged, counterfeited or falsely altered, is guilty of forgery in the third degree.

Forging United States or state stamps.

§ 517. A person who forges, counterfeits or alters any postage or revenue stamp of the United States, or any tax or revenue stamp of the state of New York, or who sells, or offers, or keeps for sale, as genuine or as forged, any such stamp, knowing it to be forged, counterfeited or falsely altered, is guilty of forgery in the third degree.

Thus amended by chap. 242, Laws of 1905.
See chap. 241, Laws of 1905, *ante*.

Officer of corporation selling, etc., forged or fraudulent scrip, etc.

§ 518. An officer, agent or other person employed by any company or corporation existing under the laws of this state, or of any other state or territory of the United States, or of any foreign government, who willfully and with a design to defraud, sells, pledges or issues, or causes to be sold, pledged or issued, or signs or procures to be signed with intent to sell, pledge or issue, or to be sold, pledged or issued, a false, forged or fradulent paper, writing or instrument, being or purporting to be a scrip, certificate or other evidence of the ownership or transfer of any share or shares of the capital stock of such company or corporation, or a bond or other evidence of debt of such company or corporation, or a certificate or other evidence of the ownership or of the transfer of any such bond or other evidence of debt, is guilty of forgery in the third degree, and upon conviction, in addition to the punishment prescribed in this title for that offense, may also be sentenced to pay a fine not exceeding $3,000.

Falsely indicating person as corporate officer.

§ 519. ´ The false making or forging of an instrument or writing purporting to have been issued by or in behalf of a corporation or association, state or government, and bearing the pretended signature of any person, therein falsely indicated as an agent or officer of such corporation, is forgery, in the same degree, as if that person were in truth such officer or agent of the corporation or association, state or government.

Terms "forge" and "forging."

§ 520. The expression "forge," "forged" and "forging," as used in this chapter, includes false making, counterfeiting and the alteration, erasure, or obliteration of a genuine instrument, in whole or in part, the false making or counterfeiting of the signature of a party or witness, and the placing or connecting together with intent to defraud different parts of several genuine instruments.

Completed unissued instruments property (larceny).

§ 536. All the provisions of this chapter apply to cases where the property taken is an instrument for the payment of money, an evidence of debt, a public security, or a passage ticket, completed and ready to be issued or delivered, although the same has never been issued or delivered by the maker thereof to any person as a purchaser or owner.

Value of passenger ticket.

§ 546. If the thing stolen is a ticket, paper or other writing, entitling or purporting to entitle the holder or proprietor thereof

to a passage upon a railway car, vessel, or other public conveyance, the price at which a ticket, entitling a person to a like
passage, is usually sold, is deemed the value thereof.

Criminally receiving property.

§ 550. A person, who buys or receives any stolen property, or
any property which has been wrongfully appropriated in such a
manner as to constitute larceny according to this chapter, knowing the same to have been stolen or so dealt with, or who corruptly, for any money, property, reward, or promise or agreement
for the same, conceals, withholds, or aids in concealing or withholding any property, knowing the same to have been stolen, or
appropriated wrongfully in such a manner as to constitute larceny under the provisions of this chapter, if such misappropria-
tion has been committed within the state, whether such property
were so stolen or misappropriated within or without the state, or
who being a dealer in or collector of junk, metals or second hand
materials, or the agent, employe or representative of such dealer
or collector, buys or receives any wire, cable, copper, lead, solder,
iron or brass used by or belonging to a railroad, telephone, telegraph, gas or electric light company without ascertaining by diligent inquiry, that the person selling or delivering the same has a
legal right to do so, is guilty of criminally receiving such property, and is punishable, by imprisonment in a state prison for not
more than five years, or in a county jail for not more than six
months, or by a fine of not more than two hundred and fifty dollars, or by both such fine and imprisonment.

Thus amended by chap. 326, Laws of 1903, taking effect July 1, 1903.
See chap. 308, Laws of 1903; section 56, Code of Criminal Procedure; section 290, Penal Code, *ante.*

Frauds in the organization of corporations.

§ 590. A person who:

1. Without authority subscribes the name of another to or
inserts the name of another in any prospectus, circular or other
advertisement or announcement of any corporation or joint-stock

association existing or intended to be formed, with intent to permit the same to be published, and thereby to lead persons to believe that the person whose name is so subscribed is an officer, agent, member or promoter of such corporation or association; or,

2. Signs the name of a fictitious person to any subscription for or agreement to take stock in any corporation, existing or proposed; or,

3. Signs to any such subscription or agreement the name of any person, knowing that such person does not intend in good faith to comply with the terms thereof, or under any understanding or agreement, that the terms of such subscription or agreement are not to be complied with or enforced; is guilty of a misdemeanor.

Fraudulent issue of stock, etc.

§ 591. An officer, agent or other person in the service of any joint-stock company or corporation formed or existing under the laws of this state, or of the United States, or of any state or territory thereof, or of any foreign government or country, who willfully and knowingly, with intent to defraud, either,

1. Sells, pledges or issues, or causes to be sold, pledged or issued, or signs or executes, or causes to be signed or executed, with intent to sell, pledges or issues, or causes to be sold, pledged or issued, any certificate or instrument purporting to be a certificate or evidence of the ownership of any share or shares of such company or corporation, or any bond or evidence of debt, or writing purporting to be a bond or evidence of debt of such company or corporation, without being first thereto duly authorized by such company or corporation, or contrary to the charter or laws under which such corporation or company exists, or in excess of the power of such company or corporation, or of the limit imposed by law or otherwise upon its power to create or issue stock or evidences of debt; or,

2. Re-issues, sells, pledges or disposes of, or causes to be re-issued, sold, pledged or disposed of, any surrendered or canceled certificates, or other evidence of the transfer or ownership of any such share or shares, is punishable by imprisonment for a term not exceeding seven years, or by a fine not exceeding three thousand dollars, or by both.

Fraud in procuring organization of corporation or increase of stock.

§ 592. An officer, agent or clerk of a corporation, or of persons proposing to organize a corporation, or to increase the capital stock of a corporation, who knowingly exhibits a false, forged or altered book, paper, voucher, security or other instrument of evidence to any public officer or board authorized by law to examine the organization of such corporation, or to investigate its affairs, or to allow an increase of its capital, with intent to deceive such officer or board in respect thereto, is punishable by imprisonment in a state prison not exceeding ten years.

Misconduct of directors of stock corporations.

§ 594. A director of a stock corporation, who concurs in any vote or act of the directors of such corporation, or any of them, by which it is intended,

1. To make a dividend, except from the surplus profits arising from the business of the corporation, and in the cases and manner allowed by law; or,

2. To divide, withdraw, or in any manner pay to the stock-holders or any of them, any part of the capital stock of the corporation; or to reduce such capital stock without the consent of the legislature; or,

3. To discount or receive any note or other evidence of debt in payment of an installment of capital stock actually called in, and required to be paid, or with intent to provide the means of making such payment; or,

4. To receive or discount any note or other evidence of debt with intent to enable any stockholder to withdraw any part of the money paid in by him on his stock; or,

5. To apply any portion of the funds of such corporation, except surplus profits, directly or indirectly, to the purchase of shares of its own stock; or,

6. (Repealed by chapter 588, Laws of 1901.)

7. (Repealed by chapter 588, Laws of 1901.)

Is guilty of a misdemeanor.

Misappropriation of property, by officer of a corporation, etc.

§ 602. A director, officer or agent of any corporation or joint-stock association, who knowingly receives or possesses himself of any property of such corporation or association, otherwise than in payment of a just demand, and with intent to defraud, omits to make, or cause or direct to be made, a full and true entry thereof, in the books or accounts of such corporation or association; and a director, officer, agent or member of any corporation or joint-stock association who, with intent to defraud, destroys, alters, multilates, or falsifies any of the books, papers, writings or securities belonging to such corporation or association, or makes or concurs in making any false entry, or omits or concurs in omitting to make any material entry in any book of accounts, or other record or document kept by such corporation or association, is punishable by imprisonment in a state prison not exceeding ten years, or by imprisonment in a county jail not exceeding one year, or by a fine not exceeding five hundred dollars, or by both such fine and imprisonment.

Thus amended by chap. 662, Laws of 1892. See chapter 692, Laws of 1892 also amending this section.

See sections 57 and 158, Railroad Law, sections 101a and 416, Penal Code, *ante;* section 611, Penal Code, *post.*

Misconduct of officers and directors of stock corporations.

§ 610. An officer or director of a stock corporation who:

1. Issues, participates in issuing, or concurs in a vote to issue

any increase of its capital stock beyond the amount of the capital stock thereof, duly authorized by or in pursuance of law; or,

2. Sells, or agrees to sell, or is directly or indirectly interested in the sale of any share of stock of such corporation, or in any agreement to sell the same, unless at the time of such sale or agreement he is an actual owner of such share; is guilty of a misdemeanor, punishable by imprisonment for not less than six months, or by a fine not exceeding five thousand dollars, or by both.

Thus amended by chap. 692, Laws of 1892.

Misconduct of officers and employes of corporations.

§ 611. A director, officer, agent or employe of any corporation or joint-stock association who:

1. Knowingly receives or possesses himself of any of its property otherwise than in payment for a just demand, and with intent to defraud, omits to make or to cause or direct to be made a full and true entry thereof in its books and accounts; or,

2. Makes or concurs in making any false entry, or concurs in omitting to make any material entry in its books or accounts; or,

Subdivision 2 thus amended by chap. 286, Laws of 1906, taking effect September 1, 1906.

3. Knowingly (1), concurs in making or publishing any written report, exhibit or statement of its affairs or pecuniary condition containing any material statement which is false, or (2), omits or concurs in omitting any statement required by law to be contained therein; or,

Subdivision 3 thus amended by chap. 286, Laws of 1906, taking effect September 1, 1906.

4. Having the custody or control of its books, willfully refuses or neglects to make any proper entry in the stock book of such corporation as required by law, or to exhibit or allow the same to be inspected and extracts to be taken therefrom by any person entitled by law to inspect the same or to take extracts therefrom.

Subdivision 4 thus amended by chap. 692, Laws of 1893.

5. If a notice of an application for an injunction affecting the property or business of such joint-stock association or corporation is served upon him, omits to disclose the fact of such service and the time and place of such application to the other directors, officers and managers thereof; or,

6. Refuses or neglects to make any report or statement lawfully required by a public officer; is guilty of a misdemeanor.

Thus amended by chap. 692, Laws of 1892.
See sections 57 and 158, Railroad Law, sections 101a, 416 and 602, Penal Code, *ante.*

Misconduct of corporate elections.

§ 613. Any person who:

1. (Repealed by chapter 588, Laws of 1901.)

2. Being entitled to vote at any meeting of the stockholders or bondholders or both of a stock corporation, sells his vote, or who issues a proxy to vote to any person for any sum of money or thing of value, except as expressly authorized by law; or,

Subdivision 2, thus amended by chap. 588, Laws of 1901.

3. Acts as an inspector of election at any such meeting and violates an oath taken by him, in pursuance of law as such inspector, or violates the provisions of an oath required by law to be taken by him as such inspector, or is guilty of any dishonest or corrupt conduct as such inspector; is guilty of a misdemeanor.

Thus amended by chap. 692, Laws of 1892.

Presumption of knowledge of corporate condition and business and of assent thereto by directors; definition.

§ 614. It is no defense to a prosecution for a violation of the provisions of this chapter, that the corporation is a foreign corporation, if it carries on business or keeps an office therefor in this state. The term "director" as used in this chapter includes any of the persons having, by law, the direction or management of the affairs of a corporation, by whatever name described. A director of a corporation or joint-stock association is deemed to have such a knowledge of the affairs of the corporation or association as to enable him to determine whether any act, proceeding or omission of its directors is a violation of this chapter. If present at a meeting of the directors at which any act, proceeding or omission of such directors in violation of this chapter occurs, he must be deemed to have concurred therein, unless he at the time causes or in writing requires his dissent therefrom to be entered on the minutes of the directors. If absent from such meeting, he must be deemed to have concurred in any such violation, if the facts constituting such violation appear on the record or minutes of the proceedings of the board of directors, and he remains a director of the corporation for six months thereafter without causing or in writing requiring his dissent from such violation to be entered on such record of minutes.

Thus amended by chap. 692, Laws of 1892.

Sale of passage tickets on vessels and railroads forbidden except by agents specially authorized.

§ 615. No person shall issue or sell, or offer to sell, any passage ticket, or an instrument giving or purporting to give any right, either absolutely or upon any condition or contingency to a passage or conveyance upon any vessel or railway train, or a berth or state-room in any vessel, unless he is an authorized agent of the owners or consignees of such vessel, or of the company running such train, except as allowed by sections six hundred and sixteen and six hundred and twenty-two; and no person is deemed an authorized agent of such owners, consignees or company, within the meaning of the chapter, unless he has received authority in writing therefor, specifying the name of the company, line, vessel or railway for which he is authorized to act as agent, and the city, town or village together with the street and street number, in which his office is kept, for the sale of tickets.

Added by chap. 506, Laws of 1897, taking effect September 1, 1897. Unconstitutional in part, 157 N. Y. See section 38, Railroad Law, *ante.*

Sales by authorized agents restricted.

§ 616. No person, except as allowed in section six hundred and twenty-two, shall ask, take or receive any money or valuable thing as a consideration for any passage or conveyance upon any vessel or railway train, or for the procurement of any ticket or instrument giving or purporting to give a right, either absolutely or upon a condition or contingency, to a passage or conveyance upon a vessel or railway train, or a berth or state-room on a vessel, unless he is an authorized agent within the provisions of the last section; nor shall any person, as such agent, sell or offer to sell, any such ticket, instrument, berth or state-room, or ask. take or receive any consideration for any such passage, conveyance, berth or state-room, excepting at the office designated in his appointment, nor until he has been authorized to act as such agent according to the provisions of the last section, nor for a sum exceeding the price charged at the time of such sale by the company, owners or consignees of the vessel or railway mentioned in the ticket. Nothing in this section or chapter contained shall prevent the properly authorized agent of any transportation company from purchasing from the properly authorized agent of any other transportation company a ticket for a passenger to whom he may sell a ticket to travel over any part of the line for which he is the properly authorized agent, so as to enable such passenger to travel to the place or junction from which his ticket shall read. Every person who shall have purchased a passage ticket from an authorized agent of a railroad company, which shall not have been used, or shall have been used only in part, may, within thirty days after the date of the sale of said ticket, present the same, unused or partly used, for redemption, at the general office of the railroad company which issued said ticket, or at the ticket office where said ticket was sold, or at the ticket office at the point to which the ticket has been used. If said ticket, wholly unused, shall be presented for redemption at the ticket office where sold, the same shall be then and there redeemed by the agent in charge of said ticket office at the price paid for said ticket. If said ticket, partly used, shall be presented for redemption at the ticket office where sold, or at the ticket office at the point to which used, the ticket agent at either of said offices, upon the delivery of said ticket, shall issue to the holder thereof a receipt, properly describing said ticket and setting forth the date of the receipt of said ticket, and the name of the person from whom received, and shall thereupon forthwith transmit said ticket for redemption to the general office. It shall be the duty of every railroad company to redeem tickets presented for redemption, as in this section provided for, promptly and within not to exceed thirty days from the date of presentation at the general office or from the date of the aforesaid receipt. A wholly unused ticket shall be redeemed at the price paid therefor. A partly used ticket shall be redeemed at a rate which shall be equal to the difference between the price paid for the whole ticket and the cost of a ticket of the same class between the points for which said ticket was actually used. Mileage books shall be redeemed within thirty days after the date of the expiration thereof in the same manner. Every railroad company which shall wrongfully refuse redemption, as in this section provided for, shall forfeit to the aggrieved party fifty dollars, which sum may be recovered, together with the amount of redemption money to which the party is entitled, in an action in any court of competent jurisdiction, together with costs; but no such action can be maintained unless commenced within one year after the cause of action accrued.

Thus amended by chap. 506, Laws of 1897, taking effect September 1, 1897. Unconstitutional in part, 157 N. Y. See section 38, Railroad Law, *ante.*

Unauthorized persons forbidden to sell certificates, receipts, etc., for the purpose of procuring tickets.

§ 617. No person other than an agent appointed, as provided in section 615, shall sell, or offer to sell, or in any way attempt to dispose of any order, certificate, receipt or other instrument,

37

for the purpose or under the pretence, of procuring any ticket
or instrument mentioned. in section 615, upon any company or
line, vessel or railway train therein mentioned. And every such
order sold or offered for sale by any such agent, must be directed
to the company, owners or consignees at their office.

Penalty.

§ 618. A person guilty of a violation of any of the provisions
of the preceding sections of this chapter is punishable by imprison
ment in a state prison not exceeding two years, or imprisonment
in a county jail not exceeding six months.

Thus amended by chap. 662, Laws of 1892.

Conspiring to sell passage tickets in violation of law.

§ 619. All persons who conspire together to sell, or attempt
to sell to any person, any passage ticket, or other instrument
mentioned in sections 615 and 616, in violation of those sections.
and all persons, who, by means of any such conspiracy, obtain,
or attempt to obtain any money, or other property, under the
pretence of procuring or securing any passage or right of passage
in violation of this chapter, are punishable by imprisonment in
a state prison not exceeding five years.

§ 619a. No transfer ticket or written or printed instrument
giving, or purporting to give, the right of transfer to any person
or persons from a public conveyance operated upon one line or
route of a street surface railroad to a public conveyance upon
another line or route of a street surface railroad, or from one
car to another car upon the same line of street surface railroad,
shall be issued, sold or given except to a passenger lawfully
entitled thereto. Any person who shall issue, sell or give away
such a transfer ticket or instrument as aforesaid to a person or
persons not lawfully entitled thereto, and any person or persons
not lawfully entitled thereto who shall receive and use or offer
for passage any such transfer ticket or instrument, or shall sell
or give away such transfer ticket or instrument to another with

intent to have such transfer ticket used or offered for passage after the time limited for its use shall have expired, shall be guilty of a misdemeanor.

Added by chap. 663, Laws of 1898.

Conspirators may be indicted, notwithstanding object of conspiracy has not been accomplished.

§ 620. Persons guilty of violating the last section may be indicted and convicted for a conspiracy, though the object of such conspiracy has not been executed.

Offices kept for unlawful sale of passage tickets, declared disorderly houses.

§ 621. All offices kept for the purpose of selling passage tickets in violation of any of the provisions of this chapter, and all offices where any such sale is made, are deemed disorderly houses; and all persons keeping any such office, and all persons associating together for the purpose of violating any of the provisions of this chapter are punishable by imprisonment in a county jail for a period not exceeding six months.

Thus amended by chap. 662, Laws of 1892.

Owners, pursers, etc., allowed to sell tickets.

§ 622. The provisions of this chapter do not prevent the actual owners or consignees of any vessel from selling passage tickets thereon; nor do they prevent the purser or clerk of any vessel from selling in his office on board of such vessel, any passage tickets upon such vessel.

Station masters, conductors, etc., allowed to sell tickets.

§ 623. The provisions of this chapter do not prevent the station master or other ticket agent upon any railway from selling in his office at any station on such railway, any passage tickets upon such railway; nor do they prevent any conductor upon a railway from selling such tickets upon the trains of such railway.

Emigrants sales and exchanges of passenger tickets.

§ 626. A person who,

1. Sells, or causes to be sold, a passage ticket, or order for such ticket, on any railway, vehicle or vessel, to any emigrant passenger at a higher rate than one and a quarter cents per mile; or,

2. Takes payment for any such ticket or order for a ticket under a false representation as to the class of the ticket, whether emigrant or first-class; or,

3. Directly or indirectly, by means of false representations, purchases or receives from an emigrant passenger any such ticket; or,

4. Procures or solicits any such passenger having such a ticket to exchange the same for another passenger ticket, or to sell the same and purchase some other passenger ticket; or,

5. Solicits or books any passenger arriving at the port of New York from a foreign country before such passenger has left the vessel on which he has arrived, or enters or goes on board any vessel arriving at the port of New York from a foreign country, having emigrant passengers on board, for the purpose of soliciting or booking such passengers; and a person or agent of a corporation employing any person for the purpose of booking such passengers before leaving the ship;

Is guilty of a misdemeanor.

" Company " defined.

§ 627. The term " company," as used in this chapter, includes all corporations, whether created under the laws of this state or of the United States, or those of any other state or nation.

Issuing fictitious bills of lading, receipts and vouchers.

§ 629. A person who:

1. Being the master, owner, or agent of any vessel, or officer or agent of any railway, express or transportation company, or

otherwise being or representing any carrier, who delivers any bill of lading, receipt or other voucher, by which it appears that merchandise of any kind has been shipped on board a vessel, or delivered to a railway, express or transportation company, or other carrier, unless the same has been so shipped or delivered and is at the time actually under the control of such carrier, or the master, owner or agent of such vessel, or of some officer or agent of such company, to be forwarded as expressed in such bill of lading, receipt or voucher; or,

2. Carrying on the business of a warehouseman, wharfinger or other depository of property, who issues any receipt, bill of lading or other voucher for merchandise of any kind which has not been actually received upon the premises of such person, and is not under his actual control at the time of issuing such instrument, whether such instrument is issued to a person as being the owner of such merchandise, or as security for any indebtedness; is guilty of a misdemeanor, punishable by imprisonment not exceeding one year, or by a fine not exceeding one thousand dollars, or by both.

Thus amended by chap. 692, Laws of 1892.

Erroneous bills of lading on receipts issued in good faith excepted.

§ 630. No person can be convicted of an offense under the last two sections, for the reason that the contents of any barrel, box, case, cask or other vessel or package mentioned in the bill of lading receipt or other voucher did not correspond with the description given in such instrument of the merchandise received, if such description corresponds substantially with the marks, labels or brands upon the outside of such vessel or package, unless it appears that the defendant knew that such marks, labels or brands were untrue.

Duplicate receipt must be marked " duplicate."

§ 631. A person mentioned in sections 628 and 629, who issues any second or duplicate receipt or voucher of a kind specified in those sections, at a time while a former receipt or voucher for the merchandise specified in such second receipt is outstanding and uncanceled, without writing across the face of the same the word "duplicate," in a plain and legible manner, is punishable by imprisonment not exceeding one year, or by a fine not exceeding $1,000, or by both.

Selling, hypothecating or pledging property received for transportation or storage.

§ 632. A person mentioned in sections 628 and 629, who sells or pledges any merchandise for which a bill of lading, receipt or voucher has been issued by him without the consent in writing thereto of the person holding such bill, receipt or voucher, is punishable by imprisonment not exceeding one year, or by a fine not exceeding $1,000, or by both.

Property demanded by process of law.

§ 634. The last two sections (§§ 632 and 633) do not apply to any case where property is demanded by virtue of legal process.

Injuries to railroad tracks, et cetera.

§ 635. A person who wilfully:

1. Displaces, loosens, removes, injures or destroys any rail, sleeper, switch, bridge, viaduct, culvert, embankment or structure or any part thereof, attached, appertaining to or connected with any railway, or by any other means attempts to wreck, destroy, or so damage any car, tender, locomotive or railway train or part thereof, while moving or standing upon any railway track in this state, as to render such car, tender, locomotive or railway train wholly or partially unfitted for its ordinary use, whether operated by steam, electricity or other motive power; or

2. Places any obstruction upon the track of any such railway; or

3. Wilfully destroys or breaks any guard erected or maintained by a railroad corporation as a warning signal for the protection of its employes; or

4. Wilfully discharges a loaded firearm or projects, or throws
a stone or other missile at a railway train, or at a locomotive,
car or vehicle standing or moving upon a railway; or

5. Wilfully displaces, removes, cuts, injures or destroys any
wire, insulator, pole, dynamo, motor, locomotive, or any part
thereof, attached, appertaining to or connected with any railway
operated by electricity, or wilfully interferes with or interrupts
any motive power used in running such road, or wilfully places
any obstruction upon the track of such railroad, or wilfully discharges a loaded firearm, or projects or throws a stone or any
other missile at such railway train or locomotive, car or vehicle,
standing or moving upon such railway; or

6. Removes a journal brass from a car while standing upon
any railroad track in this state, without authority from some
person who has a right to give such authority, is punishable as
follows: First. If thereby the safety of any person is endangered, by imprisonment for not more than twenty years. Second.
In every other case by imprisonment for not more than five years.
Thus amended by chap. 183, Laws of 1897, taking effect September 1, 1897.
See section 183a, Penal Code, *ante;* section 30, Rapid Transit Act, *post.*

Altering, etc., signal or light for railway engine or train.

§ 638. A person who, with intent to bring a vessel, railway
engine or railway train into danger, either,

1. Unlawfully or wrongfully shows, masks, extinguishes, alters
or removes a light or other signal; or

2. Exhibits any false light or signal;

Is punishable by imprisonment for not more than ten years.

Endangering life by maliciously placing explosive near building,
car, etc.

§ 645. A person who places in, upon, under, against or near
to, any building, car, vessel or structure, gunpowder or any other

explosive substance, with intent to destroy, throw down or injure the whole or any part thereof, under such circumstances, that, if the 'intent were accomplished, human life or safety would be endangered thereby, although no damage is done, is guilty of a felony.

§ 654. A person who unlawfully and willfully destroys or injures any real or personal property of another or who without authority or permission from a person who has the right to give such authority or permission, loosens any brake or blocking of any car standing on any railroad track in this state, or without like authority or permission, puts upon or runs any hand car, or other car, on any railroad track in this state, or without like authority or permission, interferes or meddles with any brake or coupling of any car while standing or moving on any rail- road track in this state, or takes any part therein, in a case where the punishment is not specially prescribed by statute, is punishable as follows:

1. If the value of the property destroyed, or the diminution in the value of the property by the injury is more than twenty- five dollars, by imprisonment for not more than four years.

2. In any other case, by imprisonment for not more than six months, or by a fine of not more than two hundred and fifty dollars, or by both such fine and imprisonment.

3. And in addition to the punishment prescribed therefor, he is liable in treble damages for the injury done, to be recovered in a civil action by the owner of such property, or the public officer having charge thereof.

Thus amended by chap. 186, Laws of 1892.

Carrying animals in a cruel manner, a misdemeanor.

§ 659. A person who carries or causes to be carried in or upon any vessel or vehicle, or otherwise, any animal in a cruel or inhuman manner or so as to produce torture, is guilty of a misdemeanor.

Throwing substance injurious to animals in public places, a misdemeanor.

§ 661. A person who willfully throws, drops or places, or causes to be thrown, dropped or placed upon any road, highway, street or public place, any glass, nails, pieces of metal, or other substance which might wound, disable or injure any animal, is guilty of a misdemeanor.

Transporting animals for more than twenty-four consecutive hours, a misdemeanor.

§ 663. A railway corporation, or an owner, agent, consignee, or person in charge of any horses, sheep, cattle, or swine, in the course of, or for transportation, who confines, or causes or suffers the same to be confined, in cars for a longer period than twenty-four consecutive hours, without unloading for rest, water and feeding, during ten consecutive hours, unless prevented by storm or inevitable accident, is guilty of a misdemeanor. In estimating such confinement, the time during which the animals have been confined without rest, on connecting roads from which they are received, must be computed. If the owner, agent, consignee, or other person in charge of any such animals refuses or neglects upon demand to pay for the care or feed of the animals while so unloaded or rested, the railway company, or other carriers thereof, may charge the expense thereof to the owner or consignee and shall have a lien thereon for such expense.

Running horses on highway a misdeameanor.

§ 666. A person driving any vehicle upon any plank road, turnpike or public highway, who unjustifiably runs the horses drawing the same, or causes, or permits them to run, is guilty of a misdemeanor.

Thus amended by chap. 539, Laws of 1904.

Definitions.

§ 669. 1. The word "animal," as used in this title, does not include the human race, but includes every other living creature;

2. The words "torture" or "cruelty" includes every act, omis-sion, or neglect, whereby unjustifiable physical pain, suffering or death is caused or permitted;   ✱   ✱   ✱   ✱   ✱   ✱   ✱

Endangering life by refusal to labor.

§ 673. A person who willfully and maliciously, either alone or in combination with others, breaks a contract of service or hiring, knowing or having reasonable cause to believe, that the probable consequence of his so doing will be to endanger human life, or to cause grievous bodily injury, or to expose valuable property to destruction or serious injury, is guilty of a misde-meanor.

Offenses not otherwise enumerated.

§ 675. Any person who shall by any offensive or disorderly act or language, annoy or interfere with any person or persons in any place or with the passengers of any public stage, railroad car, ferry boat, or other public conveyance, or who shall disturb or offend the occupants of such stage, car, boat or conveyance. by any disorderly act, language or display, although such act, conduct or display may not amount to an assault or battery, shall be deemed guilty of a misdemeanor. A person who wil-fully and wrongfully commits any act which seriously injures the person or property of another, or which seriously disturbs or endangers the public peace or health, or which openly out-rages public decency, for which no other punishment is expressly prescribed by this code, is guilty of a misdemeanor; but nothing in.this code contained shall be so construed as to prevent any person from demanding an increase of wages, or from assembling and using all lawful means to induce employers to pay such wages to all persons employed by them, as shall be a just and fair compensation for services rendered.

See subdivision 36, section 56, Code of Criminal Procedure, *ante.*

*Rapid Transit Act.

(As amended to and including the session of the Legislature of 1906.)

CHAP. 4, LAWS OF 1891, AMENDED BY CHAP. 102, LAWS OF 1892, CHAP. 556, LAWS OF 1892, CHAP. 752, LAWS OF 1894, CHAP. 519, LAWS OF 1895, CHAP. 729, LAWS OF 1896, CHAP. 616, LAWS OF 1900, CHAP. 587, LAWS OF 1901, CHAPTERS 533, 542, 544 AND 584, LAWS OF 1902, CHAPTERS 562 AND 564, LAWS OF 1904, CHAPTERS 599 AND 631, LAWS OF 1905, AND CHAPTERS 472, 606 AND 607, LAWS OF 1906.

(See provisions of Greater New York Charter, *an.*)

AN ACT to provide for rapid transit railways in cities of over one million inhabitants.

Commissioners of rapid transit; appointments; board constituted; vacancies.

§ 1. In each city having over one million of inhabitants, according to the last preceding national or state census, there shall be a board of rapid transit railroad commissioners in and for such city, which shall consist of the mayor of such city, the comptroller or other chief financial officer of such city, the president of the chamber of commerce of the state of New York, by virtue of his office, and the following named persons, to wit: William Steinway, Seth Low, John Claflin, Alexander E. Orr and John H. Starin. The members of said board shall be styled commissioners of rapid transit. Vacancies which may take place in the offices so held by the persons specifically named herein as such commissioners shall be filled by a majority vote of the remaining members of said board. Provided, however, that vacancies which

---

*See article 5, Railroad Law, *ante.*

may at any time after the first day of January, nineteen hundred
and six take place in the offices so held by the persons specifically
named herein as such commissioners, or by their successors heretofore elected, shall be filled by the mayor of such city, and any
person so hereafter appointed by the mayor of such city to fill
any such vacancy shall be a citizen of the United States and of
the state of New York and a bona fide resident of the city in
which such person is appointed. The board thus constituted
shall have and exercise the specific authority and powers hereinafter conferred and also such other and necessary powers as may
be requisite to the efficient performance of the duties imposed
upon said board by this act.

Thus amended by chap. 472, Laws of 1906.

Oath of commissioners.

§ 2. Each of the said commissioners other than the mayor
and comptroller or other chief financial officer of such city shall
take and subscribe an oath faithfully to perform the duties of
his office, which oath shall be filed in the office of the clerk of
any county within which there shall be a city of the class mentioned in the first section of this act.

Thus amended by chap. 752, Laws of 1894.

First meeting of board; by-laws and rules; quorum; record of proceedings.

§ 3. Within twenty days after the filing of the oaths of said
commissioners so required to make and file the same the
commissioners of rapid transit in respect to each of such cities
shall meet and organize as a board. The board when so organized, may frame and adopt by-laws not inconsistent with this
act, and establish suitable rules and regulations for the proper
exercise of the powers and duties hereby conferred and imposed.
and may, from time to time, amend the same. Four members
of the board shall constitute a quorum for the transaction of
business, but a less number may adjourn meetings. The said

board shall adopt a seal, and keep a record of its proceedings, which shall be a public record and be open to inspection at all reasonable times.

§ 4. The said board upon its own motion may proceed, from time to time, to consider and determine whether it is for the interest of the public and of the city in which it is appointed, that a rapid transit railway or railways for the conveyance and transportation of persons and property should be established therein, and upon the request in writing of the local authorities of any such city at any time, the said board shall proceed forth-with to consider and determine the same questions, and in each case the said board shall conduct such an inquest and investigation as may be deemed necessary in the premises. If, after any such consideration and inquest, the said board shall determine that a rapid transit railway or railways, in addition to any already existing authorized or proposed are necessary for the interest of the public, and such city, it shall proceed to determine and establish the route or routes thereof and the general plan of construction. Such general plan shall show the general mode of operation and contain such details as to manner of construction as may be necessary to show the extent to which any street, avenue or other public place is to be encroached upon and the property abutting thereon affected, and the concurrent votes of at least six members of the board shall be necessary for the purpose of determining and establishing such route or routes and plan of construction. The said board, from time to time, may locate the route or routes of such railway or railways over, under, upon, through and across any streets, avenues, bridges, viaducts, rivers, waters and lands within such city, including blocks between streets or avenues or, partly over, under, upon, through and across any streets, avenues, bridges, viaducts, and lands within such city and partly through blocks between streets or avenues; provided that the consent of the owners of one-half in value of the property bounded on and the consent also of the local authorities having control of that portion of a street, bridge, viaduct, or highway, upon which it is proposed to construct or operate such railway or railways be first obtained, or in case the consent of such property owners cannot be obtained, that the determination of three commissioners appointed by the general term of the supreme court in the district of the proposed construction, given after due hearing of all parties interested, and confirmed by the court, that such railway or railways ought to be constructed or operated, be taken in lieu of the consent of such property owners; except that no public park nor any lands or places, lawfully set apart for, or occupied by, any public building of any. city or county, or of the state of New York, or of the United States, nor those portions of Grand, Classon, Franklin avenues and Downing street in the city of Brooklyn, lying between the southerly line of Lexington avenue and northerly line of Atlantic avenue, nor that portion of Classon avenue in said city lying between the northerly line of Lexington avenue and southerly line of Park avenue, nor that portion of Washington avenue in said city lying between Park and Atlantic avenues, nor DeBevoise place, Irving place and Leffert's place, Lee avenue, Nostrand avenue, Waverly avenue, Vanderbilt avenue and Clinton avenue in said city of Brooklyn, nor that portion of the city of Buffalo lying between Michigan and Main streets, nor any part of Fifth avenue in the city of New York, nor that portion of any street or avenue which is now actually occupied by any elevated railroad structure, shall be occupied by any corporation to be organized under the provisions of this act for the purpose of constructing a railway in or upon any of such public parks, lands or places, or upon or along either of the said excepted streets or avenues. It shall be lawful for said commissioners to locate the route of a railway or railways, by tunnel under any such public parks, lands, places, rivers or waters and to locate the route of any railway to be built, under this act, across any of the streets and avenues now occupied by an elevated railroad structure in the city of New York, or across any of the streets or avenues excepted in this act at any point at which, in its discretion, the board of rapid transit railroad commissioners may deem necessary in the location of any route or routes, or under, or under and along, any of said streets or avenues now so occupied or so excepted in this act. Nothing in this act shall authorize the construction of an ele vated railway on Broadway south of Thirty-third street, nor on Madison avenue in the city of New York. It shall not be lawful to grant, use or occupy, for the purposes of an elevated railroad, except for the purpose of crossing the same, any portion of the following named streets and places in the city of New York, that is to say: Second avenue below Twenty-third street; Fourteenth street, between the easterly line or side of Seventh avenue, and the westerly side of Fourth avenue; nor Eleventh street, west of Seventh avenue, nor any part of Bank street; Nassau street; Printing House square, socalled, south of Franklin street; Park row, south of Tryon row; Broad street and Wall street.

2. The provisions of the said section four of the said act shall, with reference to any rapid transit railroad for which routes and a general plan have been heretofore adopted by the board of rapid transit railroad commissioners of any city and for the municipal construction of which a contract has been heretofore made by any city, be deemed to have been in full force as hereby amended from before the time when the routes and general plan for such railroad or railroads were so adopted by the board of rapid transit railroad commissioners.

Thus amended by chap. 564, Laws of 1904. See section 2, chap. 616, Laws of 1900.

§ 5. After any determination by said board of any such route or routes and of any general plan of construction of said railway or railways, the said board shall transmit to the board of estimate and apportionment or other board or boards of said

city having the control of any street, highway, boulevard, drive
way, bridge, tunnel, park, parkway, dock, bulkhead, wharf, pier
or public grounds or water which is within or belongs to the
city, a copy of said plans and conclusions as adopted. It shall
be the duty of such board of estimate and apportionment and of
every other such board or boards having such control, upon
receiving such copy of plans and conclusions to appoint a day
not less than one week nor more than ten days after the receipt
thereof for the consideration of such plans and conclusions, and
the said board of estimate and apportionment and every other
such board having such control shall, on the day so fixed, proceed
with the consideration thereof and may continue and adjourn
such consideration, from time to time, until a final vote shall
be taken thereon, as hereinafter provided. Within sixty days
after the copy of such plans and conclusions adopted by the
board of rapid transit railroad commissioners shall have first
been received by said board of estimate and apportionment or
such other board or boards having such control, a final vote
shall be taken thereon, by ayes and nays, according to the number of votes by law pertaining to each member of any such
board in the form of a vote upon a resolution to approve such
plans and conclusions, and to consent to the construction of a
railway or railways in accordance therewith. Upon the adoption of such a resolution by a majority vote of all the members
of the said board of estimate and apportionment or other such
board or boards having such control according to the number
of votes by law pertaining to each member of any such board
and the approval of the mayor, the said plans and conclusions
shall be deemed to have been finally consented to and adopted,
and such consent shall be deemed to be consent of the local
authorities of such city; provided, that where in any such city
the exclusive control of any street, road, bridge, viaduct, highway or avenue which is to be used or occupied by any railway or
railways constructed under the provisions of this act, is by law
vested in any local authority other than the board of estimate
and apportionment of such city, the approval of the aforesaid

plans and conclusions and the consent to the construction of a railway thereunder shall be given by such local authority in place of and if required in addition to such approval and consent by said board of estimate and apportionment and with like effect. Upon obtaining the approval and consent of the local authorities as above provided, the said board of rapid transit railroad commissioners shall also, unless such approval and consent of local authorities shall have been refused, take the necessary steps to obtain, if possible, the said consents of the property owners along the line of the said route or routes. For the purposes of this act the value of the property bounded on that portion of any street or highway in, upon, over or under which it is proposed to construct or operate such railway or railways, or any part thereof, shall be ascertained and determined from the assessment roll of the city in which the said property is situated, confirmed or completed last before the local authorities shall have given their consent as above provided. If such consents of property owners cannot be obtained, the said board may, in its own name, make application to the appellate division of the supreme court in the judicial district in which such railway is to be constructed for the appointment of three commissioners to determine and report after due hearing whether such railway ought to be constructed and operated. Two weeks' notice of such application shall be given by daily publication thereof, Sundays and holidays excepted, in six daily newspapers published in the city where such proposed railway is to be constructed, if there be so many newspapers published in said city, and if not, then in all the daily newspapers published in said city. The newspapers in which said publication shall be made shall be designated by the appellate division of the supreme court to which such application is to be made on the application of the commissioners without notice. The said appellate division, upon due proof of the publication aforesaid, shall appoint three disinterested persons who shall act as commissioners, and such commissioners within ten days after their appointment shall cause public notice to be given in the manner

38

directed by the said appellate division of their first sitting, and may adjourn from time to time until all their business is completed. Vacancies in such commission may be filled by said appellate division after such notice to persons interested as the appellate division may deem proper, and the evidence taken before as well as after such vacancy occurred shall be deemed to be properly before such commissioners. The said commissioners shall determine after public hearing of all parties interested whether such railroad ought to be constructed and operated and shall report the evidence taken to said appellate division together with a report of their determination whether such road ought to be constructed and operated, which report, if in favor of the construction and operation of such road shall, when confirmed by said court, be taken in lieu of the consent of the property owners above mentioned. Such report shall be made within sixty days after the appointment of said commissioners, unless the said court, or a judge thereof, shall extend such time. The board of estimate and apportionment of the city of New York shall, with respect to that city, be hereafter for all purposes of this act and be deemed to be the local authority in control of the streets, roads, bridges, viaducts, highways, avenues, boulevards, driveways, parks, parkways, docks, bulkheads, wharfs, piers and public grounds and waters which are within or belong to the said city; and the consent of such board of estimate and apportionment and the mayor, without the consent of the common council, board of aldermen or other board or officer of the city, shall be the only consent of local authorities required hereunder.

Thus amended by chap. 631, Laws of 1905, section 2, of said chapter 631, being as follows:

§ 2. (Chapter 631, Laws of 1905.) This act and all the amendments hereby made to the sections thereof hereby amended, shall be applicable to every grant, franchise or contract heretofore made, authorized or issued by the said board of rapid transit railroad commissioners but not yet consented to by the common council or board of aldermen of the city, as well as to all grants, franchises and contracts hereafter made, authorized or issued by the said board of rapid transit railroad commissioners.

Detailed plan; subways for pipes and wires; work at points of
sub-surface structures; expenses, how paid; as to claimed
franchises.

§ 6. When the consents of the local authorities and the property owners, or, in lieu thereof, the authorization of the said·ap-
pellate division of the supreme court upon the report of commissioners, shall have been obtained, the board of rapid transit railroad commissioners shall at once proceed to prepare detailed
plans and specifications for the construction of such rapid transit
railway or railways in accordance with the general plan of construction, including all devices and appurtenances deemed by it
necessary to secure the greatest efficiency, public convenience and
safety, including the number, location and description of stations
and plans and specifications for the suitable supports, turnouts,
switches, sidings, connections, landing places, buildings, platforms, stairways, elevators, telegraph and signal devices, and
other suitable appliances incidental and requisite to what the
said board may approve as the best and most efficient system of
rapid transit in view of the public needs and requirements, and
the said board may, in its discretion, include in said plans
provisions for galleries, ways, subways or tunnels for sewers,
gas or water pipes, electric wires and other subsurface structures
and conductors proper to be placed underground, whenever
necessary so to do, in order to permit of the proper construction of any railway herein provided for in accordance
with the plans and specifications of the said board, or for any
other purpose in furtherance of the public interest or convenience.
Stations and station approaches may be under or over streets of
the route or cross streets, and the board of aldermen, or other
legislative body, of any such city shall have power to regulate by
general or special ordinance or resolution, the erection, alteration and maintenance upon or in connection with any building
used, wholly or in part for station purposes, or approaches, or
any and all structures or parts of structures extending over the
whole or any part of any sidewalk or sidewalks adjacent thereto.

The board may, from time to time, alter such detailed plans and specifications, but always so that the same shall accord with the general plan of construction; but whenever a contract shall have been made for the construction of any railway herein provided for, no such alteration shall be made by the board without the consent of the contractor and his sureties, except as liberty shall have been reserved in such contract by said board for such alteration. Whenever the construction of any railway, depressed way, subway or tunnel under the provisions of this act shall interfere with, disturb or endanger any sewer, waterpipe, gaspipe, or other duly authorized subsurface structure, the work of construction at such points shall be conducted in the city of New York in accordance with the reasonable requirements of the commissioner of public works, and in other cities in accordance with the reasonable requirements and under the supervision of the officer or local authority having the care of and the jurisdiction or control over such subsurface structures so interfered with, disturbed or endangered. All expenses incidental to such supervision and to the work of reconstructing, readjusting and supporting any such sewer, waterpipe, gaspipe or other duly authorized subsurface structure shall be borne and paid by the company which shall have acquired the right, privilege and franchise to construct, maintain and operate such railway, pursuant to a sale of the same at public auction, as hereinafter provided, if any such sale shall be made by said board. Where under the direction of the said board or in pursuance of any general plan adopted or of any contract made by the said board, galleries, ways, subways or tunnels shall be constructed to contain sewers, pipes or other subsurface structures, the said galleries, ways, subways or tunnels shall be maintained by the said city and shall be in the care and charge of the said board and subject to such regulations as it shall prescribe not inconsistent with the provisions of this act, and any revenue derived therefrom shall be paid into the treasury of said city, except that where bonds shall have been issued to provide for the cost of construction or equipment of such rail.

roads, such amounts shall be paid to the sinking fund of the city, if there be one, or if not then into the sinking fund, to be established and created out of the annual rentals of said road, as provided in section thirty-seven of this act. Provided, however, that any person or corporation who or which at the time of the construction of the said galleries, ways, subways, or tunnels shall own pipes, subways or conduits in a street, avenue or public place in which said galleries, ways, subways or tunnels shall be constructed pursuant to this act, shall be entitled to the use of such galleries, ways, subways or tunnels for his or its said pipes, subways or conduits in the same manner as the said person or corporation shall be entitled by law to the use of such street, avenue or public place, and that no rent shall be charged for such use, except a reasonable charge to defray the actual cost of maintenance, unless such pipes, subways or conduits shall be of greater capacity than those theretofore owned by such person or corporation in said street, avenue or public place, and that, if the capacity of any such pipe, subway or conduit, so placed in the said galleries, ways, subways or tunnels shall be increased, the rent shall be charged only for such increased capacity; and provided further, that the placing in any such galleries, ways, subways or tunnels of the subways or conduits of any corporation owning subways or conduits for electrical conductors, shall not in any wise affect the right of such corporation to charge and demand such compensation or rent for the use of said subways or conduits by other corporations or individuals as is, or may be, permitted by law. Nothing in this section or contained in the act hereby amended shall be construed as granting, enlarging, changing, or in any manner validating, any right, privilege or franchise, or any claimed or alleged right, privilege or franchise, to maintain, operate, or possess any gas mains, pipes or conductors, or any conduits or conductors for transmission of electricity, or any subsurface structures of any name or nature whatever, in any street, avenue, highway or public place in such city.

Thus amended by chap. 472, Laws of 1906.

Public sale of franchise; notice thereof; terms and conditions;
    supervision of board and engineers; deposits by bidders;
    nullity of bids and rights thereunder; time for beginning and
    finishing roads; forfeiture and resale of franchise; terms as
    to organization of corporation, etc.; rejection and acceptance
    of bids; terms on resales; adjournments; term of franchise;
    proviso as to extension.

§ 7. If, after having secured the necessary consents and after
having prepared such detailed plans and specifications as are
by this act provided for, it shall not have been determined by
vote of the people as provided by sections twelve and thirteen
of chapter seven hundred and fifty-two of the laws of eighteen
hundred and ninety-four, that such railway or railways shall
be constructed for and at the expense of such city as hereafter
provided, said board shall sell at public auction in the city where
said railway or railways are to be built and for the account
and benefit of said city the right, privilege and franchise to construct, maintain and operate such railway or railways. Notice
of the time and place of such sale shall be published three times
a week for at least six successive weeks in at least three daily
newspapers published in said city. The board may prescribe all
such terms and conditions of sale as it may deem to be for the
interest of the public and of the city in which the railway or
railways are to be constructed. The advertisement of sale shall
contain only so much of the said terms, plans and specifications
for the construction as the said board may think proper, but such
advertisement must state at what place the full terms, plans and
specifications may be examined, and they shall be subject to
examination under such reasonable rules anl regulations as the
board may prescribe. The terms of sale shall provide for the
construction of the railway or railways under the supervision of
the board, and for the approval of an engineer or engineers to
be appointed, from time to time, by the board, and the corpora-

tion or corporations to be organized for the purpose of constructing and operating such railway or railways as in this act provided shall pay such engineer or engineers such salary as may,
from time to time, be fixed by the said board of rapid transit
railroad commissioners. Such engineer or engineers shall hold
their office at the pleasure of the said board. The terms of sale
shall require the successful bidder to deposit with the comptroller or chief fiscal officer of the city, in cash or approved
securities, such amount as the board may deem sufficient to constitute a guarantee of full compliance with the terms of sale
by the purchaser and by the corporation to be formed for the
purpose of building and operating said railway as hereinafter
provided. Said bids and all rights which may have been acquired
thereunder shall become null and void and of no effect, at the
option of said board, should there be a failure to organize a
corporation to exercise such rights, privileges and franchises as
required by said terms of sale and this act, or for any violation
of any of the requirements of said terms of sale which should
be complied with before such corporation is organized, and thereupon any deposit which may have been made pursuant to such
terms of sale shall be paid into the treasury of such city upon a
certificate being made and filed by said board with the public
officer with whom such deposit shall have been made, that said
bid, and all rights which may have been acquired thereunder, have
become null and void and of no effect; and said rights, privileges
and franchises shall be again sold by said board, subject to all
the provisions of this act regulating such sales. The terms of
sale shall require the construction of the road to be begun within
a time to be specified in said terms of sale, and to be finished
within a certain time thereafter, to be specified therein, and may
prescribe the time with which portions of the same shall be begun
and finished. The said terms of sale may reserve to the board
the power to extend the times for the commencement and com-

pletion of the construction of said railway, or of portions of the
same, if, in its discretion, the said board deem such extension to
be for the best interests of the city. In case the corporation
formed for the purpose of constructing said railway shall fail to
begin or finish the construction within the times for those purposes respectively limited, all rights, privileges and franchises of
such corporations to maintain and operate said railway shall be
forfeited, and upon such forfeiture being adjudged by the court
in a suit brought for that purpose in the name of the mayor,
aldermen and commonalty of the city of New York, or such other
appropriate corporate title of said city or by said board of rapid
transit railroad commissioners, then the said board shall have
power to advertise and resell said rights, privileges and franchises
and so much of the road as shall have been constructed by such
corporation; such suit shall have preference over all other cases
in all courts; and the proceeds of such resale shall be applied
first to the payment of the expenses of the resale, and then to
the discharge of any liens which may have been created upon
such property, and the balance shall be paid over to the said
corporation. The terms of sale must provide for the organization by the purchaser or purchasers of such rights, privileges
and franchises of a corporation to exercise the same, and to construct, maintain and operate such rapid transit railway or railways, with the powers and subject to the duties and liabilities
granted or imposed by this act. The said terms of sale must
also specify the amount of the capital of any such corporation,
and number of shares of capital stock which such corporation
shall be authorized to issue, the percentage to be paid in cash
by the subscribers on subscribing for such shares, the maximum
amount of the bonded indebtedness which such corporation be
authorized to incur, and which may be secured by mortgage upon
its property and franchises, and the rates of fares and freights
which such corporation may charge and collect for the carriage

of persons and property. But the rate of fare for any passenger on said railway from any point on the same northward or south-ward within the city of New York shall not exceed five cents under any provision of this act. The said board may, if it considers that the public interest requires it to do so, reject all bids and readvertise the said rights, privileges and franchises for sale, with the same or different terms of sale, as often as it may deem necessary in the interest of such city, and shall finally accept that bid which, under all circumstances, in its opinion is most advantageous to the public and such city; and no bid shall be accepted without the concurrent vote of six members of the board. The terms of sale on any such resale must contain all the provisions required by this act to be inserted in the original terms of sale. Such sale may be adjourned from time to time at the discretion of the board. All sales of such rights, privileges and franchises shall be made for a definite term of years, but the expiration of the term, if sold for a term of years, shall not impair any mortgage or other lien upon the property of such corporation or the rights of any creditor or creditors of such corporation; provided, however, that nothing herein contained shall be so construed as to extend the term for which such rights, privileges and franchises are sold.

Thus amended by chap. 752, Laws of 1894, and chap. 519, Laws of 1895.

Resale of franchise after expiration of term; purchasers; new corporation.

§ 8. Within one year, and not less than six months, prior to the expiration of any term for which such rights, privileges and franchises shall have been sold, said board shall proceed to resell the right to maintain and operate the said railway. Such sale shall be made in the manner prescribed for the original sale, and the board is empowered to make suitable provisions for securing to the corporation then operating such railway or railways suitable compensation for the railroad structure and appurtenances,

and for any other property, real or personal, which the said corporation may own or of which it may be vested at the expiration
of the term for which such rights, privileges and franchises were
sold. Any corporation theretofore organized under the provisions
of this act may be a purchaser on such resale; but if no such
corporation be the purchaser, a new corporation shall be formed
to maintain and operate said road in the manner prescribed for
the organization of a corporation on the original sale, except
that the plans and specifications according to which said railway
has been constructed need not be set out at large, but may be
referred to as forming part of the articles of association of said
new corporation.

Offices and assistants for board, etc.

§ 9. The said board may rent such offices and employ such
engineers, attorneys and other persons, from time to time, as it
may, in its discretion, deem necessary to the proper performance
by it of its duties as in this act prescribed. It may sue in the
name and behalf of the city for which it acts as a board. It
may in the name of and in behalf of the said city bring action of
specific performance or may apply by mandamus to compel the
performance within its city by any corporation or person of any
duty or obligation with reference to or arising out of the construction or operation of any railroad under, or by reason of,
any grant made or right acquired under this act or the acts
amendatory hereof or supplementary hereto, or out of or by
reason of any contract made or authorized by any board of
rapid transit commissioners within its city, or it may in behalf
of and in the name of said city bring actions to recover damages
for any violation of contract or duty, or for any wrong committed by any such corporation or person by reason of any non-
performance or violation of duty under the provisions of this
act, or under any contract or stipulation made in pursuance of

any provisions of this act. Every action or proceeding brought by the said board, and every action or proceeding in which an injunction is had or sought against the board or the said city, or against any corporation or person who or which shall have entered into a contract under the provisions of this act, or any act supplementary hereto, or amendatory hereof, by reason of any act or thing done, proposed or threatened under or by virtue of any provision of this act, or any act supplementary hereto, or amendatory hereof, or is sought against any corporation or person claiming or claiming to act under any grant or franchise under this act, or any act supplementary hereto, or amendatory hereof, and every action or proceeding in which the constitutionality of any part of this act, or of any act supplementary hereto, or amendatory hereof, shall or may be brought in question, shall have a preference above all causes not criminal on the calendar of every court, and may be brought on for trial or argument upon notice of eight days for any day of any term on which the court shall be in session.

Thus amended by chap. 519, Laws of 1895.

Appropriations for board; proceedings upon failure to appropriate amount; liability of city; audit and payment of expenditures; revenue bonds, issue of, etc.; repayment of expenses; compensation of commissioners.

§ 10. The board of estimate and apportionment or other board or public body on which is imposed the duty, and in which is vested the power, of making appropriations of public moneys for the purposes of the city government in any city in which it is proposed to construct such railway or railways shall, from time to time, on requisition duly made by the board of rapid transit railroad commissioners, appropriate such sum or sums of money as may be requisite and necessary to properly enable it to do and perform, or cause to be done and performed, the duties herein prescribed, and to provide for the compensation of such commissioners, and such appropriation shall be made forthwith upon presentation of a requisition from the board of rapid transit railroad commissioners, which shall state the purposes for which such moneys are required by the said board. In case the said board of estimate and apportionment or such other board or public body fail to appropriate such amount as the board of rapid transit railroad commissioners deem requisite and necessary, the said board of rapid transit railroad commissioners may apply to the general term of the supreme court, in the department in which the railway is to be or has been constructed, on notice to the board of estimate and apportionment, or such other board or public body aforesaid, to determine what amount shall be appropriated for the purposes required by this section, and the decision of said general term shall be final and conclusive; and no city shall be liable for any indebtedness incurred by the said board of rapid transit railroad commissioners in excess of such appropriation or appropriations. It shall be the duty of the auditor and comptroller of any such city, after such appropriations shall have been duly made, to audit and pay the proper expenditures and compensation of said commissioners upon vouchers therefor, to be furnished by the said commissioners, which payments shall be made in like manner as payments are now made by the auditor, comptroller, or other public officers, of claims against and demands upon such city; and for the purpose of providing funds with which to pay the said sums, the comptroller or other chief financial officer of said city is hereby authorized and directed to issue and sell revenue bonds of such city in anticipation of receipt of taxes, and out of the proceeds of such bonds to make the payments in this section required to be made. The amount necessary to pay the principal and interest of such bonds shall be included in the estimates of moneys necessary to be raised by taxation to carry on the busi. ness of said city, and shall be made a part of the tax levy for the year next following the year in which such appropriations are made. All expenses of the said board of rapid transit railroad commissioners, including the compensation of said commission· ers, so incurred and paid by any city as in this section provided, and for which any city shall be liable, shall be repaid, with interest, by the bidder or bidders at the public sale of the rights, privileges and franchises, as in this act provided, in case said board shall so sell the same, whose bid shall be accepted by the board of rapid transit railroad commissioners, and the terms of such sale shall specify the time when such payment shall be made, as well as the amount thereof. The commissioners, other than the mayor and comptroller or other chief financial officer of such city, shall be paid a reasonable compensation for the duties performed by them, from time to time, under the provisions of this act. The amount of such compensation shall be determined by the general term of the supreme court in the department in which said city shall be located upon application by said board after notice to the mayor of such city.

Thus amended by chap. 752, Laws of 1894.

Corporations, how organized; articles of association; approval and filing thereof; subscriptions to stock; meeting of subscribers; preference in subscriptions, etc.

§ 11. A corporation or corporations to construct and operate such rapid transit railway or railways, and to enjoy and exercise the rights, privileges and franchises in this act provided for shall be created and organized in the manner following: Articles of association shall be duly signed and acknowledged by not less than twenty-five persons, and such articles shall set forth the name of the proposed corporation and duration thereof. Said articles must also state that they are made and filed under and in pursuance of this act for the purpose of taking and exercising the rights, privileges and franchises so purchased as aforesaid, according to the terms of sale; and such terms of sale and all plans and specifications must be made a part of said articles, annexed thereto and filed therewith. The said articles must also contain such other provisions as the said board may deem requisite and necessary, not inconsistent with the terms of sale or with this act. The said articles must be approved by said board, by the concurrent vote of four members, and its approval must be indorsed thereon and attested by the seal of the board and the signature of its presiding officer, and must then be filed in the office of the secretary of state, and a duly certified copy, or a duplicate thereof, must be filed in the office of the clerk of the county in which such railway or railways are to be constructed. Immediately after the articles of association shall have been so made, approved and filed, the board of rapid transit railroad commissioners shall cause books of subscription to the capital stock of any such corporation to be opened, and shall give public notice of the opening of such books and of the time and place at which subscriptions will be received; and when the full amount of such capital stock shall have been subscribed by not less than fifty persons, and such percentage of the amount subscribed as may have been fixed by the board in the terms of sale shall have been paid in, in cash, to such bank or trust company as the board may select, the said board shall call a meeting of the subscribers for the purpose of organizing the corporation, serving upon or mailing to each subscriber a notice of such meeting at least ten days before the time appointed for holding the same; and the person or persons whose bid shall have been accepted by the said board of rapid transit railroad commissioners shall, if they elect to become subscribers to the capital stock of such corporation, be entitled to a preference for themselves and their associates in subscribing for, and in the allotment of the shares of capital stock of such corporation.

Election of first directors; by-laws to be adopted.

§ 12. At such meeting of subscribers thirteen directors of the corporation shall be elected, each of whom shall be a holder in his own right of at least one hundred shares of the capital stock of the corporation, and the board of rapid transit railroad commissioners shall appoint the the* inspectors of the first election. Each share of stock shall entitle the holder to one vote for each director. The directors so selected shall hold office for one year and until others are elected in their places. At such meeting by-laws must be adopted not inconsistent with this act; which by-laws shall, among other things, provide for:

1. The term of office of the directors elected at any subsequent meeting of stockholders, which term shall not exceed one year.

2. The manner of filling any vacancy which may occur in any office or in the board of directors.

3. The time and place of the annual meeting of stockholders.

4. The manner of calling and holding special meetings of stockholders.

5. The number of stockholders who shall attend either in person or by proxy, at any stockholders' meeting in order to constitute a quorum.

6. The officers of the corporation, the manner of their election by the directors, and their duties and powers, and among which officers there shall be included a president, a secretary and a treasurer.

7. The manner of electing or appointing inspectors of election.

8. The manner of amending the by-laws.

The by-laws may also provide for the forfeiture of shares for the non-payment of calls and for such other matters as may be deemed proper by the board of rapid transit railroad commissioners and they must be approved by a resolution of said board.

---

* So in the original.

Record of proceedings; certificate of organization; record and
    certificate to be filed; payment of deposit to corporation;
    repayment to purchaser of franchise.

§ 13. Within ten days after the said subscribers' meeting a
record of the proceedings thereof, containing a copy of the subscription list, a copy of the by-laws adopted, and the names of
the directors chosen, shall be prepared and duly certified by the
person presiding over, and person acting as secretary of said
meeting. There shall be attached thereto a certificate of the
board of rapid transit railroad commissioners, attested by its
seal and the signature of its presiding officer, that said board
has approved the by-laws adopted at the subscribers' meeting,
and that said corporation has been organized in accordance with
the provisions of this act. The said record and certificate shall
be filed by said board in the office of the secretary of state, and
a duly certified copy or duplicate thereof shall be filed in the
office of the clerk of the county in which said railway or railways
are to be built, and thereupon and upon the payment to the
state treasurer of a tax of one-eighth of one per centum of the
par value of the capital stock of said corporation, such corporation shall be deemed to be fully organized. A copy of said certificate, duly certified by the secretary of state, or by the county
clerk in whose office it is filed, shall be presumptive evidence of
the due organization of such corporation in all courts and proceedings. Upon the production of the certified copy of said certificate, and upon the order of such corporation, the bank or
trust company in which the percentage of subscriptions to the
capital stock shall have been deposited, shall pay over to any
such corporation the amount of such deposit, and said corporation shall repay to the purchaser or purchasers at the sale provided for in section seven of this act, the expenses paid by him
or them to the city pursuant to the provisions of the terms of
sale, with interest to the date of such repayment.

Modification of plans, etc.; certificates thereof; filing of certificate and modified plans.

§ 14. The said board of rapid transit railroad commissioners, if, in their judgment, the public interest requires, may, at any time after the full organization of any such corporation, by the concurrent vote of four members, authorize such corporation to alter or add to the detailed plans and specifications contained in its articles of association, provided the plans and specifications as so modified do not change the route or routes of said railway and be not inconsistent with the general plan of construction, adopted under the provisions of section four of this act, and provided also such modifications be first approved by a vote of two-thirds of the directors of said corporation present and voting at any special meeting duly called for the purpose, by written notice stating the nature of the business to be transacted at said meeting. When such authorization by the board of rapid transit railroad commissioners shall have been given, a certificate shall be prepared, and acknowledged by the president and a majority of the directors of said corporation, stating the nature of the modification, and that the same has been approved by the board of directors in the manner above set forth, to which certificate there shall be attached a copy of so much of the original plans and specifications as are to be affected by the modification, and also the plans and specifications as modified. There shall also be contained in such certificate a declaration of the approval of said board of rapid transit railroad commissioners, attested in the same manner as the certificate of full organization. The said certificate, plans and specifications shall then be filed in the office of the secretary of state, and a certified copy or duplicate thereof shall be filed in the office of the clerk in which the articles of association are filed. And thereupon said corporation shall be authorized to construct its railway or railways and appurtenances in accordance with such modified plans and specifications.

39

Principal office and place of taxation.

§ 15. Every corporation organized under this act shall have its principal office and be taxed on its property in the city where its railway or railways are situated. But no taxes of any kind or nature shall be levied or imposed upon that portion of any railway constructed under this act which is in process of construction, and not in actual operation for the transportation of passengers or freight, but this exemption from taxation during construction shall not apply to any portion or portions of said railway after the date on which said portion or portions shall have been opened to the public for the transportation of passengers or freight.

Thus amended by chap. 556, Laws of 1892.

Board of directors; vacancies and qualifications; exhibition of books.

§ 16. The affairs of said corporation shall be managed by a board of thirteen directors, who shall be chosen annually, by a majority of the votes of the stockholders voting at such election, in such manner as may be prescribed in the by-laws of the corporation, and they may and shall continue to be directors until others are elected in their places. In the election of directors, each stockholder shall be entitled to one vote for each share of stock held by him. Vacancies in the board of directors shall be filled in such manner as shall be prescribed by the by-laws of the corporation. No person shall be a director unless he shall be a stockholder owning one hundred shares of stock absolutely in his own right, and qualified to vote for directors at the election at which he shall be chosen. At every election of directors the books and papers of such corporation shall be exhibited to the meeting, provided a majority of the stockholders present shall require it.

Payment of subscriptions to stock.

§ 17. The directors shall require the subscribers to the capital stock of the company to pay the amount by them respectively subscribed in money at such times and in such installments as they may deem proper, not inconsistent with the by-laws and the articles of association.

Personal liability of stockholders; notice and commencement of action; recovery by stockholder.

§ 18. Each stockholder of any corporation formed under this act shall be individually liable to the creditors of such corporation, to an amount equal to the amount unpaid on the stock held by him, for all the debts and liabilities of such corporation, until the whole amount of the capital stock so held by him shall have been paid to the corporation; and all the stockholders of any such corporation shall be jointly and severally liable for the debts due or owing to any of its laborers and servants, other than contractors, for personal services, for thirty days' service performed for such corporation, but shall not be liable to an action therefor before an execution or executions shall be returned unsatisfied in whole or in part against the corporation, and the amount due on such execution or executions shall be the amount recoverable, with costs, against such stockholders; before such laborer or servant shall charge such stockholder for such thirty days' service, he shall give him notice in writing within twenty days after the performance of such service, that he intends so to hold him liable, and he shall commence such action therefor within thirty days after the return of such execution unsatisfied, as above mentioned; and every such stockholder against whom any such recovery by such laborer or servant shall have been had, shall have a right to recover the same of the other stockholders in said corporation, in ratable proportion to the amount of the stock they shall respectively hold.

Transfer of stock.

§ 19. The stock of every corporation formed under this act shall be deemed personal estate, and shall be transferable in the manner prescribed by the by-laws of the company, but no share shall be transferable until all previous calls thereon shall have been fully paid in.

Increase or reduction of capital; notice to stockholders; statement to be made and filed.

§ 20. Any corporation formed under this act may increase or reduce its capital stock from time to time upon obtaining the approval of the board of rapid transit railroad commissioners by a concurrent vote of four members thereof. Such increase or reduction must be approved by a vote in person, or by proxy, of two-thirds in amount of all the stockholders of the corporation, at a meeting of such stockholders called by the directors of the corporation for that purpose, by a notice in writing to each stockholder, to be served on him in the manner provided for service of the notice of the subscribers' meetings provided for in section eleven of this act. Such notice shall state the time and place of the meeting, and its object, and the amount to which it is proposed to increase or reduce the capital stock. A statement of the increase or reduction shall be signed by the president and a majority of the directors and shall be filed in the office of the secretary of state and of the clerk of the county in which the original articles of association are filed. There must be attached thereto a certificate of the approval of said board of rapid transit railroad commissioners attested in the same manner as the certificate of full organization.

Liability of certain holders of stock.

§ 21. No person holding stock in any such corporation, as executor, administrator, guardian or trustee, and no person hold-

ing such stock as collateral security, shall be personally subject
to any liability as a stockholder of such corporation; but the
person pledging such stock shall be considered as holding the
same, and shall be liable as a stockholder accordingly; and the
estate and funds in the hands of such executor, administrator,
guardian or trustee shall be liable in like manner, and to the
same extent, as the testator or intestate or the ward or person
interested in such trust fund would have been if he had been
living and competent to act, and held the same stock in his own
name.

Liability of corporation to employes of contractors; notice to be
given; actions, when commenced.

§ 22. As often as any contractor for the construction of any
part of a railway, which is in progress of construction under the
provisions of this act, shall be indebted to any laborer for thirty
or any less number of days' labor performed in constructing
said road, such laborer may give notice of such indebtedness to
said corporation in the manner herein provided; and said corporation shall thereupon become liable to pay such laborer the
amount so due him for such labor, and an action may be maintained against said corporation therefor. Such notice shall be
given by said laborer to said corporation within twenty days
after the performance of the number of days' labor for which the
claim is made. Such notice shall be in writing, and shall state
the amount and number of days' labor, and the time when the
same was performed and the name of the contractor from whom
due, and shall be signed by such laborer or his attorney, and
shall be served on an engineer, agent or superintendent employed
by such corporation having charge of the section of the road on
which such labor was performed personally, or by leaving the
same at the office or usual place of business of such engineer,
agent or superintendent with some person of suitable age. But

no action shall be maintained against any corporation under the provisions of this section, unless the same be commenced within thirty days after notice is given to such company by such laborer as above provided.

Real estate; proceedings to acquire title.

§ 23. Every such corporation shall have the right to acquire and hold such real estate or easement or other interest therein, or rights appertaining thereto, as may be necessary to enable it to construct, maintain and operate the said railway, or railways, and such as may be necessary for stations, depots, engine-house, car-houses, machine-shops and other appurtenances specified in the articles of association; and in case any such corporation can not agree with the owner or owners of such property it shall have the right to acquire title to the same in pursuance of the terms of and in the manner prescribed in title one of chapter twenty-three of the Code of Civil Procedure, known as the con-demnation law.

Corporate powers; voluntary grants; purchase of property; may cross and unite with other roads; compensation; transportation of persons and property; entry upon streets, etc.; construction and maintenance of road; excavations; parks and streets, use or occupancy of; right to borrow money and issue bonds.

§ 24. Every corporation formed under this act shall have power:

1. To take and hold such voluntary grants of real estate and other property as shall be made to it, to aid in the construction, maintenance and accommodation of its railway or railways, but the real estate received by voluntary grant shall be held and used for the purposes of such grant only.

2. To purchase, lease, hold and use all such real estate and other property as may be necessary for the construction and

maintenance of its railway or railways, and the stations or other accommodations necessary to accomplish the objects of its incorporation; but nothing herein contained shall be held as repealing or in any way affecting the act, entitled "An act authorizing the construction of railroads upon Indian lands," passed May twelve, eighteen hundred and thirty-six.

3. To cross, intersect, joint and unite its railway or railways with any other railway at any point on its route and upon the grounds of such other railway company, with the necessary turnouts, sidings and switches and other conveniences in furtherance of the objects of its connections. And every corporation whose railway is or shall be hereafter intersected by any new railway, shall unite with the owners of such new railway in forming such intersections and connections, and grant the facilities aforesaid; and if the two corporations cannot agree upon the amount of compensation to be made therefor, the same shall be ascertained and determined by commissioners to be appointed by the court, in the manner provided in this act in respect to acquiring title to real estate. And if the two corporations cannot agree upon the points and manner of such crossings and connections, the board of rapid transit railroad commissioners shall determine the same on the application of either corporation.

4. To take and convey persons and property on its railway or railways by the power or force of steam, or by any motor other than animal power, and to receive compensation therefor not inconsistent with the provisions of this act, and the terms of sale under which the said corporation shall have acquired its rights, privileges and franchises.

5. To enter upon and underneath the several streets, avenues, public places and lands designated by the said board of rapid transit railroad commissioners, and enter into and upon the soil of the same; to construct, maintain, operate and use, in accordance with the plan adopted by said board, a railway or railways

upon the route or routes and to the points decided upon, and to secure the necessary foundations and erect the columns, piers and other structures which may be required to secure safety and stability in the construction and maintenance of the railways constructed upon the plan adopted by the said board, and which may be necessary for operating the same, except that nothing in this act shall authorize the construction of a railway crossing the track of any steam railway in actual operation at the grade thereof, and it shall be lawful to make such excavations and openings along the route through which such railway or railways shall be constructed as shall be necessary from time to time; in all cases the surface of said streets around such foundations, piers and columns shall be restored to the condition in which they were before such excavations were made, as near as may be, and under the direction of the proper local authorities; and in all cases the use of the streets, avenues, places and lands designated by the said board, and the right of way through the same, for the purpose of a railway or railways, as herein authorized and provided, shall be considered, and is hereby declared, to be a public use, consistent with the uses for which the roads, streets, avenues and public places are publicly held; but no such corporation shall have the right to acquire the use or occupancy of public parks or squares in such county, or the use or occupancy of any of the streets or avenues, except such as may have been designated for the route or routes of such railway, and except such temporary privileges as the proper authorities may grant to such corporations to facilitate such construction.

6. From time to time to borrow such sums of money as may be necessary for completing and finishing or operating their railroad, and to issue and dispose of their bonds for such purposes; but the amount of such bonds outstanding at any one time shall not exceed the amount limited by the articles of association.

Thus amended by chap. 556, Laws of 1892.

Employes to wear badges.

§ 25. Every conductor, baggage master, engineer, brakeman or other servant of any railroad corporation employed in a passenger train, or at stations for passengers, shall wear upon his hat or cap a badge, which shall indicate his office, and the initial letter of the style of the corporation by which he is employed. No conductor or collector, without such badge, shall be entitled to demand or receive from any passenger any fare or ticket, or to exercise any of the powers of his office; and no officer or servant without such badge shall have authority to meddle or interfere with any passenger, his baggage or property.

Carrying of mails; extra trains therefor.

§ 26. Any corporation or person operating a railroad under any provision of this act or of any act supplementary hereto or amendatory hereof shall, when applied to by the postmaster-general, convey the mails of the United States on their road or roads respectively; and in case the parties cannot agree as to the rate of transportation therefor, and as to the time, rate of speed, manner and conditions of carrying the same, it shall be lawful for the governor of this State to appoint three commissioners, who, or a majority of them, after fifteen days' notice in writing of the time and place of meeting to the corporation, shall determine and fix the prices, terms and conditions aforesaid; but such price shall not be less for carrying said mails in the regular passenger trains than the amount which such corporation would receive as freight on a like weight of merchandise transported in their merchandise trains, and a fair compensation for the post-office car. And in case the postmaster-general shall require the mail to be carried at other hours, or at a higher speed than the passenger trains are run, the corporation shall furnish an extra train for the mail and be allowed an extra compensation for the expenses and wear and tear thereof, and for the service to be fixed as aforesaid.

Thus amended by chap. 519, Laws of 1895.

Ejection of passengers from cars.

§ 27. If any passenger shall refuse to pay his fare, it shall be lawful for the conductor of the train and the servants of the corporation to put him and his baggage out of the cars, using no unnecessary force, at any usual stopping place, on stopping the train.

Running of cars and conveyance of freight and passengers.

§ 28. Every such corporation shall start and run its cars for the transportation of passengers and property at regular times, to be fixed by public notice; and shall furnish sufficient accommodations for the transportation of all such passengers and property as shall, within a reasonable time previous thereto, be offered for transportation at the place of starting and the junction of other railroads, and at usual stopping places established for receiving and discharging way passengers and freight for that train; and shall take, transport and discharge such passengers and property at, from and to such places, on the due payment of the freight or fare legally authorized therefor; and shall be liable to the party aggrieved in an action for damages, for any neglect or refusal in the premises.

Intoxication of employes.

§ 29. If any person shall, while in charge of a locomotive engine running upon the railway of any such corporation, or while acting as the conductor of a car or train of cars on any such railroad, be intoxicated, he shall be deemed guilty of a misdemeanor.

See section 42, Railroad Law; section 41, chap. 112, Laws of 1896; section 420, Penal Code; section 56, Code of Criminal Procedure, *ante.*

Willful injury to property.

§ 30. If any person or persons shall willfully do, or cause to be done, any act or acts whatever, whereby any building, construction or work of or on any part of any railroad either

constructed or operated under any provision of this act or of
any act supplementary hereto or amendatory hereof, or under
any provision of any contract made under this act or any act
supplementary hereto or amendatory hereof, or any engine,
machine or structure, or any matter or thing appertaining to
the same, shall be stopped, obstructed, impaired, weakened,
injured or destroyed, the person or persons so offending shall
be guilty of a misdemeanor, and shall forfeit and pay to the
owner of such building, construction, works, engine, machine,
structure, matter or thing treble the amount of damages sustained in consequence of such offense.

Thus amended by chap. 519, Laws of 1895.
See sections 183a, 635, Penal Code, *ante*.

Dissolution by legislature.

§ 31. The legislature may, at any time, annul or dissolve any
corporation formed under this act; but such dissolution shall
not take away or impair any remedy given against any such corporation, its stockholders or officers, for any liability which
shall have been previously incurred.

See chap. 310, Laws of 1886, *ante*.

Power to fix connecting routes and extend lines; additional tracks and facilities; plans of construction; powers of state board of railroad commissioners, etc.

§ 32. The said board of rapid transit railroad commissioners
may also from time to time, as in this section hereinafter provided, with the approval of the board of estimate and apportionment, or other analogous local authority of such city, grant a
right or rights, franchise or franchises or enter into a contract
or contracts, upon application to said board of any railroad corporation, now or hereafter incorporated, for the purpose of constructing and operating a tunnel railroad or railroads from an
adjoining state under the North or Hudson or Harlem river to a
terminus within such city; or under the North or Hudson river
and thence transversely across and under the surface of the

borough of Manhattan and thence under the East river by the shortest practicable route; such railroad or railroads to be connected with some trunk line railroad or railroads whose terminus or termini are in this or an adjoining state, thereby forming a continuous line for the carriage of passengers and property between a point or points within such adjoining state and a point or points within the said city, provided such purpose is declared in the certificate of incorporation of such corporation. A similar grant may be made, or a similar contract or contracts entered into, upon the application of a railroad corporation, owning or actually operating a trunk line railroad whose terminus or termini are within such city, or of a railroad corporation owning or actually operating, or by the certificate of the board of rapid transit railroad commissioners hereinafter in this section mentioned required to own or actually operate, a railroad wholly or partly within said city and engaged or intended, and in said certificate so recited and required, to be, in interstate commerce in connection with a trunk line railroad and which shall have, or be required by such certificate to have a terminus or termini in said city, for the purpose of constructing and operating a railroad or railroads from such terminus or termini by the shortest practicable route to and under or over the East river or the North or Hudson river, or the Harlem river, to any point in this or an adjoining state, or to connect such terminus or termini with the railroad or terminus of any other such railroad or trunk line railroad in this state or to straighten or improve the grade or alignment of any such railroad or more directly connect any points thereon. If and when in the judgment of said board the public interests so demand, the said board may, with like approval, by the concurrent vote of six of its members fix and determine the route or routes by which any such railroad corporation making such application may so establish and construct or so extend its lines into or within said city, and may authorize any such railroad corporation to construct and operate any such railroad or connecting railroad under any lands, streets, avenues,

waters, rivers, parkways, highways or public places in the said
city, and also in the case of any such railroad or connecting railroad which is, or by the terms of the said certificate of the said
board of rapid transit railroad commissioners is required to be,
operated or used as a part of an interstate trunk line, to construct
and operate the same over and across any such lands, waters,
rivers, streets, avenues, parkways, highways or public places in
the said city, but not over and lengthwise of any streets, avenues
or highways, with all necessary sidings, platforms, stations.
facilities for access to the surface and other appurtenances and
with the right to emerge to the surface upon private lands at the
termini, and to transport over the same passengers or freight or
both, and to run over the same either passenger trains or freight
trains or mixed trains. The said board shall, with like approval,
fix and determine the locations and plans of construction of the
railroad or railroads upon such route or routes, the times within
which they shall be respectively constructed, the compensation to
be made therefor to the city by the railroad corporation to which
the grant shall be made, or with which the contract shall be entered into, and such other terms, conditions and requirements as
to the said board may appear just and proper,— provided, however, that every such grant shall be made and every such contract
entered into upon the condition that the railroad corporation to
which the grant shall be made or with which the contract shall
be entered into shall, from the time of the commencement of the
operation of any such railroad, annually pay to the said city a
sum or rental, and that the amount of such sum or rental for a
period of not more than twenty-five years, beginning with such
operation of any such railroad, shall be prescribed by the said
board in such grant or contract and that every such grant or
contract shall provide for the readjustment of the amount of
such sum or rental at the expiration of the period for which the
same shall be so prescribed and for readjustment from time to
time in the future of the amount of such annual payment at
intervals each of not more than twenty-five years. A certificate

shall be prepared by the said board, attested by its seal and the signature of its presiding officer, setting forth in detail the action taken and grant made or contract entered into by the said board with respect to such railroad or railroads and the terms, conditions and requirements aforesaid, including provisions as to the said annual payments and the future readjustments thereof. A like certificate shall be prepared in like manner upon every modification of the terms of the grant or contract as hereinafter provided. Each such certificate shall prescribe the terms and conditions of the readjustments of such annual payments and may provide for the determination of such amount upon such readjustments by arbitration or by the supreme court. Such certificate shall be delivered to said railroad corporation upon the receipt by said board of a written acceptance of the terms, conditions and requirements of the grant or contract, duly executed by said railroad corporation, so as to entitle it to be recorded. The said certificate shall be filed in the office of the secretary of state, and a duly certified copy thereof shall be filed in the office of the clerk of the county in which the said city is situated, and thereupon, and upon fulfillment by such railroad corporation, so far as it relates to such railroad or railroads, of such of the requirements and conditions as are necessary to be fulfilled in such cases, under section eighteen of article three of the constitution of this state, and upon fulfillment by such railroad corporation of such other terms, conditions and requirements enumerated in said certificate, as the said board may require to be fulfilled as a condition precedent to commencing said work, said railroad corporation shall in such cases possess in addition to its already existing franchises all the powers conferred by this act upon corporations specially formed thereunder, with respect to its railways authorized to be constructed as aforesaid, and when any route or routes, rights or franchises, shall be so fixed and determined, and a certificate as aforesaid shall have been duly filed, such railroad corporation may construct the same with all the rights, and with like effect as though the same had been a part of

the original route of its railroad then in actual operation, or as
may be provided in said certificate but in every case subject to all
the provisions and conditions of the said certificate. Every certificate prepared by the board of rapid transit railroad commissioners as aforesaid when delivered to and accepted by such railroad corporation, shall be deemed to constitute a contract between the said city and said railroad corporation, according to
the terms of the said certificate; and such contract shall be enforceable by the said board acting in the name of and in behalf
of the said city, or by the said corporation according to the terms
thereof, but subject to the provisions of this act. The terms of
such contract may from time to time, with like approval and with
the consent of such corporation, be modified by the board of rapid
transit railroad commissioners by the vote of six of its members.
But the construction and operation of such railroad or railroads
are hereby authorized only upon the condition that the consent
of the owners of one-half in value of the property bounded on,
and the consent also of the local authorities having the control
of that portion of a street or highway upon, above or under which
it is proposed to construct or operate the same, be first obtained,
provided that such local authorities shall, upon the presentation
to them of any such grant or contract, without requiring the
execution of any other agreements than those herein provided for,
either approve or disapprove the same; and every such approval,
shall be and be deemed to be, free of all limitations except those
contained in this act or the constitution of the state. In case the
consent of such property owners cannot be obtained, the appellate division of the supreme court in the department in which
such railroad or railroads are proposed to be constructed, may,
upon application, in the same manner and on the same notice
specified in section five of this act, appoint three commissioners,
who shall determine after a hearing of all parties interested,
whether the same ought to be constructed or operated, and their
determination, confirmed by the court, may be taken in lieu of the
consent of such property owners. Nothing in this act contained

shall be construed as interfering in any way with the jurisdiction, powers and duties of the board of railroad commissioners of the state of New York, nor shall any grant or contract be made hereunder affecting in any way the liabilities and obligations of the grantee or contracting railroad corporation with reference to taxation for state or local purposes. The state of New York shall not be liable for injuries to persons or property in connection with any railroad or other construction which may be authorized under the provisions of this act, nor shall the state of New York be liable for any damages in any event for any act or omission of the board of rapid transit railroad commissioners.

Thus amended by chap. 606, Laws of 1906; section 32 was first amended in 1906 by chap. 472.

Additionl franchises to railroad companies.

§ 32-a. The said board of rapid transit railroad commissioners may also from time to time, with the approval of the board of estimate and apportionment, upon aplication of any person, firm or corporation owning, leasing, constructing, or actually operating a railroad wholly or in part within the limits of the city in which the said board has power to act, if in the judgment of said board the public interests so demand, by the concurrent vote of six of the members of said board, fix and determine the route or routes by which any such person, firm or corporation may connect with other railways, or the stations thereof, or with ferries, or may extend his or its lines within said city, and may with like approval authorize any such person, firm or corporation to lay an additional track or tracks on, above, under or contiguous to a portion or the whole of the route or routes of his or its railway or railways within said city and to acquire terminal or other facilities necessary for the accommodation of the traveling public on any street or place except the place known as Battery park on which said railway shall be located; and may also with like approval authorize any such person, firm or corporation to lay his or its tracks and operate his or its railway to any terminal or terminals within the said city, and to transport over the same

passengers or freight or both, and to run over the same either
passenger trains or freight trains or mixed trains; and the said
board shall with like approval fix and determine the locations
and plans of construction of the railways upon such route or
routes and of such tracks and facilities, the times within which
they shall be respectively constructed, the compensation to be
made therefor to the city by said person, firm or corporation,
and such other terms, conditions and requirements as to the
said boards may appear just and proper, provided, however, that
every such determination, authorization and license shall be made
upon the condition that such person, firm or corporation shall
from the time of the commencement of the operation of any such
railway or track or tracks under such determination, authorization or license, annually pay to the said city a sum or rental, and
that the amount of such sum or rental for a period of not more
than twenty-five years, beginning with such operation of any such
railway, track or tracks, shall be prescribed by the said board in
such determination, authorization and license, and that every
such determination, authorization and license shall provide for
the readjustment of the amount of such sum or rental at the
expiration of the period for which the same shall be so prescribed
and for readjustment from time to time in the future, to the end
of the period of renewal, if any, of the amount of such annual
payment at intervals each of not more than ten years. No such
determination, authorization or license shall be made for a
longer period than twenty-five years but may provide for renewal
or renewals thereof not to exceed twenty years in the aggregate.
A certificate shall be prepared by the said board, attested by its
seal and the signature of its presiding officer, setting forth in
detail the action taken by the said board with respect to such
connecting or extended route or routes and such tracks and
facilities, and the terms, conditions and requirements aforesaid,
including provisions as to the said annual payments and the
future readjustments thereof. A like certificate shall be prepared
in like manner upon every modification or renewal of the terms
of the contract as hereinafter provided. Every such certificate

shall prescribe the terms and conditions of the readustments of
such annual payments and may provide for the determination of
such amount upon such readjustments by arbitration or by the
supreme court. Such certificate shall be delivered to said person,
firm or corporation upon the receipt by said board of a written
acceptance of said terms, conditions and requirements, duly
executed by said person, firm or corporation, so as to entitle it to
be recorded. The said certificates shall be filed in the office of
the secretary of state, and a duly certified copy thereof shall be
filed in the office of the clerk of the county in which the said city
is situated, and thereupon, and upon fulfillment by such person,
firm or corporation, so far as it relates to such connections, additional track or tracks, or facilities, of such of the requirements
and conditions as are necessary to be fulfilled in such cases,
under section eighteen of article three of the constitution of this
state, and upon fulfillment by such person, firm or corporation
of such other terms, conditions and requirements enumerated in
said certificate, as the said board may require to be fulfilled as a
condition precedent to commencing said work, said person, firm
or corporation shall in such cases possess in addition to existing
franchises all the powers conferred by this act upon corporations
specially formed thereunder, with respect to his or its railways
authorized to be constructed as aforesaid, and when any route or
routes, additional track or tracks, or terminal or other facilities,
shall be so fixed and determined, and a certificate as aforesaid
shall have been duly filed, such person, firm or corporation may
construct the same with all the rights, and with like effect as
though the same had been a part of the original route of his or
its railway then in actual operation or in process of construction,
except that no franchise, right or authority shall be granted
under this section to extend any railway, make any connections,
lay any additional track or tracks or acquire any terminal or
other facilities for a longer period than the original grant, franchise or contract of the railway to which such extension, connection, additional track or tracks, or terminal or other facilities

are added. The certificate or certificates prepared by the board
of rapid transit railroad commissioners as aforesaid when delivered to and accepted by such person, firm or corporation, shall
be deemed to constitute a contract between the said city and said
person, firm or corporation according to the terms of the said
certificate; and such contract shall be enforceable by the said
board acting in the name of and in behalf of the said city or by
the said person, firm or corporation according to the terms
thereof, but subject to the provisions of this act. The terms of
such contract may from time to time, with the consent of such
person, firm or corporaion be modified by the board of rapid
transit railroad commissioners by the vote of six of its members.
But the construction and operation of such connections, extensions, additional track or tracks, or facilities, are hereby authorized only upon the condition that the consent of the owners of
one-half in value of the property bounded on, and the consent
also of the local authorities having the control of that portion
of a street or highway upon, above or under which it is proposed
to construct or operate the same, be first obtained, or in case the
consent of such property owners cannot be obtained, the appellate
division of the supreme court in the district in which they are
proposed to be constructed, may, upon application, in the same
manner, and on the same notice specified in section five of this
act, appoint three commissioners, who shall determine after a
hearing of all the parties interested, whether the same ought to
be constructed or operated, and their determination, confirmed
by the court, may be taken in lieu of the consent of the property
owners. Every such certificate granting any franchise, right or
authority as aforesaid shall provide that upon the termination
thereof all the rights of property of the grantee in the streets,
avenues, parkways, highways and public places shall cease and
terminate without compensation and shall further provide that
upon such termination of such franchise, right or authority the
plant and structure together with the appurtenances thereto, of
the grantee constructed pursuant to such certificate, except rolling

stock and other movable equipment, shall become the property of the city without further or other compensation to the grantee; but such certificate may provide that upon such termination there shall be a fair valuation of the rolling stock and other movable equipment which shall be and become the property of the city on the termination of the grant on paying the grantee such valuation. The provisions of this section shall apply to any railroad or railroads constructed, constructing or contracted for under the provisions of section thirty-four of this act, and to any person, firm or corporation constructing or operating such railroad or railroads.

Added by chap. 472, Laws of 1906.

Removal of surface railway tracks, etc.; costs and charges; construction of tramways for removal of material.

§ 33. Wherever or whenever the route selected by the said board of rapid transit railroad commissioners for the construction of such railway shall intersect, cross or coincide with any railway track or tracks occupying the surface of any street or avenues, or the construction or operation of said railway shall interfere with any pipes, sewers, subways, or underground conduits or ways, any corporation organized under this act, or any contractor or person constructing any railway or part of a railway under any contract made with the board of rapid transit railroad commissioners, is hereby authorized, for the purpose of constructing the said work, to remove the track or tracks of any such surface railway or railways, or any such pipes, sewers, subways, or underground conduits or ways, but the same shall be done in such manner as to interfere as little as possible with the practical operation or workings of such surface railway or railways, or the works or business of the owners of any such pipes, sewers, subways, or underground conduits or ways, and upon the construction of such railways built under and in conformity with the provisions of this act, where such removals or changes have been made, said track or tracks, pipes, sewers, subways or underground conduits or ways shall be restored as nearly as may be to the condition in which they were previous to the construction of any such railway built under the provisions of this act, and any damages which such company or companies or owners may sustain shall be ascertained by a commission to be appointed the same as in the case where lands are taken for the purpose of a railway route or routes as hereinbefore provided in this act. For the purpose of the construction or operation of any railway under the provisions of this act, the board of rapid transit railroad commissioners may remove or cause to be removed, any pipes, sewers, subways or underground conduits or ways underneath any street, highway, park, or public place; provided, however, that the same shall be replaced as soon as practicable, either in the same position as before or in a secure and convenient position underneath such street, highway or public place, or underneath such other street, highway or public place as may be approved by the head of the department of public works of the city. Provided, however, that nothing in this section contained shall authorize the permanent removal from any street, highway, park or public place of any subways or conduits for the reception of electrical conductors which shall have been placed in such street, highway or public place prior to the construction of the rapid transit railroad, without the consent of the owner and lessee of such subway or conduit. All such removals and restorations shall be made at the proper cost and charge of such corporation, contractor or person as may have made such removals, but subject to the provisions of its, his or their contract, if any, with the board of rapid transit railway commissioners. Nothing contained in this act shall authorize any corporation formed thereunder to use the tracks of any horse railway. For the purpose of facilitating construction, and to diminish the period of occupancy of any street for the transportation of material, any contractor acting under a contract made in pursuance of this act, or of any act supplementary hereto or amendatory hereof, may, with the approval of the board of rapid transit railroad commissioners, lay upon or over the surface of any street, temporary tramways, to be used only for the removal of excavated materials or the transportation of material for use in the construction; provided, however, that any such tramway shall be forthwith removed upon the direction of the board of rapid transit railroad commissioners; and provided, further, that this provision shall not be construed to authorize the construction or operation of any street railroad or to grant to any corporation, association or individual the right to lay down railroad tracks.

Thus amended by chap. 564, Laws of 1904.

If railroad is built by city, etc.

§ 34. In case the people shall determine by vote, as provided in sections twelve and thirteen of chapter seven hundred and fifty-two of the laws of eighteen hundred and ninety-four, that any such railway or railways shall be constructed for and at the expense of such city, then and in that event it shall be the duty of said board to consider the routes, plans and specifications, if any, previously laid out and adopted by them or their predecessors, and for which the consents have been obtained referred to in section five of this act; and either to proceed with the construction of such railway or railways, and provide for the operation of the same, as hereinafter provided, or to change and modify the said routes, plans or specifications in such particulars as to said board may seem to be desirable, or from time to time and with or without reference to former routes or plans to adopt other or different or additional routes, plans and specifications for such railway or railways, provided always, that in all cases in which any such change or modification shall be of such character as to require the consents thereto referred to in section five of this act; and in all cases where other or different routes or general plans may have been so adopted the said board shall proceed to secure the consents required to be obtained by section five of this act as herein set forth. If any city has been or shall have been formed by the union or consolidation of one or more cities and other territory, and if in or for one of such cities so consolidated or united there shall have been a board of rapid transit railroad commissioners as provided in this act the board of rapid transit railroad commissioners for the said city formed by such union or consolidation shall have for and within such city so formed all the powers, and be subject to all the duties and responsibilities, which at the time of such union or consolidation belonged to the board of rapid transit railroad commissioners of the former city so as aforesaid possessing such board for or in or with respect to such former city. If in such former city the vote of the qualified electors thereof shall have been for municipal construction of rapid transit road as prescribed in sections twelve and thirteen of chapter seven hundred and fifty-two of the laws of eighteen hundred and ninety-four, then the system of municipal construction of rapid transit railways provided for in this act and all of the provisions with respect thereto in this act contained shall be applicable to, and in full force within, all the districts or boroughs and throughout the entire area of the said city formed by such union or consolidation. The board of rapid transit railroad commissioners for any city shall, prior to the time of the final grant of any franchise under the provisions of this act or the making of a contract for construction of any railroad under the provisions of this act have power to rescind and revoke any resolution or resolutions of such board adopting any routes or general plan for a rapid transit railroad adopted by such board and, in the discretion of such board, in lieu thereof to adopt new routes and general plan. Every such rescindment or revocation which shall have been heretofore made shall be deemed to have been lawful and authorized by this act as the same was prior to the present amendment hereof. As soon as such consents, where necessary, shall have been obtained for any rapid transit railroad or railroads, and the detailed plans and specifications have been prepared as provided in section six

of this act, the said board, for and in behalf of said city, shall
enter into a contract with any person, firm or corporation, which
in the opinion of said board shall be best qualified to fulfill and
carry out said contract, for the construction of such road or
roads, including such galleries, ways, subways and tunnels for
subsurface structures as said board may include in the plans for
such road or roads under the authority of section six of this act;
upon the routes and in accordance with the plans and specifications so adopted, for such sum or sums of money, to be raised
and paid out of the treasury of said city, as hereinafter provided,
and on such terms and conditions, not inconsistent with the
aforesaid plans and specifications, as said board shall determine
to be best for the public interests. The sum or sums of money
to be paid for the construction of such road or roads shall be
separately stated in the contract from the sum or sums to be paid
for any galleries, ways, subways or tunnels for subsurface structures, the construction of which is provided for in such contract.
And said board may in any case contract for the construction
of the whole road, or all the roads provided for by the aforesaid
plans in a single contract, or may by separate contracts, executed
from time to time, or at the same time, with one or more such
persons, firms or corporations provide for the construction of
parts of said road or roads or for the construction at first of two
or more tracks over a part or parts of such road or roads and
afterwards of one or more additional tracks over a part or parts
of such road or roads as the necessities of said city and the increase of its population or the advantageous and economical performance of the work may in the judgment of said board require.
The board may also, in a contract for a part of any such rapid
transit railroad, insert a provision that, at a future time, upon
the requirement of the board, the contractor shall construct the
remainder or any part of the remainder of said road, as the
growth of population or the interests of the city may, in the
judgment of the board, require, and may, in such contract, insert
a provision of a method for fixing and ascertaining at such future

time the amount to be paid to the contractor for such additional construction, and to the end of such ascertainment, may provide for arbitration or for determination by court of the amount of such compensation, or of any other details of construction which shall not be prescribed in the contract, but which shall be deemed necessary or convenient by said board. Any such contract may provide, if the public interest shall, in the opinion of the board, justify the provision, that the construction of any section or portion of the railroad included in such contract may, with the consent of the board, be suspended during the term of operation of the railroad as hereinafter mentioned, or any part of such term; provided that during such term or part of term there shall be available for use, in lieu of such portion of the road, a railroad or a portion or section thereof, which shall, with the railroad or portion of railroad constructed under such contract form a continuous and convenient route. Any such contract may be made for the construction of said road in sections, or for the construction of any section or sections thereof; and, except as herein otherwise provided, every such contract shall specify when the construction of the railroad or the section or sections thereof included therein shall be commenced in each case, and, in each case, the date of completion. The said board may by any such contract determine when and how the work of construction of the rapid transit railroad or railroads included therein shall proceed. The said board of rapid transit railroad commissioners may also provide for the equipment at public expense of such railroad or railroads in connection with the construction thereof, and may include in any contract for construction authorized by this act provision for the equipment, or any part thereof, of such railroad or railroads, but may make a separate contract or contracts for the whole or any part of such equipment with the constructing contractor or contractors or any other responsible persons, firms or corporations.

Thus amended by chap. 472, Laws of 1906.
See section 3, chap. 599, Laws of 1905.

Equipment and operation.   .

§ 34-a. The board of rapid transit railroad commissioners shall, subject to the approval of the board of estimate and apportionment, or other analogous local authority of such city, have full power and authority to provide for the maintenance, supervision, care and operation of the railroad or railroads, including the aforesaid galleries, ways, subways and tunnels for subsurface structures and all other appurtenances, constructed or to be constructed for and at the expense of such city pursuant to the provisions of this chapter, and may, with like approval, enter into a contract with any person, firm or corporation, who or which in the opinion of said board of rapid transit railroad commissioners shall be best qualified to fulfill and carry out said contract, for the equipment, or any part thereof not provided for pursuant to the next preceding section of this act, of such road or roads, at his or its own costs and expense, and for the maintenance and operation of such road or roads for a term of years to be specified in said contract and not to exceed twenty years. Every such contract shall contain such terms and conditions as to the rates or fare to be charged and the character of services to be furnished and otherwise as said board of rapid transit railroad commissioners shall deem to be best suited to the public interests, and subject to such public supervision and to such conditions, regulations and requirements as may be determined upon by said board, with like approval; provided, that in case different parts of a road shall be constructed at different times or at intervals of time, or if the contract shall provide for the use by the contractor of an existing railroad as part of a continuous route as aforesaid, then and in any such case the board of rapid transit railroad commissioners may, in its discretion, prescribe periods for the operation of the different parts of said road so that at one period of time in the future the board may be enabled to make a single operating contract or lease of the entire road. Every such contract shall further provide that the person, firm or corporation so contracting to equip, maintain and operate

said road shall annually pay into the treasury of said city, as
rental for the use of said road, a sum which shall not, except as
hereinafter provided, be less than the annual interest upon the
bonds to be issued by said city for the construction and equipment of said road as hereinafter provided for, and in addition to
said interest, a further sum which shall be equal to a percentage
of not less than one per centum upon the whole amount of said
bonds; provided, that in estimating such annual interest and
additional percentage there shall be deducted from the amount
of said bonds the amount thereof issued to pay for rights, terms,
easements, privileges or property other than lands acquired in fee,
and also the amount thereof issued to pay for the construction
of galleries, ways, subways and tunnels for subsurface structures.
And provided, further, that the said contract may, in the discretion of the said board, provide that the payment of the said
further sum of not less than one per centum upon the amount of
said bonds as aforesaid, shall begin at a date not more than five
years after the date at which the payment of rental shall begin,
and that the said annual rate, instead of one per centum, may
be a rate not less than one-half per centum for a further period
not exceeding five years; but in case the contractor shall, during
any year in which the said payment of one per centum shall be
suspended or reduced as aforesaid, earn a greater profit upon his,
its or their net capital invested in the enterprise than five per
centum, then the surplus of his, its or their earnings for such
year up to the extent of at least one per centum shall be paid as
rental as aforesaid.   Such rental and the term for the operation
of the railroad included in any such contract shall begin, as to
said road, or any section thereof, when the same shall be declared
by the board of rapid transit railroad commissioners to be completed and ready for operation.   For the purpose of estimating
such one per centum per annum upon the ascertainment of the
amount of such rental, there shall be included such portion of
the said bonds as shall have been issued to pay interest on bonds
theretofore issued under the provisions of this act, except bonds

issued to pay for rights, terms, easements, privileges or property
other than lands acquired in fee. The aforesaid annual rental
shall be paid at such times during each year as said board shall
require, and shall be applied first to the payment of the interest
on said bonds, as the same shall accrue and fall due, and the
remainder of said rental not required for the payment of said
interest shall be paid into the sinking fund, for the payment of
the city debt, if there shall be such sinking fund in said city, or,
if there be none such, then said balance of said rental shall be
securely invested, and, with the annual accretions of interest
thereon, shall constitute a sinking fund for the payment and
redemption at maturity of the bonds issued, as hereinafter provided. Any such contract may also provide for a renewal or
renewals not to exceed twenty years in the aggregate of the lease
of said road upon the expiration of the original term upon such
terms and conditions, to be approved by the board of estimate
and apportionment, or other analogous local authority of such
city, as to said board of rapid transit railroad commissioners
may seem just and proper, and may also contain provisions for
the valuation of the whole or a part of the property of said contracting person, firm or corporation, employed in and about the
equipment, maintenance and operation of said road, and for the
purchase of the same by the city, at such valuation, or a percentage of the same, should said lease not be so renewed at any
time. Such contract shall also state the date on which the operation of the road, or of any section thereof, shall commence.
The city in and for which said road shall be constructed shall
also have a first lien upon the rolling stock and other property
of said contracting person, firm or corporation, constituting the
equipment of said road and used or intended for use in the maintenance and operation of the same, as further security for the
faithful performance by such contracting person, firm or corporation of the covenant, conditions and agreements of said
contract, on his, their, or its part to be fulfilled and performed,
and in case of the breach of any such covenant, condition and

agreement said lien shall be subject to foreclosure by action, at the suit of such city, in the same manner, as far as may be, as is then provided by law in the case of foreclosure by action of mortgages on real estate. The said board of rapid transit railroad commissioners may, however, from time to time, by a concurrent vote of six of the members of said board, relieve from such lien, any of the property to which the same may attach, upon receiving additional security, which may be deemed by said board so voting to be the equivalent of that which it is proposed to release and otherwise upon such terms as to such board so voting shall seem just. The said contract shall further provide that in case of default in paying the annual sum or rental therein provided for, or in case of the failure or neglect on the part of said contracting person, firm or corporation, faithfully to observe, keep and fulfill the conditions, obligations and requirements of said contract, the said city, by its board of rapid transit railroad commissioners, may take possession of said road and the equipment thereof, and as the agent of said contracting person, firm or corporation, either maintain and operate said road, or enter into a contract with some other person, firm or corporation for the maintenance and operation thereof, retaining out of the proceeds of such operation, after the payment of the necessary expenses of operation and maintenance, the annual rental hereinbefore referred to, and paying over the balance, if any, to the person, firm or corporation with whom the first contract above mentioned was made, and if such proceeds of the operation of said road, after the payment of the necessary expenses of maintenance and operation, including the keeping in repairs of the rolling stock and other equipment, shall in any year be less than the annual rental hereinbefore referred to and provided in the first contract, then and in that case, the said contracting person, firm or corporation, and his or its bondsmen, shall be and continue (but in the case of any bond hereafter executed each bondsman only to the extent of the liability expressly assumed by him upon the bond) jointly and severally liable to the aforesaid city for the amount of such deficiency, until the end of the full term for which the said first contract was originally made. Any existing railway corporation owning or actually operating a railway wholly or in part within the limits of the city in and for which said board has power to act, and approved by the said board of rapid transit railroad commissioners, shall be competent and is hereby authorized to enter into any contract for the equipment, maintenance and operation of any railway pursuant to the provisions of this chapter, or, after such a contract shall have been made, shall be competent and is hereby authorized, with the approval of the said board, to contract with the original contractor or his assignee or assignees for the maintenance and operation (including the equipment or any part thereof) of any railway constructed or in process of construction pursuant to the provisions of this chapter, and shall have all the powers necessary to the due performance of such contract. A corporation may be organized under the railroad law of this state, for the purpose of maintaining and operating a railway (including the equipment or any part thereof) already constructed or in process of construction pursuant to the provisions of this chapter; and any corporation so organized, upon the approval in writing of the said board of rapid transit railroad commissioners, shall, in addition to the powers conferred by the general act under which such corporation is organized, be empowered, and is hereby authorized to enter into any contract permitted by law for the maintenance and operation when constructed (including the equipment or any part thereof if desired), as the case may be, of any such railway constructed or to be constructed at the expense of the city as in this act provided. The certificate of such approval shall be filed in the office of the secretary of state, and a copy thereof certified to be a true copy by the secretary of state or his deputy, shall be evidence of the fact therein stated. A corporation so organized shall not be required to procure the consent of the board of railroad commis- sioners of the state as provided for in section fifty-nine of the railroad law. Where in this section or in section thirty-four of this act the consents referred to in section five of this act are mentioned, they shall be construed to include any consent given by the commissioners appointed by the general term or appellate division of the supreme court, and confirmed by the said general term or appellate division in lieu of the consent of property owners· as hereinbefore provided.

Added by chap. 472, Laws of 1906.

Equipment and operation.

§ 34-b. If in the opinion of the board of estimate and apportionment, or other analogous local authority of such city, a contract for the equipment, maintenance and operation as provided for in the preceding section shall be inexpedient, impracticable or prejudicial to the public interest, the board of rapid transit railroad commissioners may, with the approval of the board of estimate and apportionment, or such other analogous authority, equip the said road or roads in whole or in part, for and at the public expense, by contract or contracts therefor subject to the provisions of section thirty-six of this act, and enter into a contract with any person, firm or corporation, who or which, in the opinion of said board of rapid transit railroad commissioners, shall be best qualified to fulfill and carry out said contract, for the maintenance and operation of such road or roads for a term of years to be specified in said contract, and not to exceed ten years. The provisions of the foregoing sections in respect of a contract or contracts for the equipment, maintenance and operation of such road or roads shall apply to such contract for maintenance and operation so far as such provisions are pertinent and applicable thereto except that the annual rental to be paid into the city treasury for the use of said road or roads shall be based upon the total amount of bonds issued by said city for the construction and equipment, instead of for the construction alone, of said road or roads as hereinafter provided for and that the renewal or renewal of said contract provided for therein shall not exceed in the aggregate ten years.

Added by chap. 472, Laws of 1906.

Holding contractor harmless; bond of contractor; assignment of contract, etc.

§ 34-c. Every contract for the construction or operation of such road or roads shall provide by proper stipulations and covenants on the part of the said city, that the said city shall secure and assure to the contractor, so long as the contractor shall perform the stipulations of the contract, the right to construct or to operate the road as prescribed in the contract, free of all right, claim or other interference, whether by injunction, suit for damages or otherwise, on the part of the owner, abutting owner, or other person. The person, firm or corporation bidding or contracting for the construction, equipment, maintenance or operation of the railroad or railroads included in any such contract shall make such deposit of cash or securities, and shall give a bond to said city, in such amount as said board of rapid transit railroad commissioners shall require, and with sureties to be approved by said board, who shall justify each in double the amount of his liability upon said bond. Said bond shall be a continuing security, and shall provide for the prompt payment by said contracting person, firm or corporation, of the amount of annual rental, if any, specified in the aforesaid contract, and also for the faithful performance by said contracting person, firm or corporation of all the conditions, covenants and requirements specified and provided for in said contract. In lieu of said continuing bond such contracting person, firm or corporation may, upon the approval of the said board, deposit with the comptroller or other chief financial officer of such city cash equal in amount to the entire amount of the said bond or securities which are lawful for the investment of the funds of savings banks within this state and are worth not less than the entire amount of such bond. If such bond shall have been given then after the deposit of cash and securities in lieu thereof as aforesaid, and the approval thereof by the said board, the said bond shall be surrendered by the said city to the said contracting person, firm or corporation duly canceled by the comptroller or other chief financial officer of the said city. In the event of the deposit of cash or securities as aforesaid, the contract may provide for the payment to the contractor of the income of such securities or of interest upon such moneys at a rate not higher than the highest rate received by the city upon the deposit of its funds with banks, and may also provide for withdrawal of securities so deposited upon deposit of cash or securities of the same value, provided that all such securities shall be such as are so lawful for the investment of the funds of savings banks. The said board may in or by any such contract and in its discretion require, and this act, as the same was prior to the present amendment thereof shall be deemed to have authorized the said board to have heretofore required any other security upon any such contract. No contract entered into under authority of this act shall be assigned without the written consent of the said board of rapid transit railroad commissioners, concurred in by six members of said board. The said contracting person, firm or corporation, with such written consent and upon such terms and conditions as the said board shall prescribe, may either assign the whole of such contract or separately the right or obligation to maintain and operate the said road or roads for the remainder of the term of years specified in such contract and all rights with respect to such maintenance and operation, or included in the leasing provisions of such contract, but subject to all the terms and conditions therein stated; provided, however, that the assignee or assignees shall, in and by such assignment, assume all of the obligations of the original contractor under or with respect to such leasing provisions and all obligations which relate in any way to such operation and maintenance, and provided, further, that the said board before giving its consent shall be satisfied that the pecuniary responsibility of the assignee or assignees shall be no less than that of such original contractor; and provided, further, that all of the security or securities which the city shall have received

41

for the performance by the original contractor of such leasing provisions and of all provisions of the contract with respect to such operation and maintenance shall continue in full force as provided in such contract, or any modification thereof, as security for the performance by such assignee of all obligations of the contractor under or with respect to such leasing provisions and such maintenance or operation. It shall be deemed to be part of every such contract that, in case the board of rapid transit railroad commissioners shall cease to exist, the legislature may provide what public officer or officers of the city shall exercise the powers and duties belonging to the board of rapid transit railroad commissioners under or by virtue of any such contract, and that in default of such provision, such powers and duties shall be deemed to be vested in the mayor of the city. Every such contract shall provide that if the contracting person, firm or corporation shall fail to construct, equip, maintain or operate the railway according to the terms of the contract, and shall, after due notice of its default, omit for more than a reasonable time to comply with the provisions of such contract, the board of rapid transit railroad commissioners may bring an action in the name and in behalf of the city to forfeit and vacate all the rights of such contracting person, firm or corporation under such contract, and for damages and otherwise as may be necessary for the sufficient and just protection of the rights of the city; or may, upon such terms as to the board of rapid transit railroad commissioners seem just, and with such person or corporation as to the said board may seem proper, make another operating contract and lease of the said road for the residue of the term of the contractor in default; and may bring action in the name and on behalf of the city to recover from the contractor the amount due from the contractor, less the amount which shall have been received by the city, under or by virtue of such new contract, and for all other damages sustained by the city by reason of such default.

Added by chap. 472, Laws of 1900.

Operation by the city; rate of fare; no advertisements to be allowed, etc.

§ 34-d. If in the opinion of the board of estimate and appor tionment, or other analogous local authority of such city, either a contract for equipment, maintenance and operation, or a con tract for maintenance and operation as provided for in the preceding sections would be inexpedient, impracticable or preju dicial to the public interest, the board of rapid transit railroad commissioners shall forthwith devise and prepare a plan for the maintenance and operation of such road or roads, and when said plan shall have been approved by the board of estimate and apportionment, or other analogous local authority of such city, the said board of rapid transit railroad commissioners shall maintain and operate such road or roads for and on behalf of said city. The rates of fare provided for in any operating contract or plan aforesaid shall be adjusted, fixed and readjusted always with a view to securing sufficient receipts therefrom, when added to the net revenues from such galleries, ways, subways or tunnels, and all other sources incidental or appurtenant to the use and operation of said road or roads, to provide for operating expenses, maintenance, interest on the cost, all other proper charges, and a sinking fund to discharge the bonds issued for the construction and equipment of such road or roads within a reasonable period, without recourse to taxation. Whenever it shall seem practicable to reduce rates of fare, the reduction shall in the first instance be in favor of school children, and then, next in order, in favor of all the public between six and nine o'clock ante meridian, and between four and seven o'clock post meridian, and then for all the public from five o'clock ante meridian until seven o'clock post meridian, and, lastly, for all the public at all times. No part of any road or roads or of its or their appurtenances, constructed under the authority of this act, shall be used for advertising pur poses, except that the person, firm or corporation operating such road or roads may use the structure for posting necessary infor mation for the public relative to the running of trains and to the operation of the road or roads. Nor shall any trade, traffic or occupation, other than required for the operation of said road or roads be permitted thereon or in the stations thereof, except such sale of newspapers and periodicals as may, from time to time, always with the right of revocation, be permitted by the board of rapid transit railroad commissioners.

Added by chap. 472, Laws of 1906.

Discretion as to contracts.

§ 34-e. Nothing contained in this act shall be deemed, or be construed as intending, to limit, or as limiting, in any manner, the discretion of the board of rapid transit railroad commissioners, provided in the opinion of the board of estimate and apportionment, or other analogous local authority of such city, it is expedient, practicable and in the public interest to do so, to enter into contracts for construction, equipment, maintenance and operation with the same person, firm or corporation, or for any one or more of said purposes with the same person, firm or corporation, or with different persons, firms or corporations, either in one contract or in separate contracts, and at any time or times.

Added by chap. 472, Laws of 1906.

Equipment, what contract to include; power houses.

§ 35. The equipment to be supplied by the person, firm or corporation contracting for the equipment or any part thereof, of any such road shall include all such rolling stock, motors, boilers, engines, wires, ways, conduits and mechanisms, machinery, tools, implements and devices of every nature whatsoever used for the generation or transmission of motive power and including all power houses, and all apparatus and all devices for signaling and ventilation as may be required for the operation of such road and specified in the contract for such equipment.

Thus amended by chap. 472, Laws of 1906.
See section 3 of chap. 599, Laws of 1905.

Advertising for proposals.

§ 36. The said board of rapid transit railroad commissioners before awarding any contract or contracts shall advertise for proposals for such contracts by a notice to be printed twice a week for three successive weeks in no less than four of the daily newspapers published in said city, and in such newspapers published elsewhere than in said city as said board shall determine. Such notice shall set forth and state the points within said city, between which said road or roads is or are to run, the general method of construction, the route or routes to be followed, the term of years for which it is proposed to make such contract, and such other details and specifications as said board shall deem to be proper. Said notice shall state the time and place at which said proposals will be opened, and the said board shall attend at the time and place so specified, and shall publicly open all proposals that shall have been received, but the said board shall not be bound to accept any proposals so received, but may reject all such proposals and readvertise for proposals in the manner hereinbefore provided, or may accept any of such proposals as will, in the judgment of such board, best promote the public interest, and award a contract accordingly.

Thus amended by chap. 519, Laws of 1895.

Issuance of bonds by the city; public hearing on proposed contracts.

§ 37. For the purpose of providing the necessary means for such construction, or equipment, or both, as the case may be, at the public expense, of any such road or roads, including galleries, ways, subways and tunnels for subsurface structures, and the necessary means to pay for lands, property, rights, terms, privileges and easements, whether of owners, abutting owners, or others, which shall be acquired by the city for the purposes of the construction or the operation of such road or roads as hereinafter provided, and of meeting the interest on the bonds in this section hereinafter provided for accruing thereon prior to the completion and readiness for operation of the portion of such road or roads, and the galleries, ways, subways and tunnels for subsurface structures, for the construction, or equipment of which such bonds shall have been respectively issued, the board of estimate and apportionment, or other local authority in said city, in which such road or roads are to be constructed, having power to make appropriations of moneys to be raised by taxation therein, from time to time, and as the same shall be necessary, and upon the requisition of said board of rapid transit railroad commissioners, shall direct the comptroller, or other chief financial officer of said city, and it shall thereupon become his duty, to issue the bonds of said city at such a rate of interest, not exceeding four per centum per annum, as said board of estimate and apportionment, or other local authority directing the issue of such bonds, may prescribe. Said bonds shall provide for the payment of the principal and interest in gold coin of the United States of America. They shall not be sold for less than the par value thereof, and the proceeds of the same shall be paid out and expended for the purposes for which the same are issued, upon vouchers certified by said board of rapid transit railroad commissioners. Said bonds shall be free from all taxation for city and county purposes, and shall be payable at maturity out of the sinking fund for the payment of the city debt, if there be such a sinking fund of said city; but if there be no such sinking fund, then out of a sinking fund to be established and created out of the annual rentals or revenues of said road including galleries. ways, subways, or tunnels for subsurface structures, as hereinbefore provided. But this provision that the said bonds shall be payable out of such sinking fund shall not diminish or affect the obligation of said city as a debtor upon said bonds, or any other right or remedy of any holder or owner of any such bonds. to collect the principal or interest thereof. The amount of bonds authorized to be issued and sold by this section shall not exceed the limit of amount which shall be prescribed by the board of estimate and apportionment or such other local authority having power to make appropriations of moneys to be raised by taxation; and no contract for the construction of such road or roads shall be made unless and until such board of estimate and apportion. ment or such other local authority shall have consented thereto and prescribed a limit to the amount of bonds available for the purposes of this section which shall be sufficient to meet the requirements of such contract in addition to all obligations theretofore incurred and to be satisfied from such bonds. Before finally fixing the terms and conditions of any contract for any of the purposes contained and set forth in this act, the board of rapid transit railroad commissioners of the appropriate city shall set a date or dates for a public hearing upon the proposed terms and conditions thereof, at which citizens shall be entitled to appear and be heard. 'No such hearing shall be held, however, until notice thereof shall have been published for at least two weeks immediately prior thereto in the City Record, or other official publication of the city, and at least twice in two daily newspapers published in the city, to be designated by the mayor. It shall be the duty of the board of rapid transit railroad commissioners to cause not less than five hundred copies of a draft of the proposed contract to be printed at least two weeks in advance of such hearing. The said notice of such public hearing shall state where copies of such drafts may be obtained upon payment of a fee, to be fixed by said board, but not to exceed, one dollar for each such copy. The said board may, after the hearing to be held as above required, alter, modify or amend such draft contract in any manner in its discretion.

Thus amended by chap. 607, Laws of 1906.
Section 37 was first amended in 1906 by chap. 472.

Modification of contracts and plans.

§ 38. The board of rapid transit railroad commissioners for and on behalf of the said city in which such road or roads may be constructed, may, from time to time, with the concurrence of six members of said board and the consent, in writing, of the bondsmen or sureties of the person, firm or corporation which has contracted to construct, equip, maintain or operate said road or roads, or any of them, agree with the said contracting person, firm or corporation upon changes in and modifications of said contract, or of the plans and specifications upon which said road or roads is or are to be constructed, but no change or modifications in the plans and specifications consented to and authorized pursuant to section five of this act shall be made without the further consent and authorization provided for in said section; but in no event shall the annual rental to be paid to said city, for the use of said road, be reduced below the minimum rate hereinbefore provided.

Thus amended by chap. 472, Laws of 1906.

Elevated railways in lieu of bridge approaches.

§ 38a. The board of directors of any company incorporated for the purpose of constructing, maintaining or operating a bridge or bridges connecting a city of more than one million inhabitants with any other city in this state, and by the act of incorporation of which authority shall have been conferred or intended to be conferred, to construct, maintain or operate, as a part of or in connection with its bridge, an approach or approaches thereto extending generally in an easterly and westerly direction, may determine in lieu of constructing such approach or approaches, to build, maintain and operate an elevated railway, the route of which shall be coincident with the route of such approach or approaches as defined in said act, and shall adopt a general plan for the construction thereof, and which shall show the general mode of operation, and contain such details as to manner of construction as may be necessary to show the extent to which any street, avenue, or other public place is to be encroached upon and the property abutting thereon affected, a copy of which plan shall be transmitted to the common council of the city in which the same is to be located. Such proceedings shall thereupon be had by such common council as are provided by section five of this act, as though such plans had been transmitted by the rapid transit commissioners as contemplated in said section. Provided, that where in any such city the exclusive control of any street, route, highway or avenue, which is to be occupied by any railway or railways constructed under the provisions of this section is by law vested in any local authority other than the common council

of such city, the approval of the aforesaid plans, and consent to
the construction of a railway thereunder shall be given by such
local authority in place of, and if required in addition to such
approval and consent by such common council, and with like
effect. Upon obtaining the approval and consent of the local
authorities as in said section provided, the said board of directors
shall take the necessary steps to obtain, if possible, the consent
of the property owners along the line of the said route or routes,
and all proceedings in respect of such consents or when such
consents cannot be obtained shall be similar in all respects to the
proceedings in said section provided. Any consent of the local
authorities to construct or operate such railway shall be given
only upon the condition that the rate of fare upon such elevated
railway shall not exceed five cents for each passenger, and that
payment of such fare shall entitle each passenger to or from said
elevated railroad to free transit across the bridge or bridges with
which it is intended to connect the same. When the consents of
the local authorities and the property owners, or in lieu thereof,
the authorization of the supreme court upon the report of the
commissioners shall have been obtained, and the said company
shall have accepted such condition it shall have all the powers
of corporations formed under this act, it shall be authorized to
build, construct, maintain and operate such elevated railway or
railways, but all provisions of this act, or of any act requiring
the sale of the right, privilege and franchise of constructing,
maintaining and operating such railway or railways, or requiring
a corporation or corporations to be organized for the purpose of
acquiring such right, privilege and franchise, and all other provisions of this act or of any act inconsistent with this section, are
hereby declared inapplicable to such elevated railway and to such
company. The entire route of any elevated railway constructed
under the provisions of this section shall not exceed three miles
in length, nor shall any part of said railway except at the termini

thereof be less than sixteen feet above any street, avenue or public place, or less than fourteen feet above any existing elevated railway which may be crossed, intervened or intersected thereby. The said railway may be located and constructed so as to cross any intersecting street, avenue, highway or place otherwise exempted, except that no public park shall be occupied or crossed thereby, the structure of such elevated railway shall be liable to taxation as provided by law for similar structures.

Thus amended by changing the number of the section from 38 to 38a, by chap. 519, Laws of 1895. This section was added to the law by chap. 102, Laws of 1892.

Acquisition of land, etc.

§ 39. For the purpose of constructing or operating any road for the construction or operation of which a contract shall have been made by the board of rapid transit railroad commissioners, including necessary stations and station approaches, or for the purpose of operating or securing the operation of the same free of interference and right of interference and of action and right of action for damages and otherwise, whether by abutting owners or others, or to provide, lay or maintain conduits, pipes, ways or other means for the transmission of electricity, steam, water, air or other source or means of power or of signals or of messages necessary or convenient for or in the construction or operation of such road, or for the transportation of materials necessary for such construction or operation, or to provide a temporary or permanent way or course for any such conduit, pipe or other means or source of transportation, said board for and in behalf of said city may acquire, by conveyance or grant to said city to be delivered to the said board and to contain such terms, conditions, provisos and limitations as the said board shall deem proper, or by condemnation or other legal or other proceedings, as in this act provided, any real estate and any rights, terms and interest therein, any and all rights, privileges, franchises and easements, whether of owners or abutters, or others to interfere with the construction or operation of such road or to recover

damages therefor, which, in the opinion of the board, it shall be
necessary to acquire or extinguish for the purpose of constructing and operating such road free of interference or right of interference. The word property hereinafter used shall be deemed
to include any such real estate, and any rights, terms and interest
therein, and any such rights, privileges, franchises and easements,
whether of owners, abutting owners, or others. Where any contractor for the construction or operation of any such railroad
shall require any property for such construction and operation,
such property shall be deemed to be required for a public purpose;
and with the approval of the said board of rapid transit railroad
commissioners the same may be acquired by the said contractor
in all respects as such property may be acquired by the said board
of rapid transit railroad commissioners for the said city, and all
proceedings to acquire the said property shall be conducted under
the direction and subject to the approval of the rapid transit railroad commissioners. It shall be the duty of the board whenever
any property which the city shall have acquired as provided in
this act shall be unnecessary for rapid transit purposes, to sell
and convey the same in behalf of said city, provided, however,
that no such sale or conveyance shall be made except with the
approval of the commissioners of the sinking fund of such city
or, if there be no commissioners of the sinking fund then the
other board or public body thereof having power to sell or lease
city property and provided further that the proceeds of any such
sale or conveyance shall, under the direction of the said board of
rapid transit railroad commissioners, be applied either to the
purchase of other property necessary for rapid transit purposes
or shall be applied in all respects as the payments of rental to be
made by the contractor as provided in this act. Whenever the
said rapid transit railroad commissioners for and in behalf of
the city shall have acquired or shall hereafter acquire an easement in property by conveyance or grant for the purpose of the
operation or construction of a rapid transit railroad, it may in
behalf of the city and as part consideration for the grant or con-

veyance of the easement, enter into an agreement with the grantor of such easement or right of way, giving to such grantor or his assigns, the right of lateral or other support through, in, or under the said property, or any adjoining lands or space occupied by said rapid transit railroad for any building erected or to be erected upon the land over which the easement or right of way has been obtained for the support and maintenance of any such building or buildings, provided that any structure that shall be built for the support of any such building or buildings shall be approved by said board and shall not extend in or under any street beyond the curb lines as fixed by the ordinances of the board of aldermen or other legislative body of such city.

Thus amended by chap. 472, Laws of 1906.

Entry upon lands and property.

§ 40. It shall and may be lawful for said board, and for all persons acting under its authority, to enter in the daytime into and upon any and all lands and property which it shall deem necessary to be acquired, or to which there may be appurtenant rights, terms, franchises, easements or privileges which it shall deem necessary to be acquired or extinguished by said city, for the purpose of making the maps or surveys hereinafter mentioned, and also to enter in like manner and for the same purpose upon any property adjacent to and within five hundred feet of the property to be so surveyed; and the said board shall cause three similar maps or plans to be made of each parcel of property which it may deem necessary so to be acquired, or to which there may be appurtenant rights, terms, franchises, easements or privileges necessary so to be acquired or extinguished, designating each of said parcels by a number, and upon each map or plan so made or in a memorandum accompanying the same and to be deemed part thereof the said board shall cause to be clearly indicated the particular estate or estates, rights, terms, privileges, franchises or easements to be acquired or extinguished for the purposes of this act, in relation to each and every piece or parcel of property described upon said map or plan. The said board shall have power to cause a triplicate set of maps or plans and memoranda as herein provided for to be made as often and at such times as said board shall determine, and each set of maps or plans and memoranda so made shall contain the particulars above enumerated within such district as said board shall in each case provide. The maps or plans and memoranda herein provided for, when approved and adopted by said board, shall have written thereon a certificate of such approval, signed by the members of said board adopting and approving the same, and one copy thereof shall be filed in the department of public works, or other chief executive department having principal charge of the streets, there to remain as a public record, and the other two of said maps or plans and memoranda shall be transmitted to the counsel to the corporation or other principal legal adviser of said city. The said board may from time to time make and file further maps or plans and memoranda amending those already filed, but not so as to defeat or impair any property or interest which shall have been already acquired, or to revive any interest or right which may have been already extinguished by the said city.

Thus amended by chap. 519, Laws of 1895.

Board may direct proceedings to be taken.

§ 41. Whenever and as often as the said board shall deem it to be necessary and proper that the said city should acquire any such property and shall have caused to be made, as provided in the last preceding sections, the maps or plans and memoranda specifying and defining the said property to be acquired, or to which are appurtenant the rights, terms, franchises, easements or privileges to be acquired or extinguished, and shall have certified, filed and transmitted the several copies of such maps or plans as in the last section prescribed, the said board may direct the counsel to the corporation or other principal legal adviser of said city, to take legal proceedings to acquire the same for the said city, and the said counsel to the corporation, or other principal legal adviser, shall thereupon take proceedings as in this act provided.

Thus amended by chap. 519, Laws of 1895.

Filing of maps.

§ 42. The said counsel to the corporation, or other principal legal adviser of said city, shall cause one of the maps or plans, so as aforesaid transmitted to him, to be filed in the office of the register of the county, or if there be no such register, then in the office of the county clerk of the county in which said city is situated. The map, hereinafter denominated the third map, being the other one of the two so as aforesaid transmitted to said counsel to the corporation, or other legal adviser, shall be disposed of as hereinafter provided.

This section added by chap. 752, Laws of 1894.

Application for commissioners of appraisal.

§ 43. After the said set shall have been filed as hereinbefore provided in the office of the register or county clerk of said county, the said counsel to the corporation, or other principal legal adviser, for and on behalf of the said city, shall, and he may from time to time, upon first giving the notice required by the next section of this act, apply to the supreme court at any special or general term thereof, to be held in the judicial district in which said city is situated, for the appointment of commissioners of appraisal. Upon each such application he shall present to the court a petition, signed by a majority of the members of said board and verified in the manner prescribed by law for the verification of pleadings, according to the practice of said court, setting forth the action or determination theretofore taken or had by said board, with respect to the property to be acquired, and the filing of said maps or plans and memoranda and praying for the appointment of such commissioners of appraisal. Such petition shall contain a general description of all the property to, or in or over or appurtenant to which any title, interest, right, franchise, easement, term or privilege is sought to be acquired or extinguished, and of every right, franchise, easement, or privilege sought to be acquired, by the said city for public purposes, each lot or parcel being more particularly described by a reference to the number of said lot or parcel as given on said maps, and the title, interest, right, easement, term or privilege sought to be acquired, or extinguished, to or in or over or appurtenant to each of said lots or parcels shall be stated in said petition.

Thus amended by chap. 519, Laws of 1895.

Publication of notice, or service of petition for application for appointment of commissioners of appraisal.

§ 44. The said counsel to the corporation, or other principal legal adviser, shall give or cause to be given notice by publication in two public newspapers published in the said city, or, instead of such publication, may in his discretion cause service of the petition and notice of his intention to make application to the said court for the appointment of such commissioners of appraisal, to be made in the same manner prescribed by section three thousand three hundred and sixty-two of the code of civil procedure, as amended by chapter ninety-five of the laws of eighteen hundred and ninety, such notice if published as aforesaid shall state the time and place of such application, shall briefly state the object of the application, and shall briefly describe the property sought to be acquired or affected, and refer to a fuller statement to be filed in the office of the board of rapid transit railroad commissioners, in which shall be set forth the location and boundaries of the several lots or parcels of property, and rights, franchises, easements or privileges sought to be taken or affected, and a brief statement as to each of said lots or parcels, of the title, interest, rights, easements, terms

or privileges therein or appurtenant thereto sought to be acquired
or extinguished, with a reference to the dates and places of filing
the said maps or plans and memoranda shall be a sufficient
description of the property sought to be so taken or affected.
Such notice in case of publication as aforesaid shall be so published, in said newspapers twice a week for six weeks immediately previous to the time fixed in said notice for the presentation of each petition.

Thus amended by chap. 533, Laws of 1902.

Order for appointment of commissioners.

§ 45. At the time and place mentioned in said notice, unless
the said court shall adjourn said application to a subsequent
date, and in that event at the time to which the same may be
adjourned, the court, upon due proof to its satisfaction of the
publication aforesaid, and upon filing the said petition, shall
make an order for the appointment of three disinterested freeholders, residents in said city, as commissioners of appraisal, to
ascertain and appraise the compensation to be made to the
owners of property so to be taken or extinguished for the purposes indicated in this act. Such order shall fix the time and
place for the first meeting of the commissioners.

This section added by chap. 752, Laws of 1894.

Oath of commissioners.

§ 46. The said commissioners shall take and subscribe the oath
required by the twelfth article of the constitution of the state of
New York, and shall forthwith file the same in the office of the
clerk of the county in which said city is situated.

This section added by chap. 752, Laws of 1894.

City seized in fee of land upon filing oaths.

§ 47. On filing said oath in the manner provided in the last
section, the said city shall be and become seized and possessed
in fee or absolute ownership of all those parcels of property,

rights, terms, franchises, easements and privileges which are in
the maps or plans and memoranda referred to in section forty
of this act, described as parcels of property, rights, franchises,
easements, or privileges which are to be acquired, and also shall
become seized and possessed of all the rights, terms, franchises,
easements or privileges appurtenant to any lots or parcels of
property indicated on said maps or plans as parcels in regard to
which it is deemed necessary to acquire such rights, terms,
franchises, easements or privileges, or the said rights, terms,
franchises, easements or privileges shall be extinguished as the
case may be; and the said board for the said city, may immediately or at any time or times thereafter take possession or
enter into the enjoyment of the said property, rights, terms, franchises, easements and privileges or of any part or parts thereof
without any suit or proceeding at law for that purpose and the
said board for the said city, or any person or persons acting
under their or its authority, may enter upon and use, occupy,
and enjoy in perpetuity all the parcels of property and all the
rights, terms, franchises, easements or privileges appurtenant
to any of the parcels of property and all rights, franchises, easements, and privileges, described on said maps or plans or in said
memoranda, for any of the purposes authorized and provided for
by this act. But on such filing of the said oath the said city
shall be and become forthwith liable to the respective owners of
the several parcels of property and the several rights, terms,
franchises, easements and privileges appertaining thereto, and
of the said rights, franchises, easements, and privileges acquired
as aforesaid, for the true and respective values thereof, together
with interest thereon from the time of filing the said oath, provided, however, that no such interest shall be payable to any
owner of any such property, right, term, franchise, easement or
privilege during any period during which the said city or the

42

said board of rapid transit railroad commissioners may by any resistance, whether by legal proceedings or otherwise of such owner or with his authority, be prevented from taking possession thereof or enjoying the same; and provided further, that no action shall be brought to recover the amount of such value or interest unless within eighteen months after the filing of such oath, a report shall not have been duly made by commissioners of appraisal as herein provided, or such report shall not have been confirmed by the supreme court as herein provided, so that the said city shall be liable to forthwith pay the amount by such report ascertained to be due for such value or interest.

Thus amended by chap. 519, Laws of 1895.

Powers of commissioners.

§ 48. Any one of said commissioners of appraisal may issue subpoenas and administer oaths to witnesses, and they or any one of them, in the absence of the others, may adjourn the proceedings, from time to time in their discretion, but they shall continue to meet from time to time as may be necessary to hear, consider and determine upon all claims which may be presented to them under any of the provisions of this act. In case of the death, resignation, refusal or neglect to serve of any commissioner of appraisal, the remaining commissioner or commissioners shall, upon ten days' notice, to be given by advertisement in the newspapers mentioned in section forty-four of this act, apply to the supreme court, at a special or general term thereof, to be held in the judicial district in which said city is situated, for the appointment of a commissioner or commissioners to fill the vacancy or vancancies so occasioned. In case of the death, resignation or refusal to serve of all the commissioners of appraisal, the said counsel to the corporation or other principal legal adviser to said city shall, on giving the notice required in this section, apply to the said court for the appointment of other commissioners of appraisal. It shall be the duty of the commissioners of appraisal to procure from the counsel to the corporation or other principal legal adviser the third set of maps or plans and memoranda provided for in sections forty and forty-two of this act. They shall view the property laid down on said map, and shall hear the proofs and allegations of any owner, lessee or other person in any way entitled to or interested in the property to be acquired or extinguished, or any part or parcel thereof, and also such proofs and allegations as may be offered on behalf of the said city. They shall reduce the testimony, if any, taken before them to writing, and after the testimony is closed, they, or a majority of them, all having considered the same, and having an opportunity to be present, shall, without unnecessary delay, ascertain and determine the compensation which ought justly to be made by the said city to the owners or persons interested in the property acquired or extinguished by said proceedings. The said commissioners of appraisal shall make reports of their proceedings to the supreme court, as in the next section provided with the minutes of the testimony taken before them, if any, and they shall be entitled to the payment hereinafter provided for their services and expenses, to be paid from the fund hereinafter specified. The said commissioners may make a single report or may make reports from time to time as they shall reach their several decisions as to different parcels of property.

Thus amended by chap. 519, Laws of 1895.

Report of commissioners.

§ 49. The said commissioners shall prepare a report or reports, to which shall be annexed the third set of maps or plans and memoranda referred to in section forty-two of this act and therein denominated the third set or a copy thereof certified by them. Each said report shall contain a brief description of the property so taken or affected, with a reference to the map upon which the same is required to be indicated; a statement of the sums estimated and determined upon by them, as a just compensation for the same to be made by the city to the owners or persons interested therein and the names of such owners and persons; but in all and each and every case or cases where one or more of the owners and persons interested, or their respective estates or interests, are unknown, or not fully known, to the commissioners of appraisal, it shall be sufficient for them to set forth and state in general terms the respective sums to be allowed and paid to the owners of and persons interested therein, generally, without specifying the names or estates or interests of such owner or persons interested, or any or either of them.

Thus amended by chap. 519, Laws of 1895.

Filing of reports.

§ 50. Each said report, signed by said commissioners, or a majority of them, shall be filed in the office of the clerk of the county in which said city is situated, and the commissioners of appraisal shall, in each case, notify the counsel to the corporation, or other principal adviser to said city, as soon as any such report is filed.

Thus amended by chap. 519, Laws of 1895.

Notice of presentation of report to court.

§ 51. The counsel to the corporation, or other principal legal adviser, or, in case of his neglect to do so within ten days after receiving notice of such filing, then any person interested in the proceedings, shall give notice that the said report will be pre-•sented for confirmation to the supreme court, at a special term thereof, to be held in the judicial district in which said city is situated, at a time and place to be specified in said notice. The said notice shall contain a statement of the time and place of the filing of the report, and shall be published in two daily news-papers published in such city, for at least two weeks imme-diately prior to the presentation of said report for confirma-tion.

Thus amended by chap. 519, Laws of 189?

Confirmation of report.

§ 52. The application for the confirmation of each such report shall be made to the supreme court at a special term thereof, held in the judicial district in which said city is situated. Upon the hearing of the application for the confirmation thereof, the said court shall confirm such report and make an order con-taining a recital of the substance of the proceedings in the matter of the appraisal, with a general description of the prop-erty appraised and for which compensation is to be made, and shall also direct to whom the money is to be paid, and whether or not any part thereof, and, if so, what part, is to be deposited with the comptroller or other chief financial officer of said city with the chamberlain of said city, or if there be no chamber-lain, with a bank or trust company to be designated by said court. Such report when so confirmed shall, except in the case of an appeal, as hereinafter provided, be final and conclusive, as well upon the said city as upon owners and all persons interested in or entitled to said property, and also upon all other persons whomsoever.

Thus amended by chap. 519, Laws of 1895.

Payment of awards.

§ 53. The said city shall, within four calendar months after the confirmation of any report of the commissioners of appraisal, pay to the respective owners and bodies politic or corporate mentioned or referred to in said report, in whose favor any sum or sums of money shall be estimated and reported by said commissioners, the respective sum or sums so estimated and reported in their favor respectively, with legal interest thereon from the date of filing the oath of said commissioners, and in case of neglect or default in the payment of the same within the time aforesaid, the respective person or persons or bodies politic or corporate, in whose favor the same shall be so reported, his, her or their executors, administrators, successors or assigns at any time or times after application first made by him, her or them, to the comptroller or other chief financial officer of said city for payment thereof, may sue for and recover the same, with lawful interest as aforesaid, and the costs of suit, in any proper form of action against the said city in any court having cognizance thereof, and in which it shall be sufficient to declare generally for so much money due to the plaintiff or plaintiffs therein by virtue of this act for property taken or extinguished for the purposes herein mentioned, and the report of said commissioners, with proof of the right and title of the plaintiff or plaintiffs to the sum or sums demanded shall be conclusive evidence in such suit or action.

Thus amended by chap. 519, Laws of 1895.

Payment of awards to chamberlain or bank in certain cases.

§ 54.   Whenever the owner or owners, person or persons interested in any property taken or affected in such proceeding, or in whose favor any such sum or sums or compensation shall be so reported, shall be under the age of twenty-one years, or of unsound mind or absent from the city, and also in all cases where the name or names of the owner or owners, person or persons, interested in any such property shall not be set forth or mentioned in said report, or where the said owner or owners, person or persons, being named therein, can not, upon diligent inquiry, be found, or where there are adverse or conflicting claims to the money awarded as compensation, it shall be lawful for the said city to pay the sum or sums mentioned in said report, payable, or that would be coming to such owner or owners, person or persons, respectively, with interest, as aforesaid, to the chamberlain of said city, or, if there be no chamberlain, then to any bank or trust company designated by the court in the order confirming the report of the commissioners of appraisal, to the credit of such owner or owners, person or persons, and such payments shall be as valid and effectual in all respects as if made to the said owner or owners, person or persons, interested therein, respectively, according to their just rights; and, provided, also, that in all and each and every such case and cases where any sum or sums or compensation reported by the commissioners in favor of any person or persons or parties whatsoever, whether named or not named in said report, shall be paid to any person or persons, or party or parties, whomsoever, when the same shall of right belong and ought to have been paid to some other person or persons, or party or parties, it shall be lawful for the person or persons, or party or parties, to whom the same ought to have been paid, to sue for and recover the same, with lawful interest and costs of suit, as so much money had and received to his, her or their use by the person or persons, party or parties, respectively, to whom the same shall have been so paid.

This section added by chap. 752, Laws of 1894.

Claims for compensation for property taken.

§ 55. Every owner or person in any way interested in any property taken or extinguished as contemplated in this act, if he intends to make claim for compensation for such taking or extinguishment, shall within six months after the appointment of the commissioners of appraisal exhibit to the said commissioners a statement of his claim, and shall thereupon be entitled to offer testimony and to be heard before them touching such claim and the compensation proper to be made him, and to have a determination made by such commissioners of appraisal as to the amount of such compensation. Every person neglecting or refusing to present such claim within said time shall be deemed to have surrendered his claim for such compensation, except so far as he may be entitled, as such owner or person interested, to the whole or a part of the sum of money awarded by the commissioners of appraisal as a just compensation for taking or extinguishing the property owned by said person, or in which the said person is interested.

Thus amended by chap. 587, Laws of 1901.

Payment of awards.

§ 56. Payment of the compensation awarded by said commissioners of appraisal to the persons named in their report (if not infants or persons of unsound mind), shall, in the absence of notice to the said city or other claimants to such award, protect the said city.

This section added by chap. 752, Laws of 1894.

Specified claims and special reports thereon.

§ 57. Said commissioners of appraisal may in their discretion take up any specified claim or claims, and finally ascertain and determine the compensation to be made thereon, and make a separate report with reference thereto, annexing to said report a copy of so much of the set of maps or plans and memoranda referred to in section forty-two of this act as indicates the property so reported on. Such report shall, as to claims therein specified, be the report required in this act, and the subsequent action with reference thereto, shall be had in the same manner as though no other claim were embraced in said proceeding, which, however, shall continue as to all claims upon which no such determination and report is made.

Thus amended by chap. 519, Laws of 1895.

Appeals from appraisal and report to general term.

§ 58.   Within twenty days after notice of the confirmation of
the report of the commissioners, as provided for in section fifty-
two of this act, which notice may, as to parties who have not
appeared before the commissioners, be given in the manner provided in section fifty-one of this act, either party may appeal
to the general term of the supreme court in the department in
which such commissioners were appointed, from the appraisal
and report of the commissioners and the order confirming the
same. Such appeal shall be heard upon due notice thereof being
given, according to the rules and practice of said court. On the
hearing of such appeal the court may direct a new appraisal
and determination of any question passed upon, by the same or
new commissioners, in its discretion, and from any determination of the general term either party, if aggrieved, may take an
appeal, which shall be heard and determined by the court of
appeals. In the case of a new appraisal the second report shall
be final and conclusive on all the parties and persons interested.
If the amount of compensation to be made by such city is
increased by the second report, the difference shall be paid by
the comptroller or other chief financial officer of said city, to the
parties entitled to the same, or shall be deposited with the chamberlain, or bank or trust company, as the court may direct, and
if the amount is diminished the difference shall be refunded to
the said city by the party to whom the same may have been
paid, and judgment therefor may be rendered by the court on
the filing of the second report against the party liable to pay
the same. But the taking of an appeal by any person or persons
shall not operate to stay the proceedings under this act except
as to the particular property with which the said appeal is concerned. Such appeal shall be heard upon the evidence taken
before said commissioners, and any affidavits as to irregularities,

and three printed copies of such evidence shall be furnished by
the said city to the party taking the appeal, within ten days
after the appeal is perfected, and such appeal may be heard on
the evidence so furnished, and may be taken without security
thereon.

This section added by chap. 752, Laws of 1894.

Power of court to amend defects, etc.

§ 59. The supreme court in the judicial district in which said
city is situated shall have power at any time to amend any
defect or informality in any of the special proceedings authorized by this act as may be necessary, and to direct such further
notices to be given to any party in interest as it deems proper,
and also to appoint other commissioners in place of any who
shall die, or refuse, or neglect to serve or be incapable of serving,
or be removed. And the said court may at any time remove
any commissioner of appraisal who in its judgment shall be
incapable of serving, or who shall for any reason in its judgment
be an unfit person to serve as such commissioner. The
cause of such removal shall be specified in the order making
the same. If in any particular it shall at any time be found
necessary to amend any pleading or proceeding or to supply any
defect therein arising in the course of any special proceeding
authorized by this act, the same may be amended or supplied
in such manner as shall be directed by the supreme court, which
is hereby authorized to make such amendment or correction.
Wherever in this act reference is made to the general term of
the supreme court, it shall be deemed to include the appellate
division of the supreme court for the district in which said city
is situated, whenever said general term shall be superseded
thereby.

Thus amended by chap. 519, Laws of 1895.

Property acquired deemed acquired for public use.

§ 60. All property acquired under the provisions of this act shall be and shall be deemed to have been acquired for public uses and purposes, and for the purpose of affording increased facilities for rapid transit between points within the city acquiring such property.

This section added by chap. 752, Laws of 1894.

Expense payable from proceeds of bonds.

§ 61. The moneys necessary and sufficient to be paid for any property, acquired in any manner under the provisions of this act, together with all expenses necessarily incurred in surveying, locating, and acquiring title to such property, and for surveying and locating the same, and for preparing the necessary maps and plans in connection therewith, shall be raised and paid out of the proceeds of bonds issued and sold as provided by section thirty-seven of this act, and all such expenses so incurred in surveying, locating and acquiring title, and for preparing necessary maps and plans and also those incurred as provided in the next section shall be deemed a part of and included in the cost of constructing the road or roads, the construction of which rendered it necessary to acquire the property in the course of the acquisition of which such expenses may be incurred.

Thus amended by chap. 519, Laws of 1895.

Pay of commissioners and employes.

§ 62. The commissioners of appraisal appointed in pursuance of this act shall receive as compensation the sum of ten dollars per day for each day actually employed. They may employ the necessary clerks, stenographers and surveyors. The counsel to the corporation or other principal legal adviser to said city shall, either in person or by such counsel as he shall designate for the purpose, appear for and protect the interests of the city in all such proceedings in court and before the commissioners. The fees of the commissioners and the salaries and compensation of their employes, and all other necessary expenses in and about the said proceedings provided for by this act, and such allowance for counsel fees as may be made by order of the court, and all reasonable expenses incurred by said counsel to the corporation, or other principal legal adviser of said counsel designated by him for the proper presentation and defense of the interests of said city before said commissioners and in court, shall be paid by the comptroller or other chief financial officer of said city out of the funds referred to in the last preceding section. But such fees and expenses shall not be paid until they have been taxed before a justice of the supreme court in the judicial district in which said city is situated upon five days' notice to the counsel to the corporation, or other chief legal adviser of said city. Such allowance shall, in no case, exceed the limits prescribed by section thirty-two hundred and fifty-three of the code of civil procedure.

This section added by chap. 752, Laws of 1894.

Proviso in case roads constructed at city's expense.

§ 63. In case it shall be determined by vote of the people as provided by sections twelve and thirteen of chapter seven hundred and fifty-two of the laws of eighteen hundred and ninety-four to construct by and at the city's expense, then and in that event the road or roads so constructed shall be and remain the absolute property of the city so constructing it or them, and shall be and be deemed to be a part of the public streets and highways of said city, to be used and enjoyed by the public upon the payment of such fares and tolls, and subject to such reasonable rules and regulations as may be imposed and provided for by the board of rapid transit railroad commissioners in said city.

This section added by chap. 752, Laws of 1894, and amended by chap. 519, Laws of 1895.

Construction of act.

§ 64. This act shall not be construed to repeal or in any manner affect chapter six hundred and six of the laws of eighteen hundred and seventy-five, entitled "An act to further provide for the construction and operation of a steam railway or railways in the counties of this state," or the acts amendatory thereof or supplementary thereto, or article five of chapter five hundred and sixty-five of the laws of eighteen hundred and ninety, known as the railroad law, except so far as the said acts, or either of them, would, if this act had not been passed, authorize the appointment hereafter of any commissioners applied for as provided in section one of said act of eighteen hundred and seventy-five, or in section one hundred and twenty of said act of eighteen hundred and ninety, in any city or cities containing a population of over one million inhabitants, according to the last preceding national or state census, or authorize any commissioners already appointed pursuant to the provisions of such act or acts in any such city or cities, to fix, determine or locate any new route or routes, pursuant to the provisions of either of said acts. This act shall not be construed in any manner to affect the exercise or enjoyment at any time, and from time to time hereafter, of any right or rights heretofore acquired, exercised or enjoyed by any corporation heretofore duly incorporated and organized or deriving powers and rights under the laws of this state. This act shall not affect or impair the exercise or enjoyment of any right or rights now possessed or heretofore acquired or heretofore authorized to be acquired, exercised or enjoyed by any street surface railroad corporation, except as herein otherwise expressly provided, and this act shall not be construed to repeal or in any manner affect chapter one hundred and forty of the laws of eighteen hundred and fifty, entitled "An act to authorize the formation of railroad corporations, and to regulate the same," or either of the several acts amendatory thereof or supplementary thereto. This act shall not be construed to repeal or in any manner affect chapter five hundred and sixty-five of the laws of eighteen hundred and ninety, known as the railroad law, except as hereinabove expressly provided, or except so far as the provisions of the same conflict with the provisions of this act. But nothing in this section contained shall prevent the board of rapid transit railroad commissioners from laying out a route for a railway and constructing and operating a railway, and such board shall have the right to lay out such route and construct and operate such railway, over, under, along or across any street in, along, under or over which there shall be any existing railway, provided that the routes so laid out by the said board and the railway so constructed by it shall so pass over or under or at the side of such existing railway as not to interfere with its operation.

Thus amended by chap. 472, Laws of 1906. The number of section 64 was changed from 34 to 64 by chap. 752, Laws of 1894.

As to surface railroads.

§ 65. (Section 65 repealed by chap. 472, Laws of 1906; see section 12 of said chapter as to the language in which section 65 is repealed. The number of section 65 was changed from 35 to 65 by chap. 752, Laws of 1894).
Chap. 752, Laws of 1894.

Repeal.

§ 65. All acts and parts of acts local or general inconsistent with this act are hereby repealed.

The number of this section was changed from 36 to 66 by chap. 752, Laws of 1894, and from 66 to 65 by chap. 472, Laws of 1906.

§ 66. This act shall take effect immediately.

The number of this section was changed from 37 to 67 by chap. 752, Laws of 1894, and from 67 to 66 by chap. 472, Laws of 1906.

Concurrent vote of rapid transit commissioners.

§ 10. Whenever it is expressly provided in the act hereby amended that any act of the board of rapid transit railroad commissioners shall be done by the concurrent vote of four of the members of said board, the act hereby amended is further amended so as to provide in such cases that such vote shall be that of six of such members.

Chap. 752, Laws of 1894.

Termination of commission heretofore appointed.

§ 11. The commissioners of rapid transit heretofore appointed under the act hereby amended, or who became such commissioners by its terms, upon the organization of the board which shall succeed them pursuant to said act as hereby amended, shall cease to be such commissioners and shall transfer and deliver to the board of rapid transit railroad commissioners, provided for by the act hereby amended, as so amended, all furniture, books, maps, records, plans and other papers and property of what kind soever appertaining or belonging to or in the custody of the board of which they were commissioners, or in their possession, or under their control as such commissioners, or held by them, or for which they are responsible in their official capacity. The expenses incurred by said commissioners for which an appropriation or appropriations shall have been made pursuant to section ten of the act hereby amended, shall be paid upon vouchers to be furnished by said commissioners and otherwise, as provided in said section. Said commissioners shall also be entitled to receive a reasonable compensation for the services which have been rendered by them, which may have been, or which shall be, determined on their application in the manner provided for in said section. The comptroller, or other chief financial officer of said city, is hereby authorized and directed to issue and sell revenue bonds of such city in anticipation of the receipt of taxes, and out of the proceeds of such bonds to pay said compensation so ascertained and determined, and the amount necessary to pay the principal and interest of said bonds shall be included in the tax levy of said city for the year next following the issue and sale of the same.

Chap. 752. Laws of 1894.

Submission of question of construction of road by city to electors.

§ 12. The said board of rapid transit railway commissioners shall cause the question, whether such railway or railways shall be constructed by the city and at the public expense, to be submitted to the vote of the qualified electors of the city within which such railway or railways is or are to be constructed, and to that end it shall be the duty of the said board, after completion of the detailed plans and specifications, as required by the act hereby amended, at least thirty days prior to the next general election, to file with the public officer or officers within the county in which such city is located, who may be charged with the duty of printing the ballots to be used at such election, a request that separate ballots be printed and supplied to such electors, one-half in number of which shall read: "For municipal construction of rapid transit road," and the other half in number of said ballots shall read, "Against municipal construction of rapid transit road." Upon such request being so filed, such ballots shall be printed and supplied to such electors at such general election, and separate ballot boxes shall be provided for the reception of the same in each election district within such city, and the provisions of chapter six hundred and eighty of the laws of eighteen hundred and ninety-two, entitled "An act in relation to the elections constituting chapter six of the general laws," and any act or acts amendatory thereof or supplemental thereto shall apply thereto as far as the nature of the case may allow. No ballot which may be provided under this section shall be deemed invalid by reason of any error in dimensions, style of printing, or other formal defect, or through having been deposited in the wrong ballot box, but all of such ballots shall be canvassed and returned as if such formal defect had not existed, or as if they had been deposited in the box provided for the purpose. Upon the canvass of such votes by the board of county canvassers of the county in which such city is located, it shall be the duty of said board to file with the county clerk of said county a statement which shall declare the total number of votes cast in said city "for municipal construction of rapid transit road," and the total number so cast therein "against municipal construction of rapid transit road." And the said railway or railways shall be constructed by the said city and at the public expense, if it shall be found from such statements so filed that there is a majority of the votes so cast in favor of such municipal construction.

Chap. 752. Laws of 1894.

Duty of board in case of municipal construction.

§ 13. In case the majority of votes cast at such election shall be in favor of such municipal construction of said railway or railways, it shall be the duty of said board of rapid transit railway commissioners within thirty days after the official declaration of the said vote to proceed to construct the said railway or railways, and to make and let all contracts required for the performance of the work necessary to be done and performed in and about the construction thereof. All such contracts must, before execution, be approved as to form by the counsel to the corporation, or other chief legal adviser for said city.

Chap. 752, Laws of 1894.

Act when to take effect.

§ 14. This act shall take effect immediately; except that the building of said road, or the sale of the franchises as provided for in sections seven and thirty-four of the act hereby amended, as so amended, is postponed until, and made dependent upon, the determination of that question by the vote of the people as called for by sections twelve and thirteen of this act.

Chap. 752, Laws of 1894.

43

Effect of act.

§ 14. Nothing in this act contained shall repeal, modify or alter any provision of the act hereby amended in respect of any railway or railways constructed, constructing or contracted for thereunder when this act takes effect; but the act hereby amended shall be and continue in full force and effect in respect of such railway or railways so constructed, constructing, or contracted for, as if this act had not been passed.

Chap. 472, Laws of 1906.

AN ACT to terminate the use of streets, avenues and public places in the city of New York, in the borough of Manhattan, by railroads operated by steam locomotive power at grade.

Section 1. The board of rapid transit commissioners in and for cities having over one milion inhabitants is hereby empowered and directed as speedily as possible to prepare a plan for the removal of the tracks of railways now operated by steam locomotive power, laid on, across, through or along the public streets, avenues, or public parks or places of the city of New York, in the borough of Manhattan, at grade; and to terminate the operation thereon of any railway by steam locomotive power; and to take such action in that regard as herein provided. In carrying out the duties imposed by this act, said board of rapid transit commissioners and their various officers and agents shall have and enjoy all the powers now conferred on them by chapter four of the laws of eighteen hundred and ninety-one and also amendments thereto now in force, so far as the same may be applicable to the purpose of this act, together with all the powers which any board, commissioner or public officer now has to regulate the manner of exercise on, across, through or along such streets, avenues, or public parks or places of any public franchise heretofore granted to any such steam railway·company, including the right to regulate or require changes to be made for the public convenience or benefit in the use of such streets, avenues, public parks or places by such railroad company, and all other powers in that regard expressed or implied in any such franchise granted to any such railway company so operated to operate a railroad on, across, through or along avenues, streets, or public parks or places of the borough of Manhattan.

§ 2. The said board of rapid transit commissioners is hereby empowered and instructed to prepare a plan and make an

---

* While this is a local act it is deemed of sufficient importance to print here.

agreement with any railroad company or companies now so operating a railroad by steam locomotive power in the borough of Manhattan, in the city of New York, which railroad is now operated at grade as aforesaid in said borough, said plan and agreement to provide in detail for the construction by the railroad company or companies at its or their own cost of a subway under the roadbed of the present tracks or under such other street or streets, avenues or public or private property as may be agreed upon, to which said tracks shall be removed and on which shall be operated, subject to the regulation of the board of rapid transit commissioners, a freight, passenger or freight and passenger railway business under a franchise, the terms and duration whereof shall be in such agreement fixed and determined, and such plan and agreement further to provide that as a condition of said agreement and as a part of the consideration therefor, all present franchises of every kind on, across, through and along such streets, avenues and public parks and places where said railroad is so operated by such steam locomotive power at grade shall be surrendered and canceled and the tracks thereof shall at the cost of the railroad company or companies be removed therefrom and that the right and franchise to operate said railroad thereon shall cease. The board of rapid transit commissioners may grant to said company or companies an additional franchise to lay in said subway such additional tracks as may be agreed upon and to operate thereon a freight, passenger or freight and passenger business, under such terms and for such compensation as shall be fixed by said board in said grant. It shall be further stipulated in said agreement that the consent of the board of rapid transit commissioners shall be obtained and proper compensation be fixed by said board as a condition to said company or companies making any connection or connections between said subway and other subways, to be owned or occupied by said company or companies or by any other company or companies.

§ 3. The board of rapid transit commissioners may further provide in said plan for the construction of such pipe galleries in, along and through said subway as they may deem necessary for the public use; and provide for the expense of constructing the same to be borne by the city of New York, said pipe galleries to be and remain the property of the city of New York. If the board of estimate and apportionment shall provide for the construction of pipe galleries to contain sewers, pipes or other sub-surface structures, the said galleries shall be maintained by the city of New York and shall be in the care and charge of the said board and subject to such regulations as it shall prescribe not inconsistent with the provisions of this act, and any revenue derived therefrom shall be paid into the treasury of said city. Provided, however, that any person or corporation who or which, at the time of the construction of the said galleries shall own pipes, subways or conduits in a street, avenue or public place in which said galleries shall be constructed pursuant to this act, shall be entitled to the use of such galleries for his or its said pipes, subways or conduits in the same manner as the said person or corporation shall be entitled by law to the use of such street, avenue or public place, and that no rent shall be charged for such use, except a reasonable charge to defray the actual cost of maintenance, unless such pipes, subways or conduits shall be of a greater capacity than those theretofore owned by such person or corporation in said street, avenue or public place, and that, if the capacity of any such pipe, subway or conduit so placed in the said galleries shall be increased, the rent shall be charged only for such increased capacity; and provided, further, that the placing in any such galleries of the subways or conduits of any corporation owning subways or conduits for electrical conductors, shall not in any wise affect the right of such corporation to charge and demand such compensation or rent for the use of said subways or conduits by other corporations or individuals as is, or may be permitted by law. Whenever the construction of any railway, depressed way, subway or tunnel under the provisions of this act shall interfere with, disturb or endanger any sewer, water pipe, gas pipe, or other duly authorized sub-surface structures, the work of construction at such points shall be conducted in accordance with the reasonable requirements and under the supervision of the officer or local authority having the care of and the jurisdiction or control over such subsurface structures so interfered with, disturbed or endangered. All expenses incidental to such supervision and to the work of reconstructing, readjusting and supporting any such sewer, water pipe, gas pipe or other duly authorized subsurface structure shall be borne and paid by the railroad company or companies now operating such railroad by steam locomotive power. Said plan shall provide further, the time within which such work shall be done which shall be under the supervision and the control of the board of rapid transit commissioners. The board of rapid transit commissioners shall prepare such plan, and the maps and drawings necessary thereto as speedily as possible. No agreement for the changes proposed by this act or for the plan herein provided for, shall be binding or take effect until the contract, the said plan and the maps in connection therewith, prepared by and under the direction of the board of rapid transit commissioners, shall have been submitted to the board of estimate and apportionment of the city of New York and shall have been approved by said board. Upon said approval, the said contract may be executed by the board of rapid transit commissioners and said railroad company or companies and shall thereupon be binding upon the city of New York, upon said board of rapid transit commissioners and upon said railroad company or companies. After said contract shall have gone into effect, the enforcement thereof and of the several provisions therein contained shall be a part of the duties of said board of rapid transit commissioners, which shall in its own name take such proceedings in law or in equity as may be from time to time necessary to enforce the same.

§ 4. In case the board of rapid transit commissioners shall be unable within twelve months after this act takes effect to agree as herein provided with such railroad company upon a plan as contained in the preceding section and obtain the approval thereof of the board of estimate and apportionment, the said board of rapid transit commissioners shall thereupon condemn all and any rights, privileges and franchises of any such railway company or companies to operate by locomotives using steam or other power cars or trains for carrying freight and passengers at grade on, across, through or along streets, avenues, public parks or places of the city of New York, borough of Manhattan and cause the tracks of such railroad or railroads to be removed therefrom. It shall cause to be prepared three similar maps or plans showing the streets, avenues, public parks and places on which any such railroad company now operates or has any franchise or right to operate such steam railway at grade in said city and borough and showing the location thereon of the tracks, if any, of such railway whose tracks or appurtenances or whose right to conduct such railway are to be so condemned as herein provided. Such maps or plans when adopted and approved by said board shall be disposed of in like manner as maps or plans of property to be condemned under the provisions of chapter four of the laws of eighteen hundred and ninety-one as amended; and the provisions of said chapter relative to the condemnation of property for public use, so far as the same may be applicable and not in conflict with the provisions of this act, shall apply to the proceedings to be had hereunder. Said board shall after the filing of said maps or plans direct the counsel to the corporation of the city of New York to take legal proceedings to acquire by condemnation all such valid or unlawful franchises of any such company operating such railway in said city, and the tracks and appurtenances thereof in such public streets, avenues, public parks or places as shown in said map or plans. Said counsel to the corporation shall thereupon cause to be served on the president or other officer upon whom a summons against such corporation might be served in an action of the railway corporation or corporations whose franchise or right to operate such railway or railways is to be condemned, or whose tracks or property is to be affected by such proceeding, ten days prior to the date on which the same is made returnable, notice of an application for the appointment of commissioners for the condemnation of such franchise or franchises and of such tracks or appurtenances thereto, and shall accompany such notice with a copy of a petition signed by a majority of the members of said board and verified in the manner prescribed by law for the verification of pleadings, setting forth. the action or determination theretofore taken or had by said board in respect to the franchises, rights, privileges or property to be acquired, and the filing of said maps or plans and praying for the appointment of said commissioners of appraisal for the purpose of condemning terminating and acquiring such franchises, rights, privileges and property therein specified. Said petition shall contain a general description of the franchises, grants, easements, tracks, properties or appurtenances sought to be acquired or extinguished and such notice, so served, shall be sufficient notice to such corporation without publication thereof. Said application shall be made to the supreme court at a special term in the judicial district in which said city is situated. The provisions of chapter four of the laws of eighteen hundred and ninety-one as amended relative to the acquisition of property for public uses thereunder shall apply to such application and to the appointment, powers, procedure, compensation and report of the commissioners and other public officers acting for the purpose of such condemnation under this act. Said commissioners shall take testimony and shall make a report with all convenient speed, which report shall include, among other matters deemed to be relevant and proper in such report, a statement of the source, nature and extent of each franchise, privilege or right lawfully possessed by such railway company or companies as found by them and condemned and terminated in such proceeding, the value thereof and, if more than one franchise, they shall state such values separately, a statement of the tracks, property and appurtenances so condemned and the value thereof. Such report shall fix the compensation if any, which the commissioners find to be reasonable and proper to be made to such railway company or companies for such franchise so condemned and terminated and for the tracks, property and appurtenances thereto so taken and condemned. Notice of an application to confirm such report may be given by any party thereto, by serving a copy of said report on the attorney or attorneys for the railroad corporation or corporations or upon the counsel to the corporation with notice that an application shall be made for such confirmation to the supreme court not less than ten days thereafter at a time and place therein provided and no publication of notice or of the filing of such report shall be required.

§ 5. No such franchise shall terminate nor shall the right, title or interest of such railroad company or companies in the same or in the tracks, properties or appurtenances to be condemned and acquired in such proceeding, cease or terminate until the entry of a final order made by the supreme court confirming the report of such commissioners and the court on making such order shall fix a date not more than one year thereafter on which the right to operate such railway or exercise such franchise and to use such tracks, property or appurtenances shall cease and determine, and in case an appeal be taken from such order of confirmation such time shall be further extended for a like period after the entry of an order of affirmance on such appeal. During such period it shall be lawful for such railroad company or companies to continue the use of such franchise or franchises or of the tracks, property or appurtenances sought to be condemned or acquired, as if no such proceeding had been instituted. The award, if any, made to such commissioners and confirmed by said court shall become payable on the expiration of such period with interest thereafter, and such award with the cost and expenses incident to such proceeding shall be borne and paid by the city of New York by the issue and sale of corporate stock of the city of New York, and the board of estimate and apportionment shall be authorized to issue and sell such stock as shall be necessary for such purpose, in like manner as corporate stock is by law issuable for the payment of damages awarded by commissioners of estimate and assessment in reports confirmed in proceedings taken to open streets, roads, avenues, boulevards or public parks. Such corporate stock may be authorized to be issued by said board without the concurrence or approval of any other public board or body.

§ 6. The board of rapid transit commissioners is authorized and empowered to discontinue any and all legal proceedings taken under this act for condemning such franchise or franchises and acquiring the tracks, property or appurtenances of such railway company or companies or any part thereof at any time before the confirmation of the report of the commissioners in such proceeding, if, in its opinion, the public interest requires such discontinuance and with power to cause new proceedings to be taken in such cases for the appointment of new commissioners.

§ 7. Nothing in this act contained shall be construed in any wise to abridge or affect the powers of the city of New York or of any proper and authorized board or public officer of said city to prevent the unlawful use by any railway company or corporation or* any street, avenue, public park or place in said city.

§ 8. Nothing in this act contained shall be held to affect or apply in any way to a corporation operating a steam surface railroad in the city of New York for the purpose only of transporting freight from its wharves, docks or piers to its freight yards or depots in said city over tracks not more than one-half mile in length.

§ 9. This act shall take effect immediately.

---

* So in original.

Interstate Commerce Act and Kindred Acts, as Amended to June 30, 1906.

CONTENTS.

(Showing citations.)

An act to regulate commerce, approved February 4, 1887, and in effect April 5, 1887 (24 Statutes at Large, 379; 1 Supp. to Rev. Stat. U. S., 529), as amended by an act approved March 2, 1889 (25 Statutes at Large, 855; 1 Supp. to Rev. Stat. U. S., 684), and by an act approved February 10, 1891 (26 Statutes at Large, 743; 1 Supp. to Rev. Stat. U. S., 891), and by an act approved February 8, 1895 (28 Statutes at Large, 643; 2 Supp. to Rev. Stat. U. S., 369), and by an act approved June 29, 1906 (34 Statutes at Large), and by a joint resolution approved June 30, 1906 (34 Statutes at Large).

An act in relation to testimony before the Interstate Commerce Commission, and in cases or proceedings under or connected with an act entitled an act to regulate commerce, and amendments thereto, approved February 11, 1893 (27 Statutes at Large, 443; 2 Supp. to Rev. Stat. U. S., 80).

An act defining the right of immunity of witnesses under the act entitled an act in relation to testimony before the Interstate Commerce Commission, and so forth, approved February 11, 1893, and an act entitled an act to establish the Department of Commerce and Labor, approved February 14, 1903, and an act entitled an act to further regulate commerce with foreign nations and among the States, approved February 19, 1903, and an act entitled an act making appropriations for the legislative, executive, and judicial expenses of the Government for the fiscal year ending June 30, 1904, and for other purposes, approved February 25, 1903. (34 Statutes at Large), approved June 30, 1906.

An act to further regulate commerce with foreign nations and among the States, approved February 19, 1903 (32 Statutes at Large, 847), as amended by an act approved June 29, 1906 (34 Statutes at Large).

An act to expedite the hearing and determination of suits in equity pending or hereafter brought under the act of July 2, 1890, entitled an act to protect trade and commerce against unlawful restraints and monopolies, an act to regulate commerce, or any other acts having a like purpose that may be hereafter enacted, approved February 11, 1903 (32 Stat. L., 823).

An act supplementary to the act of July 1, 1862, entitled an act to aid in the construction of a railroad and telegraph line from the Missouri River to the Pacific Ocean, and to secure to the Government the use of the same for postal, military, and other purposes, and also of the act of July 2, 1864, and other acts amendatory of said first-named act, approved August 7, 1888 (25 Stat. L., 382; 1 Supp. to Rev. Stat. U. S., 602).

An act to promote the safety of employees and travelers upon railroads by compelling common carriers engaged in interstate commerce to equip their cars with automatic couplers and continuous brakes and their locomotives with driving-wheel brakes, and for other purposes, approved March 2, 1893 (27 Statutes at Large, 531; 2 Supp. to Rev. Stat. U. S., 102), as amended by an act approved April 1, 1896 (29 Statutes at Large, 85; 2 Supp. to Rev. Stat. U. S., 455).

An act to amend an act entitled an act to promote the safety of employees and travelers, and so forth, approved March 2, 1893, and amended April 1, 1896, approved March 2, 1903 (32 Statutes at Large, 943).

An act authorizing the Commission to employ safety-appliance inspectors, approved June 28, 1902 (32 Statutes at Large, 444).

Joint resolution directing the Interstate Commerce Commission to investigate and report on block-signal systems and appliances for the automatic control of railway trains, approved June 30, 1906 (34 Statutes at Large).

An act authorizing Commission to approve system of interlocking or automatic signals on certain railroads in Indian and Oklahoma Territories, approved February 28, 1902 (32 Statutes at Large, 50).

An act requiring common carriers engaged in interstate commerce to make full reports of all accidents to the Interstate Commerce Commission, approved March 3, 1901 (31 Statutes at Large, 1446).

Joint resolution instructing the Interstate Commerce Commission to make examinations into the subject of railroad discriminations and monopolies in coal and oil, and report on the same from time to time, approved March 7, 1906 (34 Statutes at Large).

Joint resolution amending joint resolution instructing the Interstate Commerce Commission to make examinations into the subject of railroad discriminations and monopolies, and report on the same from time to time, approved March 7, 1906, approved March 21, 1906 (34 Statutes at Large).

An act concerning carriers engaged in interstate commerce and their employees, approved June 1, 1898 (30 Statutes at Large, 424).

An act to promote the security of travel upon railroads engaged in interstate commerce, and to encourage the saving of life, approved February 23, 1905 (33 Statutes at Large, 743), and regulations prescribed thereunder.

THE ACT TO REGULATE COMMERCE.

Be it enacted by the Senate and House of Representatives of the United States of America in Congress assembled, SEC. *1.* (*As amended June 29, 1906.*) That the provisions of this Act shall apply to any corporation or any person or persons engaged in the transportation of oil or other commodity, except water and except natural or artificial gas, by means of pipe lines, or partly by pipe lines and partly by railroad, or partly by pipe lines and partly by water, who shall be considered and held to be common carriers within the meaning and purpose of this Act, and to any common carrier or carriers engaged in the transportation of passengers or property wholly by railroad (or partly by railroad and partly by water when both are used under a common control, management, or arrangement for a continuous carriage or shipment), from one State or Territory of the United States, or the District of Columbia, to any other State or Territory of the United States, or the District of Columbia, or from one place in a Territory to another place in the same Territory, or from any place in the United States to an adjacent foreign country, or from any place in the United States through a foreign country to any other place in the United States, and also to the transportation in like manner of property shipped from any place in the United States to a foreign country and carried from such place to a port of trans-shipment, or shipped from a foreign country to any place in the United States and carried to such place from a port of entry either in the United States or an adjacent foreign country: *Provided, however,* That the provisions of this Act shall not apply to the transportation of passengers or property, or to the receiving, delivering, storage, or handling of property wholly within one State and not shipped to or from a foreign country from or to any State or Territory as aforesaid.

Carriers an transportatio subject to th act.

Act does no apply to tran portation wholl within on State.

Express companies and sleeping car companies included.

The term " common carrier " as used in this Act shall include express companies and sleeping car companies. The term " railroad," as used in this Act, shall include all bridges and ferries used or operated in connection with any railroad, and also all the road in use by any corporation operating a railroad, whether owned or operated under a contract, agreement, or lease, and shall also include all switches, spurs, tracks, and terminal facilities

What the terms " railroad " and " transportation " include.

of every kind used or necessary in the transportation of the persons or property designated herein, and also all freight depots, yards, and grounds used or necessary in the transportation or delivery of any of said property; and the term " transportation " shall include cars and other vehicles and all instrumentalities and facilities of shipment or carriage, irrespective of ownership or of any contract, express or implied, for the use thereof and all services in connection with the receipt, delivery, elevation, and transfer in transit, ventilation, refrigeration or icing, storage, and handling of property transported; and it shall be the duty of every carrier subject to the provisions of this Act to provide and furnish such transportation upon reasonable request therefor, and to establish through routes and just and reasonable rates applicable thereto.

Charges must be just and reasonable.

All charges made for any service rendered or to be rendered in the transportation of passengers or property as aforesaid, or in connection therewith, shall be just and reasonable; and every unjust and unreasonable charge for such service or any part thereof is prohibited and declared to be unlawful.

Free passes and free transportation prohibited.

No common carrier subject to the provisions of this Act shall, after January first, nineteen hundred and seven, directly or indirectly, issue or give any interstate free ticket, free pass, or free transportation for passengers, except to its employees and their families, its officers, agents, surgeons, physicians, and attorneys at law; to ministers of religion, traveling secretaries of railroad Young Men's Christian Associations, inmates of hospitals and charitable and eleemosynary institutions, and persons exclusively engaged in charitable and eleemosynary work; to indigent, destitute and homeless persons, and to such persons when transported by charitable societies or hospitals, and the necessary agents employed in such transportation; to inmates of the National Homes or State Homes for Disabled Volunteer Soldiers, and of Soldiers' and Sailors' Homes, including those about to enter and those returning home after discharge and boards of managers of such Homes; to necessary care takers of live stock, poultry, and fruit; to employees on sleeping cars, express cars, and to linemen of telegraph and telephone companies; to Railway Mail Service employees, post-office inspectors, customs inspectors and immigration inspectors; to newsboys on trains, baggage agents, witnesses attending any legal investigation in which the common carrier is interested, persons injured in wrecks and physicians and nurses attending such persons: *Provided,* That this provision shall not be construed to prohibit the interchange of passes for the officers, agents, and employees of common carriers, and their families; nor to prohibit any common carrier from carrying passengers free with the object of providing relief in cases of general epidemic, pestilence, or other calamitous visitation. Any common carrier violating this provision shall be deemed guilty of a misdemeanor and for each offense, on conviction, shall pay to the United States a penalty of not less than one hundred dollars nor more than two thousand dollars, and any person, other than the persons excepted in this provision, who uses any such interstate free ticket, free pass, or free transportation, shall be subject to a like penalty. Jurisdiction of offenses under this provision shall be the same as that provided for offenses in an Act entitled "An Act to further regulate commerce with foreign nations and among the States," approved February nineteenth, nineteen hundred and three, and any amendment thereof. (*See section 22.*)

From and after May first, nineteen hundred and eight, it shall be unlawful for any railroad company to transport from any State, Territory, or the District of Columbia, to any other State, Territory, or the District of Columbia, or to any foreign country, any article or commodity, other than timber and the manufactured products thereof, manufactured, mined, or produced by it, or under its authority, or which it may own in whole, or in part, or in which it may have any interest direct or indirect except such articles or commodities as may be necessary and intended for its use in the conduct of its business as a common carrier.

Any common carrier subject to the provisions of this Act, upon application of any lateral, branch line of railroad, or of any shipper tendering interstate traffic for transportation, shall construct, maintain, and operate upon reasonable terms a switch connection with any such lateral, branch line of railroad, or private side track which may be constructed to connect with its railroad, where such connection is reasonably practicable and can be put in with safety and will furnish sufficient business to justify the construction and maintenance of the same; and shall furnish cars for the movement of such traffic to the best of its ability without discrimination in favor of or against any such shipper. If any common carrier shall fail to install and operate any such switch or connection as aforesaid, on application therefor in writing by any shipper, such shipper may make complaint to the Commission, as provided in section thirteen of this Act, and the Commission shall bear and investigate the same and shall determine as to the safety and practicability thereof and justification and reasonable compensation therefor and the Commission may make an order, as provided in section fifteen of this Act, directing the common carrier to comply with the provisions of this section in accordance with such order, and such order shall be enforced as hereinafter provided for the enforcement of all other orders by the Commission, other than orders for the payment of money.

witch connec-
ns.

Switch connec-
ns may be or-
red by the
mmission.

SEC. 2. That if any common carrier subject to the provisions of this Act shall, directly or indirectly, by any special rate, rebate, drawback, or other device, charge, demand, collect, or receive from any person or persons a greater or less compensation for any service rendered, or to be rendered, in the transportation of passengers or property, subject to the provisions of this Act, than it charges, demands, collects, or receives from any other person or persons for doing for him or them a like and contemporaneous service in the transportation of a like kind of traffic under substantially similar circumstances and conditions, such common carrier shall be deemed guilty of unjust discrimination, which is hereby prohibited and declared to be unlawful. *Unjust discrimination defined and forbidden.*

SEC. 3. That it shall be unlawful for any common carrier subject to the provisions of this Act to make or give any undue or unreasonable preference or advantage to any particular person, company, firm, corporation, or locality, or any particular description of traffic, in any respect whatsoever, or to subject any particular person, company, firm, corporation, or locality, or any particular description of traffic, to any undue or unreasonable prejudice or disadvantage in any respect whatsoever. *Undue or unreasonable preference or advantage forbidden.*

Every common carrier subject to the provisions of this Act shall, according to their respective powers, afford all reasonable, proper, and equal facilities for the interchange of traffic between their respective lines, and for the receiving, forwarding, and delivering of passengers and property to and from their several lines and those connecting therewith, and shall not discriminate in their rates and charges between such connecting lines; but this shall not be construed as requiring any such common carrier to give the use of its tracks or terminal facilities to another carrier engaged in like business. *Facilities for interchange of traffic.* *Discrimination between connecting lines forbidden.*

SEC. 4. That it shall be unlawful for any common carrier subject to the provisions of this Act to charge or receive any greater compensation in the aggregate for the transportation of passengers or of like kind of property,

44

under substantially similar circumstances and conditions, for a shorter than for a longer distance over the same line, in the same direction, the shorter being included within the longer distance; but this shall not be construed as authorizing any common carrier within the terms of this Act to charge and receive as great compensation for a shorter as for a longer distance: *Provided, however,* That

Commission
has authority to
relieve carriers
from the opera-
tion of this sec-
tion. upon application to the Commission appointed under the provisions of this Act, such common carrier may, in special cases, after investigation by the Commission, be authorized to charge less for longer than for shorter distances for the transportaton of passengers or property; and the Commission may from time to time prescribe the extent to which such designated common carrier may be relieved from the operation of this section of this Act.

SEC. 5. That it shall be unlawful for any common carrier subject to the provisions of this Act to enter into any contract, agreement, or combination with any other com-

Pooling of
freights and di-
vision of earn-
ings forbidden. mon carrier or carriers for the pooling of freights of different and competing railroads, or to divide between them the aggregate or net proceeds of the earnings of such railroads, or any portion thereof; and in any case of an agreement for the pooling of freights as aforesaid, each day of its continuance shall be deemed a separate offense.

SEC. 6. (*Amended March 2, 1889. Following section substituted June 29, 1906.*) That every common carrier subject to the provisions of this Act shall file with the Commission created by this Act and print and keep open to public inspection schedules showing all the rates, fares, and charges for transportation between different points on its own route and between points on its own route and points on the route of any other carrier by railroad, by

Printing and
posting of sched-
ules of rates,
fares and charges
including rules
and regulations
affecting the
same, icing, stor-
age, and termi-
nal charges, and
freight classifi-
cations. pipe line, or by water when a through route and joint rate have been established. If no joint rate over the through route has been established, the several carriers in such through route shall file, print, and keep open to public inspection, as aforesaid, the separately established rates, fares and charges applied to the through transportation.

The schedules printed as aforesaid by any such common carrier shall plainly state the places between which prop. erty and passengers will be carried, and shall contain the classification of freight in force, and shall also state sepa. rately all terminal charges, storage charges, icing charges, and all other charges which the Commission may require, all privileges or facilities granted or allowed and any rules or regulations which in any wise change, affect, or determine any part or the aggregate of such aforesaid rates, fares, and charges, or the value of the service ren. dered to the passenger, shipper, or consignee. Such schedules shall be plainly printed in large type, and copies for the use of the public shall be kept posted in two public and conspicuous places in every depot, station, or office of such carrier where passengers or freight, respectively, are received for transportation, in such form that they shall be accessible to the public and can be conveniently inspected. The provisions of this section shall apply to all traffic, transportation, and facilities defined in this Act.

Any common carrier subject to the provisions of this Act receiving freight in the United States to be carried through a foreign country to any place in the United States shall also in like manner print and keep open to public inspection, at every depot or office where such freight is received for shipment, schedules showing the through rates established and charged by such common carrier to all points in the United States beyond the foreign country to which it accepts freight for shipment; and any freight shipped from the United States through a foreign country into the United States the through rate on which shall not have been made public, as required by this Act, shall, before it is admitted into the United States from said foreign country, be subject to customs duties as if said freight were of foreign production. *Printing and posting of schedules of rates on freight carried through a foreign country.* *Freight subject to customs duties in case of failure to publish through rates.*

No change shall be made in the rates, fares, and charges or joint rates, fares, and charges which have been filed and published by any common carrier in compliance with the requirements of this section, except after thirty days' *Thirty days' public notice of change in rates must be given.*

notice to the Commission and to the public published as aforesaid, which shall plainly state the changes proposed to be made in the schedule then in force and the time when the changed rates, fares, or charges will go into effect; and the proposed changes shall be shown by printing new schedules, or shall be plainly indicated upon the schedules in force at the time and kept open to public inspection : *Provided,* That the Commission may, in its discretion and for good cause shown, allow changes upon

Commission may modify requirements of this section. less than the notice herein specified, or modify the requirements of this section in respect to publishing, posting, and filing of tariffs, either in particular instances or by a general order applicable to special or peculiar circumstances or conditions.

Joint tariffs must specify names of carriers participating. Evidence of concurrence. The names of the several carriers which are parties to any joint tariff shall be specified therein, and each of the parties thereto, other than the one filing the same, shall file with the Commission such evidence of concurrence therein or acceptance thereof as may be required or approved by the Commission, and where such evidence of concurrence or acceptance is filed it shall not be necessary for the carriers filing the same to also file copies of the tariffs in which they are named as parties.

Copies of contracts, agreements or arrangements relating to traffic must be filed with Commission. Every common carrier subject to this Act shall also file with said Commission copies of all contracts, agreements, or arrangements with other common carriers in relation to any traffic affected by the provisions of this Act to which it may be a party.

Commission may prescribe forms of schedules. The Commission may determine and prescribe the form in which the schedules required by this section to be kept open to public inspection shall be prepared and arranged and may change the form from time to time as shall be found expedient.

No carrier shall engage in transportation unless it files and publishes rates, fares, and charges thereon. No carrier, unless otherwise provided by this Act, shall engage or participate in the transportation of passengers or property, as defined in this Act, unless the rates, fares, and charges upon which the same are transported by said carrier have been filed and published in accordance with the provisions of this Act; nor shall any carrier charge or demand or collect or receive a greater or less or different compensation for such transportation of passengers or property, or for any service in connection therewith, between the points named in such tariffs than the rates, fares, and charges which are specified in the tariff filed and in effect at the time; nor shall any carrier refund or remit in any manner or by any device any portion of the rates, fares, and charges so specified, nor extend to any shipper or person any privileges or facilities in the transportation of passengers or property, except such as are specified in such tariffs: *Provided,* That wherever the word "carrier" occurs in this Act it shall be held to mean "common carrier." *Published rates not to be deviated from.*

"Carrier" means "common carrier."

That in time of war or threatened war preference and precedence shall, upon the demand of the President of the United States, be given, over all other traffic, to the transportation of troops and material of war, and carriers shall adopt every means within their control to facilitate and expedite the military traffic. *Preference and expedition of military traffic in time of war.*

SEC. 7. That it shall be unlawful for any common carrier subject to the provisions of this Act to enter into any combination, contract, or agreement, expressed or implied, to prevent, by change of time schedule, carriage in different cars, or by other means or devices, the carriage of freights from being continuous from the place of shipment to the place of destination; and no break of bulk, stoppage, or interruption made by such common carrier shall prevent the carriage of freights from being and being treated as one continuous carriage from the place of shipment to the place of destination, unless such break, stoppage, or interruption was made in good faith for some necessary purpose, and without any intent to avoid or unnecessarily interrupt such continuous carriage or to evade any of the provisions of this Act. *Continuous carriage of freights from place of shipment to place of destination.*

SEC. 8. That in case any common carrier subject to the provisions of this Act shall do, cause to be done, or permit to be done any act, matter, or thing in this Act prohibited or declared to be unlawful, or shall omit to do any Act, matter, or thing in this Act required to be done, such

Liability of common carriers for damages. common carrier shall be liable to the person or persons injured thereby for the full amount of damages sustained in consequence of any such violation of the provisions of this Act, together with a reasonable counsel or attorney's fee, to be fixed by the court in every case of recovery, which attorney's fee shall be taxed and collected as part of the costs in the case.

Persons claiming to be damaged may elect whether to complain to the Commission or bring suit in a United States court. SEC. 9. That any person or persons claiming to be damaged by any common carrier subject to the provisions of this Act may either make complaint to the Commission as hereinafter provided for, or may bring suit in his or their own behalf for the recovery of the damages for which such common carrier may be liable under the provisions of this Act, in any district or circuit court of the United States of competent jurisdiction; but such person or persons shall not have the right to pursue both of said remedies, and must in each case elect which one of the two methods of procedure herein provided for he or they will adopt. In any such action brought for the recovery of damages the Officers of defendant may be compelled to testify. court before which the same shall be pending may compel any director, officer, receiver, trustee, or agent of the corporation or company defendant in such suit to attend, appear, and testify in such case, and may compel the production of the books and papers of such corporation or company party to any such suit; the claim that any such testimony or evidence may tend to criminate the person giving such evidence shall not excuse such witness from testifying, but such evidence or testimony shall not be used against such person on the trial of any criminal proceeding.

Penalties for violations of Act by carriers, or when the carrier is a corporation, its officers, agents, or employés: Fine and imprisonment. SEC. 10. (*As amended March 2, 1889.*) That any common carrier subject to the provisions of this Act, or, whenever such common carrier is a corporation, any director or officer thereof, or any receiver, trustee, lessee, agent, or person, acting for or employed by such corporation, who, alone or with any other corporation, company, person, or party, shall willfully do or cause to be done, or shall willingly suffer or permit to be done, any act, matter, or thing in this Act prohibited or declared to be unlawful, or who shall aid or abet therein, or shall willfully omit or fail to do any act, matter, or thing in this Act required to be done, or shall cause or willingly suffer or permit any act, matter, or thing so directed or required by this Act to be done not to be so done, or shall aid or abet any such omission or failure, or shall be guilty of any infraction of this Act, or shall aid or abet therein, shall be deemed guilty of a misdemeanor, and shall, upon conviction thereof in any district court of the United States within the jurisdiction of which such offense was committed, be subject to a fine of not to exceed five thousand dollars for each offense: *Provided,* That if the offense for which any person shall be convicted as aforesaid shall be an un-lawful discrimination in rates, fares, or charges, for the transportation of passengers or property, such person shall, in addition to the fine hereinbefore provided for, be liable to imprisonment in the penitentiary for a term of not exceeding two years, or both such fine and imprison-ment, in the discretion of the court.

Any common carrier subject to the provisions of this Act, or, whenever such common carrier is a corporation, any officer or agent thereof, or any person acting for or employed by such corporation, who, by means of false billing, false classification, false weighing, or false report of weight, or by any other device or means, shall know-ingly and willfully assist, or shall willingly suffer or per-mit, any person or persons to obtain transportation for property at less than the regular rates then established and in force on the line of transportation of such common carrier, shall be deemed guilty of a misdemeanor, and shall, upon conviction thereof in any court of the United States of competent jurisdiction within the district in which such offense was committed, be subject to a fine of not exceeding five thousand dollars, or imprisonment in the penitentiary for a term of not exceeding two years, or both, in the discretion of the court, for each offense. *Penalties for false billing, etc., by carriers, their officers or agents: Fine and imprisonment.*

Any person and any officer or agent of any corporation or company who shall deliver property for transportation *Penalties for false billing, etc., by shippers and other per-sons: Fine and imprisonment.*

to any common carrier, subject to the provisions of this
Act, or for whom as consignor or consignee any such carrier shall transport property, who shall knowingly and
wilfully, by false billing, false classification, false weighing, false representation of the contents of the package,
or false report of weight, or by any other device or means,
whether with or without the consent or connivance of the
carrier, its agent or agents, obtain transportation for such
property at less than the regular rates then established
and in force on the line of transportation, shall be deemed
guilty of fraud, which is hereby declared to be a misdemeanor, and shall, upon conviction thereof in any court
of the United States of competent jurisdiction within the
district in which such offense was committed, be subject
for each offense to a fine of not exceeding five thousand
dollars or imprisonment in the penitentiary for a term of
not exceeding two years, or both, in the discretion of the
court.

Penalties for inducing common carriers to discriminate unjustly: Fine and imprisonment. Joint liability with carrier for damages. If any such person, or any officer or agent of any such
corporation or company, shall, by payment of money or
other thing of value, solicitation, or otherwise, induce any
common carrier subject to the provisions of this Act, or
any of its officers or agents, to discriminate unjustly in
his, its, or their favor as against any other consignor or
consignee in the transportation of property, or shall aid
or abet any common carrier in any such unjust discrimination, such person or such officer or agent of such corporation or company shall be deemed guilty of a misdemeanor,
and shall, upon conviction thereof in any court of the
United States of competent jurisdiction within the district in which such offense was committed, be subject to a
fine of not exceeding five thousand dollars, or imprisonment in the penitentiary for a term of not exceeding two
years, or both, in the discretion of the court, for each
offense; and such person, corporation, or company shall
also, together with said common carrier, be liable, jointly
or severally, in an action on the case to be brought by any
consignor or consignee discriminated against in any court

of the United States of competent jurisdiction for all damages caused by or resulting therefrom.

SEC. 11. That a Commission is hereby created and established to be known as the Interstate Commerce Commission, which shall be composed of five Commissioners, who shall be appointed by the President, by and with the advice and consent of the Senate. The Commissioners first appointed under this Act shall continue in office for the term of two, three, four, five, and six years, respectively, from the first day of January, Anno Domini eighteen hundred and eighty-seven, the term of each to be designated by the President; but their successors shall be appointed for terms of six years, except that any person chosen to fill a vacancy shall be appointed only for the unexpired time of the Commissioner whom he shall succeed. Any Commissioner may be removed by the President for inefficiency, neglect of duty, or malfeasance in office. Not more than three of the Commissioners shall be appointed from the same political party. No person in the employ of or holding any official relation to any common carrier subject to the provisions of this act, or owning stock or bonds thereof, or who is in any manner pecuniarily interested therein, shall enter upon the duties of or hold such office. Said Commissioners shall not engage in any other business, vocation, or employment. No vacancy in the Commission shall impair the right of the remaining Commissioners to exercise all the powers of the Commission. (*See section 24, enlarging Commission and increasing salaries.*)

Interstate Commerce Commissioners—how appointed.

Terms of Commissioners.

SEC. 12. (*As amended March 2, 1889, and February 10, 1891.*) That the Commission hereby created shall have authority to inquire into the management of the business of all common carriers subject to the provisions of this Act, and shall keep itself informed as to the manner and method in which the same is conducted, and shall have the right to obtain from such common carriers full and complete information necessary to enable the Commission to perform the duties and carry out the objects for which

Power and duty of Commission to inquire into business of carriers and keep itself informed in regard thereto

Commission required to execute and enforce provisions of this act.

it was created; and the Commission is hereby authorized and required to execute and enforce the provisions of this Act; and, upon the request of the Commission, it shall be

the duty of any district attorney of the United States to whom the Commission may apply to institute in the proper court and to prosecute under the direction of the Attorney-General of the United States all necessary proceedings for the enforcement of the provisions of this Act and for the punishment of all violations thereof, and the

costs and expenses of such prosecution shall be paid out of the appropriation for the expenses of the courts of the United States; and for the purposes of this Act the Com-

mission shall have power to require, by subpœna, the attendance and testimoney of witnesses and the production of all books, papers, tariffs, contracts, agreements, and documents relating to any matter under investigation.

Such attendance of witnesses, and the production of such documentary evidence, may be required from any place in the United States, at any designated place of hearing. And in case of disobedience to a subpœna the Commission, or any party to a proceeding before the Commission, may invoke the aid of any court of the United States in requiring the attendance and testimony of witnesses and the production of books, papers, and documents under the provisions of this section.

And any of the circuit courts of the United States within the jurisdiction of which such inquiry is carried on may, in case of contumacy or refusal to obey a subpœna issued to any common carrier subject to the provisions of this Act, or other person, issue an order requiring such common carrier or other person to appear before said Commission (and produce books and papers if so ordered) and give evidence touching the matter in question; and any failure to obey such order of the court may be punished by such court as a contempt thereof.

The claim that any such testimony or evidence may tend to criminate the person giving such evidence shall not excuse such witness from testifying; but such evidence or testimony shall not be used against such person on the trial of any criminal proceeding.

The testimony of any witness may be taken, at the instance of a party in any proceeding or investigation depending before the Commission, by deposition, at any time after a cause or proceeding is at issue on petition and answer. The Commission may also order testimony to be taken by deposition in any proceeding or investigation pending before it, at any stage of such proceeding or investigation. Such depositions may be taken before any judge of any court of the United States, or any commissioner of a circuit, or any clerk of a district or circuit court, or any chancellor, justice, or judge of a supreme or superior court, mayor or chief magistrate of a city, judge of a county court, or court of common pleas of any of the United States, or any notary public, not being of counsel or attorney to either of the parties, nor interested in the event of the proceeding or investigation. Reasonable notice must first be given in writing by the party, or his attorney, proposing to take such deposition to the opposite party or his attorney of record, as either may be nearest, which notice shall state the name of the witness and the time and place of the taking of his deposition. Any person may be compelled to appear and depose, and to produce documentary evidence, in the same manner as witnesses may be compelled to appear and testify and produce documentary evidence before the Commission as hereinbefore provided.

Every person deposing as herein provided shall be cautioned and sworn (or affirm, if he so request) to testify the whole truth, and shall be carefully examined. His testimony shall be reduced to writing by the magistrate taking the deposition, or under his direction, and shall, after it has been reduced to writing, be subscribed by the deponent.

If a witness whose testimony may be desired to be taken by deposition be in a foreign country, the deposition may be taken before an officer or person designated by the

Marginal notes:

Testimony may be taken by deposition.

Commission may order testimony to be taken by deposition.

Reasonable notice must be given.

Testimony by deposition may be compelled in the same manner as above specified.

Manner of taking depositions.

When witness is in a foreign country.

Commission, or agreed upon by the parties by stipulation in writing to be filed with the Commission. All depositions must be promptly filed with the Commission.

Witnesses whose depositions are taken pursuant to this Act, and the magistrate or other officer taking the same, shall severally be entitled to the same fees as are paid for like services in the courts of the United States.

SEC. 13. That any person, firm, corporation, or association, or any mercantile, agricultural, or manufacturing society, or any body politic or municipal organization complaining of any thing done or omitted to be done by any common carrier subject to the provisions of this Act in contravention of the provisions thereof, may apply to said Commission by petition, which shall briefly state the facts; whereupon a statement of the charges thus made shall be forwarded by the Commission to such common carrier, who shall be called upon to satisfy the complaint or to answer the same in writing within a reasonable time, to be specified by the Commission. If such common carrier, within the time specified, shall make reparation for the injury alleged to have been done, said carrier shall be relieved of liability to the complainant only for the particular violation of law thus complained of. If such carrier shall not satisfy the complaint within the time specified, or there shall appear to be any reasonable ground for investigating said complaint, it shall be the duty of the Commission to investigate the matters complained of in such manner and by such means as it shall deem proper.

Said Commission shall in like manner investigate any complaint forwarded by the railroad commissioner or railroad commission of any State or Territory, at the request of such commissioner or commission, and may institute any inquiry on its own motion in the same manner and to the same effect as though complaint had been made.

No complaint shall at any time be dismissed because of the absence of direct damage to the complainant.

SEC. 14. (*Amended March 2, 1889, and June 29, 1906.*) That whenever an investigation shall be made by said Commission, it shall be its duty to make a report in writing in respect thereto, which shall state the conclusions of the Commission, together with its decision, order, or requirement in the premises; and in case damages are awarded such report shall include the findings of fact on which the award is made.

Commission must make report of investigations, stating its conclusions and order.

Reparation.

All reports of investigations made by the Commission shall be entered of record, and a copy thereof shall be furnished to the party who may have complained, and to any common carrier that may have been complained of.

Reports of investigations must be entered of record. Service of copies on parties.

The Commission may provide for the publication of its reports and decisions in such form and manner as may be best adapted for public information and use, and such authorized publications shall be competent evidence of the reports and decisions of the Commission therein contained in all courts of the United States and of the several States without any further proof or authentication thereof. The Commission may also cause to be printed for early distribution its annual reports.

Reports and decisions. Authorized publication competent evidence.

Publication and distribution of annual reports of Commission.

SEC. 15. (*As amended June 29, 1906.*) That the Commission is authorized and empowered, and it shall be its duty, whenever, after full hearing upon a complaint made as provided in section thirteen of this Act, or upon complaint of any common carrier, it shall be of the opinion that any of the rates, or charges whatsoever, demanded, charged, or collected by any common carrier or carriers, subject to the provisions of this Act, for the transportation of persons or property as defined in the first section of this Act, or that any regulations or practices whatsoever of such carrier or carriers affecting such rates, are unjust or unreasonable, or unjustly discriminatory, or unduly preferential or prejudicial, or otherwise in violation of any of the provisions of this Act, to determine and prescribe what will be the just and reasonable rate or rates, charge or charges, to be thereafter observed in such case as the maximum to be charged; and what regulation

Commission may determine and prescribe just and reasonable rates to be observed as maximum charges.

Commission may determine and prescribe just and reasonable regulations or practices. Commission may order carriers to cease and desist from full extent of violations found. Orders of the Commission effective as prescribed, but in not less than thirty days.

or practice in respect to such transportation is just, fair and reasonable to be thereafter followed; and to make an order that the carrier shall cease and desist from such violation, to the extent to which the Commission find the same to exist, and shall not thereafter publish, demand, or collect any rate or charge for such transportation in excess of the maximum rate or charge so prescribed, and shall conform to the regulation or practice so prescribed. All orders of the Commission, except orders for the payment of money, shall take effect within such reasonable time, not less than thirty days, and shall continue in force

Orders shall continue in force not exceeding two years, unless suspended or set aside by Commission or court.

When Carriers fail to agree on divisions of joint rate Commission may prescribe Proportion of such rate to be received by each carrier.

for such period of time, not exceeding two years, as shall be prescribed in the order of the Commission, unless the same shall be suspended or modified or set aside by the Commission or be suspended or set aside by a court of competent jurisdiction. Whenever the carrier or carriers, in obedience to such order of the Commission or otherwise, in respect to joint rates, fares, or charges, shall fail to agree among themselves upon the apportionment or division thereof, the Commission may after hearing make a supplemental order prescribing the just and reasonable proportion of such joint rate to be received by each carrier party thereto, which order shall take effect as a part of the original order.

Commission may establish through routes and joint rates.

The Commission may also, after hearing on a complaint, establish through routes and joint rates as the maximum to be charged and prescribe the division of such rates as hereinbefore provided, and the terms and conditions under which such through routes shall be operated, when that may be necessary to give effect to any provision of this Act, and the carriers complained of have refused or neglected to voluntarily establish such through routes and joint rates, provided no reasonable or satisfactory through route exists, and this provision shall apply when one of the connecting carriers is a water line.

If the owner of property transported under this Act directly or indirectly renders any service connected with such transportation, or furnishes any instrumentality used therein, the charge and allowance therefor shall be no more than is just and reasonable, and the Commission may, after hearing on a complaint, determine what is a reasonable charge as the maximum to be paid by the carrier or carriers for the service so rendered or for the use of the instumentality so furnished, and fix the same by appropriate order, which order shall have the same force and effect and be enforced in like manner as the orders above provided for in this section.

Commission may determine just and reasonable charge or allowance for service rendered by owner of property transported or for any instrumentality furnished by such owner and used in such transportation.

The foregoing enumeration of powers shall not exclude any power which the Commission would otherwise have in the making of an order under the provisions of this Act.

Enumeration of powers in this section not exclusive.

SEC. 16. (*Amended March 2, 1889. Following section substituted June 29, 1906.*) That if, after hearing on a complaint made as provided in section thirteen of this Act, the Commission shall determine that any party complainant is entitled to an award of damages under the provisions of this Act for a violation thereof, the Commission shall make an order directing the carrier to pay to the complainant the sum to which he is entitled on or before a day named.

Award of damages by Commission.

If a carrier does not comply with an order for the payment of money within the time limit in such order, the complainant, or any person for whose benefit such order was made, may file in the circuit court of the United States for the district in which he resides or in which is located the principal operating office of the carrier, or through which the road of the carrier runs, a petition setting forth briefly the causes for which he claims damages, and the order of the Commission in the premises. Such suit shall proceed in all respects like other civil suits for damages, except that on the trial of such suit the findings and order of the Commission shall be prima facie evidence of the facts therein stated, and except that the petitioner shall not be liable for costs in the circuit court nor for costs at any subsequent stage of the proceedings unless they accrue upon his appeal. If the petitioner shall finally prevail he shall be allowed a reasonable attorney's

Petition to United States court in case carrier does not comply with order for payment of money.

Findings of fact of Commission shall be prima facie evidence in reparation cases.

Petitioner not liable for costs in circuit court.

Petitioner's attorney's fees. fee, to be taxed and collected as a part of the costs of th suit. All complaints for the recovery of damages shall b

Limitation upon action. filed with the Commission within two years from the tim the cause of action accrues, and not after, and a petitior for the enforcement of an order for the payment of money shall be filed in the circuit court within one year from the date of the order, and not after: *Provided,* That claims

Accrued claims. accrued prior to the passage of this Act may be presented within one year.

In such suits all parties in whose favor the Commission may have made an award for damages by a single order

Joint plaintiffs may sue joint defendants in courts on awards of damages. may be joined as plaintiffs, and all of the carriers parties to such order awarding such damages may be joined as defendants, and such suit may be maintained by such joint plaintiffs and against such joint defendants in any district where any one of such joint plaintiffs could maintain such suit against any one of such joint defendants;

Service of process. and service of process against any one of such defendants as may not be found in the district where the suit is brought may be made in any district where such de fendant carrier has its principal operating office. In case of such joint suit the recovery, if any, may be by judgment in favor of any one of such plaintiffs, against the de fendant found to be liable to such plaintiff.

Every order of the Commission shall be forthwith

Service of order of Commission by mailing. served by mailing to any one of the principal officers or agents of the carrier at his usual place of business a copy thereof; and the registry mail receipt shall be prima faci evidence of the receipt of such order by the carrier in du course of mail.

Commission may suspend or modify order. The Commission shall be authorized to suspend o modify its orders upon such notice and in such manne as it shall deem proper.

Carriers, their agents and employees, must comply with such orders. It shall be the duty of every common carrier, its agent and employees, to observe and comply with such order so long as the same shall remain in effect.

Any carrier, any officer, representative, or agent of carrier, or any receiver, trustee, lessee, or agent of eithe of them, who knowingly fails or neglects to obey any order made under the provisions of section fifteen of this Act shall forfeit to the United States the sum of five thousand dollars for each offense. Every distinct violation shall be a separate offense, and in case of a continuing violation each day shall be deemed a separate offense.

Punishment by forfeiture for refusal to obey order of Commission under section 15.

The forfeiture provided for in this Act shall be payable into the Treasury of the United States, and shall be recoverable in a civil suit in the name of the United States, brought in the district where the carrier has its principal operating office, or in any district through which the road of the carrier runs.

Forfeiture payable into Treasury and recoverable in civil suit.

It shall be the duty of the various district attorneys, under the direction of the Attorney-General of the United States, to prosecute for the recovery of forfeitures. The costs and expenses of such prosecution shall be paid out of the appropriation for the expenses of the courts of the United States. The Commission may, with the consent of the Attorney-General, employ special counsel in any proceeding under this Act, paying the expenses of such employment out of its own appropriation.

Duty of district attorneys to prosecute.

Costs and expenses to be paid out of appropriation for court expenses.

Commission may employ special counsel.

If any carrier fails or neglects to obey any order of the Commission, other than for the payment of money, while the same is in effect, any party injured thereby, or the Commission in its own name, may apply to the circuit court in the district where such carrier has its principal operating office, or in which the violation or disobedience of such order shall happen, for an enforcement of such order. Such application shall be by petition, which shall state the substance of the order and the respect in which the carrier has failed of obedience, and shall be served upon the carrier in such manner as the court may direct, and the court shall prosecute such inquiries and make such investigations, through such means as it shall deem needful in the ascertainment of the facts at issue or which may arise upon the hearing of such petition. If, upon such hearing as the court may determine to be necessary, it appears that the order was regularly made and duly

Petition to United States courts in cases of disobedience to order of Commission other than for payment of money. Jurisdiction of court.

45

served, and that the carrier is in disobedience of the same,

Court must enforce disobeyed order if regularly made and duly served. the court shall enforce obedience to such order by a writ of injunction, or other proper process, mandatory or otherwise, to restrain such carrier, its officers, agents, or representatives, from further disobedience of such order, or to enjoin upon it, or them, obedience to the same; and in the enforcement of such process the court shall have those powers ordinarily exercised by it in compelling obedience to its writs of injunction and mandamus.

Appeal to Supreme Court of United States. From any action upon such petition an appeal shall lie by either party to the Supreme Court of the United States, and in such court the case shall have priority in hearing and determination over all other causes except criminal causes, but such appeal shall not vacate or suspend the order appealed from.

Venue of suits brought against Commission to enjoin, set aside, annul, or suspend order of Commission. The venue of suits brought in any of the circuit courts of the United States against the Commission to enjoin, set aside, annul, or suspend any order or requirement of the Commission shall be in the district where the carrier against whom such order or requirement may have been made has its principal operating office, and may be brought at any time after such order is promulgated. And if the order or requirement has been made against two or more carriers then in the district where any one of said carriers has its principal operating office, and if the carrier has its principal operating office in the District of Columbia then the venue shall be in the district where said carrier has its principal office; and jurisdiction to hear and determine such suits is hereby vested in such courts. The provisions of "An Act to expedite the hearing and determination of suits in equity, and so forth,"

Provisions of expediting act to apply. approved February eleventh, nineteen hundred and three. shall be, and are hereby, made applicable to all such suits, including the hearing on an application for a preliminary injunction, and are also made applicable to any proceeding in equity to enforce any order or requirement of the Commission, or any of the provisions of the Act to regulate commerce approved February fourth, eighteen hun.

dred and eighty-seven, and all Acts amendatory thereof
or supplemental thereto. It shall be the duty of the
Attorney-General in every such case to file the certificate
provided for in said expediting Act of February eleventh,
nineteen hundred and three, as necessary to the application of the provisions thereof, and upon appeal as therein
authorized to the Supreme Court of the United States,
the case shall have in such court priority in hearing and
determination over all other causes except criminal
causes: *Provided,* That no injunction, interlocutory
order or decree suspending or restraining the enforcement
of an order of the Commission shall be granted except on
hearing after not less than five days' notice to the Commission. An appeal may be taken from any interlocutory
order or decree granting or continuing an injunction in
any suit, but shall lie only to the Supreme Court of the
United States: *Provided further,* That the appeal must
be taken within thirty days from the entry of such order
or decree and it shall take precedence in the appellate
court over all other causes, except causes of like character
and criminal causes.

Appeal to Supreme Court.

Priority of case in Supreme Court.

No injunction or interlocutory order to be granted except after not less than 5 days' notice.

Appeal to Supreme Court from interlocutory order or decree in 30 days.

The copies of schedules and tariffs of rates, fares, and
charges, and of all contracts, agreements, or arrangements
between common carriers filed with the Commission as
herein provided, and the statistics, tables, and figures
contained in the annual reports of carriers made to the
Commission, as required by the provisions of this Act,
shall be preserved as public records in the custody of the
secretary of the Commission, and shall be received as
prima facie evidence of what they purport to be for the
purpose of investigations by the Commission and in all
judicial proceedings; and copies of or extracts from any
of said schedules, tariffs, contracts, agreements, arrangements, or reports made public records as aforesaid, certified by the secretary under its seal, shall be received in
evidence with like effect as the originals.

Rate schedules, contracts, or agreements, and carriers' annual reports filed with Commission and in custody of secretary are public records, receivable in courts and by the Commission as prima facie evidence. Certified copies or extracts therefrom also prima facie evidence.

SEC. 16a. (*Added June 29, 1906.*) That after a decision, order, or requirement has been made by the Com-

mission in any proceeding any party thereto may at any time make application for rehearing of the same, or any matter determined therein, and it shall be lawful for the Commission in its discretion to grant such a rehearing if sufficient reason therefor be made to appear. Applications for rehearing shall be governed by such general rules as the Commission may establish. No such application shall excuse any carrier from complying with or obeying any decision, order, or requirement of the Commission, or operate in any manner to stay or postpone the enforcement thereof, without the special order of the Commission. In case a rehearing is granted the proceedings thereupon shall conform as nearly as may be to the proceedings in an original hearing, except as the Commission may otherwise direct; and if, in its judgment, after such rehearing and the consideration of all facts, including those arising since the former hearing, it shall appear that the original decision, order, or requirement is in any respect unjust or unwarranted, the Commission may reverse, change, or modify the same accordingly. Any decision, order, or requirement made after such rehearing, reversing, changing, or modifying the original determination shall be subject to the same provisions as an original order.

Commission may grant rehearings.

Application for rehearing shall not operate as stay of proceedings, unless so ordered by Commission.

Commission may, on rehearing, reverse, change, or modify order.

SEC. 17. (*As amended March 2, 1889.*) That the Commission may conduct its proceedings in such manner as will best conduce to the proper dispatch of business and to the ends of justice. A majority of the Commission shall constitute a quorum for the transaction of business, but no Commissioner shall participate in any hearing or proceeding in which he has any pecuniary interest. Said Commission may, from time to time, make or amend such general rules or orders as may be requisite for the order and regulation of proceedings before it, including forms of notices and the service thereof, which shall conform, as nearly as may be, to those in use in the courts of the United States. Any party may appear before said Commission and be heard, in person or by attorney. Every

Interstate Commerce Commission. Form of procedure.

Parties may appear before the Commission in person or by attorney.

vote and official act of the Commission shall be entered of record, and its proceedings shall be public upon the request of either party interested. Said Commission shall have an official seal, which shall be judicially noticed. Either of the members of the Commission may administer oaths and affirmations and sign subpœnas.

Official seal.

SEC. 18. (*As amended March 2, 1889.*) [*See Section 24, increasing salaries of Commissioners.*] That each Commissioner shall receive an annual salary of seven thousand five hundred dollars, payable in the same manner as the judges of the courts of the United States. The Commisson shall appoint a secretary, who shall receive an annual salary of three thousand five hundred dollars, payable in like manner. The Commission shall have authority to employ and fix the compensation of such other employees as it may find necessary to the proper performance of its duties. Until otherwise provided by law, the Commission may hire suitable offices for its use, and shall have authority to procure all necessary office supplies. Witnesses summoned before the Commission shall be paid the same fees and mileage that are paid witnesses in the courts of the United States.

Salaries of Commissioners.

Secretary— how appointed; salary.

Employees.

Offices and supplies.

Witnesses' fees.

All of the expenses of the Commission, including all necessary expenses for transportation incurred by the Commissioners, or by their employees under their orders, in making any investigation, or upon official business in any other places than in the city of Washington, shall be allowed and paid on the presentation of itemized vouchers therefor approved by the chairman of the Commission.

Expenses of the Commission —how paid.

SEC. 19. That the principal office of the Commission shall be in the city of Washington, where its general sessions shall be held; but whenever the convenience of the public or the parties may be promoted, or delay or expense prevented thereby, the Commission may hold special sessions in any part of the United States. It may, by one or more of the Commissioners, prosecute any inquiry necessary to its duties, in any part of the United States, into

Principal office of the Commission.

Sessions of the Commission.

Commission may prosecute inquiries by one or more of its members in any part of the United States.

any matter or question of fact pertaining to the business of any common carrier subject to the provisions of this Act.

SEC. 20. (*As amended June 29, 1906.*) That the Commission is hereby authorized to require annual reports from all common carriers subject to the provisions of this Act, and from the owners of all railroads engaged in interstate commerce as defined in this Act; to prescribe the manner in which such reports shall be made, and to require from such carriers specific answers to all questions upon which the Commission may need information. Such annual reports shall show in detail the amount of capital stock issued, the amounts paid therefor, and the manner of payment for the same; the dividends paid, the surplus fund, if any, and the number of stockholders; the funded and floating debts and the interest paid thereon; the cost and value of the carrier's property, franchises, and equipments; the number of employees and the salaries paid each class; the accidents to passengers, employees, and other persons, and the causes thereof; the amounts expended for improvements each year, how expended, and the character of such improvements; the earnings and receipts from each branch of business and from all sources; the operating and other expenses; the balances of profit and loss; and a complete exhibit of the financial operations of the carrier each year, including an annual balance sheet. Such reports shall also contain such information in relation to rates or regulations concerning fares or freights, or agreements, arrangements, or contracts affecting the same as the Commission may require; and the Commission may, in its discretion, for the purpose of enabling it the better to carry out the purposes of this Act, prescribe a period of time within which all common carriers subject to the provisions of this Act shall have, as near as may be, a uniform system of accounts, and the manner in which such accounts shall be kept.

Said detailed reports shall contain all the required statistics for the period of twelve months ending on the

---

Margin notes:

Carriers subject to Act, and owners of railroads engaged in interstate commerce must render full annual reports to Commission; and Commission is authorized to prescribe manner in which reports shall be made and require specific answers to all questions.

What reports of carriers shall contain.

Commission may prescribe uniform system of accounts and manner of keeping accounts.

Annual reports to be filed with Commission by September 30 of each year.

thirtieth day of June in each year, and shall be made out under oath and filed with the Commission, at its office in Washington, on or before the thirtieth day of September then next following, unless additional time be granted in any case by the Commission; and if any carrier, person, or corporation subject to the provisions of this Act shall fail to make and file said annual reports within the time above specified, or within the time extended by the Commission for making and filing the same, or shall fail to make specific answer to any question authorized by the provisions of this section within thirty days from the time it is lawfully required so to do, such parties shall forfeit to the United States the sum of one hundred dollars for each and every day it shall continue to be in default with respect thereto. The Commission shall also have authority to require said carriers to file monthly reports of earnings and expenses or special reports within a specified period, and if any such carrier shall fail to file such reports within the time fixed by the Commission it shall be subject to the forfeitures last above provided.

Said forfeitures shall be recovered in the manner provided for the recovery of forfeitures under the provisions of this Act.

The oath required by this section may be taken before any person authorized to administer an oath by the laws of the State in which the same is taken.

The Commission may, in its discretion, prescribe the forms of any and all accounts, records, and memoranda to be kept by carriers subject to the provisions of this Act, including the accounts, records, and memoranda of the movement of traffic as well as the receipts and expenditures of moneys. The Commission shall at all times have access to all accounts, records, and memoranda kept by carriers subject to this Act, and it shall be unlawful for such carriers to keep any other accounts, records, or memoranda than those prescribed or approved by the Commission, and it may employ special agents or examiners, who shall have authority under the order of the Commis-

Marginal notes:

Commission may grant additional time.

Punishment by forfeiture for failure to file.

Commission may require filing of monthly and special reports.

Punishment by forfeiture for failure to file special reports.

Oath to annual reports, how taken.

Commission may prescribe forms of accounts, records, and memoranda, and have access thereto.

Carrier cannot keep other accounts than those prescribed by Commission.

Commission may employ special examiner to inspect accounts and records.

sion to inspect and examine any and all accounts, records, and memoranda kept by such carriers. This provision shall apply to receivers of carriers and operating trustees.

In case of failure or refusal on the part of any such carrier, receiver, or trustee to keep such accounts, records, and memoranda on the books and in the manner prescribed by the Commission, or to submit such accounts, records, and memoranda as are kept to the inspection of the Commission or any of its authorized agents or examiners, such carrier, receiver, or trustee shall forfeit to the United States the sum of five hundred dollars for each such offense and for each and every day of the continuance of such offense, such forfeitures to be recoverable in the same manner as other forfeitures provided for in this Act.

Any person who shall willfully make any false entry in the accounts of any book of accounts or in any record or memoranda kept by a carrier, or who shall willfully destroy, mutilate, alter, or by any other means or device falsify the record of any such account, record, or memoranda, or who shall willfully neglect or fail to make full, true, and correct entries in such accounts, records, or memoranda of all facts and transactions appertaining to the carrier's business, or shall keep any other accounts, records, or memoranda than those prescribed or approved by the Commission, shall be deemed guilty of a misdemeanor and shall be subject, upon conviction in any court of the United States of competent jurisdiction, to a fine of not less than one thousand dollars nor more than five thousand dollars, or imprisonment for a term not less than one year nor more than three years, or both such fine and imprisonment.

Any examiner who divulges any fact or information which may come to his knowledge during the course of such examination, except in so far as he may be directed by the Commission or by a court or judge thereof, shall be subject, upon conviction in any court of the United States of competent jurisdiction, to a fine of not more than five thousand dollars or imprisonment for a term not exceeding two years, or both.

That the circuit and district courts of the United States shall have jurisdiction, upon the application of the Attorney-General of the United States at the request of the Commission, alleging a failure to comply with or a violation of any of the provisions of said Act to regulate commerce or of any Act supplementary thereto or amendatory thereof by any common carrier, to issue a writ or writs of mandamus commanding such common carrier to comply with the provisions of said Acts, or any of them. *United States courts may issue mandamus to compel compliance with provisions of Act.*

And to carry out and give effect to the provisions of said Acts, or any of them the Commission is hereby authorized to employ special agents or examiners who shall have power to administer oaths, examine witnesses, and receive evidence. *Commission may employ special agents or examiners to administer oaths, examine witnesses, and receive evidence.*

That any common carrier, railroad, or transportation company receiving property for transportation from a point in one State to a point in another State shall issue a receipt or bill of lading therefor and shall be liable to the lawful holder thereof for any loss, damage, or injury to such property caused by it or by any common carrier, railroad, or transportation company to which such property may be delivered or over whose line or lines such property may pass, and no contract, receipt, rule, or regulation shall exempt such common carrier, railroad, or transportation company from the liability hereby imposed: *Provided,* That nothing in this section shall deprive any holder of such receipt or bill of lading of any remedy or right of action which he has under existing law. *Receiving common carrier liable for loss or damage on through shipments carried by it or by any connection, irrespective of contract to contrary.*

Remedies under existing law not barred.

That the common carrier, railroad, or transportation company issuing such receipt or bill of lading shall be entitled to recover from the common carrier, railroad, or transportation company on whose line the loss, damage, or injury shall have been sustained the amount of such loss, damage, or injury as it may be required to pay to the owners of such property, as may be evidenced by any receipt, judgment, or transcript thereof. *Initial carrier may have recourse upon carrier responsible for loss or damage.*

Annual reports of the Commission to Congress. SEC. 21. (*As amended March 2, 1889.*) That the Commission shall, on or before the first day of December in each year, make a report, which shall be transmitted to Congress, and copies of which shall be distributed as are the other reports transmitted to Congress. This report shall contain such information and data collected by the Commission as may be considered of value in the determination of questions connected with the regulation of commerce, together with such recommendations as to additional legislation relating thereto as the Commission may deem necessary; and the names and compensation of the persons employed by said Commission.

Persons and property that may be carried free or at reduced rates. SEC. 22. (*As amended March 2, 1889, and February 8, 1895.*) [*See section 1, 4th par.*] That nothing in this Act shall prevent the carriage, storage, or handling of property free or at reduced rates for the United States, State, or municipal governments, or for charitable purposes, or to or from fairs and expositions for exhibition thereat, or the free carriage of destitute and homeless persons transported by charitable societies, and the necessary agents employed in such transportation, or the issuance Mileage, excursion, or commutation passenger tickets. of mileage, excursion, or commutation passenger tickets; nothing in this Act shall be construed to prohibit any common carrier from giving reduced rates to ministers of religion, or to municipal governments for the transportation of indigent persons or to inmates of the National Homes or State Homes for Disabled Volunteer Soldiers, and of Soldiers' and Sailors' Orphan Homes, including those about to enter and those returning home after discharge, under arrangements with the boards of Passes and free transportation to officers and employees of railroad companies. managers of said homes; nothing in this Act shall be construed to prevent railroads from giving free carriage to their own officers and employees, or to prevent the principal officers of any railroad company or companies from Provisions of act are in addition to remedies existing at common law. Pending litigation not affected by act. exchanging passes or tickets with other railroad companies for their officers and employees; and nothing in this Act contained shall in any way abridge or alter the remedies now existing at common law or by statute, but

the provisions of this Act are in addition to such remedies: *Provided,* That no pending litigation shall in any
way be affected by this Act: *Provided further,* That **Joint inter-**
nothing in this Act shall prevent the issuance of joint **changeable five- thousand-mile tickets. Amount**
interchangeable five-thousand-mile tickets, with special **of free baggage.**
privileges as to the amount of free baggage that may be
carried under mileage tickets of one thousand or more
miles. But before any common carrier, subject to the
provisions of this Act, shall issue any such joint interchangeable mileage tickets with special privileges, as
aforesaid, it shall file with the Interstate Commerce Commission copies of the joint tariffs of rates, fares, or
charges on which such joint interchangeable mileage
tickets are to be based, together with specifications of the
amount of free baggage permitted to be carried under
such tickets, in the same manner as common carriers are
required to do with regard to other joint rates by section
six of this Act; and all the provisions of said section six **Publication of rates.**
relating to joint rates, fares, and charges shall be ob-
served by said common carriers and enforced by the
Interstate Commerce Commission as fully with regard to
such joint interchangeable mileage tickets as with regard
to other joint rates, fares, and charges referred to in said
section six. It shall be unlawful for any common carrier **Sale of tickets.**
that has issued or authorized to be issued any such joint
interchangeable mileage tickets to demand, collect, or
receive from any person or persons a greater or less compensation for transportation of persons or baggage under
such joint interchangeable mileage tickets than that required by the rate, fare, or charge specified in the copies **Penalties.**
of the joint tariff of rates, fares, or charges filed with the
Commission in force at the time. The provisions of
section ten of this Act shall apply to any violation of the
requirements of this proviso.

NEW SECTION. (*Added March 2, 1889.*) [Sec. 23.] **Jurisdiction of United States courts to issue**
That the circuit and district courts of the United States **writs of peremp- tory mandamus commanding the**
shall have jurisdiction upon the relation of any person or **movement of in- terstate traffic or**
persons, firm, or corporation, alleging such violation by a **the furnishing of cars or other**
common carrier, of any of the provisions of the Act to **transportation facilities.**

which this is a supplement and all Acts amendatory thereof, as prevents the relator from having interstate traffic moved by said common carrier at the same rates as are charged, or upon terms or conditions as favorable as those given by said common carrier for like traffic under similar conditions to any other shipper, to issue a writ or writs of mandamus against said common carrier, commanding such common carrier to move and transport the traffic, or to furnish cars or other facilities for transportation for the party applying for the writ: *Provided,* That if any question of fact as to the proper compensation to the common carrier for the service to be enforced by the writ is raised by the pleadings, the writ of peremptory mandamus may issue, notwithstanding such question of fact is undetermined, upon such terms as to security, payment of money into the court, or otherwise, as the court may think proper, pending the determination of the question of fact: *Provided,* That the remedy hereby given by writ of mandamus shall be cumulative, and shall not be held to exclude or interfere with other remedies provided by this Act or the Act to which it is a supplement.

Peremptory mandamus may issue, notwithstanding proper compensation of carrier may be undetermined.

Remedy cumulative, and shall not interfere with other remedies provided by the Act.

SEC. 24. (*Added June 29, 1906.*) That the Interstate Commerce Commission is hereby enlarged so as to consist of seven members with terms of seven years, and each shall receive ten thousand dollars compensation annually. The qualifications of the Commissioners and the manner of the payment of their salaries shall be as already provided by law. Such enlargement of the Commission shall be accomplished through appointment by the President, by and with the advice and consent of the Senate, of two additional Interstate Commerce Commissioners, one for a term expiring December thirty-first, nineteen hundred and eleven, one for a term expiring December thirty-first, nineteen hundred and twelve. The terms of the present Commissioners, or of any successor appointed to fill a vacancy caused by the death or resignation of any of the present Commissioners, shall expire as heretofore provided by

Commission to consist of seven members; terms; salaries.

Qualifications and enlargement of Commission.

law. Their successors and the successors of the additional Commissioners herein provided for shall be appointed for the full term of seven years, except that any person appointed to fill a vacancy shall be appointed only for the unexpired term of the Commissioner whom he shall succeed. Not more than four Commissioners shall be apointed from the same political party.

(*Additional provisions in Act of June 29, 1906.*)

(SEC. 9.) That all existing laws relating to the attendance of witnesses and the production of evidence and the compelling of testimony under the Act to regulate commerce and all Acts amendatory thereof shall apply to any and all proceedings and hearings under this Act. *Existing laws as to attendance of witnesses and production of evidence applicable in proceedings under this Act.*

(SEC. 10.) That all laws and parts of laws in conflict with the provisions of this Act are hereby repealed; but the amendments herein provided for shall not affect causes now pending in courts of the United States, but such causes shall be prosecuted to a conclusion in the manner heretofore provided by law. *Conflicting laws repealed. Amendments not to affect pending causes in court.*

(SEC. 11.) That this act shall take effect and be in force from and after its passage. *When Act effective.*

Joint resolution of June 30, 1906, provides: " That the act entitled 'An act to amend an act entitled "An act to regulate commerce," approved February 4, 1887, and all acts amendatory thereof, and to enlarge the powers of the Interstate Commerc Commission,' shall take effect and be in force sixty days after its approval by the President of the United States." *Time of taking effect extended 60 days (August 28, 1906).*

Public No. 41, approved February 4, 1887, as amended by Public No. 125, approved March 2, 1889, and Public No. 72, approved February 10, 1891. Public No. 38, approved February 8, 1895. Public No. 337, approved June 29, 1906. Public Res., No. 47, approved June 30, 1906.

AN ACT In relation to testimony before the Interstate Commerce Commission, and in cases or proceedings under or connected with an act entitled "An act to regulate commerce," approved February fourth, eighteen hundred and eighty-seven, and amendments thereto.

Be it enacted by the Senate and House of Representatives of the United States of America in Congress assembled, That no person shall be excused from attending and testifying or from producing books, papers, tariffs, contracts, agreements and documents before the Interstate Commerce Commission, or in obedience to the subpœna of the Commission, whether such subpœna be signed or issued by one or more Commissioners, or in any cause or proceeding, criminal or otherwise, based upon or growing out of any alleged violation of the act of Congress, entitled "An act to regulate commerce," approved February fourth, eighteen hundred and eighty-seven, or of any amendment thereof on the ground or for the reason that the testimony or evidence, documentary or otherwise, required of him, may tend to criminate him or subject him to a penalty or forfeiture. But no person shall be prosecuted or subjected to any penalty or forfeiture for or on account of any transaction, matter or thing, concerning which he may testify, or produce evidence, documentary or otherwise, before said Commission, or in obedience to its subpœna, or the subpœna of either of them, or in any such case or proceeding: *Provided,* That no person so testifying shall be exempt from prosecution and punishment for perjury committed in so testifying.

Any person who shall neglect or refuse to attend and testify, or to answer any lawful inquiry, or to produce books, papers, tariffs, contracts, agreements, and documents, if in his power to do so, in obedience to the subpœna or lawful requirement of the Commission, shall be guilty of an offense and upon conviction thereof by a court of competent jurisdiction shall be punished by fine not less than one hundred dollars nor more than five thousand dollars, or by imprisonment for not more than one year or by both such fine and imprisonment.

Public, No. 54, approved February 11, 1893.

Margin notes:

Attendance and testimony of witnesses and production of documentary evidence compulsory before the Commission, and in any case, criminal or otherwise, in the courts.

Immunity to testifying witnesses.

Perjury excepted.

Penalties: Fine or imprisonment, or both.

AN ACT Defining the right of immunity of witnesses under the Act
entitled "An act in relation to testimony before the Interstate
Commerce Commission," and so forth, approved February eleventh,
eighteen hundred and ninety-three, and an act entitled "An act
to establish the Department of Commerce and Labor," approved
February fourteenth, nineteen hundred and three, and an act
entitled "An act to further regulate commerce with foreign nations
and among the States," approved February nineteenth, nineteen
hundred and three, and an act entitled "An act making appropriations for the legislative, executive, and judicial expenses of the
Government for the fiscal year ending June thirtieth, nineteen
hundred and four, and for other purposes," approved February
twenty-fifth, nineteen hundred and three.

Be it enacted by the Senate and House of Representatives of the United States of America in Congress assembled, That under the immunity provisions in the Act
entitled "An Act in relation to testimony before the Interstate Commerce Commission," and so forth, approved
February eleventh, eighteen hundred and ninety-three, in
section six of the Act entitled "An Act to establish the
Department of Commerce and Labor," approved February fourteenth, nineteen hundred and three, and in the
Act entitled "An Act to further regulate commerce with
foreign nations and among the States," approved February nineteenth, nineteen hundred and three, and in the
Act entitled "An Act making appropriations for the legislative, executive, and judicial expenses of the Government
for the fiscal year ending June thirtieth, nineteen hundred and four, and for other purposes," approved February twenty-fifth, nineteen hundred and three, immunity *Immunity ex
tends only t*
shall extend only to a natural person who, in obedience *natural person?
who give testi*
to a subpœna, gives testimony under oath or produces *mony under sub
pœna.*
evidence, documentary or otherwise, under oath.

Public No. 389, approved June 30, 1906.

AN ACT To further regulate commerce with foreign nations and
among the States.

Be it enacted by the Senate and House of Representa- *Carrier corpo
ration as well a*
tives of the United States of America in Congress as- *officer or agen
liable to convic*
sembled, SEC. 1. (As amended June 29, 1906.) That *tion for misde
meanor.*
anything done or omitted to be done by a corporation

common carrier, subject to the act to regulate commerce and the acts amendatory thereof, which, if done or omitted to be done by any director or officer thereof, or any receiver, trustee, lessee, agent, or person acting for or employed by such corporation, would constitute a misdemeanor under said acts or under this act, shall also be held to be a misdemeanor committed by such corporation, and upon conviction thereof it shall be subject **Penalty.** to like penalties as are prescribed in said acts or by this act with reference to such persons, except as such penal-

Failure of carrier to publish rates or observe tariffs a misdemeanor. ties are herein changed. The willful failure upon the part of any carrier subject to said acts to file and publish the tariffs or rates and charges as required by said acts, or strictly to observe such tariffs until changed according to law, shall be a misdemeanor, and upon conviction thereof the corporation offending shall be subject to a fine **Penalty, fine.** of not less than one thousand dollars nor more than twenty thousand dollars for each offense; and it shall be

Misdemeanor to offer, grant, give, solicit, accept, or receive any rebate from published rates or other concession or discrimination. unlawful for any person, persons, or corporation to offer, grant, or give, or to solicit, accept or receive any rebate, concession, or discrimination in respect to the transportation of any property in interstate or foreign commerce by any common carrier subject to said act to regulate commerce and the acts amendatory thereof whereby any such property shall by any device whatever be transported at a less rate than that named in the tariffs published and filed by such carrier, as is required by said act to regulate commerce and the acts amendatory thereof, or whereby any other advantage is given or discrimination is practised. Every person or corporation, whether carrier or shipper, who shall, knowingly, offer, grant, or give, or solicit, accept, or receive any such rebates, concession, or discrimination shall be deemed guilty of a misde-

Penalty, fine or imprisonment, or both. meanor, and on conviction thereof shall be punished by a fine of not less than one thousand dollars nor more than twenty thousand dollars: *Provided,* That any person, or any officer or director of any corporation subject to the provisions of this act, or the act to regulate commerce and the acts amendatory thereof, or any receiver, trustee, lessee, agent, or person acting for or employed by any such corporation, who shall be convicted as aforesaid, shall, in addition to the fine herein provided for, be liable to imprisonment in the penitentiary for a term of not exceeding two years, or both such fine and imprisonment, in the discretion of the court. Every violation of this section shall be prosecuted in any court of the United States having jurisdiction of crimes within the district in which such violation was committed, or through which the transportation may have been conducted; and whenever the offense is begun in one jurisdiction and completed in another it may be dealt with, inquired of, tried, determined, and punished in either jurisdiction in the same manner as if the offense had been actually and wholly committed therein.

Judicial district in which cases may be prosecuted.

In construing and enforcing the provisions of this section, the act, omission, or failure of any officer, agent, or other person acting for or employed by any common carrier, or shipper, acting within the scope of his employment, shall in every case be also deemed to be the act, omission, or failure of such carrier or shipper as well as that of the person. Whenever any carrier files with the Interstate Commerce Commission or publishes a particular rate under the provisions of the act to regulate commerce or acts amendatory thereof, or participates in any rates so filed or published, that rate as against such carrier, its officers or agents, in any prosecution begun under this act shall be conclusively deemed to be the legal rate, and any departure from such rate, or any offer to depart therefrom, shall be deemed to be an offense under this section of this act.

Act of officer or agent to be also deemed act of carrier.

Rates filed or participated in by carrier shall, as against such carrier, be deemed legal rate.

Any person, corporation, or company who shall deliver property for interstate transportation to any common carrier, subject to the provisions of this act, or for whom, as consignor or consignee, any such carrier shall transport property from one State, Territory, or the District of Columbia, to any other State, Territory, or the District

46

of Columbia, or foreign country, who shall knowingly by employee, agent, officer, or otherwise, directly or indirectly, by or through any means or device whatsoever, receive or accept from such common carrier any sum of money or any other valuable consideration as a rebate or offset against the regular charges for transportation of such property, as fixed by the schedules of rates provided

Forfeiture, in addition to other prescribed penalty, of three times amount of money and value of consideration illegally received shall be paid to the United States. for in this act, shall in addition to any penalty provided by this act forfeit to the United States a sum of money three times the amount of money so received or accepted and three times the value of any other consideration so received or accepted, to be ascertained by the trial court;

Attorney-General to collect such forfeiture by civil action. and the Attorney-General of the United States is authorized and directed, whenever he has reasonable grounds to believe that any such person, corporation, or company has knowingly received or accepted from any such common carrier any sum of money or other valuable consideration as a rebate or offset as aforesaid, to institute in any court of the United States of competent jurisdiction a civil action to collect the said sum or sums so forfeited as aforesaid; and in the trial of said action all such rebates or other considerations so received or accepted for a

Period covered to be six years prior to commencement of action. period of six years prior to the commencement of the action may be included therein, and the amount recovered shall be three times the total amount of money, or three times the total value of such consideration, so received or accepted, or both, as the case may be.

Persons interested in matters involved in cases before Interstate Commerce Commission or circuit court may be made parties and shall be subject to orders or decrees. SEC. 2. That in any proceeding for the enforcement of the provisions of the statutes relating to interstate commerce, whether such proceedings be instituted before the Interstate Commerce Commission or be begun originally in any circuit court of the United States, it shall be lawful to include as parties, in addition to the carrier, all persons interested in or affected by the rate, regulation, or practice under consideration, and inquiries, investigations, orders, and decrees may be made with reference to and against such additional parties in the same manner, to the same extent, and subject to the same provisions as are or shall be authorized by law with respect to carriers.

SEC. 3. That whenever the Interstate Commerce Com. mission shall have reasonable ground for belief that any common carrier is engaged in the carriage of passengers or freight traffic between given points at less than the published rates on file, or is committing any discriminations forbidden by law, a petition may be presented alleging such facts to the circuit court of the United States sitting in equity having jurisdiction; and when the act complained of is alleged to have been committed or as being committed in part in more than one judicial district or State, it may be dealt with, inquired of, tried, and determined in either such judicial district or State, whereupon it shall be the duty of the court summarily to inquire into the circumstances, upon such notice and in such manner as the court shall direct and without the formal pleadings and proceedings applicable to ordinary suits in equity, and to make such other persons or corporations parties thereto as the court may deem necessary, and upon being satisfied of the truth of the allegations of said petition said court shall enforce an observance of the published tariffs or direct and require a discontinuance of such discrimination by proper orders, writs, and process, which said orders, writs, and process may be enforceable as well against the parties interested in the traffic as against the carrier, subject to the right of appeal as now provided by law. It shall be the duty of the several district attorneys of the United States, whenever the Attorney-General shall direct, either of his own motion or upon the request of the Interstate Commerce Commission, to institute and prosecute such proceedings, and the proceedings provided for by this act shall not preclude the bringing of suit for the recovery of damages by any party injured, or any other action provided by said act approved February fourth, eighteen hundred and eighty-seven, entitled An act to regulate commerce and the acts amendatory thereof. And in proceedings under this act and the acts to regulate commerce the said courts shall have the power to compel the attendance of witnesses,

Proceedings to enjoin or restrain departures from published rates or any discrimination prohibited by law against carriers and parties interested in traffic.

Such proceedings shall not prevent actions for recovery of damages or other action authorized by act to regulate commerce or amendments thereof.

Compulsory attendance and testimony of witnesses and production of books and papers.

both upon the part of the carrier and the shipper, who shall be required to answer on all subjects relating directly or indirectly to the matter in controversy, and to compel the production of all books and papers, both of the carrier and the shipper, which relate directly or indirectly to such transaction; the claim that such testimony or evidence may tend to criminate the person giving such evidence shall not excuse such person from testifying or such corporation producing its books and papers, but no person shall be prosecuted or subjected to any penalty or forfeiture for or on account of any transaction, matter, or thing concerning which he may testify or produce evidence, documentary or otherwise, in such proceeding: *Provided,* That the provisions of an act entitled "An act to expedite the hearing and determination of suits in equity pending or hereafter brought under the act of July second, eighteen hundred and ninety, entitled 'An act to protect trade and commerce against unlawful restraints and monopolies,' 'An act to regulate commerce,' approved February fourth, eighteen hundred and eighty-seven, or any other acts having a like purpose that may be hereafter enacted, approved February eleventh, nineteen hundred and three," shall apply to any case prosecuted under the direction of the Attorney-General in the name of the Interstate Commerce Commission.

SEC. 4. That all acts and parts of acts in conflict with the provisions of this act are hereby repealed, but such repeal shall not affect causes now pending, nor rights which have already accrued, but such causes shall be prosecuted to a conclusion and such rights enforced in a manner heretofore provided by law and as modified by the provisions of this act.

SEC. 5. That this act shall take effect from its passage.

Public, No. 103, approved February 19, 1903.

(*See additional provisions in act of June 29, 1906, p. 32.*)

Immunity to testifying witnesses.

Expediting act of Feb. 11, 1903, to apply in cases prosecuted under direction of Attorney-General in name of Interstate Commerce Commission.

Conflicting laws repealed.

AN ACT To expedite the hearing and determination of suits in equity pending or hereafter brought under the act of July second, eighteen hundred and ninety, entitled "An act to protect trade and commerce against unlawful restraints and monopolies," "An act to regulate commerce," approved February fourth, eighteen hundred and eighty-seven, or any other acts having a like purpose that may be hereafter enacted.

Be it enacted by the Senate and House of Representatives of the United States of America in Congress assembled, That in any suit in equity pending or hereafter brought in any circuit court of the United States under the act entitled "An act to protect trade and commerce against unlawful restraints and monopolies," approved July second, eighteen hundred and ninety, "An act to regulate commerce," approved February fourth, eighteen hundred and eighty-seven, or any other acts having a like purpose that hereafter may be enacted, wherein the United States is complainant, the Attorney-General may file with the clerk of such court a certificate that, in his opinion, the case is of general public importance, a copy of which shall be immediately furnished by such clerk to each of the circuit judges of the circuit in which the case is pending. Thereupon such case shall be given precedence over others and in every way expedited, and be assigned for hearing at the earliest practicable day, before not less than three of the circuit judges of said circuit, if there be three or more; and if there be not more than two circuit judges, then before them and such district judge as they may select. In the event the judges sitting in such case shall be divided in opinion, the case shall be certified to the Supreme Court for review in like manner as if taken there by appeal as hereinafter provided.

SEC. 2. That in every suit in equity pending or hereafter brought in any circuit court of the United States under any of said acts, wherein the United States is complainant, including cases submitted but not yet decided, an appeal from the final decree of the circuit court will lie only to the Supreme Court and must be taken within sixty days from the entry thereof: *Provided,* That in any case where an appeal may have been taken from the final

Margin notes:
- Expedition of cases.
- Hearing before three judges.
- Review by Supreme Court on certificate.
- Appeal to Supreme Court.
- Exception.

decree of a circuit court to the circuit court of appeals
before this act takes effect, the case shall proceed to a
final decree therein, and an appeal may be taken from
such decree to the Supreme Court in the manner now provided by law.

Public No. 82, approved February 11, 1903.

————

AN ACT Supplementary to the act of July first, eighteen hundred
and sixty-two, entitled "An act to aid in the construction of a
railroad and telegraph line from the Missouri River to the Pacific
Ocean, and to secure to the Government the use of the same for
postal, military, and other purposes," and also of the act of July
second, eighteen hundred and sixty-four, and other acts amendatory of said first-named act.

*Government
aided railroad
and telegraph
lines must them-
selves maintain
and operate.*

*Be it enacted by the Senate and House of Representa-
tives of the United States of America in Congress
assembled,* That all railroad and telegraph companies to
which the United States has granted any subsidy in lands
or bonds or loan of credit for the construction of either
railroad or telegraph lines, which, by the acts incorporat-
ing them, or by any act amendatory or supplementary
thereto, are required to construct, maintain, or operate
telegraph lines, and all companies engaged in operating
said railroad or telegraph lines shall forthwith and hence-
forward, by and through their own respective corporate
officers and employees, maintain and operate, for railroad,
Governmental, commercial, and all other purposes, telegraph lines, and exercise by themselves alone all the telegraph franchises conferred upon them and obligations
assumed by them under the acts making the grants as
aforesaid.

SEC. 2. That whenever any telegraph company which
shall have accepted the provisions of title sixty-five of the
Revised Statutes shall extend its line to any station or
office of a telegraph line belonging to any one of said railroad or telegraph companies, referred to in the first section of this act, said telegraph company so extending its
line shall have the right and said railroad or telegraph

*Connecting tele-
graph lines.*

company shall allow the line of said telegraph company so extending its line to connect with the telegraph line of said railroad or telegraph company to which it is extended at the place where their lines may meet, for the prompt and convenient interchange of telegraph business between said companies; and such railroad and telegraph companies, referred to in the first section of this act, shall so operate their respective telegraph lines as to afford equal facilities to all, without discrimination in favor of or against any person, company, or corporation whatever, and shall receive, deliver, and exchange business with connecting telegraph lines on equal terms, and affording equal facilities, and without discrimination for or against any one of such connecting lines; and such exchange of business shall be on terms just and equitable.

Equal facilities required.

SEC. 3. That if any such railroad or telegraph company referred to in the first section of this act, or company operating such railroad or telegraph line shall refuse or fail, in whole or in part, to maintain, and operate a telegraph line as provided in this act and acts to which this is supplementary, for the use of the Government or the public, for commercial and other purposes, without discrimination, or shall refuse or fail to make or continue such arrangements for the interchange of business with any connecting telegraph company, then any person, company, corporation, or connecting telegraph company may apply for relief to the Interstate Commerce Commission, whose duty it shall thereupon be, under such rules and regulations as said Commission may prescribe, to ascertain the facts, and determine and order what arrangement is proper to be made in the particular case, and the railroad or telegraph company concerned shall abide by and perform such order; and it shall be the duty of the Interstate Commerce Commission, when such determination and order are made, to notify the parties concerned, and, if necessary, enforce the same by writ of mandamus in the courts of the United States, in the name of the United States, at the relation of either of said Interstate Com-

Complaints to Interstate Commerce Commission.

Duties of the Commission where complaint is made.

Commission may institute inquiries on its own motion. merce Commissioners: *Provided,* That the said Commissioners may institute any inquiry, upon their own motion, in the same manner and to the same effect as though complaint had been made.

Duty of the Attorney-General under this act. SEC. 4. That in order to secure and preserve to the United States the full value and benefit of its liens upon all the telegraph lines required to be constructed by and lawfully belonging to said railroad and telegraph companies referred to in the first section of this act, and to have the same possessed, used, and operated in conformity with the provisions of this act and of the several acts to which this act is supplementary, it is hereby made the duty of the Attorney-General of the United States, by proper proceedings, to prevent any unlawful interference with the rights and equities of the United States under this act, and under the acts hereinbefore mentioned, and under all acts of Congress relating to such railroads and telegraph lines, and to have legally ascertained and finally adjudicated all alleged rights of all persons and corporations whatever claiming in any manner any control or interest of any kind in any telegraph lines or property, or exclusive rights of way upon the lands of said railroad companies, or any of them, and to have all contracts and provisions of contracts set aside and annulled which have been unlawfully and beyond their powers entered into by said railroad or telegraph companies, or any of them, with any other person, company, or corporation.

Penalties for failure to comply with the provisions of this act or the orders of the Interstate Commerce Commission. SEC. 5. That any officer or agent of said railroad or telegraph companies, or of any company operating the railroads and telegraph lines of said companies, who shall refuse or fail to operate the telegraph lines of said railroad or telegraph companies under his control, or which he is engaged in operating, in the manner directed in this act and by the acts to which it is supplementary, or who shall refuse or fail, in such operation and use, to afford and secure to the Government and the public equal facilities, or to secure to each of said connecting telegraph lines equal advantages and facilities in the interchange of business, as herein provided for, without any discrimination whatever for or adverse to the telegraph line of any or either of said connecting companies, or shall refuse to abide by, or perform and carry out within a reasonable time the order or orders of the Interstate Commerce Commission, shall in every such case of refusal or failure be guilty of a misdemeanor, and, on conviction thereof, shall in every such case be fined in a sum not exceeding one thousand dollars, and may be imprisoned not less than six months; and in every such case of refusal or failure the party aggrieved may not only cause the officer or agent guilty thereof to be prosecuted under the provisions of this section, but may also bring an action *Actions for damages may* for the damages sustained thereby against the company *also be brought.* whose officer or agent may be guilty thereof, in the circuit or district court of the United States in any State or Territory in which any portion of the road or telegraph line of said company may be situated; and in case of suit process may be served upon any agent of the company found in such State or Territory, and such service shall be held by the court good and sufficient.

SEC. 6. That it shall be the duty of each and every one *Duty of railroad and tele-* of the aforesaid railroad and telegraph companies, within *graph lines subject to this act* sixty days from and after the passage of this act, to file *to file copies of* with the Interstate Commerce Commission copies of all *contracts and a report with the Commission.* contracts and agreements of every description existing between it and every other person or corporation whatsoever in reference to the ownership, possession, maintenance, control, use, or operation of any telegraph lines, or property over or upon its rights of way, and also a report describing with sufficient certainty the telegraph lines and property belonging to it, and the manner in which the same are being then used and operated by it, and the telegraph lines and property upon its right of way in which any other person or corporation claims to have a title or interest, and setting forth the grounds of such claim, and the manner in which the same are being then used and operated; and it shall be the duty of each and

every one of said railroad and telegraph companies an
nually hereafter to report to the Interstate Commerce
Commission, with reasonable fullness and certainty, the
nature, extent, value, and condition of the telegraph lines
and property then belonging to it, the gross earnings, and
all expenses of maintenance, use, and operation thereof,
and its relation and business with all connecting telegraph companies during the preceding year, at such time
and in such manner as may be required by a system of
reports which said Commission shall prescribe; and if any
of said railroad or telegraph companies shall refuse or
fail to make such reports or any report as may be called
for by said Commission, or refuse to submit its books and
records for inspection, such neglect or refusal shall operate as a forfeiture, in each case of such neglect or refusal, of a sum not less than one thousand dollars nor
more than five thousand dollars, to be recovered by the
Attorney-General of the United States, in the name and
for the use and benefit of the United States; and it shall
be the duty of the Interstate Commerce Commission to
inform the Attorney-General of all such cases of neglect
or refusal, whose duty it shall be to proceed at once to
judicially enforce the forfeitures hereinbefore provided.

SEC. 7. That nothing in this act shall be construed to
affect or impair the right of Congress, at any time hereafter, to alter, amend, or repeal the said acts hereinbefore
mentioned; and this act shall be subject to alteration,
amendment, or repeal as, in the opinion of Congress, justice or the public welfare may require; and nothing herein
contained shall be held to deny, exclude, or impair any
right or remedy in the premises now existing in the United
States, or any authority that the Postmaster-General now
has under title sixty-five of the Revised Statutes to fix
rates, or, of the Government, to purchase lines as provided under said title, or to have its messages given
precedence in transmission.

Public No. 237, approved August 7, 1888.

Annual reports to the Commis-sion.

Penalties for refusal to make reports to Com-mission.

Duty of Attor-ney-General to prosecute.

Right of Con-gress to alter, amend, or repeal.

Equity rights of the Govern-ment preserved.

THE SAFETY APPLIANCE ACTS.

AN ACT To promote the safety of employees and travelers upon railroads by compelling common carriers engaged in interstate commerce to equip their cars with automatic couplers and continuous brakes and their locomotives with driving-wheel brakes, and for other purposes.

Be it enacted by the Senate and House of Representatives of the United States of America in Congress assembled, That from and after the first day of January, eighteen hundred and ninety-eight, it shall be unlawful for any common carrier engaged in interstate commerce by railroad to use on its line any locomotive engine in moving interstate traffic not equipped with a power driving-wheel brake and appliances for operating the train-brake system, or to run any train in such traffic after said date that has not a sufficient number of cars in it so equipped with power or train brakes that the engineer on the locomotive drawing such train can control its speed without requiring brakemen to use the common hand brake for that purpose.

Driving-wheel and train brakes.

SEC. 2. That on and after the first day of January, eighteen hundred and ninety-eight, it shall be unlawful for any such common carrier to haul or permit to be hauled or used on its line any car used in moving interstate traffic not equipped with couplers coupling automatically by impact, and which can be uncoupled without the necessity of men going between the ends of the cars.

Automatic couplers.

SEC. 3. That when any person, firm, company, or corporation engaged in interstate commerce by railroad shall have equipped a sufficient number of its cars so as to comply with the provisions of section one of this act, it may lawfully refuse to receive from connecting lines of road or shippers any cars not equipped sufficiently, in accordance with the first section of this act, with such power or train brakes as will work and readily interchange with the brakes in use on its own cars, as required by this act.

When carriers may lawfully refuse to receive cars from connecting lines or shippers.

Grab irons and ndholes.

SEC. 4. That from and after the first day of July, eighteen hundred and ninety-five until otherwise ordered by the Interstate Commerce Commission, it shall be unlawful for any railroad company to use any car in interstate commerce that is not provided with secure grab irons or handholds in the ends and sides of each car for greater security to men in coupling and uncoupling cars.

tandard height draw bars for eight cars.

SEC. 5. That within ninety days from the passage of this act the American Railway Association is authorized hereby to designate to the Interstate Commerce Commission the standard height of drawbars for freight cars, measured perpendicular from the level of the tops of the rails to the centers of the drawbars, for each of the several gauges of railroads in use in the United States, and shall fix a maximum variation from such standard height to be allowed between the drawbars of empty and loaded cars. Upon their determination being certified to the Interstate Commerce Commission, said Commission shall at once give notice of the standard fixed upon to all common carriers, owners, or lessees engaged in interstate commerce in the United States by such means as the Commission may deem proper. But should said association fail to determine a standard as above provided, it shall be the duty of the Interstate Commerce Commission to do so, before July first, eighteen hundred and ninety-four, and immediately to give notice thereof as aforesaid. And after July first, eighteen hundred and ninety-five, no cars, either loaded or unloaded, shall be used in interstate traffic which do not comply with the standard above provided for.

nalty for violation of the provisions of this t.

SEC. 6. (*As amended April 1, 1896.*) That any such common carrier using any locomotive engine, running any train, or hauling or permitting to be hauled or used on its line any car in violation of any of the provisions of this act, shall be liable to a penalty of one hundred dollars for each and every such violation, to be recovered in a suit or suits to be brought by the United States district attorney in the district court of the United States having jurisdiction in the locality where such violation shall have been committed; and it shall be the duty of such district attorney to bring such suits upon duly verified information being lodged with him of such violation having occurred; and it shall also be the duty of the Interstate Commerce Commission to lodge with the proper district attorneys information of any such violations as may come to its knowledge: *Provided,* That nothing in this act contained shall apply to trains composed of four-wheel cars or to trains composed of eight-wheel standard logging cars where the height of such car from top of rail to center of coupling does not exceed twenty-five inches, or to locomotives used in hauling such trains when such cars or locomotives are exclusively used for the transportation of logs.

Duty of United States district attorney.

Duty of Interstate Commerce Commission.

Exceptions to the act.

SEC. 7. That the Interstate Commerce Commission may from time to time upon full hearing and for good cause extend the period within which any common carrier shall comply with the provisions of this act.

Power of Interstate Commerce Commission to extend time of carriers to comply with this act.

SEC. 8. That any employee of any such common carrier who may be injured by any locomotive, car, or train in use contrary to the provision of this act shall not be deemed thereby to have assumed the risk thereby occasioned, although continuing in the employment of such carrier after the unlawful use of such locomotive, car, or train had been brought to his knowledge.

Employees not deemed to assume risk of employment.

Public No. 113, approved March 2, 1893, amended April 1, 1896.

NOTE.— Prescribed standard height of drawbars: Standard-gauge roads, 34½ inches; narrow-gauge roads, 26 inches; maximum variation between loaded and empty cars, 3 inches.

AN ACT To amend an act entitled "An act to promote the safety of employees and travelers upon railroads by compelling common carriers engaged in interstate commerce to equip their cars with automatic couplers and continuous brakes and their locomotives with driving-wheel brakes, and for other purposes," approved March second, eighteen hundred and ninety-three, and amended April first, eighteen hundred and ninety-six.

Be it enacted by the Senate and House of Representatives of the United States of America in Congress assembled, That the provisions and requirements of the act

Safety appliance act of Mar. 2, 1893, as amended by act of April 1, 1896, shall apply in Territories and District of Columbia. entitled "An act to promote the safety of employees and travelers upon railroads by compelling common carriers engaged in interstate commerce to equip their cars with automatic couplers and continuous brakes, and their loco-

Provisions of safety appliance acts as to couplers shall apply in all cases when couplers are brought together. motives with driving-wheel brakes, and for other purposes," approved March second, eighteen hundred and ninety-three, and amended April first, eighteen hundred and ninety-six, shall be held to apply to common carriers

Safety appliance acts shall apply to all equipment of any railroad engaged in interstate commerce. by railroads in the Territories and the District of Columbia and shall apply in all cases, whether or not the couplers brought together are of the same kind, make, or type; and the provisions and requirements hereof and of said acts relating to train brakes, automatic couplers, grab irons, and the height of drawbars shall be held to apply to all trains, locomotives, tenders, cars, and similar vehicles used on any railroad engaged in interstate commerce, and in the Territories and the District of Columbia, and to all other locomotives, tenders, cars, and

Exceptions. similar vehicles used in connection therewith, excepting those trains, cars, and locomotives exempted by the provisions of section six of said act of March second, eighteen hundred and ninety-three, as amended by the act of April first, eighteen hundred and ninety-six, or which are used upon street railways.

Power or train brakes on not less than 50 per cent of cars in trains shall be used and operated. SEC. 2. That whenever, as provided in said act, any train is operated with power or train brakes, not less than fifty per centum of the cars in such train shall have their brakes used and operated by the engineer of the locomotive drawing such train; and all power-braked cars in such train which are associated together with said fifty per centum shall have their brakes so used and operated; and, to more fully carry into effect the objects of said act, the Interstate Commerce Commission may, from time to time, after full hearing, increase the minimum percentage of cars in any train required to be operated with power or train brakes which must have their brakes used and operated as aforesaid; and failure to comply with any such requirement of the said Interstate Commerce Commission shall be subject to the like penalty as failure to comply with any requirement of this section.

Commission may increase minimum percentage of power or train brake cars to be used.

Penalty.

SEC. 3. That the provisions of this act shall not take effect until September first, nineteen hundred and three. Nothing in this act shall be held or construed to relieve any common carrier, the Interstate Commerce Commission, or any United States district attorney from any of the provisions, powers, duties, liabilities, or requirements of said act of March second, eighteen hundred and ninety-three, as amended by the act of April first, eighteen hundred and ninety-six; and all of the provisions, powers, duties, requirements, and liabilities of said act of March second, eighteen hundred and ninety-three, as amended by the act of April first, eighteen hundred and ninety-six, shall, except as specifically amended by this act, apply to this act.

Act effective Sept. 1, 1903.

Provisions, powers, duties, requirements, and liabilities specified in act of Mar. 2, 1893, and act of Apr. 1, 1896, apply to this act.

Public, No. 133, approved March 2, 1903.

Sundry civil act (appropriations) of June 28, 1902, authorizes Commission to employ "inspectors to execute and enforce the requirements of the safety-appliance act."

Employment of inspectors.

JOINT RESOLUTION Directing the Interstate Commerce Commission to investigate and report on block-signal systems and appliances for the automatic control of railway trains.

Resolved by the Senate and House of Representatives of the United States of America in Congress assembled, That the Interstate Commerce Commission be, and it is hereby, directed to investigate and report on the use of and neces-

Commission directed to investigate and report on necessity for block signals.

sity for block-signal systems and appliances for the automatic control of railway trains in the United States. For this purpose the Commission is authorized to employ persons who are familiar with the subject, and may use such of its own employees as are necessary to make a thorough examination into the matter.

Commission to
ake testimony
nd make recom-
endations. In transmitting its report to the Congress the Commission shall recommend such legislation as to the Commission seems advisable.

To carry out and give effect to the provisions of this resolution the Commission shall have power to issue subpœnas, administer oaths, examine witnesses, require the production of books and papers, and receive depositions taken before any proper officer in any State or Territory of the United States.

Public Resolution No. 46, approved June 30, 1906.

AN ACT To grant the right of way through the Oklahoma Territory and the Indian Territory to the Enid and Anadarko Railway Company, and for other purposes.

✴   ✴   ✴   ✴   ✴   ✴   ✴

SEC. 18. That when in any case two or more railroads crossing each other at a common grade shall, by a system of interlocking or automatic signals, or by any works or fixtures to be erected by them, render it safe for engines and trains to pass over such crossing without stopping, and such interlocking or automatic signals or works or Approval by
ommission of
nterlocking or
utomatic sig-
als at crossings. fixtures shall be approved by the Interstate Commerce Commissioners, then, in that case, it is hereby made lawful for the engines and trains of such railroad or railroads to pass over such crossing without stopping, any law or the provisions of any law to the contrary notwithstanding; and when two or more railroads cross each other at a common grade, either of such roads may apply to the Interstate Commerce Commissioners for permission to introduce upon both of said railroads some system of interlocking or automatic signals or works or fixtures render-

ing it safe for engines and trains to pass over such crossings without stopping, and it shall be the duty of said
Interstate Commerce Commissioners, if the system of   Common grade
works and fixtures which it is proposed to erect by said   crossings.
company are, in the opinion of the Commission, sufficient
and proper, to grant such permission. .

SEC. 19. That any railroad company which has obtained   Notice of in
permission to introduce a system of interlocking or auto- tent to use sig
matic signals at its crossing at a common grade with any   nals at crossings
other railroad, as provided in the last section, may, after
thirty days' notice, in writing, to such other railroad com- Division of cos
pany, introduce and erect such interlocking or automatic
signal or fixtures; and if such railroad company, after
such notification, refuses to join with the railroad company giving notice in the construction of such works or
fixtures, it shall be lawful for said company to enter upon
the right of way and tracks of such second company, in
such manner as to not unnecessarily impede the operation
of such road, and erect such works and fixtures, and may
recover in any action at law from such second company
one-half of the total cost of erecting and maintaining such
interlocking or automatic signals or works or fixtures on
both of said roads.

＊　　＊　　＊　　＊　　＊　　＊　　＊

Public No. 26, approved February 28, 1902.

AN ACT Requiring common carriers engaged in interstate commerce
to make full reports of all accidents to the Interstate Commerce
Commission.

*Be it enacted by the Senate and House of Representa-
tives of the United States of America in Congress assembled,* It shall be the duty of the general manager, superintendent, or other proper officer of every common carrier
engaged in interstate commerce by railroad to make to
the Interstate Commerce Commission, at its office in
Washington, District of Columbia, a monthly report,   Monthly
under oath, of all collisions of trains or where any train   ports of railwa
                                                             accidents.

or part of a train accidentally leaves the track, and of all accidents which may occur to its passengers or employees while in the service of such common carrier and actually on duty, which report shall state the nature and causes thereof, and the circumstances connected therewith.

Failure to make report within thirty days after end of any month a misdemeanor.

SEC. 2. That any common carrier failing to make such report within thirty days after the end of any month shall be deemed guilty of a misdemeanor and, upon conviction

Penalty.

thereof by a court of competent jurisdiction, shall be punished by a fine of not more than one hundred dollars for each and every offense and for every day during which it shall fail to make such report after the time herein specified for making the same.

Reports not to be used in evidence against the carrier.

SEC. 3. That neither said report nor any part thereof shall be admitted as evidence or used for any purpose against such railroad so making such report in any suit or action for damages growing out of any matter mentioned in said report.

Form of report.

SEC. 4. That the Interstate Commerce Commission is authorized to prescribe for such common carriers a method and form for making the reports in the foregoing section provided.

Public No. 171, approved March 3, 1901.

JOINT RESOLUTION Instructing the Interstate Commerce Commission to make examinations into the subject of railroad discriminations and monopolies in coal and oil, and report on the same from time to time.

Resolved by the Senate and House of Representatives of the United States of America in Congress assembled, That

Commission instructed to examine into subject of railroad discriminations in coal and oil, and make report from time to time.

the Interstate Commerce Commission be, and is hereby, authorized and instructed immediately to inquire, investigate, and report to Congress, or to the President when Congress is not in session, from time to time as the investigation proceeds —

First. Whether any common carriers by railroad, subject to the interstate-commerce act, or either of them, own or have any interest in, by means of stock ownership in other corporations or otherwise, any of the coal or oil which they, or either of them, directly or through other companies which they control or in which they have an interest, carry over their or any of their lines as common carriers, or in any manner own, control, or have any interest in coal lands or properties or oil lands or properties.

Second. Whether the officers of any of the carrier companies aforesaid, or any of them, or any person or persons charged with the duty of distributing cars or furnishing facilities to shippers are interested, either directly or indirectly, by means of stock ownership or otherwise in corporations or companies owning, operating, leasing, or otherwise interested in any coal mines, coal properties, or coal traffic, oil, oil properties, or oil traffic over the railroads with which they or any of them are connected or by which they or any of them are employed.

Interest of carriers in coal and oil lands or coal and oil traffic.

Interest of railroad officials in coal and oil lands or coal and oil traffic.

Third. Whether there is any contract, combination in the form of trust, or otherwise, or conspiracy in restraint of trade or commerce among the several States, in which any common carrier engaged in the transportation of coal or oil is interested, or to which it is a party; and whether any such common carrier monopolizes or attempts to monopolize, or combines or conspires with any other carrier, company or companies, person or persons to monopolize any part of the trade or commerce in coal or oil, or traffic therein among the several States or with foreign nations, and whether or not, and if so, to what extent, such carriers, or any of them, limit or control, directly or indirectly, the output of coal mines or the price of coal and oil fields or the price of oil.

Combination or trust in restraint of trade, or monopoly in co'l or oil traffic.

Fourth. If the Interstate Commerce Commission shall find that the facts or any of them set forth in the three paragraphs above do exist, then that it be further required to report as to the effect of such relationship, ownership, or interest in coal or coal properties and coal traffic, or oil, oil properties, or oil traffic aforesaid, or such contracts or combinations in form of trust or otherwise, or conspiracy or such monopoly or attempt to monopolize

Commission to make report.

or combine or conspire as aforesaid, upon such person or persons as may be engaged independently of any other persons in mining coal or producing oil and shipping the same, or other products, who may desire to so engage, or upon the general public as consumers of such coal or oil.

System of car supply and distribution. Fifth. That said Commission be also required to investigate and report the system of car supply and distribution in effect upon the several railway lines engaged in the transportation of coal or oil as aforesaid, and whether said systems are fair and equitable, and whether the same are carried out fairly and properly; and whether said carriers, or any of them discriminate against shippers or parties wishing to become shippers over their several lines, either in the matter of distribution of cars or in furnishing facilities or instrumentalities connected with receiving, forwarding, or carrying coal or oil as aforesaid.

Commission to suggest remedy and report facts and conclusions. Sixth. That said Commission be also required to report as to what remedy it can suggest to cure the evils above set forth, if they exist.

Seventh. That said Commission be also required to report any facts or conclusions which it may think pertinent to the general inquiry above set forth.

Information to be furnished from time to time. Eighth. That said Commission be required to make this investigation at its earliest possible convenience and to furnish the information above required from time to time and as soon as it can be done consistent with the performance of its public duty.

Public Res. No. 8, approved March 7, 1906.

JOINT RESOLUTION Amending joint resolution instructing the Interstate Commerce Commission to make examinations into the subject of railroad discriminations and monopolies, and report on the same from time to time, approved March seventh, nineteen hundred and six.

Resolved by the Senate and House of Representatives of the United States of America in Congress assembled, That joint resolution instructing the Interstate Commerce Commission to make examinations into the subject of railroad discriminations and monopolies, and report on the same from time to time, approved March seventh, nineteen hundred and six, is hereby amended by adding the following thereto:

Ninth. To enable the Commission to perform the duties required and accomplish the purposes declared herein, the Commission shall have and exercise under this joint reso- **Commission given full power to compel testimony in coal and oil investigations.** lution the same power and authority to administer oaths, to subpœna and compel the attendance and testimony of witnesses and the production of documentary evidence, and to obtain full information, which said Commission now has under the act to regulate commerce, approved February fourth, eighteen hundred and eighty-seven, and acts amendatory thereof or supplementary thereto now in force or may have under any like statute taking effect hereafter. All the requirements, obligations, liabilities, and immunities imposed or conferred by said act to regulate commerce and by "An act in relation to testimony before the Interstate Commerce Commission in cases under or connected with an act entitled 'An act to regulate commerce,' approved February fourth, eighteen hundred and eighty-seven, and amendments thereto," approved February eleventh, eighteen hundred and ninety-three, shall also apply to all persons who may be subpœnaed to testify as witnesses or to produce documentary evidence in pursuance of the authority herein conferred.

Public Res. No. 11, approved March 21, 1906.

AN ACT Concerning carriers engaged in interstate commerce and their employees.

Be it enacted by the Senate and House of Representatives of the United States of America in Congress assembled, That the provisions of this act shall apply to any **Adjustment of controversies between railroads and their employees.** common carrier or carriers and their officers, agents, and **Scope of act.** employees, except masters of vessels and seamen, as defined in section forty-six hundred and twelve, Revised Statutes of the United States, engaged in the transportation of passengers or property wholly by railroad, or partly by railroad and partly by water, for a continuous carriage or shipment, from one State or Territory of the United States, or the District of Columbia, to any other State or Territory of the United States, or the District of Columbia, or from any place in the United States to an adjacent foreign country, or from any place in the United States through a foreign country to any other place in the United States.

Terms.

—"railroad."

—"transportation."

The term " railroad " as used in this act shall include all bridges and ferries used or operated in connection with any railroad, and also all the road in use by any corporation operating a railroad, whether owned or operated under a contract, agreement, or lease; and the term " transportation " shall include all instrumentalities of shipment or carriage.

—"employees.

The term " employees " as used in this act shall include all persons actually engaged in any capacity in train operation or train service of any description, and notwithstanding that the cars upon or in which they are employed may be held and operated by the carrier under

Street railroads excepted.

lease or other contract: *Provided, however,* That this act shall not be held to apply to employees of street railroads and shall apply only to employees engaged in railroad train service. In every such case the carrier shall be responsible for the acts and defaults of such employees in the same manner and to the same extent as if said cars were owned by it and said employees directly employed by it, and any provisions to the contrary of any such lease

Responsibility of carrier on leased cars.

or other contract shall be binding only as between the parties thereto and shall not affect the obligations of said carrier either to the public or to the private parties concerned.

Chairman of Interstate Commerce Commission and Commissioner of Labor to mediate differences.

SEC. 2. That whenever a controversy concerning wages, hours of labor, or conditions of employment shall arise between a carrier subject to this act and the employees o such carrier, seriously interrupting or threatening to interrupt the business of said carrier, the chairman of the Interstate Commerce Commission and the Commissioner of Labor shall, upon the request of either party to the controversy, with all practicable expedition, put themselves in communication with the parties to such controversy, and shall use their best efforts, by mediation and conciliation, to amicably settle the same; and if such efforts shall be unsuccessful, shall at once endeavor to bring about an arbitration of said controversy in accordance with the provisions of this act.

SEC. 3. That whenever a controversy shall arise between a carrier subject to this act and the employees of such carrier which can not be settled by mediation and conciliation in the manner provided in the preceding section, said controversy may be submitted to the arbitration of a board of three persons, who shall be chosen in the manner following: One shall be named by the carrier or employer directly interested; the other shall be named by the labor organization to which the employees directly interested belong, or, if they belong to more than one, by that one of them which specially represents employees of the same grade and class and engaged in services of the same nature as said employees so directly interested: *Provided, however,* That when a controversy involves and affects the interests of two or more classes and grades of employees belonging to different labor organizations, such arbitrator shall be agreed upon and designated by the concurrent action of all such labor organizations; and in cases where the majority of such employees are not members of any labor organization, said employees may by a majority vote select a committee of their own number, which committee shall have the right to select the arbitrator on behalf of said employees. The two thus chosen shall select the third commissioner of arbitration; but, in the event of their failure to name such arbitrator within five days after their first meeting, the third arbitrator shall be named by the commissioners named in the pre-

Failure to adjust.

Board to arbitrate. How selected.

Controversies affecting different labor organizations.

Third arbitrator.

ceding section. A majority of said arbitrators shall be competent to make a valid and binding award under the provisions hereof. The submission shall be in writing, shall be signed by the employer and by the labor organization representing the employees, shall specify the time and place of meeting of said board of arbitration, shall state the questions to be decided, and shall contain appropriate provisions by which the respective parties shall stipulate, as follows:

Form of submission.

First. That the board of arbitration shall commence their hearings within ten days from the date of the appointment of the third arbitrator, and shall find and file their award, as provided in this section, within thirty days from the date of the appointment of the third arbitrator; and that pending the arbitration the status existing immediately prior to the dispute shall not be changed: *Provided,* That no employee shall be compelled to render personal service without his consent.

Stipulations of submission. Time of hearings.

Status of controversy pending arbitration.

Involuntary service.

Second. That the award and the papers and proceedings, including the testimony relating thereto certified under the hands of the arbitrators and which shall have the force and effect of a bill of exceptions, shall be filed in the clerk's office of the circuit court of the United States for the district wherein the controversy arises or the arbitration is entered into, and shall be final and conclusive upon both parties, unless set aside for error of law apparent on the record.

Filing of award in the United States circuit court.

Third. That the respective parties to the award will each faithfully execute the same, and that the same may be specifically enforced in equity so far as the powers of a court of equity permit: *Provided,* That no injunction or other legal process shall be issued which shall compel the performance by any laborer against his will of a contract for personal labor or service.

Enforcing award.

Involuntary service.

Fourth. That employees dissatisfied with the award shall not by reason of such dissatisfaction quit the service of the employer before the expiration of three months from and after the making of such award without givin

Notice of termination of service.

.thirty days' notice in writing of their intention so to quit. Nor shall the employer dissatisfied with such award dismiss any employee or employees on account of such dis· satisfaction before the expiration of three months from and after the making of such award without giving thirty days' notice in writing of his intention so to discharge.

Fifth. That said award shall continue in force as be- *Continuance in force of award.* tween the parties thereto for the period of one year after the same shall go into practical operation, and no new arbitration upon the same subject between the same employer and the same class of employees shall be had until the expiration of said one year if the award is not set aside as provided in section four. That as to individual *Individual employees not parties not bound by award.* employees not belonging to the labor organization or organizations which shall enter into the arbitration, the said arbitration and the award made therein shall not be binding, unless the said individual employees shall give assent in writing to become parties to said arbitration.

SEC. 4. That the award being filed in the clerk's office *Exceptions to award.* of a circuit court of the United States, as hereinbefore provided, shall go into practical operation, and judgment shall be entered thereon accordingly at the expiration of ten days from such filing, unless within such ten days either party shall file exceptions thereto for matter of law apparent upon the record, in which case said award shall go into practical operation and judgment be entered accordingly when such exceptions shall have been finally disposed of either by said circuit court or on appeal therefrom.

At the expiration of ten days from the decision of the *Appeal to circuit court of appeals.* circuit court upon exceptions taken to said award, as aforesaid, judgment shall be entered in accordance with said decision unless during said ten days either party shall appeal therefrom to the circuit court of appeals. In such case only such portion of the record shall be *Record.* transmitted to the appellate court as is necessary to the proper understanding and consideration of the questions of law presented by said exceptions and to be decided.

Judgment.

The determination of said circuit court of appeals upon said questions shall be final, and being certified by the clerk thereof to said circuit court, judgment pursuant thereto shall thereupon be entered by said circuit court.

Judgment by agreement.

If exceptions to an award are finally sustained, judgment shall be entered setting aside the award. But in such case the parties may agree upon a judgment to be entered disposing of the subject-matter of the controversy, which judgment when entered shall have the same force and effect as judgment entered upon an award.

Powers of arbitration.

SEC. 5. That for the purposes of this act the arbitrators herein provided for, or either of them, shall have power to administer oaths and affirmations, sign subpœnas, require the attendance and testimony of witnesses, and the production of such books, papers, contracts, agreements, and documents material to a just determination of the matters under investigation as may be ordered by the court; and may invoke the aid of the United States courts to compel witnesses to attend and testify and to produce such books, papers, contracts, agreements and documents to the same extent and under the same conditions and penalties as is provided for in the act to regulate commerce, approved February fourth, eighteen hundred and eighty-seven, and the amendments thereto.

Agreement to arbitrate.

SEC. 6. That every agreement of arbitration under this act shall be acknowledged by the parties before a notary public or clerk of a district or circuit court of the United States, and when so acknowledged a copy of the same shall be transmitted to the chairman of the Interstate Commerce Commission, who shall file the same in the office of said Commission.

Filing of agreement in office of Interstate Commerce Commission.

Agreement of individual employees to arbitrate.

Any agreement of arbitration which shall be entered into conforming to this act, except that it shall be executed by employees individually instead of by a labor organization as their representative, shall, when duly acknowledged as herein provided, be transmitted to the chairman of the Interstate Commerce Commission, who shall cause a notice in writing to be served upon the arbitrators, fixing a time and place for a meeting of said board, which shall be within fifteen days from the execution of said agreement of arbitration; *Provided, however,* That the said chairman of the Interstate Commerce Commission shall decline to call a meeting of arbitrators under such agreement unless it be shown to his satisfaction that the employees signing the submission represent or include a majority of all employees in the service of the same employer and of the same grade and class, and that an award pursuant to said submission can justly be regarded as binding upon all such employees.

SEC. 7. That during the pendency of arbitration under this act it shall not be lawful for the employer, party to such arbitration, to discharge the employees, parties thereto, except for inefficiency, violation of law, or neglect of duty; nor for the organization representing such employees to order, nor for the employees to unite in, aid, or abet, strikes against said employer; nor, during a period of three months after an award under such an arbitration, for such employer to discharge any such em- ployees, except for the causes aforesaid, without giving thirty days' written notice of an intent so to discharge; nor for any of such employees, during a like period, to quit the service of said employer without just cause, without giving to said employer thirty days' written notice of an intent so to do; nor for such organization representing such employees to order, counsel, or advise otherwise. Any violation of this section shall subject the offending party to liability for damages: *Provided,* That nothing herein contained shall be construed to prevent any em- ployer, party to such arbitration, from reducing the number of its or his employees whenever in its or his judgment business necessities require such reduction.

SEC. 8. That in every incorporation under the pro- visions of chapter five hundred and sixty-seven of the United States Statutes of eighteen hundred and eighty-five and eighteen hundred and eighty-six it must be provided in the articles of incorporation and in the constitu-

tion, rules, and by-laws that a member shall cease to be
Forfeiture of membership for violence. such by participating in or by instigating force or violence against persons or property during strikes, lockouts, or boycotts, or by seeking to prevent others from working through violence, threats, or intimidations. Members of
Liabilities. such incorporations shall not be personally liable for the acts, debts, or obligations of the corporations, nor shall such corporations be liable for the acts of members or
Appearance of corporations in arbitration proceedings. others in violation of law; and such corporations may appear by designated representatives before the board created by this act, or in any suits or proceedings for or against such corporations or their members in any of the Federal courts.

Railroads in hands of Federal receiver. Employees to be heard. SEC. 9. That whenever receivers appointed by Federal courts are in the possession and control of railroads, the employees upon such railroads shall have the right to be heard in such courts upon all questions affecting the terms and conditions of their employment, through the officers and representatives of their associations, whether incorporated or unincorporated, and no reduction of wages shall be made by such receivers without the authority of the court therefor upon notice to such employees, said
Notice of reduction of wages. notice to be not less than twenty days before the hearing upon the receivers' petition or application, and to be posted upon all customary bulletin boards along or upon the railway operated by such receiver or receivers.

Prohibition of unjust requirements as conditions to employment. SEC. 10. That any employer subject to the provisions of this act and any officer, agent, or receiver of such employer who shall require any employee, or any person seeking employment, as a condition of such employment, to enter into an agreement, either written or verbal, not to become or remain a member of any labor corporation, association, or organization; or shall threaten any employee with loss of employment, or shall unjustly discriminate against any employee because of his membership in such a labor corporation, association, or organization; or who shall require any employee or any person seeking employment, as a condition of such employment, to enter into a contract whereby such employee or applicant for employment shall agree to contribute to any fund for charitable, social, or beneficial purposes; to release such employer from legal liability for any personal injury by reason of any benefit received from such fund beyond the proportion of the benefit arising from the employer's contribution to such fund; or who shall, after having discharged an employee, attempt or conspire to prevent such employee from obtaining employment, or who shall, after the quitting of an employee, attempt or conspire to prevent such employee from obtaining employment, is hereby declared to be guilty of a misdemeanor, and, upon conviction thereof in any court of the United States of competent jurisdiction in the district in which such offense was committed, shall be punished for each offense by a fine of not less than one hundred dollars and not more than one thousand dollars. *Attempts to prevent further employment after discharge.* *Penalty.*

SEC. 11. That each member of said board of arbitration shall receive a compensation of ten dollars per day for the time he is actually employed, and his traveling and other necessary expenses; and a sum of money sufficient to pay the same, together with the traveling and other necessary and proper expenses of any conciliation or arbitration had hereunder, not to exceed ten thousand dollars in any one year, to be approved by the chairman of the Interstate Commerce Commission and audited by the proper accounting officers of the Treasury, is hereby appropriated for the fiscal years ending June thirtieth, eighteen hundred and ninety-eight, and June thirtieth, eighteen hundred and ninety-nine, out of any money in the Treasury not otherwise appropriated. *Appropriation for expenses of arbitration.*

SEC. 12. That the act to create boards of arbitration or commission for settling controversies and differences between railroad corporations and other common carriers engaged in interstate or territorial transportation of property or persons and their employees, approved October first, eighteen hundred and eighty-eight, is hereby repealed. *Repeal.*

Public No. 115, approved June 1, 1898.

AN ACT To promote the security of travel upon railroads engaged in interstate commerce, and to encourage the saving of life.

Be it enacted by the Senate and House of Representatives of the United States of America in Congress assembled, That the President of the United States be, and he is hereby, authorized to cause to be prepared bronze medals of honor, with suitable emblematic devices, which shall be bestowed upon any persons who shall hereafter, by extreme daring, endanger their own lives in saving, or endeavoring to save, lives from any wreck, disaster, or grave accident, or in preventing or endeavoring to prevent such wreck, disaster, or grave accident, upon any railroad within the United States engaged in interstate commerce: *Provided,* That no award of said medal shall be made to any person until sufficient evidence of his deserving shall have been furnished and placed on file, under such regulations as may be prescribed by the President of the United States.

SEC. 2. That the President of the United States be, and he is hereby, authorized to issue to any person to whom a medal of honor may be awarded under the provisions of this Act a rosette or knot, to be worn in lieu of the medal, and a ribbon to be worn with the medal; said rosette or knot and ribbon to be each of a pattern to be prescribed by the President of the United States: *Provided,* That whenever a ribbon issued under the provisions of this Act shall have been lost, destroyed, or rendered unfit for use without fault or neglect on the part of the person to whom it was issued, a new ribbon shall be issued to such person without charge therefor.

SEC. 3. That the appropriations for the enforcement and execution of the provisions of the Acts to promote the safety of employees and travelers upon railroads are hereby made available for carrying out the provisions of this Act.

Public, No. 98, approved February 23, 1905.

INTERSTATE COMMERCE ACT.

REGULATIONS GOVERNING THE AWARD OF LIFE-SAVING MEDALS UNDER THE FOREGOING ACT.

Made by the President of the United States on March 29, 1905.

1. Applications for medals under this act should be addressed to and filed with the Interstate Commerce Commission, at the city of Washington, D. C. Satisfactory evidence of the facts upon which the application is based must be filed in each case. This evidence should be in the form of affidavits made by eyewitnesses, of good repute and standing, testifying of their own knowledge. The opinion of witnesses that the person for whom an award is sought acted with extreme daring and endangered his life is not sufficient, but the affidavits must set forth the facts in detail and show clearly in what manner and to what extent life was endangered and extreme daring exhibited. The railroad upon which the incident occurred, the date, time of day, condition of the weather, the names of all persons present when practicable, and other pertinent circumstances should be stated. The affidavits should be made before an officer duly authorized to administer oaths and be accompanied by the certificate of some United States official of the district in which the affiants reside, such as a judge or clerk of United States court, district attorney, or postmaster, to the effect that the affiants are reputable and credible persons. If the affidavits are taken before an officer without an official seal his official character must be certified by the proper officer of a court of record under the seal thereof.

2. Applications for medals, together with all affidavits and other evidence received in connection therewith, shall be referred to a committee of five persons, consisting of the secretary of the Commission, the chief inspector of safety appliances, two inspectors of safety appliances designated by the Commission, and the clerk of the safety-appliance examining board, who shall act as clerk of the committee. This committee shall carefully consider each application presented and, after thoroughly weighing the evidence, shall prepare an abstract or brief covering the

case and file the same, together with the committee's recommendation, with the Commission, which brief and recommendation shall be transmitted by the Commission to the President for his approval. The committee may, with the approval of the Commission, direct any inspector of safety appliances in the employ of the Commission to proceed to the locality where the service was performed for which a medal is claimed, and make a personal investigation and report upon the facts of the case, which report shall be filed and made a part of the evidence considered by the committee.

3. Upon final approval of the committee's recommendation by the President the Commission shall take such measures to carry the recommendation into effect as the President may direct.

4. The Commission shall cause designs to be prepared for the medal, rosette, and ribbon provided for by the act, which designs shall be submitted to the President for his approval.

INDEX.

48